COLLECTIVE BEHAVIOR
AND
SOCIAL MOVEMENTS

COLLECTIVE BEHAVIOR AND SOCIAL MOVEMENTS

LOUIS E. GENEVIE, EDITOR

City University of New York

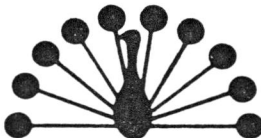

F. E. PEACOCK PUBLISHERS, INC.
ITASCA, ILLINOIS 60143

Copyright © 1978
F. E. Peacock Publishers, Inc.
All rights reserved
Library of Congress
Catalog Card No. 77-83419
ISBN 0-87581-228-7

To
EVA, DAVID and DIANE

Contents

Preface

The word *science* is used so often in its generic sense that it is easy to forget the multiplicity of meaning implied by the word. The actual work of science involves relatively isolated studies conducted by individuals working in different disciplines, each with a unique set of methodological tools and vocabulary, and each addressing a restricted professional audience. The process and progress of science is not unitary. The student or researcher attempting to keep up with the advancing edge of the social sciences must contend with the increasing quantity of work on human behavior, as well as the variety of approaches in the field. If progress is to be made in the development of a social science it is necessary to begin developing an integrated literature that is generally available. This process is quite slow at present, as individual researchers are rarely able to take into account all relevant work in a given area. Indeed, information is becoming so voluminous that the task of accumulation cannot be left to the individual researcher who is constantly beset by the day to day difficulties of the research process. One of the critical challenges for the social sciences in the coming years is the development of techniques for information collection, reduction and dissemination. This volume is a first step in that direction.

The primary purpose of this reader is to reflect the development and present state of social theory and research in the area of Collective Behavior and Social Movements. The general organization of the volume forms a chronology of the major developments in the field.

Part I, *Historical Perspectives,* illustrates the thinking of the major nineteenth century social thinkers concerned with the topic. Part II, *Theoretical and Empirical Foundations,* shows the mid-twentieth century movement toward the development of more systematic thinking about the causes and consequences of collective action. Parts III, IV, and V, *Recent Theory and Research,* are illustrative of recent developments in the field. Each of these sections is devoted to one of the general levels of explanation available to the researcher and theorist. The *micro-level* section illustrates research efforts which seek explanations for collective behavior on the level of individual attributes or characteristics. Those articles organized under the heading *macro-level research* seek explanations for collective action based primarily on the attributes of larger units of analysis such as cities or nations. The *mid-level* section contains articles that are primarily concerned with the attributes of organizations, neighborhoods or primary groups, in attempting to explain the emergence of collective behavior.

The limitations imposed by time and space have made this volume of readings necessarily incomplete. No book could include everything of importance in the field of collective behavior, and during the editing process it was necessary to eliminate many deserving works rather arbitrarily. Those articles that were selected for inclusion have been highly edited. Most of the difficult statistical material has been removed from the recent research sections, and the advanced student is advised to check the original version of these articles if the edited copy creates interest. To make the volume more readable, footnotes have been moved to the end of each article. In addition, although individual bibliographies have been eliminated from each article, all references appear in a master bibliography which is included at the end of the volume.

Louis E. Genevie

New York City
November 1977

Acknowledgments

Few volumes reveal the cooperative nature of social science as does one of this kind. I wish to acknowledge my personal debt to Professor Edgar F. Borgatta whose encouragement made this work possible. I also wish to thank Richard Berk and Robert Evans whose comments on earlier drafts of the organization proved helpful. My appreciation is also due to Michelle Epstein and Sarah Bobson who assisted in the collection of the theoretical and research materials, and to Maria Maldonado who made sure that some semblance of order was maintained as I sifted through the hundreds of books and articles that were reviewed; and to Eva Margolies and Paulette Pierce who were kind enough to read preliminary drafts of the introductory material. My thanks are also due to the staff at Peacock, including my editor, Tom LaMarre, who encouraged the inclusion of whatever material I thought necessary. And last, but in no way least, I wish to thank the authors and publishers of the material included in the volume whose cooperation made this work a reality. Each of these persons added considerably to the quality of this volume. As for the faults that remain, I claim full credit.

Introduction

Toward a Definition of the Field

All society rests upon the maintenance of common definitions and shared imagery. At the same time, these definitions and the social relations that emerge from them are constantly undergoing transformation. The dynamic process of change exists in all society, from the smallest social unit, through various organizational and institutional configurations, to entire cultures. The study of collective behavior is the study of the processes through which individuals in society develop new, as well as change existing patterns of interaction. In this way, collective behavior is viewed as the mediating force of social change.

Underlying the analysis of all forms of collective behavior is the identification of the processes through which norms governing human behavior emerge. The phenomenon under consideration include those patterns of interaction that emerge in situations where individuals lack adequate guides for conduct. Such situations usually occur when individuals view existing social circumstances negatively, and challenge the legitimacy of existing norms, but can also occur when environmental conditions change rapidly, such as during natural disasters. Once existing norms become inadequate, individuals in interaction with one another attempt to develop understanding of one another's perceptions, expectations and programs of action and, in doing so, strive to forge new definitions and complementary behavioral patterns.

TABLE 1
A Continuum of Normative Regulation

ORGANIZED GROUP BEHAVIOR		COLLECTIVE BEHAVIOR				
Institutional Behavior	Small Group Interaction	The Public	Social Movements	Revolutionary Uprisings	Crowds	Panic
		Extent of Normative Regulations				
Behavior Regulated by Traditional Norms and Organization			Behavior Not Regulated by Traditional Norms and Organization			

Although all forms of collective behavior are characterized by lack of adequate guides to conduct, the *extent* to which norms are absent varies considerably from situation to situation. The distinction between collective behavior and other forms of group behavior is neither categorical nor absolute and might be more clearly conceptualized by considering the continuum elaborated in Table 1.

The extreme left of the continuum is representative of highly structured behavior such as those interactions that take place between individuals occupying institutional or organizational roles. In such situations, individual behavioral options are limited, consensus with respect to norms is high, and there is little tolerance for deviance. As we move toward the right side of the continuum, we encounter behavior in small groups that, although still regulated by established norms, is much less formal and not subject to the rigid control of institutionalized roles.

Further to the right along the continuum, the adequacy of traditional norms governing patterns of interaction diminishes, and the construction or reconstruction of social reality begins. On this side of the continuum, we find the *Public,* where relevant social issues are identified and discussed, and the convergence or divergence of opinions, attitudes and courses of action can be observed. Moving farther to the right side of the continuum, we find the emergence of *Social Movements,* which are organized and guided by general social norms to varying degrees, and usually directed at modifying a limited number of values, attitudes or behaviors in the society that are perceived as undesirable. Farther toward the right side of the continuum are *revolutionary movements,* which like *Social Movements* exhibit varying degrees of organization, but, unlike social movements, are usually directed at restructuring the form of most political, economic or social patterns in the society. Toward the far right side of the continuum is crowd behavior, the prototype of collective behavior, where individual action has traditionally been thought to be largely spontaneous and unstructured; and finally panic behavior, the most unstructured, ephemeral and rarest form of collective action.

We see, then, that collectivities, or the groups in which collective behavior takes place, are not guided in a direct fashion by the larger society, nor are there any organizational guidelines or norms to follow in structuring behavior. Every collectivity has members, but there are no clearly defined procedures for recruiting, selecting, or identifying them. Collectivities usually form around a specific value, goal or issue, but there is usually little forethought concerning the nature of the goal or the probability of goal attainment, and no well defined procedures for making group decisions. This is not to imply that no coordination exists between members. In fact, some minimal interaction is necessary before a collectivity of any kind can be said to exist. And while some degree of organization may exist within the group, the division of labor, leadership and norms guiding behavior arise from the interaction among group members, and not through identification with some element in the larger social structure.

TABLE 2
A Comparison of Formal Groups and Three Major Forms of Collective Behavior

	Comparative Characteristic				
	Size	Duration	Organizational Characteristics	Reason for Development	Implications for Social Change
Formal Groups	Unlimited; actual size dependent upon goals and resources available to achieve them.	Unlimited	Strong organization; clear goals; leadership; hierarchy; division of labor; well defined procedures for selecting leaders and members; behavior structured by traditional norms.	Fulfill a specific social need directly or indirectly related to the survival of the group.	The force of stability
Publics	Unlimited; actual size dependent upon nature of the issues addressed, and the means of communication available.	Unlimited	Limited or non-existent, although the professional press can be thought of as having a loosely structured leadership role.	The need for a forum where social alternatives are identified, evaluated and expressed.	Preliminary; may effect attitudes and opinions about various social issues which in turn may lead to individual or social change.
Crowds	Some variation, but generally limited by environmental characteristics such as the size of the room or other area where the group happens to congregate.	Transitory; limited by the finite energy of the participants and the reaction of social control forces.	Minimal; behavior not structured by traditional norms; membership and leadership transitory; little, if any division of labor or hierarchy; behavior structured by norms that emerge from group interaction.	Desire or need to change social or environmental circumstances and achieve goals defined as obtainable through immediate group action.	Little direct change can be attributed to crowd activity in modern society. But crowd behavior often stimulates other social forces that can have substantial impact.
Social Movements	Considerable variation; primarily dependent upon nature of the movement and its relationship to the larger society.	Considerable variation; primarily dependent upon the nature of the movement to the larger society to suppress or incorporate movement goals.	Considerable variation; for all but the most radical movements however, organization, goals, hierarchy, leadership and membership requirements become defined over time, and in some instances movements develop into formal groups.	Desire or need to change specific social or environmental circumstances and achieve goals defined as obtainable through long range planning, organization and group action.	Success dependent upon the nature of the movement and its relationship to the larger society; some movements directly influence social patterns (e.g. Women's Movement, Temperance Movement, Civil Rights Movement), while other have little direct effect on social behavior (Millenarian Religious groups).

This is not to imply that collective behavior never takes place within the structure of everyday social life. In fact, collective behavior can and does occur at any time and in all forms of social structure, even in the institutional setting. In formal organizations, attempts to create or clarify goals or expectations are usually of brief duration, and differences are usually settled within the confines of existing structural restraints. When consensus concerning a particular issue, definition, expectation or behavioral pattern cannot be reached, however, and individuals mobilize on the basis of mutually desirable positions, one of the major forms of collective behavior is likely to occur. While some elementary form of collective behavior is present in every social encounter, the processes through which social definitions arise or change can best be observed in situations that involve one or more of the fundamental elements of instability: crisis, conflict, novelty or choice.

In addition to the extent of normative structure in a particular situation, the nature and form of collective behavior is also influenced by two additional characteristics: first, the importance of the questioned or ambiguous norm to the survival of the individual or the society; and second, the immediacy with which decisions must be made and action taken in the situation in order to avert harm and maximize positive outcomes. For example, in life and death situations that require immediate action, such as during a fire or other natural disaster, loosely organized crowd behavior is likely to occur. In situations perceived as not requiring immediate response and more long term institutional modification, social or revolutionary movements often emerge.

Considerable variation exists in the form of inchoate social organization that develops during collective behavior. The major types of collective behavior, publics, crowds and social movements, differ as much from one another as each does from formal groups. Similarly, considerable variation exists within each major type of collectivity: All publics, crowds and social movements are not alike. Since such a wide range of behavior falls within the domain of the field, a comparison of some of the similarities and differences between the three major types of collectivities will be useful in completing the general definition of collective behavior.

As has been noted thus far, all collective behavior differs from formal group activity in that the norms governing behavior in collectivities emerge from the interaction among participants, whereas in formal groups there is considerable reliance on traditional norms, expectations and behavioral patterns. Formal groups and various types of collectivities also differ on a number of other dimensions. For illustrative purposes, five major characteristics have been chosen for comparison: size, duration, organizational development, factors influencing the emergence of the behavior and the implications that each type of behavior has for social change. Although these characteristics are by no means exhaustive, they do represent an adequate basis for comparison. Table 2 is a summary of the differences between formal groups and the major forms of collective behavior across each of these dimensions and should be studied carefully in order to gain a clear understanding of the variety of behavior within the field and how behavior in collectives differs from behavior in formal social groups.

The Public

A public is defined as a group of individuals who are divided on some issue or set of issues and because of their mutual interest are engaged in some form of communication. Publics exist because of the need or desire in human society to identify, evaluate and express opinions about various problems, issues and social alternatives. The scientific community might be thought of as an *issue specific public,* while all members of a society are potential members of the *general public:* Interest in and communication about a relevant issue constitutes membership. In this way the general public might be thought of as the preliminary forum of social change, where individuals form and change opinions, attitudes and values which in turn may lead to future modification of behavioral patterns.

Although communication must exist before an aggregation of persons can be defined as a public, it need not be direct. In fact, most persons in a public never engage in face to face communication. Although there are exceptions, the boundaries of publics are quite fluid: The collectivity expands when more individuals become interested enough in a particular issue to enter into discussion, and contracts when individuals no longer feel the need to participate. Therefore, there is no inherent limitation on a public's size. The actual size at any point in time depends on the extent to which the issues addressed are relevant to members of the larger society from which the public recruits members, and on the means of communication available to members. When the issues addressed are of vital importance to the larger society and individuals have easy access to the means of communication, a public is likely to become large and exist over a long period of time.

Most publics are not organized, although there are numerous exceptions, such as professional and scientific publics whose organizations serve as links between members of these communities. The organization that exists in the general public is usually indirect, such as the political party organizations that exist in countries where most members of the society are accorded suffrage. While no direct organization exists in the general public, the professional press, which controls the public communication network, can be thought of as having a particularly powerful leadership role, although how this power can be used for specific purposes is largely unknown. Aside from this loosely defined form of leadership, no organizational hierarchy exists in the general public.

The Crowd

The crowd is a group of persons in close physical proximity who have gathered because of a need or desire to change some aspect of the environment not adequately addressed by traditional norms and known patterns of behavior. Goals may emerge from the interaction of crowd members and are usually defined as obtainable through some form of *immediate* group action. Traditionally, behavior under such circumstances has been defined as emotional, irrational and essentially unpredictable. In recent years however, there has been a movement in the discipline toward the conceptualization of crowd behavior as more closely related to routine forms of social behavior: Individuals in interaction with one another attempt to formulate the most appropriate course of action by developing understanding of one another's perceptions, expectatons and programs of action under the constraint of the need or desire for immediate response in the situation.

Unlike behavior in the public, interaction in the crowd involves face to face communication. Loosely defined goals or points of focus emerge, and a minimal level of organizational structure, usually consisting of one or more leaders and their followers, develops from the interaction of crowd members. The size of the crowd is limited by the area available in which to congregate. Crowds are transitory in nature. Their existence over time is limited by the finite energy of the participants, coupled with the reaction of social control forces to the actions of the crowd.

Although some crowds that develop during the course of routine social interaction such as sports' audiences and religious assemblies, the crowds of primary interest to those who study collective behavior occur outside the range of routine social situations. Of primary interest are those crowds that are encountered during such events as riots and looting, as well as those that occur during fires, earthquakes or other natural disasters.

In modern society little long term social change can be directly attributed to crowd activity, although crowd behavior often stimulates other social forces that have substantial impact on the form, rate and substance of social change. For example, the racial disturbances that occurred in American cities during the late 1960s did not result in direct, substantive change. The riots did however, bring the social and economic plight of the Black inner-city resident to the attention of the general public, and the ensuing debate over such issues as the meaning of *equal opportunity* has yet to subside.

Social Movements

Social movements are collectivities that develop out of a desire on the part of a relatively large number of individuals to change or resist change in some aspect of the environment and to achieve goals defined as obtainable through continuity in planning, organization, leadership and group action. Because goals are defined as obtainable through long range planning and organization, all social movements, by definition, develop some form of organizational structure, hierarchy and membership requirements. But these organizational characteristics vary considerably from movement to movement: Some movements develop a minimal structure, while others become more bureaucratized over time, and in some instances develop into formal organizations.

Social movements vary considerably in terms of size and existence over time. To a large extent, both their size and duration are contingent upon the nature of the goals and ideology that develop in the group, and the relationship of the movement to the society of which it is a part. In addition, the ability of the larger society to incorporate or suppress movement goals is also an important factor influencing movement size and duration.

Social movements also vary considerably in terms of their effect on patterns of interaction in the larger society. Some movements promote change; others are designed to resist change. Some movements, such as the Women's Movement and the Civil Rights Movement in America, effect social change in a direct manner. Other movements, such as the various millenarian religious movements that have achieved some notoriety during the 1970s, have little or no direct effect on the society as a whole.

Summary

In comparing the major types of collective behavior across a number of important analytic dimensions, we see that tremendous variation exists within the set of behaviors that fall under the rubric of collective behavior. Individual experience in publics, crowds and social movements differs markedly, and the social processes involved in each situation are also substantially different. Yet each form of collective behavior shares the underlying process that forms the foundation of the field as a distinct discipline: the search for shared definition, for a common imagery and understanding that is consistent with the needs and desires of individuals in society.

The Organization of the Collection

The organization of this volume emerged from a study of the field of collective behavior. As the collection and preliminary organization of theoretical and research materials progressed, two major classificatory schemes developed, and these have been merged to form the structure of the volume. The first organizing concept is a chronological ordering of work in the area into three distinct *developmental stages*. The work presented in Part I, *Historical Perspectives,* reflects the first of three developmental stages in the field. Representing material written prior to 1930, this section includes the work of LeBon, de Tocqueville, Park and Burgess, and Simmel. In addition, the work of George Rudé, a contemporary historian, is also included in this section as a critique of the work of this era. The second developmental stage of the field, illustrated in Part II, *Theoretical and Empirical Foundations,* occurred roughly between 1930 and 1960. During this period Herbert Blumer, Hadley Cantril and Neil Smelser laid the theoretical foundations for the study of collective behavior by carefully setting forth the diverse set of concepts in the field in a systematic, observable fashion. The works of Vander Zanden, Turner, Surace, Hopper and Quarantelli are illustrative of the new interest in theory testing and validation that emerged during this period, brought about largely by these theoretical foundations.

Beginning in the mid-1960's the volume of research on collective behavior mushroomed; this was, to a large extent, due to the increase in civil disorders that occurred in America during that time. This material, illustrated in Parts III, IV, and V, is representative of recent theory and research in the field. The work selected for these sections of the volume is illustrative of the current theoretical perspectives and research methodologies in the field, and includes research by sociologists, psychologists, and economists.

In addition to the evolutionary development that has taken place in the field over time, a second classificatory scheme involving what might be termed the *level of analytic thought* also became evident while collecting and organizing work in the area. Three distinct analytic approaches, each with particular strengths and weaknesses have been applied to the analysis of collective behavior, and each forms a separate part of the recent work included in this volume. Each approach narrows the focus of the researcher or theorist by implicitly or explicitly specifying the *unit of analysis* to which a particular theory applies or on which data were collected and analyzed. Part III of this volume focuses on *micro-level* theory and research which seeks explanations for collective behavior on the level of individual processes, characteristics and attributes. By focusing on the individual as the primary analytic unit, the scope of analysis is limited to the characteristics of persons engaged in various forms of collective behavior and the patterns of interaction between individuals in collective behavior situations. Illustrating work on this level, Part III focuses on two major topics: the nature of the processes and patterns of interaction involved in crowd activity and the process of commitment to social movements. Part IV, *Mid-level Theory and Research,* focuses on organizational and institutional characteristics related to collective behavior. While this section of the volume is primarily concerned with organizational characteristics and processes inherent in social movements, analyses of elementary forms of collective behavior, viewed from an organizational or institutional perspective, are also included.

Part V is illustrative of macro-level analyses that focus primarily on the overall characteristics of cities, nations and entire cultures related to collective behavior. Macro-level analyses have added to our understanding of the social and cultural forces that affect individual and organizational behavior, as well as to our understanding of the processes related to national and international stability.

The student is now invited to turn to the collection of theoretical and research articles. Introductory material has been provided at the beginning of each section which summarizes the essential points in each article and also points out a number of the important links between the articles in each section.

I. Historical Perspectives

Introduction

This part of the volume, with one exception, is devoted to the early speculative work in collective behavior that characterized the beginnings of social science. Many of the observations and interpretations included here have not withstood the careful inspection of scientific analysis and should be approached with a critical eye. It should also be kept in mind, however, that the application of scientific method begins with an idea, and, despite a lack of systematic information, the early thinkers developed numerous concepts that remain important today.

The section begins with LeBon's (1) description and analysis of crowd behavior. LeBon was one of the early pioneers in collective behavior, and is often referred to as the founder of the field. *The Crowd,* first published in 1896, remains one of the classic readings in the area. LeBon was one of the first to view the crowd not merely as an aggregate of individuals but rather as a single entity with a unique psychology. Within this framework, the important analytic focus in explaining crowd behavior is the characteristics of the crowd itself, as opposed to the characteristics of individual members. LeBon argues, for example, that the crowd possesses a *collective mind* that emerges from the interaction of individuals. In the crowd situation, individual traits are greatly weakened, and as a result individuals behave in radically different ways than they would under routine circumstances. Although much of LeBon's work is outdated, his contribution remains a fertile source of propositions concerning the nature of crowd behavior.

Tarde's (2) work, originally published around the turn of the century, focuses on the definition, inception and development of *the public* and *public opinion.* The author defines the public as a group of persons who, although not in direct interaction with one another, communicate knowledge and ideas of mutual interest and concern. Publics may take the form of specialized groups, such as scientific or philosophical publics. But there also exists a more general public, concerned with a wide range of societal issues. Tarde traces the beginnings of the public and public opinion to the invention of the printing press and the proliferation of printed material, combined with the increased need of individuals in modern society to communicate common information and concerns. In addition, the author examines the role of journalists in the development and transformation of public opinion, as well as the general significance of public opinion in understanding social change.

Park and Burgess (3), writing a quarter century after LeBon and Tarde, extend the conceptual domain of the field by including not only crowd behavior, but all behavior not governed by established norms. In their work presented here, the authors argue that the spontaneity and unstructured nature of collective behavior is the primary difference between collective behavior and other forms of social interaction. Employing this definition, the authors include interaction in the crowd, the public, and certain forms of small group and organizational behavior in their definition of the field. In addition, they distinguish between interaction patterns within each of these collectivities, as well as showing how each differs from more formalized patterns of interaction.

Georg Simmel (4) is rarely cited as one of the early contributors to the field of collective behavior. Yet his classic analysis of the relationship between the size of the group and the nature of the relationships between group members has particular relevance for the discipline. Simmel argues persuasively that the nature of social interaction is, to a large extent, a function of the number of persons in the group and that this relationship is operative in all interaction, irrespective of content. His discussion of the limitations and potentialities that exist when a change in group size occurs is important in understanding the underlying group processes influencing behavior in crowds and less ephemeral collectivities. Focusing on the differences between interaction in the dyad and the triad, Simmel shows how the addition of another person to the dyad changes the nature of the possible relationships that can develop, and how this expansion or delimitation of available behaviors affects individual action in all types of social situations.

While Simmel's work is important in its focus on the general dynamics of human interaction, the work of Alexis de Tocqueville (5) is important for its contribution to the understanding of societal level processes that influence revolutionary behavior. De Tocqueville argues that revolutions are the inevitable outcome of long periods of social development. Within this framework, revolutions are the inevitable outcome of certain forms of societal evolution. Although the author sees political or economic repression as the root of revolution, he argues that these phenomena must be evaluated within the context of the social development of the society. Because changes in the beliefs, sentiments and customs of individuals occur at each stage of development, more socially advanced countries have a greater likelihood of even further development that may take the form of revolution. Applying his theory to the French Revolution of 1789, de Tocqueville points out that prior to 1789 the French peasants had made considerable progress in breaking down the more repressive aspects of feudalism, and compared to other European countries, France was more tolerant and progressive, both economically and politically. On the basis of *absolute* repression alone, one would have expected a revolution to have occurred, in countries like Germany, where feudalism was still the dominant social, political and economic force in the late eighteenth century. De Tocqueville argues that in order to understand why the revolution took place in France it is necessary to evaluate the repression in France in terms of the tolerance for repression on the part of individuals in the society. Because of their history of social development, the French were unwilling to accept the repressive aspectives of their society even though they had more freedom than other less advanced societies, hence the revolution.

The work of George Rudé (6) concludes this part of the volume. Although Rudé is a contemporary historian, his work is included here because it is one of the few critiques of earlier approaches to the study of crowd behavior in pre-industrial societies. In characterizing the pre-industrial crowd, Rudé points to three major factors that tended to accompany incidences of crowd behavior: economic difficulties, political turmoil, and millenarian religious ideas. Although the author finds similarities between the factors influencing crowd behavior throughout history, he argues that all incidences of crowd behavior must be analyzed within their historical contexts in order to gain insight into the particular pattern of social forces that influence crowd behavior at any particular point in time.

1.

Gustave LeBon

THE MIND OF THE CROWDS

In its ordinary sense the word "crowd" means a gathering of individuals of whatever nationality, profession, or sex, and whatever be the chances that have brought them together. From the psychological point of view the expression "crowd" assumes quite a different signification. Under certain given circumstances, and only under those circumstances, an agglomeration of men presents new characteristics very different from those of the individuals composing it. The sentiments and ideas of all the persons in the gathering take one and the same direction, and their conscious personality vanishes. A collective mind is formed, doubtless transitory, but presenting very clearly defined characteristics. The gathering has thus become what, in the absence of a better expression, I will call an organized crowd, or, if the term is considered preferable, a psychological crowd. It forms a *single being,* and is *subjected to the law of the mental unity of crowds.*

A psychological crowd once constituted, it acquires certain provisional but determinable general characteristics. To these general characteristics there are adjoined particular characteristics which vary according to the elements of which the crowd is composed, and may modify its mental constitution. Psychological crowds, then, are susceptible of classification; and when we come to occupy ourselves with this matter, we shall see that a heterogeneous crowd—that is, a crowd composed of dissimilar elements—presents certain characteristics in common with homogeneous crowds—that is, with crowds composed of elements more or less akin (sects, castes, and classes)—and side by side with these common characteristics particularities which permit of the two kinds of crowds being differentiated.

But before occupying outselves with the different categories of crowds, we must first of all examine the characteristics common to them all.

It is not easy to describe the mind of crowds with exactness, because its organization varies not only according to race and composition, but also according to the nature and intensity of the exciting causes to which crowds are subjected. The same difficulty, however, presents itself in the psychological study of an individual. It is only in novels that individuals are found to traverse their whole life with an unvarying character. It is only the uniformity of the environment that creates the apparent uniformity of characters. I have shown elsewhere that all mental constitutions contain possibilities of character which may be manifested in consequence of a sudden change of environment.

It being impossible to study here all the successive degrees of organization of crowds, we shall concern ourselves more especially with such crowds as have attained to the phase of complete organization. In this way we shall see what crowds may become, but not what they invariably are. It is only in this advanced

Reprinted with permission of Macmillan Publishing Co., Inc., from "The Mind of the Crowd" in *The Crowd* by Gustave LeBon. Published in the United States by Macmillan Publishing Co., Inc.

phase of organization that certain new and special characteristics are superposed on the unvarying and dominant character of the race; then takes place that turning already alluded to of all the feelings and thoughts of the collectivity in an identical direction. It is only under such circumstances too, that what I have called above the *psychological law of the mental unity of crowds* comes into play.

Among the psychological characteristics of crowds there are some that they may present in common with isolated individuals, and others, on the contrary, which are absolutely peculiar to them and are only to be met with in collectivities. It is these special characteristics that we shall study, first of all, in order to show their importance.

The most striking peculiarity presented by a psychological crowd is the following: Whoever be the individuals that compose it, however like or unlike be their mode of life, their occupations, their character, or their intelligence, the fact that they have been transformed into a crowd puts them in possession of a sort of collective mind which makes them feel, think, and act in a manner quite different from that in which each individual of them would feel, think, and act were he in a state of isolation. There are certain ideas and feelings which do not come into being, or do not transform themselves into acts except in the case of individuals forming a crowd. The psychological crowd is a provisional being formed of heterogeneous elements, which for a moment are combined, exactly as the cells which constitute a living body form by their reunion a new being which displays characteristics very different from those possessed by each of the cells singly.

It is easy to prove how much the individual forming part of a crowd differs from the isolated individual, but it is less easy to discover the causes of this difference.

To obtain at any rate a glimpse of them it is necessary in the first place to call to mind the truth established by modern psychology, that unconscious phenomena play an altogether preponderating part not only in organic life, but also in the operations of the intelligence. The conscious life of the mind is of small importance in comparison with its unconscious life. The most subtle analyst, the most acute observer, is scarcely successful in discovering more than a very small number of the unconscious motives that determine his conduct. Our conscious acts are the outcome of an unconscious substratum created in the mind in the main by hereditary influences. This substratum consists of the innumerable common characteristics handed down from generation to generation, which constitute the genius of a race. Behind the avowed causes of our acts there undoubtedly lie secret causes that we do not avow, but behind these secret causes there are many others more secret still which we ourselves ignore. The greater part of our daily actions are the result of hidden motives which escape our observation.

Men the most unlike in the matter of their intelligence possess instincts, passions, and feelings that are very similar. In the case of everything that belongs to the realm of sentiment—religion, politics, morality, the affections and antipathies, etc.—the most eminent men seldom surpass the standard of the most ordinary individuals. From the intellectual point of view an abyss may exist between a great mathematician and his bootmaker, but from the point of view of character the difference is most often slight or non-existent.

It is precisely these general qualities of character, governed by forces of which we are unconscious, and possessed by the majority of the normal individuals of a race in much the same degree—it is precisely these qualities, I say, that in crowds become common property. In the collective mind the intellectual aptitudes of the individuals, and in consequence their individuality, are weakened. The heterogeneous is swamped by the homogeneous, and the unconscious qualities obtain the upper hand.

Different causes determine the appearance of these characteristics peculiar to crowds, and not possessed by isolated individuals. The first is that the individual forming part of a crowd acquires, solely from numerical considerations, a sentiment of invincible power which allows him to yield to instincts which, had he been alone, he would perforce have kept under restraint. He will be the less disposed to check himself from the consideration that, a crowd being anonymous, and in consequence irresponsible, the sentiment of responsibility which always controls individuals disappears entirely.

The second cause, which is contagion, also intervenes to determine the manifestation in crowds of their special characteristics, and at the same time the trend they are to take. Contagion is a phenomenon of which it is easy to establish the presence, but that it is not easy to explain. It must be classed among those phenomena of a hypnotic order, which we shall shortly study. In a crowd every sentiment and act is contagious, and contagious to such a degree that an individual readily sacrifices his personal interest to the collective interest. This is an aptitude very contrary to his nature, and of which a man is scarcely capable, except when he makes part of a crowd.

A third cause, and by far the most important, determines in the individuals of a crowd special characteristics which are quite contrary at times to those presented by the isolated individual. I allude to that suggestibility of which, moreover, the con-

tagion mentioned above is neither more nor less than an effect.

To understand this phenomenon it is necessary to bear in mind certain recent physiological discoveries. We know to-day that by various processes an individual may be brought into such a condition that, having entirely lost his conscious personality, he obeys all the suggestions of the operator who has deprived him of it, and commits acts in utter contradiction with his character and habits. The most careful observations seem to prove that an individual immerged for some length of time in a crowd in action soon finds himself— either in consequence of the magnetic influence given out by the crowd, or from some other cause of which we are ignorant —in a special state, which much resembles the state of fascination in which the hypnotized individual finds himself in the hands of the hypnotizer. The activity of the brain being paralyzed in the case of the hypnotized subject, the latter becomes the slave of all the unconscious activities of his spinal cord, which the hypnotizer directs at will. The conscious personality has entirely vanished; will and discernment are lost. All feelings and thoughts are bent in the direction determined by the hypnotizer.

Such also is approximately the state of the individual forming part of a psychological crowd. He is no longer conscious of his acts. In his case, as in the case of the hypnotized subject, at the same time that certain faculties are destroyed, others may be brought to a high degree of exaltation. Under the influence of a suggestion, he will undertake the accomplishment of certain acts with irresistible impetuosity. This impetuosity is the more irresistible in the case of crowds than in that of the hypnotized subject, from the fact that, the suggestion being the same for all the individuals of the crowd, it gains in strength by reciprocity. The individualities in the crowd who might possess a personality sufficiently strong to resist the suggestion are too few in number to struggle against the current. At the utmost, they may be able to attempt a diversion by means of different suggestions. It is in this way, for instance, that a happy expression, an image opportunely evoked, have occasionally deterred crowds from the most bloodthirsty acts.

We see, then, that the disappearance of the conscious personality, the predominance of the unconscious personality, the turning by means of suggestion and contagion of feelings and ideas in an identical direction, the tendency immediately to transform the suggested ideas into acts; these we see, are the principal characteristics of the individual forming part of a crowd. He is no longer himself, but has become an automaton who has ceased to be guided by his will.

He possesses the spontaneity, the violence, the ferocity, and also the enthusiasm and heroism of primitive beings, whom he further tends to resemble by the facility with which he allows himself to be impressed by words and images—which would be entirely without action on each of the isolated individuals composing the crowd—and to be induced to commit acts contrary to his most obvious interests and his best-known habits.

It is for these reasons that juries are seen to deliver verdicts of which each individual juror would disapprove, that parliamentary assemblies adopt laws and measures of which each of their members would disapprove in his own person. Taken separately, the men of the French Revolutionary Convention were enlightened citizens of peaceful habits. United in a crowd, they did not hesitate to give their adhesion to the most savage proposals, to guillotine individuals most clearly innocent, and,

contrary to their interests, to renounce their inviolability and to decimate themselves.

It is not only by his acts that the individual in a crowd differs essentially from himself. Even before he has entirely lost his independence, his ideas and feelings have undergone a transformation, and the transformation is so profound as to change the miser into a spendthrift, the sceptic into a believer, the honest man into a criminal, and the coward into a hero.

The conclusion to be drawn from what precedes is, that the crowd is always intellectually inferior to the isolated individual, but that, from the point of view of feelings and of the acts these feelings provoke, the crowd may, according to circumstances, be better or worse than the individual. All depends on the nature of the suggestion to which the crowd is exposed.

The leaders of crowds

As soon as a certain number of living beings are gathered together, whether they be animals or men, they place themselves instinctively under the authority of a chief.

In the case of human crowds the chief is often nothing more than a ringleader or agitator, but as such he plays a considerable part. His will is the nucleus around which the opinions of the crowd are grouped and attain to identity. He constitutes the first element in the organization of heterogeneous crowds, and paves the way for their organization in sects; in the meantime he directs them. A crowd is a servile flock that is incapable of ever doing without a master.

The leaders we speak of are more frequently men of action than thinkers. They are not gifted with keen foresight, nor could they be, as this quality generally conduces to doubt and inactivity. They are especially recruited from the ranks of those morbidly nervous, excitable, half-deranged persons who are bordering on madness. However absurd may be the idea they uphold or the goal they pursue, their convictions are so strong that all reasoning is lost upon them. Contempt and persecution do not affect them, or only serve to excite them the more. They sacrifice their personal interest, their family—everything. The very instinct of self-preservation is entirely obliterated in them, and so much so that often the only recompense they solicit is that of martyrdom. The intensity of their faith gives great power of suggestion to their words. The multitude is always ready to listen to the strong-willed man, who knows how to impose himself upon it. Men gathered in a crowd lose all force of will, and turn instinctively to the person who possesses the quality they lack.

The arousing of faith—whether religious, political, or social, whether faith in a work, in a person, or an idea—has always been the function of the great leaders of crowds, and it is on this account that their influence is always very great. Of all the forces at the disposal of humanity, faith has always been one of the most tremendous, and the Gospel rightly attributes to it the power of moving mountains. To endow a man with faith is to multiply his strength tenfold. The great events of history have been brought about by obscure believers, who have had little beyond their faith in their favor. It is not by the aid of the learned or of philosophers, and still less of sceptics, that have been built up the great religions which have swayed the world, or the vast empires which have spread from one hemisphere to the other.

In every social sphere, from the highest to the lowest, as soon as a man ceases to be isolated he speedily falls under the influence of a leader. The majority of men, especially among the masses, do not possess clear and reasoned ideas on any subject whatever outside their own specialty. The leader serves them as guide. It is just possible that he may be replaced, though very inefficiently, by the periodical publications which manufacture opinions for their leaders and supply them with ready-made phrases which absolve them of the trouble of reasoning.

The leaders of crowds wield a very despotic authority, and this despotism indeed is a condition of their obtaining a following. It has often been remarked how easily they extort obedience, although without any means of backing up their authority, from the most turbulent section of the working classes. They fix the hours of labor and the rate of wages, and they decree strikes, which are begun and ended at the hour they ordain.

At the present day these leaders and agitators tend more and more to usurp the place of the public authorities in proportion as the latter allow themselves to be called in question and shorn of their strength. The tyranny of these new masters has for result that the crowds obey them much more docilely than they have obeyed any Government. If in consequence of some accident or other the leaders should be removed from the scene, the crowd returns to its original state of a collectivity without cohesion or force of resistance. During the last strike of the Parisian omnibus employees the arrest of the two leaders who were directing it was at once sufficient to bring it to an end. It is the need not of liberty but of servitude that is always predominant in the soul of crowds. They are so bent on obedience that they instinctively submit to whoever declares himself their master.

These ringleaders and agitators may be divided into two clearly defined classes. The one includes the men who are energetic and possess, but only intermittently, much strength of will, the other the men, far rarer than the preceding, whose strength of will is enduring. The first-mentioned are violent, brave, and audacious. They are more especially useful to direct a violent enterprise suddenly decided on, to carry the masses with them in spite of danger, and to transform into heroes the men who but yesterday were recruits. Men of this kind were Ney and Murat under the First Empire, and such a man in our own time was Garibaldi, a talentless but energetic adventurer who succeeded with a handful of men in laying hands on the ancient kingdom of Naples, defended though it was by a disciplined army.

Still, though the energy of leaders of this class is a force to be reckoned with, it is transitory, and scarcely outlasts the exciting cause that has brought it into play. When they have returned to their ordinary course of life the heroes animated by energy of this description often evince, as was the case with those I have just cited, the most astonishing weakness of character. They seem incapable of reflection and of conducting themselves under the simplest circumstances, although they had been able to lead others. These men are leaders who cannot exercise their function except on the condition that they be led themselves and continually stimulated, that they have always as their beacon a man or an idea, that they follow a line of conduct clearly traced. The second category of leaders, that of men of enduring strength of will, has, in spite of a less brilliant aspect, a much more considerable influence. In this category are to be found the true founders of religions and great undertakings: St. Paul, Mahomet, Christopher Columbus, and de Lesseps, for example. Whether they be intelligent or narrow-minded is of no importance: the world belongs to them. The persistent will-force they possess is an immensely rare and immensely powerful faculty to which everything yields. What a strong and continuous will is capable of is not always properly appreciated. Nothing resists it; neither nature, gods, nor man.

2.

Gabriel Tarde

THE PUBLIC AND PUBLIC OPINION

The public

Not only does a crowd attract and exert an irresistible pull on the spectator, but its

Abridged from Gabriel Tarde, *On Communication of Social Influence,* chaps. 16-17, Terry Clark (ed.) (Heritage of Sociology Series), University of Chicago Press, 1969, with permission of the editor and publisher.

From *L'Opinion et la foule* (Paris: Alean, 1922: originally published 1901), pt. 1, "Le Public et la foule," pp. 1-62, with elisions.

very name has a prestigious attraction for the contemporary reader, encouraging certain writers to use this ambiguous word to designate all sorts of human groupings. It is important to put an end to this confusion, and notably not to confuse the crowd with the *public,* a word in itself subject to various interpretations but which I shall attempt to define precisely. We speak of the public at a theater, the public at some assembly, and here public means crowd. But this is neither the sole nor even the primary meaning, and while the importance of this type of public has declined or remains static, the invention of printing has caused a very different type of public to appear, one which never ceases to grow and whose indefinite extension is one of the most clearly marked traits of our period. There is a psychology of crowds[1]: there remains to be developed a psychology of the public, understood in this other sense as a purely spiritual collectivity, a dispersion of individuals who are physically separated and whose cohesion is entirely mental. Where the public comes from, how it arises and develops; its varieties and relationships with those who are its directors; its relationships to the crowd, to corporations, to states; its strength for good or evil, and its ways of acting and feeling—this is what we plan to investigate in this study.

Neither in Latin nor Greek is there any word which is the equivalent of what we mean by public. There are words to designate the masses, the gathering of armed or unarmed citizens, the electoral body, and all types of crowds. But what writer of antiquity thought of talking about his public? None of them ever knew anything other than his *audience* in rooms rented for public readings, at which the poets contemporary to Pliny the Younger gathered a small sympathetic crowd. As for the few scattered readers of manuscripts copied by hand and existing in perhaps a dozen copies, they, unlike the present-day readers of a newspaper or even, sometimes, of a popular novel, were not aware of forming a social aggregate. Was there a public in the Middle Ages? No, but there were fairs, pilgrimages, tumultuous multitudes dominated by pious or belligerent emotions, angers or panics. The public could begin to arise only after the first great development in the invention of printing, in the sixteenth century. The transportation of force over distance is nothing compared to this transportation of thought across distance. Is not thought the social force *par excellence?* The public as such only began to assume a definite form under Louis XIV. But although at that time there were crowds as torrential as at present, and as sizable, at royal coronations, the great holidays, and the demonstrations provoked by periodic famine, the public was scarcely anything beyond a narrow elite of "gentlefolk" (*honnêtes gens*) reading their monthly gazette, reading books, a small number of books written for a small number of readers. And the majority of these readers were in Paris, if not at court.

In the eighteenth century, this public grew rapidly and became fragmented. I do not think that there was a philosophical public distinct from the general literary public before Bayle, because I do not apply the term public to a group of scholars—united, it is true, despite their dispersion in various provinces or countries, by their preoccupation with similar investigations and the reading of the same writings, but so few in number that they can keep up an active correspondence and draw from these personal relationships the principal sustenance for their scientific communion. A special public does not take shape until that time—difficult to specify—when men given to the same study were too numerous to know each other personally and felt themselves bound only by impersonal communications of sufficient frequency and regularity. In the second half of the eighteenth century, a political public arose, grew, and soon overflowed and absorbed all the other publics—literary, philosophical, and scientific—just as a river absorbs its tributaries. Until the Revolution, however, the life of the public has little intensity of its own and only acquires importance through the life of the crowd, to which it is still connected, and through the very lively activity of the salons and cafés.

The true advent of journalism, hence that of the public, dates from the Revolution, which was one of the growing pains of the public. . . .

The revolutionary public was above all Parisian; outside Paris its influence was weak. Arthur Young, in his famous journey, was struck by seeing the public newspapers so little circulated even in the cities. Of course, this observation applies to the beginning of the Revolution; a little later it would be much less true. Until the end of the Revolution, however, the absence of rapid communication posed an insurmountable obstacle to the intensity and propagation of the life of the public. How could newspapers, arriving only two or three times a week and then a week after their publication in Paris, give readers in the south of France that feeling of immediacy and awareness of simultaneous unanimity without which the reading of a newspaper does not differ essentially from the reading of a book? It remained for our century, through its perfected means of locomotion and instantaneous transmission of thought from any distance, to give all publics the indefinite extension of which they are capable and which contrasts them so sharply with crowds. The crowd is the social group of the past; after the family it is the oldest of all social groups. Whatever its form, standing or seated, immobile or on the march, it is incapable of extension beyond a limited area; when its leaders cease to keep it in hand, when the crowd no longer hears their voices, it breaks loose. The biggest audience ever seen was in the Coliseum, and even that did not exceed 100,000 persons. . . .

But the public can be extended indefi-

nitely, and since its particular life becomes more intense as it extends, one cannot deny that it is the social group of the future. Thus three mutually auxiliary inventions—printing, the railroad, and the telegraph—combined to create the formidable power of the press, that prodigious telephone which had so inordinately enlarged the former audiences of orators and preachers. I therefore cannot agree with that vigorous writer, Dr. LeBon, that our age is the "era of crowds." It is the era of the public or of publics, and that is a very different thing. . . .

Up to a certain point, a public is confused with what we call a *world,* "the literary world," "the political world," and so forth, except that this idea implies personal contact such as an exchange of visits or receptions among those who are part of this world: this contact need not exist among the members of the same public. From the crowd to the public is an enormous leap, as we have already seen, even though the public comes in part from a type of crowd, from the orators' audience.

Between the two there are many other instructive differences which I have not yet pointed out. One can belong—and in fact one always does belong—simultaneously to several publics, as to several corporations or sects: one can only be part of one crowd at a time. From this follows the far greater intolerance of crowds, and consequently of nations dominated by the spirit of crowds, because one is completely taken over, irresistibly drawn along by a force with no counterbalance: hence the advantage of the gradual substitution of publics for crowds, a transformation which is always accompanied by progress in tolerance, if not in skepticism. Admittedly, it often happens, that an overexcited public produces fanatical crowds which run around in the streets crying "long live" or "death" to anything at all. In this sense the public could be defined as a potential crowd. But this fall from public to crowd, though extremely dangerous, is fairly rare; and without questioning whether or not these crowds which have arisen from publics are a little less brutal, on the whole, than crowds preceding any public, it remains evident that the opposition of two publics, always ready to fuse along their indistinct boundaries, is a lesser danger to social peace than the encounter of two opposing crowds. . . .

It has been contested, wrongly but not without a deceptive appearance of reason, that every crowd has a leader and that in fact it is often the crowd that leads its chief. But who will contest the fact that every public has someone who inspires it and is sometimes its creator? What Sainte-Beuve said of genius, that "genius is a king who creates his people," is especially true of the great journalist. How often one sees publicists create their own public![2] For Edouard Drumont to resuscitate anti-semitism it was necessary that his initial attempts at agitation respond to a certain state of mind among the population; but as long as no voice made itself heard, echoed and expressed this state of mind, it remained purely individual, with little intensity and even less contagion, unaware of itself. He who expressed it created it as a collective force, artificial perhaps, yet nonetheless real. I know of areas in France where the fact that no one has ever seen a single Jew does not prevent antisemitism from flowering, because people there read antisemitic papers. Nor did the socialist state of mind or the anarchist state of mind amount to anything before a few famous publicists, Karl Marx, Kropotkin, and others, expressed them and put them into circulation. Accordingly it is quite understandable that the individual stamp of its promoter's genius is more marked on a public than the genius of its nationality,

and that the opposite is true of the crowd. . . .

It may be objected that a newspaper reader is much more in control of his intellectual freedom than a lost individual swept up in a crowd. He can think about what he reads, in silence, and despite his ordinary passivity he may change newspapers until he finds the one that suits him or that he thinks will suit him. On the other hand, the journalist seeks to please him and to keep him. Statistics of circulation and subscriptions are excellent thermometers, which are often consulted and which warn the editors of the lines of behavior and thought to follow. The public, then, sometimes reacts on the journalist, but he is continually acting on his public. After a few trial runs, the reader has chosen his paper, the paper has selected its readers, there has been mutual selection, hence mutual adaptation. The one has a paper which pleases him and flatters his prejudices and passions; the other has hold of a reader to his liking, docile and credulous, whom he can easily direct with a few concessions to his positions, analogous to the oratorical precautions of the ancient orators. A crowd is, in general, much less homogeneous than a public; it always swells with many bystanders—simply curious or semi-involved —who are momentarily caught up and assimilated but succeed in making it difficult for the incoherent elements to achieve a common direction. . . .

As every supplier has two sorts of clientele, one fixed and the other floating, there are also two sorts of publics for newspapers and journals: a consolidated stable public and a floating, unstable public. The proportion of these two is very unequal from one newspaper to the next; for the older newspapers, organs of old parties, the second group does not count, or scarcely so, and I agree that here the action of the publicist is singularly hindered by the intolerance of the organization he has entered and from which he will be driven by a manifest dissidence. On the other hand, when it does occur in such a situation, his action is extremely durable and penetrating. Note, finally, that faithful publics traditionally loyal to a paper tend to disappear, being increasingly replaced by more mobile publics on which the talented journalist often has a more effective, if not more lasting, hold. This evolution of journalism can rightly be lamented, because firm publics make for honest and convinced publicists, just as capricious publics make for light, versatile, unsettling publicists; but this evolution certainly seems irresistible at present and not easily reversible, and one can see the growing resources of social power it opens up for writers. It may be that this evolution results in increasing subservience of mediocre publicists to the whims of their public, but it certainly subjugates the public more and more to the despotism of important publicists. Far more than statesmen, these men make opinion and lead the world.

Indeed, one has only to open one's eyes to see that the division of a society into publics, an entirely psychological division which corresponds to differences in states of mind, tends not to substitute itself for, but to superimpose itself more and more visibly and effectively on, divisions along economic, religious, aesthetic, political lines, and divisions into corporations, sects, professions, schools, or parties. It is not uniquely the crowds of old, the audiences of orators and preachers, that are dominated or enlarged by their corresponding publics—the parliamentary and religious publics; there is not one sect that does not wish to have its own newspaper in order to surround itself with a public extending far beyond it, causing a sort of

mobile atmosphere in which it will be bathed, a collective awareness by which it will be illuminated. And we cannot say of this awareness that it is a simple *epiphenomenon,* in itself inefficacious and inactive. Nor is there any profession, be it small or large, that does not want its own newspaper or review as well, as each corporation in the Middle Ages had its chaplain or its habitual preacher, and each class in ancient Greece its regular orator.

This transformation of any and all groups into publics can be explained by an increasing need for sociability, which necessitates the regular communication of the associates by a continual current of common information and enthusiasms. It is therefore inevitable, and it is important to seek the consequences that it has, or in all probability will have, on the destiny of the groups thus transformed, on their duration, their solidity and strength, their battles and alliances. . . .

The relative force of existing social aggregates is also singularly modified by the intervention of the press. First of all, note that the press is far from favoring a preponderance of professional classifications. The professional press, the one dedicated to the interests of the judicial, industrial, or agricultural worlds, is the least read, the least interesting, the least active, except when dealing with strikes or politics in the guise of work. What does visibly emphasize and give preponderance to the press is social division into groups by theoretical ideas, aspirations, and feelings. Interests are only expressed—and this is to its credit—when disguised or sublimated into theories and passions: even when it arouses excitement over these ideas, the press spiritualizes and idealizes them: and however dangerous this transformation may sometimes be, it is basically a fortunate one. Ideas and passions may foam up when they clash, they are still less irreconcilable than interests.

Religious or political parties are those social groups over which the newspapers have the greatest hold and to which they give the most prominence. Mobilized into publics, parties come apart, reform and transform themselves with a rapidity that would have stupefied our ancestors. And it must be agreed that their mobilization and mutual interlacing are hardly compatible with the regular functioning of English-type parliamentarianism. This is a small misfortune, but one which forces a profound modification of the parliamentary system. Sometimes the parties are reabsorbed and destroyed in a few years. Sometimes they grow to unheard-of porportions, in which case they acquire enormous, but only temporary, force. They take on two characteristics not previously seen in them: they become capable of interpenetration and internationalization. They interpenetrate easily because, as we said above, each of us does or can belong to several publics at once. They become international because the winged words of the papers easily cross borders which were never crossed by the voice of the famous orator or party leader.[3]

Thus, whatever the nature of the groups into which a society is fragmented, be they religious, economic, political, or even national, the public is in some way their final state and, so to speak, their common denominator. Everything is reduced to this entirely psychological group of states of mind in the process of perpetual mutation. It is remarkable that the professional aggregate, based on the mutual exploitation and adaptation of desires and interests, has been affected most deeply by this civilizing transformation. In spite of all the dissimilarities that we have noted, the crowd and the public, those two extremes of social evolution,[4] have in common the

bond between the diverse individuals making them up, which consists not in *harmonizing* through their very diversities, through their mutually useful specialties, but rather in reflecting, fusing through their innate or acquired similarities into a simple and powerful *unison* (but with how much more force in the public than in the crowd!), in a communion of ideas and passions which, moreover, leaves free play to their individual differences.

Public opinion

Opinion is to the modern public what the soul is to the body, and the study of one leads us naturally to the other. Might one object that public opinion has always existed whereas the public, as defined here, is fairly recent? This is certainly true, but we shall soon see how little this objection amounts to. What is opinion? How is it born? What are its various sources? While growing, how is it articulated, and by being articulated, how does it grow still further—a phenomenon illustrated by its contemporary modes of expression, universal suffrage and journalism? What is its productivity and its social significance? How is it transformed? And toward what common outlet, if there is one, do its multiple currents converge? It is to these questions that we shall essay a few answers.

Let us first say that in the word *opinion* two things are generally confused which are intermingled in practice, but which a careful analysis must distinguish: opinion proper, a totality of judgments; and the general will, a totality of desires. It is primarily but not exclusively opinion taken in the first sense that will concern us here.

However great the importance of opinion, its role must not be exaggerated. Let us try to circumscribe its domain. Opinion should not be confused with two other parts of the social mind, which both feed and limit it, and which are in perpetual border disputes with it. One is Tradition, a condensed and accumulated extract of what was the opinion of those now dead, a heritage of necessary and salutatory prejudices frequently onerous to the living. The other is what I take the liberty of calling by the collective and abbreviated name Reason. This I understand to be the relatively rational although often unreasonable personal judgments of an elite which isolates itself, reflects, and emerges from the popular stream of thought in order to dam it up or direct it. Originally priests, then philosophers, scholars, lawyers—councils, universities, law courts— are successively or simultaneously the incarnation of these resistant and directive judgments, which are clearly differentiated both from the passionate and sheeplike enthusiasms of the multitudes and from their own innermost motives or age-old principles. Well before an opinion is experienced as such, the individuals who comprise a nation are aware of possessing a common tradition and knowingly submit to the decisions of judgments deemed superior. Thus of the three branches of the public mind, Opinion is the last to develop but also the most apt to grow after a certain time; and it grows at the expense of the two others. No national institution can resist its intermittent assaults; there is not one individual judgment that does not tremble and stutter in the face of its threats or demands. Which of its two rivals does Opinion most impair? This depends on who is in control of Opinion. When those in control are part of the reasoning elite, they sometimes raise up Opinion like a battering ram to breach the ramparts of tradition, enlarging them through destruction, an act not without danger. But when the direction of the multitude is left to the firstcomers, it is easier for them, leaning on tradition, to rouse opinion against

reason, which nevertheless triumphs in the end.

All would be for the best if opinion limited itself to popularizing reason in order to consecrate it in tradition. Today's reason would thus become tomorrow's opinion and the day after tomorrow's tradition. But instead of serving as a link between its neighbors, Opinion likes to take part in their squabbles and sometimes, becoming intoxicated with new and fashionable doctrines, it pillages established ideas or institutions before it is able to replace them; sometimes, under the authority of Custom, it expulses or oppresses rational innovators, or forces them to don the hypocritical disguise of traditionalist livery.

These three forces differ as much in their causes and effects as in their natures. They work together, but very unequally and variably, to create the *value* of things; and value is very different according to whether it is primarily a question of custom or of style, or of reasoning. Later we shall affirm that conversation at all times, and the press, which at present is the principal source of conversation, are the major factors in opinion, without counting, of course, tradition and reason, which never cease to have part in it and to leave their stamp on it. The factors[5] of tradition, besides opinion itself, are family education, professional apprenticeship, and academic instruction, at least on an elementary level. In all the judicial, philosophical, scientific, and even ecclesiastical coteries where it develops, reason has as its characteristic sources observation, experience, inquiry, or in any case reasoning, deduction based on subject matter.

The battles or the alliances of these three forces, their clashes, their reciprocal trespassing, their mutual action, their multiple and varied relations are one of the keen interests of history. Social life has nothing more intestine but also nothing more productive than this long travail of often bloody opposition and adaptation. Tradition, which is always national, is more restricted between fixed limits than Opinion, but infinitely more profound and stable, for opinion is something as light, as transitory, as expansive as the wind, and always striving to become international, like reason. It can be said, in general, that the cliffs of tradition are endlessly eroded by the flow of opinion's unebbing tide. Opinion is all the stronger because tradition is weaker, which is not to say that then reason too is weaker. In the Middle Ages reason, represented by the universities, the councils, and the courts of justice, had much more strength than today to resist and repress popular opinion: it had much less strength, it is true, to fight and reform tradition. The misfortune is that contemporary Opinion has become omnipotent not only against tradition (which is serious enough) but also against reason—judicial reason, scientific reason, legislative or political reason, as the opportunity occurs. If Opinion has not invaded the laboratories of scholars—the only inviolable asylum up to now—it overwhelms tribunes of the judiciary, it submerges parliaments, and there is nothing more alarming than this deluge, whose end is not in sight.

Now that we have delimited Opinion, let us essay a better definition.

Opinion, as we define it, is a momentary more or less logical cluster of judgments which, responding to current problems, is reproduced many times over in people of the same country, at the same time, in the same society.

All these conditions are essential. It is also essential that each of these individuals be more or less aware of the similarity of his judgments with those of others: for if each one thought himself isolated in his evaluation, none of them would feel himself to be (and hence would not be) bound in close association with others like himself (unconsciously like himself). Now, in order for the consciousness of this similarity of ideas to exist among the members of a society, must not the cause of this similarity be the manifestations in words, in writing, or in the Press, of an idea that was individual at first, then gradually little by little generalized? The transformation of an individual opinion into a social opinion, into Opinion, is due to public discourse in classical times and in the Middle Ages, to the press of our own time, and at all times, most particularly, to those private conversations which we shall soon be discussing.

We say Opinion, but for every problem there are always two opinions. One of the two, however, manages to eclipse the other fairly quickly by its more rapid and striking brilliance or else because, even though less widespread, it is the more clamorous of the two.[6]

Every age, even the most barbaric, has had an opinion, but it has differed profoundly from what we call by that name. In the clan, in the tribe, even in the classical or medieval city everyone knew everyone else personally, and when, in private discussion or the speeches of orators, a common idea was established, it did not appear like a stone fallen from heaven, of impersonal and hence so much more prestigious origin: for each person the idea was linked to the tone of voice, the face, of the person from whom it had come, a person who lent it a living visage. For the same reason it served as a link only between people who, seeing and speaking to each other every day, were never deceived about each other.

For as long as the state did not extend beyond the ramparts of the city or, at most, the borders of a small canton, opinion thus formed, original, and strong,

strong sometimes against tradition itself but especially against individual judgments, played in men's government the preponderant role of the chorus in Greek tragedy, a role often assumed by modern opinion, which is of quite another origin, in our large states or in our immense and growing federations. But in the enormously long interval separating these two historical phases, the importance of opinion underwent an enormous depression, which can be explained by its disintegration into local opinions unaware of each other and without liaison.

In a feudal state, such as medieval England or France, each village, each town had its internal dissensions, its own politics. And the currents of ideas, or rather the eddies of ideas which whirled around inside these enclaves, were as different from one place to another as they were alien and indifferent to one another, at least in normal times. Not only were local politics absorbing in these places, but to the extent, the small extent, that there was interest in national politics, it was only among acquaintances, and there was only the vaguest notion of the way in which the same questions were resolved in neighboring villages. It was not Opinion that existed but thousands of separate opinions with no continuous link between them.

This link was not provided until the advent, first, of books, and then (and with greater efficacy) newspapers. The periodical press enabled these primary groups of similar individuals to form a secondary and far superior aggregate, whose units were closely bound without personal contact. From this situation arose important differences—among others, this one: in the primary groups the voices *ponderantur* rather than *numerantur,* while in the secondary and much larger group, adhered to blindly by individuals who cannot see one another, voices can only be counted and

not weighed. Unconsciously the press thus worked to create the strength of numbers and to reduce that of character, if not of intelligence.

At the same time it suppressed the conditions which made possible the absolute power of the governing group. This power was greatly favored, in actuality, by the local splitting of opinion: even more, it found here its raison d'être and justification. What kind of a country is it whose various regions, cities, towns are not linked by a collective consciousness of their unity of views? Is it really a nation? Is it anything more than a geographical or, at most, political expression? Yes, it is a nation but only in the sense that political submission of these various factions of a realm to the same chief is already nationalism. In the France of Philip the Fair,[7] for example, with the exception of a few rare occasions when a common danger preoccupied all the cities and fiefs, there was no *public mind* (*esprit public*), there were only local minds aroused separately by their own fixed ideas or passions. But through his administrators the king was aware of these diverse states of mind; he assembled them in his person, as it were, and in his own summary knowledge of them, which served as a basis for his plans, he thus unified them.

It was a fragile unification, an imperfect one, to be sure, which gave to the king only a vague awareness of what was general in local preoccupations. His person was the only area of their mutual penetration. When the Estates-General were convened, a new step was taken toward the nationalization of regional and local opinion. In the mind of each deputy these opinions met, and found themselves similar or dissimilar; and the entire country, its eyes on its deputies, interested to a small (infinitely smaller than today) degree in their work, then created the unusual (at that time) spectacle of a nation aware of itself. And this intermittent, exceptional consciousness was very vague, as well as slow and obscure. The meetings of the Estates-General were not public. In any case, for want of a press the discussions were not published, and, lacking even postal service, letters could not make up for this absence of newspapers. In short, it became known through sometimes distorted news passed from mouth to mouth, after weeks and months, from travelers on horseback and on foot, wandering monks and merchants, that the Estates-General had met, and that they had considered such and such a subject—and that was all.

Note that the members of these assemblies, during their short and infrequent meetings, themselves formed a local group, the site of an intense local opinion, born contagiously from meeting man to man, from personal relationships, from reciprocal influences. And it was owing to this superior, temporary, elective local group that the inferior, permanent hereditary local groups composed of relatives or traditional friends in the towns and fiefs felt themselves united in transitory alliance.

The development of the mails by multiplying first public then private correspondence, the development of highways by multiplying new contacts between people, the development of permanent armies by making soldiers from all the provinces fraternize with each other, and finally the development of courts by drawing the aristocratic elite from all corners of the earth to the monarchical center of the nation—all had the effect of gradually developing the public mind (*l'esprit public*). But it remained for the printing press to extend this great work to the fullest. It was for the press, once it had reached the stage of newspaper, to make national, European, even cosmic, any-thing local which, despite its possible intrinsic interest, formerly would have remained unknown beyond a limited range. . . .

Let us try to be more precise. In a large society divided into nations, subdivided into provinces, fiefs, and cities, international opinion, arising every now and then, has always existed, even before the press: beneath international opinion are national opinions, still intermittent but already more frequent; beneath national opinions are the almost continuous regional and local opinions. These are the superimposed strata of the public mind. But the proportions of these diverse layers have varied considerably with regard to importance and depth, and it is easy to see how. The farther back one goes into the past, the more local opinion is predominant. The work of journalism has been to nationalize more and more, and even to internationalize, the public mind.

Journalism both sucks in and pumps out information, which, coming in from all corners of the earth in the morning, is directed, the same day, back out to all the corners of the earth, insofar as the journalist defines what is or appears to be interesting about it, given the goals he is pursuing and the party for which he speaks. His information is in reality a force which little by little becomes irresistible. Newspapers began by expressing opinion, first the completely local opinion of privileged groups, a court, a parliament, a capital, whose gossip, discussions, or debates they reproduced; they ended up directing opinion almost as they wished, modeling it, and imposing the majority of their daily topics upon conversation.

Notes

1. "Psychologie des foules," which Tarde uses here, is usually rendered as mass or mob psychology;

in keeping with Tarde's thought in this essay, we have given the more literal translations.—Ed.

2. Will it be said that if every publicist creates his public every sizable public creates its publicist? This second proposition is much less true than the first; there are large groups which for many years do not succeed in bringing forward the writer adapted to their true orientation. Such is the case with the Catholic world at present.

3. Certain large newspapers, the *Times*, the *Figaro*, and certain journals have their public spread throughout the entire world. The religious, scientific, economic, and aesthetic *publics* are essentially and constantly international; religious, scientific, etc. crowds are so only rarely, in the form of a congress. And the congresses could only become international because they were preceded in this direction by their respective publics.

4. The family and the horde are the two points of departure of this evolution. But the horde, the gross,

pillaging band, is only the crowd in motion.

5. This word *factor* (*facteur*) is ambiguous: it means *channel* or *source*. Here it means channel, because conversation and education only transmit the ideas which constitute opinion or tradition. *Sources* are always individual initiatives, small or great inventions.

6. However widespread an opinion may be, it is never *manifest* if it is moderate; but however narrowly held a violent opinion may be, it is very *manifest*. Now the "manifestations," expressions which are at once all-inclusive and very clear, play an immense role in the fusion and interpenetration of opinions of various groups and in their propagation. It is the most violent opinions which, through manifestation, are soonest and most clearly aware of their coexistence, and thus their expansion is strangely favored.

7. 1268-1314, king of France who convoked the first Estates-General (1302).—Ed.

3.

Robert E. Park and Ernest W. Burgess

COLLECTIVE BEHAVIOR

A collection of individuals is not always, and by the mere fact of its collectivity, a society. On the other hand, when people come together anywhere, in the most casual way, on the street corner or at a railway station, no matter how great the social distances between them, the mere fact that they are aware of one another's presence sets up a lively exchange of influences, and the behavior that ensues is both social and collective. It is social, at the very least, in the sense that the train of thought and action in each individual is influenced more or less by the action of every other. It is collective in so far as each individual acts under the influence of a

mood or a state of mind in which each shares, and in accordance with conventions which all quite unconsciously accept, and which the presence of each enforces upon the others.

The amount of individual eccentricity or deviation from normal and accepted modes of behavior which a community will endure without comment and without protest will vary naturally enough with the character of the community. A cosmopolitan community like New York City can and does endure a great deal in the way of individual eccentricity that a smaller city like Boston would not tolerate. In any case, and this is the point of these observations, even in the most casual relations of life, people do not behave in the presence of others as if they were living alone like Robinson Crusoe, each on his individual island. The very fact of their

Originally published in Robert E. Park and Ernest W. Burgess, *Introduction to the Science of Sociology* (Chicago: University of Chicago Press, 2d ed., 1924), pp. 865-78, with the permission of the publisher.

consciousness of each other tends to maintain and enforce a great body of convention and usage which otherwise falls into abeyance and is forgotten. Collective behavior, then, is the behavior of individuals under the influence of an impulse that is common and collective, an impulse, in other words, that is the result of social interaction.

I. Social unrest and collective behavior

The most elementary form of collective behavior seems to be what is ordinarily referred to as "social unrest." Unrest in the individual becomes social when it is, or seems to be, transmitted from one individual to another, but more particularly when it produces something akin to the milling process in the herd, so that the manifestations of discontent in A communicated to B, and from B reflected back to A, produce the circular reaction.

The significance of social unrest is that it represents at once a breaking up of the established routine and a preparation for new collective action. Social unrest is not of course a new phenomenon; it is possibly true, however, that it is peculiarly characteristic, as has been said, of modern life. The contrast between the conditions of modern life and of primitive society suggests why this may be true.

The conception which we ought to form of primitive society, says Sumner, is that of small groups scattered over a territory. The size of the group will be determined by the conditions of the struggle for existence and the internal organization of each group will correspond (1) to the size of the group, and (2) to the nature and intensity of the struggle with its neighbors.

Thus war and peace have reacted on each other and developed each other, one within the group, the other in the intergroup relation. The

closer the neighbors, and the stronger they are, the intenser is the warfare, and then the intenser is the internal organization and discipline of each. Sentiments are produced to correspond. Loyalty to the group, sacrifice for it, hatred and contempt for outsiders, brotherhood within, warlikeness without—all grow together, common products of the same situation. These relations and sentiments constitute a social philosophy. It is sanctified by connection with religion. Men of an others-group are outsiders with whose ancestors the ancestors of the we-group waged war. The ghosts of the latter will see with pleasure their descendants keep up the fight, and will help them. Virtue consists in killing, plundering, and enslaving outsiders.[1]

The isolation, territorial and cultural, under which alone it is possible to maintain an organization which corresponds to Sumner's description, has disappeared within comparatively recent times from all the more inhabitable portions of the earth. In place of it there has come, and with increasing rapidity is coming, into existence a society which includes within its limits the total population of the earth and is so intimately bound together that the speculation of a grain merchant in Chicago may increase the price of bread in Bombay, while the act of an assassin in a provincial town in the Balkans has been sufficient to plunge the world into a war which changed the political map of three continents and cost the lives, in Europe alone, of 8,500,000 combatants.

The first effect of modern conditions of life has been to increase and vastly complicate the economic interdependence of strange and distant peoples, i.e., to destroy distances and make the world, as far as national relations are concerned, small and tight.

The second effect has been to break down family, local, and national ties, and emancipate the individual man.

When the family ceases, as it does in the city, to be an economic unit, when parents and children have vocations that not only intercept the traditional relations of family life, but make them well nigh impossible, the family ceases to function as an organ of social control. When the different nationalities, with their different national cultures, have so far interpenetrated one another that each has permanent colonies within the territorial limits of the other, it is inevitable that the old solidarities, the common loyalties and the common hatreds that formerly bound men together in primitive kinship and local groups should be undermined.

A survey of the world today shows that vast changes are everywhere in progress. Not only in Europe but in Asia and in Africa new cultural contacts have undermined and broken down the old cultures. The effect has been to loosen all the social bonds and reduce society to its individual atoms. The energies thus freed have produced a world-wide ferment. Individuals released from old associations enter all the more readily into new ones. Out of this confusion new and strange political and religious movements arise, which represent the groping of men for a new social order.

II. The crowd and the public

Gustave LeBon, who was the first writer to call attention to the significance of the crowd as a social phenomenon,[2] said that mass movements mark the end of an old regime and the beginning of a new.

"When the structure of a civilization is rotten, it is always the masses that bring about its downfall."[3] On the other hand, "all founders of religious or political creeds have established them solely because they were successful in inspiring crowds with those fanatical sentiments which have as result that men find their happiness in worship and obedience and are ready to lay down their lives for their idol."[4]

The crowd was, for LeBon, not merely any group brought together by the accident of some chance excitement, but it was above all the emancipated masses whose bonds of loyalty to the old order had been broken by "the destruction of those religious, political, and social beliefs in which all the elements of our civilization are rooted." The crowd, in other words, typified for LeBon the existing social order. Ours is an age of crowds, he said, an age in which men, massed and herded together in great cities without real convictions or fundamental faiths, are likely to be stampeded in any direction for any chance purpose under the influence of any passing excitement.

LeBon did not attempt to distinguish between the crowd and the public. This distinction was first made by Tarde in a paper entitled "Le Public et la foule," published first in *La Revue de Paris* in 1898, and included with several others on the same general theme under the title *L'Opinion et la foule* which appeared in 1901. The public, according to Tarde, was a product of the printing press. The limits of the crowd are determined by the length to which a voice will carry or the distance that the eye can survey. But the public presupposes a higher stage of social development in which suggestions are transmitted in the form of ideas and there is "contagion without contact."[5]

The fundamental distinction between the crowd and the public, however, is not to be measured by numbers nor by means of communication, but by the form and effects of the interactions. In the public, interaction takes the form of discussion. Individuals tend to act upon one another critically; issues are raised and parties form. Opinions clash and thus modify and moderate one another.

The crowd does not discuss and hence it does not reflect. It simply "mills." Out of this milling process a collective impulse is formed which dominates all members of the crowd. Crowds, when they act, do so impulsively. The crowd, says LeBon, "is the slave of its impulses."

"The varying impulses which crowds obey may be, according to their exciting causes, generous or cruel, heroic or cowardly, but they will always be so imperious that the interest of the individual, even the interest of self-preservation, will not dominate them."[6]

When the crowd acts it becomes a mob. What happens when two mobs meet? We have in the literature no definite record. The nearest approach to it are the occasional accounts we find in the stories of travelers of the contacts and conflicts of armies of primitive peoples. These undisciplined hordes are, as compared with the armies of civilized peoples, little more than armed mobs. Captain S. L. Hinde in his story of the Belgian conquest of the Congo describes several such battles. From the descriptions of battles carried on almost wholly between savage and undisciplined troops it is evident that the morale of an army of savages is a precarious thing. A very large part of the warfare consists in alarms and excursions interspersed with wordy duels to keep up the courage on one side and cause a corresponding depression on the other.[7]

Gangs are conflict groups. Their organization is usually quite informal and is determined by the nature and imminence of the conflicts with other groups. When one crowd encounters another it either goes to pieces or it changes its character and becomes a conflict group. When negotiations and palavers take place as they eventually do between conflict groups, these two groups, together with the neutrals who have participated vicariously in the conflict, constitute a public. It is possible that the two opposing savage hordes which seek, by threats and boastings and

beatings of drums, to play upon each other's fears and so destroy each other's morale, may be said to constitute a very primitive type of public.

Discussion, as might be expected, takes curious and interesting forms among primitive peoples. In a volume, *Iz Derevni: 12 Pisem* ("From the Country: 12 Letters"), A. N. Engelgardt describes the way in which the Slavic peasants reach their decisions in the village council.

In the discussion of some questions by the *mir* [organization of neighbors] there are no speeches, no debates, no votes. They shout, they abuse one another—they seem on the point of coming to blows; apparently they riot in the most senseless manner. Some one preserves silence, and then suddenly puts in a word, one word, or an ejaculation, and by this word, this ejaculation he turns the whole thing upside down. In the end, you look into it and find that an admirable decision has been formed and, what is most important, a unanimous decision. . . . (In the division of land) the cries, the noise, the hubbub do not subside until everyone is satisfied and no doubter is left.[8]

III. Crowds and sects

Reference has been made to the crowds that act, but crowds do not always act. Sometimes they merely dance or, at least, make expressive motions which relieve their feelings. "The purest and most typical expression of simple feeling," as Hirn remarks, "is that which consists of mere random movements."[9] When these motions assume, as they so easily do, the character of a fixed sequence in time, that is to say when they are rhythmical, they can be and inevitably are, as by a sort of inner compulsion, initiated by onlookers. "As soon as the expression is fixed in rhythmical form its contagious power is incalculably increased."[10]

This explains at once the function and social importance of the dance among primitive people. It is the form in which they prepare for battle and celebrate their victories. It gives the form at once to their religious ritual and to their art. Under the influence of the memories and the emotions which these dances stimulate the primitive group achieves a sense of corporate unity, which makes corporate action possible outside of the fixed and sacred routine or ordinary daily life.

If it is true, as has been suggested, that art and religion had their origin in the choral dance, it is also true that in modern times religious sects and social movements have had their origin in crowd excitements and spontaneous mass movements. The very names which have been commonly applied to them—Quakers, Shakers, Convulsionaires, Holy Rollers—suggest not merely the derision with which they were at one time regarded, but indicate likewise their origin in ecstatic or expressive crowds, the crowds that *do not act.*

All great mass movements tend to display, to a greater or less extent, the characteristics that LeBon attributes to crowds. Speaking of the convictions of crowds, LeBon says:

When these convictions are closely examined, whether at epochs marked by fervent religious faith, or by great political upheavals such as those of the last century, it is apparent that they always assume a peculiar form which I cannot better define than by giving it the name of a religious sentiment.[11]

LeBon's definition of religion and religious sentiment will hardly find general acceptance but it indicates at any rate his conception of the extent to which individual personalities are involved in the excitements that accompany mass movements.

A person is not religious solely when he worships a divinity, but when he puts all the resources of his mind, the complete submission of his will, and the whole-souled ardour of fanaticism at the service of a cause or an individual who becomes the goal and guide of his thoughts and actions.[12]

Just as the gang may be regarded as the perpetuation and permanent form of "the crowd that acts," so the sect, religious or political, may be regarded as a perpetuation and permanent form of the orgiastic (ecstatic) or expressive crowd.

"The sect," says Sighele, "is a crowd *triee,* selected, and permanent; the crowd is a transient sect, which does not select its members. The sect is the *chronic* form of the crowd; the crowd is the *acute* form of the sect."[13] It is Sighele's conception that the crowd is an elementary organism, from which the sect issues, like the chick from the egg, and that all other types of social groups "may, in this same manner, be deduced from this primitive social protoplasm." This is a simplification which the facts hardly justify. It is true that, implicit in the practices and the doctrines of a religious sect, there is the kernel of a new independent culture.

IV. Sects and institutions

A sect is a religious organization that is at war with the existing mores. It seeks to cultivate a state of mind and establish a code of morals different from that of the world about it and for this it claims divine authority. In order to accomplish this end it invariably seeks to set itself off in contrast with the rest of the world. The simplest and most effective way to achieve this is to adopt a peculiar form of dress and speech. This, however, invariably makes its members objects of scorn and derision, and eventually of persecution. It would probably do this even if there was no assumption of moral superiority to the rest of the world in this adoption of a peculiar manner and dress.

Persecution tends to dignify and sanctify all the external marks of the sect, and it becomes a cardinal principle of the sect to maintain them. Any neglect of them is regarded as disloyalty and is punished as heresy. Persecution may eventually, as was the case with the Puritans, the Quakers, the Mormons, compel the sect to seek refuge in some part of the world where it may practice its way of life in peace.

Once the sect has achieved territorial isolation and territorial solidarity, so that it is the dominant power within the region that it occupies, it is able to control the civil organization, establish schools and a press, and so put the impress of a peculiar culture upon all the civil and political institutions that it controls. In this case it tends to assume the form of a state, and become a nationality. Something approaching this was achieved by the Mormons in Utah. The most striking illustration of the evolution of a nationality from a sect is Ulster, which now has a position not quite that of a nation within the English empire.

This sketch suggests that the sect, like most other social institutions, originates under conditions that are typical for all institutions of the same species; then it develops in definite and predictable ways, in accordance with a form or entelechy that is predetermined by characteristic internal process and mechanisms, and that has, in short, a nature and natural history which can be described and explained in sociological terms. Sects have their origin in social unrest to which they give a direction and expression in forms and practices that are largely determined by historical circumstances; movements which were at first inchoate impulses and aspirations gradually take form; policies are defined, doctrine and dogmas formulated; and eventually an administrative machinery and efficiencies are developed to carry into effect policies and purposes. The Salvation Army, of which we have a more adequate history than of most other religious movements, is an example.

A sect in its final form may be described, then, as a movement of social reform and regeneration that has become institutionalized. Eventually, when it has succeeded in accommodating itself to the other rival organizations, when it has become tolerant and is tolerated, it tends to assume the form of a denomination. Denominations tend and are perhaps destined to unite in the form of religious federations—a thing which is inconceivable of a sect.

What is true of the sect, we may assume, and must assume if social movements are to become subjects for sociological investigation, is true of other social institutions. Existing institutions represent social movements that survived the conflict of cultures and the struggle for existence.

Sects, and that is what characterizes and distinguishes them from secular institutions, at least, have had their origin in movements that aimed to reform the mores—movements that sought to renovate and renew the inner life of the community. They have wrought upon society from within outwardly. Revolutionary and reform movements, on the contrary, have been directed against the outward fabric and formal structure of society. Revolutionary movements in particular have assumed that if the existing structure could be destroyed it would then be possible to erect a new moral order upon the ruins of the old social structures.

A cursory survey of the history of revolutions suggests that the most radical and the most successful of them have been religious. Of this type of revolution Christianity is the most conspicuous example.

V. Classification of the materials

The materials in this chapter have been arranged under the headings: (a) social contagion, (b) the crowd, and (c) types of mass movements. The order of materials follows, in a general way, the order of institutional evolution. Social unrest is first communicated, then takes form in crowd and mass movements, and finally crystallizes in institutions. The history of almost any single social movement—woman's suffrage, prohibition, protestantism—exhibits in a general way, if not in detail, this progressive change in character. There is at first a vague general discontent and distress. Then a violent, confused, and disorderly, but enthusiastic and popular movement arises. Finally the movement takes form; develops leadership, organization; formulates doctrines and dogmas. Eventually it is accepted, established, legalized. The movement dies, but the institution remains.

a) Social contagion

The ease and the rapidity with which a cultural trait originating in one cultural group finds its way to other distant groups is familiar to students of folklore and ethnology. The manner in which fashions are initiated in some metropolitan community, and thence make their way, with more or less rapidity, to the provinces is an illustration of the same phenomenon in a different context.

Fashion plays a much larger role in social life than most of us imagine. Fashion dominates our manners and dress but it influences also our sentiments and our modes of thought. Everything in literature, art or philosophy that was characteristic of the middle of the nineteenth century, the "mid-Victorian period," is now quite out of date and no one who is intelligent now-a-days practices the pruderies, defends the doctrines, nor shares the enthusiasms of that period. Philosophy, also, changes with the fashion and Sumner says that even mathematics and science do the same. Lecky in his history of Rationalism in Europe describes in great detail how the belief in witches, so characteristic of the Middle Ages, gradually disappeared with the period of enlightenment and progress.[14] But the enlightenment of the eighteenth century was itself a fashion and is now quite out of date. In the meantime a new popular and scientific interest is growing up in obscure mental phenomena which no man with scientific training would have paid any attention to a few years ago because he did not believe in such things. It was not good form to do so.

But the changes of fashion are so pervasive, so familiar, and, indeed, universal phenomena that we do not regard the changes which they bring, no matter how fantastic, as quite out of the usual and expected order. Gabriel Tarde, however, regards the "social contagion" represented in fashion (imitation) as the fundamental social phenomenon.[15]

The term social epidemic, which is, like fashion, a form of social contagion, has a different origin and a different connotation. J. F. C. Hecker, whose study of the Dancing Mania of the Middle Ages, published in 1832, was an incident of his investigation of the Black Death, was perhaps the first to give currency to the term.[16] Both the Black Death and the Dancing Mania assumed the form of epidemics and the latter, the Dancing Mania, was in his estimation the sequel of the former, the Black Death. It was perhaps this similarity in the manner in which they spread—the one by physical and the other by psychical infection—that led him to speak of the spread of a popular delusion in terms of a physical science. Furthermore, the hysteria was directly traceable, as he believed, to the prevailing conditions of the time, and this seemed to put the manifestations in the world of intelligible and controllable phenomena, where they could be investigated.

It is this notion, then, that unrest which manifests itself in social epidemics is an indication of pathological social conditions, and the further, the more general, conception that unrest does not become social and hence contagious except when there are contributing causes in the environment—it is this that gives its special significance to the term and the facts. Unrest in the social organism with the social ferments that it induces is like fever in the individual organism, a highly important diagnostic symptom.

b) The crowd

Neither LeBon nor any of the other writers upon the subject of mass psychology has succeeded in distinguishing clearly between the organized or "psychological" crowd, as LeBon calls it, and other similar types of social groups. These distinctions, if they are to be made objectively, must be made on the basis of case studies. It is the purpose of the materials under the general heading of "The 'Animal' Crowd," not so much to furnish a definition, as to indicate the nature and sources of materials from which a definition can be formulated. It is apparent that the different animal groups behave in ways that are distinctive and characteristic, ways which are predetermined in the organism to an extent that is not true of human beings.

One other distinction may possibly be made between the so-called "animal" and the human crowd. The organized crowd is controlled by a *common purpose* and acts to achieve, no matter how vaguely it is defined, a common end. The herd, on the other hand, has apparently no common purpose. Every sheep in the flock, at least

as the behavior of the flock is ordinarily interpreted, behaves like every other. Action in a stampede, for example, is collective but it is not concerted. It is very difficult to understand how there can be concerted action in the herd or the flock unless it is on an instinctive basis. The crowd, however, responds to collective representations. The crowd does not imitate or follow its leader as sheep do a bellwether. On the contrary, the crowd *carries out the suggestions of the leader,* and even though there be no division of labor each individual acts more or less in his own way to achieve a common end.

In the case of a panic or a stampede, however, where there is no common end, the crowd acts like a flock of sheep. But a stampede or a panic is not a crowd in LeBon's sense. It is not a psychological unity, nor a "single being," subject to "the mental unity of crowds.[17] The panic is the crowd in dissolution. All effective methods for dispersing crowds involve some method of distracting attention, breaking up the tension, and dissolving the mob into its individual units.

c) Types of mass movements

The most elementary form of mass movement is a mass migration. Such a mass movement displays, in fact, many of the characteristics of the "animal" crowd. It is the "human" herd. The migration of a people, either as individuals or in organized groups, may be compared to the swarming of the hive. Peoples migrate in search of better living conditions, or merely in search of new experience. It is usually the younger generation, the more restless, active, and adaptable, who go out from the security of the old home to seek their fortunes in the new. Once settled on the new land, however, immigrants inevitably remember and idealize the home they have left. Their first disposition is to reproduce as far as possible in the new world the institutions and the social order of the old. Just as the spider spins his web out of his own body, so the immigrant tends to spin out of his experience and traditions, a social organization which reproduces, as far as circumstances will permit, the organization and the life of the ancestral community. In this way the older culture is transplanted and renews itself, under somewhat altered circumstances, in the new home. That explains, in part, at any rate, the fact that migration tends to follow the isotherms, since all the more fundamental cultural devices and experience are likely to be accommodations to geographical and climatic conditions.

In contrast with migrations are movements which are sometimes referred to as crusades, partly because of the religious fervor and fanaticism with which they are usually conducted and partly because they are an appeal to the masses of the people for direct action and depend for their success upon their ability to appeal to some universal human interest or to common experiences and interests that are keenly comprehended by the common man.

The Woman's Christian Temperance Crusade, referred to in the materials, may be regarded, if we are permitted to compare great things with small, as an illustration of collective behavior not unlike the crusades of the eleventh and twelfth centuries.

Crusades are reformatory and religious. This was true at any rate of the early crusades, inspired by Peter the Hermit, whatever may have been the political purposes of the popes who encouraged them. It was the same motive that led the people of the Middle Ages to make pilgrimages which led them to join the crusades. At bottom it was an inner restlessness, that sought peace in great hardship and inspiring action, which moved the masses.

Somewhat the same widespread contagious restlessness is the source of most of our revolutions. It is not, however, hardships and actual distress that inspire revolutions but hopes and dreams, dreams which find expression in those myths and "vital lies," as Vernon Lee calls them,[18] which according to Sorel are the only means of moving the masses.

The distinction between crusades, like the Woman's Temperance Crusade, and revolutions, like the French Revolution, is that one is a radical attempt to correct a recognized evil and the other is a radical attempt to reform an existing social order.

Notes

1. W. G. Sumner, *Folkways* (Boston, 1906), pp. 12-13.
2. Scipio Sighele, in a note to the French edition of his *Psychology of Sects,* claims that his volume, *La Folla delinquente,* of which the second edition was published at Turin in 1895, and his article "Physiologie du succès," in the *Revue des Revues,* October 1, 1894, were the first attempts to describe the crowd from the point of view of collective psychology. LeBon published two articles, "Psychologie des foules" in the *Revue scientifique,* April 6 and 20, 1895. These were later gathered together in his volume *Psychologie des foules,* Paris, 1895. See Sighele, *Psychologie des sectes,* pp. 25, 39.
3. Gustave LeBon, *The Crowd: A study of the popular mind.* (New York, 1900), p. 19.
4. *Ibid.,* p. 83.
5. *L'Opinion et la foule* (Paris, 1901), pp. 6-7.
6. *The Crowd,* p. 41.
7. Sidney L. Hinde, *The Fall of the Congo Arabs* (London, 1897), p. 147. Describing a characteristic incident in one of the strange confused battles Hinde says: "Wordy war, which also raged, had even more effect than our rifles. Mahomedi and Sefu led the Arabs, who were jeering and taunting Lutete's people, saying that they were in a bad case, and had better desert the white man, who was ignorant of the fact that Mohara with all the forces of Nyange was camped in his rear. Lutete's people replied: 'Oh, we know all about Mohara; we ate him the day before yesterday.'" This news became all the more depress-

ing when it turned out to be true. See also Hirn, *The Origins of Art*, p. 269, for an explanation of the role of threats and boastings in savage warfare.

8. Robert E. Park and Herbert A. Miller, *Old World Traits Transplanted* (New York, 1921), Document 23, pp. 32-33.

9. Yrjo Hirn, *The Origins of Art* (London, 1900), p. 87. A psychological and sociological inquiry.

10. *Ibid.*, p. 80.

11. LeBon, p. 82.

12. *Ibid.*, p. 83.

13. Scipio Sighele, *Psychologie des sectes* (Paris, 1898), p. 46.

14. W. E. H. Lecky, *History of the Rise and Influence of the Spirit of Rationalism in Europe* (New York, 1866), vol. I.

15. See Gabriel Tarde, *Laws of Imitation*.

16. J. F. C. Hecker, *Die Tanzwuth, eine Volkskrankheit im Mittelater.* (Berlin, 1832.) See Introduction of *The Black Death and the Dancing Mania*. Translated from the German by B. G. Babington. Cassell's National Library. (New York, 1888.)

17. LeBon, p. 26.

18. Vernon Lee [pseud.], *Vital Lies* (London, 1912). Studies of some varieties of recent obscurantism.

4.

Georg Simmel

THE NUMBER OF PERSONS AS DETERMINING THE FORM OF THE GROUP

In respect to the fundamental problem which appears to me solely to form the basis of a sociology as a distinct science, I indicate here merely that this problem rests upon the distinction between the content or purpose of socializations, and the form of the same. The content is economic or religious, domestic or political, intellectual or volitional, pedagogic or convivial. That these purposes and interests, however, attain to realization in the form of a society, of the companionship and the reciprocity of individuals, is the subject-matter of special scientific consideration. That men build a society means that they live for the attainment of those purposes in definitely formed interactions. If there is to be a science of society as such, it must therefore abstract those forms from the complex phenomena of societary life, and it must make them the subject of deter-

mination and explanation. Those contents are already treated by special sciences, historical and systematic; the relationships, however, of men to each other, which in the case of the most diverse purposes may be the same, and in the case of like purposes may be most various—these have not as yet been the subject-matter of a particular science; and yet such a science, when constituted, would for the first time make manifest what it is which makes the society—that is, the totality of historical life—into society.

It will be conceded at the first glance, without hesitation, that the sociological structure of a group is essentially modified by the number of the individuals that are united in it. It is an everyday experience— yes, it is almost to be construed from the most general social-psychological presuppositions—that a group of a certain extent and beyond a certain stage in its increase of numbers must develop for its maintenance certain forms and organization which it did not previously need; and that,

Abridged from Simmel, Georg. "The Number of Members as Determining the Sociological Form of the Group," *American Journal of Sociology*, 1902, 1-46 and 158-96, with permission of the publisher.

on the other hand, more restricted groups manifest qualities and reciprocal activities which, in the case of their numerical extension, inevitably disappear. A double significance attaches itself to the quantitative determination: first, the negative significance that certain forms which are necessary or possible from the contents or the conditions of life can come to realization only before or after a certain numerical extension of the elements; the positive significance that other forms are promoted directly through definite and purely quantitative modifications of the group. As a matter of course, these do not emerge in every case, but they depend upon other social circumstances in the group. The decisive matter, however, is that the forms in question never spring from these latter conditions alone, but are produced from them only through the accompanying numerical factor. Thus it may be demonstrated that quite or nearly communistic formations have up to the present day been possible only in relatively small circles, while they have always failed in large groups. The presumption of such socialistic groups—namely, justice in the distribution of effort and of enjoyment—can no doubt be established in a small group, and, what is at least quite as important, it can be observed and controlled by the individuals. What each does for the totality, and wherewith the totality rewards him, is in such cases close at hand, so that comparison and equalization easily occur. In a great group this practice is hindered, particularly by the unavoidable differentiation of persons within it, of their functions and of their claims. A very large number of people can constitute a unity only with decisive division of labor, not merely on the obvious grounds of economic technique, but because this alone produces that interpenetration and interdependence of persons which puts each through innumerable intermediaries in combination with each, and without which a widely extended group would break apart on every occasion. Consequently the more intimate the unity demanded in the same, the more exact must be the specialization of individuals, in order that the individuals may be the more immediately responsible to the whole, and the whole may be dependent upon the individuals. The communism of a great community would thus promote the sharpest differentiation of the personalities, which would naturally extend over and beyond their labor, to their feeling and desiring. Hence a comparison of services with each other, of rewards with each other, and equilibration of the two, is infinitely difficult; but upon this the feasibility of approximate communism for small, and therefore undifferentiated circles rests. What limits such circles, under advanced culture, by a sort of logical necessity, so to speak, to restricted numerical extent, is their dependence upon goods which under their peculiar productive conditions can never be furnished.

A previously calculated, mechanically working life-system, in which every detail is regulated according to general principles, can be applied, to be sure, in a small circle which can draw from a greater one whatever it requires for the establishment of its internal equilibrium. But human needs appear to contain an accidental or incalculable element, and this fact permits their satisfaction only at the cost of carrying on parallel activities which produce countless irrational and unavailable by-products. A circle, therefore, which avoids this, and confines itself to complete responsibility and utility in its activities, must always remain minute, because it has need of a greater group in order to be reinforced with the requisite capacity for life.

Small and centripetally organized groups usually call out and employ to their full extent the energies available within them; in greater groups, on the other hand, much more energy, not merely absolutely but also relatively, remains in a latent condition. The demand of the whole does not seize upon every member constantly and completely, and it permits much power to remain unused which then, in extreme cases, may be mobilized and actualized. The decisive thing in this case is, as indicated, the social centripetalism, that is, the ratio in which the energies present in the society are harnessed for its purposes. When it, therefore, occurs that a lower and smaller group allows its members much autonomy and independence, the latter then often develop energies which are not used socially, and, therefore, in case the appeal to the common interests occurs, they represent a considerable available recourse. This was for a long time the case, for example, with the nobility of the Scotch highlands. Likewise, on the other hand, where dangers, which demand an unused quantity of social energy, are excluded by the circumstances, means of numerical limitation, which extend even beyond endogamy, may be quite appropriate. The dangers of the quantitative limitation are provided against by the external conditions of the life of the group, and their consequences for its inner structure.

Where the small group absorbs the personalities in considerable measure into its unity, especially in political groups, it strives, precisely for the sake of its unity, for definiteness of status toward persons, material tasks, and other societies. The large group, with the number and variety of its elements, demands or tolerates such definiteness much less. It is precisely that absence of organs, or reserves, of undefined and transitional elements, which makes modification and adaptation difficult for them, and, apart from their external conditions, forces them, on account of their fundamental sociological configuration, much oftener to confront the question, "To be or not to be?"

By the side of such tendencies in small circles I cite, with the same unavoidable arbitrary selection from innumerable cases, the following for the sociological characterization of greater circles. I start from the fact that these, compared with smaller circles, seem to show an inferior degree of radicalism and obstinacy of attitude. This, however, requires a limitation. Precisely where great masses must be set in motion in political, social, and religious movements, they show a ruthless radicalism, a victory of the extreme parties over the mediating. This is primarily for the reason that great masses are always filled merely with simple ideas, and can be led by such only. What is common to many must for that reason be of a sort which the lowest, most primitive minds among them can entertain. And even higher and more differentiated personalities will approach each other in great numbers, not in the more complicated and highly elaborated, but only in the relatively simple universal human conceptions and impulses. Since, however, the actualities in which the ideas of the mass strive to become practical are always articulated in a very multifold way, and are composed of a great assemblage of very divergent elements, it follows that simple ideas can work only in an entirely one-sided, ruthless, and radical fashion. This fact is accentuated in case the behavior of a crowd in actual physical contact is in question. Under such circumstances, the innumerable suggestions working back and forth produce an extraordinarily intense nervous excitement, which often deprives the individual of his senses, and drags him along as though he were unconscious. It inflates every impulse, often in a freakish manner, and makes the mob the prey of the most passionate personality in its number. This melting of masses into *one* feeling, in which all peculiarity and reserves of personalities are suspended, is naturally in its content so thoroughgoing, so radical, so alien to all mediation and consideration, that it would lead to sheer impracticabilities and destructions, if it did not usually find its end at an earlier stage from inner wearinesses and reactions, the consequence of this one-sided exaggeration. More than that, the masses, in the sense now in mind, have little to lose. On the contrary, they believe, so to speak, that they have everything to gain. This is the situation in which most of the restraints of radicalism habitually fall away; in this unorganized mass which consists of human beings with their immediate reciprocities, without a super-individual unity and form, those indefinitenesses, many-sidednesses, and mediatorial phenomena are lacking through which the great community ordinarily is distinguished from the small one. In order to form themselves upon the periphery of a community, they need precisely a stable center of the same, an objective social form and interest, in excess of the merely subjective and momentary unification of the elements.

Thus it is to be observed in general that small parties are more radical than large ones, of course within the limits which the ideas constituting the party prescribe. The radicalism here meant is immediately sociological; that is, it is marked by the unreserved dedication of the individual to the tendency of the group, by the sharp delimitation of the same against neighboring structures which is necessary to the self-preservation of the group, by the impossibility of taking up into the externally narrow frame a multitude of far-reaching endeavors and thoughts. The radicalism which is peculiarly such in its content is to a considerable degree independent of the sort here in mind. The unqualified coherence of the elements, upon which the possibility of radicalism rests sociologically, loses power to maintain itself as more and more varied individual elements are introduced with numerical accretion. For that reason professional labor coalitions, whose purpose is the improvement of the conditions of labor in detail, know very well that they lose in actual coherence with increase of extent. In this case, however, numerical extension has, on the other hand, the tremendous significance that every added member frees the coalition from a competitor, perhaps underbidding and thereby threatening it in its existence. There occur evidently quite special life-conditions for a group which constitutes itself inside of a large group, and subordinate to its idea, and when its idea realizes its purpose only in so far as it unites in itself all elements which fall under its presuppositions. In such cases the rule usually holds: "He that is not for me is against me"; the personality outside of the group to which it, in accordance with the claims of the latter, so to speak, ideally belongs, does the group a very positive injury, through the mere indifference of nonattachment. This is the case whether, as among labor coalitions, through competition, or when it reveals to those standing outside of the group the boundaries of its power, or when the group only comes to real existence by the inclusion of all the elements concerned, as in the case of many industrial syndicates. In case, therefore, the question of completeness, which is by no means always in point, confronts a group—that is, the question whether all elements to which its principle extends are also actually included in it—then the consequences of this *complete-*

ness must be carefully distinguished from those consequences which follow from its size alone. To be sure, the group will also be larger if it is complete than if it is incomplete; but not this association as a quantity, but the problem dependent immediately upon that, viz., whether with that quantity the group fills out therewith a prescribed scheme, may be so important for the group that, as in the case of labor coalitions, the disadvantages in cohesion and unity, following from mere increase of numbers, may stand in direct antagonism and counterpoise with the advantages of increasing completeness.

In general we may, in a very essential degree, explain the structures which are peculiar to large communities, as such, from the fact that they produce with these structures a substitute for the personal and immediate cohesion which is peculiar to the smaller circles. In the case of the large group, the question is one of correlating centers which are channels and mediators of the reciprocal action of the elements, and which thus operate as independent bearers of the societary unity, after this is no longer produced by immediate relationship of person to person. For this purpose magistracies and representatives grow up, laws and symbols of the group-life, organizations and social generalizations. At this point I have only to emphasize their connection with the numerical point of view. They all occur purely and maturely, so far as the main point is concerned, only in large circles, i.e., as the abstract form of group-dependence, whose concrete form can no longer exist after a certain extension of the community has been reached. Their utility, ramifying into a thousand social qualities, rests in the last analysis upon numerical presuppositions. The character of the superpersonal and objective with which such incorporations of the group-energies face the individual is de-

rived directly from the *multiplicity* of the variously operative individual elements; for only through their multiplicity is the individual element in them paralyzed, and from the same cause the universal mounts to such a distance from the individual that it appears as something existing entirely by itself, not needing the individual, and possibly even antagonistic to the individual—somewhat as the *concept,* which, composed of singular and various phenomena of the common, is the higher above everyone of these details, the more it includes; so that precisely the universal ideas which rule the greatest circumference of particulars—the abstractions with which metaphysics reckons—attain a life apart, whose norms and developments are often alien, or hostile, to those of the tangible particulars. The great group thus gains its unity—as it expresses itself in its organs and in its law, in its political ideas and in its ideals—only at the price of a wide distance of all those structures from the individual, his views and needs, which find immediate activity and consideration in the social life of a small circle. From this relation there arises the typical difficulty of organizations in which a series of minor combinations are included within a larger one; viz., the fact is that the situations can be readily seen, and treated with interest and care, only close at hand; while, on the contrary, only from the distance which the central position holds can a just and regular relation of all the details to each other be established. The relationships of person to person, which constitute the life-principle of smaller circles, are not easily compatible with the distance and coolness of the objective-abstract norms without which the great group cannot exist.

The unity and the correlating form of the great group, as contrasted with its elements and their primary socializations, come into existence only through negations. Social actions and regulations evolve in many ways the character of negativity in the degree of their numerical inclusiveness. In the case of mass actions, the motives of individuals are often so different that their unification is possible in the degree in which their content is merely negative and destructive. The unrest which leads to great revolutions is always nursed from so many, and often directly opposing, sources that their focalization upon a positive aim would be impossible. The erection of the latter is usually the task then of the smaller circles, and of the energy of individuals who separate from each other in countless private undertakings, while these individuals united in a mass have worked in sweeping and destructive fashion. The same trend appears in the results of wide appeals to popular suffrage, which are so often, and almost incomprehensively, negative.

* * *

Perhaps the connection between the enlargement of the circle and the negative character of its determinations shows itself most decisively in the following: The more generally, that is, for the greater circle, the norm is applicable, the less is its observance characterizing and significant for the individual; while the failure to observe it is usually accompanied by especially severe and notable consequences. This is particularly the case, in the first place, in the intellectual realm. The theoretical understanding, without which there could be no human society, rests upon a small number of generally recognized, although of course not abstractly conscious, norms which we designate as logical principles. They constitute the minimum of that which must be recognized by all who want to hold commerce with each other. Upon this basis rests the most fleeting consensus of individuals least acquainted with each

other, as well as the daily association of the most intimate.

What is common to these circles and the most primitive, with which for us social history begins, is nothing else than numerical paucity. The life-forms which earlier sufficed for the entire community-circle have, with the growth of the latter, withdrawn themselves to its subordinate divisions, for these contain now the possibilities of personal relationships, the approximate equality of level of the members, the common interests and ideals, in the presence of which one may confide social regulation to so precarious and ambiguous a species of norm as customary morality is. With increasing quantity of the elements, and of the therewith unavoidable independence of the same, these limitations disappear for the circle as a whole. The peculiar constraining power of custom becomes for the state too little, and for the individual too much. The former demands greater guarantees, the latter greater freedom; and only with those sides with which each element belongs to intermediate circles is it still socially controlled through custom.

To this correlation which attaches the difference of the social form of custom from that law, to the quantitative variation of the communities, there are obvious exceptions. Within the particular state many modes of action are established as law which in external relationships, that is, within the largest circle, must be consigned to the looser form of custom. The resolution of the contradiction is very simple: The size of the circle demands the legal form naturally only in that relation in which the manifoldness of its elements *is composed into a unity*. The social unity is a graduated idea; the spirit and purpose of various circles demand various degrees in the closeness and strength of their unity; so that the social form of regulation which is demanded by a certain quantity of the circle, with respect to the degree of the unity which it is to achieve may still be the same with different quantities. The significance of the numerical conditions is thus not impaired if a greater circle, on account of its special tasks, may or must content itself without giving legal forms to its rules, just as in other cases is possible only to a smaller circle.

It is evident that the concepts "greater and smaller circle" are of a very crude scientific order, entirely indefinite and fluctuating, and properly applicable in general only in order to point out the dependence of the sociological form-character of a group upon its quantitative limitations. It cannot serve in any way to show more exactly the actual proportion which exists between the former and the latter. Nevertheless it is perhaps not in all cases impossible to make out this proportion more exactly. In the thus far observed formations and relationships any attempt to assign precise numerical values would evidently be, for any stage of our knowledge that can be foreseen, a completely fantastic undertaking. But within certain limits even now traits of those socializations may be cited which exist between a limited number of persons, and which are characterized by this limitation.

The isolate

The numerically simplest formation which can at all be designated as social reciprocities appear to occur in the case of reactions between two elements. Yet there is a structure still simpler in external appearance, which belongs in sociological categories, namely, however paradoxical and essentially contradictory it seems, the isolated individual man. As a matter of fact, the processes which produce forma-tions in the case of a duality of elements are often simpler than those necessary for the sociological characterization of the integer. In the case of these latter we have to do chiefly with two here pertinent phenomena: isolation and freedom. The mere fact that an individual is in no sort of reciprocal relationship with other individuals is, of course, not sociological, but it also does not fill out the entire concept of isolation. This concept rather, in so far as it is emphasized and is essentially significant, signifies by no means merely the absence of all society, but rather the existence of society in some way represented and afterward inhibited. Isolation receives its unequivocal positive meaning as long-distance effect of society—whether as echo of past or anticipation of future relationships; whether as longing after society or as voluntary turning away from it. The isolated man has not the same characteristics as if he had been from the beginning the only inhabitant of the world; but socialization, even if it is only that with the negative coefficient, determines *his* condition also. The whole joy and the whole bitterness of isolation are merely various reactions upon socially experienced influences. Either is a reciprocal effect from which the one member, after production of definite consequences, is really excluded and further lives and further works only ideally in the mind of the other member. In this connection there is decided significance in the well-known psychological fact that the feeling of loneliness seldom occurs so decidedly and importunately in actual physical isolation as when one is conscious of being a stranger and without attachments among many physically quite adjacent people. For the configuration of a group much depends upon whether it favors or even renders possible such loneliness within its limits. Close and intimate communities do not permit such inter-cellular vacuums in their structure. As we speak, however, of a social deficit, which is produced in fixed proportions to the societary conditions—the anti-social phenomena of the miserable, the criminal, the suicides—in like manner a given quantity and quality of societary life produces a certain number of temporarily or chronically solitary existences, which, to be sure, the statistician cannot so exactly as in these other cases express in arithmetical terms. In another way isolation becomes sociologically significant, so soon as it ceases to consist in a relationship which is a play within an individual between himself and another definite group, or group-life in general; but is rather a pause or a periodic differentiation within one and the same relationship. This is important in relationships which from their fundamental idea are aimed at permanent negation of isolation, as in the chief instance of monogamous marriage. So far as in the structure of this relation the finest subjective shadings express themselves, there is an essential difference whether man and wife, with the complete happiness of life in common, have still preserved for themselves the pleasure in isolation, or whether their relation is never interrupted by devotion to solitude—either because the habit of being together has taken from solitude its charm, or because an absence of essential assurance of love makes such interruptions feared as dangers or as infidelities. Thus isolation, apparently confined to a single person, consisting in the negation of sociality, is really a phenomenon of very positive sociological significance; not merely from the side of the agent, in whom it presents, as a conscious affection, an entirely determinate relation to society, but also through the decisive characteristic which its occurrence, both as cause and as

effect, lends to large groups as well as to the most intimate relationships.

The dyad

The sociological formation which is *methodologically* simplest is that between *two* elements. It furnishes the scheme, the germ, and the material for countless more complex formations; although its sociological significance by no means rests merely upon its extensions and its multiplications. It is rather itself a socialization, in which not only many forms of socialization realize themselves, purely and characteristically, but the limitation to a duality of the elements is, indeed, the condition under which alone a certain series of forms of relationship can emerge. The typically sociological nature of the same appears then not only in the fact that the greatest manifoldness of the individualities and of the combining motives does not alter the similarity of these formations, but rather that these sometimes occur quite as typically between pairs of groups —families, states, combinations of various sorts—as between pairs of single persons.

The peculiar conferring of characteristics upon a relationship through the duality of persons concerned in it is exhibited by everyday experiences. For instance, how differently a common lot, an undertaking, an agreement, a shared secret binds each of two sharers, from the case when even only three participate. The specific character of this difference is determined by the fact that the relationship, as a unity composed of its individuals, as a special structure beyond these, has a different bearing upon each of its participants from that of a more complicated structure to each of its members. However it may appear to third parties as an independent, superindividual unity, yet, as a rule, that is not the case for its participants, but each regards himself in antithesis only with the other, but not with a collectivity extending beyond him. The social structure rests immediately upon the one and the other. The departure of each single individual would destroy the whole, so that it does not come to such a super-personal life of the whole that the individual feels himself independent; whereas, even in the case of an association of only three, if one individual departs, a *group* may still continue to exist.

There are, nevertheless, exceptions to this character of the dual groupings, the most decisive of which seems to appear in the case of that relationship which depends most definitely upon the dyad type, that is, monogamous marriage. The by no means rare fact that among thoroughly worthy persons decidedly unfortunate marriages occur, and very fortunate ones between defective persons, points at once to the fact that this structure, however *dependent* it is upon each of the members, still may have a character which coincides with that of neither associate. If, for example, each of the wedded pair suffers from vagaries, difficulties, and unavail-abilties, but at the same time understands how to localize these upon himself, while he invests in the marital relationship only his best and purest, and thus holds the relationship free from all the discounts which affect himself as a person, this may immediately be to the credit merely of the partner in marriage as a person, but never-theless arises from it the feeling that mar-riage is something superpersonal, some-thing in itself worthy and sacred, which stands over and above the unsanctity of each of its elements. Since within a rela-tionship the one is sensitive only on the side toward the other, and behaves only with regard to him, his qualities, although they are, of course, always his own, never-

theless attain a quite different shading, status, and meaning from that which they have when, referring only to the proper *ego,* they weave themselves into the total complexity of the *ego.* Hence for the con-sciousness of each of the two the relation-ship may crystallize to an entity outside of himself, which is more and better—under certain circumstances also worse—than himself; something toward which he has obligations, and from which there come to him, as from an objective existence, bene-fits and injuries.

Something sociologically similar might be pointed out, furthermore, in the duality of partners in a business. Although the formation and operation of the partner-ship rest, perhaps, exclusively upon the cooperation of these two personalities, yet the subject-matter of this co-operation, the business or the firm, is an objective struc-ture, toward which each of its components has rights and duties—in many respects not otherwise than any third party. Yet this has a sociological meaning different from that in the case of marriage; for the business is something from the beginning separated from the persons of those who carry it on, and indeed in the case of a duality of such persons this is not other-wise true than in the case of one alone or many. The reciprocal relationship of the business associates has its purpose outside of itself; whereas in the case of marriage it is within itself. In the former instance the relationship is the means for the gaining of certain objective results; in the latter every-thing objective appears really only as a means for the subjective relationship. It is the more observable that in marriage, nevertheless, the objectivity and self-reliance of the group-structure, which are otherwise more foreign to groups of two, psychologically increase in contrast with immediate subjectivity.

One constellation, however, of extreme

sociological importance is wanting in every grouping of two, while it is in principle open to every group of larger numbers, namely, the *shifting* of duties and responsibilities upon the impersonal structure, which so often, and not to its advantage, characterizes social life. This occurs in two directions. Every totality which is more than a mere juxtaposition of given individuals has an indefiniteness of its boundaries and of its power which easily tempts us to expect from it all sorts of achievements that really belong to the separate members. We turn them over to the society, as we very often, in pursuance of the same psychological tendency, postpone them to our own future, whose nebulous possibilities give room for everything, or will accomplish, by spontaneously growing strength, everything which the present moment is not willing to take upon itself. In the precise circumstances in question, the power of the individual is transparent, but for that very reason it is also clearly limited, while in contrast with it is always the somewhat mystical power of the totality, of which we therefore easily expect, not only that the individual cannot perform, but also what he would not care to perform, and, moreover, with the feeling of the full legitimacy of this transfer. Quite as dangerous, however, as on the side of omission is membership in a totality also on the side of commission. Here the point is not merely the increase of impulsiveness and the exclusion of moral restraint, as they appear in the case of the individual in a crowd, and lead to those mass-crimes in which even the legal responsibility of the participants is debatable, but the point is that the true or the ostensible interest of a community justifies or constrains the individual in undertakings for which he would not be willing to bear the responsibility as an individual. Economic combinations make demands of

such shameless egoism, colleagues in office wink at such crying malfeasances, corporations of political or of scientific nature exercise such monstrous suppressions of individual rights, as would be impossible in the case of an individual if he were responsible for them as a person, or at least they would put him to shame. As a member of a corporation, however, he does all this with untroubled conscience, because in that case he is anonymous and feels himself covered and, as it were, concealed by the totality. There are few cases in which the distance of the social unity from the elements which constitute it is so great. It is perceptible and operative to a degree which descends almost to caricature.

It was necessary to indicate this reduction of the practical worth of personality, which inclusion in a group often occasions for the individual, in order that, by exclusion of this factor, we might characterize the dyad-group. Since in this case each element has only another individual by its side, but not a multiplicity which ultimately constitutes a higher unity, the dependence of the whole upon himself, and consequently his co-responsibility for all collective action, is made perfectly visible. He can, to be sure, as happens frequently enough, shift responsibility upon his associate, but the latter will be able to decline the same much more immediately and decisively than can often be done by an anonymous whole, which lacks the energy of personal interest or the legitimate representation requisite for such cases. Moreover, just as the one of two constituting a group cannot hide himself behind the group in cases of positive action, no more can he claim the group for his excuse in cases of culpable inaction. The energies with which the group very indefinitely and very partially, to be sure, but still very perceptibly, overtops the individual cannot in this instance reinforce the individual inadequacy, as in the case of larger combinations; for, however manifoldly two combined individuals accomplish more than two that are isolated, yet the decisive factor in this case is that each must actually perform something, and that, when he refuses to do this, only the other remains, without any superindividual energy such as, even in the case of a combination of only three, is in some measure present. The significance of this detail resides, however, by no means merely in the negative, in that which it excludes; from it grows rather a close and special modulation of the union of two. Precisely the fact that each knows he can depend only upon the other, and upon nobody else, gives to such a combination— for example, marriage, friendship, and even more external combinations up to political adjustment of two groups—a special consecration; each element in them is, in respect to its sociological destiny and everything dependent upon this, much more frequently made to confront the alternative of all or nothing than in other associations.

The triad

The tri-unity as such appears to produce three sorts of typical group-forms, which on the one hand are not possible with two elements, on the other hand, in case of a number greater than three, are either likewise excluded, or are merely extended quantitatively without changing their form-type.

1. The unpartisan and the mediator

It is a highly effective sociological fact that the common relationship of isolated elements to a potentiality existing outside of themselves produces a unification between them.

In the most significant case of bipartite combinations, namely, monogamous marriage, the child or the children, or a third element, may often exercise the function of holding the whole together. In the case of many nature peoples, the marriage is only considered actually complete or as indissoluble when a child is born. The ground for this rests, of course, in the value which the child has for the man, and in his inclination, sanctioned by statute or custom, to disown a childless wife. The actual result, however, is that this third additional element really for the first time closes the circle by binding the two others together. This may occur in two forms. Either the existence of the third element immediately produces or strengthens the attachment of the two, as for example, when the birth of a child increases the love of the parents for each other, or, at least, that of the man for the wife, or the relation of each one of the two to the third produces a new and *indirect* attachment between them, as the common cares of parents for a child universally signify a bond which must always lead beyond this child, and does not consist of sympathies which could spare this intermediate station. This coming into existence of essential socialization out of three elements, while the two elements of themselves offer resistance to socialization, is the reason why many essentially disharmonious married pairs wish for no children. It is the instinct that therewith a circle would be closed, within which they would be bound closer together—and that not externally alone, but also in the profounder psychic strata—than they are inclined to be. It is by no means a contradictory case if sometimes very intimate and passionate unions prefer to be childless. In such instances the immediate attachment is so strong that if a third element were to enter the circle, even though it is indirectly an element of cohesion, it would stimulate consciousness not so much of the attachment, which already exists in its highest degree, but rather of the indirectness of the relation through the third factor, which would thus operate relatively as an interruption. We must not overlook the fact, which is of the highest importance for all human attachment, that every mediation inserts itself *between* the elements which are to be combined, and thus separates in the very act of uniting them. When mediation is no longer necessary, this factor of interposition and separation, latent in every mediation, is accentuated: where mediation is superfluous, it is for that very reason worse than superfluous, and becomes quite as obnoxious as where its unifying function as such is not desired.

Another variation of mediation occurs when the third element functions as a nonpartisan. In that case the mediator will either secure a consensus of the other two colliding elements, in which instance the mediator seeks to eliminate himself, and only to bring to pass that the two disunited or ununited parties may unite directly; or he acts as arbitrator and attempts to reconcile to each other the conflicting claims, and to eliminate whatever in them is irreconcilable. We find boards of conciliation in which the parties, under the presidency of a nonpartisan, put an end to quarrels by conferences. The mediator in this form brings about reconciliation, to be sure, only when, in the belief of both parties, the circumstances in themselves indicate the advantage of peace; in a word, when the real situation in itself justifies peace. Apart from matter-of-course removal of misunderstandings, appeals to good intentions, etc., the way is prepared

for progress of this belief among the parties, through the mediation of the nonpartisan, somewhat in the following manner: While the nonpartisan holds the claims and the arguments of the one party before the other, they lose the tone of that subjective passion which produces the like on the other side. Here appears, in a wholesome way, what is so often to be regretted; namely, that the feeling which accompanies a psychic content within its first agent, within a second, to whom this content is transferred, is considerably weakened. For that reason recommendations and testimonials which must first pass several intermediate persons are so often impotent, even if their objective content comes with no real diminution to the person who is to give the final decision. In the transfer affective imponderabilities are lost which not only insufficient actual reasons replace, but even sufficient ones supply with the impulse for realization. This fact, which is highly significant for the development of purely psychical influences, brings to pass, in the simple case of a third mediating social element, that the modulations of feeling which accompany the demand, because they are formulated from one unpartisan side and represented to the other, suddenly fall away from the material content, and thus the circle fatal to all conciliation is avoided, viz., that the intensity of the one provokes that of the other, and then the latter reacts to increase the violence of the first, and so on until there is no stopping-place. More than this, each party not merely hears more objective statement, but each must also express himself more objectively than in the case of immediate confronting of the contestant. For now it is an object to each party to win over the mediator also to its standpoint. Where the third party is not arbitrator, but merely the leader of the attempted reconciliation, and must constantly hold himself this side of actual decision, whereas the arbitrator finally takes a decided position on one side, this winning of the mediator's approval can be hoped for only on the basis of the most real grounds. Within the range of sociological technique there is nothing which so effectively promotes the uniting of conflicting parties as their objectivity; that is, the attempt to let the bare material-content underneath the complaints and demands speak for itself— to put it in philosophic terms, to let the objective spirit of the party standpoint speak—so that the persons appear only as the irrelevant vehicles of the same. The personal form in which objective contents are subjectively living must pay for its warmth, its shading, its depth of feeling, with the keenness of the antagonism which it produces in cases of conflict; the toning down of this personal factor is the condition upon which agreement and understanding are attainable between the opponents; and this is the case especially because only under such conditions does each party actually perceive what the other *must* insist upon. Psychologically expressed, the problem is that of reducing the volitional form of antagonism to the intellectual: the understanding is everywhere the principle of consensus; upon it as a basis there may be accommodation of those things which, upon the basis of feeling and of final appeal to the will, irreconcilably repel each other. The mediator's office is, then, to promote this reduction, to represent it at the same time in himself, or, otherwise expressed, to constitute a sort of central station which, in whatever form the controverted material may come in from one side, may give it out to the other side only in objective form, and may hold back everything over and above the objective which needlessly encourages strife carried on without mediation.

For the analysis of community life it is important to make clear that the constellation just characterized constantly occurs in all groups which count more than two elements, even where the mediator is not specially chosen, and is not, as such, particularly known or designated. The group of three is here only type and scheme. All cases of mediation finally reduce to its form. There is no community of threes, from the conversation for an hour up to family life, in which there does not presently occur dissension, now between this pair, now between that, harmless or acute, momentary or permanent, of theoretical or practical nature, and in which the third does not exercise a mediatorial function. This occurs countless times in quite rudimentary ways, perhaps only in suggestive fashion, mixed with other actions and reciprocal relationships from which it is impossible to abstract the mediating function distinctly. Such mediations need not occur in words: a gesture, a way of listening, the quality of feeling which proceeds from a person, suffices to give to this dissent between two others a direction toward consensus, to make the essentially common underneath an acute difference of opinion perceptible, to bring this into the form in which it will most easily exert its proper influence. The issue need by no means be a real strife or struggle. It is rather the thousand easy varieties of opinion, the jarring of an antagonism of natures, the emergence of quite momentary antitheses of interest or feeling, which color the fluctuating form of every association, and is constantly modified in its course by the presence of the third party, who almost of necessity exercises the mediatorial function. This function passes around among the three elements in rotation, so to speak, since the ebb and flow of associated life constantly realize this form in the case of every possible combination of the elements.

The nonpartisanship demanded for mediation may have two sorts of pre-condition. The third party is nonpartisan if he is either beyond the interests and opinions which separate the others and is thus untouched by them, or if he shares in *both* in equal degrees. The former case is the simplest, and it involves the smallest number of complications.

The position of the nonpartisan tends to more complicated formation when he owes his position to equal participation in the contradictory interests instead of to indifference to both. A mediatorial status upon this basis is often made possible when a personality belongs locally to another circle of interests from that which is immediately concerned with the material question. The difficulty of such position of mediator usually consists in the fact that the equality of his interest for both parties, his essential equilibrium of interest, is not securely demonstrable, and is often enough suspected by *both* parties. A still more difficult and often tragic situation occurs, however, when it is not such separated interest-provinces of the third party with which he is attached to each of the others, but when his *whole* personality is close to both. This case is most sharply defined when the object of struggle cannot be distinctly objectified, and the essential significance of the struggle is only an excuse or an accidental occasion for deeper personal incompatibilities. In such a case the third party, who is intimately united by love or duty, by destiny or habit, with each of the two in equal degrees, will be directly consumed by the conflict much more than if he placed himself upon one of the two sides. This is all the more the case

since in these instances the equilibrium of his interests, which permits no one-sided decision, usually leads to no successful mediation, because reduction to a merely material antithesis is impossible. This is the type of very many family conflicts. Whereas the mediator who is nonpartisan through equal distance from the contestants can with relative ease do justice to both, he who is mediator by reason of equal nearness to both will find it very much more difficult, and will come personally into the most painful dualism of feeling.

Herewith is the transition given to the second form of unification by means of the nonpartisan: that is, to arbitration. So long as the third party works as a real mediator, the ending of the conflict rests finally in the hands of the parties themselves. By choice of the arbitrator they have put this ultimate decision out of their own hands. They have at the same time projected their purpose of conciliation beyond themselves. It has become a person in the arbitrator, whereby it attains special distinctness and energy in contrast with the antagonistic forces. The voluntary appeal to an arbitrator, to whom the parties subordinate themselves *a priori,* presupposes a greater subjective confidence in the objectivity of the judgment than any other form of decision, for even before the civic court the action of the appellant only proceeds from confidence in the justness of the decision (since he regards that decision as just what is favorable to himself); the respondent must take part in the process, whether he believes in the nonpartisanship of the judge or not. Arbitration, however, occurs, as was said, only through this belief on *both* sides. In principle mediation is differentiated from arbitration very sharply by the difference thus pointed out, and the more official the conciliatory action is, the more tenaciously will this differentiation be kept in mind, from the conflicts between capitalists and laborers mentioned above, to those of high politics, in which the "friendly offices" of a government, for the adjustment of a conflict between two others, are something quite different from the function of arbitrator which the ruler of a third land is sometimes invited to undertake.

On the whole, in accordance with all the foregoing, the existence of the nonpartisan serves to promote the stability of the group; as provisional representative of the intellectual energy, in contrast with the momentary disposition of the parties to be controlled more by will and feeling, he reinforces these parties, so to speak, to completeness of the psychic unity which resides in the life of the group. He is, on the one side, the retarding factor opposed to the impulsiveness of the other, while, on the contrary, he may carry and lead the movement of the whole group in case the antagonism of the two other elements would paralyze its energy. Nevertheless, this result may be transformed into its opposite. In case of the assumed correlation the elements of the group that are intellectually most endowed will especially incline to nonpartisanship, because cool intelligence is likely to find light and shade on both sides, and is not likely to find objective equity wholly on either side. Consequently the most intelligent elements are often unable to exert influence upon the decision of conflicts, although such influence from precisely such a quarter were highly to be wished. Just such elements as these should throw their weight into the balance when the group must choose between yes and no, since with their help the balance would be the more likely to incline toward the right side. If, therefore, nonpartisanship does not contribute to practical mediation, the consequence will be that through its connection with the intellectuality of the group the decision will be left to the play of the more foolish, or at least the more prejudiced, forces of the group.

2. The *tertius gaudens*

The nonpartisanship of the third element has benefited or injured the group as a whole, in the combinations thus far discussed. The mediator and the arbitrator alike wish to preserve the group unity against the danger of disruption. The nonpartisan, however, may use his relatively superior status in a purely egoistic interest. While in the former cases he acted as a means to the ends of the group, in this case, on the contrary, he makes the reciprocal occurrences between the parties and between himself and the parties a means for his own ends. Here we have to do not always with previously consolidated structures, in the social life of which this occurrence emerges by the side of others, but now the relationship between the parties and the nonpartisan is often formed *ad hoc*. Elements which otherwise constitute no reciprocal unity may come into conflict; a third, previously unattached to both alike, may seize, by means of a spontaneous action, the opportunities which this conflict gives to him, the nonpartisan, and thus may set up a purely precarious reciprocity, whose vitality and richness of forms may for each element be entirely out of proportion to the fluidity of its constitution.

I note, without further discussion, two forms of the *tertius gaudens,* because the reciprocity within the tetrad, with the typical forms of which we are here concerned, does not appear very characteristically in these instances. Rather is the significant thing in these cases a certain passivity, which rests either upon the two contestants or upon the third element. The forms are these: In the first place the advantage of the third may be produced by the fact that the two others hold each other reciprocally in check, and he can now make a gain which one of these two would otherwise contest with him. The quarrel brings about in this instance merely a paralyzing of forces which, if they could, would turn against the third. The situation in this case thus really suspends the reciprocity between the three elements, instead of establishing it, without on that account, it must be added, excluding the most appreciable results for all three. We have to treat the intentional production of this situation in the case of the next configuration of threes. In the second place, advantage may accrue to the third party merely because the action of the one contending party realizes this advantage for purposes of its own, and without the necessity of using any initiative on the part of the person reaping the advantage. The type for this form is furnished by the benefactions and the promotions which a party may confer upon a third, merely for the sake of thereby embarrassing the opposing party.

The formations of this type which are more essential at this point, result when the third party, for reasons of prudence respecting his own interests, adopts an attitude of practical support toward the one party (that is, not merely by way of intellectual decision, as in the case of the arbitrator) and from this attitude derives his mediate or immediate gain. Within this form there are two chief variations: namely, two parties are hostile to each other, and for that reason compete for the favor of a third; or two parties compete for the favor of a third, and are for that reason hostile to each other. This difference has specially important bearings upon the further development of the constellation.

If an already existing hostility makes in the direction of an attempt by each party to get the favor of the third, the decision of this competition, that is, the attachment of the third to the one party, will really mean the beginning of the conflict. On the other hand, in case the two elements independent of each other seek the favor of a third, and this constitutes the ground of their hostility, of their partisanship, the final assignment of this favor, which is in this case end, not means, of the strife, will terminate the same. The decision is reached, and further hostility is therewith made meaningless. In both cases the advantage of nonpartisanship, with which the *tertius* originally stood in antithesis with the other two, consists in the fact that he can set his own *conditions* for the decision. Where, for any reason, this assignment of conditions is denied to him, the situation does not bring to him the complete advantage.

3. Divide *et empera*

In these combinations of the triad scheme we have to do with an existing or an emerging conflict of two elements, from which the third derives an advantage; it is now a variation to be regarded as separate, although it is in reality not always separable, that the third instigates the difference intentionally, in order to gain a controlling situation. It is also to be premised in this case that the triple number is, as a matter of course, only the minimum number of the elements requisite for this formation, and consequently it may serve as the most simple scheme. The essential fact here in question is that two elements are opposed to a third, and in this opposition they are either combined with each other or dependent upon each other, and that the third is able to set in motion *against each other* the two powers which are combined *against him.* The consequence is, then, that they either hold the balance against each other, so that he, undisturbed by the two, may follow his advantage, or that they reciprocally so weaken each other that neither of them can withstand the superior power of the third. I proceed to characterize a few steps of the scale in which one may arrange the phenomena here in question. The most simple occurs when a superior power prevents the uniting of elements which do not positively attempt to form such a union, but still *might* perhaps make such an attempt. The prophylactic prevention of unification operates more distinctly in case there exists a direct endeavor for union. This preventing of combination between the elements attains, instead of a merely prohibitive, an active form in case the third party instigates jealousy between them. We have not here in mind the cases in which he instigates hostilities between the other two in order to produce at their cost a new order of things; but the facts here in question are frequently conservative tendencies, the third party tries to maintain his already existing prerogative through preventing a dreaded coalition of the two others, by means of jealousy between them, at the beginning or at least early in the course of the development of the combination beyond its first elements. There is especial likelihood of utilizing this constellation in case the two personalities to be restrained from combination already possess certain competencies. These furnish the appropriate objects of jealousy. For that reason this technique of *divide et impera* is not easily applicable in the case of personalities low in the social scale or without property. The baldest form of *divide et impera,* the instigation of positive struggle between two elements, may have its purpose in the relation of the third party either to these two, or to an object

existing outside of them. The latter occurs in case one of three candidates for an office understands how to instigate the two others against each other, in such a way that by gossip and slander, which each of them sets in motion against the other, they spoil each other's chances.

In case, finally, the purpose of the third does not reside in an object, but in the immediate control of the two other elements, two sociological points of view are essential.

(1) Certain elements are so formed that they can be successfully opposed only by similar elements. The will to subjugate them finds no proper point of attack in themselves, so that the only thing remaining is, as it were, to divide them against themselves, and to maintain between the divisions a struggle which they now can carry on with homogeneous weapons, until they are sufficiently weakened, and so may fall a prey to the third party. Precisely those who by likeness of interests are brought together best know reciprocally each other's weaknesses and their vulnerable points, so that the principle of *similia similibus*—the annihilation of a condition by producing a similar condition—may here be produced in the widest degree. Although reciprocity and unification may best be obtained with a certain degree of qualitative variation, because reinforcement, consolidation, organically differentiated life can thus result, reciprocal disturbance seems to succeed best in case of qualitative likeness, apart, of course, from so great quantitative superiority in the energy of the one party that the terms of correlation are a matter of utter indifference. The whole category of enmities of which fraternal strife is the extreme derives its radically destructive character precisely from the fact that experience and knowledge, just like the instincts which have their source in the same radical unity,

place in the hands of each the most deadly weapon against this very opponent. That which constitutes the basis of the relationship of similars to each other—namely, knowledge of the external situation, and ability to enter sympathetically into the subjective situation—this is evidently quite as much the means of the deepest wounds, which do not allow any opportunity for attack to escape, and it leads, since by its very nature it is reciprocal, to the most utter destruction. Consequently struggle of like against like, the division of the enemy into two, qualitatively homogeneous parties, is one of the most thorough realiza-

tions of *divide et impera.*

(2) Where it is not possible for the oppressor to have his purposes carried out so exclusively by his victims themselves, where he must himself enter into their struggle, the scheme is very simple. He simply supports the one until the other is a practically eliminated factor, whereupon the former is his easy prey. This support is most advantageously given to the one who of himself is the stronger. This policy may be carried out in the more negative form, that the more powerful, in a complex of elements which is to be suppressed, may merely be protected.

5.

Alexis de Tocqueville

THE OLD REGIME AND THE FRENCH REVOLUTION

What did the French Revolution accomplish?

The aim of the Revolution was not, as once was thought, to destroy the authority of the Church and religious faith in general. Appearances notwithstanding, it was essentially a movement for political and social reform and, as such, did not aim at creating a state of permanent disorder in the conduct of public affairs or (as one of its opponents bitterly remarked) at "methodizing anarchy." On the contrary, it sought to increase the power and jurisdiction of the central authority. Nor was it intended, as some have thought, to change

From Alexis de Tocqueville. *The Old Regime and the French Revolution.* Trans. by Stuart Gilbert, Garden City, New York: Doubleday and Co., Inc., 1955, pp. 19-32, 203-11. Reprinted by permission of the publisher.

the whole nature of our traditional civilization, to arrest its progress, or even to make any vital change in the principles basic to the structure of society in the Western World. If we disregard various incidental developments which briefly modified its aspect at different periods and in different lands, and study it as it was essentially, we find that the chief permanent achievement of the French Revolution was the suppression of those political institutions, commonly described as feudal, which for many centuries had held unquestioned sway in most European countries. The Revolution set out to replace them with a new social and political order, at once simple and more uniform, based on the concept of the equality of all men.

This in itself was enough to constitute a thorough-paced revolution since, apart from the fact that the old feudal institutions still entered into the very texture of the religious and political institutions of almost the whole of Europe, they had also given rise to a host of ideas, sentiments, manners, and customs which, so to speak, adhered to them. Thus nothing short of a major operation was needed to excise from the body politic these accretions and to destroy them utterly. The effect was to make the Revolution appear even more drastic than it actually was, since what it was destroying affected the entire social system.

Radical though it may have been, the Revolution made far fewer changes than is generally supposed, as I shall point out later. What in point of fact it destroyed, or is in process of destroying—for the Revolution is still operative—may be summed up as everything in the old order that stemmed from aristocratic and feudal institutions, was in any way connected with them, or even bore, however faintly, their imprint. The only elements of the old regime that it retained were those which had always been foreign to its institutions and could exist independently of them. Chance played no part whatever in the outbreak of the Revolution; though it took the world by surprise, it was the inevitable outcome of a long period of gestation, the abrupt and violent conclusion of a process in which six generations had played an intermittent part. Even if it had not taken place, the old social structure would nonetheless have been shattered everywhere sooner or later. The only difference would have been that instead of collapsing with such brutal suddenness it would have crumbled bit by bit. At one fell swoop, without warning, without transition, and without compunction, the Revolution effected what in any case was bound to happen, if by slow degrees.

Why feudalism had come to be more detested in France than in any other country

At first sight it may appear surprising that the Revolution, whose primary aim, as we have seen, was to destroy every vestige of the institutions of the Middle Ages, should not have broken out in countries where those institutions had the greatest hold and bore most heavily on the people instead of those in which their yoke was relatively light.

At the close of the eighteenth century serfdom had not yet been completely abolished anywhere in Germany; indeed, in most parts of that country the peasants were still literally bound to the land, as they had been in the Middle Ages. The armies of Frederick II and Maria Theresa were composed almost entirely of men who were serfs on the medieval pattern.

In most German states in 1788 the peasant was not allowed to quit his lord's estate; if he did so, he was liable to be tracked down wherever he was and brought back in custody. He was subject to the jurisdiction of his lord, who kept a close eye on his private life and could punish him for intemperance or idleness. He could neither better his social position, change his occupation, nor even marry without his master's consent, and a great number of his working hours had to be spent in his master's service. The system of compulsory labor, known in France as the *corvée,* was in full force in Germany, and in some districts entailed no less than three days' work a week. The peasant was expected to keep the buildings on his lord's estate in good repair and to carry the produce of the estate to market; he drove his lord's carriage and carried his messages. Also he had to spend some years of his youth in his lord's household as a member of the domestic staff. However, it was possible for the serf to become a landowner, though his tenure was always hedged round with restrictions. He had to cultivate his land in a prescribed manner, under his lord's supervision, and could neither alienate nor mortgage it without permission. In some cases he was compelled to sell its produce, in others forbidden to sell it; in any case he was bound to keep the land under cultivation. Moreover, his children did not inherit his entire estate, some part of it being usually withheld by his lord.

In France such conditions had long since passed away; the peasants could move about, buy and sell, work, and enter into contracts as they liked. Only in one or two eastern provinces, recent annexations, some last vestiges of serfdom lingered on; everywhere else it had wholly disappeared. Indeed, the abolition of serfdom had taken place in times so remote that its very date had been forgotten. However, as a result of recent research work it is now known that as early as the thirteenth century serfdom had ceased to exist in Normandy.

Meanwhile another revolution, of a different order, had done much to improve the status of the French peasant; he had not merely ceased to be a serf, he had also become a landowner. Though this change had far-reaching consequences, it is apt to be overlooked, and I propose to devote some pages to this all-important subject.

Until quite recently it was taken for granted that the splitting up of the landed estates in France was the work of the Revolution, and the Revolution alone; actually there is much evidence in support of the contrary view. Twenty years or more before the Revolution we find complaints being made that land was being subdivided to an unconscionable extent. "The practice of partitioning inheritances," said Turgot, writing at about this time, "has

gone so far that a piece of land which just sufficed for a single family is now parceled out between five or six sons. The result is that the heirs and their families soon find that they cannot depend on the land for their livelihood and have to look elsewhere." And some years later Necker declared that there was "an inordinate number" of small country estates in France.

In a confidential report made to an Intendant shortly before the Revolution I find the following observations: "Inheritances are being subdivided nowadays to an alarming extent. Everybody insists on having his share of the land, with the result that estates are broken up into innumerable fragments, and this process of fragmentation is going on all the time." One might well imagine these words to have been written by one of our contemporaries.

Then, as in our own day, the peasant's desire for owning land was nothing short of an obsession and already all the passions to which possession of the soil gives rise in present-day France were active. "Land is always sold above its true value," a shrewd contemporary observer remarked, "and this is due to the Frenchman's inveterate craving to become a landowner. All the savings of the poorer classes, which in other countries are invested in private companies or the public funds, are used for buying land."

It was chiefly along the Rhine that at the close of the eighteenth century German farmers owned the land they worked and enjoyed almost as much freedom as the French small proprietor; and it was there, too, that the revolutionary zeal of the French found its earliest adepts and took more permanent effect. On the other hand, the parts of Germany which held out longest against the current of new ideas were those where the peasants did not as yet enjoy such privileges—and this is, to my mind, a highly suggestive fact.

Thus the prevalent idea that the break-up of the big estates in France began with the Revolution is erroneous; it had started long before. True, the revolutionary governments sold the estates owned by the clergy and many of those owned by the nobility; however, if we study the records of these sales (a rather tedious task, but one which I have on occasion found rewarding) we discover that most of the parcels of land were bought by people who already had land of their own. Thus, though estates changed hands, the number of landowners was increased much less than might have been expected. For, to employ the seemingly extravagant, but in this case correct, expression used by Necker, there were already "myriads" of such persons.

What the Revolution did was not to parcel out the soil of France, but to "liberate" it—for a while. Actually these small proprietors had much difficulty in making a living out of the land since it was subject to many imposts from which there was no escaping.

How, given the facts set forth thus far, the Revolution was a foregone conclusion

My object in this final chapter is to bring together some of those aspects of the old regime which were depicted piecemeal in the foregoing pages and to show how the Revolution was their natural, indeed inevitable, outcome.

When we remember that it was in France that the feudal system, while retaining the characteristics which made it so irksome to, and so much resented by, the masses, had most completely discarded all that could benefit or protect them, we may feel less surprise at the fact that France was the place of origin of the revolt destined so violently to sweep away the last vestiges of that ancient European institution.

Similarly, if we observe how the nobility after having lost their political rights and ceased, to a greater extent than in any other land of feudal Europe, to act as leaders of the people, had nevertheless not only retained but greatly increased their fiscal immunities and the advantages accruing to them individually; and if we also note how, while ceasing to be the ruling class, they had remained a privileged, closed group, less and less (as I have pointed out) an aristocracy and more and more a caste—if we bear these facts in mind, it is easy to see why the privileges enjoyed by this small section of the community seemed so unwarranted and so odious to the French people and why they developed that intense jealousy of the "upper class" which rankles still today.

Finally, when we remember that the nobility had deliberately cut itself off both from the middle class and from the peasantry (whose former affection it had alienated) and had thus become like a foreign body in the State: ostensibly the high command of a great army, but actually a corps of officers without troops to follow them—when we keep this in mind, we can easily understand why the French nobility, after having so far weathered every storm, was stricken down in a single night.

I have shown how the monarchical government, after abolishing provincial independence and replacing local authorities by its nominees in three quarters of the country, had brought under its direct management all public business, even the most trivial, I have also shown how, owing to the centralization of power, Paris, which had until now been merely the capital city, had come to dominate France —or, rather, to embody in itself the whole kingdom. These two circumstances, peculiar to France, suffice to explain why it was that an uprising of the people could overwhelm so abruptly and decisively a monarchy that for so many centuries had successfully withstood so many onslaughts and, on the very eve of its downfall, seemed inexpugnable even to the men who were about to destroy it.

In no other country of Europe had all political thought been so thoroughly and for so long stifled as in France: in no other country had the private citizen become so completely out of touch with public affairs and so unused to studying the course of events, so much so that not only had the average Frenchman no experience of "popular movements" but he hardly understood what "the people" meant. Bearing this in mind, we may find it easier to understand why the nation as a whole could launch out into a sanguinary revolution, with those very men who stood to lose most by it taking the lead and clearing the ground for it.

Since no free institutions and, as a result, no experienced and organized political parties existed any longer in France, and since in the absence of any political groups of this sort the guidance of public opinion, when its first stirrings made themselves felt, came entirely into the hands of the philosophers, that is to say the intellectuals, it was only to be expected that the directives of the Revolution should take the form of abstract principles, highly generalized theories, and that political realities would be largely overlooked. Thus, instead of attacking only such laws as seemed objectionable, the idea developed that *all* laws indiscriminately must be abolished and a wholly new system of government, sponsored by these writers, should replace the ancient French constitution.

Moreover, since the Church was so closely bound up with the ancient institutions now to be swept away, it was inevitable that the Revolution, in overthrowing the civil power, should assail the established religion. As a result, the leaders of the movement, shaking off the controls that religion, law, and custom once had exercised, gave free rein to their imagination and indulged in acts of an outrageousness that took the whole world by surprise. Nevertheless, anyone who had closely studied the condition of the country at the time might well have guessed that there was no enormity, no form of violence from which these men would shrink.

Never had religious tolerance, the lenient use of power and kindness toward one's neighbor been preached so earnestly and, to all appearances, so generally practiced as in the eighteenth century. Even the rules of war, last resort of the will to violence, had been humanized. Yet it was in this humanitarian climate that the most inhuman of revolutions took its rise. Nor must it be thought that these amiable sentiments were merely feigned; once the Revolution had run its headlong course, these same feelings came to the fore again and promptly made their presence felt not only in legislation but in all the doings of the new government.

This contrast between theory and practice, between good intentions and acts of savage violence, which was a salient feature of the French Revolution, becomes less startling when we remember that the Revolution, though sponsored by the most civilized classes of the nation, was carried out by its least educated and most unruly elements. For, since the members of the cultured elite had formed a habit of keeping to themselves, were unused to acting together, and had no hold on the masses, the latter became masters of the situation almost from the start. Even where the people did not govern *de facto* and directly, they set the tone of the administration. And in view of the conditions in which these men had been living under the old regime, it was almost a foregone conclusion how they now would act.

Actually it was to these very conditions that our peasantry owed some of their outstanding qualities. Long enfranchised and owning some of the land he worked, the French peasant was largely independent and had developed a healthy pride and much common sense. Inured to hardships, he was indifferent to the amenities of life, intrepid in the face of danger, and faced misfortune stoically. It was from this simple, virile race of men that those great armies were raised which were to dominate for many years the European scene. But their very virtues made them dangerous masters. During the many centuries in which these men had borne the brunt of nation-wide misgovernment and lived as a class apart, they had nursed in secret their grievances, jealousies, and rancors and, having learned toughness in a hard school, had become capable of enduring or inflicting the very worst.

It was in this mood that gripping the reins of power, the French people undertook the task of seeing the Revolution through. Books had supplied them with the necessary theories, and they now put these into practice, adjusting the writers' ideas to their lust for revenge.

Toward the close of the old régime these two passions were equally sincerely felt and seemed equally operative. When the Revolution started, they came in contact, joined forces, coalesced, and reinforced each other, fanning the revolutionary ardor of the nation to a blaze. This was in '89, that rapturous year of bright enthusiasm, heroic courage, lofty ideals—untempered, we must grant, by the reality of experience: a historic date of glorious memory to which the thoughts of men will turn with admiration and respect long after those who witnessed its achievement, and we ourselves, have passed away. At the time the French had such proud confidence in the cause they were defending, and in themselves, that they believed they could reconcile freedom with equality and interspersed democratic institutions everywhere with free institutions. Not only did they shatter that ancient system under which men were divided into classes, corporations, and castes, and their rights were even more unequal than their social situations, but by the same token they did away with all the more recent legislation, instituted by the monarchy, whose effect was to put every Frenchman under official surveillance, with the government as his mentor, overseer, and, on occasion, his oppressor. Thus centralization shared the fate of absolute government.

But when the virile generation which had launched the Revolution had perished or (as usually befalls a generation engaging in such ventures) its first fine energy had dwindled; and when, as was but to be expected after a spell of anarchy and "popular" dictatorship, the ideal of freedom had lost much of its appeal and the nation, at a loss where to turn, began to cast round for a master—under these conditions the stage was set for a return to one-man government. Indeed, never had conditions been more favorable for its establishment and consolidation, and the man of genius destined at once to carry on and to abolish the Revolution was quick to turn them to account.

Actually there had existed under the old régime a host of institutions which had quite a "modern" air and, not being incompatible with equality, could easily be embodied in the new social order—and all these institutions offered remarkable facilities to despotism. They were hunted for among the wreckage of the old order and duly salvaged. These institutions had formerly given rise to customs, usages, ideas, and prejudices tending to keep men apart, and thus make them easier to rule. They were revived and skillfully exploited; centralization was built up anew, and in the process all that had once kept it within bounds was carefully eliminated. Thus there arose, within a nation that had but recently laid low its monarchy, a central authority with powers wider, stricter, and more absolute than those which any French King had ever wielded. Rash though this venture may have been, it was carried through with entire success for the good reason that people took into account only what was under their eyes and forgot what they had seen before. Napoleon fell but the more solid parts of his achievement lasted on; his government died, but his administration survived, and every time that an attempt is made to do away with absolutism the most that could be done has been to graft the head of Liberty onto a servile body.

On several occasions during the period extending from the outbreak of the Revolution up to our time we find the desire for freedom reviving, succumbing, then returning, only to die out once more and presently blaze up again. This presumably will be the lot for many years to come of a passion so undisciplined and untutored by experience; so easily discouraged, cowed and vanquished, so superficial and short-lived. Yet during this same period the passion for equality, first to entrench itself in the hearts of Frenchmen, has never given ground; for it links up with feelings basic to our very nature. For while the urge to freedom is forever assuming new forms, losing or gaining strength according to the march of events, our love of equality is constant and pursues the object of its desire with a zeal that is obstinate and often blind, ready to make every conces-

sion to those who give it satisfaction. Hence the fact that the French nation is prepared to tolerate in a government that favors and flatters its desire for equality practices and principles that are, in fact, the tools of despotism.

To those who study it as an isolated phenomenon the French Revolution can but seem a dark and sinister enigma; only when we view it in the light of the events preceding it can we grasp its true significance. And, similarly, without a clear idea of the old régime, its laws, its vices, its prejudices, its shortcomings, and its greatness, it is impossible to comprehend the history of the sixty years following its fall. Yet even this is not enough; we need also to understand and bear in mind the peculiarities of the French temperament.

When I observe France from this angle I find the nation itself far more remarkable than any of the events in its long history. It hardly seems possible that there can ever have existed any other people so full of contrasts and so extreme in all their doings, so much guided by their emotions and so little by fixed principles, always behaving better, or worse, than one expected of them. At one time they rank above, at another below, the norm of humanity; their basic characteristics are so constant that we can recognize the France we know in portraits made of it two or three thousand years ago, and yet so changeful are its moods, so variable its tastes that the nation itself is often quite as much startled as any foreigner at the things it did only a few years before. Ordinarily the French are the most routine-bound of men, but once they are forced out of the rut and leave their homes, they travel to the ends of the earth and engage in the most reckless ventures. Undisciplined by temperament, the Frenchman is always readier to put up with the arbitrary rule, however harsh, of an autocrat than with a free, well-ordered government by his fellow citizens, however worthy of respect they be. At one moment he is up in arms against authority and the next we find him serving the powers-that-be with a zeal such as the most servile races never display. So long as no one thinks of resisting, you can lead him on a thread, but once a revolutionary movement is afoot, nothing can restrain him from taking part in it. That is why our rulers are so often taken by surprise; they fear the nation either too much or not enough, for though it is never so free that the possibility of enslaving it is ruled out, its spirit can never be broken so completely as to prevent its shaking off the yoke of an oppressive government. The Frenchman can turn his hand to anything, but he excels in war alone and he prefers fighting against odds, preferring dazzling feats of arms and spectacular successes to achievements of the more solid kind. He is more prone to heroism than to humdrum virtue, apter for genius than for good sense, more inclined to think up grandiose schemes than to carry through great enterprises. Thus the French are at once the most brilliant and the most dangerous of all European nations, and the best qualified to become, in the eyes of other peoples, an object of admiration, of hatred, of compassion, or alarm—never of indifference.

France alone could have given birth to revolution so sudden, so frantic, and so thoroughgoing, yet so full of unexpected changes of direction, of anomalies and inconsistencies. But for the antecedent circumstances described in this book, the French would never have embarked on it; yet we must recognize that though their effect was cumulative and overwhelming, they would not have sufficed to lead to such a drastic revolution elsewhere than in France.

Thus I have brought my readers to the threshold of this memorable revolution; for the present I shall halt at this point, though I may perhaps go further in a subsequent work and study not its causes but the French Revolution itself and endeavor to appraise the new social order which issued from it.

6.

George Rudé

THE PRE-INDUSTRIAL CROWD

As long as the crowd in history was considered unworthy of serious attention, it was natural that the study of its motives should have been somewhat superficial.

Explanations of why the crowd rioted or rebelled have naturally tended to vary with the social attitudes or *values* of the writer. To those to whom the crowd's actions were wholly reprehensible, the crowd would appear to be prompted by the basest motives, by the lure of loot, gold, rape, or the prospect of satisfying other lurking criminal instincts. To those to whom the crowd seemed, on balance, to be an object worthy of sympathy or compassion rather than of reprobation (though this would vary with the occasion), noble ideals, particularly those of sound middle-class and liberal inspiration, would play an important part. To others again, those whom Marx in his day termed the proponents of a "vulgar" materialism, short-term economic factors seemed the most valid explanation of all types of popular unrest, and every disturbance became almost by definition a hunger riot, or *émeute de la faim.*

None of these explanations are wholly without merit, yet all are either superficial or misleading. Why this is so will, I hope, appear in the course of the present chapter. But a preliminary word needs to be said about the first of these interpretations, which, being the most pervasive of the three, calls for a separate comment. Its underlying assumption appears to be that the masses have no worthwhile aspirations of their own and, being naturally venal, can be prodded into activity only by the promise of a reward by outside agents or "conspirators." "In most popular movements," writes Mortimer-Ternaux, a historian of the French Revolutionary Terror, "money plays a greater role than feeling or conviction (*la passion*)"; and Taine and his school offer similar explanations of why the Bastille fell or the French monarchy was overthrown. But such a view, with its evident social bias, was by no means the invention of these writers: on the contrary, it receives ample confirmation from the opinions of contemporary observers. For as long as no serious attempt was made to probe the deeper aspirations of the poor, their periodic outbursts in riot or rebellion were liable to be attributed to the machinations of a political opponent or a "hidden hand."

Such an attitude was shared by all in authority, whether aristocratic or middle class, conservative, liberal, or revolutionary, though the sort of outbreak that might, exceptionally, be condoned would naturally vary from one class or party to the other. Where Sir Robert Walpole, the King's Chief Minister, attributed the riots of 1736 in England to a Jacobite conspiracy and some of his agents spoke darkly of "high church" or "popish priests," Lord Granville, an opposition peer, was willing to ascribe such "tumults" to "oppression." Again, where George III's ministers and their agents hinted that the Gordon Riots might have been instigated by French or American gold, some opposition leaders were inclined to blame the government itself for deliberately fostering riot as a pretext for calling in the army and imposing martial law. Indeed it was common in eighteenth-century England for one party to accuse the other of "raising a Mob." In France, Voltaire, being a critic of aristocracy and a friend of Turgot, convinced himself that the grain-rioters of 1775 were in the pay of Turgot's enemies at Court. During the French Revolution, both revolutionary leaders and their royalist or aristocratic opponents were remarkably liberal with such charges when it suited them: Montjoie, a royalist journalist, claimed to have first-hand proof (which proved to have little foundation) that the Réveillon rioters of 1789 had been bribed with *louis d'or;* and Girondins and Jacobins alike were disposed to believe that food rioters like those that invaded Paris grocery shops in February 1793 had been paid by agents of Pitt or the "aristocrats." Thirty or forty years later, such simple explanations had lost much of their force: we have but to read English parliamentary debates on the Luddites and Chartists to appreciate the difference; but, throughout the eighteenth century, the police—the French perhaps more stubbornly than the English—clung to their conviction that the twin agents of riot and rebellion were bribery and "conspiracy."

[Such] explanations, even where they contain a more solid substance of truth, are grossly oversimplified. The crowd may riot because it is hungry or fears to be so, because it has some deep social grievance, because it seeks an immediate reform or the millennium, or because it wants to destroy an enemy or acclaim a "hero"; but it is seldom for any single one of these reasons alone. Of course, it would be ludicrous to reject the simple and obvious answers merely because they are so. Economic motives, for example, may be presumed to be dominant in strikes and food riots, as political issues play a part of varying importance in both radical reform movements and movements directed against radical reform, such as the Priestley riots in Birmingham in 1791. When Cornish tin miners or West Country weavers burn down their employer's house or mill or destroy his machinery in the course of an industrial dispute, we need no particular powers of divination to conclude that, whatever the form of disturbance, it is higher wages that they are after. Similarly, when food rioters threaten bakers, invade markets, and rip open sacks of flour or grain, we may assume that the real purpose is not so much to intimidate or destroy as to bring down the price of food. Again, when Parisians assault and capture the Bastille and Londoners "pull down" Catholic houses and chapels, we must suppose that they intended to do precisely this. In looking for motives we must, therefore, not be so subtle or devious as to ignore the overt or primary intention.

The latter, however, only gives us a clue to the general nature of a disturbance; and here we are not so much concerned with this as with what prompted people, often of different social groups, occupations, and

beliefs to take part in the event. Even if the immediate or overt motives leap to the eye, we still have to explore those that lie beneath the surface; and if persons of differing classes or creeds are involved, some may be impelled by one motive and some by another. Motives will, therefore, vary not only between one action and the next but between different groups participating in the same disturbance. Even so we shall become hopelessly confused if we do not attempt to make some distinction between what we may term dominant and underlying motives or beliefs. Here, for the sake of clarity, it is proposed to divide the former into "economic" and "political" and to consider what part they played, both separately and in association, in the activities of the pre-industrial crowd.

Let us begin with those disturbances in which economic issues were clearly paramount. Such were food riots (at this time, the most frequent of all), strikes, peasant attacks on châteaux, the destruction of gates and fences, the burning of hayricks and the wrecking of industrial and agricultural machinery. These account, as we have seen, for the vast majority of disturbances in which the pre-industrial crowd in France and England was actively engaged. And in these we must assume (unless we have evidence to the contrary) that the common people of town and countryside were impelled by the urge to maintain or improve living standards, to raise or prevent reductions in wages, to resist encroachments on their holdings in land or their rights of common pasture, to protect their means of livelihood against the threat of new mechanical devices, and, above all, to ensure a constant supply of cheap and plentiful food. Yet bad, even abysmal, economic conditions were not an automatic "trigger" to disturbance. In England, strikes and trade-union activity tended to occur not at moments of deepest trade depression and unemployment, but rather on the upswing of a boom: as in 1792, 1818, 1824, and 1844-6 (the year 1768 appears to have been an exception). During the French Revolution, we noted, the most protracted industrial disputes were those of 1791 and 1794, which were years of comparative prosperity; and that when runaway inflation and unemployment set in, as in the winter of 1794-5, strikes came to an end and food riots took over. Food riots, unlike strikes, were the direct product of bad harvests and trade depression, rising prices and shortage of stocks; but they did not necessarily occur at the peak of a cycle of rising prices: we saw rather that they tended, as in the largest disturbances of their kind before 1789—those of 1766 in England and 1775 in France—to arise as the result of a sudden sharp upward movement leading to shortage and panic buying. Again, strikes, food riots, and peasant movements, even when the prevailing issues were purely economic, might take place against a political background that gave them a greater intensity or a new direction. In London in 1768, already existing industrial disputes were touched by the Wilkite political movement: we find striking weavers and coal heavers acclaiming John Wilkes; and, in France in 1789, it seems unlikely that the peasants would have chosen that particular moment to settle accounts with their landlords if the general political conditions had not been what they were.

Conversely, economic motives often impinged on movements that were, in their essence, political. City riots, upon which political issues usually obtruded, frequently took place against a background of rising prices or food shortage: we saw examples from Paris in 1720, 1752, and 1788, and from London in 1736, 1768, and 1794; though, here, the Gordon Riots and the later Wilkite disturbances appear to have been exceptions. Similarly, the French revolutions of 1830 and 1848 broke out during periods of food shortage and trade depression; and we have noted the particular part played by the unemployed in Paris in June 1848. The same intrusion of economic issues is evident in English disturbances of the early nineteenth century; Professor Rostow has vividly illustrated the point in his "social tension chart" for the years 1790 to 1850.

On such occasions, the shortage and high price of bread and food appear to have acted as a stimulus to popular participation in movements that were ostensibly concerned with other objects and issues. During the first French Revolution concern for the price of bread runs like a constant thread through every phase of the struggle of parties and through nearly every one of the great popular *journées,* and accounts, perhaps more than any other factor, for the unity and militancy of the Parisian sans-culottes. The revolutionary crisis of 1789 broke out against a backcloth of steeply rising bread prices: we saw how the peasant movement began with raids on markets, millers, and granaries before turning into a war against the landlords; and the Réveillon rioters, who destroyed the houses of two unpopular manufacturers, also raided food shops and demanded a reduction in the price of bread. In October, the women of the markets who marched to Versailles to fetch the royal family to Paris chanted as they marched (or, at least, so tradition has it), "let us fetch the baker, the baker's wife and the little baker's boy"; and Barnave, in describing the day's proceedings to his *Dauphinois* constituents, wrote that while "the bourgeoisie" were mainly preoccupied with the political issues, "the people" were equally concerned with the shortage of food. The outbreak of war brought further problems: not only bread, but meat, wine, coffee, and sugar began to disappear from the shops, and in Paris food riots preceded or accompanied each one of the political *journées* of 1792 and 1793. In September 1793, as we saw, it was as the direct result of the popular agitation in the markets, streets, and Sections that the National Convention adopted the law of the General Maximum that placed a ceiling on the prices of most necessities. And, after the Jacobins had fallen and the *maximum* had been abandoned, the insurgents of May 1795 wore on their caps and on their blouses the twin slogans, "The Constitution of 1793" and "Bread."

We are certainly not arguing that short-term economic factors eclipsed all others and that all popular movements of this period, even such politically oriented movements as those of the French Revolution, were really food riots in disguise. We saw in an earlier chapter that even before 1789 the political ideas of the *parlements* in Paris and of the Common Council of the City of London played a part in popular disturbance. Mr. Edward Thompson claims that the London crowd of the 1760s and 1770s "had scarcely begun to develop its own organization or leaders" and, that, having little theory distinct from that of its middle-class "managers," was as yet an unreliable instrument of radical policies. This is true enough, and the proof lies in the fact that the same crowd that had shouted for "Wilkes and Liberty" in 1768 was, a dozen years later, directing its energies into channels that were hardly propitious for the radical cause—destroying Catholic houses and chapels. Nevertheless, the political lessons learned were not entirely forgotten, and they revived and were enriched under the impact of the French Revolution. For, both in England and France, the Revolution of 1789, by posing sharply in their multiform aspects

the new concepts of the "rights of man" and the "sovereignty of the people," added a new dimension to popular disturbance and gave a new content to the struggle of parties and classes.

Some historians have doubted the depth of the penetration of these political ideas among the common people. Professor Cobban, for example, has questioned the importance of the circulation of a few political slogans, for (he writes) "one knows how easily a crowd can be taught to chant these and how little serious political content they can have." This would be true enough if it were only a matter of mouthing borrowed slogans, though even these were of some importance in mustering popular support for a radical cause: it is surely significant, for example, that even before the Estates General assembled at Versailles on May 5, 1789, Parisian crowds had taken up the rallying cry of *Vive le Tiers Etat!* and (like Arthur Young's peasants of a few months later) given it a special meaning of their own. And such ideas and slogans were certainly not kept on ice, as it were, for the great political occasions: on the contrary, there is ample evidence that they permeated ever more deeply and widely as the Revolution progressed. Already in August 1789, we find a journeyman gunsmith arrested at Versailles for speaking slightingly of General Lafayette supporting his claim to a fair hearing with an appeal to the "rights of man"; and Malouet, a hostile observer, relates how at this time chairmen at the gates of the National Assembly were eagerly discussing the rights and wrongs of the case for a royal right of "veto." A year later, the democrats of the Cordeliers Club were forming popular clubs and societies through which they began to give systematic instruction to small craftsmen and wage earners in the more advanced revolutionary doctrines; and, in police records, we read of journeymen and domestic servants subscribing to the radical press and even taking out subscriptions to the more exclusive Jacobin Club. Under this impetus, the sans-culottes not only formed political organizations of their own but later, when they dominated the Paris Sections and Commune, began to advance policies and solutions that proved highly embarrassing to their Jacobin allies. And not only that; for, having assimilated their ideas, they gave them a new content that corresponded more with their own interests than with those of their middle-class teachers.

Millenarial and religious ideas also clearly played a part in popular disturbance. The millennium might assume a secular or a religious form, though (unlike the Wesleyan ideal) it was generally to be realized on earth rather than in heaven. Millenarial fantasies no doubt underlie many of the actions of the poor in the course of the French Revolution; but in none are they so clearly evident as in the sudden upsurge of hope aroused among them by the news that the Estates General should meet in the summer of 1789. The news fostered what French historians since Taine have called *la grande espérance:* the hope that, at last, past promises would be fulfilled and the burdens, particularly the hated *taille,* lifted off the peasants' backs, and that a new golden era would begin. The state of exaltation thus engendered equally produced its corollary, the conviction, once these hopes appeared to be endangered, that their realization was being frustrated by a *complot aristocratique.* This dual phenomenon, it has been argued, does a great deal to explain the almost mystical fervor with which the *menu peuple* pursued their "aristocratic" enemies during the Revolution. Or, as in England, millenarial fantasies might be clothed in the poetic imagery of Blake's

"Jerusalem" or the apocalyptic extravagances of a Richard Brothers, whose *Revealed Knowledge of the Prophesies and Times* was published in London in early 1794. This was a time when Jacobin ideas were still making headway among the "lower orders"; and it has been suggested that men like Brothers, who interlaced their talk of "the whore of Babylon" and the "Antichrist" with denunciations of the high and mighty, may have nourished similar political aspirations to those nourished by Tom Paine's *The Rights of Man.* But millenarial ideas, while they might, under certain circumstances, stimulate rather than weaken an already existing political movement, might equally act as an antidote to popular militancy or as a consolation for a political defeat. This may have been the case in France after Waterloo and, in England in 1838, in the strange affair of "the battle in Bossenden Wood."

In the latter case, a number of Kentish laborers believed implicitly that their leader, the spurious Sir William Courtenay, was the Messiah. But this is only one guise in which the religious motive may appear in riots. At other times, though overtly proclaimed, it might not be so profound as it was made to appear; or conversely it might lie submerged beneath the surface of events. Of the first kind "No Popery" riots, "High Church" attacks on Methodist or Presbyterian meeting halls and chapels, and urban "Church and King" explosions are obvious examples. Quite apart from their social undercurrents, such movements were never quite what they seemed. We have seen that the ill-assorted slogans "destruction to Presbyterians" and "No Popery" appeared side by side in the Birmingham riots; and one of those sentenced to death for his part in the Gordon Riots said, when questioned: "Damn my eyes, I have no religion;

but I have to keep it up for the good of the cause." It is not so much that in such movements the religious element is non-existent or a mere cloak for other issues (though this was firmly believed by some contemporaries) as that in them religious, social, and political motives are bewilderingly interwoven. Perhaps, in view of their proclaimed purpose to maintain an established Church as part of an established order, we should treat them less as religious movements than as anti-radical political demonstrations.

The case is somewhat different where a dissenting religious tradition serves as an undercurrent rather than as a proclaimed object of disturbance. In London and England's West Country, in particular, religious dissent and popular radicalism had had a long association; and Methodism, even when it professed to stave off riot and lay up its treasures solely in heaven, brought with it a new fervor and moral purpose that, sooner or later, were bound to leave their mark on popular social movements. Such was certainly the case in England and Wales in the disturbances of 1830 and the 1840s: in the "Swing" and Rebecca riots and in the Welsh Chartist movement Protestant nonconformity, both Wesleyan and other, played a part.

Nor must we assume that such secular, rationalist ideas as the "rights of man" and other products of the Enlightenment would, when they gripped the common people, necessarily serve as an antidote to religion. This was no doubt the intention of many rationalist thinkers and middle-class and aristocratic reformers or revolutionaries in England and France in the eighteenth century; and there were moments during the French Revolution when they appeared to have been successful. Certainly, the monopoly and authority of

the established Catholic Church were successively undermined and broken—and these were never fully recovered; and Parisian crowds demonstrated to shouts of *A bas la calotte!* ("Down with the priests!") and played a part at the height of the "de-christianization" movement in the autumn of 1793, in closing down every church in the city. Yet the popular anti-religious (as distinct from the anticlerical) movement was comparatively short lived; as late as June 1793, Parisians in the revolutionary Faubourg St. Antoine demonstrated for the right to preserve the traditional Corpus Christi procession; and Robespierre himself sought to win further popular support for the Revolutionary Government by launching a brand-new religious cult, the Cult of the Supreme Being. This was only the most highly publicized of numerous attempts to effect a fusion between religion and the current political ideas. In many districts, the people took the initiative themselves and the Revolution saw a remarkable upsurge of new religious cults; and solemn ceremonies, accompanied by all the *mystique* of the old religious practices, were dedicated to new local "saints" or to the great popular martyrs of the Revolution, Marat, Chalier, and Lepeletier. Yet once the Revolution was over, such cults appear to have left few traditions; and neither they nor the reestablished Catholic Church, nor the religious minority groups, appear to have played any significant part in the revolutions of 1830 and 1848.

Thus, gradually, the pattern of popular protest, and the ideas that underlay it, would suffer a sea-change. In 1848, this process was by no means completed; but the new "industrial" crowd, with its richer stock of forward-looking concepts, was already clearly visible on the horizon.

II. Theoretical and Empirical Foundations

Introduction

A number of descriptive and speculative accounts of collective behavior were published after 1925, but it was not until 1938 when LaPiere's work, *Collective Behavior,* was published that a full volume was devoted to the subject. Blumer's (7) work, first published the following year, has since served as one of the major analytic models in the field. In the portion of his work presented here, Blumer identifies what he refers to as "elementary collective groupings," and in doing so sets forth the major conceptual units in collective behavior. The author distinguishes between various types of crowds and the stages of their formation, as well as the relationship of individual members to different types of collectivities. Blumer's differentiation between the crowd, the public, the mass, and social movements, and his specification of the relationship of each of these groups to the individual, did much to clarify the major conceptual units in the field, and also provided the basis for numerous research efforts.

Smelser (8) focuses on the nature of individual and group processes in collective behavior, as well as the relationship of collective behavior to social change in general. Of critical importance in understanding Smelser's theory is his differentiation between collective behavior and his general theory of social change that he terms *social action.* In his theory of social action, the author argues that when available resources in a society are inadequate for alleviating social strain, social action in the form of structural reorganization occurs. When strain is present, specific solutions within the existing social structure are first attempted. For example, individuals experiencing financial difficulties may attempt to increase their income or decide to spend their available resources more efficiently. If such solutions fail, there is a tendency to move from specific solutions to advocating more general social reorganization. Individuals unable to solve their financial difficulties through specific solutions within existing economic institutions, begin to view change in these institutions as the primary means of easing their difficulties. Once the "appropriate level of generality" has been reached, reorganization of the relevant social structure occurs, and new principles guiding behavior are developed. Based on these principles, individuals then formulate specific behavioral solutions aimed at reducing stress.

Smelser argues that collective behavior differs from this general process of social change in that when the appropriate level of generality relevant to alleviating stress is reached, individuals engaging in collective behavior develop a strong belief in the *generalized solution,* and expect that specific behavioral solutions will somehow emerge. Smelser calls this the "short-circuiting effect" in which collective mobilization takes the form of belief or wishful thinking, bypassing the specific steps necessary to make general solutions operational. Within this model, collective behavior is seen as the "action of the impatient," because action develops before specific resources for alleviating strain have been fully identified and mobilized.

Although Smelser's differentiation between "collective behavior" and "social action" is arbitrary and has not gained general acceptance in the field, his work still deserves critical attention in that it is the only comprehensive statement available that attempts to develop a theory of collective behavior within the framework of a general theory of social change.

The Langs' work (9) focuses on the evolution of, and dynamics within, social movements. The authors argue that successful social movements move through four major stages of development: The first, a period of social unrest often characterized by crowd behavior, is followed by a period of "popular excitement" during which the objectives of the movement are identified and clarified; the third stage of the typical social movement is characterized by the development of an organization, with the beginnings of a division of labor, criteria for membership, and other characteristics common to formal organizations; the last stage of movement evolution, institutionalization, is characterized by the development and maintenance of a bureaucratic structure. These stages of development should be viewed as general categories, as the precise nature of the events that occur during each stage varies considerably from movement to movement. For example, the Langs note that the "style of organization" varies considerably between social movements, and they outline the major factors influencing the type of organization, such as the goals of the movement, and the extent of opposition the movement encounters. In addition, the authors discuss the types of leaders and the characteristics of the participants found at each stage of social movements.

In contrast to the sociological approach employed by Blumer, Smelser, and the Langs, Cantril (10) focuses on the psychological processes important in understanding collective behavior. In his work presented here, the author discusses the concept of individual susceptibility to suggestion in relation to commitment to social movements. Central to his argument is the notion that individuals interpret events in their environment within a specific "frame of reference" which is the means by which "sense" is made of events in relation to other available information. According to Cantril, the degree of individual susceptibility is determined by the extent to which the individual desires an interpretation of a particular situation, coupled with an inability to formulate an adequate interpretation of the situation within a current frame of reference. The author points out that leaders of social movements are likely to use slogans and catch-all phrases that express general dissatisfaction, and encourage oversimplified courses of action, thus providing a simplified framework for interpreting complex events. The author argues that an individual who desires an interpretation of a particular set of circumstances will be highly susceptible to the rhetoric of a strong leader who can provide an interpretation of the situation that brings a sense of order to his world.

The work of Blumer, Smelser, Cantril, and the Langs can be viewed as initial attempts to explain collective behavior in general social and psychological terms. Although many aspects of the theories proposed by these authors have proven inaccurate in light of recent research, their work provides a framework for relating the diverse concepts in the field, as well as forming the basis for future research efforts.

The remaining articles in this part of the volume illustrate attempts at theory verification and conceptual clarification that took place during the 1950s. Hopper (11), for example, applies Blumer's theoretical framework to the study of the stages of the revolutionary process. In defining the ways in which revolutionary movements reorganize societal institutions in order to meet individual needs, the author identifies mechanisms for the expression of discontent, the types of leaders likely to emerge, as well as the forms of collective behavior most likely to lead to revolution.

The work of Turner and Surace (12) is exemplary of attempts to clarify the role of symbols in crowd behavior. Addressing the role of unambiguous symbols and their relationship to uniform crowd behavior, the authors argue that symbols perceived as unambiguously negative account for the similarity of emotional response from crowd participants. This uniformity of emotional response is, in turn, likely to result in actions that would usually be stifled or diverted by prevailing norms. Focusing on the role that unambiguous symbol development played in the outbreak of violence against Mexicans in California in 1943, the authors studied the context in which the term "Mexican" was used in the *Los Angeles Times* over a ten year period prior to the riots. Turner and Surace thought that as the riots drew nearer, the term "Mexican" would be stripped of all positive and ambivalent connotations, until it came to evoke unambiguously negative feelings in the community. Although this did not occur, the authors report that three years prior to the riots, the term "Zoot-Suiter," referring to a particular type of dress and hairstyle worn by members of the Mexican community, began to appear in newsprint. Thus, the authors conclude that although the term *Mexican* was used in neither more positive nor more negative contexts, the term "Zoot-Suiter," which was unambiguously negative, provided the basis for uniform emotional response and subsequent crowd behavior.

Vander Zanden's (13) work calls for a broadening of the definition of social movements to include those movements which attempt to resist change as well as those whose primary purpose is to effect change. This author points out that the emergence of a social movement may, but does not necessarily, bring about change. Frequently, social movements trigger the rise of opposing movements and the interaction between the two will have a substantial effect on the speed, extent and nature of resulting social change. After carefully analyzing the definition of social movements, Vander Zanden argues that countermovements, such as the one in the South after the 1954 Supreme Court desegregation ruling, should be viewed as true social movements. In addition to definitional clarification, Vander Zanden's contribution did much to enlarge the scope of theoretical development in the area by pointing out the necessity of *general* concepts and theoretical propositions that encompass all behaviors within a given domain.

Quarantelli's article (14) was one of the pioneering efforts in developing the notion that even the most ephemeral crowd behavior, panic, is not as random or irrational as once thought. This author outlines the processes involved in the panic situation, and proposes a number of ways to explain the behavior of panic participants. He argues that considerable cognitive skill is involved in such situations, and that although individuals generally ignore social solutions to their difficulty, they are not necessarily behaving irrationally. For example, individuals facing immediate danger from fire, may be acting quite reasonably in choosing to flee the scene, rather than attempting to put the fire out. In fact, their behavior may be the most appropriate course of action in the situation.

Turner's work (15) concludes Part II and outlines the significant issues and areas of research in the field that emerged during the 1950s. The author designates five major areas in need of further research: the processes through which decisions are made in the collective situation; the relationship between institutional authority and collective behavior; the relationship between changes in the value structure of society and the occurrence of collective behavior; the significance of counter movements; and the role of symbols in crowd behavior. As we approach the recent research in the field, Turner's article serves as a benchmark for measuring the progress that has been made over the last two decades.

7.

Herbert Blumer

ELEMENTARY COLLECTIVE GROUPINGS

The crowd

Much of the initial interest of sociologists in the field of collective behavior has centered on the study of the crowd. This interest was lively particularly towards the end of the last century, especially among French scholars. It gained its most vivid expression in the classical work, *The Crowd,* by Gustave LeBon. This work and others have provided us with much insight into the nature and behavior of the crowd, although much still remains unknown.

Types of crowds

It is convenient to identify four types of crowds. The first can be called a *casual* crowd, as in the instance of a street crowd watching a performer in a store window. The casual crowd usually has a momentary existence; more important, it has a very loose organization and scarcely any unity. Its members come and go, giving but temporary attention to the object which has awakened the interest of the crowd, and entering into only feeble association with one another. While the chief mechanisms of crowd formation are present in the casual crowd, they are so reduced in scope and weak in operation, that we need not concern ourselves further with this type of crowd. A second type may be designated as the *conventionalized crowd,* such

as the spectators at an exciting baseball game. Their behavior is essentially like that of casual crowds, except that it is expressed in established and regularized ways. It is this regularized activity that marks off the conventional crowd as a distinct type. The third type of crowd is the *acting,* aggressive crowd, best represented by a revolutionary crowd or a lynching mob. The outstanding mark of this type of crowd is the presence of an aim or objective toward which the activity of the crowd is directed. It is this type of crowd which is the object of concern in practically all studies of the crowd. The remaining type is the *expressive* or "dancing" crowd, such as one sees in the case of carnivals or in the beginning stage of many religious sects. Its distinguishing trait is that excitement is expressed in physical movement primarily as a form of release instead of being directed toward some objective. We shall consider the acting crowd, and then the expressive crowd.

Formation of crowds

The essential steps in the formation of a crowd seem to be quite clear. First is the occurrence of some exciting event which catches the attention and arouses the interest of people. In becoming preoccupied with this event and stirred by its excitatory character, an individual is already likely to lose some of his ordinary self-control and to be dominated by the exciting object. Further, this kind of experience, by arousing impulses and feelings, establishes a condition of tension

"Elementary Collective Groupings" (with minor deletions) by Dr. Herbert Blumer from *Principles of Sociology,* 3rd edition, edited by Alfred McClung Lee. Copyright © 1969 by Barnes & Noble, Inc. Used by permission of Harper & Row Publishers, Inc.

which, in turn, presses the individual on to action. Thus, a number of people stimulated by the same exciting event are disposed by that very fact to behave like a crowd.

This becomes clear in the second step—the beginning of the milling process. The tension of individuals who are aroused by some stimulating event, leads them to move around and to talk to one another; in this milling the incipient excitement becomes greater. The excitement of each is conveyed to others, and, as we have indicated above, in being reflected back to each, is intensified. The most obvious effect of this milling is to disseminate a common mood, feeling, or emotional impulse, and also to increase its intensity. This leads to a state of marked rapport wherein individuals become sensitive and responsive to one another and where, consequently, all are more disposed to act together as a collective unit.

Another important result may come from the milling process, and may be regarded as the third important step in the formation of the acting crowd. This step is the emergence of a common object of attention on which the impulses, feelings, and imagery of the people become focused. Usually the common object is the exciting event which has aroused the people; much more frequently, however, it is an image which has been built up and fixed through the talking and acting of people as they mill. This image, or object, like the excitement, is common and shared. Its importance is that it gives a common orientation to the people, and so provides a common objective to their activity. With such a common objective, the crowd is in a position to act with unity, purpose, and consistency.

The last step may be thought of as the stimulation and fostering of the impulses that correspond to the crowd objective, up to the point where the members are ready to act on them. This nurturing and crystallizing of impulses is a result of the interstimulation that takes place in milling and in response to leadership. It occurs primarily as a result of images that are aroused through the process of suggestion and imitation, and reinforced through mutual acceptance. When the members of a crowd have a common impulse oriented toward a fixed image and supported by an intense collective feeling, they are ready to act in the aggressive fashion typical of the acting crowd.

The acting crowd

It should be noted, first, that such a group is spontaneous and lives in the momentary present. As such it is not a society or a cultural group. Its action is not preset by accepted conventions, established expectations, or rules. It lacks other important marks of a society such as an established social organization, an established division of labor, a structure of established roles, a recognized leadership, a set of norms, a set of moral regulations, an awareness of its own identity, or a recognized "we-consciousness." Instead of acting, then, on the basis of established rule, it acts on the basis of aroused impulse. Just as it is, in this sense, a noncultural group, so likewise it tends to be a nonmoral group. In the light of this fact it is not difficult to understand that crowd actions may be strange, forbidding, and at times atrocious. Not having a body of definitions or rules to guide its behavior and, instead, acting on the basis of impulse, the crowd is fickle, suggestible, and irresponsible.

This character of the crowd can be appreciated better by understanding the condition of the typical member. Such an individual loses ordinary critical understanding and self-control as he enters into rapport with other crowd members and becomes infused by the collective excitement which dominates them. He responds immediately and directly to the remarks and actions of others instead of interpreting these gestures, as he would do in ordinary conduct. His inability to survey the actions of others before responding to them carries over to his own tendencies to act. Consequently, the impulses aroused in him by his sympathetic sharing of the collective excitement are likely to gain immediate expression instead of being submitted to his own judgment. This explains why suggestion is so pronounced in the crowd. It should be noted, however, that this suggestibility exists only along the line of the aroused impulses; suggestions made contrary to them are ignored. This limiting of the area of suggestibility, but with an intensification of the suggestibility inside of these limits, is a point which is frequently overlooked by students of crowd behavior.

The loss of customary critical interpretation and the arousing of impulses and excited feelings explain the queer, vehement, and surprising behavior so frequent among members of a genuine crowd. Impulses which ordinarily would be subject to a severe check by the individual's judgment and control of himself now have a free passage to expression. That many of these impulses should have an atavistic character is not strange, nor, consequently, is it surprising that much of the actual behavior should be violent, cruel, and destructive. Further, the release of impulses and feelings which encounter no restraint, which come to possess the individual, and which acquire a quasi-sanction through the support of other people, gives the individual a sense of power, of ego-expansion, and of rectitude. Thus, he is likely to experience a sense of invincibility and of conviction in his actions.

It should be borne in mind that this state of the members of the crowd is due to their extreme rapport and mutual excitement; and, in turn, that this rapport in the acting crowd has become organized around a common objective of activity. Common focusing of attention, rapport, and individual submergence—these exist as different phases of one another, and explain the unity of the crowd and the general character of its behavior. We should note that individuals may be physically present in a crowd yet not participate sympathetically in its process of shared excitement; such individuals are not true members of the crowd.

To prevent the formation of a mob or to break up a mob it is necessary to disrupt the milling process so that attention ceases to be focused collectively on one object. This is the theoretical principle underlying crowd control. Insofar as the attention of the members is directed toward different objects, they form an aggregation of individuals instead of a crowd united by intimate rapport. Thus, to throw people into a state of panic, or to get them interested in other objects, or to get them engaged in discussion or argumentation represents different ways in which a crowd can be broken up.

Our discussion of the crowd has presented the psychological bond of the crowd, or the spirit, that may be called "crowdmindedness," to use a felicitous phrase of E. A. Ross.[1] If we think in terms of crowd-mindedness, it is clear that many groups may take on the character of a crowd without having to be as small in size as in the instance of a lynching mob. Under certain conditions, a nation may come to be like a crowd. If the people become preoccupied with the same stirring event or object, if they develop a high state of mutual excitement marked by no disagreement, and if they have strong impulses to act toward the object with which they are preoccupied, their action will be like that of the crowd. We are familiar with such behavior on a huge scale in the case of social contagion, like that of patriotic hysteria.

The expressive crowd

The distinguishing feature of the acting crowd, as we have seen, is the direction of the attention toward some common objective or goal; the action of the crowd is the behavior gone through to reach that objective. In contrast, the expressive crowd has no goal or objective—its impulses and feelings are spent in mere expressive actions, usually in unrestrained physical movements, which give release to tension without having any other purpose. We see such behavior in a marked form in the saturnalia, the carnival, and the dancing crowds of primitive sects.

Comparisons with the acting crowd

In explaining the nature of the expressive crowd we should note that in formation and fundamental character it is very much like the acting crowd. It consists of people who are excited, who mill, and who in doing so, spread and intensify the excitement. There develops among them the same condition of rapport marked by quick and unwitting mutual responsiveness. Individuals lose awareness of themselves. Impulses and feelings are aroused, and are no longer subject to the constraint and control which an individual usually exercises over them. In these respects the expressive crowd is essentially like the acting crowd.

The fundamental difference is that the expressive crowd does not develop any image of a goal or objective, and, consequently, suggestion does not operate to build up a plan of action. Without having an objective toward which it might act, the crowd can release its aroused tension and excitement only in physical movement. Stated tersely, the crowd has to act, but it has nothing toward which it can act, and so it merely engages in excited movements. The excitement of the crowd stimulates further excitement which does not, however, become organized around some purposive act which the crowd seeks to carry out. In such a situation the expression of excited feeling becomes an end in itself; the behavior, therefore, may take the form of laughing, weeping, shouting, leaping, and dancing. In a more extreme expression, it may be in the form of uttering gibberish or having violent physical spasms.

Rhythmic expression

Perhaps the most interesting feature of this expressive behavior, as it is carried on collectively, is that it tends to become rhythmical; so that with sufficient repetition and with the existence of sufficient rapport, it takes on the form of people's acting in unison. In more advanced form it comes to be like a collective dance; it is this aspect that leads one to designate the expressive crowd as a dancing crowd. It may be said that just as an acting crowd develops its unity through the formation of a common objective, the expressive crowd forms its unity through the rhythmical expression of its tension.

This feature is of outstanding significance, for it throws considerable light on the interesting association between "dancing" behavior and primitive religious sentiment. To illustrate this point, let us consider the experience of the individual in such a crowd.

The individual in the expressive crowd

The stimulation that the individual receives from those with whom he is in rapport lessens his ordinary self-control and evokes and incites impulsive feelings which take possession of him. He feels carried away by a spirit whose source is unknown, but whose effect is acutely appreciated. There are two conditions which are likely to make this experience one of ecstasy and exaltation, and to seal it with a sacred or divine stamp. The first is that the experience is cathartic in nature. The individual who has been in a state of tension, discomfort, and perhaps anxiety, suddenly gains full release and experiences the joy and fullness that come with such relief. This organic satisfaction unquestionably yields a pleasure and exhilaration that makes the experience momentous. The fact that this mood has such complete and unobstructed control over the individual easily leads him to feel that he is possessed or pervaded by a kind of transcendental spirit. The other condition which gives the experience a religious character is the approval and sanction implied in the support coming from those with whom he is in rapport. The fact that others are sharing the same experience rids it of suspicion and enables its unqualified acceptance. When an experience gives complete and full satisfaction, when it is socially stimulated, approved, and sustained, and when it comes in the form of a mysterious possession from the outside, it easily acquires a religious character.

The development of collective ecstasy

When an expressive crowd reaches the height of such collective ecstasy, the tendency is for this feeling to be projected upon objects which are sensed as having some intimate connection with it. Thereupon such objects become sacred to the members of the crowd. These objects may vary; they may include persons (such as a religious prophet), the dance, a song, or physical objects which are felt to be linked with the ecstatic experience. The appearance of such sacred objects lays the basis for the formation of a cult, sect, or primitive religion.

Not all expressive crowds attain this stage of development. Most of them do not pass beyond the early milling or excited stage. But implicitly, they have the potentiality of doing so, and they have most of the characteristic features even though they be in a subdued form.

Like the acting crowd, the expressive crowd need not be confined to a small compact group whose members are in immediate physical proximity of one another. The behavior which is characteristic of it may be found on occasion in a large group, such as the nation-wide public.

Evaluation

A brief evaluation of the acting crowd and the expressive crowd can be made here. Both of them are spontaneous groupings. Both of them represent elementary collectivities. Their form and structure are not traceable to any body of culture or set of rules; instead, such structures as they have, arise indigenously out of the milling of excited individuals. The acting crowd focuses its tension on an objective and so becomes organized around a plan of action; the expressive crowd merely releases its tension in expressive movement which tends to become rhythmical and establishes unity in this fashion. In both crowds the individual is stripped of much of his conscious, ordinary behavior, and is rendered malleable by the crucible of collective excitement. With the breakdown of his previous personal organization, he is in a position to develop new forms of conduct and to crystallize a new personal organization along new and different lines. In this sense, crowd behavior is a means by which the breakup of the social organization and personal structure is brought about, and at the same time is a potential device for the emergence of new forms of conduct and personality. The acting crowd presents one of the alternative lines for such reorganization—the development of aggressive behavior in the direction of the purposive social change. We shall view this line of reorganization as giving rise to a political order. The expressive crowd stands for the other alternative—the release of inner tension in conduct which tends to become sacred and marked by deep sentiment. This might be regarded as giving rise to a religious order of behavior.

The mass

We are selecting the term *mass* to denote another elementary and spontaneous collective grouping which, in some respects, is like the crowd but is fundamentally different from it in other ways. The mass is represented by people who participate in mass behavior, such as those who are excited by some national event, those who share in a land boom, those who are interested in a murder trial which is reported in the press, or those who participate in some large migration.

Distinguishable features of the mass

So conceived, the mass has a number of distinguishable features. *First,* its membership may come from all walks of life, and from all distinguishable social strata; it may include people of different class position, of different vocation, of different cultural attainment, and of different wealth. One can recognize this in the case of the mass of people who follow a murder trial. *Second,* the mass is an anonymous group, or more exactly, is composed of anonymous individuals. *Third,* there exists little interaction or exchange of experience between the members of the mass. They are usually physically separated from one another, and, being anonymous, do not have the opportunity to mill as do the members of the crowd. *Fourth,* the mass is very loosely organized and is not able to act with the concertedness or unity that marks the crowd.

The role of individuals in the mass

The fact that the mass consists of individuals belonging to a wide variety of local groups and cultures is important. For it signifies that the object of interest which gains the attention of those who form the mass is something which lies on the outside of the local cultures and groups; and therefore, that this object of interest is not defined or explained in terms of the understandings or rules of these local groups. The object of mass interest can be thought of as attracting the attention of people away from their local cultures and spheres of life and turning it toward a wider universe, toward areas which are not defined or covered by rules, regulations, or expectations. In this sense the mass can be viewed as constituted by detached and alienated individuals who face objects or areas of life which are interesting, but which are also puzzling and not easy to understand and order. Consequently, before such objects, the members of the mass are likely to be confused and uncertain in their actions. Further, in not being able to communicate with one another, except in limited and imperfect ways, the members of the mass are forced to act separately, as individuals.

Society and the mass

From this brief characterization it can be seen that the mass is devoid of the features of a society or a community. It has no social organization, no body of custom and tradition, no established set of rules or rituals, no organized group of sentiments, no structure of status roles, and no established leadership. It merely consists of an aggregation of individuals who are separate, detached, anonymous, and thus, homogeneous as far as mass behavior is concerned. It can be seen, further, that the behavior of the mass, just because it is not made by pre-established rule or expectation, is spontaneous, indigenous, and elementary. In these respects, the mass is a great deal like the crowd.

In other respects, there is an important difference. It has already been noted that the mass does not mill or interact as the crowd does. Instead, the individuals are separated from one another and unknown to one another. This fact means that the individual in the mass, instead of being stripped of his self-awareness is, on the other hand, apt to be rather acutely self-conscious. Instead of acting in response to the suggestions and excited stimulation of those with whom he is in rapport, he acts in response to the object that has gained his attention and on the basis of the impulses that are aroused by it.

Nature of mass behavior

This raises the question as to how the mass behaves. The answer is in terms of each individual's seeking to answer his own needs. The form of mass behavior, paradoxically, is laid down by individual lines of activity and not by concerted action. These individual activities are primarily in the form of selections—such as the selection of a new dentifrice, a book, a play, a party platform, a new fashion, a philosophy, or a gospel—selections which are made in response to the vague impulses and feelings which are awakened by the object of mass interest. Mass behavior, even though a congeries of individual lines of action, may become a momentous significance. If these lines converge, the influence of the mass may be enormous, as is shown by the far-reaching effects on institutions ensuing from shifts in the selective interest of the mass. A political party may be disorganized or a commercial institution wrecked by such shifts in interest or taste.

When mass behavior becomes organized, as into a movement, it ceases to be mass behavior, but becomes societal in nature. Its whole nature changes in acquiring a structure, a program, a defining culture, traditions, prescribed rules, an in-group attitude, and a we-consciousness. It is for this reason that we have appropriately limited it to the forms of behavior which have been described.

Increasing importance of mass behavior

Under conditions of modern urban and industrial life, mass behavior has emerged in increasing magnitude and importance. This is due primarily to the operation of factors which have detached people from their local cultures and local group settings. Migration, changes of residence, newspapers, motion pictures, the radio, education—all have operated to detach individuals from customary moorings and thrust them into a new and wider world. In the face of this world, individuals have had to make adjustments on the basis of largely unaided selections. The convergence of their selections has made the mass a potent influence. At times, its behavior comes to approximate that of a crowd, especially under conditions of excitement. At such times it is likely to be influenced by excited appeals as these appear in the press or over the radio— appeals that play upon primitive impulses, antipathies, and traditional hatreds. This should not obscure the fact that the mass may behave without such crowdlike frenzy. It may be much more influenced by an artist or a writer who happens to sense the vague feelings of the mass and to give expression and articulation to them.

Instances of mass behavior

In order to make clearer the nature of the mass and of mass behavior, a brief consideration can be given to a few instances. Gold rushes and land rushes illustrate many of the features of mass behavior. The people who participate in them usually come from a wide variety of backgrounds; together they constitute a heterogeneous assemblage. Thus, those who engaged in the Klondike Rush or the Oklahoma Land Boom came from different localities and areas. In the rush, each individual (or at best, family) had his own goal or objective so that between the participants there was a minimum of cooperation and very little feeling of allegiance or loyalty. Each was trying to get ahead of the other, and each had to take care of himself. Once the rush is under way, there is little discipline, and no organization to enforce order. Under such conditions it is easy to see how a rush turns in to a stampede or a panic.

Mass advertising

Some further appreciation of the nature of mass behavior is yielded by a brief treatment of mass advertising. In such adver-

tising, the appeal has to be addressed to the anonymous individual. The relation between the advertisement and the prospective purchaser is a direct one—there is no organization or leadership which can deliver, so to speak, the body of purchasers to the seller. Instead, each individual acts upon the basis of his own selection. The purchasers are a heterogeneous group coming from many communities and walks of life; as members of the mass, however, because of their anonymity, they are homogeneous or essentially alike.

Proletarian masses

What are sometimes spoken of as the proletarian masses illustrate other features of the mass. They represent a large population with little organization or effective communication. Such people usually have been wrested loose from a stable group life. They are usually disturbed, even though it be only in the form of vague hopes or new tastes and interests. Consequently, there is a lot of groping in their behavior—an uncertain process of selection among objects and ideas that come to their attention.

The public

We shall consider the public as the remaining elementary collective grouping. The term *public* is used to refer to a group of people (*a*) who are confronted by an issue, (*b*) who are divided in their ideas as to how to meet the issue, and (*c*) who engage in discussion over the issue. As such, it is to be distinguished from a public in the sense of a national people, as when one speaks of the public of the United States, and also from a *following,* as in the instance of the "public" of a motion-picture star. The presence of an issue, of discussion, and of a collective opinion is the mark of the public.

The public as a group

We refer to the public as an elementary and spontaneous collective grouping because it comes into existence not as a result of design, but as a natural response to a certain kind of situation. That the public does not exist as an established group and that its behavior is not prescribed by traditions or cultural patterns is indicated by the very fact that its existence centers on the presence of an issue. As issues vary, so do the corresponding publics. And the fact that an issue exists signifies the presence of a situation which cannot be met on the basis of a cultural rule but which must be met by a collective decision arrived at through a process of discussion. In this sense, the public is a grouping that is spontaneous and not pre-established.

Characteristic features of the public

This elementary and spontaneous character of the public can be better appreciated by noticing that the public, like the crowd and the mass, is lacking in the characteristic features of a society. The existence of an issue means that the group has to act; yet there are no understandings, definitions, or rules prescribing what that action should be. If there were, there would be, of course, no issue. It is in this sense that we can speak of the public as having no culture—no traditions to dictate what its action shall be. Further, since a public comes into existence only with an issue it does not have the form or organization of a society. In it, people do not have fixed status roles. Nor does the public have any we-feeling or consciousness of its identity. Instead, the public is a kind of amorphous group whose size and membership varies with the issue; instead of having its activity prescribed, it is engaged in an effort to arrive at an act, and therefore forced to *create* its action.

The peculiarity of the public is that it is marked by disagreement and hence by *discussion* as to what should be done. This fact has a number of implications. For one thing, it indicates that the interaction that occurs in the public is markedly different from that which takes place in the crowd. A crowd mills, develops rapport, and reaches a unanimity unmarred by disagreement. The public interacts on the basis of interpretation, enters into dispute, and consequently is characterized by conflict relations. Correspondingly, individuals in the public are likely to have their self-consciousness intensified and their critical powers heightened instead of losing self-awareness and critical ability as occurs in the crowd. In the public, arguments are advanced, are criticized, and are met by counterarguments. The interaction, therefore, makes for opposition instead of the mutual support and unanimity that mark the crowd.

Another point of interest is that this discussion, which is based on difference, places some premium on facts and makes for rational consideration. While, as we shall see, the interaction may fall short by far of realizing these characteristics, the tendency is in their direction. The crowd means that rumor and spectacular suggestion predominate; but the presence of opposition and disagreement in the public means that contentions are challenged and become subject to criticism. In the face of attack that threatens to undermine their character, such contentions have to be bolstered or revised in the face of criticisms that cannot be ignored. Since facts can maintain their validity, they come to be valued; and since the discussion is argumentative, rational considerations come to occupy a role of some importance.

Behavior patterns of the public

Now we can consider the question as to how a public acts. This question is interesting, particularly because the public does not act like a society, a crowd, or the mass. A society manages to act by following a prescribed rule or consensus; a crowd, by developing rapport; and the mass, by the convergence of individual selections. But the public faces, in a sense, the dilemma of how to become a unit when it is actually divided, of how to act concertedly when there is a disagreement as to what the action should be. The public acquires its particular type of unity and manages to act by arriving at a collective decision or by developing a collective opinion. It becomes necessary to consider now the nature of public opinion and the manner of its formation.

The public, the crowd, and the mass

Before concluding the discussion of the public, it should be pointed out that under certain conditions the public may be changed into a crowd. Most propaganda tends to do this, anyway. When the people in the public are aroused by an appeal to a sentiment which is common to them, they begin to mill and to develop rapport. Then, their expression is in the form of public sentiment and not public opinion. In modern life, however, there seems to be less tendency for the public to become the crowd than for it to be displaced by the mass. The increasing detachment of people from local life, the multiplication of public issues, the expansion of agencies of mass communication, together with other factors, have led people to act increasingly

by individual selection rather than by participating in public discussion. So true is this, that in many ways the public and the mass are likely to exist intermingled with one another. This fact adds confusion to the scene of contemporary collective behavior and renders analysis by the student difficult.

Collective groupings and social change

In the discussion of elementary collective groupings we have considered the acting crowd, the expressive crowd, the mass, and the public. There are other primitive groupings which we can mention here only briefly, such as the panic, the stampede, the strike, the riot, the "popular justice" vigilante committee, the procession, the cult, the mutiny, and the revolt. Most of these groupings represent variations of the crowd; each of them operates through the primitive mechanisms of collective behavior which we have described. Like the four major types which we have considered, they are not societies, but operate outside of a governing framework of rules and culture. They are elementary, natural, and spontaneous, arising under certain fit circumstances.

The appearance of elementary collective groupings is indicative of a process of social change. They have the dual character of implying the disintegration of the old and the appearance of the new. They play an important part in the development of new collective behavior and of new forms of social life. More accurately the typical mechanisms of primitive association which they show have a significant role in the formation of a new social order.

It is to this problem of the formation of a new social order, that we shall now devote ourselves. Our task will be to consider primarily the social movements by which new kinds of collective behavior are built up and crystallized into fixed social forms.

Social movements can be viewed as collective enterprises seeking to establish a new order of life. They have their inception in a condition of unrest, and derive their motive power on one hand from dissatisfaction with the current form of life, and on the other hand, from wishes and hopes for a new scheme or system of living. The career of a social movement depicts the emergence of a new order of life. In its beginning, a social movement is amorphous, poorly organized, and without form; the collective behavior is on the primitive level that we have already discussed, and the mechanisms of interaction are the elementary, spontaneous mechanisms of which we have spoken. As a social movement develops, it takes on the character of a society. It acquires organization and form, a body of customs and traditions, established leadership, an enduring division of labor, social rules and social values—in short, a culture, a social organization, and a new scheme of life.

Our treatment of social movements will deal with three kinds — general social movements, specific social movements, and expressive social movements.[2]

General social movements

By general social movements we have in mind movements such as the labor movement, the youth movement, the women's movement, and the peace movement. Their background is constituted by gradual and pervasive changes in the values of people—changes which can be called cultural drifts. Such cultural drifts stand for a general shifting in the ideas of people, particularly along the line of the conceptions which people have of themselves, and of their rights and privileges. Over a period of time many people may develop a new view of what they believe

they are entitled to—a view largely made up of desires and hopes. It signifies the emergence of a new set of values, which influence people in the way in which they look upon their own lives. Examples of such cultural drifts in our own recent history are the increased value of health, the belief in free education, the extension of the franchise, the emancipation of women, the increasing regard for children, and the increasing prestige of science.

Indefinite images and behavior

The development of the new values which such cultural drifts bring forth involves some interesting psychological changes which provide the motivation for general social movements. They mean, in a general sense, that people have come to form new conceptions of themselves which do not conform to the actual positions which they occupy in their life. They acquire new dispositions and interests and, accordingly, become sensitized in new directions; and, conversely, they come to experience dissatisfaction where before they had none. These new images of themselves, which people begin to develop in response to cultural drifts, are vague and indefinite; and correspondingly, the behavior in response to such images is uncertain and without definite aim. It is this feature which provides a clue for the understanding of general social movements.

Characteristics of general social movements

General social movements take the form of groping and unco-ordinated efforts. They have only a general direction, toward which they move in a slow, halting, erratic yet persistent fashion. As movements they are unorganized, with neither established leadership nor recognized membership, and little guidance and control. Such a movement as the women's movement, which has the general and vague aim of the emancipation of women, suggests these features of a general social movement. The women's movement, like all general social movements, operates over a wide range—in the home, in marriage, in education, in industry, in politics, in travel—in each area of which it represents a search for an arrangement which will answer to the new idea of status being formed by women. Such a movement is episodic in its career, with very scattered manifestations of activity. It may show considerable enthusiasm at one point and reluctance and inertia at another; it may experience success in one area, and abortive effort in another. In general, it may be said that its progress is very uneven with setbacks, reverses, and frequent retreading of the same ground. At one time the impetus to the movement may come from people in one place, at another time in another place. On the whole the movement is likely to be carried on by many unknown and obscure people who struggle in different areas without their striving and achievements becoming generally known.

A general social movement usually is characterized by a literature, but the literature is as varied and ill-defined as is the movement itself. It is likely to be an expression of protest, with a general depiction of a kind of utopian existence. As such, it vaguely outlines a philosophy based on new values and self-conceptions. Such a literature is of great importance in spreading a message or view, however imprecise it may be, and so in implanting suggestions, awakening hopes, and arousing dissatisfactions. Similarly, the "leaders" of a general social movement play an important part—not in the sense of exercising directive control over the movement,

but in the sense of being pace-makers. Such leaders are likely to be "voices in the wilderness," pioneers without any solid following, and frequently not very clear about their own goals. However, their example helps to develop sensitivities, arouse hopes, and break down resistances. From these traits one can easily realize that the general social movement develops primarily in an informal, inconspicuous, and largely subterranean fashion. Its media of interaction are primarily reading, conversations, talks, discussions, and the perception of examples. Its achievements and operations are likely to be made primarily in the realm of individual experience rather than by noticeable concerted action of groups. It seems evident that the general social movement is dominated to a large extent by the mechanisms of mass behavior, such as we have described in our treatment of the mass. Especially in its earlier stages, general social movements are likely to be merely an aggregation of individual lines of action based on individual decisions and selections. As is characteristic of the mass and of mass behavior, general social movements are rather formless in organization and inarticulate in expression.

The basis for specific social movements

Just as cultural drifts provide the background out of which emerge general social movements, so the general social movement constitutes the setting out of which develop specific social movements. Indeed, a specific social movement is usually a crystallization of much of the motivation of dissatisfaction, hope, and desire awakened by the general social movement and the focusing of this motivation on some specific objective. A convenient illustration is the antislavery movement, which was, to a considerable degree, an individual expression of the widespread humanitarian movement of the nineteenth century. With this recognition of the relation between general and specific social movements, we can turn to a consideration of the latter.

Specific social movements

The outstanding instances of this type of movement are reform movements and revolutionary movements. A specific social movement is one which has a well-defined objective or goal which it seeks to reach. In this effort it develops an organization and structure, making it essentially a society. It develops a recognized and accepted leadership and a definite membership characterized by a "we-consciousness." It forms a body of traditions, a guiding set of values, a philosophy, sets of rules, and a general body of expectations. Its members form allegiances and loyalties. Within it there develops a division of labor, particularly in the form of a social structure in which individuals occupy status positions. Thus, individuals develop personalities and conceptions of themselves, representing the individual counterpart of a social structure.

A social movement, of the specific sort, does not come into existence with such a structure and organization already established. Instead, its organization and its culture are developed in the course of its career. It is necessary to view social movements from this temporal and developmental perspective. In the beginning a social movement is loosely organized and characterized by impulsive behavior. It has no clear objective; its behavior and thinking are largely under the dominance of restlessness and collective excitement. As a social movement develops, however, its behavior, which was originally dis-persed, tends to become organized, solidified, and persistent. It is possible to delineate stages roughly in the career of a social movement which represent this increasing organization. One scheme of four stages has been suggested by Dawson and Gettys.[3] These are the stage of social unrest, the stage of popular excitement, the stage of formalization, and the stage of institutionalization.

Stages of development

In the first of these four stages people are restless, uneasy, and act in the random fashion that we have considered. They are susceptible to appeals and suggestions that tap their discontent, and hence, in this stage, the agitator is likely to play an important role. The random and erratic behavior is significant in sensitizing people to one another and so makes possible the focusing of their restlessness on certain objects. The stage of popular excitement is marked even more by milling, but it is not quite so random and aimless. More definite notions emerge as to the cause of their condition and as to what should be done in the way of social change. So there is a sharpening of objectives. In this stage the leader is likely to be a prophet or a reformer. In the stage of formalization the movement becomes more clearly organized with rules, policies, tactics, and discipline. Here the leader is likely to be in the nature of a statesman. In the institutional stage, the movement has crystallized into a fixed organization with a definite personnel and structure to carry into execution the purposes of the movement. Here the leader is likely to be an administrator. In considering the development of the specific social movement our interest is less in considering the stages through which it passes than in discussing the mechanisms and means through which such a movement is able to grow and become organized. It is convenient to group these mechanisms under five heads: (1) agitation, (2) development of *esprit de corps,* (3) development of morale, (4) the formation of an ideology, and (5) the development of operating tactics.

The role of agitation

Agitation is of primary importance in a social movement. It plays its most significant role in the beginning and early stages of a movement, although it may persist in minor form in the later portions of the life-cycle of the movement. As the term suggests, agitation operates to arouse people and so make them possible recruits for the movement. It is essentially a means of exciting people and of awakening within them new impulses and ideas which make them restless and dissatisfied. Consequently, it acts to loosen the hold on them of their previous attachments, and to break down their previous ways of thinking and acting. For a movement to begin and gain impetus, it is necessary for people to be jarred loose from their customary ways of thinking and believing, and to have aroused within them new impulses and wishes. This is what agitation seeks to do. To be successful, it must first gain the attention of people; second, it must excite them, and arouse feelings and impulses; and third, it must give some direction to these impulses and feelings through ideas, suggestions, criticisms, and promises.

Agitation operates in two kinds of situations. One is a situation marked by abuse, unfair discrimination, and injustice, but a situation wherein people take this mode of life for granted and do not raise questions about it. Thus, while the situation is potentially fraught with suffering and protest, the people are marked by inertia. Their views of their situation

incline them to accept it; hence the function of the agitation is to lead them to challenge and question their own modes of living. It is in such a situation that agitation may create social unrest where none existed previously. The other situation is one wherein people are already aroused, restless, and discontented, but where they either are too timid to act or else do not know what to do. In this situation the function of agitation is not so much to implant the seeds of unrest, as to intensify, release, and direct the tensions which people already have.

Agitators seem to fall into two types corresponding roughly to these two situations. One type of agitator is an excitable, restless, and aggressive individual. His dynamic and energetic behavior attracts the attention of people to him; and the excitement and restlessness of his behavior tends to infect them. He is likely to act with dramatic gesture and to talk in terms of spectacular imagery. His appearance and behavior foster the contagion of unrest and excitement. This type of agitator is likely to be most successful in the situation where people are already disturbed and unsettled; in such a situation his own excited and energetic activity can easily arouse other people who are sensitized to such behavior and already disposed to excitability.

The second type of agitator is more calm, quiet, and dignified. He stirs people not by what he does, but what he says. He is likely to be a man sparing in his words, but capable of saying very caustic, incisive, and biting things—things which get "under the skin" of people and force them to view things in a new light. This type of agitator is more suited to the first of the social situations discussed—the situation where people endure hardships or discrimination without developing attitudes of resentment. In this situation, his function is to make people aware of their own position and of the inequalities, deficiencies, and injustices that seem to mark their lot. He leads them to raise questions about what they have previously taken for granted and to form new wishes, inclinations, and hopes.

The function of agitation, as stated above, is in part to dislodge and stir up people and so liberate them for movement in new directions. More specifically, it operates to change the conceptions which people have of themselves, and the notions which they have of their rights and dues. Such new conceptions involving beliefs that one is justly entitled to privileges from which he is excluded, provide the dominant motive force for the social movement. Agitation, as the means of implanting these new conceptions among people, becomes, in this way, of basic importance to the success of asocial movement.

A brief remark relative to the tactics of agitation may be made here. It is sufficient to say that the tactics of agitation vary with the situation, the people, and the culture. A procedure which may be highly successful in one situation may turn out to be ludicrous in another situation. This suggests the problem of identifying different types of situations and correlating with each the appropriate form of agitation. Practically no study has been conducted on this problem. Here, one can merely state the truism that the agitator, to be successful, must sense the thoughts, interests, and values of his listeners.

The development of *esprit de corps*

Agitation is merely the means of arousing the interest of people and thus getting them to participate in a movement. While it serves to recruit members, to give initial impetus, and to give some direction, by itself it could never organize or sustain a movement. Collective activities based on mere agitation would be sporadic, disconnected, and short-lived. Other mechanisms have to enter to give solidity and persistency to a social movement. One of these is the development of *esprit de corps*.

Esprit de corps might be thought of as the organizing of feelings on behalf of the movement. In itself, it is the sense which people have of belonging together and of being identified with one another in a common undertaking. Its basis is constituted by a condition of rapport. In developing feelings of intimacy and closeness, people have the sense of sharing a common experience and of forming a select group. In one another's presence they feel at ease and as comrades. Personal reserve breaks down and feelings of strangeness, difference, and alienation disappear. Under such conditions, relations tend to be of co-operation instead of personal competition. The behavior of one tends to facilitate the release of behavior on the part of others, instead of tending to inhibit or check that behavior; in this sense each person tends to inspire others. Such conditions of mutual sympathy and responsiveness obviously make for concerted behavior.

Esprit de corps is of importance to a social movement in other ways. Very significant is the fact that it serves to reinforce the new conception of himself that the individual has formed as a result of the movement and of his participation in it. His feeling of belonging with others, and they with him, yields him a sense of collective support. In this way his views of himself and of the aims of the movement are maintained and invigorated. It follows that the development of *esprit de corps* helps to foster an attachment of people to a movement. Each individual has his sentiments focused on, and intertwined with, the objectives of the movement. The resulting feeling of expansion which he experiences is in the direction of greater allegiance to the movement. It should be clear that *esprit de corps* is an important means of development solidarity and so of giving solidity to a movement.

How is *esprit de corps* developed in a social movement? It would seem chiefly in three ways: the development of an in-group—out-group relation, the formation of informal fellowship association, and the participation in formal ceremonial behavior.

The In-Group—Out-Group Relation. The nature of the in-group—out-group relation should be familiar to the student. It exists when two groups come to identify each other as enemies. In such a situation each group regards itself as the upholder of virtue and develops among its members feelings of altruism, loyalty, and fidelity. The out-group is regarded as unscrupulous and vicious, and is felt to be attacking the values which the in-group holds dear. Before the out-group the members of the in-group not only feel that they are right and correct, but believe they have a common responsibility to defend and preserve their values.

The value of these in-group—out-group attitudes in developing solidarity in a social movement is quite clear. The belief on the part of its members that the movement is being opposed unjustly and unfairly by vicious and unscrupulous groups serves to rally the members around their aims and values. To have an enemy, in this sense, is very important for imparting solidarity to the movement. In addition, the "enemy" plays the important role of a scapegoat. It is advantageous to a movement to develop an enemy; this development is usually in itself spontaneous. Once made, it functions to establish *esprit de corps.*

Informal Fellowship. Esprit de corps is formed also in a very significant way by the development of informal association on the basis of fellowship. Where people can come together informally in this way they have the opportunity of coming to know one another as human beings instead of as institutional symbols. They are then in a much better position to take one another's roles and, unwittingly, to share one another's experience. It seems that in such a relationship, people unconsciously import and assimilate into themselves the gestures, attitudes, values, and philosophy of life of one another. The net result is to develop a common sympathy and sense of intimacy which contributes much to solidarity. Thus, we find in social movements the emergence and use of many kinds of informal and communal association. Singing, dancing, picnics, joking, having fun, and friendly informal conversation are important devices of this sort in a social movement. Through them, the individual gets a sense of status and a sense of social acceptance and support, in place of prior loneliness and personal alienation.

Ceremonial Behavior. The third important way in which social movements develop *esprit de corps* is through the use of formal ceremonial behavior and of ritual. The value of mass meetings, rallies, parades, huge demonstrations, and commemorative ceremonies has always been apparent to those entrusted with the development of a social movement; the value is one that comes from large assemblages, in the form of the sense of vast support that is experienced by the participant. The psychology that is involved here is the psychology of being on parade. The individual participant experiences the feeling of considerable personal expansion and therefore has the sense of being somebody distinctly important. Since this feeling of personal expansion comes to be identified with the movement as such, it makes for *esprit de corps*. Likewise, the paraphernalia of ritual possessed by every movement serves to foster feelings of common identity and sympathy. This paraphernalia consists of a set of sentimental symbols, such as slogans, songs, cheers, poems, hymns, expressive gestures, and uniforms. Every movement has some of these. Since they acquire a sentimental significance symbolizing the common feelings about the movement, their use serves as a constant reliving and re-enforcement of these mutual feelings.

Esprit de corps may be regarded, then, as an organization of group feeling and essentially as a form of group enthusiasm. It is what imparts life to a movement. Yet just as agitation is inadequate for the development of a movement, so is mere reliance on *esprit de corps* insufficient. A movement which depends entirely on *esprit de corps* is usually like a boom and is likely to collapse in the face of a serious crisis. Since the allegiance which it commands is based merely on heightened enthusiasm, it is likely to vanish with the collapse of such enthusiasm. Thus, to succeed, especially in the face of adversity, a movement must command a more persistent and fixed loyalty. This is yielded by the development of morale.

The development of morale

As we have seen, *esprit de corps* is a collective feeling which gives life, enthusiasm, and vigor to a movement. Morale can be thought of as giving persistency and determination to a movement; its test is whether solidarity can be maintained in the face of adversity. In this sense, morale can be thought of as a group will or an enduring collective purpose.

Morale seems to be based on, and yielded by, a set of convictions. In the case of a social movement these seem to be of three kinds. First is a conviction of the rectitude of the purpose of the movement. This is accompanied by the belief that the attainment of the objectives of the movement will usher in something approaching a millennial state. What is evil, unjust, improper, and wrong will be eradicated with the success of the movement. In this sense, the goal is always overvalued. Yet these beliefs yield to the numbers of a movement a marked confidence in themselves. A second conviction closely identified with these beliefs is a faith in the ultimate attainment, by the movement, of its goal. There is believed to be a certain inevitability about this. Since the movement is felt to be a necessary agent for the regeneration of the world, it is regarded as being in line with the higher moral values of the universe, and in this sense as divinely favored. Hence, there arises the belief that success is inevitable, even though it be only after a hard struggle. Finally, as part of this complex of convictions, there is the belief that the movement is charged with a sacred mission. Together, these convictions serve to give an enduring and unchangeable character to the goal of a movement and a tenacity to its effort. Obstructions, checks, and reversals are occasions for renewed effort instead of for disheartenment and despair, since they do not seriously impair the faith in the rectitude of the movement nor in the inevitability of its success.

It is clear from this explanation that the development of morale in a movement is essentially a matter of developing a sectarian attitude and a religious faith. This provides a cue to the more prominent means by which morale is built up in a movement. One of these is found in the emergence of a saint cult which is to be discerned in every enduring and persisting social movement. There is usually a major saint and a series of minor saints, chosen from the popular leaders of the movement. Hitler, Lenin, Marx, Mary Baker Eddy, and Sun Yat-sen will serve as convenient examples of major saints. Such leaders become essentially deified and endowed with miraculous power. They are regarded as grossly superior, intelligent, and infallible. People develop toward them attitudes of reverence and awe, and resent efforts to depict them as ordinary human beings. The pictures or other mementos of such individuals come to have the character of religious idols. Allied with the saints of a movement are its heroes and its martyrs. They also come to be regarded as sacred figures. The development of this whole saint cult is an important means of imparting essentially a religious faith to the movement and of helping to build up the kind of convictions spoken of above.

Similar in function is the emergence in the movement of a creed and of a sacred literature. These, again, are to be found in all persisting social movements. Thus, as has been said frequently, *Das Kapital* and *Mein Kampf* have been the bibles respectively of the communist movement and of the National Socialist movement. The role of a creed and literature of this sort in imparting religious conviction to a movement should be clear.

Finally, great importance must be attached to myths in the development of morale in a social movement. Such myths may be varied. They may be myths of being a select group or a chosen people; myths of the inhumanity of one's opponents; myths about the destiny of the movement; myths depicting a glorious and millennial society to be realized by the movement. Such myths usually grow out of, and in response to, the desires and hopes of the people in the movement and acquire by virtue of their collective character a solidity, a permanency, and an

unquestioned acceptance. It is primarily through them that the members of the movement achieve the dogmatic fixity of their convictions, and seek to justify their actions to the rest of the world.

The development of group ideology

Without an ideology a social movement would grope along in an uncertain fashion and could scarcely maintain itself in the face of pointed opposition from outside groups. Hence, the ideology plays a significant role in the life of a movement; it is a mechanism essential to the persistency and development of a movement. The ideology of a movement consists of a body of doctrine, beliefs, and myths. More specifically, it seems to consist of the following: *first,* a statement of the objective, purpose, and premises of the movement; *second,* a body of criticism and condemnation of the existing structure which the movement is attacking and seeking to change; *third,* a body of defense doctrine which serves as a justification of the movement and of its objectives; *fourth,* a body of belief dealing with policies, tactics, and practical operation of the movement; and, *fifth,* the myths of the movement.

This ideology is almost certain to be of a twofold character. In the first place, much of it is erudite and scholarly. This is the form in which it is developed by the intellectuals of the movement. It is likely to consist of elaborate treatises of an abstract and highly logical character. It grows up usually in response to the criticism of outside intellectuals, and seeks to gain for its tenets a respectable and defensible position in this world of higher learning and higher intellectual values. The ideology has another character, however—a popular character. In this guise, it seeks to appeal to the uneducated and to the masses. In its popular character, the ideology takes the form of emotional symbols, shibboleths, stereotypes, smooth and graphic phrases, and folk arguments. It deals, also, with the tenets of the movement, but presents them in a form that makes for their ready comprehension and consumption.

The ideology of a movement may be thought of as providing a movement with its philosophy and its psychology. It gives a set of values, a set of convictions, a set of criticisms, a set of arguments, and a set of defenses. As such, it furnishes to a movement (*a*) direction, (*b*) justification, (*c*) weapons of attack, (*d*) weapons of defense, and (*e*) inspiration and hope. To be effective in these respects, the ideology must carry respectability and prestige—a character that is provided primarily by the intelligentsia of the movement. More important than this, however, is the need of the ideology to answer to the distress, wishes, and hopes of the people. Unless it has this popular appeal, it will be of no value to the movement.

The role of tactics

We have referred to tactics as the fifth major mechanism essential to the development of a social movement. Obviously the tactics are evolved along three lines: gaining adherents, holding adherents, and reaching objectives. Little more can be said than this, unless one deals with specific kinds of movements in specific kinds of situations. For, tactics are always dependent on the nature of the situation in which a movement is operating and always with reference to the cultural background of the movement. This functional dependency of tactics on the peculiarity of the situation helps to explain the ludicrous failures that frequently attend the application of certain tactics to one situation even though they may have been successful in other situations. To attempt revolutionary tactics these days in terms of the tactics of two centuries ago would be palpably foolish. Similarly, to seek to develop a movement in this country in terms of tactics employed in a similar movement in some different cultural setting would probably bring very discouraging results. In general, it may be said that tactics are almost by definition flexible and variable, taking their form from the nature of the situation, the exigencies of the circumstances, and the ingenuity of the people.

We can conclude this discussion of the five mechanisms considered merely by reiterating that the successful development of a movement is dependent on them. It is these mechanisms which establish a program, set policies, develop and maintain discipline, and evoke allegiance.

Reform and Revolution

Mention has been made of the fact that specific social movements are primarily of two sorts: reform and revolutionary movements. Both seek to effect changes in the social order and in existing institutions. Their life-cycles are somewhat similar, and the development of both is dependent on the mechanisms which we have just discussed. However, noteworthy differences exist between the two; some of these differences will now be indicated.

The two movements differ in the *scope of their objectives*. A reform movement seeks to change some specific phase or limited area of the existing social order; it may seek, for example, to abolish child labor or to prohibit the consumption of alcohol. A revolutionary movement has a broader aim; it seeks to reconstruct the entire social order.

This difference in objective is linked with a *different vantage point of attack*. In endeavoring to change just a portion of the prevailing social order, the reform movement accepts the basic tenets of that social order. More precisely, the reform movement accepts the existing mores; indeed, it uses them to criticize the social defects which it is attacking. The reform movement starts with the prevailing code of ethics, and derives much of its support because it is so well grounded on the ethical side. This makes its position rather unassailable. It is difficult to attack a reform movement or reformers on the basis of their moral aims; the attack is usually more in the form of caricature and ridicule, and in characterizing reformers as visionary and impractical. By contrast, a revolutionary movement always challenges the existing mores and proposes a new scheme of moral values. Hence, it lays itself open to vigorous attack from the standpoint of existing mores.

A third difference between the two movements follows from the points which have been made. A reform movement has *respectability*. By virtue of accepting the existing social order and of orienting itself around the ideal code, it has a claim on existing institutions. Consequently, it makes use of these institutions such as the school, the church, the press, established clubs, and the government. Here again the revolutionary movement stands in marked contrast. In attacking the social order and in rejecting its mores, the revolutionary movement is blocked by existing institutions and its use of them is forbidden. Thus, the revolutionary movement is usually and finally driven underground; whatever use is made of existing institutions has to be carefully disguised. In general, whatever agitation, proselytizing, and maneuvers are carried on by revolutionary movements have to be done outside the fold of existing institutions. In the event that a reform movement is felt as challenging too seriously some powerful

class or vested interests, it is likely to have closed to it the use of existing institutions. This tends to change a reform movement into a revolutionary movement; its objectives broaden to include the reorganization of the institutions which are now blocking its progress.

The differences in position between reform and revolutionary movements bring in an important distinction in their *general procedure and tactics.* A reform movement endeavors to proceed by developing a public opinion favorable to its aims; consequently, it seeks to establish a public issue and to make use of the discussion process which we have already considered. The reform party can be viewed as a conflict group, opposed by interest groups and surrounded by a large inert population. The reform movement addresses its message to this indifferent or disinterested public in the effort to gain its support. In contradistinction, the revolutionary movement does not seek primarily to influence public opinion, but instead tries to make converts. In this sense it operates more like a religion.

This means some difference as to groups among which the two movements respectively conduct their agitation and seek their adherents. The reform movement, while usually existing on behalf of some distressed or exploited group, does little to establish its strength among them. Instead, it tries to enlist the allegiance of a middle-class public on the outside and to awaken within them a vicarious sympathy for the oppressed group. Hence, generally, it is infrequent that the leadership or membership of a reform movement comes from the group whose rights are being espoused. In this sense a revolutionary movement differs. Its agitation is carried on among those who are regarded as in a state of distress or exploitation. It endeavors to establish its strength by bringing these people inside of its ranks. Hence, the revolutionary movement is usually a lower-class movement operating among the underprivileged.

Finally, by virtue of these characteristic differences, the two movements diverge in their functions. The primary function of the reform movement is probably not so much the bringing about of social change, as it is to reaffirm the ideal values of a given society. In the case of a revolutionary movement, the tendency to dichotomize the world between those who have and those who have not, and to develop a strong, cohesive, and uncompromising group out of the latter, makes its function that of introducing a new set of essentially religious values.

A concluding remark may be made about specific social movements. They can be viewed as societies in miniature, and as such, represent the building up of organized and formalized collective behavior out of what was originally amorphous and undefined. In their growth a social organization is developed, new values are formed, and new personalities are organized. These, indeed, constitute their residue. They leave behind an institutional structure and a body of functionaries, new objectives and views, and a new set of self-conceptions.

Notes

1. E. A. Ross, *Social Psychology* (New York: Macmillan Co., 1908).

2. Attention is called, in passing, to spatial movements, such as nomadic movements, barbaric invasions, crusades, pilgrimages, colonization, and migrations. Such movements may be carried on as societies, as in the case of tribal migrations; as diverse peoples with a common goal, as in the case of the religious crusades of the Middle Ages; or as individuals with similar goals, as in most of the immigration into the United States. Mechanisms of their collective operation will be dealt with in the following discussion of social movements. In themselves, such movements are too complicated and diversified to be dealt with adequately here.

3. C. A. Dawson and W. E. Gettys, *Introduction to Sociology* (Rev. ed.; New York: Ronald Press Co., 1935, chap. 19).

8.

Neil J. Smelser

THE NATURE OF COLLECTIVE BEHAVIOR

The general nature of structural reorganization

When strain exists, we might say that the components of social action are out of order and require fixing. How, *in general,* is strain overcome? How is social action repaired? By outlining the general charac-

Reprinted with permission of Macmillan Publishing Company, from *Theory of Collective Behavior,* pp. 67-78, by Neil J. Smelser.

ter of the process of reorganizing the components of action, we shall be able to specify the nature of collective behavior. To facilitate our discussion we have reproduced Table 1—the components of social action in full detail.

The general principle for reconstituting social action is this: when strain exists attention shifts to the higher levels of the components to seek resources to overcome this strain. We may characterize this

TABLE 1
Levels of Specificity of the Components of Action

Level	Values	Norms	Mobilization of motivation for organized action	Situational facilities
1	Societal values	General conformity	Socialized motivation	Preconceptions concerning causality
2	Legitimization of values for institutionalized sectors	Specification of norms according to institutional sectors	Generalized performance capacity	Codification of knowledge
3	Legitimization of rewards	Specification of norms according to types of roles and organizations	Trained capacity	Technology, or specification of knowledge in situational terms
4	Legitimization of individual commitment	Specification of requirements for individual observation of norms	Transition to adult role-assumption	Procurement of wealth, power, or prestige to activate Level 3
5	Legitimization of competing values	Specification of norms of competing institutional sectors	Allocation to sector of society	Allocation of effective technology to sector of society
6	Legitimization of values for realizing organizational goals	Specification of rules of cooperation and coordination within organization	Allocation to specific roles or organization	Allocation of effective technology to roles or organizations
7	Legitimization of values for expenditure of effort	Specification of schedules and programs to regulate activity	Allocation to roles and tasks within organization	Allocation of facilities within organization to attain concrete goals

More specific (left vertical axis)

More specific ⟶

process in the language of Table 1 by saying that, in the search for solutions to conditions of strain, people turn their attention either *upward* or *to the left,* or *both.*

To illustrate the *upward* movement we shall consider a situation of strain in American society which was particularly acute during the first two years or so following the launching of the first Russian Sputnik in the fall of 1957. Because Americans judged that progress in the conquest of space was important for our international prestige, the pressure to produce successful space vehicles was great. Yet we could not assemble the facilities to put even a modest capsule into orbit. We were uncertain whether a military or civilian agency was better suited to develop a space program, and how resources should be allocated to

develop the best space equipment in the shortest time. Thus serious strains began to build up at the operative levels of the Facilities Series (Levels 5-7 of Table 1).

How might these strains have been overcome? We could have encouraged the space program by increasing its budget and by giving political authorization to various space agencies to move ahead quickly. Such action would have invested greater financial and political resources in the space effort. Formally, this kind of action can be described as a movement *up* the Facilities Scale to Level 4 in order to overcome the strains at the lower levels.

This movement to Level 4, however, would have been satisfactory *only if* we had already possessed an adequate technology for producing the appropriate kinds of space vehicles. In fact, we did not. Merely to allocate more funds and greater authority to space agencies would not have been enough. It was necessary to move higher in the Facilities Scale in an attempt to improve our technology (Level 3).

Yet technology alone might not have been enough. Some persons felt that without "basic research" we were inherently limited in our ability to develop an effective space program. What is basic research? It is the production of *scientific knowledge itself,* on which new technology can be built. Formally, basic research means activity at Level 2 of the Facilities Series; this activity is more generalized than the production of technology. The principle of moving up the levels of generality, then, is that when any given level (e.g., technology) reaches a limit and becomes inadequate to deal with the condition of strain, it is necessary to move to the next higher level (e.g., basic research) in order to broaden the facilities for attacking the strain.

One more level of generality goes beyond Level 2. In the flurry of excitement, dismay, and self-criticism after the Russians launched their first Sputnik, some persons felt that American society has the wrong "approach" to scientific endeavor. American society, it was felt, is too pragmatic. Historically we have had to rely on European scientists for high-level theory in mathematics and physics; we, as technicians, have applied this theory, not created it. To develop a really advanced space program it is necessary to *go beyond* the basic research possible in our system; it is necessary to create a new outlook, perhaps even a new philosophy (Level 1). Only then would we generate fundamental scientific knowledge (Level 2) and apply it down the line through technology (Level 3) and investment (Level 4) to the world of operations (Levels 5-7).

The reduction of strains such as the unfulfilled demand for an adequate space program frequently lies in the *generaliza-*

tion of facilities. If facilities at one level are inadequate, attention turns to the next higher level. After reconstitution occurs at the higher level, moreover, the new higher-level facilities must be reapplied back down the line to the lower levels. New basic research must be converted into new technology; new investment and authorization must be given this new technology; new agencies must be set up or old ones modified, and so on. For any given empirical case of strain, the exact level of generality which must be reconstituted to overcome the strain depends on two things: (*a*) the seriousness of the initial conditions of strain, and (*b*) the adequacy of the existing facilities at each level to meet the conditions of strain.

To illustrate the process of generalization *to the left* in Table 1, we shall consider the strains occasioned by a major financial crisis and business depression. Many persons lose their jobs, others their fortunes. Strain concentrates on the deprivation of rewards (Mobilization Series) and on the disorganization of norms governing market behavior (Normative Series).[1] How can such conditions of strain be attacked? The first line of attack would be to punish those individuals—e.g., financiers or government officials—who behaved irresponsibly. This reaction concentrates on the Mobilization Series. It is not too drastic from the standpoint of the total system, for it merely withholds rewards from *particular* agents who presumably behaved imprudently or dishonestly enough to bring on an economic crisis.

A more general solution would be to pass laws and regulations which affect not only those who behaved irresponsibly in the past, but also all others who might do so in the future. An example would be to place restrictions on those speculative practices that were to blame for the financial collapse. Thus the slogan "there ought to be a law" is more drastic than the slogan "throw the rascals out" because it is more general in its applicability. The former deals with the Normative Series rather than with particular agents.

Even more general is a solution that brings the values of the economic system itself into question. The most drastic attack on the system that produces economic crises and business depressions would be to do away with the system itself and bring some sort of socialistic values to bear. This solution is more far-reaching than merely passing laws and regulations, for it means reorganizing the values by which the laws and regulations are legitimized.

What happens, then, to social action when strain exists? Attempts are made to move to higher-level components, reconstitute them, then incorporate the new principles back into the more concrete, operative levels of social action. In the event of failure at one level of generality, moreover, the tendency is to "appeal to an even higher court" in an attempt to understand and control the action that is under strain at the lower levels. This process of generalization moves toward the higher levels of each individual component, toward the higher-level components (norms, values), or both. Having generalized to higher levels, attempts are then made to work "back down the line." Attempts are made to generalize, then respecify; the components of action are first *destructured*, then *restructured*.[2] Many instances of social change can be interpreted according to this scheme.[3]

Collective behavior as generalized behavior

Collective behavior involves a generalization to a high-level component of action. Like many other kinds of behavior, it is a search for solutions to conditions of strain by moving to a more generalized level of resources. Once the generalization has taken place, attempts are made to reconstitute the meaning of the high-level component. At this point, however, the critical feature of collective behavior appears. Having redefined the high-level component, people do not proceed to respecify, step by step, down the line to reconstitute social action. Rather, they develop a belief which "short-circuits" from a very generalized component *directly* to the focus of strain. The accompanying expectation is that the strain can be relieved by a direct application of a generalized component. From a slightly different perspective, collective behavior is a *compressed* way of attacking problems created by strain. It compresses several levels of the components of action into a single belief, from which *specific operative solutions* are expected to flow. An episode of collective behavior itself occurs when people are mobilized for action on the basis of such a belief. Thus our formal characterization of collective behavior is this: *an uninstitutionalized[4] mobilization for action in order to modify one or more kinds of strain on the basis of a generalized reconstitution of a component of action.*

In the following chapter we shall discuss hysterical and wish-fulfillment beliefs. Both beliefs arise in a situation of strain (for example, danger to life, threat of loss of funds). Both beliefs also constitute redefinitions of the situation of strain. In these redefinitions some aspect of the situation is selected and attributed a *power* or *force* (Facilities Level 1)[5] that is sufficiently generalized to *guarantee the outcome* of the situation at hand. This outcome may be a catastrophe (produced by the negative forces envisioned in a hysterical belief) or a blessing (produced by the positive forces envisioned in a wish-fulfillment belief). The force may be felt to reside in any object, event, action, or verbal formula. The defining characteristic of such a force is that it will guarantee the outcome of an ambiguous situation of strain. Such a force operates, moreover, without reference to the many steps of respecification that must intervene between generalized force and concrete situation to make the force genuinely operative.

Take the space example again. We would consider it a wish-fulfillment belief if a body of persons subscribed to the following: *If only* we concerned ourselves with purifying and reaffirming the American way of life, we would not be experiencing frustrations in the development of operative space vehicles. This assumes that generalized facilities—"the American way"—will guarantee a specific solution and that the intervening steps of scientific codification, technological specification, investment, and so on, will follow. In reality each of these steps contributes in transforming the American way into particular successes. The hypothetical faith in the American way alone, however, short-circuits many of these necessary steps, and thus constitutes a compressed solution to the problem of facilities.

We shall find this "if only" mentality in the beliefs associated with all forms of collective behavior. For instance, in the norm-oriented movement, we shall find extraordinary results promised if only certain reforms are adopted, and (on the negative side) gloomy predictions of decay and collapse if the sources of strain are not attacked quickly and vigorously. *Adherents to such movements exaggerate "reality"* because their action is based on beliefs which are both *generalized and short-circuited.*

In the detailed expositions that comprise the rest of the volume we shall expand and document our characterization of collective behavior. We can suggest already, however, why collective behavior displays some of the crudeness, excess, and eccentricity that it does. By short-circuiting from high-level to low-level components of social action, collective episodes by pass many of the specifications, contingencies, and controls that are required to make the generalized components operative. Furthermore, "solutions" to situations of strain that are produced by the riot and craze are sometimes "irresponsible" because the headlong attempt to apply generalized beliefs to specific situations disregards many existing moral and legal restrictions and violates the interests and integrity of many individuals and groups.

Collective behavior, then, is the action of the impatient. It contrasts with the processes of social readjustment that do not short-circuit the journey from generalized belief to specific situations. Historically, collective behavior is closely associated with processes of structural reorganization of the components of action. In fact, episodes of collective behavior often constitute an early stage of social change[6]; they occur when conditions of strain have arisen, but before social resources have been mobilized for a specific and possibly effective attack on the sources of strain.[7] This is one reason for defining collective behavior as uninstitutionalized; it occurs when structured social action is under strain and when institutionalized means of overcoming the strain are inadequate. We might note that certain types of social control operate as an intermediary between these short-circuited collective episodes and orderly social change. Social control blocks the headlong attempts of collective episodes to bring quick results; if social control is effective, moreover, it channels the energy of collective outbursts into more modest kinds of behavior.

Exclusion of other phenomena from the field of collective behavior

According to our definition, any instance of collective behavior must contain the following: (*a*) uninstitutionalized (*b*) collective action, (*c*) taken to modify a condition of strain (*d*) on the basis of a generalized reconstitution of a component of action. The term "collective behavior" has in the past been applied to many types of behavior which have one or several, but not all, of these characteristics. For this and other reasons, "collective behavior . . . is obviously a catchall for various phenomena that do not readily fit into conceptions of institutional order."[8] We shall now mention several types of behavior—some of which have been called collective behavior—which we do not intend to encompass by our technical definition:

(1) Collective reaffirmations of values, rituals, festivals, ceremonials, and rites of passage. By these we mean, for example, the homecoming, the alumni rally, the salute to the flag, the patriotic demonstration on holidays, the ritual rebellion, and the revelry which frequently accompanies such occasions.[9] Even though these celebrations may provide the setting for genuine collective outbursts—e.g., the patriotic demonstration that turns into a riot—they are not in themselves examples of collective behavior. True, they are based often on generalized values such as the divine, the nation, the monarchy, or the *alma mater*. True, they are collective. True, they may release tensions generated by conditions of structural strain. The basic difference between such ceremonials

and collective behavior—and the reason for excluding them—is that the former are institutionalized in form and context. The index of their institutionalization is that such events are often scheduled for definite times, places, and occasions,[10] and are shrouded in formal rituals such as chants, or semi-formal "ways of celebrating," such as drinking, whooping, marching, and so on. Such celebrative activities are well described by the phrase "conventionalization of the crowd."[11] The beliefs on which they are based are not assembled as quick solutions for problems arising out of structural strain. Ceremonial activities are occasions for periodic reaffirmation of existing generalized components of action rather than the creation of new components.

We may illustrate the difference between ceremonial behavior and collective behavior further by reference to two aspects of the same episode of behavior. The worker-socialist movements that have developed in the history of American labor are episodes of collective behavior, since they involve *unprecedented* and *uninstitutionalized* mobilization of action to abolish many institutional norms (and even values) of industrial capitalism, and to establish corresponding social forms envisioned in the socialist ideology. We must exclude from our definition, however, their collective songs, pledges to solidarity, initiation rites, and so on, because they are significant primarily as regularized reaffirmations of the established values and symbols of the movement itself. Thus, even though we include such social movements as instances of collective behavior, we do not include the ceremonies that build up within movements.

Empirically some types of behavior are on the borderline between collective behavior and ceremonial behavior. Let us examine lynching, for instance. In some cases it is a genuine hostile outburst, closely related to economic and status deprivation.[12] As such it would fit the definition of collective behavior. Lynching also has been, both in the West and the South, a quasi-institutionalized form of justice to replace weak civil regulations or general conditions of political disorganization.[13] Furthermore, some evidence indicates that lynching was in part a ritual to reaffirm old Southern values and to defy the North during Reconstruction and post-Reconstruction times.[14] Finally, as the term "lynching bee" connotes, it is possible that lynching was a kind of periodic, partially organized entertainment or release of tension for people who "crave some excitement, some interest, some passionate outburst."[15] The multiple significance of lynching should remind us that in many cases history does not always produce instances that fit neatly into our analytic definition of collective behavior. We must examine carefully the context of the event in question before we decide upon its relevance for study.

(2) The audience. Let us consider both the casual and intentional audiences. An example of the first is a gathering of passers-by to watch construction crews at work, the second an audience at a symphony. We would exclude the "watchers" as an instance of collective behavior on several grounds: (a) The common object on which they focus is not generalized in a technical sense. It is simply men and machinery at work. (b) In all likelihood structural strain does not underlie the gathering. (c) No modification of any component of action is envisioned. In the case of the symphony audience, they may gather on the basis of generalized esthetic symbols; in addition, the music may have certain tension-release

functions. Still, the audience is an institutionalized form. Persons gather at fixed times and places, even evoke enthusiastic "bravos" at selected moments. Both the street throng and the audience provide common settings for genuine collective episodes such as the panic or the riot.[16] This is true, however, not because the audience itself is an instance of collective behavior, but rather because the audience situation provides geographical proximity and ease of communication and mobilization (as contrasted with other more dispersed situations).

(3) Public opinion. In general the term "public opinion" refers to a body of significant ideas and sentiments about controversial issues.[17] This kind of opinion is related to our definition of collective behavior in two ways: (a) Collective episodes may constitute a part of total "public opinion." In the 1880's and 1890's, for instance, a significant part of American public opinion was a product of collective movements—the Farmers' Alliance, the Grange, and the Populists—which gripped many parts of the agricultural population. (b) Public discussion of an issue may contribute to the rise of episodes of collective behavior. For instance, the spread and discussion of information on the danger of radioactive fall-out may produce widespread fears and perhaps a number of movements to prevent testing. Despite these links between public opinion and our definition of collective behavior, we do not treat public opinion as a type of collective behavior; it lies on a different conceptual level.[18]

(4) Propaganda is the "expression of opinion or action . . . deliberately designed to influence opinions or actions of . . . individuals or groups with reference to predetermined ends."[19] Propaganda is related to collective behavior in several

ways: (a) It may be an attempt to create attitudes that will inspire collective outbursts. An example is the broadcasts to enemy populations in wartime with the intention of aggravating the dissatisfactions and discomforts from which they are suffering already. (b) Propaganda may attempt to prevent the rise of beliefs which could produce collective outbursts. Government propaganda that exaggerates the prosperous condition of a starving population is an example. (c) Reform and revolutionary movements themselves may use propaganda to gain adherents. Thus, propaganda may be a discouragement to, an encouragement to, or an adjunct of collective behavior. Propaganda does not, however, qualify as a type of collective behavior as we define the term. Often it is institutionalized—as in advertising, political campaigning, or political control— even though its aim may be to stir uninstitutionalized behavior. Even when it is the adjunct of a reform or revolutionary movement, propaganda is not the act of collective mobilization; it is one instrument by which participants in the movement hope to convince others and mobilize them for action.

(5) Crime. Individual crime poses no problems for classification, since it is not collective. What about organized crime? In many cases it flatly violates institutionalized property and personal rights.[20] In addition, crime often springs from conditions of social strain such as poverty and broken families.

Why, then, is organized crime not a form of collective behavior? In criminal activity no attempt is made to *reconstitute* a component of action on the basis of a generalized belief. Organized robbery, for instance, differs from a reform movement to change property laws in two senses: (a) In one sense criminals *accept* the

existing social arrangements more than do adherents of the reform movement. They do not attempt to redefine or modify the general definition of property. Rather, crime feeds on existing property arrangements by stealing, pilfering, extorting, and blackmailing. Criminals attempt to subvert or avoid authority rather than change its form. Furthermore, a band of criminals offers no institutional "solutions" for the social problems created by the conditions of strain underlying criminal activity. (b) In another sense, criminals *reject* the social order more than adherents of the reform movement. The former wish to break the law as such. Reformers are not interested in illegality for its own sake; they desire to reject *but also to substitute* new institutional definitions. Participants in collective episodes may break the law—as in the riot or revolutionary outburst—but the aim of the outburst is not simply to profit from defiance. In collective behavior, law-breaking is generally a concomitant of a headlong attempt to modify some component of social action. Criminal activity, then, may be an aspect of collective behavior, but crime alone does not constitute collective behavior. The criminal act of robbery, for instance, differs radically from the prison riot of convicted criminals. The latter is generally a protest against the conditions of prison life with the implication that these conditions should be modified.[21]

(6) Individual deviance such as hoboism, addiction, or alcoholism. Although such behavior has social and psychological origins similar to those of collective behavior, much deviance poses no problem of classification because it is individual, not collective. Furthermore, such behavior—like crime—does not involve any envisioned change in the components of social action. On occasion the use of

drugs is an aspect of a collective movement—as in the Peyote cults among the American Indians—but it is not the use of the drug which makes the movement an instance of collective behavior. Rather it is the belief in the regeneration of a social order that gives the movement its distinctive character as a collective episode.

Notes

1. Above, pp. 54-62.
2. This principle of generalization followed by respecification has been identified in studying the organism's reaction to stress, learning processes, personality development, and problem-solving processes in small groups. Cf. H. Selye, *The Story of the Adaptation Syndrome* (Montreal, 1952), pp. 15-71, 203-25; Parsons, Bales, *et al., Family, Socialization and Interaction Process*, Chs. IV, VII; R. F. Bales, "How People Interact in Conferences," *Scientific American*, Vol. 192 (1955), pp. 31-35.
3. For an attempt to apply this logic to historical sequences during the Industrial Revolution in Great Britain, cf. Smelser, *Social Change in the Industrial Revolution*.
4. Above, pp. 8-9 for an initial contrast between established behavior and collective behavior. The "uninstitutionalized" character of collective behavior is also implied by the fact that the high level component is redefined or reconstituted.
5. Above, p. 41.
6. For statements of this sort of relationship between collective behavior and social change, cf. Blumer, "Collective Behavior," in Lee (ed.), *op. cit.*, p. 169; H. Gerth and C. W. Mills, *Character and Social Structure* (New York, 1953), p. 429; E. B. Reuter and C. W. Hart, *Introduction to Sociology* (New York, 1933), p. 527.
7. For an account of the timing of collective outbursts in these terms, cf. Smelser, *Social Change in the Industrial Revolution*, Chs. II, III, XV, especially pp. 29-32.
8. Gerth and Mills, *Character and Social Structure*, p. 455.
9. E.g., E. Shils and M. Young, "The Meaning of the Coronation," *Sociological Review*, New Series, Vol. 1 (1953), pp. 63-81. For a brief discussion of the "demonstration" as mass behavior, cf. Dawson and Gettys, *An Introduction to Sociology*, p. 775. For descriptions of festive holiday celebrations, cf. F. T. Tinker and E. L. Tinker, *Old New Orleans: Mardi Gras Masks* (New York, 1931), pp. 66-69; W. W. Fowler, *The Roman Festivals of the Period of the Republic* (London, 1899), pp. 270-272; A Munthe,

The Story of San Michele (London, 1930), pp. 470-477. For an account of the ritual rebellion, cf. M. Gluckman, *Rituals of Rebellion in South-east Africa* (Manchester, 1954), pp. 20-31. Further examples of collective celebrations are found in LaPiere, *Collective Behavior*, pp. 464-481.
10. For example, military or athletic victories are celebrated in this way. As LaPiere notes, much revelrous behavior involves "carrying out socially designated formulas." Even that revelry which "does not occur at socially designated times," such as honoring the chieftain or religious leader, picnics, etc., is heavily burdened with stylized and ritual elements. *Collective Behavior*, pp. 465-466.
11. Turner and Killian, *Collective Behavior*, pp. 143-161.
12. For such background conditions, cf. H. Cantril, *The Psychology of Social Movements* (New York, 1941), pp. 110-113; Commission on Interracial Cooperation, *The Mob Still Rides* (Atlanta, 1935), p. 5. Also C. I. Hovland and R. R. Sears, "Minor Studies of Aggression: VI. Correlation of Lynchings with Economic Indices," *The Journal of Psychology*, Vol. 9 (1940), pp. 301-310. For a convincing critique of Hovland and Sears' statistical methods, cf. A Mintz, "A Re-examination of Correlations between Lynchings and Economic Indices," *Journal of Abnormal and Social Psychology*, Vol. 41 (1946), pp. 154-160.
13. J. E. Cutler, *Lynch Law* (New York, 1905), pp. 82, 137 ff.; W. Cash, *The Mind of the South* (Garden City, N.Y., n.d.), pp. 124-126.
14. Cash, *The Mind of the South*, p. 128.
15. F. Tannenbaum, quoted in K. Young, *Source Book for Social Psychology* (New York, 1927), pp. 524-525.
16. For a discussion of some of the ways of changing an audience into a crowd, cf. W. D. Scott, *The Psychology of Public Speaking* (New York, 1926), pp. 180-182.
17. Cf. Blumer, "Collective Behavior," in Lee (ed.), *op. cit.*, pp. 191-193.
18. For discussion of the relations between public opinion and norm-oriented movements, below, pp. 273-274.
19. Definition from the Institute for Propaganda Analysis quoted in A. M. Lee and E. B. Lee, *The Fine Art of Propaganda* (New York, 1939), p. 15; cf. also L. W. Doob, *Propaganda* (New York, 1935), p. 89.
20. Quasi-institutionalized forms of crime such as protection rackets, dope or gambling rings, etc., that are organized with full knowledge and cooperation of political authorities are not by any criteria instances of collective behavior.
21. Cf. F. E. Hartung and M. Floch, "A Sociopsychological Analysis of Prison Riots: An Hypothesis," *Journal of Criminal Law, Criminology, and Police Science*, Vol. 47 (1956-57), pp. 51-57.

9.

Kurt Lang and Gladys Engel Lang

THE DYNAMICS OF SOCIAL MOVEMENTS

Organization, strategy, and tactics

Though a movement as such is not organized, it faces structural problems that must be solved if it is to survive. The manner in which these problems are met usually entails some organization and rules in terms of which to meet future contingencies. The major structural problems are:

1. Regularizing the relations between leaders and followers.
2. Developing an appropriate type of leadership.
3. Determining the hierarchy of leaders and functionaries.
4. Organizing of a staff.
5. Co-ordinating the relations among various groups within the movement.
6. Setting the criteria for full membership in the core group, including the duties and obligations of such membership.
7. Co-ordinating the activities of the movement in its dealings with other groups and outsiders in general—that is, developing and executing a strategy and tactics.[1]

Since social movements pass through several phases in the course of their development, the problems as well as the characteristic ways of dealing with them differ from phase to phase.

The careers of social movements

Several characteristic sequence patterns have been used to depict the career of a social movement. They have in common the notion that every movement passes through an incipient phase, a phase in which it organizes, and finally a stable phase when the forms have become fixed. The scheme of Dawson and Gettys is probably best known.

1. A period of social unrest with the agitator as the typical leader.
2. The period of popular excitement in which the vision of the prophet or the objective defined by the reformer spreads by contagion.
3. The stage of formal organization, headed by an administrator, with the beginnings of a division of labor, formal criteria of membership, etc.
4. The stage of institutionalization, when the movement, now bureaucratized, is represented by a statesman.[2]

If at any point in its career leadership fails to measure up to the contingencies confronting it, a movement will fail. Actually the study of abortive social movements may bolster our understanding of their mechanics considerably more than the concern with sequence patterns. One such abortive movement was Coxey's Army of the Unemployed (the Commonwealth Movement) which marched toward Washington, D.C., in 1894 to demand relief but never got beyond its popular phase. Technocracy, a mushrooming doctrine during the depression of the 1930's, disappeared as suddenly as it rose to prominence. With regard to many fascist and nativist groups in the United States in the same period, Shils suggests that they never got off the ground because their

From Kurt Lang and Gladys Engel Lang, *Collective Dynamics*, pp. 507-42, Thomas Y. Crowell Company, 1961, with permission of the publisher and authors.

leaders, though reflecting the collective paranoia of their followers, lacked the requisite organizational skills to launch a larger movement.[3]

Some kind of administrative superstructure is undoubtedly necessary if a movement is to survive and enlarge its following. With this in mind, Robert Michels, observing the socialist parties of Europe as they evolved from the socialist movement, formulated his "iron law of oligarchy." He reasons that leadership will always treat the organization—that is, the administrative apparatus, the party press, the electoral system, etc.—as instruments for perpetuating their power, notwithstanding the democratic ideology of the movement. According to Michels, "it is organization which gives birth to the dominion of the elected over the electors, of the mandataries over the mandators, of the delegates over the delegators. Who says organization says oligarchy."[4]

In a study of the Canadian Commonwealth Federation, an agrarian socialist movement in the Canadian prairies during the great depression, Lipset noted an extremely high degree of membership participation and few oligarchal tendencies.[5] The geographic dispersal of members in the agrarian region necessitated a decentralization of activities. The movement had to rely heavily on local initiative, and a high proportion of the members were functionaries in its various activities. Mediating organizations serve as bases from which to oppose the encroachments of central oligarchy. A lack of bureaucratized leadership is also claimed for the Moral Rearmament movement; perhaps the explanation lies in the same tendency to seek "guidance" in local groups.

The reverse of oligarchy is factionalism, a problem responsible for the demise of many movements. Factionalism is most likely to develop when there are many bases of power while a central apparatus through which control can be exercised has not yet fully developed. Operating under conditions of illegality in small groups, the Bolsheviks developed many divergent factions, notwithstanding an official ideology that called for democratic centralism. Many of the leaders carried their private following into the new Soviet apparatus. But as long as the personality of Lenin was dominant, factionalism was held in check. The bitterness of the struggle that followed his death was enhanced by the inability of secondary leaders to step down and accept Stalin's control of the party apparatus. It can be hypothesized that factional, as opposed to oligarchic, tendencies will be more pronounced when there are (a) many private and personal bases of power and (b) no approved institutional means for gracefully surrendering positions of power.

What is called, for lack of a better term, the "style of organization" refers to the general mode of regulating relations within a movement, resolving its conflicts, and meeting external contingencies. Among the factors that affect the style of organization are:

1. The *degree of opposition* the movement encounters. A movement operating under strong threat is likely to develop a quasi-military style of organization. This is imperative for a movement that wishes to survive illegality. But even a religious movement, like the Jehovah's Witnesses, confronted by a hostile world and threatened with suppression because of refusal to recognize state authority, adopts both a military type of organization and military terminology.

2. The *social position of its followers*. The style of organization tends to be adapted to what followers expect. For example, a movement based on the middle classes will generally tend to rely on parliamentary procedure in the conduct of its internal business and on official channels of communication to effect its ends. On the other hand, European workers liked to

use the intimate form of address provided by their native tongues and the appellation of "comrade."

3. The *aims of the movement*. An inward movement that aims at moral regeneration is likely to involve every one of its members. Since active proselytizing is required of every convert, the movement will be organized in such a way as to give each follower some kind of task, to let him know just what his role is. By contrast, a movement working toward a highly specific objective rarely involves its followers as deeply in its activities. Its organization may be so haphazard that members, recruited and anxious to contribute, cannot find out how to go about doing so.

4. The *cultural ethos* of the society. Styles of organization reflect the country and the period in which a movement emerges. Messianic movements of the nativist variety, aimed at extirpating Western influence, usually adopt the old tribal forms of organization in every detail. Or, if a tradition for democratic organization exists, the leadership of the movement is likely to offer opportunities for participation at the grassroots level.

5. The *type of leader*. A charismatic leader is more likely to have an appointed staff. Where the movement is headed by a statesman or an administrative type of leader—that is, in its later phases—both the leader and his lieutenants are likely to be elected. As the charismatic element in leadership declines, the staff is bound primarily to the organization; its loyalty can be readily transferred to new leaders.

Strategy and tactics refer to the manner in which a social movement goes about achieving its objective. The over-all design for action represents its strategy. Tactics, on the other hand, have to do with the manner of meeting day-to-day contingencies, such as attracting and holding members, exerting pressure on the opposition, choosing one's propaganda targets, etc. Strategy and tactics not only are interdependent but in fact often fuse.

Strategies are often classified according to the means favored for action. Inward movements place their greatest reliance on education and on individual proselytizing, although they have often reinforced their conversion efforts with threats and force. The strategy of outward movements is usually designed to move large masses, not individuals. The manner in which pressure is applied varies among these movements. Some rely primarily on negotiation and pressure carefully applied; some make extensive use of mass propaganda and demonstrations; finally, some use various degrees of "force," such as mass boycotts, strikes, and other pressure tactics, as their strategy. The distinction among strategies based predominantly on education, on mobilizing mass support through propaganda, and on force seems meaningful.

Some movements are specifically identified by their strategy. The strategy of passive resistance, utilized against the British by the Indian nationalists under Gandhi, has since been exported to South Africa and to the American South. Its aim is to solicit moral support when open resistance would be immediately suppressed. It has also been repeatedly adopted by movements with pacifist overtones. On occasion, the hunger strike, popularized by Gandhi's religious fastings to wrest concessions from the British, has also been used as a tactic by individuals belonging to movements fundamentally different in spirit from Gandhi's. Its great advantage, as recognized for example by the Zionists in Israel, lies in the way it fixes public attention on the moral struggle, in which the person fasting represents a rallying point for the movement.

Still other distinctions among strategies make use of the degree of "gradualism." One speaks not only of revolutionary versus reform goals but also of two types of strategy. The strategy that aims to achieve its objective by means of some dramatic uprising (e.g., a general strike, a march on Washington) not only appears revolutionary but may actually, because of its implications, be so. The reformist strategy aims to achieve its goals by the constant pyramiding of specific achievements, however trivial each in itself may seem. To each strategy there usually corresponds some particular set of tactics. But a movement relying on a revolutionary strategy often finds it useful to hide its true intent and make extensive use of "reform" tactics. Sometimes a given set of tactics becomes divorced from its end and becomes an end in itself, but, on the whole, tactics are more subject to change than strategy; they must be constantly adapted to meet the demands of new situations.

The dramatic success of some social movements is attributed primarily to their tactics. For example, the phenomenal growth of the Jehovah's Witnesses indicates the success of the tactic of door-to-door visiting. Each Witness is a minister, and as such he acts as a house-to-house visitor, convinced that he is a trained servant of God, in possession of an absolute and final truth that must be accepted on invincible and divine authority. The movement's success at persuasion, rather than its high morale in response to persecution from outside, best explains its success. Another example of success due to superior tactics was the successful political lobbying of the Anti-Saloon League.

Tactics used successfully by one movement are frequently taken over by others. Once the sitdown strike had met with success in the Auto-Lite plant in Toledo, Ohio, it was quickly adopted by rubber, automobile, and steel workers in 1936, whence it spread to France as a favored tactic in the Popular Front days.[6] Sometimes tactics spread by imitation, because of their past success, even when local circumstances seem altogether unfitting. As we have pointed out, after 1917 the American communist movement modeled

its strategy on the Russian Revolution. The wonderment was how the Bolsheviks, numbering only eleven thousand members in all Russia as late as May, 1917, were able to seize power five months later. The answer, it seemed, must be found in their tactics. "If great numbers were not necessary, the revolution in every country [they reasoned] was much closer than anyone had dared to hope," leaving out of account all the particular circumstances that made Russia different from the United States.[7]

In comparing movements, one finds few tactical innovations, except those that rely on modern technological means, such as the media of mass communication. For example, the idea that converts could be held only if organized into small prayer groups was already known to and widely applied by John Wesley over two hundred years ago. It is a tactic essentially similar to that employed by Moral Rearmament to gain converts and by Alcoholics Anonymous to regenerate alcoholics. Likewise, one finds that Billy Graham's only major addition to the tactics used by Billy Sunday in his revival some forty years earlier was the widespread use of television, not available to his predecessor. Billy Sunday, in his turn, had served a successful apprenticeship under the Reverend Dwight Moody, a famed revivalist in the preceding generation.[8]

Finally, it must be recognized that tactics are directed as much to maintaining the internal stability of a movement as to the achievement of its concrete objective. Demonstrations, strikes, efforts to seek out converts, etc., are often necessary if morale and faith in the movement's mission is to be maintained. Because of the ideology and psychological fabric that hold a movement together, its leadership often has little choice as to means. Tradeunionists, trained in a tradition of militancy, will agree to strike even if economic conditions are unfavorable and public resentment seems likely to result in punitive action.

Ideology

The content of the official doctrines for which a movement stands are collectively designated as its ideology. Included in the ideology of a social movement would be the following:

1. A *statement of purpose* defining the general objective of the movement and giving the premise on which it is based.
2. A *doctrine of defense*—that is, the body of beliefs that serves as a justification for the movement and its activities.
3. An *indictment*, a criticism, and a condemnation of existing social arrangements.
4. A general *design for action* as to how the objective is to be achieved.
5. Certain *myths* that embody the emotional appeals, a promise of success (based on a revolution or an "objective" law of history), its heroes, and the many folk arguments that are taken seriously.[9]

Attention to the structural aspects of a movement should never lead one to ignore its ideology. The sociological significance of ideology lies in the clues it provides for linking a specific group to a more general ideological current. Such connections are sometimes established by tracing the ideological antecedents of a core group. Furthermore, the study of ideology—that is, the targets at which criticism is aimed and the ultimate goals espoused—helps to identify the class whose interests the ideology reflects. For example, in studying any socialist group, one needs to relate it to the broader socialist movement as well as to identify the groups it most strongly idealizes. Similarly, the Populist revolt in the West, the Wisconsin Progressive movement, and McCarthyism had their roots in the same geographic area; to some extent they also attacked the same targets,

an affinity that analysis of ideology is able to reveal.

Ideology is not only more than the specific program of a movement but also something different. A program is the official face a movement presents to the outside, a platform on the basis of which it seeks support. During periods of active agitation, many people join in support of a movement solely because they agree with some part of its program, without being fully aware of its ideology. Moreover, just as a social movement has various categories of follower, it also may have more than one ideology. The existence of several sets of ideologies side by side in the same movement is due to these factors:

1. One ideology is, as Blumer suggests, for the inner circle, especially the erudite and scholarly intellectuals, and the other, a more simplified version, is for popular consumption. The latter is slanted toward a large body of followers who are judged incompetent to comprehend the complex social philosophies, theologies, economic theories, or scientific evidence that underlie the exoteric doctrine. Could the Single-Taxer be expected to understand, or even have first-hand acquaintance with, the economic theories of Henry George? or the rank-and-file Communist to master Marxian economics? or the opponent of nuclear testing to comprehend fully the scientific basis on which an evaluation of the harmful effects of fallout must be made? The more complex the esoteric doctrine of the inner circle, the more will its popularized version differ from it. But in these instances we are really dealing with different presentations or versions of the same ideology.

2. The exoteric doctrine often hides the diversity of interests that underlie the movement. Hence the "official" doctrine may serve to provide a semblance of the unity required for common action. The ideology of the Massachusetts Know-Nothings, already mentioned, helped a movement consisting of several core groups to maintain a common front, even though several interests were represented, each seeking the same goal for different reasons. The abortive movement (the Progressive Party) that in 1948 sought to elect Henry Wallace

President of the United States was made up of many diverse elements. Among them were many liberals and New Dealers of the moderate "left," who had never favored Truman over Wallace as a running mate for Roosevelt in 1944 and wished for a third party to represent the interests of liberals and labor. A second element consisted of persons with pacifist inclinations, concerned over worsening relations with the Soviet Union. A third core of followers consisted of Communists and their fellow-travelers who sought a forum for their pro-Soviet policy. The ideology espoused by the group covered these divergent interests, but once the degree of control achieved by the Communists became evident, the "movement" fell apart.

3. The ideology presented to the mass of followers is a "mask" for the real beliefs of the inner core. Its "real" ideology is hidden from all but the initiated. Almond discusses in some detail the esoteric and the exoteric doctrines as they apply to Communist followers.[10] But fascist, Nazi, and other movements seeking mass support for a conspiracy, no less than the Communists, have used two ideologies as well as many front organizations. For instance, the real intent and ideology of the Coughlinite movement was successfully hidden from the mass of its followers for some time. Father Charles E. Coughlin's radio talks at first gained him a considerable following among working people, including Negroes and Jews. Through his National Union for Social Justice, he campaigned against the gold standard and depicted the World Court as the fountainhead of evil. Both his headquarters and greatest source of strength was the auto capital, Detroit, and he also had a sizable following in other industrial cities. When in 1936 the United Auto Workers launched an organizing drive in Flint, Michigan, their organizers found that many of their new recruits were ardent Coughlinites. Also a number of auto locals had endorsed the radio priest's sixteen-point program and were contributing funds to him. They continued to receive advice from him on union tactics and organizing strategy. It was only after the violent strike against General Motors in the fall of 1936 that union members began to discern his real intent. Coughlin, despite repeated requests from strikers, failed to raise his voice to support them.[11] The anti-Semitic nature of the movement became clear only when he began to preach driving the "money changers" from the temple. His National Union was not publicly exposed as pro-fascist and pro-Nazi in ideology until some time later.

Unifying forces

Symbols and actions supplement ideology as unifying forces binding the participants together. Bonds that develop out of common emotions toward a social object, whether common love or common hate, are as important as belief in a principle. Every movement has its heroes as well as its villains.

The sense of positive identification with a movement, pride in belonging and in its accomplishments, which are so essential to its persistence, constitute the *esprit de corps* of a movement. A movement develops the proper spirit by directing all positive emotions into group-relevant symbols. Largely this is a function of experiences shared over time. But *esprit de corps* also is developed through practices that increase the involvement of members in the movement. Its fellowship is advanced by initiation rites, designed to enhance the superiority of insiders, by various kinds of ceremonial behavior, by opportunities for informal fellowship, by cultivating special forms of expressive behavior. Songs in particular have been effective unifying agents. The Cold Water Army advanced the temperance cause immeasurably by the way it employed both songs and the kind of oratory that was a substitute for vaudeville. Referring to the temperance orator, Jensen wrote,[12]

Generally this Demosthenes was a reformed old soak, and one of them was famous for the child he planted in the audience. When he reached his peroration: "As for the rum seller, my friends, what name black enough shall we call him?" the shrill voice would shriek, "Devil! Devil!" and the audience would sob its amens.

Some movements, such as the I.W.W., the colorful "Wobblies," have been "singing" movements. Their songs (e.g., "Joe Hill," "Solidarity Forever," "Casey Jones") are now part of trade-union tradition throughout the English-speaking world.

The effect of the villain on the unity of a mass movement seems fundamentally different from that of the idol. Whereas the latter evokes sentiments that become attached to the movement, the invocation of the devil serves primarily to move the collectivity to action. Hoffer has insisted that mass movements can rise and spread without a belief in a God but never without a belief in a devil.[13] Actually, hate suffices to unite a group of followers in outbursts of violence, but hate alone does not enable a movement to develop a permanent identity and a positive program, once the accumulated emotion has spent itself, unless new devils are found. An enemy promotes unity within a movement torn by inner dissension, but only when the internal forces that hold it together are present. Hence, the typical follower of mass movements about whom Hoffer writes quickly abandons one movement for another when it fails.

The crystallization of permanent nuclei that survive the particular eruption of unrest requires the development of a lore, which includes saints, heroes, legends of successful action, forms of expressing fellowship, as well as villains against whom to unite. The lore of a movement includes more than rumors about conspiracies and immorality on the part of the enemy. The morale of a movement depends on a belief in one's rightness, invincibility, and a willingness to sacrifice. *Esprit de corps* and morale are intimately connected, but whether *esprit de corps* is actually translatable into morale can be established only during periods of adversity. High morale enables a movement to weather a setback. Hate, though necessary, never accounts for the *persistence* of a *collective* enterprise when it encounters obstacles.

Social movements effect conversions because they assimilate their followers into a compact body, which offers at once fellowship and rallying points. In the inward movement, the hostility is internalized, leading the participant to make strict demands on himself but to fight a devil with love. This permits a movement to accept converts; the ability to win sinners from the enemy is a mark of one's own superiority. By implanting in its members a deprecating attitude toward outsiders, a focus on the future, and an unquestioning belief in the movement (e.g., fanaticism), movements are able to rally followers.

To understand a social movement it is always necessary to refer to the opposition it encounters. By definition a social movement always represents some unrecognized interest. Unless there is some degree of opposition, the mass of potential followers will not develop the zeal, the opposition, the conviction, and the fanaticism necessary for the success of a social movement. In this case, there is no need to combine with others in a collective effort toward fundamental change in the social order, since aspirations can be channeled into private goals.

The historian usually finds the beginnings of a social movement in some specific event: the prophet who had a vision; the meeting of a small group to launch a sectarian association; or some spontaneous collective action, such as the challenge of a mob to constituted authority. The sociologist explaining a movement is more likely to point to the general social unrest and to seek underlying causes in the social structure. Neither of the two constitutes a full explanation of how a *movement* itself was launched. A movement arises when the general situation is favorable, and at the same time it gets its impetus from some specific person or event. There are several ways in which the diffuse unrest comes to congeal into a collective enterprise that promises remedy for a widely recognized social ill.

Early leaders

To say how a social movement began is often difficult since the original instigators become known only through the successful groups. Furthermore, what is known about them is usually distilled in the glorification of early struggles by those who inherit the movement and lay claim to its tradition. The early leaders best remembered are most likely to be those who, canonized as martyrs and heroes, served best to unify the followers. It does not follow that they played the most significant role in the formation of the movement or that the deeds recorded about them were typical for those early activists who sparked the movement. For example, people remember Carry A. Nation for her saloon-smashing fame. Mrs. Nation's career has been chronicled and we are told that the death of her husband, a physician, from acute alcoholism accounts for her participation in the crusade.[14] It is much more difficult to track down the background of such early temperance workers as Mrs. Eliza Jane Trimble Thompson, of Hillsboro, Ohio, known as "Mother" Thompson, first leader of the Crusade Movement, which later became the Woman's Christian Temperance Union. Published sources do tell us that she felt herself called to duty through a conversion experience.[15]

This holds true of many other movements. The importance of the role played by Louis Fraina in the foundation of the American Communist Party was until 1957 almost undocumented and his life shrouded in mystery.[16] Much work has been done on the life of Hitler, but little is known of other leaders with whom he joined in the very early days of the movement. Martov, leader of the Russian Menshiviks and an important figure in the early history of Russian socialism, also remains obscure because he did not participate in the successful uprising that culminated in the Russian Revolution.

Speaking generally, social movements get their impetus from instigators or initiators who supply examples, from the active direction of a recognized leader or core group, from a small group or leader who offers a solution (ideology or plan) for their unfocused sentiments, or from any combination of these.

Where the initial impetus comes from an *example,* the behavior imitated must appear to be a solution to the problem the mass following shares. The instigator setting the example may be either an individual or a collectivity. In either case, the example set is followed because it holds promise of success.

Leadership differs from instigation by example inasmuch as the leader initiates group action for a following. His *directives* are accepted as solutions because of the faith, trust, and authority he enjoys.

The impetus to a social movement may come from the way *the situation is defined.* An ideology that explains the sources of frustration and offers a plan promising relief is congruent with the dispositions of the potential following. Under conditions of extreme discontent, many solutions, however illogical, may be accepted because they seem to define the situation in a plausible manner.

As a movement changes, the kind of leadership demanded also changes. At the beginning, a movement requires agitators—that is, persons who are able to "stir things up." But the agitator is not enough. A movement needs a man of vision to show the way, a prophet. The prophet is in a sense still an agitator, but he is above all capable of painting a utopia from which the hope for the movement derives. The administrator becomes more important as the movement grows and spreads. His major function is to co-ordinate the movement and supervise its apparatus. Finally, the statesman is the politician who adroitly moves within the realm of the possible and helps the movement gain its objective.[17]

Leadership Roles. Although the kinds of tasks required of each leader vary as the movement passes through different phases, it seems incorrect to identify a specific type of leader with each phase. In many religious or quasi-religious movements—for example, the Muslims, a black supremacy movement—the leader during its agitational phase is a charismatic prophet to whom almost mystical qualities are imputed. But in another very similar movement, the United African Nationalist Movement, the head of the movement acts as a statesman, making contact with other groups in the United States and the Middle East. The agitational function is taken over by professional agitators who go out on the street and stir up the people on Harlem streetcorners from soap boxes.[18] A division of labor makes possible the cultivation of an image that may be out of line with the major activity of the movement.

If a social movement built essentially around one person is to survive his death or fall from grace, provision must be made for an heir apparent. The continuing success of the movement represented by Father Divine depends largely on a belief in his immortality. A cult, based on myths concerning his survival, has been built

up.[19] By contrast, the Jehovah's Witnesses, brought into being by the persuasive preaching of Charles Taze Russell, never focused all attention on a single personality. The International Bible Students, formed in response to the message of this lay preacher, could be transformed from a sect into a full-scale religious movement only because the personal charisma of its leader was played down. Russell's successor, J. F. Rutherford, a lawyer who in 1931 gave the society the name by which it is now known, also stayed very much in the background. Stroup claims that he was almost a secret personality, much as Father Divine has become for his followers. But unlike Father Divine, Rutherford was an excellent administrator, with a good head for finance. When the scandal of his divorce rocked the movement, it survived because hate for the devil was a more important unifying force than faith in and attachment to a personal prophet. Nathan H. Knorr, Rutherford's successor, also sought anonymity, directing the attention of the followers to Jehovah God.[20]

It is rare for a single individual to survive the transformation of a social movement through its active agitational phase and its more organized phase. To be able to do so requires unusual adaptability. Margaret Sanger's birth-control movement seems to have been guided throughout by the person who initiated it. Mrs. Sanger's role as leader changed through the years, but she continued to remain as its head. Under her guidance, the movement has coalesced into an organization, so that its fortunes no longer depend on her survival.[21] Many one-man movements, especially those of unclear origin built around the message of a particular prophet, do not survive the death of the leader unless they develop an effective apparatus.

An analogous phenomenon is the co-optation of leaders trained in one movement by another movement that succeeds and displaces it, provided the leadership roles are similar. The history of the women's rights movement is replete with women who were "trained" in the Abolition and temperance movements. Lucretia Coffin Mott began as a crusader for Abolition; Amelia Jenks Bloomer had agitated for temperance as had Susan B. Anthony and the Reverend Antoinette Brown. Others had been leaders of socialist and religious sects. Similarly, many American leaders of the communist movement were trained in the 1912-1913 strikes of the Paterson and Lawrence mills, protests led by the International Workers of the World. Among them were John Reed, Louis C. Fraina, and Elizabeth Gurley Flynn.

Recruitment. Many reform leaders are persons whose social position provides a certain amount of leisure time and whose training stresses humanitarian ideals and an aristocratic sense of responsibility as their brother's keeper. Leaders of this sort have seldom been recruited from among the persons who stand to benefit directly from the reform. Convicted criminals are not likely to head movements for penal reform; the wives of habitués of the workingmen's saloons did not spearhead the prohibition movement. Nor was a destitute mother of fifteen children likely to spark the birth-control movement. On the contrary, women of better-than-average education, secure in economic status, and seeking a socially useful outlet for their energies, have provided a high proportion of the leaders in American reform movements.

Movements seeking to attain revolutionary goals by mobilizing mass support have often recruited leaders from among the young and discontented "intellectuals" of a society—the students and professionals—and, to some extent, from among the self-schooled underprivileged. The dissatisfied intelligentsia have been the traditional reservoir of "revolutionary" leadership. Blind and fanatical dedication seems most typical of the social categories whose intellectual discontent and rebelliousness find support in sectarian associations that provide the ideology for or become the core group of revolutionary mass movements.

Consequently, the leadership potential for social movements depends on the social structure. An increase in education without a corresponding increase in opportunities for the educated fosters a revolutionary leadership—for example, observe the radical movements led by students in many underdeveloped countries. Similarly, where economic development swells the ranks of the middle classes but fails to inculcate the newly risen with a humanitarianism typical of the oldfashioned Tory, few leaders will arise to launch new moral and social crusades. Redress will be sought from private institutions and government agencies already established rather than by agitating for new causes.

The following

The "movement" characteristic of a collective enterprise hinges on its capacity to inspire support from a large following. Still, generalization about the follower as a unitary type is difficult and probably unwarranted. Several distinctions among followers are suggestive, including the phase of the movement in which they join; their proximity to the core group; and the degree of involvement and commitment to the cause.

Active core versus periphery

There is a "division" of labor among the followers of every social movement. A central core of followers, the true believers about whom Hoffer writes, perform the routine work and dedicate what spare time they have to the movement. Some of them consider themselves leaders, but in fact they only do the work. Opposed to this cadre is the larger rank and file of the movement, who "march" along. The majority of them are loyal; they attend meetings, participate in activities, believe its ideology, and learn its songs and slogans. Beyond them is a much larger periphery of individuals, not clearly either in or outside the movement. They act as a "cheering" section, whose support can be mobilized on occasion. Although their connection to the movement is tenuous, they are crucial to its success.

Because no clear criteria of membership exist to identify them, the mass following has often been overlooked in favor of the core membership. Among the most useful studies of the mass following is Selznick's study of the fellow-travelers in the American Communist Party.[22] The loyalty of more peripheral followers can be great, although psychological commitment probably declines with distance from the core. Thus, one may infer that of all followers the most strongly committed to a movement are its paid workers, however menial their task. Because their livelihood is tied to the movement, and sometimes because they literally live in it, these "functionaries" find it hardest to get out.

The degree of involvement

Involvement is itself a variable tied to psychological commitment. There are objective indices by which involvement can be determined. The degree of involvement helps to distinguish among followers, while movements as such can be distinguished by the degree to which followers are involved.

Participation that entails a complete rupture of previous associations means total commitment. The "totalitarian" character, irrespective of its ideology, of a movement is revealed when the recruit must give up and radically break with his prior life to dedicate himself to the cause. The more totalitarian a movement in this sense, the more does the act of affiliation constitute a conversion.

Inward movements (moral crusades) seem to effect this total commitment in a manner somewhat different from outward movements (crusades for institutional reform). The inward movement structures the relationship of its members with outsiders in terms of some tenet of morality. Only the small sects (e.g., the various utopian communities) withdraw their followers entirely from normal social relations. Those that seek to proselytize shape their relations in terms of their need to contact outsiders. A central core of full-time workers may give up their worldly goods to the movement in exchange for comradeship and room and board. The outward movement is more likely to require a complete commitment on the part of all but the most peripheral followers. In an underground movement, such demands are made for the sake of security. But the right of a movement to regulate friendships and employment and to demand severance of family ties, if they contradict its objectives, is unquestioned if complete dedication is a criterion for active participation.

Reform movements rarely attract the completely dedicated true believer. Though a movement successfully pursuing reform goals must have its share of full-time workers, some of whom spend their entire life working for its cause, they are not required to give up contact with the "outside." The fellowship they find in the movement does not require sacrificing other friendships, and often they are induced to join a movement only by friends who are already in it. An exception to this rule of limited commitment is found in some movements with reform goals that many consider a threat to the social order—for example, movements to eliminate discrimination in the South or the reforms advocated by the early labor movement. Participants in such movements, finding themselves socially ostracized, singled out for rough treatment, and even threatened with physical violence, etc., must choose between full commitment or dropping out entirely. Where such opposition tactics fail to destroy a movement, the members who remain will be a select group displaying exceptional morale. The history of the labor movement, in particular, upholds the validity of this proposition.

Both the degree of involvement and the number from whom complete dedication is demanded change as a movement passes through various phases. The degree of involvement is probably highest during the early phases. Early converts are often people fired by enthusiasm who, because of their zeal, are willing to pay the price of ostracism. At the same time, the fellowship developed in a movement during its active phase, when it attracts true believers, makes a break easier. The support a movement promises the perpetual "outsider" makes him want to belong and thereby escape frustrations experienced in his previous life. But as movements lose their spontaneous quality and a division of labor evolves, the involvement demanded from the majority of members can be expected to decline. Similarly, when objectives, once considered radical, become respectable, high commitment is no longer instrumental in achieving them.

The size of a movement is also likely to affect the involvement demanded. As it grows, control of all participants becomes less possible. As it reaches out for mass support it requires at crucial moments, the criteria of membership are often watered down. The mobilized masses cannot be controlled. With success, the motives of followers also change.

A strategic adaptation to a specific situation sometimes radically transforms the hold a movement has on its membership. A movement dedicated to the achievement of revolutionary goals may, as a temporary tactic, seek mass support by emphasizing specific reform goals. To do this, it will have to reduce its demands on potential followers. An interesting example is the transformation of the Communist Party in the United States during World War II into a movement dedicated simply to Soviet-American friendship. Since it demanded little from new recruits, save dedication to co-operation in the Allied war effort, membership in the C.P.U.S. between 1941 and 1944 approximately doubled.[23] Initiation into the now respectable movement entailed no break with one's circle of intimates. The new recruit was expected to be neither a dedicated revolutionist nor a political activist but had only the vaguest of political responsibilities. He was required only to "agree with the platform" and apply it wherever he was active, to participate in some phase of war, not party, work, to read the party press, and to pay dues to some branch. Attendance at meetings was not compulsory.[24]

The low degree of involvement exacted from the new recruit had a profound effect on the commitment of long-term party members.

Gone were the days when the members were bound by the closest fraternal and ideological bonds into a community of the elect (or as some almost seemed to feel, a consecrated family) . . . Instead as a . . . Communist leader would recall, "The rank and file were once again tasting the joy of being accepted by all groups. The party line made it possible during this period for ordinary members to be merely human beings and to act naturally, for their neighbors were now less frightened, and even listened to Communists explain how they were on the side of the American people."[25]

After the war the thousands of new members recruited in the name of Soviet-American friendship dropped out. As members, they had never left the "outside world," their involvement in the movement having been so negligible. But long-time active and dedicated Communists were similarly softened by the minimal demands made upon them. In the war years they had once more known respectability and the compensations it brought. Many of them defected once outside pressures again built up against the party; psychologically they could no longer take total involvement.[26]

Notes

1. Adapted from Rudolph Heberle, *Social Movements* (New York: Appleton-Century-Crofts, Inc., 1951), p. 273f.
2. Dawson and Gettys, *op. cit.*, Hopper, *op. cit.*, in his study of revolutionary movements, indicated the form of collective behavior characteristic of each of Dawson and Gettys' stages.
3. Edward A. Shils, "Authoritarianism—Right and Left," in R. Christie and Marie Jahoda (eds.), *Studies in the Scope and Method of the Authoritarian Personality* (Glencoe, Ill.: The Free Press, 1954).
4. Robert Michels, *Political Parties* (Glencoe, Ill.: The Free Press, 1949).
5. Seymour M. Lipset, *Agrarian Socialism* (Berkeley, Calif.: University of California Press, 1950).
6. Among many useful studies of the sitdown strike movement are: Edward Levinson, *Labor on the March* (New York: Harper & Brothers, 1938); Irving Howe and B. J. Widick, *The UAW and Walter Reuther* (New York: Random House, 1949), especially chap. 2; Rose Pesotta, *Bread Upon the Waters* (New York: Dodd, Mead & Co., 1945), especially chaps. 19-23.
7. Draper, *op. cit.*, p. 104.
8. William G. McLoughlin, *Billy Sunday Was His Real Name* (Chicago: The University of Chicago Press, 1955).
9. Adapted from Herbert Blumer, "Social Movements," in A. M. Lee (ed.), *New Outline of the Principles of Sociology* (New York: Barnes & Noble, Inc., 1946), chap. 22.
10. Gabriel Almond, *The Appeals of Communism* (Princeton, N.J.: Princeton University Press, 1954).
11. Discussion of the Coughlin loyalties of auto workers is found in Henry Kraus, *The Many and the Few* (Los Angeles, Calif.: The Planten Press, 1947). In their book Howe and Coser, *op. cit.*, refer to Kraus's interpretation of the Flint strike as highly biased and suspect. Whatever conflicts there may be among various writers in their interpretations of leadership—the role of the Reuther boys, etc.—Kraus's remarks on Coughlinism seem valid.
12. Jensen, *op. cit.*, p. 49.
13. Eric Hoffer, *The True Believer* (New York: The New American Library of World Literature, Inc., 1958), p. 86.
14. Stewart H. Holbrook, *Dreamers of the Dream* (Garden City, N.Y.: Doubleday and Company, Inc., 1957), p. 99f.; Jensen, *op. cit.*
15. Haynes, *op. cit.*
16. Theodore Draper, *The Roots of American Communism* (New York: The Viking Press, Inc., 1957), I.
17. Dawson and Gettys saw the agitator as typical of the period of social unrest, the prophet-reformer characteristic of the stage of popular excitement, the administrator leading the period of formal organization, and the statesman leading in the final phase when a movement becomes institutionalized. This typology is often cited, C. A. Dawson and W. E. Gettys, *Introduction to Sociology,* (rev. ed.; New York: The Ronald Press Company, 1935), chap. 19.
18. From a television script, "The Hate That Hate Produced," produced by Mike Wallace (WNTA-TV, New York City, July 22, 1959, 8:00-10:00 P.M., E.D.T.).
19. Rumors keep springing up that Father Divine is actually dead. Whether or not he is, and wherever he is, it seems likely that the believers will carry on since, dead or alive, he is immortal.
20. Herbert H. Stroup, *Jehovah's Witnesses* (New York: Columbia University Press, 1945); Marcus Bach, "The Startling Witnesses," *Christian Century,* LXXIV (February 13, 1957), pp. 197-99.
21. There were a number of movements sponsoring birth-control. Mrs. Sanger's, in the United States, became Planned Parenthood. See Lawrence Lader, *The Margaret Sanger Story and the Fight for Birth Control* (Garden City, N.Y.: Doubleday & Company, Inc., 1955).
22. Philip Selznick, *The Organizational Weapon; A Study of Bolsehvik Strategy and Tactics* (Santa Monica, Calif.: Rand Corporation, 1952).
23. Irving Howe and Lewis Coser, *The American Communist Party: A Critical History, 1919-1957* (Boston: Beacon Press, Inc., 1957), p. 407.
24. Ibid., pp. 420ff.
25. Ibid.
26. Ibid., p. 431.

10.

Hadley Cantril

CONDITIONS OF SUGGESTIBILITY

A person is susceptible to suggestion when (1) he has no adequate mental context for the interpretation of a given stimulus or event or (2) when his mental context is so rigidly fixed that a stimulus is automatically judged by means of this context and without any examination of the stimulus itself. The first condition results from bewilderment; the second from the "will to believe."

In general, the psychology of suggestion has been traditionally explained almost entirely in terms of the latter condition, the stereotyped nature of certain values and opinions. The former condition, however, is perhaps even more important for our understanding of social movements and must be analyzed in some detail.

Although the essential characteristic of this first condition is the lack of an appropriate standard or frame for interpretation, such a variety of states of mind may accompany this characteristic that it is useful to distinguish among at least three different ways in which people may be suggestible because they are puzzled. (*a*) They may be bewildered and consciously desire some standard or frame; (*b*) they may be bewildered but may not consciously realize that they are seeking some solution to their predicament; or (*c*) they may realize their condition, try to make some examination of the interpretations offered them, but have no adequate way to determine whether or not these interpretations are

reliable. The discussion of suggestion examines these conditions in more detail.

Conditions of suggestibility

1. Lack of adequate mental context:
   a. With a desire to find out appropriate interpretation.
   b. With no realization that an interpretation is being sought.
   c. With a desire to check interpretations but an inability to do so.
2. Fixed mental context.

(I*a*) *An individual has no standard of judgment or frame of reference adequate to interpret a given situation and wants some standard or frame of reference.* A person simply is puzzled, knows that he is puzzled, and would like to get things straightened out in his own mind. People in such a condition have no reliable signposts in their mental contexts by means of which they can test an explanation given them. And because they are eager to free themselves from a state of indecision and bewilderment, they are unusually likely to accept whatever interpretation is offered as long as it seems plausible, that is, as long as it does not conflict with any standard they feel they can rely on. Thus the curious child who asks, "What causes the wind?" may believe whatever his parents tell him; the ignorant, perplexed and anxious citizen may accept uncritically the oversimplified schemes of a crackpot utopian.

There are two important variables to this particular psychological condition of suggestibility. One is the extent to which a mental context is lacking that would

Abridged from Hadley Cantril, *The Psychology of Social Movements,* Robert E. Krieger Publishing Company, 1973, pp. 64-77, with permission of the publisher.

provide any sort of anchorage for interpretation; the other is the intensity of the desire for interpretation. Both of them are prerequisites: a person must both lack an adequate mental context and possess a certain desire for interpretation. Yet the degree to which an individual is suggestible may vary according to either variable alone. For example, if two people have an equal desire to increase the national wealth of this country, the person with even a rudimentary knowledge of economics will be less likely to believe in the efficacy of simple inflationary schemes than the person who thinks valuable money can be turned out indefinitely by the printing press. On the other hand, if two people have equally inadequate mental contexts, the individual who is extremely anxious to know how to orient himself in a given situation that may have important consequences for him will be more likely to accept a hearsay rumor than the individual who is not so personally involved. Thus the Germans, in their march through the Low Countries and northern France in the summer of 1940, had their agents in distant towns spread the news that nearby villages had just fallen into German hands. The people in the towns, anxious to know the course of a war which might at any moment threaten their lives, readily believed the false news, became panicky, and started their trek west, thus congesting the roads used by advancing Allied troops the way the Germans wanted them to. Obviously, people in towns much farther removed from the scene of hostilities who knew just as much or just as little as the unfortunate Dutch, Belgians, or French would not have been so suggestible.

As we shall see later in our discussions of various social movements, it is these critical situations that furnish fertile soil for the emergence of the mob leader, the

potential dictator, the revolutionary or religious prophet, or others with new and untried formulae. Such leaders arise because they provide people with an interpretation that brings order into their confused psychological worlds. The clever leader will sense the causes of dissatisfaction, will realize which old loyalties remain unshaken and which are being seriously challenged. He will spread among the confused and eager souls a rationalization that, from their points of view, combines the best of the old and the best of the new—the new usually being some concrete proposal, some apparent way out of what had been a dilemma, some statement or program which seems to crystallize for the followers their own disorganized, contradictory worries and aspirations.[1] Frequently the solutions offered are highly oversimplified and the leader himself may suspect that they are unworkable. But he also knows that, without such simplification, his proposals will be incomprehensible, will only prolong confusion.

Among the tools of the leader during any critical situation when people are highly suggestible are slogans and symbols. These are short-cut rationalizations which fire the imagination and spread because they somehow express the dissatisfactions from which people have been suffering and at the same time imply a new direction and purpose. The chances are "that the more correctly and the more objectively a set of slogans expresses the underlying forces in a critical situation, the more vital and lasting they will prove to be."[2] Such slogans as the "No Taxation without Representation" of the American Revolution, the "Liberty, Equality, and Fraternity" of the French Revolution, the "Peace, Bread, and Land" of the Russian Revolution all helped to give meaning to bewildered people. During the early days of the second World War when the

Germans were apparently still wondering what the war was for, a correspondent reported that Hitler had conferred with party chiefs to find some way of "translating Germany's war aims into concrete, effective slogans with meaning for the German people."[3]

Symbols, such as flags, insignia, or caricatures of the enemy, are further short cuts crowded with meaning. People seem to get worked up into a higher emotional pitch when they are reacting to symbols than to general programs or ideologies. The anti-New Dealer will probably hate some specific person who symbolizes the New Deal more than he will hate the whole complex of legislation which composes the New Deal; the Communist will probably despise the capitalist more than capitalism; the anti-Semite will probably get more angry when he talks about "the Jew" or a specific Jew than when he talks about "Jews"; the believer in democracy will no doubt dislike Hitler more than National Socialism. The probable explanation for this rather common behavior of normal individuals is that specific objects or persons are much easier to conceptualize, to focus attention on, than are more general and complex causes of dissatisfaction. Such symbols furnish a definite objective toward which action, if only verbal, can be directed. If an enemy cannot be concretized, then the emotion aroused by thoughts of the enemy will probably be a vague anxiety or fear rather than a specific anger or hatred. And since anger and hatred, rather than anxiety and fear, are more likely to lead to positive, purposive action, the leader will make every attempt to personalize the system, the nation, the evil against which he is rebelling. Christianity had its "devil"; England its "Hun" and "Jerry"; Nazi Germany its "plutocrat."

It would be quite false to assume that slogans and symbols of all kinds are entirely the work of clever propagandists, scheming warmongers, politicians, or idealistic leaders. Popular slogans and symbols are frequently created by the people themselves. They spread not so much because of any organized effort of a given group but because they provide a very definite psychological function. No amount of advertising or publicity can sell a slogan or a symbol if it does not fit the social context.

It is during these critical situations, too, that "escapist" solutions of one brand or another are likely to arise. Some people may regress to a rationalization which once brought them satisfaction, but which they had discarded or outgrown because it did not seem to square with the conditions or forces of the modern world. In times of social tension, for example, it is not difficult to understand the huge popular sale of certain books that advocate a return to religion or to the good old days.[4] Other people may accept some streamlined model of escape that simply avoids central social problems, such as moral rearmament, Christian Science, or mental telepathy.

It is not surprising at critical times to find that individual differences, in the usual sense of the term, are comparatively unimportant in determining whether or not a given person will be suggestible to a new rationalization. Innate capacities, expressive traits, or temperamental characteristics play a minor role when an individual is caught in a critical situation where a reordering of values is in the air.[5] To be sure, these individual differences will determine whether or not the person will be a clever or stupid, neat or slovenly, cheerful or grouchy member of what may be a new social movement that has arisen at a critical time. Almost any large political, religious, or social movement probably contains about the same number of extroverts, submissive souls, borderline morons, or neurotics as these characteristics would be measured by current tests. Republicans and Democrats, Fascists and Communists, Catholics and Protestants, prohibitionists and non-prohibitionists, nudists and decency leaguers—all would undoubtedly be found to have their rough, statistical share of personality traits and capacities no matter how vehemently they might deny that their group's membership contained any people with traits that society values as less desirable. Whatever differences might eventually be discovered would almost certainly be insufficient to ascribe as the main reason for the affiliation of the members. Whether or not a person becomes a member of a particular organization or movement will be determined essentially by his personal values as these are acquired from experience and knowledge and by his derivative ego drives and frames of reference.[6]

(I*b*) *An individual not only lacks an adequate frame of reference or standard of judgment by means of which he may orient himself but he also lacks even the awareness that he needs and is seeking a new frame of reference.* In such instances it never occurs to the individual to evaluate the alternative solutions offered, to question the notion that a proposed explanation or a course of action might not be the only one possible. Whatever solution is proposed, whatever interpretation first "occurs" to the individual, will be unhesitatingly accepted and acted upon. In this extreme condition, created by the lack of any internal structuration, the law of primacy may be considered operative: the interpretation accepted is the interpretation the individual is first aware of. The interpretation may not be held for any great length of time but it at least furnishes a temporary orientation.

There are various reasons why an individual may react in this irrational fashion. All may be illustrated from evidence obtained in the study of a Hallowe'en broadcast, purporting to describe an invasion from Mars, which frightened so many people in this country in 1938.[7] For some persons, the situation portrayed by the radio drama appeared so immediate and so urgent that their first thought was to escape or to prepare to deal with the monsters. "We'd better do something instead of just listen," said one woman. So she started to pack. Another woman reported, "I wasn't frightened until they said the gas was within a few miles of us." Other people immediately resigned themselves to the situation so that any attempt to check the program, like any other possible course of action, seemed pointless. "What difference does it make?" reflected a high-school girl. Others were so overwhelmed by environmental pressures that they lapsed from their normal skepticism. Frightened relatives or friends telephoned or rushed into the homes of uninformed persons who promptly turned on their radios only to have the harrowing reports confirmed. Still others were extremely susceptible because of a pattern of personality characteristics. People who felt insecure, who constantly worried, who lacked self-confidence, who were fatalistic were more readily frightened than others.

(I*c*) *An individual's mental context fails to provide him with a needed interpretation or with any reliable standards by means of which he can make a desired check on alternative interpretations offered.* This condition differs markedly from the one just mentioned. For in this instance the individual is not only aware that he is trying to select a new interpretation but also he further realizes that, because none of his present frames or standards are completely relevant, he should try to validate new interpretations before accepting them as the basis for orientation. But for any one of several reasons, he fails to make a thorough check and finally he accepts the general frame of reference or specific standard of judgment offered.

These reasons may also be illustrated from the panic resulting from the supposed Martian invasion. Some people attempted to check their own interpretation against data which were themselves already influenced by the interpretation they were trying to check. Thus certain people who were moderately disturbed by the news telephoned friends, who were also disturbed, to ask them what they thought. Other people tried to verify their interpretation by making certain observations which they then proceeded, however, to rationalize as consistent with the interpretation they thought they were checking. Thus, while one person would look out the window, see no cars on the street, and conclude that they had all been destroyed, a second person would look out the window, see the street full of cars and conclude that everyone was driving to safety. Still other people very genuinely sought to validate the interpretation presented but simply did not have sufficiently rich and well-grounded standards of judgment to know whether or not the evidence they uncovered was reliable. When they turned their dials to other stations they thought the other stations might not yet know about the disaster; when they saw the program listed as a drama in the newspaper, they thought it was not the same program. How, for example, can the average citizen, no matter how sincere his motives, conclusively prove one way or the other who sunk the *Athenia* or which belligerent power first violated Norwegian territorial neutrality in the second World War?

(2) A more familiar condition of suggestibility arises *when an individual's mental context is so patterned that a stimulus or interpretation presented is thoroughly consistent with the frames of reference and standards of judgment that constitute the mental context.* In this instance, the stimulus is experienced by the individual as thoroughly consistent with what he already thinks or "knows." It is therefore accepted. Frequently this type of suggestibility is reduced to the simplicity of a conditioned response. An individual may react to the word "Fascist" or "Red" without the slightest knowledge of what these symbols stand for, without being able to relate them to anything in his mental or behavioral repertoire except the response he has already learned. But by no means is all such suggestion explicable on the theory that specific responses to specific stimuli have been learned. Men show an ability to generalize on the basis of accepted frames of reference, to interpret entirely new stimuli and situations by means of their existing standards, to take the initiative in imitating the behavior of others when that behavior is useful in preserving or enhancing their status. The Lynds report, for example, that "Middletown's working class appears today to be less sure of many of the old values than is the business class; but in Middletown they have developed no ideology of their own, and they lack security on any basis of their own, such as labor organization. Hence, doubtful and uncertain, they tend to straggle after the wealthier, pace-setting fellow citizens in their affirmations of established values in the midst of confusion."[8]

The operation of this type of suggestibility is apparent to everyone. The ardent New Dealer enthusiastically approves each new foreign and domestic policy of President Roosevelt; the Communist accepts, without qualification, proposals which have the stamp of party leaders; the conservative gleefully welcomes, and repeats as his own, specific rationalizations of his general frame of reference provided him by paid columnists;[9] the Bible-beating fundamentalist cheers the pronouncements of any scientist who states that the world was made and is controlled by God; the American Legionnaire routinely condemns anyone who deviates from that brand of Americanism which insures his own place in the world.

The extent to which individuals are suggestible under this condition will depend, for one thing, upon the breadth of their frames of reference, the inclusiveness of the assumptions on which the frames are based. Thus a person who has acquired a thoroughly liberal point of view will reflect his liberalism in accepting the suggestions that new political parties, new moral codes, new fashions, and new religions be tolerated.[10] Whether the point of view is based on knowledge and experience or whether it has merely been accepted uncritically from the culture is irrelevant *if* it adequately provides the desired meaning to the individual. The Jesuit and the unschooled, backwoods Baptist preacher are both likely to accept some fresh evidence of God's omnipotence; the learned economist of the laissez-faire school and the propertied corner grocer are both likely to disapprove proposals for cooperative stores; the naive aviation enthusiast and the skillful airplane designer are both likely to believe in the possibility of stratosphere planes; the erudite musicologist and the untutored radio listener are both likely to accept Beethoven's music as good. As we shall see directly, this by no means implies that the knowledge or factual basis, upon which frames of reference are based, is never conducive to a higher threshold of suggestibility. But it does imply that when a

frame of reference is tenaciously held, knowledge and facts serve chiefly as stepping stones for more elaborate rationalizations.[11]

Another determinant of the extent to which this condition of suggestibility will hold in any given instance is, as we have stated before, the personal significance of the frames of reference, the degree to which the values from which they are derived involve the ego. The more the self, the me, is sustained or enhanced by a suggestion, the greater the likelihood that it will be accepted. Thus the Jesuit, the learned economist, the airplane designer, and the musicologist just mentioned all have personal, vested interests in the points of view they defend. When a person has no such vested interests, or when he feels completely secure, then he can afford to be tolerant and more openminded. We find, for example, that college students who are the children of middle-class parents are more intolerant than college students whose parents are wealthy[12]; that first- or second-generation immigrants are often most insistent on the passage of teachers' oath bills or other legislation designed to promote "Americanism." Both the student with a middle-class background and the naturalized citizen are hanging more tenuously to a status they cherish: the middle-class student who has hopefully identified himself with the values of the upper class does not want his aspirations questioned; the immigrant has to make up in fervor what he lacks in background.

Conditions of suggestibility. Discussions of the psychology of suggestion all too frequently define suggestion in some terms such as "the acceptance of a proposition for belief or action in the absence of critical thought processes." Such definitions, with phrases like "the absence of critical thought" or the "lack of active intelligence," completely beg the question and leave the crux of the problem very much up in the air. We have tried here to show more precisely what is meant by these terms and what psychological relationships between the individual and his environment account for this "absence of critical thought." Another danger in many of the "explanations" of suggestion is that their proponents entirely neglect the psychological problems merely by stating that people are susceptible to "prestige suggestion" or to "majority opinion."

Take, for example, the question of suggestibility to majority opinion. This has often been demonstrated in experiments,[13] and is often exhibited in everyday life. But this suggestibility to majority opinion is always highly relative, dependent upon the particular circumstances of the situation, cut across by numerous other influences that may be operative at the moment, and circumscribed by what the individual regards as the majority in *his* world. If people are suggestible to majority opinion, why, for example, did they not vote for Landon in 1936, when the widely publicized Literary Digest poll showed Landon the choice of the majority? Why do we still have two major political parties in the United States? Why do members of minority groups continue fervently to preach their causes when they know public opinion is ranged against them? Why do new values ever arise at all? Majority opinion is probably effective as a suggestion only when an individual has no clearly structured mental context adequate to interpret a situation and when the majority opinion does not conflict with other frames of reference or ego values. Neither the opinionated, financially insecure conservative nor the more tolerant, wealthy utility executive is likely to accept the suggestion of government ownership and operation of electric power even if the great majority of people should want it.

The effectiveness and limitations of suggestibility to majority opinion can only be understood if one has some knowledge of the mental contexts, the needs, the aspirations, and the social setting within which majority opinion penetrates. The same considerations hold for "prestige suggestion." The term explains nothing unless we know the reasons for the prestige.[14]

The psychology of suggestion is sometimes further obscured by loose generalizations to the effect that children, women, primitive peoples, fatigued or excited persons are more suggestible than others. Although all these statements may be true, they are true only within a certain context, and our psychological understanding is not enlarged by mere statements that age, sex, or certain physiological conditions affect suggestibility. These are only substitute indices with psychological counterparts that remain to be discovered. If, under certain circumstances, children and women are found to be more suggestible, further psychological probing would probably reveal that they had fewer pertinent standards of judgment and frames of reference to use in the particular interpretations presented to them. If fatigued or excited individuals are found to be more suggestible, then the problem remains to determine how these conditions affect mental context and motivation. All too frequently psychologists, particularly those interested in measuring and testing rather than in understanding, are willing to accept as "explanation" a correlation between observable behavior and some sociological or physiological index. Such findings are of immense value but they are only propaedeutic to psychological explanation.

Critical ability. The reverse side of the psychology of suggestion is the psychology of critical ability. Critical ability may be defined as the *capacity to evaluate a stimulus in such a way that a person is able to understand its inherent characteristics and to judge and act appropriately.* To say that a person is highly suggestible is to say that he lacks critical ability. But to say that a person is highly suggestible *because* he lacks critical ability and to say nothing more is to indulge in the tautology we have just condemned. Under what conditions does an individual possess critical ability?

If it is, as we have said, the opposite of suggestibility, it should therefore emerge when the individual's mental context and motivation contrast to the conditions we have described as underlying suggestibility: (I*a*) If all other things are equal, people who have standards of judgment or frames of reference, which they feel can be relied upon to interpret a given stimulus or event, are likely to display critical ability to some extent. The greater the relevant knowledge or experience upon which standards are based, the greater will be the individual's critical ability. The modern physician is more likely to give his patient appropriate remedies than is the medicine man of a primitive tribe.

(I*b*) People who have no standards of judgment or frames of reference appropriate to interpret a given stimulus, people who desire some interpretation, but who have developed a *readiness to question* the interpretations offered them, show critical ability. In such instances, critical ability will be proportional to skepticism. In the Martian broadcast, for example, it was found that educated people who had learned not to take everything at its face value were least disturbed by the fanciful news.[15]

(I*c*) People who are not able to interpret a given event directly by means of existing standards or frames may, nevertheless, have other tangential standards or frames which they can rely on and which they can use as trustworthy pegs to test evidence which they gather. Thus the majority of people who tuned in late to the Martian broadcast, who at first did not know what to make of it, but who checked by referring to the newspaper or by turning to other stations, accepted as reliable standards of judgments the newspaper's listing of a drama, "War of the Worlds" or the news-gathering efficiency of other stations which would also surely report such a major catastrophe. (2) When people have a mental context so patterned that a stimulus or interpretation seems thoroughly consistent with it but also have sufficient insight to know their own biases and prejudices, to check the interpretation and if necessary to enlarge or alter their mental contexts, then they may be said to have critical ability. This critical ability due to "self-objectification" is probably the rarest form of all.[16] For more than any other condition that might give rise to critical ability, this one is bound up with ego drives, the desire for status and self-regard which we have already shown act as blinders for the ordinary mortal who so often is unaware of the things he takes for granted.[17]

Notes

1. Leaders in the scientific, literary, or art world often arise under the same circumstances. Kenneth Burke contends, for example: "Psychoanalysis effects its cures by providing a new perspective that dissolves the system of pieties lying at the roots of the patient's sorrow or bewilderments. It is an *impious* rationalization, offering a fresh terminology of motives to replace the patient's painful terminology of motives. Its scientific terms are wholly incongruous with the unscientific nature of the distress. By approaching the altar of the patient's unhappiness with deliberate irreverence, by selecting a vocabulary which specifically violates the dictates of style and taboo, it changes the entire nature of his problems, rephrasing it in a form for which there is a solution." *Permanence and Change,* New York: New Republic, 1935, 164 f.

2. M. Sherif, The psychology of slogans. *J. Abn. & Soc. Psychol.,* 1937, **32,** 461.

3. Joseph Barnes, *New York Herald Tribune,* Oct. 23, 1939.

4. A public opinion survey reported by the Psychological Corporation on the question "Do you think religion is losing or gaining influence in the United States?" shows an increase of 23% from 1940 to 1942 in the number of people who say religious influence is growing.

5. For some experimental evidence on this point, see M. Sherif, A study of some factors in perception, *Arch. Psychol.,* 1935, 187; S. E. Asch, H. Block, M. Hertzman, Studies in the principles of judgments and attitudes. *J. Psychol.,* 1938, **5,** 219-251.

6. We are not implying here that temperamental traits and intellectual capacities are *never* important in their determination of allegiance to old or to new standards. Occasionally, as with an extremely submissive, introverted, timid person who eschews any cause advocating violence, personality traits may directly affect participation in a certain movement and directly affect the selection of values which become part of the ego. But, as was pointed out in chs. 1 and 2, the more usual condition would seem to be that these capacities and temperamental traits are exhibited *within* a mental context and motivational system.

7. Hadley Cantril, *The Invasion from Mars, op. cit.*

8. Robert S. Lynd and Helen Lynd, *Middletown in Transition,* New York: Harcourt, Brace, 1937, 493.

9. Hadley Cantril, The role of the radio commentator, *Publ. Opin. Quart.,* 1939, **3,** 654-663.

10. G. B. Vetter, The measurement of social and political attitudes and the related personality factors, *J. Abn. & Soc. Psychol.,* 1930, **25,** 149-189.

11. See K. Diven, Aesthetic appreciation test, in H. A. Murray, *op. cit.,* 447-453.

12. S. P. Rosenthal, Change of socio-economic attitudes under radical motion picture propaganda, *Arch. Psychol.,* 1934, No. 166.

13. C. H. Marple, The comparative suggestibility of three age levels to suggestion of groups vs. expert opinion, *J. Soc. Psychol.,* 1933, **4,** 176-186; C. E. Smith, A study of the autonomic excitation resulting from the interaction of individual opinion and group opinion. *J. Abn. & Soc. Psychol.,* 1936, **3,** 138-164.

14. M. Sherif, A study of some factors in perception, *op. cit.,* 47-52.

15. Hadley Cantril, *Invasion from Mars, op. cit.,* ch. 5.

16. Allport, *Personality, op. cit.,* 220-225.

17. This does not mean that a person who is completely devoid of any personal point of view, completely "objective" in the popular sense, has the greatest critical ability. As James pointed out, "If you want an absolute duffer in an investigation, you must, after all, take the man who has no interest whatever in its results: he is the warranted incapable, the positive fool. The most useful investigator, because the most sensitive observer, is always he whose eager interest in one side of the question is balanced by an equally keen nervousness lest he become deceived." *The will to believe and other essays in popular philosophy.* New York: Longmans, Green, 1896, 21. For a discussion of objectivity in social psychology, see Hadley Cantril and Daniel Katz, The problem of objectivity in the social sciences, *The Psychology of Industrial Conflict* (edited by George Hartmann and T. Newcomb), New York: Dryden, 1939, 9-19.

11.

Rex D. Hopper

THE REVOLUTIONARY PROCESS:
A FRAME OF REFERENCE FOR
THE STUDY OF REVOLUTIONARY MOVEMENTS

The hypothesis discussed herein is an example of the use of what is known as the *natural history* approach to the study of human behavior. This approach when applied to revolutionary movements has yielded the postulate that such movements pass through four stages in their development: the Preliminary Stage of Mass (Individual) Excitement, the Popular Stage of Crowd (Collective) Excitement and Unrest, the Formal Stage of Formulation of Issues and Formation of Publics, and the Institutional Stage of Legalization and Societal Organization.[1]

To prevent what we are here doing from being judged as merely another in a series of clever surmises, it is important to realize that the hypothesis just formulated has a history. By collating the work of such pioneer students as Sorokin, Edwards, Gettys, Blumer, and Brinton, it is possible to draw a general picture of revolutionary behavior in which the nature and interrelationships of the different aspects of a revolutionary movement are rather clearly indicated.[2] The full force of this remark will be lost unless it is remembered that such a generalized description is a neces-

sary prerequisite to any attempt at control; that no such generally accepted description exists at present; that the fragmentary contributions of the works just mentioned represent research on empirical data rather than "armchair philosophizing"; and that the following outline of the natural history of revolutionary movements is a synthesis of research already done and not the personal creation of the writer.

Before undertaking to outline the revolutionary process, it is necessary to undergird such a description of revolutionary behavior with a brief statement of the way *human* behavior looks to contemporary students of the "science of human relationships." In answer to the question, "What is human behavior?" there is an increasing tendency to reply that *human* behavior is a function of the development of socially-acquired attitudes toward culturally-held values.[3]

What does this point of view mean when applied to the analysis of the revolutionary process? Expressed otherwise, what happens when one social order collapses and another emerges? It means, first, that any social order or society may be viewed as a sort of moving equilibrium of culturally held values and socially-acquired attitudes. In relation to the culture, social order, then, consists of a system of relatively orderly values. From the point of view of the people living in the culture and responding to its values, a social order consists of a system of commonly held

Reprinted from *Social Forces,* Volume 28, March 1950, pp. 270-79. "A Frame of Reference for the Study of Revolutionary Movements" by Rex D. Hopper. Copyright © The University of North Carolina Press.

The writer especially wishes to acknowledge his indebtedness to W. E. Gettys and Herbert Blumer in much that follows. The contribution made by this paper consists chiefly in the attempt to synthesize the insights of earlier students of the problem.

tendencies to act toward a given system of values. Thus men call the times orderly, speak of social order and organization, and believe that they live in a *cosmos* when the values deposited in their culture satisfy the attitudes in terms of which they tend to act. On the other hand, men deem the times to be out of joint, speak of social disorder and disorganization, and fear that they live in a *chaos* when the values deposited in their culture no longer satisfy their attitudes.

It means, second, that social order is disturbed and the process of social disorganization sets in when for any reason at all attitudes and values begin to diverge.

It means, third, that social change has taken place if and when social disorganization eventuates in the reorganization of attitudes and/or values.

It means, fourth, that significant social change always has to do with change on the institutional level—that is, with changes in the attitudes-values that are deemed to be basically important. Changes on this level are very disturbing and result in great disorganization and unrest until the changed attitudes and their corresponding values have been worked into the institutional structure of the culture and a new social order has been built. Therefore, an understanding of the process of social change on this level is imperative to those interested in doing something about social change.

It means, finally, that *revolutionary* change is precisely that kind of social change which occurs when the basic institutional (i.e., legally enforced) values of a social order are rejected and new values accepted.

We may now ask what a revolutionary movement looks like when historical events are reexamined in terms of the hypothesis which the events themselves have suggested to trained observers. Ar-

ranged in terms of the postulated four stages and in a fashion designed to indicate the interdependence of the various features of the movement during each stage, the answer runs as follows.

I. The preliminary stage

Of mass (individual) excitement and unrest

Characteristic Conditions. In this stage socio-psychological conditions (meaning simply the traits which people tend to manifest in a society where a revolutionary movement may be getting under way) may be grouped under six headings, so arranged as to reveal a socio-psychological sequence or orderliness.

1. General restlessness which manifests itself in:
   a. Wish repression
   b. Development of a balked disposition mind-set
   c. Restless behavior of individuals
   d. Increase in crime, vice, insanity, suicide, agitation, and travel (wandering individuals of all classes, and emigration)
2. The development of class antagonisms as shown by:
   a. The increase in wealth, intelligence, and power of "repressed groups"
   b. The separation of economic power from political power and social distinction
   c. The development of a condition wherein men of ability are shut out from careers of any consequence
3. Marked governmental inefficiency
4. Reform efforts on the part of the government
5. Cultural drift in the direction of revolutionary change
6. Spread and socialization of restlessness as evidenced by:
   a. Increased tension, cramp, and irritation
   b. Increased talk of revolution
   c. Wandering of attention from one individual, object, or line of action to another

It is suggested that this arrangement of the dominant characteristics of the preliminary stage portrays what happens as a *society* breaks up into a *mass*, a process that is necessarily preliminary to the initiation of a revolutionary movement.

Typical Process. How may people like this be expected to behave? Or, what process is *typical* of the Preliminary Stage? They will be susceptible to the *milling* process or "circular interaction" as it is sometimes called.

Borrowed from the language of the cattle ranch, the term is used to describe a type of interaction among people that is quite comparable to the "milling" of a herd of cattle.[4] On the human level milling results from vaguely apprehended unrest on the one hand and from confusion regarding goals on the other. When translated into the terms used in our earlier description of the nature of human behavior, this means that milling occurs in the early stages of the process by which disparity is produced between the attitudes of a group and their social values. This disparity is initially expressed by a sort of unorganized and unformulated restlessness, the causes of which are unknown, hence unrecognized. The diffused nature of the discontent makes impossible the projection of any plan of action and accounts for the random character of behavior at this stage as well as the uncertainty with reference to the ends toward which action should be directed.

Effective Mechanisms. How may people so behaving be influenced? What mechanisms or devices must be employed by those presuming to positions of leadership in the Preliminary Stage? In general terms, of course, the mechanisms employed to control people must be suited to their dominant mood. When applied to the present problem this means that

people who exhibit the socio-psychological characteristics already outlined can be influenced by such devices as agitation, suggestion, imitation, propaganda, et cetera. It also means that those men will emerge as leaders who are most able and skilled in the use of such control devices. Thus it may be said that the dominant socio-psychological conditions determine both the nature of the leadership and the choice of mechanisms of social control.

Types of Leaders. What kind of leader will potential "revolutionists" follow? This stage belongs to the *agitator* and, as Blumer has shown, there are two types of agitators who correspond to the two types of situations in which they function.[5]

The first situation is one marked by abuse, unfair discrimination, and injustice, but a situation wherein people take this mode of life for granted and do not raise questions about it. Here the function of agitation is to lead people to challenge and question their mode of living. It serves to create unrest. Hence the agitator is the calm, dignified type who stirs the people not by what he does, but by what he says. Such potential leaders are always present in any society but they never exercise decisive influence unless the situation is *really* characterized by abuses, discrimination, and injustice. And such leaders function very early in the development of a revolutionary movement and are only recognized as real leaders after the fact, so to speak.

If factors—including the activities of the type of agitation just mentioned and which we need not pause to discuss—are favorable, the second type of situation may develop. It is one wherein people are already aroused, restless, and discontented, but where they either are too timid to act or do not know what to do. Here the function of the agitator is to intensify, release, and direct tensions which people already have. Hence the agitator himself is a different type. He is excitable, restless, and aggressive. Such leaders emerge much later in the Preliminary Stage and are much more familiar to us.

Dominant Social Form. In what sort of groupings do such people as we have been describing act? In other words, what is the *form* of elementary collective behavior, or the sort of behavior characteristic of the Preliminary Stage of a revolutionary movement?

It is suggested that possible participants in such a movement constitute a "psychological mass," a form of human collective behavior with the following features: first, the people composing it come from all walks and levels of life; second, the mass is made up of anonymous persons, responding to common influences but unknown to each other; third, because they are unknown to each other, there is little interaction or exchange of experience between the members of the mass; fourth, there is little or no organization on the level of mass behavior.[6]

In short, the nature of the mass is determined by what the people composing it are like. And the people behave as they do because of the characteristics they share. Thus persons who participate in mass behavior do so because the objects of interest which gain their attention lie outside of the local culture and groups and are something for which the mores of the local groups offer inadequate explanations. In consequence, the members of the mass are detached and alienated individuals, both with reference to the mores of their old culture and the new objects of attention. They are in a marginal position. A disparity of attitudes and values has developed and the process of social disorganization has set in.

II. The popular stage

Of crowd (collective) excitement and unrest

Whether a movement passes from the preliminary stage of mass (individual) excitement and unrest into this stage depends on the nature of developments in the first stage. The hypothesis under examination does not postulate an inevitable sequence of events. Quite to the contrary, it recognizes that in a variety of ways a possible movement may be indefinitely postponed or completely redirected. For example, governments sometimes use war with another nation as a device for keeping down threatened internal disturbances. Or the unrest may be drained off in nonpolitical directions. This seems to have happened in England when the development of Methodism redirected a movement that might have had catastrophic revolutionary effects.

However, failure to deal with the underlying causes of unrest and discontent will mean that the evolution of the movement will continue. If it does, the basic sociopsychological conditions typical of the second stage will emerge and their general nature is suggested by the name given to the period. It is a time of the *popularization* of unrest and discontent; a time when the dissatisfaction of the people results in the development of *collective excitement.* It is not implied that unrest and discontent become popular in the sense that they spread to every last man in the population. Rather, popularization takes place among those psychologically prepared to share in the movement. On the part of the opposition, the very popularization of unrest and discontent serves to intensify their resistance to the spread of the movement. Thus popularization in one section of the population is paralleled by resistance in another.

This is the stage when individuals participating in the mass behavior of the preceding stage become aware of each other. Their negative reactions to the basic factors in their situation are shared and begin to spread. Unrest is no longer covert, endemic, and esoteric; it becomes overt, epidemic, and exoteric. Discontent is no longer uncoordinated and individual; it tends to become focalized and collective.

Characteristic Conditions. In consequence of all this, the socio-psychological conditions typically present in this stage can be classified under six headings.

1. The spread of discontent and the contagious extension of the several signs of unrest and discontent as manifested in:
   a. Increased activity
   b. Growing focus of attention
   c. Heightened state of attention
2. The transfer of allegiance of the intellectuals, including:
   a. Wish reformulation
   b. Loss of faith in their leadership on the part of the repressed classes and the loss of faith in themselves on the part of the leaders
   c. Spread of rumor and scandal and the development of a literature of exposure
   d. Emergence of the "good man fallacy"
   e. Identification of a guilty group, focusing of attention on it, and the development of an "advertising offensive" against it
   f. Development of an "oppression psychosis"
3. The fabrication of a social myth with these allied characteristics:
   a. Creation of collective illusions, myths, and doctrines
   b. Emergence of the economic incentive to revolutionary action
   c. Development of a tentative object of loyalty[7]
4. The emergence of conflict with the out-group and the resultant increase in in-group consciousness
5. The organization of the discontented for

the purpose of remedying the threatened or actual breakdown of government
6. The presentation of revolutionary demands which if granted would amount to the abdication of those in power

Typical Processes. With reference to the processes functioning at this level, there is a marked intensification of milling. But it is not quite so random and aimless. People develop more definite notions of the causes of their difficulties and of what should be done to resolve them. This intensification and speeding up of the milling process results in so changing it that *social contagion* and *collective excitement* are better terms for describing what is going on. The attention is being caught and riveted and the people are becoming emotionally aroused and more likely to be carried away by impulses and feelings. Hence collective excitement serves to integrate unrest and discontent, break down old behavior patterns, and prepare the way for new patterns of behavior. Where collective excitement is intense and widespread there is also the possibility of social contagion; that is, there occurs the relatively rapid, unwitting, and non-rational dissemination of a mood, impulse, or form of conduct.

Social contagion, then, is simply an intense form of milling and collective excitement in which rapport is established. These processes serve to unite the individuals of the mass into the crowd and so lay the foundations for further development.

Effective Mechanisms. It is necessary again to remind ourselves that the four stages of a revolutionary movement are not clear-cut and mutually exclusive. No such claim has ever been made for them. The concept "stage" is simply a means of describing dominant tendencies and makes no pretense of dealing with absolutely delimited periods.

This reminder is particularly desirable when considering the processes and mechanisms of the Popular Stage. Milling continues, though there is a basic, if subtle, change. There is a focusing of attention on a tentative objective to be realized that was absent in the previous stage. Agitation, suggestion, imitation, and propaganda continue in use. But the change in the nature of the processes gives new direction to the mechanisms already in operation and calls into play certain additional devices.

Of these the effort to develop *esprit de corps* is especially important. Leaders who desire to intensify rapport as a means of transforming a mass of individuals into a psychological and/or acting crowd will employ *esprit de corps* as a means of social control. That is, they will foster it as a way of organizing and integrating loyalty to the movement—as a way of making people feel that they belong together and are identified with and engaged in a common undertaking. It is at once evident that *esprit de corps* is very necessary as a means of developing unity and solidarity in a movement. Its use prevents disintegration and permits the organization of unrest and discontent in such fashion as to forward the evolution of the movement. It is achieved through promoting the in-group relationship, the formation of informal fellowship associations, and participation in informal ceremonial behavior.

Another important mechanism that is brought into use at this stage has been called the "social" or "revolutionary" myth. In order to mobilize unrest and discontent and prepare for action, the people must be led to believe that they are on the march toward a New Order—a potential Utopia which it is their duty to help actualize.

In addition to these two major devices and as aids to their realization rumor,

scandal, a literature of exposure, pamphlets, plays, protests, and many other mechanisms are also employed.

Types of Leaders. The conditions of the period and the skills requisite to the use of the necessary mechanisms determine the requirements for successful leadership. Thus the Popular Stage provides opportunity for the talents of the *prophet* and the *reformer*.

The prophet feels set apart or called to leadership; that he has a special and separate knowledge of the causes of unrest and discontent which the agitator has already brought to the attention of the people. He speaks with an air of authority, revealing a new message and a new philosophy of life, though always in general terms. He formulates and promulgates the social myth. He uses his belief in himself and his confidence in his message as a means of articulating the hopes and wishes of the people.

The reformer is a somewhat different type. He is produced by and is reacting to the same basic conditions, but the nature of the reaction is different and it is likely, too, that he appears somewhat later than the prophet, whose aims are general and vague. The reformer attacks specific evils and develops a clearly defined program; he attempts to change conditions in conformity with his own conceptions of what is good and desirable.

Dominant Social Form. The above brings us to the consideration of the social form typical of the Popular Stage. For the fact that the mass of the first stage evolves into the crowd of the second is the most obvious difference between the two.

Blumer's description of the process of crowd formation merits quotation:

The essential steps in the formation of the crowd seem to be quite clear. First is the occurrence of some exciting event which catches the attention and arouses the interest of the people. In becoming preoccupied with this event, and stirred by its excitatory character, an individual is already likely to lose some of his ordinary self-control and to be dominated by the exciting object. Thus, a number of people stimulated by the same exciting object are disposed by that very fact to behave like a crowd. This becomes clear in the second step . . . the beginning of the milling process. . . . The most obvious effect of this milling is to disseminate a common mood, feeling, or emotional impulse, and also to increase its intensity. The third important step . . . is the emergence of a common object of attention on which the impulses, feelings, and imagery of the people become focused. With such a common objective, the crowd is in a position to act with unity, purpose, and consistency. The last step may be thought of as the stimulation and fostering of the impulses that correspond to the crowd objective, up to the point where the members are ready to act on them.[8]

It should be pointed out that there are two major types of crowds. The *psychological* crowd is formed in the first two steps of the process just outlined, is the work of the agitator and, of necessity, precedes the *acting* crowd. The acting crowd emerges in the third and fourth steps and is led by the prophet and reformer.

It remains only to remark that the evolution of the mass into the crowd is the result of the changing socio-psychological situation and the work of the leadership. Given the characteristics present, the processes operative, and effective leadership the crowd emerges as the form within which collective behavior goes on.

III. The formal stage

Of the formulation of issues and formation of publics

Transition from the Popular to the Formal Stage marks a crucial point in the development of a revolutionary movement. *Esprit de corps* must be buttressed by

devices designed to develop group morale and ideology if disintegration is to be avoided. Furthermore, collective excitement and social contagion are not adequate to serve as the processual foundation for enduring social change. For this the formulation of issues and the formalization of procedures are demanded. In other words, the roots of the movement must strike deeper than sensationalism, sentimentalism, fashion, and fad. It must come to appeal to the essential desires of the people.

Characteristic Conditions. The typical characteristics found at this stage may be classified in terms of the two major developments which occur.

1. The fixation of motives (attitudes) and the definite formulation of aims (values). This major characteristic is paralleled by these developments:
   a. A struggle between the conservative, moderate, and radical factions of the revolutionary group; the continuation of the in-group–out-group conflict, and the intensification of class antagonisms
   b. The moderate faction gains control to the accompaniment of these typical events:
      1) Release of prisoners
      2) Apparent co-operation of reformers and revolutionists
      3) Abortive attempts of the radicals to seize power
      4) Radical-conservative coalition attacks on the reformers
      5) Evidence of manifest incompetence on the part of the reformers
   c. The reformers are confronted with three typical handicaps:
      1) Fear of armed invasion
      2) Fear of internal rebellion
      3) Political inexperience
   d. The desertion of lukewarm supporters
   e. The elimination of the conservatives by the reformers
   f. A movement toward the "left," or an "uncontrollable swing of the masses toward radicalism"

g. The emergence of the typical "perversions"

h. The development of a set of norms formally stated in dogma and formally expressed in ritual, together with a marked increase in the use of shibboleths

i. The fusion of patriotism and the social myth elevates the radical to power

j. The radicals are also confronted with three typical dangers:
   1) The danger of conservative opposition and foreign invasion or intervention
   2) Domestic insurrection
   3) Political inexperience

2. The development of an organizational structure with leaders, a program, doctrines, and traditions. This is accompanied by:
   a. The increasing recognition of organizational breakdown and governmental inefficiency
   b. The development of a condition of dual sovereignty
   c. The occurrence of an immediate precipitating factor and the seizure of power by the radicals
   d. The presence of conflict within the ranks of the radicals
   e. The formation of a provisional government
   f. A "lull" between the seizure of power by the radicals and the initiation of the Reign of Terror
   g. The use of the Reign of Terror as a control technique

Typical Processes. Because of the character of the events of this stage the behavior of the participants in the movement may be described under three headings: (1) discussion and deliberation, (2) formulation, and (3) formalization.

Since the terms discussion and deliberation are self-defining they are introduced here only to show the interrelation of the different phases of a revolutionary movement. Given the typical events, interaction *must* take the form of discussion and deliberation, and the public is the social form within which such interaction must

take place. In other words, this is the stage when issues emerge with reference to which there are differences of opinion. Publics form to discuss these issues. Discussion as a process is marked by the effort to interpret the issues under debate, by dispute, and by the dominance of conflict relations. This results in the participants becoming more self-conscious and critical. This, in turn, makes for opposition and disagreement and places a premium on the careful consideration of pertinent facts and produces arguments and counter-arguments.

The process of formulation may be thought of as both a continuation and a result of discussion. In the give and take of argument over and critical analysis of possible lines of action with reference to the issues under examination, policies begin to take shape and programs are formulated.

As the movement proceeds through the third stage a development occurs that may be called formalization. That is, wishes (attitudes) that have been reformulated, goals (values) that have emerged, and policies that have been developed get worked into the mores of the participants and become a formal part of their behavior in preparation for subsequent institutionalization.

Effective Mechanisms. In general, the mechanisms characteristic of this stage are those devices that are effective in developing group morale and ideology.

Morale is the device by which a developing movement is given cohesion, solidarity, and unity—just the qualities needed for its on-going. It roots in three convictions: (1) that the purposes and objectives of the movement are right and just and that victory will initiate a sort of Golden Age; (2) that these purposes will actually and ultimately be realized, with all the intense motivation deriving from this faith; and

(3) that these purposes represent a sacred responsibility which must be fulfilled.

The ideology of a movement consists in a body of doctrines, beliefs, and myths which provide direction and the ability to withstand the opposition of out-groups. The following elements are usually present: (1) a statement of the objectives, purposes, and premises of the movement; (2) a body of criticism and condemnation of the existing social order which the movement is attacking and seeking to change; (3) a body of defense doctrine serving to justify the movement; (4) a body of belief dealing with policies, tactics, and practical operations; and (5) the myths of the movement. From all this it is evident that it is the function of an ideology to give an answer to the unrest and discontent of the people. Unless such an answer is provided the movement cannot move forward.

On a slightly different level propaganda—"the deliberately evoked and guided campaign to induce people to accept a given view"—[9] is also of major importance at this stage.

There is no thought of presenting here a complete list of possible mechanisms. Rather, the important point to be established is that, whatever mechanisms are employed, they serve to facilitate the process of formalization. Various types of leaders and various types of mechanisms combine to realize this end. Historians, apologists, poets, hymnologists, and propagandists use the radio, the press, pamphlets, books, the stage, the movie, the platform, the pulpit, cartoons, posters, slogans, banners, insignia, and so forth to carry the movement along its way.

Types of Leaders. As might be expected in view of the nature of the period, leadership is in the hands of statesmen. That is, the leaders are those who are able to formulate policies and will attempt to carry social policy into practice. They are those who are skilled in estimating and evaluating the nature and direction of the prevailing social forces. They are those who will try to understand and champion the beliefs and convictions that have become established in the thinking of the people. They are those who will propose the program which promises to resolve the issues and realize the objectives of which the people have become aware.

Dominant Social Form. As already intimated, all this goes on in a *public*. Because of the interdependent character of the different features of a revolutionary movement, discussion and deliberation, formulation and formalization can only occur in a public; these processes cannot function in a mass or a crowd.

A public is marked by the presence of the discussion of, and a collective opinion about, an issue. The following statement, contrasting a public and a society, gives an excellent picture of both:

A public comes into existence because of an issue with reference to which there is no recognized procedure; a society, in contrast, is marked by rules and regulations that prescribe procedure. That is, a society possesses a culture; whereas a public emerges precisely because the culture has no solution to the issue which has caused the public to form. It follows from the above that a society has form and organization which a public lacks. Finally, the members of a society have fixed status roles and a well-developed we-feeling; in contrast the public is a kind of amorphous group whose size and membership varies with the issue. Instead of having its activity prescribed, it is engaged in an effort to arrive at an act and therefore forced to create its action.[10]

IV. The institutional stage

Of legalization and societal organization

We come now to the final stage in the development of a revolutionary movement:

the period in which institutionalization takes place. If the revolutionaries are to avoid the stigma of permanent classification as "rebels" this must occur. That is, the out-group must finally be able to *legalize* or *organize* their power; they must become the in-group of the structure of political power. When the attitudes and values of the revolutionary leadership have thus become the legal and political foundation of social organization, a new *society* has been formed and the revolution has been consummated.

Characteristic Conditions. The socio-psychological conditions which indicate that a revolution is moving from the Formal into the Institutional Stage may be classified as *causal* or transitional and *resultant* or accommodative.

1. Causal characteristics:
   a. Psychological exhaustion which undermines the emotional foundations of the revolution
   b. Moral let-down and return to old habits (attitudes), including "escape recreation" and the re-emergence of graft, speculation, and corruption, become deterrents to continued revolutionary behavior
   c. Great economic distress, amounting almost to chaos, demands a settling down
2. Resultant characteristics:
   a. End of the Reign of Terror; granting of amnesty; return of exiles; repression of extremists; and search for scapegoats
   b. Increase in powers of central government, frequently resulting in dictatorship
   c. Social reconstruction along lines of the old social structure but with the new principles (values) essentially intact
   d. Dilution of the revolutionary ideal; transformation of evangelistic fervor for social change into the desire for conquest; transformation of the "revolutionary sect" into a "political denomination"
   e. Re-accommodation of church and state
   f. "Reaction to the reaction" represented by escape recreation
   g. The revolution becomes attitudinally es-

tablished and develops a permanent organization that is acceptable to the current mores; that is, it is institutionalized.

Notes

1. As applied to all organized social movements this hypothesis was advanced first by W. E. Gettys and employed by him in the study of the development of Methodism in England.—Carl Dawson and W. E. Gettys, *Introduction to Sociology* (rev. ed., New York: Ronald Press, 1934), pp. 708-09.
2. P. A. Sorokin, *The Sociology of Revolution* (Philadelphia: J. P. Lippincott, 1925); L. P. Edwards, *Natural History of Revolution* (Chicago: University of Chicago Press, 1927); Gettys, *op. cit.*; Herbert Blumer, "Collective Behavior" in *An Outline of the Principles of Sociology*, R. E. Park, ed. (New York: Barnes and Noble, 1939); Crane Brinton, *The Anatomy of Revolution* (New York: W. W. Norton, 1938).
3. An attitude is any socially-acquired tendency to act. A value is any culturally-held object of interest. Attitudes-values, then, are the basic social elements.
4. Blumer offers an excellent description of milling. See *op. cit.*, Part IV, pp. 224-28.
5. *Op. cit.*, pp. 260-61.
6. Blumer, *op. cit.*, pp. 241-45.
7. The materials listed under items two and three are presented as they were derived from the writings of previous students. The present writer believes that if they are arranged as follows they reveal what might be termed the "natural history of the process of the transfer of allegiance of the intellectuals":

1. With the passage of time a social system initially considered to be socially advantageous comes to be seen as repressive. The repression is felt first by the "inarticulate masses" who do not understand the causes of it. After a period of time, the "intellectuals" are infected with the discontent of the masses and begin to search for the causes of the repression. "The repressors neither feel the repression nor, except in rare cases, understand its causes."
2. This shift of the intellectuals leads both them and the public to become victims of the "bad-man-good-man fallacy." That is, they lose their respect for and faith in the individuals who at the time have control of the societies, and conclude that their difficulties result from the fact that their leaders are bad men. This leads to the conclusion that good men should be placed in control. So, such changes are demanded and are frequently effected with the result that the good individuals, like their "bad" predecessors, fail and lose their popularity.
3. However, in a society ripe for revolution this fallacious diagnosis does not lead men astray for long. Renewed search leads to the conclusion that

"the real cause of the unrest is to be found in certain archaic elements of the social order," and these archaic elements are then seen to be associated with the activities of "some group or order of men."

4. Having identified what seems to be the real foundation of the repression, the intellectuals believe themselves to be under obligation to inform the public. So they seek to focus the dissatisfaction of the public on what they believe to be the source of the trouble.

5. The agitation of the intellectuals provokes a typical "period of discussion" which is characterized by the use of many methods and the results of which depend, of course, on who wins. If the intellectuals are correct in their analysis, and if the repressors are unsuccessful in their efforts to avert, direct, postpone, or abort the revolutionary movement, two developments typically occur: (1) The repressed group becomes afflicted with what has been called the "oppression psychosis," and (2) "the repressors gradually lose faith in themselves and in their cause."

6. If the foregoing occurs the time is ripe for a revolutionary upheaval if one more important factor is injected into the interactional situation: a "dynamic," a *raison d'etre* is necessary and this is provided by the fabrication of the social myth, the product of the minds of the intellectuals.

8. *Op. cit.*, p. 234.
9. Blumer, *op. cit.*, pp. 250-52.
10. Blumer, *op. cit.*, pp. 245-46.

12.

Ralph Turner and Samuel J. Surace[1]

ZOOT-SUITERS AND MEXICANS: SYMBOLS IN CROWD BEHAVIOR

The purpose of this paper is to test a hypothesis concerning the symbols with which a hostile crowd designates the object of its action. The hypothesis is that hostile crowd behavior requires an unambiguously unfavorable symbol, which serves to divert crowd attention from any of the usual favorable or mitigating connotations surrounding the object. The hypothesis has been tested by a content analysis of references to the symbol "Mexican" during the ten-and-one-half-year period leading up to the 1943 "zoot-suit riots" in Los Angeles and vicinity.

Theory and hypothesis[2]

The hypothesis under examination is related to two important characteristics of

From Ralph H. Turner and Samuel J. Surace, "Zoot-Suiters and Mexicans: Symbols in Crowd Behavior." *The American Journal of Sociology* 62, July 1956, 14-20, with permission of the publisher.

crowd behavior. First, crowd behavior is *uniform* behavior in a broad sense, in contrast to behavior which exposes the infinitely varied attitudes of diverse individuals. Many attitudes and gradations of feeling can be expressed in a group's actions toward any particular object. However, the crowd is a group expressing *one* attitude, with individual variations largely concealed.

In non-crowd situations uniform behavior may be achieved by majority decision, acceptance of authority, or compromise of some sort. But crowd behavior is not mediated by such slow and deliberate procedures. Within the crowd there is a readiness to act *uniformly* in response to varied suggestions, and, until such readiness to act has spread throughout the crowd's recruitment population, fully developed and widespread-acting crowd behavior is not possible.

The response in the community to

shared symbols is crucial to this uniformity of action. Ordinarily, any particular symbol has varied connotations for different individuals and groups in the community. These varied connotations prevent uniform community-wide action or at least delay it until extended processes of group decision-making have been carried out. But, when a given symbol has a relatively uniform connotation in all parts of the community, uniform group action can be taken readily when the occasion arises. To the degree, then, to which any symbol evokes only one consistent set of connotations throughout the community, only one general course of action toward the object will be indicated, and formation of an acting crowd will be facilitated.

Second, the crowd follows a course of action which is at least partially sanctioned in the culture but, at the same time, is normally inhibited by other aspects of that culture. Mob action is frequently nothing more than culturally sanctioned punishment carried out by unauthorized persons without "due process." Support of it in everyday life is attested to in many ways. Organizations such as the Ku Klux Klan and other vigilante groups act as self-appointed "custodians of patriotism" and are fairly widely accepted as such. The lynching of two "confessed" kidnapers in California in 1933 was given public sanction by the then governor of the state on the grounds of its therapeutic effect on other would-be criminals.[3] The legal system in America implicitly recognizes these supports by including statutes designed to suppress them.

Hostile acting crowd behavior can take place only when these inhibiting aspects of the culture cease to operate.[4] Conflict between the norms sanctioning the crowd's action and the norms inhibiting it must be resolved by the neutralization of the inhibiting norms.

There is normally some ambiguity in the connotations of any symbol, so that both favorable and unfavorable sentiments are aroused. For example, even the most prejudiced person is likely to respond to the symbol "Negro" with images of both the feared invader of white prerogatives and the lovable, loyal Negro lackey and "mammy." The symbol "bank robber" is likely to evoke a picture of admirable daring along with its generally unfavorable image. These ambiguous connotations play an important part in inhibiting extreme hostile behavior against the object represented by the symbol.

The diverse connotations of any symbol normally inhibit extreme behavior in two interrelated ways. First, the symbol evokes feelings which resist any extreme course of action. A parent, for example, is normally inhibited from punishing his child to excess, because affection for him limits the development of anger. Pity and admiration for courage or resolute action, or sympathy for a course of action which many of us might like to engage in ourselves, or charity toward human weakness usually moderate hostility toward violators of the mores. So long as feelings are mixed, actions are likely to be moderate.

Second, the mixed connotations of the symbol place the object *within the normative order,* so that the mores of fair play, due process, giving a fair hearing, etc., apply. Any indication that the individual under attack respects any of the social norms or has any of the characteristics of the in-group evokes these mores which block extreme action.

On the other hand, unambiguous symbols permit immoderate behavior, since there is no internal conflict to restrict action. Furthermore, a symbol which represents a person as outside the normative order will not evoke the in-group norms of fair play and due process. The dictum that "you must fight fire with fire" and the conviction that a person devoid of human decency is not entitled to be treated with decency and respect rule out these inhibiting norms.

We conclude that a necessary condition for both the uniform group action and the unrestricted hostile behavior of the crowd is a symbol which arouses uniformly and exclusively unfavorable feelings toward the object under attack. However, the connotations of a symbol to the mass or crowd do not necessarily correspond exactly with the connotations to individuals. The symbol as presented in the group context mediates the overt expression of attitudes in terms of sanction and the focus of attention. The individual in whom a particular symbol evokes exclusively unfavorable feelings may nevertheless be inhibited from acting according to his feelings by the awareness that other connotations are sanctioned in the group. Or the individual in whom ambivalent feelings are invoked may conceal his favorable sentiments because he sees that only the unfavorable sentiments are sanctioned. He thereby facilitates crowd use of the symbol. Furthermore, of all the possible connotations attached to a symbol, the individual at any given moment acts principally on the basis of those on which his attention is focused. By shielding individuals from attending to possibly conflicting connotations, the unambiguous public symbol prevents the evocation of attitudes which are normally present. Thus, without necessarily undergoing change, favorable individual attitudes toward the object of crowd attack simply remain latent. This process is one of the aspects of the so-called restriction of attention which characterizes the crowd.

While unambiguous symbols are a necessary condition to full-fledged crowd behavior, they may also be a product of the earlier stages of crowd development. In some cases sudden development of a crowd is facilitated by the pre-existing linkage of an already unambiguous symbol to the object upon which events focus collective attention. But more commonly we suspect that the emergence of such a symbol or the stripping-away of alternative connotations takes place cumulatively through interaction centered on that object. In time, community-wide interaction about an object takes on increasingly crowd-like characteristics in gradual preparation for the ultimate crowd action. It is the hypothesis of this paper that *overt hostile crowd behavior is usually preceded by a period in which the key symbol is stripped of its favorable connotations until it comes to evoke unambiguously unfavorable feelings.* [5]

The "zoot-suit riots"

Beginning on June 3, 1943, Los Angeles, California, was the scene of sporadic acts of violence involving principally United States naval personnel, with the support of a sympathetic Anglo community, in opposition to members of the Mexican community which have come to be known as the "zoot-suit riots." "Zooter" referred mainly to two characteristics. First, zoot suits consisted of long suit coats and trousers extremely pegged at the cuff, draped full around the knees, and terminating in deep pleats at the waist.[6] Second, the zooters wore their hair long, full, and well greased.

During the riots many attacks and injuries were sustained by both sides.[7] Groups of sailors were frequently reported to be assisted or accompanied by civilian mobs who "egged" them on as they roamed through downtown streets in search of victims.[8] Zooters discovered on city streets were assaulted and forced to disrobe amid the jibes and molestations of the crowd. Streetcars and busses were stopped and searched, and zooters found therein were carried off into the streets and beaten. Cavalcades of hired taxicabs filled with sailors ranged the East Side districts of Los Angeles seeking, finding, and attacking zooters. Civilian gangs of East Side adolescents organized similar attacks against unwary naval personnel.

It is, of course, impossible to isolate a single incident or event and hold it responsible for the riots. Local, state, and federal authorities and numerous civic and national groups eventually tried to assess blame and prevent further violence. The most prominent charge from each side was that the other had molested its girls. It was reported that sailors became enraged by the rumor that zoot-suiters were guilty of "assaults on female relatives of servicemen."[9] Similarly, the claim against sailors was that they persisted in molesting and insulting Mexican girls. While many other charges were reported in the newspapers, including unsubstantiated suggestions of sabotage of the war effort,[10] the sex charges dominated the precipitating context.

Method

In the absence of any direct sampling of community sentiment in the period preceding the riots, it is assumed that the use of the symbol "Mexican" by the media of mass communication indicates the prevalent connotations. Any decision as to whether the mass media passively reflect community sentiment, whether they actively mold it, or whether, as we supposed, some combination of the two processes occurs is immaterial to the present method. Ideally we should have sampled a number of mass media to correct for biases in each. However, with the limited re-

sources at our disposal we chose the *Los Angeles Times,* largest of the four major newspapers in the Los Angeles area. It is conservative in emphasis and tends away from the sensational treatment of minority issues. In the past a foremost romanticizer of Old Mexico had been a prominent member of the *Times* editorial staff and board of directors.[11]

In order to uncover trends in the connotation of the symbol under study, one newspaper per month was read for the ten and one-half years from January, 1933, until June 30, 1943. These monthly newspapers were selected by assigning consecutive days of the week to each month. For example, for January, 1933, the paper printed on the first Monday was read; for February, the paper printed on the first Tuesday was read. After the seven-day cycle was completed, the following months were assigned, respectively, the *second* Monday, the *second* Tuesday, etc. To avoid loading the sample with days that fell early in the first half of the month, the procedure was reversed for the last half of the period. Then, to secure an intensive picture of the critical period, consecutive daily editions were read for one month starting with May 20, 1943, through June 20, 1943. This covered approximately ten days before and after the period of violence. Any editorial, story, report, or letter which had reference to the Mexican community or population was summarized, recorded, and classified.[12] The articles were placed in five basic categories: favorable themes, unfavorable themes, neutral mention, negative-favorable mention and zooter theme.[13]

1. *Favorable:* (*a*) Old California Theme. This is devoted to extolling the traditions and history of the old rancheros as the earliest California settlers. (*b*) Mexican Temperament Theme. This describes the Mexican character in terms of dashing romance,

TABLE 1
Favorable and Unfavorable Mention of "Mexican" During Three Periods

Period	Favorable Themes	Unfavorable Themes	Percentage Favorable
January, 1933—June, 1936	27	3	90
July, 1936—December, 1939	23	5	82
January, 1940—June, 1943	10	2	83
Total	60	10	86

bravery, gaiety, etc. (c) Religious Theme. This refers to the devout religious values of the Mexican community. (d) Mexican Culture Theme. This pays homage to Mexican art, dance, crafts, music, fifth of May festivities, etc.

2. *Unfavorable:* (a) Delinquency and Crime Theme. This theme includes the specific mention of a law violator as "Mexican," associating him with marihuana, sex crimes, knife-wielding, gang violence, etc. (b) Public Burden Theme. This attempts to show that Mexicans constitute a drain on relief funds and on the budgets of correctional institutions.

3. *Neutral:* This is a category of miscellaneous items, including reports of crimes committed by individuals possessing obvious Mexican names but without designation of ethnic affiliation.

4. *Negative-Favorable:* This category consists of appeals which *counter* or *deny* the validity of accusations against Mexicans as a group. For example: "Not all zoot-suiters are delinquents; their adoption by many was a bid for social recognition"; "At the outset zoot-suiters were limited to no specific race. . . . The fact that later on their numbers seemed to be predominantly Latin was in itself no indication of that race" (*Los Angeles Times,* July 11, 1943, Part 1, p. 1).

5. *Zooter Theme:* This theme identifies the zooter costume as "a badge of delinquency." Typical references were: "reat pleat boys," "long coated gentry," coupled with mention of "unprovoked attacks by zoot-suited youths," "zoot-suite orgy," etc. Crime, sex violence, and gang attacks were the dominant elements in this theme. Almost invariably, the zooter was identified as a Mexican by such clues as "East Side hoodlum," a Mexican name, or specific ethnic designation.

If the hypothesis of this paper is to be supported, we should expect a decline in the favorable contexts of the symbol "Mexican." The change should serve to produce the type of symbol suggested by the hypothesis, a symbol dominated by unambiguously unfavorable elements.

Findings

The favorable and unfavorable themes are reported alone in Table 1 for the ten and one-half years. The table by itself appears to negate our hypothesis, since there is no appreciable decline in the percentage of favorable themes during the period. Indeed, even during the last period the mentions appear predominantly favorable, featuring the romanticized Mexican. However, there is a striking decline in the total number of articles mentioning the Mexican between the second and third periods. Treating the articles listed as a fraction of all articles in the newspapers sampled and using a sub-minimal estimate of the total number of all articles, the t test reveals that such a drop in the total number of articles mentioning Mexicans could have occurred by chance less than twice in one hundred times. We conclude, then, that the decline in total favorable and unfavorable mentions of "Mexican" is statistically significant.

While the hypothesis in its simplest form is unsubstantiated, the drop in both favorable and unfavorable themes suggests

TABLE 2
Distribution of All Themes by Three Periods

Period	Per-centage Favorable	Per-centage Unfavorable	Per-centage Neutral	Percentage Negative-Favorable	Per-centage Zooter	Total Per-centage	Total Num-ber
January, 1933 — June, 1936	80	9	11	0	0	100	34
July, 1936 — December, 1939	61	13	23	3	0	100	38
January, 1940 — June, 1943	25	5	32	8	30	100	40

a shift away from *all* the traditional references to Mexicans during the period prior to the riots. If it can be shown that an actual substitution of symbols was taking place, our hypothesis may still be substantiated, but in a somewhat different manner than anticipated.

From the distribution of all five themes reported in Table 2 it is immediately evident that there has been no decline of interest in the Mexican but rather a clear-cut shift of attention away from traditional references. The straightforward favorable and unfavorable themes account for 89, 74, and 30 per cent of all references, respectively, during the three periods. This drop and the drop from 61 to 25 per cent favorable mentions are significant below the 1 per cent level. To determine whether this evidence confirms our hypothesis, we must make careful examination of the three emerging themes.

The *neutral* theme shows a steady increase throughout the three periods. While we have cautiously designated this "neutral," it actually consists chiefly of unfavorable presentations of the object "Mexican" without overt use of the symbol "Mexican." Thus it incorporates the unfavorable representation of Mexican, which we assume was quite generally recognized throughout the community, without explicit use of the symbol.

The *negative-favorable* theme, though small in total numbers, also increased. At first we were inclined to treat these as favorable themes. However, in contrast to the other favorable themes, this one documents the extent of negative connotation which is accumulating about the symbol "Mexican." By arguing openly against the negative connotations, these articles acknowledge their widespread community sanction. When the implicitly favorable themes of romantic Mexico and California's historic past give way to defensive assertions that all Mexicans are not bad, such a shift can only reasonably be interpreted as a rise in unfavorable connotations.

The most interesting shift, however, is the rise of the *zoot-suit* theme, which did not appear at all until the third period, when it accounts for 30 per cent of the references. Here we have the emergence of a new symbol which has no past favorable connotations to lose. Unlike the symbol "Mexican," the "zoot-suiter" symbol evokes no ambivalent sentiments but appears in exclusively unfavorable contexts. While, in fact, Mexicans were attacked *indiscriminately* in spite of apparel (of two hundred youths rounded up by the police on one occasion, very few were wearing zoot suits),[14] the symbol "zoot-suiter" could become a basis for unambivalent community sentiment supporting hostile crowd behavior more easily than could "Mexican."

It is interesting to note that, when we consider only the fifteen mentions which appear in the first six months of 1943, ten

TABLE 3
Distribution of All Themes from May 20
to June 20, 1943

Theme	Percentage of All Mentions*
Favorable	0
Unfavorable	0
Neutral	3
Negative-favorable	23
Zooter	74
Total	100

* Total number = 61.

are to zooters, three are negative-favorable, two are neutral, and none is the traditional favorable or unfavorable theme.

In Table 3 we report the results of the day-by-day analysis of the period immediately prior, during, and after the riots. It shows the culmination of a trend faintly suggested as long as seven years before the riots and clearly indicated two or three years in advance. The traditional favorable and unfavorable themes have vanished completely, and three-quarters of the references center about the zooter theme.

From the foregoing evidence we conclude that our basic hypothesis and theory receive confirmation, but not exactly as anticipated. The simple expectation that there would be a shift in the relative preponderance of favorable and unfavorable contexts for the symbol "Mexican" was not borne out. But the basic hypothesis that an unambiguously unfavorable symbol is required as the rallying point for hostile crowd behavior is supported through evidence that the symbol "Mexican" tended to be displaced by the symbol "zoot-suiter" as the time of the riots drew near.

The conception of the romantic Mexican and the Mexican heritage is deeply ingrained in southern California tradition.

The Plaza and Olvera Street in downtown Los Angeles, the Ramona tradition, the popularity of Mexican food, and many other features serve to perpetuate it. It seems quite probable that its force was too strong to be eradicated entirely, even though it ceased to be an acceptable matter of public presentation. In spite, then, of a progressive decline in public presentation of the symbol in its traditional favorable contexts, a certain ambivalence remained which prevented a simple replacement with predominantly unfavorable connotations.

Rather, two techniques emerged for circumventing the ambivalence. One was the presenting of the object in an obvious manner without explicit use of the symbol. Thus a Mexican name, a picture, or reference to "East Side hoodlums" was presented in an unfavorable context. But a far more effective device was a new symbol whose connotations at the time were exclusively unfavorable. It provided the public sanction and restriction of attention essential to the development of overt crowd hostility. The symbol "zoot-suiter" evoked none of the imagery of the romantic past. It evoked only the picture of a breed of persons outside the normative order, devoid of morals themselves, and consequently not entitled to fair play and due process. Indeed, the zoot-suiter came to be regarded as such an exclusively fearful threat to the community that at the height of rioting the Los Angeles City Council seriously debated an ordinance making the wearing of zoot suits a prison offense.[15]

The "zooter" symbol had a crisis character which mere unfavorable versions of the familiar "Mexican" symbol never approximated. And the "zooter" symbol was an omnibus, drawing together the most reprehensible elements in the old unfavorable themes, namely, sex crimes, delinquency, gang attacks, draft-dodgers, and the like and was, in consequence, widely applicable.

The "zooter" symbol also supplied a tag identifying the object of attack. It could be used, when the old attitudes toward Mexicans were evoked, to differentiate Mexicans along both moral and physical lines. While the active minority were attacking Mexicans indiscriminately, and frequently including Negroes, the great sanctioning majority heard only of attacks on zootsuiters.

Once established, the zooter theme assured its own magnification. What previously would have been reported as an adolescent gang attack would now be presented as a zoot-suit attack. Weapons found on apprehended youths were now interpreted as the building-up of arms collections in preparation for zoot-suit violence.[16] In short, the "zooter" symbol was a recasting of many of the elements formerly present and sometimes associated with Mexicans in a new and instantly recognizable guise. This new association of ideas relieved the community of ambivalence and moral obligations and gave sanction to making the Mexicans the victims of widespread hostile crowd behavior.

Notes

1. Judith Cahn Hart assisted greatly in the collecting and processing of data for this paper.
2. The authors owe much to Herbert Blumer for the background of ideas from which the present theory and hypothesis have been developed.
3. Cf. *Literary Digest,* CXVI (December 9, 1933), 5.

4. This statement and the general hypothesis of this paper are but expressions of the more general proposition that all crowd behavior reflects the neutralization of normally inhibiting phases of the culture in which it occurs.
5. There are other factors in the etiology of crowd behavior. The symbol with specified characteristics is hypothesized as merely an essential link in the causal chain and is itself an index of aggravated conditions in the community. The "zoot-suit riots" occurred within a larger social context characterized by violent racial and ethnic turmoil. Nationally, 1943 witnessed more race riots than any other year since the period immediately following World War I. California had recently undergone the experience of Japanese evacuation and rearoused alarm over the possibility that some Japanese-Americans might be relocated in the state. A full accounting for the riot would have to include these and several other conditions.
6. The zoot suit apparently developed in the East and was associated with the Negroes in Harlem. But in southern California, Mexican youth became the recognized wearers of this garb.
7. For a popular report of the incident see Carey McWilliams in the *New Republic.* CVIII (June 21, 1943), 818-20.
8. *Los Angeles Times,* June 8, 1943, Part I, p. 1.
9. *Ibid.,* June 7, 1943, Part II, p. 1.
10. *Ibid.,* June 10, 1943, Part I, p. A.
11. Harry Carr, author of *Old Mother Mexico* (Boston: Houghton Mifflin Co., 1931).
12. The unit of count in the present paper is the entire article, report, or item. A weighting for location and length might have indicated additional findings. For a discussion of this point see Bernard Berelson, *Content Analysis in Communications Research* (Glencoe, Ill.: Free Press, 1952).
13. In judging references to be favorable or unfavorable, it was asked whether the report tended to encourage (*a*) an increase or a decrease in social distance between the reader and the Mexican and (*b*) a definition of the Mexican as an asset or a liability to the life of the community. A full list of themes and subthemes appears in this reading.
14. *Los Angeles Times,* June 9, 1943, Part I, p. A.
15. *Ibid.,* June 10, 1943, Part I, pp. 1, A.
16. For an interesting account relative to this point see Donald M. Johnson, "The Phantom Anesthetist of Mattoon: A Field Study of Mass Hysteria," *Journal of Abnormal and Social Psychology,* XL (April, 1945), 175-86.

13.

James W. Vander Zanden

RESISTANCE AND SOCIAL MOVEMENTS

Sociologists and anthropologists have long been interested in the tenacity of culture and its slowness to change. Representative of this concern are Tylor's "survivals," Bagehot's "cake of custom," Tönnies' "sitte," Sumner's "mores and folkways," Boas' "cultural inertia," and Ogburn's "cultural lag." Common to these concepts is the notion that once a pattern of social relationships has been established, it tends to carry on unchanged, except as the dynamics of other social forces operate to undermine it.

Closely associated with the study of cultural persistence is the study of resistance to social change. The one, however, should not be confused with the other. Resistance is not simply a function of cultural persistence. Resistance implies behavior on the part of some or all of the members of society, either passive or active, which is directed toward the rejection or circumvention of a social change.

Except perhaps for Bernhard J. Stern in his studies of resistance to medical and technological change,[1] writers have concerned themselves with resistance primarily as a by-product of other work and interests. Thus Veblen and Marx in their respective analyses of "vested interests" and the "bourgeoisie" treated resistance to social change as it originated from particular groups within society. There have

From James W. Vander Zanden, "Resistance and Social Movements," *Social Forces*, 37, May 1959, 312-15, with permission of the publisher.

I have profited considerably in discussing the ideas in this paper with Dr. Guy B. Johnson and Dr. Rupert B. Vance of the University of North Carolina.

also appeared various descriptive accounts of social movements with a predominantly resistance orientation.[2] And some aspects of nativistic phenomena studied by anthropologists have possessed characteristics of resistance movements.[3] However, in most nativistic movements the revivalistic rather than the perpetualistic component appears to be the dominant theme, e.g., the Ghost Dance among the Plains Indians.[4]

Unfortunately sociologists in the field of social movements have tended to neglect these materials and the phenomenon of resistance in their studies. "Social movement" traditionally has been defined in a manner which would automatically exclude movements resisting social change. This has been the product of either explicitly or implicitly treating social movements as agencies seeking to bring about social change, often of a fundamental sort.[5] Thus the work which has emerged in the field is a study of reformistic and revolutionary movements.

Representative of the reformistic orientation are the following concepts of a social movement:

The main criterion of a social movement . . . is that it aims to bring about *fundamental changes in the social order*, especially in the basic institutions of property and labor relationships.—*Rudolf Heberle.*[6]

Social movements can be viewed as collective enterprises to establish a new order of life.—*Herbert Blumer.*[7]

. . . a social movement is circumscribed by pluristic behavior functioning as organized mass-effort directed toward *a change of established folkways or institutions.—Theodore Abel.*[8]

. . . social movements may be distinguished from other phenomena on the basis of the kind of goal to which they are committed. Unlike social institutions, their purpose is *change,* whether of relationships, norms, beliefs, or all of these. . . . But without some change in view there is no social movement.—*C. Wendell King.*[9]

To narrow the concept of a social movement in this manner is to preclude an area of fruitful research and to close the door upon a good deal of the social dynamics in movement and social change. In fact, the study of social movement within such a context becomes to a considerable degree sterile. Little more is involved than a struggle on the part of the reform effort to overcome cultural persistence. Very often there is more involved than the mere tenacity of culture. Movement frequently begets countermovement. Between the two a dynamic interrelation occurs.

In short, social movements do not initiate social change merely because they arise. They often stimulate the rise of movements opposed to the change, and between the two a more or less prolonged struggle takes place. Thus in order to understand the ultimate outcome, itself a transitory phase, it is not enough to study the change-oriented movement. A study of the countermovement and the resultant interaction of the movements is essential to such analysis.

Countermovement frequently influences the speed, degree, and nature of the social change. In fact as a consequence of the interaction between the movements and the processes which flow from it, the net result or product is rarely the complete fulfillment of the goal or goals of the parties involved. In some instances the outcome is totally different from the originally conceived goals, i.e., it is not a mere quantitative mixing of aspects of the opposing programs but a completely new qualitative entity. Likewise the resistance often serves to gradualize the process of social change. In so doing it functions to prevent sharp and sudden social dislocations within a society and to provide for a less traumatic or precipitous transition and adjustment to the new.

Illustrative of the phenomena of movement and countermovement is the southern white resistance movement to integration which arose following the Supreme Court's May 17, 1954, school desegregation ruling. It is a countermovement which has arisen in defense of southern race patterns in the wake of the challenge from the integration movement, a movement which in its organized aspect includes the National Association for the Advancement of Colored People, the united AFL-CIO labor movement, the nation's major church bodies (although a few southern denominations are at most only lukewarm supporters), the major political parties through their platform statements and the declarations of their spokesmen, various minority organizations such as B'nai B'rith, many civic organizations, and probably most formidable of all, the federal government via the national administration and the judiciary.

Some may question whether the southern white resistance in fact constitutes a social movement. In dealing with this matter the most satisfactory and definitive criteria of a social movement are probably those which can be abstracted from Rudolf Heberle's work.[10] They are the following:

1. ". . . it aims to bring about fundamental changes in the social order, especially in the basic institutions of property and labor relationships."
2. A consciousness of group identity and

solidarity is necessary along with an awareness of common sentiments and goals.

3. It is "always integrated by a set of constitutive ideas, or an ideology . . .".

4. They contain among their members groups that are formally organized, but the movements *as such* are not organized groups.

5. ". . . they are, as a rule, large enough to continue their existence even if there should be a change in the composition of the membership."

6. They are not short-lived but have duration.

Let us apply these criteria to the present southern white resistance. First, Heberle's "main criterion"[11] is that a social movement aims to bring about fundamental changes in the social order. This criterion of course is not met by the southern white resistance. Some may argue, however, that it is applicable, there being merely a question of semantics at issue. Thus it may be argued that in effect the southern whites are seeking to alter the *status quo,* i.e., the Supreme Court school ruling constitutes for the nation the new *status quo,* a *status quo* which the South is attempting to overturn.

But to argue in this manner is to obscure the picture and to lose sight of what is actually taking place. First, segregation *is* the pattern of race relations in the South and the Court's ruling where effected will *alter* this pattern, i.e., in some areas one will find desegregated schools. Secondly, the southern movement is essentially "resistance" oriented. This is how it conceives of itself and in turn is perceived by the nation.[12]

The second feature suggested by Heberle is that a social movement possesses a consciousness of group identity and solidarity along with an awareness of common sentiments and goals. Involved here is the existence of a "we-feeling" among the members of the movement. Without making an attempt to delineate

any degree of the intensity of the "we-feeling,"[13] the southern white resistance qualifies as a social movement under this criterion on two counts: first, the consciousness of identity and solidarity of the white southerner as a "white" distinguished from the subordinately defined "Negro" and the awareness of the common goal of preserving white supremacy; and secondly, the consciousness of identity and solidarity of the white southerner as a "Southerner" distinguished from the "Yankee" and the awareness of the common goal of "defending the southern way of life." The struggles waged in the past four years by the South, together with a number of sharp, well-publicized encounters between the forces of integration and segregation have undoubtedly served to intensify and heighten this southern white consciousness and awareness. Its highest form of expression has been in the organized activities of southern governmental leaders and resistance organizations.

Heberle's third criterion of a social movement is that it possesses an ideology. The body of ideas giving the southern white resistance its intellectual and ideological cohesion revolve about the Negro (white supremacy) and states' rights. It is epitomized by the two mottoes found in the emblem of the Citizens Councils: "STATES RIGHTS—RACIAL INTEGRITY."

The fourth characteristic is that although containing groups which are formally organized, the movement as such is not an organized group. More than 90 resistance organizations[14] have sprung up in the South in the wake of the Supreme Court ruling, some such as the Mississippi Association of Citizens Councils claiming 65 chapters and 80,000 members. But the movement is more inclusive than organized groups in the customary usage of the term, i.e., structured, formalized organizations. Included have been a wide variety of activities ranging from the legal maneuverings of state governors and legislators to mass petition signings and letters to the editors.

With regard to Heberle's fifth characteristic, size, the southern resistance again qualifies as a social movement. The resistance forces are large enough to continue the movement's existence even if there should be a change in the composition of the membership. Technically "membership" here could be construed to be applicable to only the organized aspects of the movement, but to do so would seem to be contradictory to the fourth feature. Here the question of sufficient size will be interpreted to mean that there is a collective effort on the part of a *considerable number of persons within a given society* to deal with a situation which they perceive to be a problem and that this number is sufficient to give the movement durability. In this instance the southern white resistance is a regional movement with deep historical roots and traditions embracing wide sections of its white population.

Finally, according to Heberle, a social movement is not short-lived but has duration, a feature closely related to the previous one. The present resistance qualifies with regard to this criterion on two counts. First, the movement is already four-and-a-half-years old and gives every promise of continuing vitality in the years ahead. Second, the present resistance cannot be divorced from its history with roots extending to the foundation of our nation It can best be understood as merely one episode in a social movement embracing some 150 years. During this time it has gone through many forms in terms of organized expressions, issues, tactics, and leadership. Over the years it has repeatedly risen and ebbed. But knitting the whole together over time have

been the two central questions: the Negro and states' rights.

Thus the southern white resistance qualifies as a social movement with regard to all Heberle's criteria but the first, namely it does not seek to *initiate* social change. But if a social movement is defined and approached exclusively in terms of its altering the *status quo,* what is to be done with those "movements" which seek to preserve the *status quo*? It is suggested that a more satisfactory definition of a social movement would be the following: *A social movement is a more or less persistent and organized effort on the part of a considerable number of members of a given society either to change a situation which they define as unsatisfactory or to prevent change in a situation which they define as satisfactory.*

The southern white resistance which has developed in the past few years and its historical predecessors probably are not unique or peculiar phenomena. A scanning of the pages of history reveal many others, e.g., the movement in opposition to the Roosevelt New Deal, the bootlegging and speakeasy movement during Prohibition, and the resistance movements in Nazi-occupied countries.

It should be noted that occasionally movements begin with a predominantly resistance orientation but as time progresses, particularly as a consequence of the dynamic interplay of movement and countermovement, become transformed into offensive, anti-*status quo* movements. This appears to be especially characteristic of nationalistic movements. Thus, for example, such Irish secret societies of the seventeenth, eighteenth, and early nineteenth centuries as the Defenders, White Boys, and Ribbonmen, oriented toward resistance to various British colonial measures and to the abuses of British landlords, were the precursors of the Irish independence movement represented organizationally by groups such as the Irish Republican Brotherhood, Fenians and Sinn Fein. By the same token, anti-*status quo* movements may become transformed into movements with considerable defensive, resistance qualities as witness the case of the Hungarian Communists, especially during late 1956 and early 1957.

The study of resistance to social change is undoubtedly one which offers great promise for further sociological research and study. In a world characterized by tremendous social change and upheavals, in which the dynamics of movement and countermovement have become increasingly inescapable in their day-to-day consequences, it becomes a phenomenon with a growing challenge for sociologists.

Notes

1. Bernhard J. Stern, *Social Factors in Medical Progress* (New York: Columbia University Press, 1927); Bernhard J. Stern, "Resistance to the Adoption of Technological Innovations," in *Technological Trends and National Policy,* Report of the Subcommittee on Technology to the National Resources Committee (Washington: Government Printing Office, 1937), pp. 39-66; and Bernhard J. Stern, *Society and Medical Progress* (Princeton: Princeton University Press, 1941). In these works Stern is primarily concerned with the social factors impeding medical and technological progress. Theodore K. Noss has sought to apply the Stern analysis in the resistance to socal innovations. See: Theodore K. Noss, Resistance to Social Innovations as Found in the Literature Regarding Innovations which Have Proved Successful (unpublished doctoral dissertation, University of Chicago, Chicago, 1940).

2. See for example: Guy B. Johnson, "A Sociological Interpretation of the New Ku Klux Movement," *The Journal of Social Forces,* 1 (May 1923), pp. 440-45.

3. Ralph Linton, "Nativistic Movements," *American Anthropologist* (n.s.), 45 (April-June 1943), pp. 230-40.

4. Bernard Barber, "Acculturation and Messianic Movements," *American Sociological Review,* 6 (October 1941), pp. 663-69; Alexander Lesser, *The Pawnee Ghost Dance Hand Game* (New York: Columbia University Press, 1933); and Melville J. Herskovits, *Acculturation* (New York: J. J. Augustin Publisher, 1938), pp. 75-103.

5. Some writers also include here the effort to revive or restore social forms that have existed in the past. See, for example, Seba Eldridge and Associates, *Fundamentals of Sociology* (New York: Thomas Y. Crowell Company, 1950), pp. 426-27. But to revive or restore a moribund mode is quite different from the effort to preserve and prevent changes in *existing* patterns and institutions.

6. Rudolf Heberle, *Social Movements* (New York: Appleton-Century-Crofts, Inc., 1951), p. 6. Italics mine.

7. Herbert Blumer, "Social Movements," in A. M. Lee (ed.), *New Outline of the Principles of Sociology* (New York: Barnes & Noble, 1946), p. 199. Italics mine.

8. Theodore Abel, "The Pattern of a Successful Political Movement," in Logan Wilson and William L. Kolb, *Sociological Analysis* (New York: Harcourt, Brace and Company, 1949), p. 828. Italics mine.

9. C. Wendell King, *Social Movements in the United States* (New York: Random House, 1956), pp. 25-26. For other similar concepts see Eldridge and Associates, *op. cit.,* pp. 425-26; Hans Gerth and C. Wright Mills, *Character and Social Structure* (New York: Harcourt, Brace and Company, 1953), p. 438; and Arnold W. Green, *Sociology* (2nd ed.; New York: McGraw-Hill Book Company, 1956), p. 530.

10. Heberle, *op. cit.,* pp. 6, 7, 8, 11, 269.

11. *Ibid.,* p. 6.

12. Frequent use is made of the terms "resist" and "resistance" by white southerners in speeches, resolutions, publications, articles, etc.

13. Heberle never makes the degree explicit although he cites one reason for excluding "short-lived group actions, such as a 'wildcat strike,' a race riot or *coup d'etat"* from the social movement category as lacking a sufficient "intensity of the we-feeling." Rudolf Heberle, "Observations on the Sociology of Social Movements," *American Sociological Review,* 14 (June 1949), p. 350.

14. James W. Vander Zanden, The Southern White Resistance Movement to Integration (unpublished doctoral dissertation, University of North Carolina, Chapel Hill, 1958), pp. 437-40.

14.

E. L. Quarantelli

THE BEHAVIOR OF PANIC PARTICIPANTS

Sociologists and social psychologists have long lamented the lack of a systematic set of empirically based generalizations and conceptualizations in the area of crowd behavior. Those activities encompassed by the term "panic" have especially been represented by a very slim body of non-speculative research and an almost nonexistent set of theoretical propositions. Consequently, it is the aim of this paper to present some general observations based on field data, concerning certain aspects of this form of collective behavior.[1]

Two conceptions of panic participants

In the literature the term "panic" is used to refer to many things. Thus, one finds it applied to such divergent behavior as a single individual's unrealistic anxieties to a group's ill-coordinated activities; at times its referent ranges from paralysis of action to a wild outburst of flight. However, the fact that the concept is commonly used in an ambiguous and vague way need not detain us here. Attempts at a conceptual clarification of the varying kinds of socially disorganizing and personally disrupting types of behavior characterized as panic have been presented elsewhere. For our purposes, panic can be conceived of as involving actual (or attempted) physical flight. The term will be used in this sense throughout the paper.

What of the behavior of the participant in this form of flight activity? One conception fairly well dominates the thinking of most individuals who have dealt with the phenomena. At least, a widely accepted image of the panic participant can be discerned. It is that, generally speaking, the panicky person is an individual who has been fairly well divested of all or almost all of his socially acquired characteristics. He is thought of as behaving in a completely irresponsible or antisocial manner, blindly trampling over people in a way analogous, if not completely similar, to the way animals act in a wild and chaotic stampede. The fleeing is visualized as irrational and nonfunctional or maladaptive to the dangerous situation. The uncritically acting participant is conceived as having little awareness of how or why he is running, or often, because of his emotional state of terror, what he is running from.

As Strauss in a broader context has indicated, such a conception of the panic participant implies a "layer-cake version of response organization."[2] In a crisis or emergency situation the veneer of culture or of social living is seen as cast off with the hidden-beast-in-man coming to the fore. In most respects, this conception views the panic participant as one who has lost his humanness, who has been stripped down to sheer emotional reaction, or who has reverted to an animal-like level of response.

That this image of panic behavior is commonly held by most sociologists is not surprising, for actually it represents but a

From E. L. Quarantelli, "The Behavior of Panic Participants." *Sociology and Social Research* 41, January 1957, pp. 187-94, with permission of the publisher.

logical extension of the supposed behavior of crowd members. The individual in the crowd (especially an acting crowd) is generally characterized as acting irrationally and in an uncontrolled fashion, as responding uncritically to stimulations and suggestions, as interacting on the primitive level of emotional contagion, etc. And since panic is thought of as an extreme form of crowd behavior, it follows that the behavior of panic participants should be thought of as exhibiting in most extreme form the attributed characteristics of individuals in a crowd.

A somewhat different position regarding crowd (and consequently panic) behavior is taken in this paper. The viewpoint here assumed is part of the growing conviction among some students of crowd behavior that the social primitivization usually attributed to the behavior of an individual in a crowd, at the very least, is a vast oversimplification if not actual conceptual distortion of the behavior that occurs. This emerging viewpoint is possibly best summed up in the following quotation which notes that, whatever "eccentric" or "deviant" form human behavior may take, it still is "the result of particular imagery, of particular definitions of situations, of interaction that still involves high order sign behavior, including complex and socialized emoting, perceiving, and remembering."[3] In short, the behavior of crowd members necessarily involves very intricate, socially learned modes of responses.

The behavior of panic participants may be conceived of in a similar way. Whatever else panic behavior may involve, it does represent the behavior of a socialized individual, perceiving and thinking in socially defined and supported ways, reacting to socially interpreted situations, and interacting with and giving meanings to the actions of still other social beings.

Therefore, panic behavior must be understood in such terms and not by recourse to an explanation basically involving nonsocial factors.

Aspects of panic behavior

Certain aspects of panic behavior will now be stated in a series of propositions or hypotheses that may serve as bases for further research.

1. The panic participant perceives a specific threat to physical survival. He defines the panic-producing situation as highly and personally threatening. Whether this is arrived at individually or through interaction with others, the situation is defined as involving a direct threat to one's very physical existence. This is a different experience from that where a threat to the ego may be perceived but where the threat is not conceived of in personal bodily terms (e.g., in becoming bankrupt).

Moreover, the panic participant is aware of what he is afraid *of*. In contrast to the anxiety-stricken person who is unable to label any object in the environment to account for his sense of terror, the panic-stricken person is able to designate the object or event to which he is reacting with fear. Actually, it is only because he can name the threat and localize it in time and space that the panic participant is even able to orient himself so that he can flee. Without a specific object from which an orientation could be taken, physical withdrawal would be an impossibility. An undefined object cannot be perceived as threatening, much less fled from.

2. The panic participant is future-threat rather than past-danger oriented. His attention is focused on what may occur rather than on what has happened. His thinking is not oriented toward such dangers as have already been experienced, but instead is focused on the possibility of

becoming blocked off from escaping from an impending threat. Especially salient in his thought is the anticipation of possible entrapment. Furthermore, the threat is perceived as having immediate effects, at most within a time span of several minutes. A rapid reaction of some sort is considered necessary in order to survive the quickly anticipated consequences of the threat.

However, that the panicky individual reacts toward very immediately rising threats rather than retrospective dangers does not mean that there necessarily exists an objective threat. In fact, the realness or illusoriness of the peril is, as far as a panicky reaction is concerned, of little import. Regardless of the objective circumstances, it is how the person defines the situation and is supported in his definition by others that determines his reaction. Thus, panicky reactions will occur in situations involving no real threat simply because a threat is perceived as possible. Similarly, the calmness of people in certain objectively threatening situations frequently stems from a discrepancy between the actual situation and their mutually supporting definition of it as nonthreatening.

3. The panic participant is acutely self-conscious and fearful. In contrast to the reactions involved in the behavior of most crowd members, the panic participant is acutely self-conscious. The more threatening he defines the situation, the greater his awareness of himself. Fear brings with it a sharp visualization of self being threatened.

However, the panicky reaction is characterized not so much by the presence of fear as by unchecked fear. As is illustrated by the behavior of combat soldiers, a person may feel extreme fear for his physical safety and yet maintain a high degree or even complete control over his impulse to flee from the threatening situation. An individual gives overt expression to his fear only if he comes to feel that he (and others that may be with him) are helpless and powerless to cope with the threat. A complete focalization upon the idea of escaping from the immediate area of threat will especially come to the fore if the individual perceives himself as being dependent solely on his own efforts for the attainment of safety.

4. The panic participant is relatively aware of his activities. The focalization of thought on escape accompanied by a loss of control over fear does not mean that a panicky person is completely unresponsive to other objects in the situation or that he just runs in a headlong stampede. On the contrary, a panicky individual orients his fleeing and modifies his behavior in terms of the circumstances he believes are facing him. Thus, a panic participant does not blindly or randomly run into objects; if possible he goes around obstacles in his path. An attempt is made to go through a door before an attempt is made to flee through a window, etc. Panic flight is directed toward the goal of getting away from the area of danger. The oft-noticed convergence of fleeing persons in a collective panic frequently occurs because individuals, seeing others flee in one direction, assume that escape is possible in that direction.

Sometimes a panicky person may appear to move in the direction of the threat and further endanger himself, e.g., by running toward sheets of flame. However, this is not blind and irrational fleeing as it overtly may appear. Generally what is involved in such instances is that the threatened person believes the only way to safety lies in that direction (e.g., in the belief or knowledge that there is a door behind the flames). The person is thus simply orienting his behavior to the situation as he or others define it for him, perceiving and responding to those elements in the situation which are relevant to his attempt to escape.

Similarly a panicky person does not continue running till physical exhaustion sets in. The characteristically short duration of panic flight to a great extent stems from the fact that the panicky person runs only as long as he conceives of himself as still within the danger area and exposed to the consequences of the threat. To the extent that he or others for him redefine the situation as nonthreatening, the flight immediately ceases.

5. The panic participant is nonrational in his flight behavior. That panic flight involves a degree of awareness on the part of a participant does not mean that it is a highly rational activity in the sense of its involving the weighing of alternative courses of action that might be followed in the situation. On the other hand, the thinking of the panicky person is not "irrational" if by that is meant anything in the way of faulty or illogical deductions from given premises. From the position of an observer with a much broader perspective of the total situation, this may appear to be the case. However, from a participant's viewpoint, given his necessarily more limited perspective of only certain portions of all the circumstances involved, no such interpretation of irrationality is warranted. To the panicky person, his flight appears to him quite appropriate to the situation as he perceives and defines it at that time, however he may retrospectively evaluate it.

Rather than being rational or irrational, the behavior of a panic participant is nonrational. In the face of an immediate possibility of personal annihilation, the potential courses of action available range from direct individual or collective attack to movement away from the endangering object. The panicky person, thinking only of escaping, makes no overt attempt to cope directly with the threat other than to flee from it. He does not engage in other activity designed to bring the threat under control. The panic participant is nonrational, not because of a failure to think or because of illogical thinking, but simply because of the extreme focalization of his thought and consequent overt activity to remove himself from the threatening area.

6. The panic participant's flight is not necessarily nonfunctional or maladaptive. Because a panicky reaction is nonrational, it is not always nor necessarily personally and collectively inappropriate to the situation.

That a panicky person flees and makes no direct attempt to cope with the threat does not make his behavior necessarily nonfunctional. Frequently, running away is the most adaptive course of action that the person could take in the particular situation. Thus, to flee from a building where the ceiling is threatening to collapse as a result of earthquake shocks, is on most occasions the most appropriate behavior possible. In such instances the flight is functional, if functionality under such circumstances is thought of as behavior which from an over-all viewpoint is appropriate to the maintenance of the life of a threatened individual.

Likewise, the panicky person's behavior is not necessarily collectively maladaptive. There are many occasions where flight simultaneously engaged in by a number of persons not only is individually functional but also has no inappropriate social consequences. People can run out of houses without having any or very little bodily contact of a destructive sort with one another. In fact, it is only very rarely, and almost always because of the presence of physical barriers, that panicky individuals may proceed to knock one another down and to trample over each other. Such collectively maladaptive activity, however, is highly atypical and is definitely not characteristic of the behavior of panicky persons.

The conception of panic flight as being nonfunctional or maladaptive actually conceals a hindsight normative judgment which cannot be considered here. Suffice it to say that panic behavior sometimes (and more often) is functional and adaptive and sometimes it is not. If the latter, it is generally so because of specific physical circumstances that prevent individuals from fleeing unhampered or unhampering others.

7. The panic participant acts in a nonsocial manner in his flight behavior. The panicky person acts in a nonsocial way in that he disregards the usual social relationships and interaction patterns that guide behavior. Even the strongest primary group ties may be shattered and the most socially expected behavior patterns ignored. Thus, a panicky mother may run out and leave her child in a house that she thinks is going to explode.

The panicky person is very highly self-centered, thinking only of saving himself. In this sense, panic flight represents very highly individualistic behavior. It involves completely individual as against collective activity in reacting to the problem of escaping from a threat. In its total absence of concerted group action, panic behavior thus represents nonsocial behavior at its zenith.

This nonsocial aspect may be short lived, but it is one of the major characteristics which distinguish panic flight from nonpanic withdrawal behavior. In the case of nonpanic withdrawal, confused and ill-coordinated activity may be manifested, but the conventional social roles and the normal interactional patterns are not totally disregarded. Thus, when a plane hit an apartment house in one disaster, most families evacuated as units, neighbors were warned, alternative courses of action were discussed, etc. People acted in an erratic and partially unorganized fashion, but, unlike when people are panicky, most of their behavior was in terms of the group norms that ordinarily guided their activities. Such excited flight is only superficially similar to panic flight.

In stating that the panicky reaction is nonsocial, there is no implication that the panic participant regresses to infantile reaction patterns or reverts to purely reflexive or biologically given ways of reacting. That is not so. Learned motor patterns of action are not forgotten by the panicky individual. Thus, in certain situations where it is physically possible, the panicky person may manifest flight by driving vehicles, swimming, digging, riding horses, etc. He maintains the learned neuromuscular coordinations effective for the carrying out of complex motor activities, as well as the capacity for perceiving, remembering, thinking, etc., in socially learned ways as was indicated earlier. The nonsocial aspect of the panicky reaction is primarily in regard to failures to play conventional social roles and to follow the expected interactional patterns.

Social interaction

The utmost importance of the nature of the interaction that occurs prior to and during panic flight should be especially stressed. In the case of collective panics, it is through individuals interacting with one another that there occurs a cognitive clarification of what the situation is and what can or cannot be done about it. Social interaction is basic in bringing about the definition of the crisis situation as a threatening one. It plays a major part in reinforcing the definition of the situation as one in which only flight is possible. Finally, panic flight frequently terminates as a result of the interaction among the participants, leading them to perceive themselves as out of the danger area. And possibly most important of all, it is frequently the presence and response of other persons that motivates individuals to control their fears, consequently diminishing the possibility of panicky reactions.

Conclusion

The behavior of panic participants does not represent a primitivization of responses. The panicky reaction is an attempt to adjust to an unexpected and action-demanding circumstance by nonrational and nonsocial individualistic flight. Such behavior nevertheless is, in terms of an earlier quotation, "the result of particular imagery, of particular definitions of situations, of interaction that still involves high order sign behavior,[4] including complex and socialized emoting, perceiving, and remembering." The seven propositions advanced in this paper represent an attempt to illustrate this fact—that a once socialized person even under extreme stress does not regress to the "brute level," but rather shifts to an individualistic solution of the crisis while continuing to use socially learned modes of responses in the process.

Notes

1. Acknowledgment is made to the National Opinion Research Center, University of Chicago, for permission to use the interview data on which this article is in part based. The research by NORC was undertaken under a contract with the Army Chemical Center, Department of the Army. However, the opinion and conclusions expressed in this article are those of the author and do not necessarily represent the views of NORC, the Army Chemical Center, or the Department of the Army. For a partial summary of the NORC studies see Charles Fritz and Eli Marks, "The NORC Studies of Human Behavior in Disaster," *Journal of Social Issues,* 10 (3rd issue, 1954), 26-41.

2. Anselm L. Strauss, "Concepts, Communication, and Groups," in Muzafer Sherif and M. O. Wilson (eds.), *Group Relations at the Crossroads* (New York: Harper & Brothers, 1953), p. 107.

3. Strauss, *op. cit.,* p. 109. His discussion is not specifically directed to crowd behavior. Rather it questions the validity of conceiving human beings as biological organisms upon which layers of social norms have been imposed, with the norms becoming inoperative in time of stress. However, logically extended, this criticism is equally applicable to most conceptions of the behavior of crowd members.

4. Strauss, *ibid.*

15.

Ralph H. Turner

NEEDED RESEARCH IN COLLECTIVE BEHAVIOR

Dealing with collective behavior

Less than two decades have passed since collective behavior began to progress beyond the provocative observations of men like LeBon, Bagehot, and E. A. Ross and historical studies like those of Edwards and Raper.[1] Research in collective behavior has turned toward more specific theory testing with such interview investigations as the Lazarsfeld public opinion studies, Cantril's *Invasion from Mars*, and Shibutani's analysis of pre-evacuation rumors among American Japanese.[2] As part of the growing movement for laboratory study of small groups, J. R. P. French attempted to induce panic under controlled observation, and G. E. Swanson attempted to create the conditions essential to test a series of propositions regarding the acting crowd.[3] Ambitiously carrying the laboratory approach to whole cities, Stuart Dodd studied rumor process following mass leaflet drops.[4] The largest program of research in the field today is the ongoing study of community response to disaster by interdisciplinary teams using a battery of methods.[5]

Relatively little of the current and recent investigation stems from a primary interest in building a theory of collective behavior. While valuable use can often be made of studies which examine some phenomenon of collective behavior incidentally to the study of political parties, community

From Ralph H. Turner, "Needed Research in Collective Behavior." *Sociology and Social Research* 42, July 1958, pp. 461-65, with permission of the publisher.

resources in disaster, or race relations, the findings are often peripheral rather than crucial for collective behavior. Light shed on causes for the mass attitudes which underlie rioting does not necessarily clarify the essential conditions and processes through which attitudes eventuate in collective action. Usual research techniques are probably more effective in exploring individual panic and disorganization than in clarifying the phenomenon of collective panic. Distortions in transmitting information may be studied microscopically in the laboratory without reproducing the atmosphere distinctive to rumor.

By contrast, S. Frank Miyamoto has endeavored to determine in one instance the conditions essential to converting local discontent into collective protest.[6] And in a unique experimental approach to panic, Putney and Cadwallader have shown the spontaneous emergence of a collective defense against incipient panic.[7] Following the lead of such investigators, research is needed which will focus specifically on key problems in the development of comprehensive theory in collective behavior. Four such problems will be suggested and briefly discussed.

(1) Decision-making in collective behavior

The first problem about which little is understood is decision-making in collective behavior. The stereotyped view of the crowd as almost mechanically transmitting attitudes through suggestion, of the public as a context of individual decision-making, and of the social movement as

147

precommitted to a cause has precluded viewing these phenomena as contexts for collective decision. The process in collective behavior is in some respects unique, since it takes place without the each-to-all interaction of the small group or the fairly well defined formal and informal channels of institutional decision. Beyond demonstrating the fairly obvious facts that decision-making takes place partially in small groups and is not altogether independent of institutional communication networks, research is needed which will clarify the uniquenesses.

As an example of a problem in collective behavior decision-making we may cite the manner in which small group discussion is incorporated into an inclusive decision in an incipient crowd. A few tentative observations might afford a starting point for investigation. In the crowd in its early stages many small knots of speakers and listeners are linked by a goodly number of circulating individuals who glean and relay comments as they pass from group to group. While each knot is a small group, it differs from the conventional small group in its constantly changing membership. Each knot is oriented to the presence of the other groups and guided in its discussion by at least an undertone of feeling that one of the other knots may have the answers that are sought. Because of this orientation and because of the changing membership, discussion consists largely of repeating anecdotes and judgments which define attitudes. As compared with conventional small groups, it may be supposed that decisions are guided disproportionately by the weight of repetition and the search for support among groups.

In a somewhat different fashion the social movement likewise consists of many smaller groups linked through a sense of being part of a larger entity and by both official and unofficial "messengers" who represent to each group the supposed views of other such groups. Top movement leadership is concerned with controlling the decisions of these groups and coordinating them while still encouraging enough spontaneity so that members will work enthusiastically in the movement's behalf. Disputes among the groups or between leadership and the groups frequently plague movements. The process by which an effective movement-wide decision is reached warrants serious investigation.

(2) Relations between collective behavior and institutional authority

A second research area concerns the relations between collective behavior and institutional order and authority. In societies with effective and accepted central authority, collective behavior with serious implications for change is not likely to occur unless the collectivities can command use of the institutionalized means for putting forward their charges and programs. The relation of mob action to sanction by constituted authority has been dramatized in the recent events of Little Rock, Arkansas, and earlier noted in connection with the 1943 Detroit race riot and many others. But the prevalent approach to social movements is still to regard them as spontaneous developments of protest reflecting mass feelings. An alternative hypothesis is the following. Endemic mass discontent and protest blossom into powerful movements when they become useful to groups who already hold legitimate power in society. The latter provide the emergent movements with the necessary access to legitimate means for promoting their cause. Thus the paradox of the sudden growth of the C.I.O. at the depths of the depression when the bargaining power of organized labor should have been least is understandable in light of its usefulness to the newly-victorious Democratic party, seeking to consolidate its political control.

The recent rise and decline of McCarthyism affords an excellent opportunity to test such a hypothesis. Extended analysis from the point of view that changes in the American socioeconomic structure provoked a mass increase in susceptibility to McCarthyite appeals is already on hand.[8] Remaining for examination is the hypothesis that variations in mass susceptibility were unimportant, but that important leaders in the Republican party saw in McCarthy a useful tool in discrediting the Democratic administration and consequently made available to him the means to attract and hold a following. McCarthy's decline would then reflect, not the lessening of grass-roots susceptibility, but denial of access to these same means when the party achieved power and found him a liability.

(3) Relation of change in social values to collective behavior

Among the most elusive yet crucial topics is the third problem, the processes and conditions of change in social values and their precise relationship to developments in collective behavior. Beneath what people conceptualize and openly acknowledge is a sense of value which makes them uncomfortable or gratified in the course of events, often without comprehending the reason. While certain gross convergences between mass values and the directions of collective behavior have long been hypothesized, more complex relationships to specific instances of such behavior remain for investigation. For example, the decline of a social system has often been accompanied by sporadic mob action in defense of the old way of life. This mob action may be viewed in a different light from that which has been customary. There is some evidence to suggest that during the last century the mass sense of value had changed to a point that the United States color caste was defended more out of desperation than out of deep conviction. The periodic lynchings may have served chiefly as desperate attempts to rediscover the archaic sense of value embedded in the system within the special situation of the lynching crowd and supporting diffuse crowd.

(4) Significance of countermovements

Likewise, the internal stresses and weaknesses of many countermovements merit study oriented about the hypothesis that the members and leaders must largely operate with an ideology which does not find support in their own strong sense of value. Their fear of the kind of people whom they identify with the opposed movement and their unwillingness to let change take place until they are prepared to direct it lend the vitality of desperation to their actions. Such an interpretation renders comprehensible such extreme swings as from the 1936 Landon conservatism to the 1940 Willkie liberalism within the Republican party. It also affords an explanation for those surprising instances in which an apparently powerful countermovement drops to insignificance after one impressive defeat.

(5) Role of symbols in collective behavior

A final area worthy of focused study is the formation, transformation, and function of symbols in collective behavior. While a number of generalizations are available concerning the characteristics of successful symbols in collective behavior, there is some historical reporting on the emergence of symbols in crisis behavior, and the function of in-group symbols in unifying groups has been explored; the processes of acceptance and rejection of symbols have not been examined in detail. A careful comparative study of the emergence and transformations of specific symbols in the crowd, fashion and fad, and social movements would be of great value.

Notes

1. Gustave LeBon, *The Crowd* (London: T. F. Unwin, 1897); Walter Bagehot, *Physics and Politics* (first published in 1869); E. A. Ross, *Social Psychology* (New York: The Macmillan Company, 1908); Lyford P. Edwards, *The Natural History of Revolution* (Chicago: University of Chicago Press, 1927); Arthur F. Raper, *The Tragedy of Lynching* (Chapel Hill: University of North Carolina Press, 1933).

2. Hadley Cantril, Hazel Caudet, and Herta Herzog, *Invasion from Mars* (Princeton: Princeton University Press, 1940); Tamotsu Shibutani, "Rumors in a Crisis Situation" (unpublished M.A. thesis, University of Chicago, 1944).

3. J. R. P. French, "Organized and Unorganized Groups Under Fear and Frustration," in Kurt Lewin et al., *Authority and Frustration,* University of Iowa Studies in Child Welfare, XX: 231-307; Guy E. Swanson, "A Preliminary Laboratory Study of Acting Crowd," *American Sociological Review,* 18: 522-333, 1953.

4. Stuart Dodd, "Testing Message Diffusion in Controlled Experiments," *American Sociological Review,* 18: 410-16, 1953.

5. National Research Council Committee on Disaster Studies, Washington, D.C., various reports.

6. Frank Miyamoto, "An Interactional Approach to Intergroup Conflict," *Research Studies of the State College of Washington,* 19: 121-24, 1951.

7. Snell W. Putney and Mervyn L. Cadwallader, "An Experiment in Crisis Interaction," *Research Studies of the State College of Washington,* 22: 94-102, 1954.

8. Daniel Bell, ed., *The New American Right* (New York: Criterion Books, 1955).

III. The Individual as Primary Unit of Analysis: Micro-level Processes in Collective Behavior and Social Movements

Introduction

Recent work in collective behavior utilizing the individual as the primary unit of analysis focuses on two major topics: the nature of the social and psychological processes in crowd behavior, and the process of recruitment and commitment to social movements. Historically, individual behavior in the crowd has been conceptualized as essentially emotional and irrational. The articles selected for Part III illustrate the emerging perspective which views crowd behavior as involving the same basic processes as more routine forms of social interaction. However, little empirical work has been aimed at identifying the underlying causes of individual participation in the crowd, and although this is not surprising in light of the theoretical and methodological difficulties such research faces, it does point to the need for further research in the area.

Because social movements are less transitory than crowds, work in this area has proven more amenable to the standard array of theoretical perspectives and research methodologies in the social sciences. Considerable effort has been directed at developing a model of individual participation, and the material on social movements presented here is illustrative of this work.

Berk (16) begins this part of the volume by challenging the traditional notion in collective behavior which states that individuals tend to behave in irrational ways in crowd situations. Utilizing the basic concepts of *game theory*, this author proposes a new approach to the study of crowd behavior, arguing that individuals in the crowd exercise considerable cognitive skill and in doing so, attempt to coordinate their behavior with the behavior of others in the crowd in order to produce personally rewarding outcomes. Crowd participants tend to make rational assessments of the degree of group support for their positions while formulating appropriate courses of action. Berk argues that the primary difference between collective behavior and more routine forms of social interaction is the speed with which decisions must be made and the scarcity of information upon which to base those decisions. The author also points out that one of the major advantages of utilizing a game theory perspective is that it allows for the incorporation of many key concepts in the field. "Milling," for example, can be viewed as the process by which individuals in a collectivity attempt to identify their position relative to other participants in order to determine the best course of action. "Uniform crowd behavior" can be viewed as the result of the participants' agreement that a certain course of action is of mutual benefit.

Like Berk, McPhail (17) also challenges the notion that individual behavior in collective situations differs substantially from other forms of social interaction. While elementary forms of collective behavior have traditionally been characterized by their spontaneity and simplicity, McPhail's analysis of a student walkout indicates that the participants were involved in a continual process of gauging one another's behavior and formulating their own behavior in terms of their perception of group support.

Haan's (18) analysis of moral reasoning processes in civil disorder situations focuses on the difference between what individuals predict they will do in

hypothetical situations involving moral reasoning, and what they actually do
when confronted with real life situations. This author interprets the differences
found between reasoning about hypothetical situations and behavior in real
situations to psychological structures and the possibility that some individuals
may not have understood the hypothetical situation clearly. However, within the
framework of the discussions presented by Berk and McPhail it is not surprising
that most individuals are unable to accurately predict their behavior prior to
actual involvement in a particular situation, since the best course of action can
only be determined once the behavior of other participants in the collectivity is
known. Of course, a totally utilitarian argument is not fully accurate either
because some individuals are able to predict their behavior prior to actual
involvement. More work in this area would be useful in separating the relevant
psychological and sociological processes operating in collectivities.

Brissett (19) criticizes those who have studied collective behavior for what he
views as a lack of sensitivity to the symbolic nature of interaction between
individuals. In analyzing the relationship between the traditional approach to
the study of collective behavior and the interactionist perspective, the author
argues that the primary analytic focus in the study of collective behavior, as well
as any other form of human behavior, should be the symbolic exchange between
individuals in the group. Although a focus on the role of symbols in
understanding human behavior is undoubtedly important, operationalizing
symbolic content has proven very difficult, and the author offers no suggestions
for alleviating this difficulty. Nevertheless, such critiques are helpful in pointing
out the difficulties involved in the scientific study of human behavior, and
should be acknowledged as worthy of further thought, despite the present state
of development in the field.

The work introduced thus far has dealt with general issues concerning relatively short-lived processes in crowd behavior. As collectivities are extended over
time, however, social movements tend to develop and different research interests and strategies emerge. Two of the primary concerns of those who have
studied social movements have been the related processes of recruitment and
commitment, and the studies that follow address these issues. Morrison (20)
utilizes the concept of *relative deprivation* to explain participation in social
movements. According to this perspective, when individual expectations are not
met, a state of tension or cognitive dissonance results. When this happens it is
possible for individuals to modify their expectations and thereby reduce tension.
Social movement participation becomes likely when individuals do not modify
their expectations and communicate their tensions to others experiencing
similar dissatisfaction.

Lofland (21) supports Morrison's argument that tension is one of the
important predispositions to participation in social movements. However, in his
study of converts to a millenarian religious movement, this author found two
additional characteristics that differentiated between those who joined the
movement and those who did not: a religious problem solving perspective,
together with an active search to discover solutions to problems within that
perspective. Lofland's additional criteria emerge from his analysis of the three

major problem solving perspectives available to persons in modern society: the *psychiatric*, the *political*, and the *religious*. Those utilizing the psychiatric perspective think that the best way to ease frustration is to alter their perceptions or expectations of themselves or of those around them. Those whose major problem solving orientation is political tend to view the social structure as the primary source of their problems, and advocate social reorganization as the primary solution. And those favoring a religious perspective tend to see their problems as well as the solutions to them as emanating from unseen "other worldly" sources.

Lofland found that those who adhere to the psychiatric or conventional political problem solving perspectives were not likely to be included among the converts in his study. Those who did convert had retained a propensity to impose religious meaning on events, although they had discarded conventional religious outlooks. In addition, this author found that the converts were more likely than those who did not convert to be actively searching for an adequate religious perspective to ease tension and somehow bring order to their perceptions of the world.

Commitment to a social movement is not the only possible outcome of adherence to a religious or political problem solving perspective, however. Such beliefs, in combination with environmental conditions, can also lead to other forms of collective behavior, such as participation in radical political action or riots. Paige (22) argues that the interaction between an individual's belief that personal action can affect political solutions, and trust in the existing political structure is one of the primary determinants of participation in radical politics. Using data on riot participants in Newark, New Jersey, this author concludes that rioting can be viewed as a form of *disorganized political protest*, engaged in by those who have become highly distrustful of existing political institutions, but who, at the same time, perceive political activity as the primary solution to their difficulties.

Although the individual's perception of immediate social, economic and political circumstances is undoubtedly important in understanding participation in collective behavior, other less immediate processes are also evident. Portes (23), for example, presents data suggesting that radical political behavior is dependent upon *differential socialization*, that is, the consistent exposure to radical political thought and action over time. But this author warns against over generalization, pointing out that the socialization process is, to a great extent, contingent upon larger structural circumstances such as the type of economic and political systems that exist in the society.

Weiss (24) adds a psychological dimension to the concept of commitment in his discussion of defection from social movements and subsequent recruitment to new movements. In his discussion of the process of re-recruitment, this author applies one of the central postulates of learning theory which states that the effects of learning are generally transferable to similar situations. In relating this concept to social movement participation, Weiss argues that if a movement, perceived as positive by its members becomes unavailable, commitment to the most similar available movement is likely to occur. In addition, the author points out that re-recruitment is also contingent upon the cause(s) of defection (if other than the nonavailability of the movement), the mediating psychological processes related to the cause, and the characteristics of available movements. For example, defection may occur when an individual is not rewarded for his beliefs or participation in a particular movement. In this situation, the mediating process of *extinction*, that is, the decreased tendency to perform a particular behavior, becomes operative. When extinction occurs, the negative feelings engendered during this experience are likely to be carried over to subsequent experiences and make recruitment to a similar movement less likely.

Although Weiss focuses exclusively on the overall process of defection and re-recruitment to social movements, learning theory might also be applied to understanding participation in various activities within social movements, such as the pro-Viet-Nam war demonstration Lin (25) studied. In developing a model of the communication processes involved in the recruitment of demonstration participants, Lin reports that participation in a demonstration is more closely associated with the extent of the individual's prior involvement with the social movement sponsoring the demonstration, than with a commitment to the specific goals of the demonstration. Within the learning theory framework, it is reasonable to assume that if overall involvement in the social movement has been rewarding, individuals will expect specific activities promoted by the movement to also be rewarding. Since Lin's data suggest that such expectations are not connected with the specific goals of the activity, we can assume that the decision to participate is, to a large extent, influenced by past rewards gained from the general overall commitment to the movement. It should be noted, however, that this argument (as well as Weiss's) is subject to the general problem inherent in psychological explanation; that is, where does the motivating force, in this case reward for movement participation, originate? Why do some individuals feel "rewarded" for participation in social movements while others do not? Often the answers to such questions are rooted in the process of social interaction and in the larger structural forces which effect societal members.

One of the neglected areas in collective behavior is the relationship between the individual and larger societal forces, such as the mass media. Singer's (26) study, which concludes Part III, focuses on the effect of the mass media and other communication processes on individual participation in the 1967 Detroit riot. In his study of 500 riot participants, the author found two primary communication processes that served to inform potential participants of the nature and location of the riot: a highly developed interpersonal communication network in the ghetto coupled with the local broadcast media. Singer's work suggests that the mass media may have increased the number of riot participants by preparing the community for the riot by broadcasting information about riots in the other cities and, once the riot had begun, by informing potential participants about the location and nature of the activity. Of course, this is not to say that the broadcast media *intentionally* caused an intensification of the riot. However, these findings do point to the fact that the behavior of individuals and organizations often has unintended results. And the mass media are not alone in their potential for unintentionally affecting behavior. Governmental agencies responsible for social control often respond to riot situations in a way that actually intensifies the riot. For example, a governor may order the National Guard to help control a riot situation, with the intention of displaying sufficient force to convince the participants to end the riot. While it is possible that such action could result in an end to the riot, it is also possible that such action could result in an escalation of the riot, especially if the original causes of the situation are perceived to be linked to governmental actions. Under these circumstances, the participants may become even more committed to the riot, and individuals not previously involved may begin to see the riot as an answer to the problems confronting them.

16.

Richard A. Berk

A GAMING APPROACH TO CROWD BEHAVIOR

Social science analyses which try to incorporate human mental processes are fraught with problems. The very existence of "mind" as a distinct structure has been debated at length with no resolution (Hook, 1960). Could we agree on useful definitions, there would remain a host of epistemological issues since inferences about psychological conditions must necessarily be drawn from observed indicators.

Nowhere has controversy about mental processes been more salient than in theories of crowd behavior. Turner and Killian note that the issues of "group mind" and "irrationality" thread the literature, and the debates have been often marked by "semantic confusion, obvious oversimplification, and sheer dogmatism" (Turner and Killian, 1972:6). At one extreme is the early work by LeBon (1960) and Freud (1957) who viewed crowd participants as creatures of passion, acting on impulse, and unable to exercise the most elementary forms of cognition. In marked contrast is work by game theorists (Raiffa, 1970, Schelling, 1963) who apply prescriptive strategies for decisions under uncertainty and risk to explain certain group processes. Brown (1965) and Berk

From Richard A. Berk, "A Gaming Approach to Crowd Behavior," *American Sociological Review* 1974, Vol. 39 (June), pp. 355-73 with permission of the publisher and author.

I wish to mention the crucial aid provided by Alan Berger in collecting the data. I also want to acknowledge the assistance of Howard S. Becker, John Walton, John I. Kitsuse, Deborah Lubeck, and Dianne LaFaver. Finally, the ASR referees, the people you love to hate, deserve mention for their thorough, insightful, and often blistering comments.

(1972b) have applied gaming approaches to actual crowds.

Despite varying assessments of the psychological states of crowd members, the dominant view in social science emphasizes emotion, suggestion, and irrationality (Couch, 1968). Smelser defines all collective behavior in terms of "generalized beliefs" (Smelser, 1962: 8) clearly implying crippled cognition. Turner (1964) emphasizes "suggestibility" which Turner and Killian (1972: 80) characterize as a "tendency to respond uncritically to suggestions that are consistent with the mood, imagery and conception of appropriate action that have developed and assumed normative character." Earlier, Blumer (1946) argued that crowds evolve through "circular reaction . . . a type of interstimulation wherein the response of one individual reproduces the stimulation that has come from another individual and in being reflected back to this individual reinforces the stimulation." He compared crowds to stampeding cattle, claiming that all collective behavior participants react uncritically to each other and the environment. Shibutani (1966) and Klapp (1972) also employ Blumer's circular reaction, while Canetti (1966) simply takes the dominance of emotion as given.

Unfortunately, this preoccupation with crowd irrationality has reinforced a type of social inequality Becker (1967) calls the "hierarchy of credibility." He argues that societies habitually give credence to the views of people in "superordinate positions" while dismissing the views of "subordinates." Becker's insights can be usefully extended if we recognize that credibility is not only a concomitant of high status, but one of its props. Labeling rioting subordinates as impulsive and irrational diverts blame from environmental causes of unrest and places it squarely on riot participants. Subordinate grievances may be discounted because they stem from emotion, contagion, and misperceptions of reality. Hence, many popular analyses of crowd behavior support superordinate interests. Equally important, the veracity of these traditional views is at best equivocal.

This paper develops an approach in which crowd participants (1) exercise a substantial degree of rational decision-making and (2) are not defined a priori as less rational than in other contexts. Decision Theory (Raiffa, 1970; Chernoff and Moses, 1959; Luce, 1959), a prescriptive strategy for maximizing one's rewards and/or minimizing costs in a given situation, provides the foundation for my perspective. To begin, Raiffa lists five steps which should precede a decision to act:

1) List the viable options available to you for gathering information, for experimentation, and for action;
2) List the events that may possibly occur;
3) Arrange in chronological order the information you may acquire and the choices you may make as time goes on;
4) Decide how well you like the consequences that result from the various courses of action open to you;
5) Judge what the chances are that any particular uncertain event will occur (Raiffa, 1970:x).

Though not intended as a description of behavior, Raiffa asserts that the strategy is also not a "positive theory of behavior for a superintelligent, fictitious being; nowhere in our analysis shall we refer to the behavior of an 'idealized, rational, economic man,' a man who always acts in a perfectly consistent manner as if somehow

there were embodied in his nature a coherent set of evaluation patterns that cover any and all eventualities" (Raiffa, 1970). Consequently, one might use Raiffa's criteria of rationality to gauge the cognitive processes of crowd members (and people in general). Note that empirically this formulation is more credible than classical game theory which must assume that information is "perfect."

How descriptive is Raiffa's view? In defending the empirical relevance of rational behavior as a "calculating, value-maximizing strategy of decision," Schelling observes "that even among the emotionally unbalanced among certified 'irrationals' there is often observed an intuitive appreciation of the principles of strategy, or at least of particular applications of them." For example, "the inmates of mental hospitals often seem to cultivate, deliberately or instinctively, value systems that make them less susceptible to disciplinary threats and more capable of exercising coercion themselves" (Schelling, 1963: 17).

Similarly, a variety of research argues that groups and individuals whose ability to reason has been disparaged, in fact exercise considerable cognitive skill. For example, Short and Strodtbeck (1964) argue that conflict behavior among teenage gang members is often calculated. Fleisher (1966) develops and supports an economic theory which suggests that property crimes committed by juvenile delinquents are motivated primarily by rational self-interest. Sjoquist (1973) proposes an elaborate econometric model to predict when potential criminals will choose to engage in crimes against property. Using variables reflecting such calculations as the probability of getting caught, the estimated dollar value of stolen goods, and costs of incarceration in time and money, Sjoquist explains a surprising amount of variance in property crime rates across a sample of cities. In a case study of prison inmates, Sykes (1970) finds considerable evidence for rational adjustments to prison and attempts to manipulate the environment. Lemert (1962) argues that paranoia may be far more a function of careful reality testing than mental health experts have recognized. Finally, Goffman (1969) examines a diverse cross-section of human interaction and concludes that commonly people strategically manipulate each other.

Raiffa's formulation is supported by some studies of crowds. Fogelson (1971) asserts that American civil disorders often involved attempts to communicate inner city grievances to the wider white society. Case studies of particular civil disorders have revealed calculative, systematic looting (Hayden, 1967; Cohen and Murphy, 1966; Gilbert, 1968). Berk and Aldrich (1972), using both cross-sectional and longitudinal data from a large sample of ghetto retail merchants, found a strong association between some types of merchants and commercial establishments and high store victimization rates during inner city rioting. These patterns of vandalism suggested conscious selection of targets by rioters. Finally, Berk's (1972b) case study of racial confrontation found that groups of black and white inner city teenagers consciously weighed a variety of costs and benefits associated with strategies of attack.

Even when decisions must be made rapidly, one can make a case for Raiffa's cognitive processes. The driver of an automobile on a crowded freeway rapidly makes many complex decisions as traffic patterns shift. These judgments are approximate solutions to complicated problems in mechanics. That such decision processes are aided by previous experience should not obscure the fact that people can consider a variety of complex events quickly.

It is also important to emphasize the distinction between Raiffa's *process* conception of rationality and the *results* of that process. One can be rational and wrong at the same time. (In fact, in Bayesian applications the central issue is the iterative steps through which inaccurate assessments are improved.) While trying to overtake and pass a truck, for example, one might approximate sound Decision Theory, yet miscalculate the speed of an oncoming car. Further, irrationality and rationality lie on a continuum. To the degree that one uses the steps in Decision Theory, one can describe levels of rationality.

An alternative approach—collective decision-making through gaming

Elaborations of Decision Theory for a gaming approach to crowds come from two traditions. The first is reflected in work by Brown (1965), Luce (1959), Raiffa (1970), Schelling (1966), Short and Strodtbeck (1964), Goffman (1970) and Luce and Raiffa (1967). These authors discuss ways individuals may select actions with "mini-max" or "best" payoffs when the outcomes *fundamentally depend on the actions of others*. A second tradition treats informal Collective Decision-Making (Shibutani, 1948; Turner and Killian, 1957; Shibutani, 1966). Though Collective Decision-Making has been applied in somewhat different (though not necessarily contradictory) ways by various authors, all use the concept to explain how concerted "spontaneous" action develops. Possibly the best known application to crowds is Shibutani's analysis of the growth of rumor in response to an excessive demand for news (Shibutani, 1966). However, collective decision-making can be reformulated and extended to encompass a wider range of crowd behavior.

Beginning with the *individual* as the

unit of analysis, one can postulate that crowd members are engaged in a "game" in which each "player's" payoff matrix depends on the actions of others on the scene. Opportunities to be highly satisfied depend on people acting in unison.

One person cannot easily undertake a lynching, nor can one inmate liberate a prison. In addition, even where very few can carry out a group's goals, typically, the potential costs per person decrease as the numbers of participants increase. In short, one of the defining characteristics of crowd behavior may be how the payoff matrices interlock.

For example, assume that situation "A" contains two types of people—"militants" and "moderates." Each anticipates certain payoffs for the activity of "trashing" under two conditions: support for the action from the crowd and no crowd support. The "militant" generally thinks that trashing is a positive outcome, while the "moderate" thinks that trashing is a negative outcome (economists call these tastes"). In addition, the payoff for each is a function of whether others will trash or engage in actions which support trashing. Looking first at the matrix for the militant, the best outcome involves trashing with others. To trash alone would involve high costs (he/she could easily be singled out and arrested), and not to trash while others did so would be to see a desired activity occur but lose the satisfaction of participating (one might also lose face). Finally, if no one trashed, an opportunity would be lost.

The moderate matrix is quite different. Some anti-war activity, but not trashing, is desired. The best outcome is not to trash and have others not trash, a result which would mean essentially no activity (given only a choice with respect to trashing). Since a moderate cannot control all the other crowd members, the best choice is not to trash because, for various reasons,

the other cells have higher costs.

Situation "A" produces a difficult problem for the militant. If the crowd members are primarily moderates, the modal crowd action will be not to trash. Given this outcome, a militant's best choice is not to trash. Therefore, the militants must discover how moderate the crowd is. If the crowd is largely militant (how "largely" will be discussed later) he/she can begin to trash anticipating group support. If not, he/she must either forego trashing or try to *alter the payoff matrices of the moderates,* so that trashing becomes a desired outcome for them. He/she might do so by persuading them, presenting new "facts" or using other techniques (Berk, 1972b).

The best solution for a militant in situation "B" has people staying on the scene, since that would retain the trashing alternative. Hence, moderate and militant individuals are in conflict. Given the two "programs" (trashing or marching away), the good militant solutions are bad for moderates, and vice versa.[1]

Despite the conflict, militants and moderates have some common goals. Both want to encourage concerted anti-war action and realize that group support must be generated. Hence, the possibility of negotiation develops. If both types of individuals can find activities which will reward enough actors, that program can be carried out. Though not the most desirable for either group, it may be the only proposal having mass support.

In summary, each individual in the crowd is faced with a series of decisions. Options for actions are noted, the likelihood for various events assessed, preferences are constructed and eventually the "best" outcome selected. In a group context, all these processes depend on others in the crowd. Hence, one can view milling before concerted action as a period in which these assessments are made and in which payoff matrices are communicated, alternative action suggested and negotiated settlements reached. Crowds will continue to mill until mutually satisfactory solutions occur and are widely known. (These settlements may involve a range of acceptable actions.)[2] If compromises are unnecessary because consensus is wide, group activity will begin as soon as the consensus becomes common knowledge. Note that common knowledge is necessary since few crowd members will gamble on group support when the costs for acting alone are high.

While the matrices describe how crowd members might assess potential outcomes, they must be extended to explain how a crowd member decides to initiate action (e. g., trashing). Since one of the two matrix dimensions involves the existence of group support, before deciding on a course of action, *each individual must gauge whether group support is likely.* In other words, the matrix is a necessary but insufficient calculation for a crowd member. Each must also assess the probability (in a Bayesian sense) that as he/she begins to act group support will be present.

The other matrix dimension involves calculating payoffs for acting or not acting with and without group support. The anticipated payoff in each cell should be seen as a "net" assessment based on a variety of individual utilities. Not everyone is considering the same components or necessarily weighing similar components identically.

Also, if the probability of support is high, a crowd member will be very likely to act, even if the difference in rewards between acting and not acting is small. Further, if probability of support is zero or if acting does not produce greater payoffs (regardless of support) than not acting, the crowd member will not act. Finally, if regardless of crowd support the payoff for acting is less than for not acting, the expression is inappropriate; but one would

nevertheless predict that the individual will not act.

Because both independent variables are unobservable mental states, this formulation is fraught with epistemological problems. Anticipated rewards and costs is probably the stickier of the two; it is explicitly a grab-bag of motivational expectations, presented as a *net* assessment. Though these judgments involve a crucial stage in Raiffa's Decision Theory (attaching preferences to various courses of action), there is no attempt here to specify causes, components or processes. Consequently, they remain a "black-box" with few mechanisms to attach to observed phenomena. Analyses of their impact risk circularity. (That is, a person who is observed beginning to act in a crowd may have his/her actions "explained" in terms of higher anticipated rewards.) In order to avoid circularity (though the epistemological issues remain) measurements of net anticipated rewards and costs must be made prior to an individual's action. This might be done by simply asking participants what they think will happen, or inferring the impact on motives of prior external events. For example, one might compare the actions of crowd participants who heard a speech at a rally with those who did not. However, since the components of anticipated rewards and costs are not well specified and clearly linked to the environment, such operationalizations remain vulnerable.[3]

Probability of support, a listing of events with their likelihood of occurrence, is less problematic for analysis. First, it is explicitly tied to the environment; and its relations with external events will shortly be specified in detail. Hence, there will be a better theoretical basis from which to make inferences. Second, the Decision Theory perspective assumes considerable homogeneity in the ways people assess their environments. The notion of interpersonal strategy suggested not only by game theorists but many observers of human interaction would be absurd unless actors in strategic situations used similar processes in evaluating their environment. For example, Goffman's analyses of impression management (1959) necessarily assume that people can play the "game" and that in general the processes and "rules" are widely understood and used. If this perspective has merit, the epistemological issues are simplified because variability in actor perceptions can be attributed largely to the environment. Third, while anticipated rewards and costs involve summary preferences based on many different factors, probability of support isolates a single issue, analogous to a "condition" in the context of conditional probability. Given a certain chance of support, what's the best action?

In two places in the equation the term "probability" is used. "Probability" is conceptualized in the Bayesian sense as an indicator of "the uncertainty a person has about whether an event will occur" (Iversen, 1970: 191), and is fundamentally different from the relative frequency interpretations of classic probability and statistics. A Bayesian approach implies three processes. First, the actor (either the person in a crowd or the social scientists evaluating the equation) specifies two or more outcomes that could occur. Second, an assessment of the likelihood of occurrence is attached to each outcome. Finally, empirical evidence is considered which alters the estimates of the likelihood of occurrence. Hence, the Bayesian view suggests an iterative procedure consistent with Decision Theory in which the accuracy of projected outcomes is continually reassessed. This is not to argue that crowd participants actually use Bayesian procedures to estimate population parameters. Rather, the underlying processes are roughly similar. Obviously, even if a crowd

member knew how to undertake a formal Bayesian analysis, few of the necessary assumptions about his data could be met (Savage, 1968; Schmitt, 1969).

"Support" can be defined as *actions by crowd members which decrease the anticipated costs for a given individual.* What actions serve this function are determined by the specific activities whose payoffs are being considered. For example, for an individual weighing an attack on a police formation, support would probably involve actions diluting a police response directed at that crowd member (e. g., increasing anonymity).

What environmental conditions might affect the probability of support? Four such variables are discussed, assuming ceteris paribus. In Bayesian terms, these influence the types and quality of samples from which judgments of likelihood of support are made.[4]

1. The number of people acting in ways which support the desired actions of the given individual

The effect of this variable may be "S" shaped (a logistic function) such that it alters the probability of support mostly through changes in its middle ranges (a tipping effect). If only a few people are acting, the effect on perceived support may be minimal. When most are acting the probability of support is already high (depending on other factors listed below). In other words, a specific functional form is postulated.

2. The visibility of the acting people

If a crowd member is not aware that others are engaged in supportive actions, obviously variable #1 (the number of people acting) can have no impact on the probability of support. The variable suggests an important role for the environment in which the crowd is located as well as the crowd's physical arrangement in space.

First, a crowd's shape affects the visibility of crowd member activity. For example, a crowd which weaves through several city blocks will prevent many crowd members from seeing any action around a corner. Each crowd member's view will depend on his/her location in relation to acting people. Consequently, not only will some crowds have structures which affect overall (aggregate) visibility, but crowd members may have differing abilities to see.

Second, crowd density will affect visibility. Its impact may be bell shaped: dense crowds and sparse crowds will substantially undercut the effect of crowd activity on perceived support. In high density crowds, it will be difficult to see more than a few neighboring individuals. Sparse crowds provide an unobstructed view, but much of the support inherent in group action is lost. Certain important advantages of concerted action are negated as density decreases because one is virtually acting alone. Note that again a functional form is suggested.

Third, actions near the center of the crowd will be more easily seen by more people than actions on the fringes because the average (per person) distance from the events will be shorter. In addition, if the existence of supportive actions is spread by word of mouth, the information will spread more rapidly because the lines of communication will be, on the average, shorter.

Fourth, the amount of light will obviously affect what can be seen. Visibility will be greater during the day than at night unless artificial light is present. This might seem a trivial point were artificial light not a manipulatable factor and, hence, relevant for social control. Indeed, the common use of bright search lights (at night) to intimidate crowds may actually facilitate mobilization.

Fifth, parts of a crowd may be at lower (or higher) elevation. Persons acting at points of high elevation will be more easily seen than those acting at lower elevations. The implications for aspiring leaders are clear.

3. Ease of interpreting the actions of others as supportive

Not only must people be seen acting, but their behavior must be understood as supporting the desired activities of the given crowd member (i. e., reducing the costs). There are several conditions which should aid each individual in deciding that the actions of others are supportive. In general, these factors simplify the interpretative task.

First, if the behavior has symbolic components that communicate its meaning, ease of interpretations will be enhanced. Throwing a bag of urine at a policeman, for example, may carry a much clearer message than shoving some unidentified onlooker.

Second, behavior previously explained will be more easily interpreted than novel, undefined behavior. Thus, once the actions of civil disorder participants had been widely publicized, throwing a brick through a ghetto merchant's window could take on a protest meaning that might not have existed previously (Fogelson, 1971).

Third, the more homogeneous the actions the easier the interpretation. There is simply less complexity to assimilate.

Fourth, the behavior of known people will be more easily interpreted than the actions of strangers. If a person is familiar, there will be more information with which to impute meaning.

Fifth, behavior which is similar to what a given individual desires will be more easily interpreted. The crowd member can more easily put himself in the other's shoes and understand actions, motives and intent.

Sixth, behavior that is explained to crowd members will be more easily interpreted. In addition, if the explanation is consistent with norms (emergent or otherwise), it will be more readily understood. Here the role of "leaders" may be important since they can sometimes gain the attention of crowd members and interpret behavior.

4. The proximity of acting people[5]

People acting near a given crowd member will be more likely to increase the probability of support for several reasons. First, they will be more visible. Second, potential strength in numbers differs if allies are proximate or at some distance. Crowd members will sense more support from actions nearby because charging "alone" into a police line, for example, with "support" from others a block away will closely approximate action with no support. Third, if a crowd is fairly dense, the only people visible to each individual will be those close by. Hence, if neighbors begin to act and if these are the only people visible, a crowd member might mistakenly think that the entire crowd was involved. His "sample" might indicate unanimity missing in the crowd as a whole.

Turning now to the crowd as the unit of analysis, our model about individuals provides some insight into the aggregate. (The term "aggregate" is *not* meant to imply that a crowd is just a sum of individuals.) First, crowds will probably differ in the mix of anticipated rewards and costs, the "average" gap between rewards and costs for various outcomes, and the "average" probability of supportive behavior. These three dimensions might be useful in developing a typology of crowds. Earlier typologies such as Smelser's (1962) have touched on some of the qualities noted here, but the emphasis was largely on the different kinds of homogeneous motives.

In a recent example of this focus, Marx (1972) distinguishes between issue oriented and issueless riots.

A second application in the aggregate involves the speed with which crowd activities begin. Some crowds mill for long periods of time, others initiate action almost immediately. This might be understood through the "average" gap between anticipated rewards and costs and the "average" probability of support. For example, crowds in which people tend to anticipate far larger rewards than costs for acting and in which the probability of support is high will more quickly initiate action. Or, crowds in which most people arrive with similar payoff matrices involving a small set of desired actions will begin to act quickly since few negotiations are necessary. The only task is to produce a common awareness of the similar goals.

A third application might explain which group activities are selected. One could look at the mix of anticipated payoffs and the processes through which interactions between crowd members alter expected outcomes. For example, the role of "agitators" or *agent provocateurs* might be explained through the ways they alter existing payoff matrices, introduce new proposals, and affect probability of support. One of the key functions of agitators might be to communicate crowd payoff matrices by moving about and bringing "news" of what others were "planning" to do. In a sense this is an organizer role facilitating a rapid collective decision with little recourse to emotional appeals. Such analyses would clearly emphasize the emergent nature of crowd behavior in which concerted action is a function not only of what people brought to the scene,[6] but of the environment, interpersonal negotiations, and means of communication.

Fourth, the notion of collective decision-making could be clarified. Our model suggests that collective decision making in crowds involves a process through which each individual decides to implement action. Since this decision rests on expectations of what others will do, enough crowd members must arrive at parallel assessments which make action for all a good bet before activity is likely to begin. The aggregate decisions can be meaningfully described as collective because the payoff matrices are interlocking and crowd members must communicate their intentions. Unless crowd members arrive at *mutually* beneficial solutions to their payoff matrices and create *common* awareness of these solutions, crowd behavior will not occur.

Finally, it might be possible to move toward a more useful definition of collective behavior. There is wide agreement that collective behavior involves relatively spontaneous, transitory behavior by people in close proximity to one another. Differences in definition often rest on the mechanisms through which concerted activity develops. The gaming approach suggests that to the degree that the actions of people in crowds become coordinated, one must consider the role of interlocking payoff matrices. What may distinguish crowds from some other kinds of informal, transitory groups (e. g., passive audiences) is the common realization that each person's payoffs depend fundamentally on the actions of others on the scene. However, a definition based in part on this characteristic should not limit collective behavior to what are conventionally called crowds. It might well apply to aspects of political conventions, legislatures, and meetings in more formal organizations where concerted action is desired but where formal procedures, existing norms and/or current interpersonal relationships are perceived inadequate. Further, such a definition would imply a multi-dimensional continuum, not fixed boundaries between collective behavior and other phenomena.[7]

The core of this approach to crowds postulates that there is nothing fundamentally different about cognitive processes in crowds from those in other circumstances.[8] Further, crowd participants, like members of any group, must accomplish the fundamental tasks of fulfilling individual and mutual needs. However, crowds seeking concerted action are affected by factors which often differ (in degree) from those faced by other groups. Besides the interlocking payoff matrices which may vary somewhat from interlocking payoff matrices in other aggregates, crowd members must orchestrate collective activity in situations which contain unusual opportunities and constraints. Hence, a more detailed examination of collective decision-making in crowds must consider some of the following factors that are possibly more salient for crowds than other groups.

1. Crowd members typically have to operate with incomplete and unreliable information. The relatively unstructured environment coupled with an absence of formal data collection procedures means that accurate assessments will be difficult even for the most perceptive participants. Additionally, crowd activity constantly redefines itself, so information must be continually updated. This low-quality information will clearly have important effects on decision-making, and may help explain, in part, alleged "irrational" behavior in crowds.

2. Collective decision-making requires communication between participants. However, communication is a difficult undertaking in crowds. No formal communication structure or network exists, and there are few rules about whom to believe. In addition, participants must gauge many different inputs at once, the language may be unclear (a mix of verbal, symbolic and behavioral styles), and, the system contains considerable "noise."

3. Crowd members rarely have prior

agreements on what constitutes a decision. There is no established "voting" mechanism (e.g., voice volume, silence, actual behavior consistent with a decision), and no agreement on the definition of a "decision."

4. Crowd members undertake decision-making with people who may be very highly motivated and hence impatient to act. This high motivation results from several circumstances. Crowds sometimes function as a "court of last resort," so crowd members are apt to be angry and frustrated. Because crowd behavior often is negatively sanctioned, fear of punishment may screen out all but the most highly motivated (self-selection). The very gathering of a crowd may raise expectations and focus attention on some set of goals (psychologists would call this an effect of the "goal-gradient"). Milling before collective action may itself produce frustration. Finally, the risks involved in much crowd activity may induce fear which many psychologists argue can raise the overall level of motivation.

5. Crowd members operate under extreme time pressure. There must be quick rewards or the participants, lacking loyalty and commitment, will disperse.

In summary, all group members must decide on their organizational goals and on the procedures by which the group is to function. Typically, they gather on several occasions to hammer out process and their purpose for being. In contrast, crowd members typically must "get themselves together" and implement goal-directed action during their first and only meeting. Even under the most favorable of circumstances, this would be extremely difficult; and crowds operate in problematic environments. It is these difficulties rather than crippled mental capacities that may account for "irrational" crowd behavior.

Conclusions

There need be no contradiction between gaming perspectives and emergent norm theory. It is apparent that some collective definitions evolve and that group pressures somewhat constrain crowd members. However, it seems misleading to assume that the "suggestion" fostered by emergent norms cripples the cognitive abilities of participants or that people in crowds are somehow less able than people in other circumstances to examine their situation critically. If there are important differences (probably in degree) in the ways individual judgments are made, it would seem to be more a function of the problematic environments in which crowds operate than any fundamental change in the capacity to reason.

Second, the gaming perspective fills important gaps in emergent norm theory. Close reading of Turner (1964) and Turner and Killian (1972) suggest that they never address systematically or in depth where the norms came from. Crowds seem to exist in an almost featureless plain where the physical environment and the motives of individual crowd members are nearly irrelevant. The theoretical emphasis is on the role of evolving norms in shaping crowd behavior, not why a particular norm, or set of norms, is originally considered. In other words, their analysis begins after certain interpretations and proposals have been introduced. By failing to address motives or responses to the environment, they leave the impression that almost *any* set of norms can be superimposed. The only reality for crowd members is the normative reality.

Third, gaming perspectives and emergent norm approaches imply very different, though probably complementary psychological mechanisms. The former involve a conscious calculus in which the best anticipated outcomes are selected. Concerted action develops in crowds because of apparent mutual benefit. The latter rests on the unconscious tendency to accede to group norms. Concerted action involves a kind of self-fulfilling prophecy in which norms shape behavior because they reflect underlying shared understandings, which are in turn further supported by behavioral conformity.

In conclusion, perhaps the most fruitful way to conceptualize crowd behavior is through a notion of collective innovation. As Weller and Quarantelli (1973) suggest, collective behavior can be characterized by concerted group activity when previous norms and/or social relationships fail to meet immediate needs. This paper describes one set of mechanisms through which such coordination might occur. However, while Turner and Killian focus on normative issues, and the gaming perspective emphasizes rational attempts to gain optimal outcomes, ultimately the relative salience of these and other factors is an empirical question. Equally important will be how these processes interact. An inclusive theory of collective behavior will have to address such complexity.

Notes

1. Given *only* information reflected in the payoff matrices, the solution is indeterminant. A solution requires assessments of group support for alternative activities without which actors cannot ascertain which column in the matrices is appropriate. That judgment will be discussed shortly.

2. A consensus does not mean that everyone will engage in exactly the same actions. It means that a certain range of activities will be defined as acceptable and other activities defined as unacceptable. As in all normative judgments, the boundaries of acceptable activity will not be perfectly delineated. While some actions will clearly be classified, others will not. This is consistent with detailed observations of crowds in which crowd members do many different things. The looting of a store, for example, will often involve considerable division of labor.

3. Until this variable is more clearly specified, it might be necessary to test the formulation by relying primarily on variability in probability of support and the dependent variable. Under these conditions one could resort to plausible assumptions about "tastes," ceteris paribus qualifiers, rough ordinal measures of anticipated rewards and costs, or analyses at some aggregate level where means could be employed. One of the nice characteristics of using a mean is that as

N becomes large, individual idiosyncracies tend to cancel out and hence, eliminate much of the complexity making the variable problematic to begin with. Alternatively, it might be possible to use one series of empirical instances to establish tentative values of anticipated rewards and costs based on accurate predictions (assuming plausible measures of the other two variables) and then use these values in later instances while assessing if the predictions are still accurate. Various combinations of these strategies are commonly used by econometricians (e.g., Sjoquist, 1973).

4. These variables will not be presented in a formalized style. Their relations with each other are probably complex, requiring various kinds of ceteris paribus qualifiers and simultaneous equations for detailed analysis. Such equations could have been generated; but with no data to suggest the functional form of the relationships, the mathematics would have been "spuriously specific." (Credit Peter H. Rossi with that characterization.) Hence, the decision not to imply more rigor than actually exists. One important consequence is that the formulation presented cannot accurately be labeled a theory.

5. This variable was first suggested by John I. Kitsuse and Sarah Fenstermaker Berk.

6. People might bring prior expectations, hopes based on other crowd experiences and a variety of other notions, such as commitment to other people or groups in the crowd.

7. Weller and Quarantelli (1973) have recently stressed that what is commonly called a crowd may be but one type (and not even prototypical) of collective behavior. They suggest a two dimensional scheme involving the degree to which relevant norms and social relationships between collective behavior participants are emergent. Though I have emphasized individuals here more than they might like, I see no contradiction between their views and mine. They argue that behavior in groups should be labeled "collective" (as opposed to "institutionalized") to the degree that the mediating norms and/or the relationships between participants evolve at the scene. This paper addressed the next question. Given that habitual mechanisms (normative and interpersonal) fail to apply to a particular situation, how does concerted activity develop?

8. The assumption that crowd behavior is fundamentally like other kinds of human activity is certainly challengeable. However, for the sake of parsimony and in reaction to some traditional approaches to collective behavior, I am attempting to see how much of crowd behavior can be understood in terms applicable in a wide variety of circumstances before I introduce unique processes such as "social facilitation" (Allport, 1924) into the analysis. One consequence is that a definition of crowd behavior (as categorically distinct from other kinds of behavior in groups) becomes problematic and possibly not desirable.

17.

Clark McPhail

STUDENT WALKOUT: A FORTUITOUS EXAMINATION OF ELEMENTARY COLLECTIVE BEHAVIOR*

Sociologists have traditionally separated crowd behavior, if not all elementary collective behavior, from routine social behavior. The separation has involved more than the recognition that behavior patterns can differ substantively in the crowd vis-à-vis the routine social encounter. More frequently than not, distinctively different explanatory principles have been employed to account for the behavior patterns in these substantively separated areas.[1]

One of the most influential interpretations of collective behavior for the past two decades has been that of Herbert Blumer. He clearly separates the principles by which he accounts for conventional social behavior from those which he introduces to account for collective behavior.

From one point of view practically all group activity can be thought of as collective behavior. Group activity means that individuals are acting together in some fashion; that there is some fitting together of the different lines of individual conduct. In this sense, group activity is a collective matter. In the classroom, for example, there is a division of labor between the teacher and the students. The students act in expected ways and the teacher, likewise, has a different kind of activity which is expected of him. The activities of the different students and of the teacher fit together to form orderly and concerted group conduct.[2]

. . . the great bulk of collective behavior among human beings occurs because people have common understandings and expectations.[3]

On the other hand:

A highly excited mob, a business panic, a state of war hysteria, a condition of social unrest represent instances of collective behavior which are [not] of this character. In these instances, the collective behavior arises spontaneously and is not due to pre-established understandings or traditions.[4]

Blumer refers to these phenomena as elementary forms of collective behavior.

Its elementary nature is suggested by its short life, its spontaneity, its simple forms of emotional interplay, its lack of the delicate and complicated alignment that occurs between self-conscious individuals, and its lack of any intricate organization.[5]

Based on this characterization, Blumer developed a separate set of explanatory principles to account for this different behavior. These separate principles emphasize spontaneous and "circular reaction" among individual participants resulting in the development of homogenous patterns of behavior.[6] This emphasis has directed

From Clark McPhail, "Student Walkout: A Fortuitous Examination of Elementary Collective Behavior," *Social Problems*, 16:4 (Spring, 1969), pp. 441-55. Reprinted by permission of The Society for the Study of Social Problems and the author.

* Revised version of a paper presented at the annual meetings of The Midwest Sociological Society, 1967. The critical reading and suggestions of Robert L. Stewart, Carl J. Couch, and Charles W. Tucker have been incorporated into the present version. The data were provided by students at a midwestern college in 1965. The participation and contribution of all the aforementioned persons is gratefully acknowledged.

the attention of students of collective behavior away from the principles Blumer employs to account for routine social behavior, viz., the fitting together of individual lines of conduct in terms of the common expectations and understandings of the participants.

The present paper is addressed to two questions concerning the traditional treatment of elementary collective behavior by sociologists in general and by Blumer in particular. First, are different principles of explanation required for the substantively different patterns which may be observed in collective versus routine social behavioral settings? Second, are the principles Blumer employs to account for social behavior restricted to such routine settings as the classroom?

Recent theoretical treatments of collective behavior have emphasized convergence with interpretations of more routine social behavior. Smelser[7] and Turner[8] have developed or applied explanatory principles which they contend are applicable to both collective and routine social behavioral settings. Irrespective of the merits of their somewhat different sets of explanatory principles, credit is due their attempts to develop parsimonious approaches to human social behavior across substantively different areas. The present paper is an additional effort toward such parsimonious development.[9]

Descriptions of and reports by participants in panic crowds and disaster situations question the restriction of many of Blumer's explanatory principles to routine social behavioral settings.[10] Participants report attention to one another's behavior and the construction of coordinated, differential, and similar lines of behavior based upon those cues.[11] Such illustrative evidence questions the separation of routine from collective behavioral phenomena maintained by Blumer's position. The present paper presents data which further challenge such a separation.

The principles of social behavior suggested by Mead, Blumer, and others of their theoretical persuasion, require attention to what people do with and in relation to one another. In routine encounters, the regularities in participants' behavior toward one another are based upon shared identifications and expectations for regularities in the behavior of persons so identified.[12] As long as the behavior of each participant permits the other participants to maintain their identification of and claims upon one another, their respective performances will be coordinated in routine fashion. An ongoing course of coordinated behavior can be deflected by an act or acts of the participants or by some intruder. When the complementary activities of the participants are deflected, a problematic situation is said to exist. A fundamental sociological notion is that the responses of the participants to the deflecting act or acts will determine the resolution of the problematic course of action; it may continue, or it may be terminated, modified, or replaced with a different course of action.[13]

An empirical examination of these views requires observations of: 1) participants fitting together a routine sequence of behaviors; 2) the deflection of that sequence of behaviors[14]; and 3) participants' efforts at resolving the problematic sequence of behaviors. Most frequently, problematic lines of coordinated behavior resume their original form with only minor adjustments. Less frequently participants are unable to fit together either their previous routine or some alternate line of behaviors and must, consequently, go their separate ways. On other occasions, alternated lines of behavior are fitted together in the construction of a new course of collective behavior. Opportunities are rare to observe such sequences and to obtain detailed data about and/or from participants during and immediately after their routine behaviors are deflected. Such an opportunity was recently afforded the present writer.

Source and analysis of data

While lecturing to a class of 25 students, all but two members of the class walked out of the room ten minutes before the end of the writer's lecture. The lecturer recovered in a sufficiently brief period of time to contact the majority of the students on the same afternoon as the walkout. Detailed written reports were obtained from 21 of the students involved, including the two students who did not walk out. Verbatim statements were extracted from these reports to construct a description of the sequence of events.[15] These descriptive data, provided by the participants, are used to outline and illustrate some rudimentary principles of human social behavior in routine and non-routine situations. The theoretical framework within which these principles are developed is briefly outlined in the following section.

Theoretical perspective

Students of social behavior frequently use such expressions as the aligning, coordinating, or fitting together of the respective lines of behavior of participants. How this fitting together is accomplished remains a central question. George H. Mead suggested that human beings accomplish this by calling out in themselves the response of the other to their own conduct.[16] Two classes of behaviors are viewed as central to this anticipatory process of "taking the attitude of the other:" designating behaviors and prescribing behaviors.[17] Designating behaviors locate and identify acting units.[18] Designating behav-

iors are the answers given to questions such as "Who am I?," "Who are we?," "Who is he?," "Who are they?," and "What is that?" To establish the identities of acting units is to construct a relationship between the namer and the named.[19] Thus, designating behaviors establish social relationships. Prescribing behaviors specify some course of action toward or from designated acting units and thus provide the substantive content of social relationships. Prescribing behaviors are answers given to the question: "What is expected from designated acting units and what may be done to them?"

Congruent designating and prescribing behaviors among acting units make possible the coordination of their respective individual lines of behavior.[20] Further, a coordinated line of behavior will be maintained or will recur until rendered problematic by some deflected action.[21] Ordinarily, then, social relationships between students and teachers, husbands and wives, or majority and minority group members are performed in routine fashion. In the absence of deflecting actions, designating and prescribing behaviors continue and permit the ongoing coordination of individual lines of behavior.

It is clear that some departures from conventional performances are ignored or squelched and participants continue in their respective, complementary lines of behavior.[22] Nonetheless, the departure from routine performances gives evidence to all who observe that such action can be taken; the response of participants to that action determines whether it will be continued, modified, or terminated.[23] Garfinkel's research on the routine grounds of everyday activities clearly illustrates the deflecting consequences of violating common expectations for participants' behaviors in routine social encounters.[24] The performance of a line of conduct which

departs from what is expected of or prescribed for a designated acting unit can
deflect the coordination of behaviors
among participants. Gross and Stone's research suggests that such departures can
require altered identifications of perform-
ers. As a consequence, "when inappropriate identities are established or appropriate identities are lost, role performance
is impossible."[25] Thus, alternate designations can and do deflect the coordination
of behaviors. Garfinkel's specification of
the sequence of actions necessary to transform the "public identity" of a person illustrates the consequences of alternate
designating behaviors for social relationships and contingent coordinated behavior.[26] The following reports of participants
in a classroom walkout suggest that the interdependence of designations, prescriptions, and performances are of central
importance for maintaining an old or developing a new line of coordinated behavior.

Routine and new lines of behavior

*New lines of coordinated behavior are
initiated in response to the deflection of
previous lines of behavior.* One type of deflection is a performance which departs
from what is routinely prescribed.

R.08 . . . the idea of staging a classroom walkout first came when the professor told the
class about an experiment in which the
lecturer nonchalantly left the room in the
middle of the class and in the middle of a
sentence.

R.10 . . . the professor mentioned the fact that
he had considered walking out of class
during a lecture and not returning. He
not only said he had considered doing it,
he demonstrated by walking out the door
how he would have done it.

It was noted earlier, however, that the
response to the deflection is crucial in de-

termining whether the problematic course
of action will be continued, modified,
terminated, or replaced. *The development
of a new line of coordinated behavior requires the proposal and organization of
those behaviors by at least some of the
participant acting units.* Without that
organization, a new line of coordinated
behavior cannot develop.

R.16 . . . several of us were walking to class
and discussing the feasibility of 'out experimenting the experimenter' and walking out of class in the middle of a lecture.
. . . On this day, however, our professor
arrived just after we'd taken our seats
and there was no time to discuss the idea
with the rest of the class.

On a subsequent day, the proposal and
organization of the new line of coordinated
behavior did develop among some of the
participant acting units.

R.16 When we reached the class, our professor
had not arrived, so we sat around talking
about what a beautiful day it was, and
how none of us felt like studying. At this
time a girl suggested asking the professor
if we could have class . . . in the union so
we could all get a cup of coffee. Suddenly,
I remembered our idea from the preceding class period. "Hey," I broke in, "He's
not here yet; today would be a perfect
day to stage the walkout."

Turner[27] and Couch[28] have recently discussed a rather prevalent misconception
about the spontaneity of new patterns of
coordinated behavior. They suggest a continuity between old and new lines of behavior. One aspect of that continuity,
noted above, is that the latter emerges or
develops in response to some deflection of
the former. Another aspect is that *new
lines of coordinated behavior always involve a new or different sequencing of old
elements of behavior, skill, and/or knowledge.* Whether the new pattern of behavior
involved preparing and hurling a molotov

cocktail, taking an item from a store and walking out with it, or walking out of a classroom, the component activities do not spontaneously emerge; rather, there is a new and different sequencing of the component behaviors.

Establishing new relationships

If routine patterns of coordinated behavior are the product of routine social relationships, then new patterns of coordinated behavior must be similarly produced. Routine social relationships can impede if not preclude participation in new lines of social behavior.[29] If the person is to participate in a new line of behavior with others, old relationships must be altered or replaced. *New relationships among participant acting units are required for the development and implementation of a new line of coordinated behavior.*[30]

In his discussion of the construction of a new line of conduct, Ralph Turner has mentioned, in order, the following three factors: a concern on the part of participants with rules; attempts to define the situation; and determination of leaders who will legitimate the rules and initiate action.[31] While each of these phenomena *may* occur, the order of their appearance and consequence must be somewhat different from that suggested by Turner. In line with my earlier comments, designating behaviors locate and differentiate "leaders" from "other participants" and thus make all designated acting units liable for corresponding prescriptions for behavior. These acts constitute a "definition of the situation." Thus, *new relationships are established by new or alternate designations of participant acting units.*[32]

The reports of the participants in the walkout included new or alternate designations of both professor and students.

These designations established new relationships among the students as well as between the students and the professor. The following report illustrates some of the acts involved in establishing a new relationship among the students.

R.11 When I walked into the classroom . . . I could tell something was going on. There were relatively few students in the room but most of them were whispering to each other. After a minute or so [Ann] turned to me and whispered: "The whole class is going to walk out at 1:40 to see what the professor will do." I thought that was a good idea so I said, "That's cool; do you think everybody will do it?" She said, "Yeah, [R.16] started it."

Nine of the 21 respondents designated R.16 as "the leader" and/or "a senior sociology major who had taken several courses with the professor and knew him quite well." While this was in fact erroneous, it served to designate R.16 as one who could propose such an alternate course of action. Similarly, designating acts were taken which constructed an alternate relationship between the students and the professor. The professor was designated as one who had suggested walking out of class earlier himself; as one supportive of students "experimenting" with ideas acquired in classes; and as one deserving of the walkout given his own past manipulations of students in similar situations.

R.04 . . . the professor would realize that this was a sort of experiment, that we had only missed eight minutes of class, and would merely laugh the whole thing off as a combination student prank and experiment pertaining to the subject matter of the course.

R.05 After all, a lot of other experiments were instigated by the professor around town and on campus. . . . It seemed only right and natural that we try an experiment on him, especially one which he himself had suggested.

R.16 There were a few people who worried about whether the professor would be angry, but we decided if we left at 1:45, only five minutes before the class was supposed to end, he would not be too upset; besides, he himself had experimented on many classes.

The students clearly designated the professor as one toward whom a new line of behavior could be taken. At the same time, however, the students scheduled their performance of the new line of behavior sufficiently late in the lecture period so that it would preclude the professor's designation of them as totally disinterested or irresponsible.

R.19 . . . a time for the walkout had to be decided upon and 1:15 was suggested as a possibility. But someone remarked that this was too early and the professor might be irritated if we left that early. Next the time of 1:45 was suggested and everyone semed to agree that it was a good time because it was near the end of the period and we wouldn't miss too much of the lecture material.

Proposals for and commitments to a new line of behavior

The suggestion was made earlier that at least some of the participant acting units must be involved in the proposal and organization of a new line of behavior to assure its development. The participants' reports indicate that all the students were not involved in the proposal and organization of the walkout.

R.02 Although the girls asked everyone who was in the class *early* if they would walk out of the class at "a quarter to two" and most answered that they would, it appeared to me that many students did not know beforehand what was coming. (Respondent's emphasis.)

R.20 I was asked, "Say, do you know about the walkout?" and then was asked, "Well, are you going to do it?" At this point I had still not heard any attempted formulation of the purpose of the walkout or any true confirmation that it was an . . . experiment. These thoughts had an influence on my reply, which amounted to a series of noncommittal mumblings, ending up with, "I don't see any purpose in it."

It should come as no surprise that R.20 did not participate in the walkout and that R.02 was the last student to leave the room at the time of the walkout.

R.20's report suggests another aspect of the organization of a new line of coordinated behavior, namely, the presence or absence of overt acts of commitment to participate in the new line of behavior. Public declarations of intention to commit some line of action involve a self-designation in the presence of others who can place appropriate claims on one who is so designated. Thus, *the successful implementation of a new line of coordinated conduct is directly related to the commitments which acting units make to one another to perform the new line of conduct.*[33]

R.21 Many of us enthusiastically joked about . . . [the walkout] . . . but [R.16] asked• seriously if we'd go along with it. Students looked around at each other first, then most affirmed the action either vocally or with some gesture. I myself said I'd go anytime but not first.

Sixteen of the 21 participants mentioned their intention, at this point, to take part in the walkout; less than half this number, however, reported a public statement of commitment to participate in the new line of behavior. An important consideration, then, is the proportion of participants who must make public commitments in order for the new line of behavior to be implemented, and the manner in which that proportion is secured.

R.14 Then someone turned to me and said, "Will you go along with it?" Without much thought about purpose or consequence I said I would. My only thoughts were that if *everyone else was going to do it, it would be safe for me to do it also,* and I did not want to hold out and ruin it for the other people. (Emphasis supplied.)

The preceding participant's report of attention to an inferred majority in the formulation of his own decision to walk out, points to an important phenomenon in the development of a new line of collective behavior. Turner suggests that "if the ability to carry out a [new or unusual] course of action successfully is often a consideration in judging it legitimate, the apparent power of the crowd adds to its displacements of the usual behavioral anchorages."[34] The course of action at issue here is the student's public commitment to participate in the walkout. Following Turner's reasoning, as more students followed this course of action without deflection in the form of challenge or dissent, the course of action was increasingly viewed as legitimate. It may be the case that the proportion of students taking the action, i.e., the size of the majority, is not so important as the absence of challenge or dissent to the course of action. Asch's research, for example, showed that a majority of three produced as much compliance as a majority of 10-15. However, he also found that a majority of three without a dissenter produced more compliance than a majority of eight with one dissenter.[35] A tentative principle summarizing the foregoing suggests that *when any proportion of acting units engage in a course of action which is not deflected, the likelihood of compliance on the part of the remaining acting units is increased.* This appears to provide behavioral referents for what Turner and other students have referred to as "the apparent power of the crowd."[36]

Synchronizing new lines of behavior

Even though the participants agreed that the new line of conduct should take place near the end of the forthcoming lecture period, there was no consensus as to the specific time at which the walkout would occur nor was there any specification of a keynoting activity or acting unit. Six of the 21 reports mentioned 1:40, 11 mentioned 1:45, and the rest made no mention or indicated confusion about the time of the walkout. Congruent designating and prescribing behaviors, establishing "who" will do "what," are necessary for the coordination of individual lines of conduct. In addition, the specification of "when" acting units will perform is necessary in order to synchronize their respective lines of behavior. For example, students are expected to be seated in the classroom, to direct their attention to the front of the room, take notes, refrain from talking, etc. However, these behaviors are prescribed for specified time frames designated by such activities as the ringing of a bell, a professor's actions, etc. Similarly, students are expected to leave the classroom at the end of a specified time frame which is designated by the ringing of a bell, a professor's action, etc. Without the timing of these prescribed performances, the routine coordination of behaviors would be impossible. The independent deviation of one or two students from this routine does not deflect the continued coordination of behaviors among others, e.g., some students may arrive late, look out the window, or leave early without disturbing the class routine. But, if the late arrival, looking out the window, or early departure is a joint enterprise involving the fitting together of two or more individual lines of conduct, some synchronizing of these lines of conduct must be consensually established. The participants in the walkout did not attend to this aspect of constructing the new line of action and their failure to do so handicapped the smooth implementation of their plan.

Routine relationships and behaviors

The specification of a keynoting activity or acting unit might have been accomplished had the professor not arrived at this point. His arrival initiated the classroom routine which in turn interrupted the planning activities of the students.

R.07 When the professor entered, students immediately prepared to take notes and because of the standard atmosphere that existed (class behavior seemed to be like any other day), I completely forgot about the intended walkout.

R.19 Since I was sitting in the front of the room, I became very engrossed with the lecture of the day and hardly noticed the time go by.

R.18 I didn't think about the walkout very much (I was busy taking notes) until a few moments before we were supposed to leave.

So far as the professor observed, the students' behavior seemed to be like any other day. Correspondingly, 11 of the 21 participants, including the three quoted above, reported that they had given the majority of their attention to the lecture and had forgotten about what had been planned. On the other hand, eight of the participants reported difficulty in concentrating on the lecture or in forgetting about the pending walkout.

R.12 The thought of the walkout ruined all lines of concentration for me and I continued to stare out the window. . . . It was such a beautiful day outside I just wanted to get out in it. I thought about how tired I was and lit a cigarette so that I wouldn't fall asleep.

R.09 Once the plan had been formed, it was extremely difficult to sit through 45 minutes of class.

Even these participants, however, did not behave in a manner noticeably different from the rest. The result was to facilitate the continuation of routine classroom behaviors and to leave the tasks of establishing the time of departure and the keynoting activities incomplete.

The professor lectured during the first 30 minutes of the class period. This activity elicited attention to him and made it difficult for students to further organize their departure. After the first 30 minutes, at about 1:30, the professor shifted from lecturing to answering questions from and asking questions of students about the lecture. This not only permitted students to attend to each other but required that they do so. It also allowed students to look at a clock or at watches and thus to take up again the problem of synchronizing. Correspondingly, some of the participants reported giving attention to time at this point.

R.19 When I finally glanced at my watch, it was 1:30.

R.07 I suddenly remembered our intentions as I glanced down at my watch—it was 1:30.

After the question and answer session proceeded for approximately ten minutes, the professor shifted back to the final portion of his lecture. Again this shift in his activity deflected the students' activities. One student reports:

R.16 As the appointed time drew close, I grew more nervous and excited. At 1:40 [ten minutes prior to the end of the period] I glanced to my left and panicked as I saw one of the girls toward the back begin to fold up her notebook and get her books together. I tried to signal her that she was too early and that we weren't leaving until 1:45, but I only succeeded in confusing her. She began looking around for validation. Since no one else in the class appeared to be getting ready to depart, she merely sat with her hands folded and her books in a pile. At this point, I began to get very nervous wondering if others in the class were similarly confused, and if so, would they still have the courage to take part.

The approximate time for the walkout was approaching but the absence of a specified time or keynoting action to synchronize the participants' individual lines of action proved problematic. Prior to the lecture, 16 of the 21 students reported their intention to participate in the walkout near the end of the period. However, as that point approached, 13 of the 21 reported doubts: whether or not the walkout would now occur; who would have the courage to take the first step; whether others would participate; or whether they would themselves participate.

R.12 At 1:40 no one moved, I started to put my things away quietly so that the professor wouldn't notice anything. [Fran] did the same thing and so did some of the other kids around me. But still, no one moved. Well, I wasn't going to be the first to go because I thought maybe they had changed their minds and wouldn't follow.

R.11 One point is important, however. I didn't want to initiate action when the plan was endangered by some changes in the planned time for the walkout. I suppose now that I wanted to slip back into the established routine, instead of doing something drastic . . .

R.09 I wanted to do it, but I didn't want to be the leader. I wondered if everyone else would walk out or if they would just sit there. Part of me hoped we'd just forget the idea and yet I wanted to get up and leave.

Implementing a proposed line of behavior

When acting units have committed themselves to a line of coordinated action but have not specified procedures by which their respective actions will be synchro- *nized, the coordinated action cannot develop.* In such situations the attention of the acting units will invariably be directed to one another rather than to the object of the proposed action. Participants may then claim prior commitments of one another in the form of reminders, challenges, or taunts.

R.18 At 1:40, several people were still looking around, apparently waiting for someone to take a line of action. I was hesitant about initiating the walkout by myself, preferring to let someone else make the first move. At this point, [R.06], sitting next to me, and I asked each other something like, "Well, are we going to leave or not?" Then we both got up simultaneously and began walking toward the door . . . I'm not sure whether or not I would have initiated the walkout by myself. I know that I would have been hesitant.

The confederate keynoter reports:

R.06 Before the walkout, I weighed the pro's and con's of getting out from my desk. I figured that if no one followed I'd go straight to the professor's office and wait for him. [R.18] and I looked at each other, said, "Shall we?" and left the room. My thoughts at the time were directed at the doorknob, turning it, and getting out. To my delightful surprise, once I did get out I noticed everyone was coming.

Altogether, 18 of the 21 participants report their attention to the actions of their fellows prior to their own departure from the classroom.

R.14 A general restlessness began as people started closing their notebooks and the boy who had taken the leadership position on himself stood up. . . . I knew that he had to be followed or the whole plan would fall through. In a matter of seconds everyone was up and heading for the door, so my momentary hesitation was gone and I felt secure in the knowledge that I was not alone.

R.19 I then waited for more students to leave

before I made any preparation to leave. I guess I was waiting for my . . . activity to be confirmed by more students. As soon as I saw other students leaving I grabbed my books as fast as I could and headed for the door.

R.11 Then several others, among them [Joyce] and her girlfriend stood up, too, and within seconds most of the class was nervously on its feet, . . . We exchanged grins to affirm each others' behavior. I stood up and put on my coat. Then I saw that [Ann] was still sitting down; so I said, "Come on, it's gonna work!" and she got up too and walked out.

"Human group life consists of the fitting together of the lines of action of the participants."[37] An examination of these data suggests that this fundamental principle holds for new as well as routine lines of social behavior. Contrary to Blumer's position that any new line of collective (i.e., social) behavior ". . . arises spontaneously and is not due to pre-established understanding or traditions,"[38] these data suggest that social behavior is not spontaneous; rather, acts are taken in relation to acts. Further, "shared understandings" are continually, although not continuously, constructed in the actions of participants with one another.[39] The preceding participants' reports have clearly demonstrated this to be the case for the lines of action taken by the students in relation to one another.

Unanticipated consequences

An examination of the response of the professor to the students' new line of collective action suggests another fundamental principle. *The development of a new line of conduct toward an acting unit not implicated in its proposal and organization is facilitated by that acting unit's continued performance of old lines of conduct and/or disorganized response to the new line of conduct.*

R.04 [The professor] was not upset when he saw the two boys stand up to leave, for there are many times when students will have to leave classes early for a number of common reasons. When the entire class followed, however, his sentences became disconnected until he finally stopped speaking with a bewildered expression on his face. He made no attempt to try to stop the class and seemed stunned, merely wanting an explanation of what was going on.

R.18 At no time did the professor attempt to stop the walkout. If he had become upset and ordered the class to return, I'm sure we would have done so.

R.07 The professor's reaction was unexpected —"Hey, did the bell ring already?"—and then as we were almost out [of the room] "Well, I'll finish the lecture for you two." These two comments, especially the first one, coupled with the look on his face, had a sort of sanctioning effect on me. I can remember thinking as I was walking, that if he had said or made some kind of dissenting word or objection that our action might have been different.

The behavior of the professor was deflected by the early departure of the two students who were seated near the back of the classroom. Such a departure, as noted above, is not unusual. Unfortunately, the professor made reference to the departure in the context of his comments. Alluding to some just-mentioned incidents of violent gang behavior, the professor wryly remarked: "I hope I didn't offend you two with the examples" and then glanced back at his lecture notes. When he looked up again, the entire class, save two, was either rising to its feet or on the way out the back door of the classroom. His next responses were: "What—what's going on, is class over already?" and "Hey, did the bell ring already?" "Did my watch stop?"

The professor's responses had two significant consequences for the development of the new line of behavior. First, his comments to the two keynoting students clearly indicated to the remaining students that the time for the walkout had arrived. The comments had the unanticipated consequence of synchronizing the participants' respective lines of behavior. Second, the sputtering and stammering of the professor, in his attempt to account for the behavior which had been deflected—his own—did nothing to render problematic the developing new line of behavior undertaken by the students. Quite the contrary, his actions facilitated the development of the new line of behavior.

The deviant cases

Two students did not join their fellows in the new line of behavior. An examination of the acts which they took at the time the walkout was proposed and organized, as well as their actions at the time of implementation, provides a partial explanation of their deviant performance. One of the two deviants had initially agreed to participate in the walkout. As the lecture period developed, however, he reports a reconsideration of that intention.

R.21 When [R.16] suggested the walkout, I consented uncritically. However, after the class began, the situation became questionable to me. I first wondered what the purpose of the walkout was. If no one stayed, the professor would simply leave and nothing would be accomplished [i.e., we wanted to observe his reactions] . . . I began to wonder if [R.16] was trying some experiment on her own, or if she was a confederate of the professor in some type of study. . . . As the time grew near, I started feeling uncomfortable. My stomach grew tense.

When the keynoting action was taken and the majority of the students had followed course, the same student—sitting in the back row of the classroom—gave the following report.

R.21 When the students filed out, I felt very conspicuous; nervous but defiant. I no-

ticed [R.20] and wondered if he was going to leave. When he didn't I felt a little relieved. Still my face was stinging and I couldn't understand much of what the professor said.

The reader will recall that R.20 declined to commit himself to participate in the walkout when this line of action was proposed and organized prior to the lecture period. He had arrived late and had not ". . . heard any attempted formulation of the purpose of the walkout or any true confirmation that it was an . . . experiment." This student, sitting in the front row of the classroom, reported the following:

R.20 Realization of the start of the walkout came when I heard a great rustling behind me and almost simultaneously I saw the professor look at his watch [and] say, "What—what's going on, is class over already?" In about one to two minutes the room was empty with the exception of myself and another student. The professor was bewildered and I was uncontrollably blushing. I remember turning around to the other remaining student [R.21] and raising my hands in a bewildered expression. By this action I think I was looking for some sort of confirmation or support for my actions. I believe he replied with almost the same actions.

And what of the professor's subsequent actions? One of the departing students, quoted earlier, recalled the professor's comments to the remaining students: ". . . as we were almost out [of the room, he said], 'Well, I'll finish the lecture for you two.'" The professor did have five minutes of prepared comments remaining and there were two students left to listen to those comments. "In the classroom . . . there is a division of labor between the teacher and the students. The students act in expected ways and the teacher, likewise, has a different kind of activity which is expected of him."[40] Had all the students left, there would have been no one to teach; had the teacher left, the remaining students would have had no one to study. While this does not provide a conclusive interpretation, the interdependence of the respective behaviors of the professor and students cannot be ignored.

Summary

The reports of participants in a classroom walkout have been used to construct the sequence of events involved in deflecting routine and constructing new lines of social behavior. These data provide an empirical record of the initiation and development of an elementary form of collective behavior. Repeated examples are provided of some rudimentary principles of social behavior which have previously been restricted to the ongoing construction of routine lines of social behavior. The applicability of these principles to the production, maintenance, and alteration of social behavior in routine and collective behavioral settings follows Turner's suggestions. The examination of collective behavior events may possibly ". . . undermine all of the traditional dynamic distinctions between collective behavior and organizational behavior and suggest that no special set of principles is required to deal with this subject matter."[41]

Notes

1. E. A. Ross, *Social Psychology*, New York: Macmillan, 1908; R. E. Park, "Collective Behavior," in E. R. A. Seligman, editor, *Encyclopedia of the Social Sciences*, New York: Macmillan, 1930, 31, p. 631; H. A. Blumer, "Collective Behavior," in A. M. Lee, editor, *Principles of Sociology*, New York: Barnes and Noble, 1946; R. H. Turner and L. M. Killian, *Collective Behavior*, Englewood Cliffs, N.J.: Prentice-Hall, 1957; K. Lang and G. E. Lang, *Collective Dynamics*, New York: Crowell, 1961; T. Shibutani, "Suggestibility and Behavioral Contagion," in his *Improvised News*, Indianapolis: Bobbs-Merrill, 1966, pp. 95-128. The influence of LeBon on this American tradition is quite clear. Each of those cited

above makes extensions and refinements of LeBon's ideas but maintains his separation and separate explanations of collective behavior from conventional human behavior. G. LeBon, *La Psychologie des Foules*, Paris: Olean, 1895; *The Crowd*, New York: Viking, 1960.

2. Blumer, *op. cit.*, p. 167.

3. *Ibid.*, p. 168.

4. *Ibid.*

5. H. Blumer, "Collective Behavior," in J. B. Gittler, editor, *Review of Sociology*, New York: Wiley, 1957, p. 131.

6. Blumer, 1946, *op. cit.*, pp. 170-171.

7. N. J. Smelser, *Theory of Collective Behavior*, New York: Free Press, 1963, p. 23.

8. R. H. Turner, "Collective Behavior," in R. E. L. Faris, editor, *Handbook of Modern Sociology*, Chicago: Rand McNally, 1964, p. 384.

9. Another recent effort to accomplish such a convergence is R. R. Dynes and E. L. Quarantelli, "Group Behavior Under Stress: A Required Convergence of Organizational and Collective Behavior Perspectives," *Sociology and Social Research*, 52 (1968), 416-428.

10. W. H. Form and C. P. Loomis, "The Persistence and Emergence of Social and Cultural Systems in Disaster," *American Sociological Review*, 21 (1956), pp. 180-185. E. L. Quarantelli, "The Behavior of Panic Participants," *Sociology and Social Research*, 41 (1957), pp. 187-194, and "Images of Withdrawal Behavior in Disasters: Some Basic Misconceptions," *Social Problems*, 8 (1960), 68-79.

11. Human beings fit together similar and different lines of behavior in routine and problematic situations. Attention must be given to one's behavior in relation to that of another when fitting together the similar behaviors involved in exiting a classroom, walking through shopping center malls, or turning over an automobile. The same is true when fitting the different behaviors together necessary for a symphony orchestra performance, for purchasing cigarettes from a clerk, engaging in sexual intercourse, or engaging in a fist-fight.

12. N. Foote, "Identification as a Basis for a Theory of Motivation," *American Sociological Review*, 16 (1951), 14-21.

13. G. H. Mead, *The Philosophy of the Act*, Chicago: U. of Chicago, pp. 82-83. An extension of this line of reasoning to interpret the production and development of interest groups is found in N. Foote and C. W. Hart, "Public Opinion and Collective Behavior," in M. Sherif and M. O. Wilson, editors, *Group Relations at the Crossroads*, N.Y.: Harper, 1953, pp. 308-333.

14. If the assumption is granted that human beings are continuously active, then only portions of activity are deflected and in turn modified, replaced, or terminated at any one time, i.e., total activity is terminated only in death.

15. All statements included in the descriptive se-

quence of events should be considered representative unless otherwise indicated. Where appropriate, the proportion of respondents citing a particular phenomenon is indicated. The names of persons mentioned by respondents have been replaced by pseudonyms. The numbers preceding the verbatim statements are respondent code numbers, e.g., R. *01-21*, and are not to be confused with frequencies.

16. G. H. Mead, "The Genesis of the Self and Social Control," *International Journal of Ethics*, 35 (1924-1925), pp. 251-277.

17. Robert L. Stewart first directed my attention to the importance of designating and prescribing behaviors and suggested many of the basic ideas stated in this paper concerning the consequence of those classes of behaviors in the organization of social behavior.

18. I am using the term designating behavior as synonymous with but more generic than such prevalent terms as identification, naming, and labeling. For a similar usage see Charles W. Morris, *Signification and Significance*, Cambridge: M.I.T., 1964, pp. 1-15.

19. A. Strauss, following K. Burke, discusses naming as an act of relational placement. See, respectively, *Mirrors and Masks*, Glencoe: Free Press, 1959, p. 19; and *A Grammar of Motives*, N.Y.: Prentice-Hall, 1945, p. 24.

20. Blumer's formulation allows for congruent designating and prescribing behaviors and consequent coordinated behavior, but only in routine settings. Blumer, *op. cit.* The writer's observations of the behaviors taken *among* demonstrators with regard to police (and presumably among police with regard to demonstrators) suggest that presence or absence of congruent designating and prescribing behaviors is consequential for coordination of behavior in these non-routine settings as well.

21. W. Catton argues that an axiom of inertia is fundamental for a naturalistic sociology. Such an axiom holds that a pattern of social behavior will continue to manifest itself at unaltered rates unless some social force modifies the pattern or rate. *From Animistic to Naturalistic Sociology*, N.Y.: McGraw-Hill, 1966, p. 235. My preference is to explicitly attend to the behaviors of individual and collective acting units, vis-à-vis "social forces," which can deflect coordinated lines of behavior.

22. T. Scheff suggests that much "residual deviance" is either transitory or denied. "The Role of the Mentally Ill and the Dynamics of Mental Disorder," *Sociometry*, 26 (1963), pp. 441-442. Some evidence bearing on this is M. Yarrow *et al.*, "The Psychological Meaning of Mental Illness in the Family," *Journal of Social Issues*, 11 (1955), pp. 12-24. See Table 2: "Wives' Initial Interpretations of the Husband's Behavior."

23. Labeling theory has emphasized the importance of other's designations for the stabilization of deviant behavior. See Scheff, *op. cit.*, p. 451. These designating or labeling behaviors are of consequence,

however, in terms of the alteration in relationships between designators and designated and the alteration in coordinated performances permitted, required, or precluded by the relationship. New or alternate designations may permit or preclude the continued coordination of similar performances, may permit or require the coordination of alternate performances, or may preclude any coordination of similar or alternate performances in terms of the relationship established by the designations. From this perspective the reciprocity of participants' responses to a deviant performance must be examined rather than assigning singular responsibility for the outcome to the behavior of the designator or the designated.

24. H. Garfinkel, "Studies in the Routine Grounds of Everyday Activities," *Social Problems*, 11 (1961), pp. 225-250.

25. E. Gross and G. Stone, "Embarrassment and the Analysis of Role Requirements," *American Journal of Sociology*, 70 (1964), p. 3.

26. H. Garfinkel, "Conditions of Successful Degradation Ceremonies," *American Journal of Sociology*, 61 (1956), pp. 420-424.

27. Turner, *op. cit.*, p. 384.

28. C. J. Couch, "Collective Behavior: An Examination of Some Stereotypes," *Social Problems*, 15 (Winter, 1968), pp. 310-322.

29. G. Marx reports data showing an inverse relationship between implication in religious activities and support for militant civil rights activities. "Religion: Opiate or Inspiration," *American Sociological Review*, 32 (1967), pp. 64-72.

30. Couch, *op. cit.*, p. 320.

31. Turner, *op. cit.*, p. 395.

32. This seems to be a fundamental principle in H. Garfinkel's discussion of successful degradation ceremonies, *op. cit.*

33. H. S. Becker, "Notes on the Concept of Commitment," *American Journal of Sociology*, 62 (1960), pp. 32-40. Empirical evidence bearing on the consequence of commitments to others is found in R. R. Blake and J. S. Mouton, "Loyalty of Representatives to Ingroup Positions during Intergroup Competition," *Sociometry*, 24 (1961), p. 181.

34. Turner, *op. cit.*, p. 386. This notion dates back as early as LeBon's statement that "An isolated individual knows well enough that alone he cannot set fire to a palace or loot a shop [but making him a part of a crowd] . . . *he is conscious of the power given him by number . . .*" *op. cit.*, p. 38. (Emphasis supplied.) It is interesting to note that on this point, LeBon contradicts his contention that members of a crowd are not conscious of their actions.

35. S. Asch, "Effects of Group Pressure Upon the Modification and Distortion of Judgments," in H. Proshansky and B. Seidenberg, editors, *Basic Studies in Social Psychology*, N.Y.: Holt, Rinehart and Winston, 1966, pp. 309 and 310.

36. It remains an empirical question as to what proportion of participants in a crowd must follow a course of action *in the presence of deflection*, before

compliance is forthcoming from the remaining participants. Casual observations suggest that although some participants may initially express reservations about pursuing a new course of action, these deflections are squelched or ignored as an increasing proportion of participants advocate or pursue the new course of action.

37. H. Blumer, "Reply to Woelfel, Stone and Farberman," *American Journal of Sociology,* 72 (1967), p. 411.
38. Blumer, 1947, *op. cit.,* p. 167.
39. Strauss, *op. cit.,* p. 25.
40. Blumer, *op. cit.,* p. 167.
41. Turner, *op. cit.,* p. 384.

18.

Norma Haan

HYPOTHETICAL AND ACTUAL MORAL REASONING IN A SITUATION OF CIVIL DISOBEDIENCE

Although the number of significant studies recently generated by the cognitive theory of moral development is impressive, almost all this work is based on subjects' reasoning in regard to hypothetical dilemmas, those designed by Kohlberg (1969). A question important to the further development and refinement of the theory needs to be kept in mind: What are the patterns of correspondence between reasoning, deciding, and acting in actual situations of moral conflict and reasoning about hypothetical situations? This question is more than a matter of "good" design or of validating an instrument by

From Norma Haan, "Hypothetical and Actual Moral Reasoning in a Situation of Civil Disobedience," *Journal of Personality and Social Psychology* 32, August 1975, pp. 255-70. Copyright 1975 by the American Psychological Association. Reprinted by permission of the publisher and the author.

The original research was funded by grants to Brewster Smith, Jeanne Block, and Norma Haan from the Rosenberg Foundation of San Francisco and the Foundations' Fund for Research in Psychiatry. The present work was supported by U.S. Public Health Service Grant HD 1650, directed by Paul Mussen.

Requests for reprints should be sent to Norma Haan, Institute of Human Development, University of California, Berkeley, 1203 Edward Chace Tolman Hall, Berkeley, California 94720.

behavioral criteria; it is rather a consideration of the conditions under which people actualize their structural capacities in both thought and action. Most work has assumed that the stage used in hypothetical reasoning is the same as the stages used in situational reasoning and action—or at least that the two are associated—whereas instances of moral courage might be described as cases in which the stages of situational reasoning and action are higher than the stage of hypothetical reasoning, and moral default as cases in which they are lower than the stage of hypothetical reasoning. Moreover, the circumstances that support or diminish the accuracy of equating actual reasoning with action are not known. These issues concern the inter-regulation of cognition and action and are addressed in this report with a variety of information, which includes actual moral reasoning and the action choices of Berkeley students in regard to the sit-in of the Free Speech Movement (FSM) at the campus administration building in 1964.

These issues are also addressed in the work by Turiel and Rothman (1972), which employed an experimental paradigm wherein children were confronted with immediate but relatively mild, contrived moral dilemmas and were asked to make both cognitive and behavioral choices. This procedure and its variants (see Turiel, 1966, 1974) have yielded critical understandings of normative stage development and transition for the conventional moral level. The focus here, however, is not primarily on development, but rather on the implications of intense situational involvement as it affects young adults' regulation of hypothetical and actual moral thinking and action choice. It is expected that systematic discrepancies sometimes occur among the moral levels that people use when they think about what a hypothetical person should do, when they think about what *they* should do, and when they act. Further, it is assumed that these discrepancies will not only be associated with people's moral capacity but also with their more general ability to cope with the complexity, intensity, and content of particular situations.

Since civil disobedience is used in this study as the action criterion, and it is not one that reasonable people can immediately accept as a moral action, more needs to be said about it and activism generally. Although moral protest must always be activist in the sense of intervening in an ongoing course of events, activism is not necessarily a moral behavior. It may be undertaken for nonmoral reasons that are merely personally preferred or capricious. However, as reported (Haan, Smith, & Block, 1968), activism was a statistically frequent choice of Bay Area principled students as compared to conventionally moral students during the 1960's.[1] The previously published findings were based on subjects whose moral reasoning was stage homogeneous (approximately one half of a sample of 900); later study that included all subjects with moral scores sharpened

the contrast.[2] Roughly 70% of a number of different activist groups, but only 46% to 26% of various nonactivist groups, used principled thinking as a major or minor way of deciding hypothetical moral issues. Fishkin, Keniston, and MacKinnon (1973) recently reported a replication of this general finding in a study of activism arising from the bombing of Cambodia.

Nevertheless, the nature of student activism during the 1960s was group protest, and not all persons are disposed to join or to act in groups. In fact, further examination of the original data (Haan & Block, Note 2) indicated that morally conventional activists differed from conventional nonactivists in seeing themselves as impulsive, socially skillful, and indulged by their parents. Both were group affiliative, but the nonactivists joined social rather than political groups. Principled nonactivists differed from principled activists regarding themselves as more tender, reserved and sensitive, and in comparison they were not group affiliative.

These findings indicated that nonmoral personal predispositions affect and thereby confound the criterion of activism as moral action. At the same time common social logic dictates that the principled person should protest in a situation of clear violation of his principles if he is to maintain self-consistency (integrity); however, group action is not required. Moreover, in the judgment of citizens, legal systems, and wise men, ultimate moral responsibility rests with the individual.

Nevertheless, the criterion of activism, and here the civil disobedience of the Free Speech Movement, had methodological and substantive advantages: the FSM crisis was local particular, and vivid in its impact on a large number of people. The act was the climax of a campus situation that had endured forty months in great complexity and heat (after new campus regulations were announced that would sharply restrict political activity), and almost all those arrested must have expected that they would be. Consequently, it can be expected that most students were informed and deliberate in their choice. Few were able to be nonpartisan as the situation became one of "no exit." Moreover, there was considerable campus consensus about the rightness of the act. Campus polls (Lyons, 1965) showed that about 70% of the students became pro-FSM, and in the end the University of California Academic Senate voted 824 to 115 to support a series of resolutions that were widely regarded as affirming the arguments of the Free Speech Movement. Although a majority consensus neither decides the rightness of an act nor the moral level of any individual's action, all matters considered and for the purposes of this empirical study of group trends, it appeared reasonable to work with the assumption that in general few doubted that a distinctively moral action of objective and personal expense had been taken, whether they agreed on its value or not. The polarization of this issue meant that those who did not sit in had probably also examined the moral grounds of their positions. The task here is to understand how students of various persuasions structured their moral thinking and their action decisions as these relate to their hypothetical thinking, which is taken as the baseline.

Hypotheses and questions

Features of the situation

The public debate of the student leaders, faculty, and administrators from September to December was often couched in morally principled terms; however, the majority (68%) of the students were not morally principled. Thus the speakers' and listeners' structuring of the situation did not often match. This is a naturalistic instance of disequilibrium, the vehicle of development conceptualized and investigated by Langer (1969) for cognitive progress and by Turiel (1969) for moral progress. It was expected, then, that gains from hypothetical to actual moral reasoning might occur, irrespective of the students' ideological position.

Second, since the moral theory is concerned with the evolution of increasingly differentiated structures, little attention has been given to the possible effects of ideological disagreement on the development of moral forms (see Alker & Poppen, 1973; Keasey, 1973, for exceptions). It seems possible, however, that an action taken for reasons of ideological stance could subsequently stimulate more adequate forms of moral justification. This would be most likely if the person is in developmental flux and/or in an inescapable situation where no choice is in essence a choice, since the conflict might be more adequately resolved by the emergence of more differentiated moral forms. On this count, too, gain might be generally expected, especially among those students who had taken a clear position.

Finally, the situational stress needs to be considered. Stress is commonly expected to result in decrement in function; however, moral action, even when personally expensive, can also represent a move to greater clarity and calm. Thus stress could work to produce either decrements or increments in the students' moral levels.

Developmental status of the subjects as young adults

Given the situational necessity of moral self-examination, it was expected that students who reasoned at the same stage for the hypothetical and FSM situations would be those who had stably consummated their moral development. Presumably, two different states could account for such stability: (a) a defensive closedness to further disequilibrium and termination at a lower stage or (b) the capacity to integrate moral decision and action so as to structure the authority-affronting situation in principled terms.

Some students could be expected to be in developmental flux. Kohlberg and Kramer (1969) report that progress continued until the late twenties with a longitudinal sample, and Haan (1974) found like changes in a follow-up study of Peace Corps Volunteers. The disquieting situational features should then lead the developmentally ready students to use higher stage forms in reasoning about the FSM, but according to the theory this readiness should be prefigured in their hypothetical reasoning by some minor use of higher stage forms.

The use of a lower stage to structure the FSM situation is not an instance of regression, since hypothetical reasoning, as an indicant of capacity, is maintained. In this context, loss is likely to be an encapsulated structural disorganization related to personal reactions that results in manifest dysfunctioning specific to this real-life, stressful situation. Blatt (1970) reports that black adolescents use lower stages in reasoning about conflicts involving society than they do in thinking about interpersonal relations, and Kohlberg, Scharf, and Hickey (1973) report that lower stages are used by prisoners when they reason about prisons. Thus the loss of phenomenon probably cannot be understood solely in moral terms. The stressed person may remain latently at his achieved moral stage and may use it again in less complex, trying situations. Presumably, unresolved moral stress would be evidenced by a failure to complement one's convictions with action or by continuing indecision.

Method

Subjects

The present sample was drawn from a larger one of 394 Berkeley undergraduates who were enrolled during the FSM crisis and who participated several months later in a study of student activism. Various reports of analyses that included additional subjects from San Francisco State University and the Peace Corps have been made (for the most general descriptions see Block, Haan, & Smith, 1969; Haan et al., 1968; Smith, Haan, & Block, 1970). The sub-sample of 310 Berkeley students chosen here met several criteria: Their answers to the FSM questions were in sufficient detail to be scored, and either the same score was given to each subject by two judges working independently ($n=290$) or both judges' designations resulted in a clear classification of the subject as having maintained parity, gained, or lost in relationship to his hypothetical reasoning ($n=20$). Subjects were contacted from the following groups: the FSM arrestees, the California Conservatives for Political Action (an activist, Ayn Rand group), Young Democrats, Young Republicans, and a cross-sample randomly drawn from the registration files (ns for the various groups can be seen in Table 2). Although personal contact was made with the leaders of each group— except for the randomly drawn sample— letters were written to almost all potential subjects, and data collection forms were sent and returned in the mail. As a result,

TABLE 1

Examples of Scoring Guides for Moral Reasoning about the Free Speech Movement (FSM) Sit-In: Pro and Con Positions

Pro	Con
Stage 2	
Focuses on the students' needs, denies sit-in harmed the University; says it worked; needs to retaliate against manipulative authorities.	Sit-in was a tool that didn't make sense since power lay with the authorities.
Stage 3	
Sit-in was both right and wrong, but the motives were good; necessary because authorities were unfeeling about needs.	Other, more peaceful means could have been used; authorities knew students' best interests and would have responded if they were approached reasonably.
Stage 4	
Sit-in was instrumental to the pursuit of social values and goals which form a coherent unit; new authorities were needed.	FSM's violation of rules made the sit-in wrong; the system provides orderly means for redress that should not be disrupted.
Stage 5	
Authorities broke social contracts with the students, making it mandatory that the students sit in as a dialogue for establishing new understandings.	Concern that FSM didn't use legitimate means to attain objectives; students could leave; their enrollment was an agreement to live by the University's rules.
Stage 6	
Focuses on the objective values of civil rights; differentiates moral and legal obligations to justify this civil disobedience.	Trust is always conditional even in an ideal society; an individual authority revoked agreements, so that disobedience to the institution was neither logical nor ideal.

response rate was not high (roughly 50%), so neither Berkeley students nor particular subsamples are well represented.

Data

Data included five of the moral interview stories designed by Kohlberg (1969), the FSM moral questions, biographical information, reports of political-social beliefs of self and family, Q-sorted descriptions of self and ideal self, and the Child Rearing Practices Report,[3] a retrospective Q-sorted description of mothers' and fathers' techniques. Five questions were asked about the Free Speech Movement (e.g., "Do you think it was right or wrong for the students to sit in? Why or why not?" "Suppose an authority doesn't keep

his agreement; what then is the extent and nature of one's own obligation? Explain your position.").

A condensed scoring guide defining the pro and con ideological positions for each stage is shown in Table 1. Reliability of scoring, based on the weighted modal stage scores of two judges, was .82 for the hypothetical stories and .72 for the FSM questions. The protocols were masked for sample membership. To increase the number of subjects, those who used mixed stages of moral reasoning were classified according to their major, predominant stage and grouped with those whose reasoning was more stage homogeneous. Subjects who used the same stage of reasoning for the hypothetical and FSM situations will be called the equal group;

those who used higher stages for the Free Speech Movement, the gain group; and those who used lower stages for the Movement, the loss group.

Results

Sex differences

Sex differences in moral change patterns were analyzed within each stage of hypothetical reasoning and for all stages combined. Although more women gained (45%) compared to men (36%), none of the differences were significant; consequently, most subsequent analyses were done with men and women combined.

Moral change groups' variations in use of minor stages

The extent of variation in stage use across the five hypothetical stories was calculated for each moral change group

TABLE 2
Distribution of Moral Change Patterns by Contact Sample and Moral Stages (Hypothetical Reasoning)

Stage (Hypothetical)	Loss		Equal		Gain		Total	% Stage (Hypothetical) within subsample
	n	%	n	%	n	%	n	
Total Sample								
2	0	0	5	13	33	**87**	38	12
3	2	3	26	28	63	**69**	91	29
4	27	29	43	46	24	26	94	30
5	30	**43**	26	38	13	19	69	22
6	(10)	(55)	(8)	(45)	—	—	(18)	6
Total[a, b]	59	20	100	34	133	**46**	292	100
FSM arrestees								
2	0	0	3	18	14	**82**	17	21
3	2	8	6	23	18	**69**	26	32
4	3	25	0	0	9	**75**	12	15
5	**8**	31	8	31	10	38	26	32
6	(4)	(33)	(8)	**(66)**	—	—	(12)	—
Total[b]	13	16	17	21	51	**63**	81	100
Cross-sample								
2	0	0	2	14	12	**86**	14	9
3	0	0	17	32	37	**68**	54	36
4	17	29	29	**50**	12	21	58	38
5	14	**56**	9	36	2	8	25	17
6	(4)	**(100)**	(0)	(0)	—	—	(4)	—
Total[b]	31	21	57	38	63	**42**	151	100
Conservatives/Republicans								
2	0	0	0	0	5	**100**	5	11
3	0	0	2	29	5	**71**	7	16
4	5	25	13	**45**	2	10	20	44
5	5	38	7	**54**	1	8	13	29
6	(1)	(100)	(0)	(0)	—	—	(1)	—
Total[b]	10	22	22	**49**	13	29	45	100

Note: Numbers in boldface represent the highest values obtained.
[a] Democrats (n=16) are included in these calculations.
[b] Stage 6 users are excluded from all summary calculations.

considered as an entity. Although the assigned stage accounted for approximately 45% of the reasoning for the entire sample, the gain subjects did use a greater proportion of higher stage reasoning than the other two (a total of 43% compared to the equal group's 24% and the loss group's 33%). Consequently, higher stage FSM reasoning for the gain group may reflect a readiness to develop, prefigured in their hypothetical thought and then energized by the crucial nature of the situation. Note, however, that the reverse was not true for the loss group, which actually used *more* higher stage as well as less lower stage thinking than the equal group (lower stage thinking was 24% for the loss group, 28% for the equal, and 14% for the gain group). Consequently, the FSM reasoning of the loss subjects appears to be a disjunctive response to the situation, not predictable from their hypothetical thinking. The results for the gain subjects accord with the theory, whereas those for the loss subjects do not.

General patterns of moral change by
stages of hypothetical reasoning

More students (46%) reasoned about the FSM situation in higher stage terms than maintained parity (34%) or used lower stage forms (20%), as can be seen in Table 2. This difference significantly departs from a chance split ($\chi^2 = 40.97$, $p \leq .01$). The predominance of the gain pattern is consistent with assumptions discussed earlier that certain aspects of the situation and the participants should generally stimulate moral progress.

Consideration of the change patterns for each stage shown in Table 2 indicates that (a) no student used Stage 1 for structuring the FSM situation, which is not unexpected for a university population; (b) gain

was the predominant trend for those who used Stages 2 and 3. However, some users of Stages 2 and 3 may have been in flux and confused and thereby misidentified by the standard scoring system, but may then have resolved their confusions to reveal their latent capacity in the FSM questions (see Haan, 1971; Haan, Stroud, & Holstein, 1973; and Turiel, 1974, for empirical examinations of young adults who are probably transitional between the conventional and principled levels and who temporarily use relativistic thinking that has superficial similarity to Stage 2 thinking; similar phenomena may occur with Stage 3); (c) the majority of Stage 4 users maintained equality between their hypothetical and actual reasoning; and (d) students representing both principled stages split fairly evenly between the equality and loss patterns.

Although the more specific meanings of these results are yet to be explicated, they do suggest that students of different moral stages structured this authority-defying situation in divergent ways. The results could be thought to represent a regression toward the mean, but the main findings of moral stage research with regard to the developmental status of young adults, as well as other more controlled analyses to be reported in this article, make this statistical explanation untenable.

Patterns of moral changes by
stages of hypothetical reasoning
within contact samples

The moral change patterns for the four main groups are also shown in Table 2. (15 Democrats are not included; many of them were civilly disobedient and thus became members of the FSM sample.) The differences in moral change patterns were significant when the FSM arrestees were compared with the cross-sample, $\chi^2(2) = 9.63$, $p \leq .10$, and with the Conservatives/Republicans, $\chi^2(2) = 12.91$, $p \leq .05$, but the comparison between the cross-sample and Conservatives/Republicans was not.

Attention to the individual stages shows that gain was the predominant trend for FSM arrestees of all stages, while only Stage 2 and [. . .] improved their reasoning, an indication that a pro ideology in itself does not explain the gain pattern.

Turning to Stage 4, as a more differentiated construction of authority's moral relationships to followers, we find highly significant differences. The most salient trend is that 67% of the con Stage 4 users were stable, unlike their ideological companions at Stage 3. An anti-FSM attitude could be well supported by Stage 4 thinking in ideological alliance with the university authorities. However, a sizable proportion (46%) of the neutral Stage 4 users lost. A main concern of Stage 4 reasoning is the formal regulation and order of society. Since this situation was neither ordered nor regulated, apolitical Stage 4 users may not have known where to turn. At the same time their sophisticated forms would have kept them concerned with the problem of civil disobedience.

It is congruent with the special nature of conventional moral structures that ideological position relates to the change patterns, since conventional formulations depend heavily on external guidance. For the Stage 3 individual the ultimate locus of his responsibility is his loyalty to others; for the Stage 4 the locus is his commitment to extant social systems. This is not to say that principled persons are disloyal or uncommitted to systems; rather, the hierarchical organization of principled reasoning is more differentiated, and moral responsibility lies in the moral principles of the self.

Personal-social constructions of self and parents

Analyses of the personal-social data permit further evaluation of the likelihood that the change patterns can be attributed to three different phenomena—developmental readiness, developmental stabilization, and the defensive compartmentalization of the self. Analyses of variance were done following adjustments to remove the effects of two covariates: the moral stage of hypothetical reasoning and the degree of political conservatism-radicalism. The stages of hypothetical reasoning were controlled because the subsamples had varying distributions as well as unequal change patterns. Political stance was controlled so that the results would not simply reflect relationships between personality and politics. Thus the intent was to consider the personal-social conditions of movement in the most general sense. It should be noted that the young people's task of describing themselves and their parents by means of Q sorts produces personal constructions that do not necessarily or accurately represent their social realities. (Block et al., 1969, reported modest correlations of .37 and .40 between young people's descriptions of their parents and their parents' own self-descriptions.) All of these measures, like other self-reports (or any other behavior for that matter, as discussed in Haan, 1965), are determined by the individual's immediate motivations and his ego strategies of task engagement and self-disclosure. Q sorting is a process that involves the construction of social formulations, just as moral reasoning involves the construction of prescriptive, ideal formulations.

Equivalence compared with change (gain or loss). No significant demo-

TABLE 3
Personal-Social Differences Between Equal and Change Groups

	Male equal group higher (n = 43)	All male changers higher (n = 100)[a]	Female equal group higher (n = 44)	All female changers higher (n = 78)[a]
Parental agreement	Agree with mother** and father** about student demonstrations			
Source of influence			Personal influence: mother** Political influence: teachers*** Ethical influence: mother*	Personal influence: older friends*
Self	Idealistic*	Conventional** Calm** Foresightful* Considerate** Tolerant* Sensitive*	Considerate*** Fair, just**	Talkative*
Ideal	Courageous** Guilty*	Self-confident*** Responsive* Dominating** Masculine*	Generous** Reserved** Fair, just* Orderly*	Independent** Self-confident** Dominating*
Mother	Let me know she was angry with me** Encouraged me to do my best*	Expected gratitude from me*** Expected me to control my feelings*** Thought children should be seen, not heard** Helped me when I was teased* Thought bad things could happen to me*	Children should be seen, not heard* Believed in early toilet training* Taught me not to cry at an early age* Enjoyed seeing me eat* Children shouldn't play without supervision*	Found it difficult to punish me** Great deal of conflict between us** Let me make my own decisions* Gave me family duties*
Father	Let me take chances, try new things*** Believed competitive games were good*** Withheld sexual information until I could understand** Let me know when he was angry* Children shouldn't keep secrets*	Tended to spoil me**** Didn't want me to play rough games*** Shared warm, intimate times with me*** Too wrapped up in his children** Worried about my health** Gave me comfort when I was upset* Kept me away from different values*	Liked time for himself*** Always knew where I was*** Important for me to play outdoors** Placed my mother's wishes ahead of my own* Punishment would find me if I were bad* Kept me away from different values*	Shared warm, intimate times with me*** Was sorry to see me grow*** Threat punishment more than giving it** Greatest satisfactions from children* Let me make my own decisions* Bad things could happen to me* Had family duties to perform*

[a] Gain and loss groups combined.
  * $p < .10$.
 ** $p < .05$.
 *** $p < .01$.
 **** $p < .001$.

graphic differences were found between the equal and change groups of either sex. Both equal groups report greater political-social compatibility with their parents: The men agreed with them about student demonstrations (whether pro or con), and the women attributed personal and ethical influence to their mothers as well as political influence to their teachers (see Table 3). The few self and ideal qualities that differentiate the groups suggest that equals of both sexes generally saw themselves as relatively judicious and autonomous and less reactive to interpersonal situations than the change groups. A variation of this theme distinguished their contrasting constructions of their parents. Both equal groups described their parents' child-rearing position and attitudes as not only clear and well defined but also as relatively detached. In contrast, both change groups saw their parents as being emotionally entangled with them—warm and intimate but intrusive and ambivalently disciplinary. Thus the subjects' constructions of self and parents are consistent both with the equal group's maintenance of moral stability at all stages and with the changers' situational reactivity and consequent readiness to shift their forms of their reasoning and choice of action.

Gain and loss groups compared. The members of the male gain group, compared to the loss group, saw themselves as interpersonally critical and unforgiving as well as guilty and disjointed. They rejected, even on an ideal basis, interpersonal warmth and commitment and wanted to be more *individualistic* and *foresightful.* They described their parental relationships as containing some conflict. Difficulties with their mothers centered on social-political issues, whereas their paternal relations lacked warmth and were defined by anger and contentiousness in regard to discipline and control. Men in the loss group, on the other hand, described themselves most positively, particularly in the interpersonal realm. Their ideal-self characteristics reiterate this regard but also suggest a degree of social vulnerability: *needs approval, talkative, reserved, competitive,* and *masculine.* They described their parents, particularly their fathers, as unusually protective, involved, and demonstrably loving, perhaps even cloying.

Altogether, then, the male students' personal-social constructions clearly contrast: The gain group took an adversary role with their parents ˙and the world, particularly in regard to matters of authority and intellectual difference, whereas the loss group saw themselves in a remarkably open, even exposed, interpersonal position, regarding themselves and their parents as particularly intimate, considerate, and loving. The gain group's constructions are consistent with their developmental readiness; they appear ready to question authority and conventional regulation (the level of their anger is not absolutely great; the result is due more to the loss group's low scores). The loss group's constructions appear not to be anticipated by the moral theory. If anything, their personal description seems compatible with Stage 3 morality, but this effect was controlled, and there were only two Stage 3 subjects in the loss group. An interpretation based on an interaction of ego capacity and stress suggests that their loss may have resulted from a disrupted expectancy that the world of authority was in loco parentis and as responsive to their openhanded ingratiation as they felt their parents to be. During the crisis, suppositions of harmony with authority became patently unsupportable, if for no other reason than the necessity of choosing which authority to follow.

Turning now to the results for the women, we can see that those who gained saw themselves as open, interpersonally reactive, sensitive personalities. This theme was repeated in their ideal-self descriptions along with several other virtues that seem necessary self-views for wishing oneself to be moral: *empathic, idealistic, genuine, fair,* and *just.* They described their mothers as supportive and willing to consider their preferences, although they believed their fathers often exerted more disciplinary force. Neither parent was seen as having urged their daughters to be competitive. The loss group members saw themselves as controlled and proud, and they idealized self-denial. Their mothers were more educated and viewed as ethically influential, disciplining, and powerful. Both parents urged their daughters to compete.

Unlike the men's, the women's gains are associated with a positive view of their parents. Thus the possibility presents itself that the women's gains were energized by the situational challenge rather than by the opportunity to resolve a developmentally transitional need to criticize authority, as appeared to be the case with the men. The women's loss, associated as it was with a self-denying, controlled view of self and a description of their mothers as influential, authoritative, and prodding, seems to suggest that their daughters may not have been able to conceive of themselves as having either individual responsibility or the need to make comprehensive moral decisions in an authority-defying situation.

Altogether then, gain for both men and women seems to be based on a latent but evocable capacity consistent with the theory's view of developmental readiness in this age group. However, the use of less mature forms in reasoning about the Free Speech Movement represents a shift that is not expected by the theory. Loss in men was related to an unrealistic denial of social complexities and they had no need to accommodate. Since the arrested Stage 6 users structured the situation as one of individual moral responsibility, it was consistent with their ideology and their decision to become civilly disobedient, so that they, too, maintained equality.

In effect, these equal subjects of different stages integrated their actual and hypothetical reasoning and their action choices as they saw the situation through the filter of their various ideological positions. Turiel and Rothman (1972) had suggested that the sufficiency of structural organization at higher stages should make for greater integration of reasoning with action. In fact, there is some evidence to support this supposition with the pro-FSM subjects if we assume that such a position led logically to civil disobedience. Among the pro-FSM students 54% of the principled ones sat in, whereas 60% of the nonprincipled did not (excluding the probably misidentified Stage 2 users: $\chi^2 = 2.89$, $p \leq .10$). However, the Turiel and Rothman study assumed all other nonmoral factors to be equal. In the FSM situation personal-social constructions and ideology appeared to function defensively to select information and action, with the consequence that the integration of action and thought occurred at lower stages as well.

Loss typified pro-FSM students who did not sit in, particularly Stage 5 and the few Stage 6 users, as well as the neutral Stage 4 users. The loss group was generally characterized by distinctive personal-social constructions, suggesting they had particular difficulties and hesitancies in dealing with authority conflict and disobedience. I suggest they were involved in dilemmas that were more affective and social than moral, with the result that they became inconsistent and disorganized in their moral thinking about the Free Speech Movement.

The thrust of these analyses is that there are systematic differences—apparently attributable to nonmoral characteristics of the participants—between giving a story character fictitious moral advice and formulating and acting on advice for oneself. The hypothetical stage provided a baseline for understanding the presented form of FSM reasoning when the organization of action choice, the nonmoral aspects of ideology, and personal-social constructions were taken into account. It may eventually turn out that there are structural elements embedded in ideological and personality attributes that reciprocally interact with moral structures to achieve more comprehensive equilibrations than we are now able to see. However, people are not always equilibrated, particularly young adults and persons in the midst of social upheavals. Moreover, equilibration can be "artificial" and achieved at the cost of factual and logical distortion and the diminution of the self. Whatever the case, the present results make it clear that in nonhypothetical circumstances moral structures are more often qualified—attenuated or elaborated—than not.

It is not the main job of moral theory to account for nonmoral conditions that may be merely associated with various stages; there is ample work yet to be done in explicating the taxonomy of normative stage progression and transition. When nonmoral conditions alter moral constructions by selecting and filtering informational input, thereby affecting accommodation, the question becomes one of understanding function and not merely one of cataloging deviance. The FSM situation was most intense, but then, actual moral dilemmas of consequence often are. If function is so readily disturbed, moral theory, more than cognitive theory, will have to take this aspect of its subject matter into account.

Notes

1. The term *principles* refers to Stages 5 and 6 as they are described in the Kohlberg (1969) system; conventional refers to Stages 3 and 4.
2. Haan, N., & Block, J. H. *Further examination of the relationship between activism and morality.* Unpublished manuscript, 1969. (Available from Norma Haan, Institute of Human Development, University of California, Berkeley, 1203 Edward Chace Tolman Hall, Berkeley, California 94720.)
3. Block, J. H. *The child-rearing practices report.* Institute of Human Development, University of California, Berkeley, 1965. (Mimeo)

19.

Dennis Brissett

COLLECTIVE BEHAVIOR: THE SENSE OF A RUBRIC[1]

There exists among contemporary sociologists a general hesitancy to adopt the term "collective behavior" as a label for a distinct type of social action. Even those authors writing specifically on subjects traditionally labeled "collective behavior"[2] invariably attempt to apologize for their use of the term. The authors of two such treatises,[3] unable to justify its use, therefore adopt other terms. This uneasiness with the term "collective behavior" seems to warrant critical examination to locate its conditions. On this basis, the uneasiness can perhaps be dispelled, or at least defended.

It is commonplace to observe that each investigator of social life approaches that life from a particular frame of reference. This perspective is, for the most part, circumscribed by the vocabulary with which he chooses to speak about that world. An extremely important consequence of such a vocabulary is the manner in which the terminology clusters certain behaviors together—how, in other words, social action is typed. Such classification is basic to inquiry and, in effect, explicitly recognizes that not all behavior is of the same kind and, further, that theory formulated to explain one kind of behavior will not be applicable to another, and that therefore each kind must be studied separately.

One of the problems with vocabularies is, however, that they tend to persist over

From Dennis Brissett, "Collective Behavior: The Sense of a Rubric," *American Journal of Sociology* 74, June 1968, pp. 70-78. Reprinted by permission of the publisher, the University of Chicago Press.

time. Therefore, classificatory schemes formulated on the basis of earlier perspectives in sociology still have, in some cases, currency in present-day thinking. One such instance is that typology which has as one of its basic classes "collective behavior." I will attempt to show in this paper the irrelevance of such a typology when one is operating out of an increasingly significant school of thought in contemporary social psychology.[4] It is hoped that the consequent uselessness of the rubric "collective behavior" will become apparent in the process of this analysis.[5]

The traditional paradigm

The classificatory scheme to be examined here seems to rest upon two crucial distinctions formulated by early sociologists: one had the consequence of defining the boundaries of the discipline; the second, the function of distinguishing, within the subject matter of sociology itself, two major kinds of behavior. The first of these distinctions was that concerning "individual behavior" and "group behavior." By making these two forms of action at least analytically distinct from one another, sociologists were able to claim that the latter was worthy of study in its own right. In group life, unique patterns, unique regularities of action were said to be discernible. In fact, Émile Durkheim[6] went so far as to declare that properties of groups were the only true "social facts" and, therefore, the only proper subject matter for sociology. Indeed, it was believed that a study of group life would yield a more complete understanding of human behavior than would a simple preoccupation with individual action. The human being was seen, then, in the sociological perspective, as a member of various groups and not, as some would have it, a spontaneous, autonomous individual.

The second basic distinction developed by the early sociologists involved a contrast between conscious, purposeful, intentional, sometimes rational behavior for which persons could be held responsible and behavior which was seemingly unintentional, without purpose, and for which persons could not be held responsible.[7] Actually, this distinction, like so many in the social sciences, had a very pronounced one-sided character. Only the former element was explicitly delineated. The latter merely "grew" residually. It was a distinction that was probably best articulated by George Herbert Mead[8] in his discussion of the social self. Here Mead explicitly distinguished between behavior that is circumscribed by the expectations of others (the "me") and behavior that is spontaneous, unpredictable, and not so circumscribed (the "I"). The reflective, purposeful, intentional[9] "me" is construed as the social dimension of the self. It is that element of the self that is built upon the expectations and reactions of others. Mead, it appears, attempted to extend this social dimension as an explanation for all behavior but, reaching an analytical impasse, invoked the spontaneous, uncontrollable "I" to account for behaviors not adequately accounted for by the "me."[10] This, it seems, was the tack generally taken by sociologists in the early twentieth century. A social explanation was sought and, if found, was elaborated to its limits. What then could not be explained by way of the social was ascribed to the psychological and biological realm. It was then quite tautologically asserted that statements of regularities made about the one realm of behavior (the social) could not be applied to the others (the biological and psychological) and vice versa. This distinction between social behavior and other kinds of behavior, as articulated by Mead and elaborated by the more culturally oriented sociologists, seems basically one of distinguishing between normative and non-normative kinds of behavior. The distinction is premised on an idea of a decision-making, socially motivated type of man versus an individual seemingly driven by either psychological, biological, or unknown forces.[11] To be normative, in this context, is not necessarily to be conforming to specific norms but, rather, to be oriented toward the expectations of others.

These two distinctions together form the basis for the following paradigm:

	NORMATIVE	NON-NORMATIVE
Individual	Normal	Abnormal
Group	Cultural	Collective

The question arises now as to whether this particular way of classifying human behavior is indeed of any relevance to the dramaturgical model of present-day social psychology.

To begin with, in the current universe of discourse of the dramaturgical social psychologist, the differentiation between individual behavior and group behavior does not have currency as a working distinction. Rather, the principal concern is with the social relationship, the actor and his other(s). The traditional idea of a group, although partially incorporated into the conceptualization of a social relationship, is not of direct relevance. An attempt is seemingly being made to break down the dualism between the individual and the group in much the same manner that

Gabriel Tarde[12] once did. The emphasis of dramaturgical social psychology, particularly in the writings of Erving Goffman,[13] is placed on interaction, not on the characteristics (be these individual or group) of the actors. The seeming historical ignorance of equating "group behavior" with "social behavior" is cast out. The methods of dramaturgical social psychology are not concerned with contrasting the psychological individual with the sociological group. The study of groups, both large and small, is in fact usually apportioned to the area of social organization. The behavior of persons is itself looked upon as a social production, as something that does not and cannot exist outside of that person's encounters with others. Therefore, the conceptualization of man versus the group and the accompanying idea of differing propositions applying to one but not the other, although a valid manner of approaching human behavior, is not considered relevant by the dramaturgical social psychologists.

The second distinction, that of the normative and non-normative, is also a notion that does not have a great deal of currency at the present time. If, as John Dewey[14] said, man "is an active being and that is all there is to be said on that score," then speculation as to the normative conditions antecedent to behavior becomes unnecessary. Dewey's statement, if logically extended, prods social psychologists to examine the consequences of behavior and not to spend time speculating as to the determinants of behavior, whether these determinants be cast in a biological, psychological, or sociological vocabulary. The normative-non-normative distinction, therefore, pales in importance. The image of a conscious, expectation-oriented man is incongruous with the notion that people simply act, and, during and after action, formulate reasons for their activity.

In this light, the matter of people's motivation changes from a context of rationalism to one of rationalizing. Motives are divorced from their traditional aura of causation. The alleged "real" reasons why people are said to act become of little relevance,[15] at least with reference to explaining the behavior of the people to whom they are ascribed. However, the reasons the actors and others ascribe to their activity become of prominent importance in terms of the career of the ongoing interaction. In other words, the avowals and imputations of motives are seen as having definite consequences for the maintenance or non-maintenance of social relationships. In this perspective, motives are seen as words that either justify a certain activity or at least enable the actor or others to feel that they understand the activity.[16] As such, they are of extreme importance in the handling or mishandling of one's identity. If identity is understood to mean the person as socially situated,[17] the relation of it to motives becomes particularly clear. For instance, Ernest Becker's[18] depiction of clinical depression illustrates that significant deviant identities are often built simply on one's avowal of certain motives, these being, in the case of depression, a "vocabulary of worthlessness." In the more general case, the identity of deviant seems most readily given to persons whose behavior is liable to the ascription of certain kinds of motives.[19] Sometimes, in fact, the inability on the part of the individual to articulate an acceptable motive for his behavior seems to lead to his being placed in the ominous identity of being mentally ill.[20] The point of all this can perhaps best be summarized by paraphrasing a very old truism of sociology: Motives believed to be true are true only in their consequences.

Thus, it no longer seems helpful to think of one type of behavior as a product of decisions made on the basis of socially current expectations and being, therefore, socially motivated, and another as the consequence of other than normative decisions. This issue is no longer at stake; the distinction, in a manner of speaking, does not exist for the dramaturgical social psychologist.[21]

Therefore, social psychology, as currently practiced by the dramaturgists, discards both distinctions upon which the rubric "collective behavior" is based. In so doing, it seems to render nil the utility of such a term in its vocabulary. However, this is not to declare that the use of the term "collective behavior" and its concomitant conceptualization entails an invalid approach to social behavior. Rather, it is simply to admit that working within the rubric obscures certain considerations that seem particularly relevant to the questions of present-day social psychology. Moreover, this is not to minimize the contributions of those who have labored in the areas of behavior traditionally circumscribed by the rubric "collective behavior." In fact, social psychologists would do well to pay particular attention to the character of the behaviors that have been isolated and studied by those interested in the traditional problem of collective behavior, since a number of important dimensions of human activity have been made prominent.[22] Indeed, it might be said that the dramaturgical model of human behavior has incorporated into its perspective many images of human activity unearthed in the study of crowds, masses, audiences, and the like. It is the contributions of the collective behaviorists to which we now turn our attention, first in terms of their specific relation to dramaturgical sociology, and second with reference to their general importance to sociology as a whole.

Contributions of the collective behavior tradition

It seems, initially, that the dramaturgical model has borrowed from the tradition of collective behavior certain defining elements of its subject matter. Historically, the majority of sociologists have tended to study the static, orderly, enduring forms of human activity and have thereby evolved an explanation of human behavior that is couched in such a context. However, those who have been interested in collective behavior have brought to attention the intermittent, ephemeral, and uncertain character of much that men do. They have pointed to the short-lived panic, the transitory mob, the volatile crowd. In so doing, they have been drawn to those behaviors that fall outside the "structure," the pattern of societal activity. In the process of their concern, they have evolved explanations of behavior that minimize the influence of the social structure. As a consequence, their thinking has been directed to the immediate situation in which "collective behavior" occurs. The concrete physical setting is examined with reference to its implications for human behavior. Furthermore, what occurs in the situation is seen as having consequences for the career of the interaction and is not said to be determined by contingencies removed from the situation.[23] Consequently, the study of behavior careers is given prominence, whether these careers be in the context of an acting crowd, a panic, or the entire process of collective behaving.[24]

This astructural concern with the immediate and the transitory has led the collective behaviorists to isolate forms of interaction that are based on other than cultural[25] kinds of communication, and also to appreciate the importance of emotion in man's behavior. Such concepts as collective excitement, circular reaction, social contagion, incitation, suggestibility, and others, have been advanced to explicitly recognize the acultural and, at the same time, emotional dimension of interaction. In like manner, the interpersonal relation becomes of extreme salience. In the relatively acultural realm of collective behavior, the personal character of much that men do becomes of great importance. The deterministic character of structural relations recedes in influence.

These elements characterizing the study of collective behavior: (1) a concern for the transitory and concrete aspects of social relations, (2) an explicit recognition of "interactional careers," (3) the acultural position, (4) the emphasis on emotion, and (5) the concern with interpersonal relations, seem also to characterize the dramaturgical model of social psychology. For instance, the insistence that social psychologists can study profitably the "situational" and leave well alone the "merely situated"[26] forms of human behavior indicates their concern for the immediate and sometimes transitory situation. That the activity of manipulating props, equipment, and so forth, serves to define situations illustrates the extreme importance of the physical setting. It is, however, in the relatively acultural emphasis on careers in interpersonal relations that the dramaturgical model exhibits its closest affinity to the perspective employed in the study of collective behavior. The dramaturgists define their field of inquiry not in terms of the traditional preoccupation with cultural behavior but in terms of the more appropriate and inclusive notion of meaningful behavior.[27] In so doing, they reject the rhetoric of cultural determinism inherent in culturology. In the dramaturgical sense, to be symbolic is not to be cultural, but to be meaningful. Inasmuch as meaning arises in the responses made to phenomena, their interest is confined to the consequences and not the antecedents of behavior. In their involvement with the consequences, they seem to dwell most on the interpersonal kind of relation.[28] Interpersonal relations become the ascribed locus of most human activity. The development and maintenance of a self is examined, for the most part, in the matrix of a person's interpersonal encounters. Identities established in interpersonal relations are construed, moreover, as having specifiable careers.[29] The relevant episodes and turning points in these careers are described in a context of adult as well as childhood socialization.[30] The element of emotion, affect, becomes again important, as the career of the interpersonal identity seems qualified most readily by mood.[31]

Besides this close affiliation to the dramaturgical model, the study of collective behavior has made numerous contributions to the broader field of sociology. First of all, and most generally, the investigation into collective behavior has led to a re-evaluation of the notion of social cohesion. In the characterization of the differing types of human association—the crowd, the public, and the audience—the nature of the social bond is found to differ widely. The manner in which people are held together—how they behave or act in concert—seems, on the basis of this work, decidedly to involve a multiplicity of elements.

On a large scale also, the nature of collective behavior is such that a preoccupation with social change, with emergent forms of behavior, and with the creative has become imminent. This concern with the "new" forms of social life was, until quite recently, almost entirely in the province of collective behavior.

Another area in which the study of collective behavior has conducted inquiry of central importance to general sociology is that of social disorganization. In their involvement with the socially undesirable—the supposedly unconscious in man—and the unconventional, the collective behaviorists have directed a great deal of attention to the prevalence and relevance of values in human behavior. Although a direct analysis of values themselves has not been conducted, the origins and consequences of such have been richly investigated. A perusal of the literature on collective behavior would indeed seem mandatory for anyone about to embark on a thoroughgoing analysis of values.

Closely related to its preoccupation with values, the study of collective behavior seems to have reached the point where a re-examination of what is involved in the notion of goal direction is called for. For instance, many forms of collective behavior are said not to be goal directed. In fact, Turner and Killian,[32] at one point, speak of collective behavior as that which is not directed toward explicit goals. The "expressive crowd," for example, is often held to exist for itself, since no goal outside itself is recognized. However, the objection can be raised that doing something merely for the sake of doing it is most assuredly a goal. If such is admitted, however, the utility of the concept—goal—is appreciably diminished. In any case, this and other such questions raised by the work of the collective behaviorists should be examined, as much of present-day sociology rests on the premise that man is a goal-directed creature.[33]

Still another issue that has become problematic through the study of collective behavior is that of distinguishing between the normal and abnormal in human behavior. Such work as that on *folie à deux*, dancing mania, and other phenomena, pointed to by Ernest Gruenberg[34] in *Explorations in Social Psychiatry*, raises important issues concerning the division between normal and pathological behavior—for one, whether or not sheer prevalence is sufficient to convert an abnormal activity into a normal one.

Conclusions

In summary then, although the rubric "collective behavior" does not seem to have a useful place in the vocabulary of the dramaturgical social psychologist, it has quite obviously affected the course of both present-day social psychology and sociology in general. Perhaps, however, the principal achievement of those operating under the rubric of "collective behavior" has not been in terms of their direct contributions to either social psychology or sociology. Paradoxically, it lies in what the collective behaviorists, in one sense, did not accomplish. This lack of accomplishment can perhaps best be seen as an inability on their part to appreciate the social nature of individuals, or at least the social nature of the behavior of individuals. Throughout the writings of those interested in collective behavior, the individual is seen as a psychological mechanism. His behavior, at least his collective behavior, is seen as a reflection of his individualistic, socially unadulterated components. Indeed, collective behavior is characterized as a primitive, elementary, autonomously individual, non-social kind of phenomenon.[35] Throughout the writings, to be social is seemingly equated with being cultural, the acultural realm being conspicuously individualistic. Such a characterization raises the general question, then, of just what or when behavior is social or, perhaps better, sociological. Social psychologists have done much to extend the realm of social to include behaving individuals, but much work in this area remains to be done. Perhaps by directly confronting the argument of collective behavior, social psychologists can better define and elaborate that peculiar circumstance of being social.

Notes

1. I am grateful to Robert P. Snow, Ramon Oldenburg, and Gregory P. Stone for comments on this manuscript.

2. There is another use of the term "collective behavior" which involves equating collective behavior with all social behavior or interaction. This formulation and its attendant problems will not be directly examined in this paper. However, Herbert Blumer, in his examination of collective behavior, discusses this use and also articulates a definition of collective behavior in terms of its being a separate division of sociological inquiry (Herbert Blumer, "Collective Behavior," in Alfred McClung Lee [ed.], *Principles of Sociology* [New York: Barnes & Noble, 1955]).

3. Kurt Lang and Gladys Lang, *Collective Dynamics* (New York: Thomas T. Crowell Co., 1961); and R. Brown, "Mass Phenomena," in G. Lindsey (ed.), *Handbook of Social Psychology* (Cambridge: Addison-Wesley Publishing Co., 1954).

4. This is in reference to the dramaturgical school of social psychology referred to by Manford Kuhn in his "Major Trends in Symbolic Interaction Theory in the Past Twenty-five Years," *Sociological Quarterly* (Winter, 1964), pp. 61-84.

5. In a recent book, and from a perspective much different than will be taken here, Neil Smelser has attempted to solve many of the problems raised by the relative autonomy of the field of collective behavior. He has done this by defining collective behavior so that it "can be classified and analyzed under the same conceptual framework as all social behavior" (Neil Smelser, *Theory of Collective Behavior* [New York: Free Press, 1963], p. 21).

6. Émile Durkheim, *The Rules of Sociological Method* (Chicago: University of Chicago Press, 1938).

7. This distinction is often mistakenly construed as one between a rational and an irrational man. However, the fact of the matter is that the actor who is responsible for his behavior may or may not act in a rational manner. The essential point is that some behavior is imputed by others to be affected by the actor's reflection, while other activity is said merely to occur without there being any imputation of thinking to the actor. It is assumed that, when people reflect, they reflect, at least in part, on the social consequences of their acts and that this reflection is in reference to social expectations of some sort. Their behavior, therefore, is construed as normative.

8. George H. Mead, *Mind, Self, and Society* (Chicago: University of Chicago Press, 1934).

9. In line with previous thinking, it does not seem necessary or worthwhile to term this aspect of the self "rational," although some authors have seen fit to do so, and then to criticize Mead for his rationalistic bias.

10. This is not to say that Mead intended to do this but only to recognize that his work may be interpreted in this way. I am well aware of arguments to the contrary.

11. There arises the immediate problem here of considering the deterministic force of social norms. It is a prevalent idea in sociology that the norms of social organization may coerce or influence an individual's behavior to the extent that he is habitually conforming. In the face of this, the distinction here rests upon three notions: (1) that a norm (particularly conformity to a norm) should be looked upon as having a career. At some time in the career of conformity to certain norms, at least in contemporary society, the person probably had the alternative of not conforming. That this conformity then became regularized is of little relevance in this context, although it may be of extreme significance in others. (2) That habitual conformity to some norms is taken as an indication by others that one is being purposeful and intentional and, moreover, is responsible for his behavior. The ire of being unintentional, purposeless, and irresponsible is evoked only when one deviates from particular norms, that is, when one's behavior is ascribed the label of "non-normative." (3) That persons' awareness and/or acknowledgment of norms should not necessarily be construed as an indication of rigorous adherence to those norms.

12. Gabriel Tarde, *The Power of Imitation* (New York: Henry Holt, 1903); and Gabriel Tarde, *Social Laws* (New York: Macmillan Co., 1899). Tarde recognized that the behavior of individuals was imitative and therefore inherently social. According to Tarde, "inventions" did not come into existence, did not have social consequences, until they were imitated. Tarde insisted that social life was a multiplication process and not, as Durkheim and others would have it, a transformation process. Therefore, it was unnecessary for Tarde to posit a psychological individual and a transforming group process. Behaving individuals were, by definition, social. All significant human behavior was interaction.

13. Erving Goffman, *Encounters* (Indianapolis: Bobbs-Merrill Co., 1961); and Erving Goffman, *Behavior in Public Places* (New York: Free Press, 1963).

14. John Dewey, *Human Nature and Conduct* (New York: Our Modern Library, 1930).

15. We are speaking here, for the most part, of the set of motives that have been assembled by social scientists. Somehow, these motives are thought of as the "true" motives of human behavior. As discussed previously, the species "normative," in all of its varied manifestations, was at one time the primary "true motive" espoused by sociologists. Sociological explanation was couched in a normative vocabulary. The point of the present perspective is that such scientific motives are not necessarily "truer" than the more pedestrian motives and that they are simply the artifact of a relationship between the actor and one particular, and we might add, somewhat isolated, audience (the scientific observer). Because they have definite consequences in the actor-scientist relationship does not make them the only real motives. This seems particularly important in light of the fact that "real" motives are usually, if not always, equated with causes.

Therefore, the fact that sociologists have claimed that individuals orient their actions to the expectations of others should not be taken by itself to mean that such orientation is a universal determinant of human behavior. Rather, such a claim should be seen as arising out of the nature of the sociological pursuit. The characteristic mode of operation in sociology has been a process of remaining objective and distant from the behavior under scrutiny. At such a vantage point, it seems relatively easy to lose one's sense of relativism and to see one's own sociological motives as the true ones and, therefore, as the causes of the behavior. However, given the methodological tack becoming prominent again in social psychology, it seems that a more relativistic approach is possible. Herbert Blumer's dictum that the sociologist "must take the role of the acting unit whose behavior he is studying" (Herbert Blumer, "Society as Symbolic Interaction," in A. Rose [ed.], *Human Behavior and Social Processes* [Boston: Houghton Mifflin Co., 1962]) naturally leads the sociologist to an appreciation of the many "others" to whom the individual actor is related. It leads him, furthermore, to a consideration of the extreme relativity of motivational statements.

This is not to say that scientific motives are of no significance whatsoever. Obviously they are often incorporated into the behavior of the acting human being and are found quite serviceable. But this is precisely the point—their importance lies in their consequences, not in their supposed reality as antecedents.

16. This function of motives has long been recognized by a small number of students, particularly by Kenneth Burke, who has spoken brilliantly of the grammar and rhetoric of motives (Kenneth Burke, *A Grammar of Motives* [New York: Prentice-Hall, Inc., 1945]; and Kenneth Burke, *A Rhetoric of Motives* [New York: Prentice-Hall, Inc., 1950]). Quite recently, psychologists have also adopted this very relativistic dimension of motivation. The prodigious amount of work done under the banner of "cognitive

dissonance" seems to underscore vividly an image of a rationalizing, rather than a rational, human being.

17. Gregory P. Stone, "Appearance and the Self," in A. Rose, *op. cit.,* pp. 86-118.

18. Ernest Becker, *The Revolution in Psychiatry* (Glencoe, Ill.: Free Press, 1964).

19. Frank Hartung speaks of an "irresistible impulse" in *Crime, Law and Society* (Detroit: Wayne State University Press, 1965); and Donald Cressey of compulsive crime in "Role Theory, Differential Association, and Compulsive Crime," in A. Rose (ed.), *op. cit.,* pp. 443-67.

20. Thomas Scheff's discussion of "residual rules" is very relevant to this issue (Thomas Scheff, *Being Mentally Ill* [Chicago: Aldine Publishing Co., 1966]).

21. With the dissolution of this distinction, the issue of "individual responsibility," so important in the contemporary psychiatric-legal debate, takes on a new dimension. The notion of responsibility indeed undergoes a socialization process whereby responsibility is placed in the context of the social relationship, not in the heads or hearts of the actors. Goffman, in advancing the idea of the moral obligation of social relationships (Erving Goffman, *The Presentation of Self in Everyday Life* [Garden City, N.Y.: Doubleday Anchor, 1959]), and Riesman, in talking of the character of other-directed tolerance (David Riesman [with Nathan Glazer and Reuel Denney], *The Lonely Crowd* [Garden City, N.Y.: Doubleday Anchor, 1953]), have isolated very important types of this responsibility. Currently, Ernest Becker (*op. cit.*) and Thomas Szasz (*The Myth of Mental Illness* [New York: Hoeber-Harper, 1961]) seem involved in clarifying this extremely tenuous idea of responsibility. That responsibility, very much like Harry Stack Sullivan's personality, requires an "other" for its reality is illustrated by Thomas Scheff in his discussion of the negotiable character of responsibility (Thomas Scheff, "The Negotiation of Reality: The Process of Assessing Responsibility," unpublished manuscript).

22. This might be due to the "interested observation" of most sociologists in this area. The study of collective behavior, from the time of LeBon, has always had a "Chicago School" flavor, unlike some other area of sociological inquiry.

23. This often leads to a kind of circular reasoning, the best example being LeBon's logic that characteristics of crowd behavior are at the same time causes of crowd behavior. This problem of tautology only arises, however, when one injects a causal or deterministic bent to the argument.

24. For an early and valuable statement concerning careers, see the discussion of natural history in Robert Park and Ernest Burgess, *Introduction to the Science of Sociology* (Chicago: University of Chicago Press, 1921).

25. The word that is traditionally used here is "symbolic." However, the tack taken here is that the distinction between symbols and natural signs is, in this context, spurious. This is because it is believed

that the symbolic aspect of an object emerges in communication and that if something takes on meaning (in the form of response) that something is symbolic. It is not, however, in the traditional usage of the term, necessarily cultural.

26. Goffman, *Behavior in Public Places*.

27. Stone, *op. cit.*

28. Some little evidence that this emphasis on interpersonal relations is a correct one, at least with respect to contemporary society, can be gleaned from the writings of numerous commentators on the modern scene. Particularly David Riesman, in his crude typology of societies and characters in *The Lonely Crowd*, seems to lend support to this view. Riesman's relevance in this context is his insistence that the present other-directed society has a very different character than tradition- and inner-directed types. His point seems to be that modern man is neither pulled strongly by a neat web of cultural values as he was in the tradition-directed era nor is he constrained by the (work) structure to the extent which he was in the society of inner direction. The implication is that the behavior of modern man may be best understood if seen in the context of an other-directed, interpersonalizing round of life. It might be said, in the light of Riesman's categorization, that the dramaturgical model, in this instance, has extended the scope of the perspective of the collective behaviorists. The study of collective behavior emphasized the acultural, astructural at a time when almost all behavior was confined by culture and

structure. The dramaturgical model has simply elaborated this perspective to fit the present, where it seems much more behavior is of an acultural, astructural cast.

29. See, for instance, Erving Goffman, "The Moral Career of the Mental Patient," *Psychiatry*, Vol. XXII (May, 1959); and Howard Becker, *Outsiders: Studies in the Sociology of Deviance* (Glencoe, Ill.: Free Press, 1963).

30. Anselm Strauss, *Mirrors and Masks* (Glencoe, Ill.: Free Press, 1959).

31. Stone, *op. cit.*

32. Ralph H. Turner and Lewis M. Killian, *Collective Behavior* (Englewood Cliffs, N.J.: Prentice-Hall, Inc., 1957).

33. See H. Schmalenbach, "The Sociological Category of Communion," in Talcott Parsons *et al.*, *Theories of Society* (Glencoe, Ill.: Free Press, 1961), pp. 331-47, particularly his discussion of Weber's types of social action.

34. Ernest Gruenberg, "Socially Shared Psychopathology," in Alexander Leighton, John A. Clausen, and Robert Wilson (eds.), *Explorations in Social Psychiatry* (New York: Basic Books, 1957).

35. At least at certain points in its development. Some kinds of collective behavior, i.e., crowds and masses, seem to retain this character throughout their career; other kinds, such as public and mass movements, seem to lose these characteristics as they develop.

20.

Denton E. Morrison

SOME NOTES TOWARD
THEORY ON RELATIVE DEPRIVATION,
SOCIAL MOVEMENTS, AND SOCIAL CHANGE

It is now commonplace to use relative deprivation explicitly or implicitly as a central variable in the explanation of social movements, and thus also to explain the processes of social change that are

Excerpts from "Some Notes Toward Theory on Relative Deprivation, Social Movements, and Social Change," by Denton E. Morrison and reprinted from *American Behavioral Scientist* Vol. 14, No. 5 (May/June 1971) pp. 675-90 by permission of the publisher, Sage Publications, Inc.

engendered by social movements.[1] The basic notion is that feelings of deprivation, of discontent over one's situation, depend on what one *wants* to have; that is, deprivation occurs in relation to desired points of reference, often "reference groups," rather than in relation to how little one has. In turn, social movements are thought to emerge and flourish when groups of persons experience relative deprivation. Indeed, much evidence supports this view. For instance, it is clear that persons who have experienced steady and abject poverty are not as likely as others to be involved in movements of protest and change, particularly others who have experienced some improvements in their situation and who assumedly want those improvements to continue (Pinard, 1967).

However, much of the evidence relevant to the connection of relative deprivation and social movements is *indirect* evidence (see, for example, Grindstaff, 1968). It is clear evidence *against* absolute deprivation, but not definitive evidence *for* relative deprivation, since data on the feeling-states of individuals are usually not offered. Often, in those cases where data on individual attitudes are offered, both data and theory on the processes by which individuals acquire feelings of relative deprivation and on the way in which relative deprivation is related to the beliefs and attitudes about social change that characterize participants in social movements, are lacking. Further, accounts that attempt to explain social movements by relative deprivation often contain little evidence, theory, or even speculation on the structural conditions that give rise to relative deprivation.

The notion of a social movement used in this paper (and implicitly in most accounts that involve relative deprivation as a crucial explanatory variable) is that of a primarily *power-oriented* movement: a deliberate, voluntary effort to organize individuals to act in concert to achieve group influence to make or block changes. In power-oriented movements, in contrast with participation-oriented movements (like the Pentecostal movement), group actions are not in and of themselves viewed as primary sources of the benefits or gratifications desired by individual participants (see Killian, 1964:

448-452). Rather, coordinated group actions are thought to be the necessary means to obtaining from some elements in the larger social context the changes desired by the participants, as in the labor and the civil rights movements.

A further specification is that this analysis applies particularly to power movements in relatively open, democratic societies that stress individual mobility, though many of the notions have broader application. In addition, the analysis probably applies more to what Smelser (1963) has termed "norm-oriented" movements (changes *within* the system that involve the means to more basic values) than to "value-oriented" movements (basic goal changes *of* a system), though broader relevance is implied.

Relative deprivation and social movements

The basic notion of relative deprivation needs elaboration in two important ways before the sense in which the discontent that arises from relative deprivations is suitably described: the desires involved must become (1) legitimate expectations that are (2) perceived as blocked.

Legitimate expectations

In relative deprivation theory, a person not only desires a given goal, but he also feels that he has a *right* to obtain that goal, that he *deserves* it, at least under certain conditions. These conditions will here generically be termed his "investments." The investments that give rise to feelings that a goal is legitimately expected can be either ascribed or achieved statuses or roles, or the actions that constitute the means by which statuses and roles are achieved. Naturally, before a goal can be legitimately expected, we must presuppose contacts of the kind and intensity that establish the awareness, the desirability, and the possibility of certain goal-states. The general process by which desires become legitimate expectations involves, beyond this, learning that certain investments *are* generally rewarded by certain outcomes, so that it becomes expected that such investments *should* be so rewarded. Such learning is probably most poignant when actual behavioral reinforcement is involved—for example, experiencing promotion and income increases as a result of certain investments in energy, effort, education, and seniority. But we also know that expectations can be formed and legitimized by identification with persons and groups whose investments are perceived as similar to and, thus, no more deserving of, certain awards than one's own but whose actual returns are greater. Thus one comes legitimately to expect returns equivalent to persons in such "reference groups."[2]

Blocked expectations

Relative deprivation also involves the notion that a negative discrepancy between what one legitimately expects and what one has will generate discontent only to the extent that there is a high perceived probability that the discrepancy will not be reduced—i.e., a high probability of blockage. This, in fact, is the social-psychological definition of "deprivation." If one expects something and thinks he will get it, he does not feel "deprived" of it.

An expectation, however, always has a time dimension—the belief that a goal will be reached within a certain time, i.e., approached at a certain rate. Thus, to have a legitimate expectation and at the same time have a high perceived probability of blockage requires, in general, that the perception of blockage probability must increase rather suddenly. This is because there is an interactive relation-

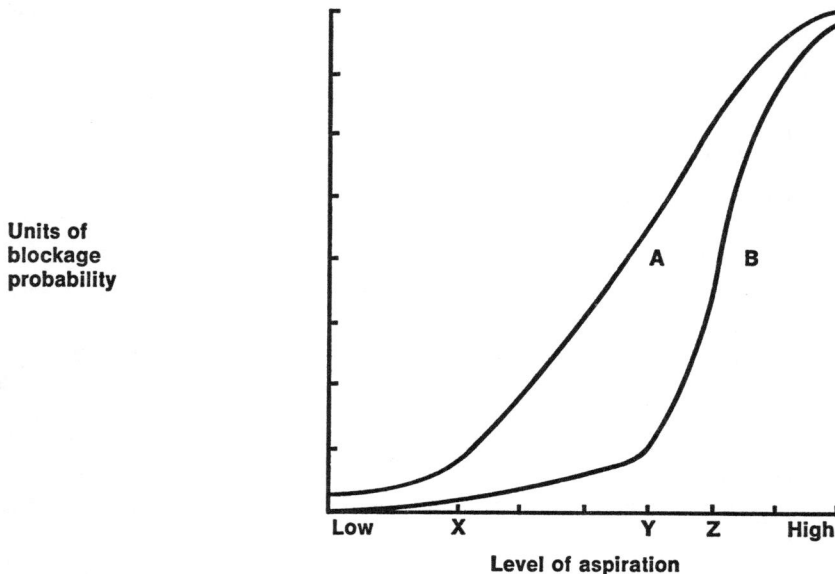

Figure 1. Hypothetical Relationship of Aspiration Level and Probability of Blockage

ship, a relationship of a mutual feedback, adjustment, and learning between the development of a legitimate expectation (i.e., the translation of a desire into a legitimate expectation) and the subjective as well as the objective probability that the expectation will be fulfilled. Where the probability that a given desire will not be fulfilled has been high over a period of time and remains high, the desire does not develop into a legitimate expectation. Thus, legitimate expectations tend over time to be for those desires that have a relatively low probability of blockage; i.e., the opportunities for realizing such desires have been relatively good; increases in blockage probability must involve a declining ratio of opportunities in relation to desires. Since actual levels of blockage probability are unknown, blockage probability is perceived to be high to the extent that increases in blockage probability exceed increases in aspiration ("aspiration" is the absolute magnitude of the desire).[3]

These notions can be illustrated by Figure 1, where the hypothetical curves represent differing opportunity structures for reaching aspirations of varying magnitudes. While it is doubtless accurate to interpret the vertical axis as representing the *level* of blockage probability, the specific interpretation here, in keeping with the rationale above, is that it represents units of blockage probability. It is assumed, then, in Figure 1 that all social systems provide some region where the curve is relatively flat and low, i.e., where increasing aspirations bring relatively small increases in the probability of blockage. Where relatively large increases in aspiration bring relatively small increases in the probability of blockage, the flat and low portion of the curve is a lengthy one, as in Curve B.

One way in which sudden increases in blockage can come about in terms of Figure 1 is the situation in which, for a certain constant level of aspiration, opportunities decline because the opportunity curve itself suddenly changes in a way that restricts opportunities—for instance, Curve B changes to Curve A for aspiration Y. In a previous context, I have termed this phenomenon "decremental deprivation" (Morrison and Steeves, 1967). Examples are situations in which a depression or recession takes opportunities away from persons, or where social, institutional, or legal changes take opportunities away, as in the confiscating of lands from elites in developing countries, or, perhaps, the situation of small businessmen in the United States in recent years. Such situations are those that are typically involved in movements to block changes or to bring about changes that will restore a former condition—i.e., rightist or reactionary movements.

The opposite, "aspirational deprivation," occurs when the magnitude of aspiration increases to a much greater extent than opportunities for realizing the increased aspiration. This can involve an increase in aspiration that is (1) large (for instance, X to Y on Curve A) or (2) small (Y to Z on B), as long as the aspiration moves through some crucial point in the opportunity structure, i.e., where the curve "suddenly" changes from flat to steep. These are the situations that are typically involved in movements *for* change—i.e., liberal or leftist movements. Case 1 is probably best exemplified by the "revolution of rising expectations" in developing countries, where, through contacts with developed countries and internal social changes, new reference groups are suddenly obtained. Case 2 is the situation in discontinuous stratification systems where, for those in any given stratum, there are somewhat severe hurdles that might be surmounted before the next higher stratum can be entered. Some examples might be passage from blue-collar to white-collar work, from worker to manager or owner, and from jobs and salaries usually available for women or for Blacks to those that are available mainly for men and for whites (see Form and Geschwender, 1962: 237).

The creation of dissonance

Summarizing what has been said thus far, relative deprivation involves a special type of cognitive dissonance in which there develops the belief in a legitimate expectation and, simultaneously, the discrepant belief that there is a high probability that the expectation will not be fulfilled.[4] Because legitimate expectations are thought by their possessors to be "deserved," the specific feelings of dissonance that arise are that this situation is one of "injustice" or "inequity."[5] Such feelings can only arise when the belief in a high blockage probability comes about suddenly; otherwise, the legitimate expectation would not develop. For decremental deprivation, the intensity of the dissonance will depend on the rate at which opportunities decline for a given level of aspiration. For aspirational deprivation, the intensity of dissonance may or may not involve a great or sudden increase in aspiration, depending on the shape of the opportunity curve and where a person's aspiration level is when a higher aspiration is required. But, in general, the intensity of dissonance will be a function of the rate at which the perception of blockage probability for a legitimate expectation increases.

Dissonance is a psychologically upsetting state that generates attempts to reduce the dissonance. One possible alternative for lowering the dissonance created by relative deprivation is to interpret the blockage as due to individual shortages of talent, luck, resources, motivation, and the like. This, in effect, amounts to a person saying that in his particular case the expectation is not legitimate, that his investments are not adequate. In this case, a failure to achieve an aspiration is viewed, as Turner (1969: 391) says, as a misfortune rather than as an injustice. Thus a person may simply lower his aspiration or he may engage in attempts to change his investments by trying to develop his talents, resources, or motivation. Another possible alternative for reducing the dissonance is to lower one's interpretation of the probability of blockage—that is, to believe that, with a little patience, one's investments will be adequately rewarded. Still another possible mode for resolving the dissonance is for a person to change his situation, to attempt to get into a context where his investments are more likely to be rewarded, as, for instance, in rural to urban migration.

When relative deprivation results in involvement in a power-oriented movement, none of these alternatives for dissonance reduction is taken. Rather, both the beliefs in the legitimate expectation and in a high probability of blockage are maintained. The belief in blockage is translated into a belief in *structural blockage,* and attempts at dissonance reduction take the form of belief in a *structural solution.* Individuals come to see themselves as part of a *group* with legitimate expectations that are blocked by some aspect of the larger social structure outside the group; there is an attempt to remove the source of the dissonance by organized group action to change the structural source of the blockage.[6] Note, however, that it would be inaccurate to say that a power movement attempts directly or immediately to lower dissonance; indeed, a social movement depends on maintaining its participants in a state of tension and upset over their situation. The dissonance is not psychologically disabling for the individual because its effect is overridden by the belief that the blockage will be removed by group action (structural faith), and by the belief that some feature of the larger social structure outside the individual can be blamed for the blockage (structural blame).

The beliefs in structural blockage and structural solution are, then, simultaneously the psychology that emerges and develops when a power-oriented movement comes into being, the kinds of beliefs that are diffused to recruit persons to participate in the movement, and the major features of the ideology of the movement: the legitimate expectations of a group are substantially blocked, the source of the blockage is in the social structure, and the group acting in concert can and will change the social structure to remove the blockage.

The structural conditions for the emergence of social movements

We have already outlined the kinds of structural conditions that are related to high relative deprivation, namely, rapid social changes of the sort that (a) increase contacts and communication between persons in different social strata and which launch many persons on trajectories of upward social mobility (aspirational deprivation), or (b) decrease opportunities (decremental deprivation), or (c) "a" followed rapidly by "b"—the latter is the Davies' "J curve" notion (1962, 1969), called "progressive deprivation" by Gurr (1970: 52-56).

The main structural conditions that increase the probability that beliefs in structural blockage and structural solution will emerge and spread when high relative deprivation is experienced (i.e., increase the probability of emergence of a power-oriented movement) would seem to be the following:

(1) *A large population experiencing the relative deprivation* increases the chances that varying interpretations will be made of any given situation, and, particularly, that leadership potential will exist among some of those who develop notions of structural blockage and structural solution.

(2) *Close interaction, communication, and proximity* are necessary so that similarity of situation can be better observed and so that interpretations of structural blockage and structural solution can be reinforced and refined into a coherent ideology when they arise. (Conditions 1 and 2 together suggest that a certain "density" of relative deprivation is necessary for movement emergence.)

(3) *High role and status commonality* is, of course, related to the "class consciousness" that is a part of all movements. It is more difficult to interpret a blockage as due to individual causes when many similar persons experience the same blockage. Also, when investments cannot be altered and rewards are inequitable, as with ascribed roles and statuses such as sex and race, individual solutions to blockage have inherently low appeal.

(4) *A stratification system with clear strata boundaries and visible power differences between the strata* increases the likelihood that the blockages lie in the nature of the stratification system, that they will be interpreted as such, and that structural interpretations of the necessary changes will develop accordingly.

(5) *The presence of much voluntary association activity in a society* is important because the notion of a structural solution is not likely to emerge where there are no precedents for the view that society can be changed by voluntary group efforts. In addition, voluntary associations tend to create in any society a residue of leader-

ship and organizational skills that are crucial for getting a movement off the ground.

Problems of movement recruitment, growth, and effectiveness

The decision to cast one's lot with *any* group that is seeking (rather than concretely providing) gains is, as Olson (1965) points out, a difficult one, since, in a group endeavor, the individual incurs costs over and above those he must bear in acting in an individual capacity, and yet the increased benefits from the group activity are problematic. Indeed, Olson argues convincingly that a large group must (a) employ separate and selective incentives—i.e., benefits other than the main ones the group is organized to seek (for instance, recreational, expressive, or insurance benefits in a union)—or (b) coercion to get and keep members. While Olson's analysis is not intended specifically to apply to power-oriented social movements, his points are clearly relevant to such movements, perhaps even more so than to other voluntary groups. This is because the costs of participation in a power movement are typically very high in relation to immediate outcomes. In addition to the economic costs in the diversion of time, energy, and resources (often dues) away from individual routes to rewards in organizational and proselytizing activities, social costs and risks are incurred because movements involve an essentially unconventional—a radical—interpretation of social reality. And there is no guarantee at all that the structural solution will ever provide substantial benefits to the participants, much less short-run benefits or benefits greater than can be obtained by individual activity.

Thus, once a movement emerges—in the sense of a core of initial adherents who

are in varying degrees the leaders of the movement—the recruitment of additional loyal adherents becomes the movement's immediate aim and, increasingly, its most perplexing problem. The recruitment of a relatively large number of loyal adherents is of central import because the power of the movement depends on the support it can command both in terms of sheer quantity of members and in terms of its ability to count on the supporters to act in concert.

Summary and conclusion

Social movements create social change, but they are also created by social changes that take away opportunities or create expectations faster than opportunities for reaching the expectations are created, resulting in relative deprivation. The latter situation would appear to be particularly important in the developing countries, where, in almost Malthusian fashion, expectations for modern life styles grow geometrically through contacts with developed countries, while opportunities grow arithmetically. Thus, the "revolution of rising expectations" may only be a temporary euphemism for an impending explosion of discontent and power-oriented movements in these countries. It is also worth considering that this phenomenon operates for awakening and underdeveloped sectors of developed countries, such as for the Blacks in the United States (Feierabend et al., 1969: 673-677).

Power-oriented movements are uniquely concerned with group, often "class," mobility and thus involve interpretations of structural blockage and structural solution. However, the social changes that create relative deprivation and the structural conditions that are conducive to interpretations of structural blockage and structural solutions do not affect potential movement benefactors equally. Therefore, movement members must be vigorously recruited and maintained by the leaders through incentives that are separate from the movement's goals or by coercion. The former results in the familiar phenomenon of movements becoming conservative, and the latter results in the coercive tendencies of movements, including violence.

Notes

1. See, for example, much of the literature summarized in Gurr (1970).
2. See Adams (1965) for an elaboration and an attempt at formalization of these notions.
3. By this conception, two men with salaries of $6,000 and $8,000 who both want to make $10,000 have the same level of aspiration. Anticipating the discussion below, they may, of course, be on different opportunity curves, so that an increase in their as-piration from $10,000 to $12,000 may mean a sudden increase in blockage for one and not for the other. This conception of aspiration is different from the earlier one in Morrison and Steeves (1967).
4. See Geschwender (1968) for a thoughtful discussion of the relationship of relative deprivation to cognitive dissonance and to status consistency.
5. It is also a situation of inequity, of course, when investments are overrewarded. Thus it is worth considering the notion that feelings of social guilt are a product of overreward and that such feelings may help account for the frequent phenomenon wherein a movement receives considerable support, even leadership, from those who would not themselves benefit if the movement achieved its goals. For some relevant theory on overreward, see Adams (1965); Anderson et al. (1969).
6. Aberle (1962) has hypothesized that millenial movements arise when relative deprivation is high and structural blockage is perceived, but no chance of changing the social order to relieve the deprivation is perceived. It would seem to be the case, then, that participation-oriented movements arise when the deprivations are perceived to be of a personal nature —i.e., structural blockage is not perceived.

21.

John Lofland

INDIVIDUAL DISPOSITIONS TO CONVERSION

In this article, I shall present a model of the conversion process through which persons came to see the world in terms set by the perspective of the Divine Precepts.

The logical and methodological structure of the analysis is based on a developmental conception.[1] That is, I will offer a series of more or less successively accumulating factors, which in their total combination would seem to account for conversion to the DP's. Seven such factors will be presented, all of which together seem both necessary and sufficient cause for conversion to occur.

The sequential arrangement of the conditions may be conceived as a funnel; that is, as a structure which systematically reduces the number of persons who can be considered available for recruitment and at the same time increasingly specifies who is available. At least theoretically, since the mission of this band of world savers was to convert America, all persons in this country could be considered as targets. Each condition thus serves both to narrow the range of people available and to show why only a handful of them ultimately responded to the DP call.

From John Lofland, "Individual Dispositions to Conversion" published by Prentice Hall in *Dooms-day Cult*, 1966. Reprinted by permission of the author.

Furthermore, the temporal order in which conditions are met may vary. Typically, and perhaps ideally, the conditions develop as presented. However, the ordering principle has been one of *activation* rather than of temporal occurrence alone. That is to say, some conditions may pre-exist for a considerable time prior to their becoming relevant to DP conversion, or they may develop only in time to accomplish conversion. The time of activation is the same in either case.

How can one determine when a person has *really* in some deep sense taken up a different perspective? The most obvious evidence is of course his own declaration that he has done so. This frequently takes the form of a tale of regeneration, about how terrible life was before and how wonderful it is now.[2] But verbal claims alone are insufficient, because they are easily made and just as easily falsified. Indeed, several persons who professed belief in the DP's were regarded as insincere by all core members.[3] However, a display of loyalty and commitment, such as giving time, energy, and money to the DP enterprise, invariably brought ratification of the conversion from all core members. But to require such a display as a necessary indication of true conversion raises problems too. A few persons who made only verbal professions were universally regarded as converts by core members. To avoid this difficulty, I shall distinguish between two classes, or degrees, of conversion: *verbal converts,* those fellow travelers and followers who professed belief and were accepted by core members as sincere, but who took no active role in the DP enterprise; and *total converts*, who exhibited their commitment through deeds as well as words.

The data indicate that, up to a point, the same factors account for both types of conversion. In my initial discussion the two groups will be treated together. Later I shall attempt to show how failure to transform verbal into total conversion is a consequence of the failure of the last stage in the conversion sequence to develop.

A model of conversion

To account for the process by which persons come to be world savers for the DP, I shall be concerned with two types of conditions or factors. The first type, which may be called *predisposing conditions,* comprises attributes of persons *prior* to their contact with the cult. In current sociological language, these may be thought of as background factors operating to produce a pool of appropriate persons from which the DP converts may be drawn. However, it is unfortunate that a convention has grown up in sociology of treating various kinds of demographic characteristics, structural and/or personal frustrations, and so forth, as reasonably complete accounts of factors that "push" people into groups that are dedicated to protest against the prevailing social order. Not that these factors are unimportant, or that such models are inaccurate, but they are woefully incomplete. One might put the character of their incompleteness in a Meadian paraphrase of T. S. Eliot: Between the impulse and the act falls the shadow.

The second type of conditions concerns this shadowy area, the contingencies of social situations. By *situational contingencies* I refer to those conditions that develop through direct confrontation and interaction between the potential convert and DP members, conditions that can lead to the successful recruitment of persons already well disposed toward the enterprise. Many of those who qualified for conversion on the basis of predispositional factors entered into interpersonal relationships with the DP's, but because the proper situational conditions were not met, they did not convert.

Let us now turn to a discussion of each of the factors operating within these two classes.

I. Tension

It would seem that no model of human conduct entirely escapes some concept of tension, strain, frustration, deprivation, or the like, as a factor in accounting for action. And not surprisingly, even the most cursory examination of the life situations of converts over the years before they embraced the DP reveals that they labored under what they at least *perceived* to be considerable tension.

This tension is best characterized as a felt discrepancy between some imaginary, ideal state of affairs and the circumstances in which they actually saw themselves. It is suggested that such acutely felt tension is a necessary but far from sufficient condition for conversion. It provides some disposition to act. But tension may be resolved in a number of ways (or remain unresolved). Hence to know that these people were in a tension situation says little about *what* action they might take.

Just as there can be myriad consequences of tension, so too can the sources be disparate. Some discovered, concrete varieties were: unrealized longing for wealth, knowledge, fame, or prestige; hallucinatory activity for which the person lacked any successful definition; frustrated sexual and marital relations; homosexual guilt; acute fear of face-to-face interaction; disabling and disfiguring physical conditions; and, perhaps of a slightly different order, a frustrated desire

for a significant, even heroic, religious status—to "know the mind of God intimately"—and to be a famous agent for His divine purposes.[4]

Some of these tensions may be sketched in the form of brief life histories of a few central believers. The case of Miss Lee, the Messiah's emissary in America, illustrates the theme of aspiring to be an important religious figure.

Miss Lee was born and raised in Korea and converted to Chang's cult in 1954, when she was thirty-nine. During her early teens she was subject to fits of depression and used to sit on a secluded hilltop and seek spirit contacts. She began receiving visions, hearing voices, and generally hallucinating, a pattern she was to maintain thereafter. Her teenage mystical experiences convinced her that she had a special mission to perform for God. Hence, at the age of nineteen, she entered a Methodist seminary in Japan. She was immediately disenchanted by the "worldly concern" of the seminarians and the training she received, although she stuck out the five-year course. Prior to entering the seminary, she had become engrossed in the spiritualistic writings of Emmanual Swedenborg, who soon began to appear to her in visions. Her estrangement from conventional religious roles was so great that upon graduation from the seminary she, alone among her classmates, refused ordination. She returned to Korea at the start of World War II, and by 1945 was a professor of social welfare at a denominational university in Seoul. In 1949 the Methodist Board of Missions sent her to a Canadian university for further theological training. There she wrote her thesis on Swedenborg, who continued to visit her in spirit form. In Canada, as in Japan, she was bitterly disappointed by the "neglect of things of the spirit," raised concern among the faculty by constantly hiding to pray and seek visions (often in the dorm basement), and occasionally stole away to Swedenborgian services. Her spirits continued to tell her that she was a religious figure of great importance. Returning to academic life in Korea, she fell ill with chronic diarrhea and eventually nephritis, both of which resisted all medical treatment. After two years of this, her health was broken and she was completely bedridden. At this time her servant took her to see Chang.

Thus is summarized the portrait of a desperately estranged spinster, with secret convictions of grandeur, frequent heterodox hallucinations, and failing health, who felt herself inextricably immersed in the mundane affairs of modern religious bureaucracy.

It would appear that problems we find among them (converts) are not *qualitatively* different or distinct from those presumably experienced by a significant, albeit unknown, proportion of the general population. Their peculiarity, if any, appears to be *quantitative;* that is, preconverts felt their problems to be acute and experienced high levels of tension concerning them over rather long periods of time.

It might in fact be said that from the point of view of an outside observer, their circumstances were in general not massively oppressive. One can probably find among the general population large numbers of people laboring under tensions that would seem to be considerably more acute and prolonged.

Perhaps the strongest qualitative characterization of tension supportable by the data is that pre-converts felt themselves frustrated in their various aspirations and *experienced* the tension rather more acutely and over longer periods than most do.

Obviously, explanation cannot rest here, for such tensions could have resulted in any number of other resolutions, and in fact they usually do. Thus these unresolved problems in living are only part of the necessary scenery, but the props, the stage itself, and the drama of conversion remain to be constructed.

II. Types of problem-solving perspectives

On the basis of the first factor alone, only those without enduring, acute tensions are ruled out as potential DP converts. Since conversion is hardly the only response to problems, it is important to ask what else these people could have done, and why they didn't.

It seems likely that there were very few converts to the DP's for the simple reason that people have a number of conventional and readily available alternative ways of defining and coping with their problems. By this I mean that they have alternative perspectives, or rhetorics, that specify the nature and sources of problems and offer some program for their resolution. There are many such alternatives in modern society, but I shall briefly describe three particular types: the *psychiatric,* the *political,* and the *religious.* In the first, the origin of problems is typically traced to the psyche, and manipulation of the self is advocated as a resolution to problems. Political solutions, mainly radical, locate the sources of problems in the social structure and advocate its reorganization as a solution. The religious perspective tends to see both sources and solutions to difficulties as emanating from an unseen, and in principle unseeable, realm.

The first two rhetorics are both secular and are the most often used in contemporary society. It is no longer appropriate to regard recalcitrant and aberrant actors as possessed of devils. Indeed, modern religious institutions, in significant measure, offer secular, frequently psychiatric rhetorics concerning problems in living. The predominance of secular definitions of tension is a major source of loss of potential converts to the DP. Most people with acute tensions "get the psychiatric word" especially, either by defining themselves as grist for its mill or by being forced into it. Several persons met other conditions of the model but had adopted a psychiatric definition of their tensions and failed to convert. The following case is striking in this regard.

Thirty-year-old *Freda*, a divorcee with a history of mental hospitalization and profuse hallucinations, met Minnie in a chance encounter on a local bus. A college graduate, she was living in a women's residence hall in State U. City and working as a secretary, all the while longing to get married again. She was unsuccessfully participating in local, organized matchmaking groups or lonely hearts clubs and taking numerous university extension courses. She said that she had no close friends and was, in fact, observed to be a very unhappy young woman, noticeably "at loose ends." Minnie and she began to associate extensively. Holding back the more bizarre DP assertions, Minnie gradually worked Freda into the DP view of history and the modern world. Freda became very fond of Minnie. To anticipate the model somewhat, Freda met the conditions of tension, cult-affective bonds, and low extra-cult bonds. She had recently been unemployed and was still at a turning point. However, she did not have a religious perspective. After nine years of psychotherapy she was a veritable fount of psychiatric self-conception. Otherwise she was an excellent candidate for conversion.

In a few cases, persons were ambivalent about psychiatric self-images, and the DP came into direct competition with the mental hospital. Thus in one exaggerated instance, Leo, an ex-GI, literally alternated residence between the DP headquarters and the psychiatric ward of the veterans hospital, never seeming able to decide once and for all which rhetoric to adopt for his circumstances.

All pre-converts seemed surprisingly uninformed about conventional psychiatric and political perspectives for defining their problems. Perhaps largely because of their backgrounds (many were from small towns and rural communities), they had long been accustomed to defining the world in religious terms. Although conventional religious outlooks had been discarded by all pre-converts as inadequate, "spiritless," "dead," etc., prior to contact with the DP's, *the general propensity to impose religious meaning on events had been retained.*

Even within these constrictions in the available solutions for acutely felt problems, a number of alternative responses still remain. First, it must be recognized that people can persist in stressful situations and do little or nothing to reduce their discomfort. This is something that students of social life too often tend to underestimate. The case of Minnie, for example, gives an idea of the way in which tension can be sustained for years with no remedial activity. Except for the emergence of certain situational factors, this tension would doubtless never have erupted.

Second, people often take specifically problem-directed action to change those portions of their lives that are troublesome, without at the same time adopting a different world view to interpret them. Thus, for example, Bertha and Minnie Mae might have simply divorced their husbands, and presumably Lester could have embraced homosexuality. Clearly many pre-converts attempted such action (Merwin *did* start a boarding house, Elmer *did* attend college, etc.) but none found a successful direct solution to his difficulties.

Third, there exists a range of maneuvers that "put the problem out of mind." In general these constitute compensations for, or distractions from, problems in living. Such maneuvers include addiction to the mass media, preoccupation with childrearing, or immersion in work. More spectacular bypass routes are alcoholism, suicide, promiscuity, and the like. A number of such tentative strategies have been mentioned above in the case histories of pre-converts. Recall, for example, the summer of 1959, when Minnie Mae, Alice, and Bertha hung around the general store during the day getting high on beer. One is forced to wonder whether if this activity had occurred in a more urban setting, with bars and strange men available, their subsequent lives might not have been very different.

In any event, it may be assumed not only that many people with tensions explore these strategies, but also that some succeed and hence become unavailable as potential DP recruits.[5]

III. Religious seekership

Whatever the reasons, pre-converts failed in their attempts to find a successful way out of their difficulties through any of the strategies outlined above. Thus their need for solutions persisted, and their problem-solving perspective was restricted to a religious outlook. However, all pre-converts found that conventional religious institutions failed to provide adequate solutions. Subsequently, each came to see himself as a seeker, a person searching for some satisfactory system for interpreting and resolving his discontent. Given their generally religious view of the world, all pre-converts had, to a greater or lesser extent, defined themselves as looking for an adequate religious perspective and had taken some action to achieve this end.

Some went from church to church and prayer group to prayer group, routing their religious seeking through relatively conventional institutions. A male convert in his early twenties recounted:

My religious training consisted of various denominations, such as Baptist, Methodist, Congregationalist, Jehovah's Witnesses, and Catholicism. Through all my experiences, I refused to accept . . . religious dogma . . . because it was Truth I was seeking, and not a limited belief or concept.

Likewise, over the years Lee surreptitiously participated in a variety of little Korean tongues-speaking and prophetic groups, attended Swedenborgian churches while in Canada, and was an ardent student of all manner of heterodox figures. Bertha also attended a variety of church services and prayer meetings, giving allegiance to none. And while bedridden for a year as a result of a car accident, Leo had taken up the Bible and read it numerous times searching for "spiritual meaning." Upon recovery he had "church hopped," looking for religious definition.

Others began exploring the occult, reading the voluminous literature of the strange, the mystical, the spiritual, and tentatively trying a series of occult groups, such as Rosicrucians, spiritualists, and the various divine sciences. Ludwig and Lester assiduously attended spiritualist churches and read religious-metaphysical books in search of the higher philosophy in terms of which they could understand spirits and themselves. Elmer laboriously waded through books on spiritualism, flying saucers, various "new" Bibles, treatises on witchcraft and hypnotism, and occult periodicals; visited mediums; attended flying saucer clubs; and perused Hindu and East-West mutant world views. In working next to Merwin eight hours a day, Elmer introduced him to this range of topics, which Merwin soon accepted as viable formulations. He, too, became an avid follower of the occult-metaphysical.

Witness too the spiritual travails of the following couple:

In April, 1960, my wife and I . . . [began] to seek a church connection. [We] began an association with Yokefellow, a spiritual growth organization in our local church. My whole religious outlook took on a new meaning and a broader vision. I grew emotionally and spiritually during the next two and a half years.

However, as I grew, many spiritual things remained unanswered and new questions came up demanding answers which Yokefellow and the Church seemed not to even begin to touch upon. . . . My wife and I became interested in the revelation of Edgar Cayce and the idea of reincarnation, which seemed to answer so much. We read searchingly about the Dead Sea Scrolls, we decided to pursue Rosicrucianism, we read books on the secret disclosures to be gained from Yogi-type meditation. The more we searched, the more questions seemed to come up. Through Emmet Fox's writings I thought I had discovered a path through Metaphysics which through study would give me the breakthrough I longed for.

Or the seekership might display some amalgam of conventional and unusual religious conceptions, as illustrated in this sad tale told by a male convert:

I was reared in a Pentecostal church and as a child was a very ardent follower of Christianity. Because of family situations, I began to fall away and search for other meanings in life. This began . . . when I was about twelve years old. From that time on, my life was most of the time an odious existence, with a great deal of mental anguish. These last two years have brought me from church to church trying to find some fusion among them. I ended up going to Religious Science in the morning and fundamentalist in the evening.

Floundering about in the area of the religious was accompanied by two fundamental beliefs that define more specifically the ideological components of the religious-seeker pattern. Although concrete pre-convert beliefs varied a good deal, all of them espoused the following religious-seeker postulates about the nature of ultimate reality.

First, there was believed to be an active supernatural realm from which spirits of some variety could intervene in the material world. Such entities could, at least sometimes, break through from the beyond and impart information, cause "experiences," or take a hand in the course of events.

Second, there was espousal of a teleological conception of the universe, a belief that there exists a purpose for which every object and event is created. This included general notions, such as that the earth is as it is in order to meet the needs of man, and that man manifests the physical structure he does in order that he might do the things he does. More important, man himself as a phenomenon must be on earth because somewhere, sometime, somehow, it was decided that Homo sapiens should exist to *fulfill a purpose* or purposes. And of course this also applies to individuals, each of whom has some purpose and some sort of "job" to perform.

Typically, the positing was little more specific than this, or at least more specific terms of espousal were only tentatively held. The religious seeking itself was in terms of finding some more detailed formulation of and answers to these vague, existential axes. [6]

A few words on the general question of the importance of prior beliefs in effecting conversion are necessary at this point. A number of discussions of conversion have placed relatively great emphasis on the existence of a strong congruence between previous ideology and a given group's appeal. [7] Others seem to treat the degree of congruence as unimportant so long as the ideology is seen as embodied in what appears to be a successful movement. [8] Both views are extreme. [9]

The data suggest that only the two *gross*

kinds of congruence that make up the ideology of religious seekership were necessary for conversion to the DP. Presumptively important items, such as a more or less fundamentalist belief in Christianity, millenarian expectations, and hallucinatory experience, were far from universal among pre-converts. Although some believed in a vaguely defined "New Age" that would appear gradually, most *became* apocalyptic pre-millenarian (in the sense of a New Age soon and suddenly) rather than choosing the DP as an outlet for previously held eschatological hopes. The role of these gross points of congruence is suggested in the DP's substantive appeals to pre-converts.

Active spirits were rampant in the DP view of reality. Converts lived with an immediate sense of unseen forces operating upon and intervening in the physical order (e.g., the weather) and human affairs, from the relations among nations, through the latest national disaster, down to their moment-to-moment lives. Nothing occurred that was not related to the intentions of God's or Satan's spirits.

For persons holding a teleological conception of reality, the DP doctrines had the virtue of being grandly teleological and offering a minute and lawful explanation of the whole of human history. They systematically revealed and defined the hidden meaning of individual lives that had lacked coherence and purpose. The ideology of course explained all hallucinatory behavior in terms of spirit manifestations and of how these spirits had been preparing the pre-convert to be able to see the truth of the DP.

Although acute and enduring tensions in the form of frustrated aspirations are not an ideological component, in the sense of being a more abstract postulate about the nature of reality, it should be noted here that the DP also offered a proximate

and major payoff. Converts were assured of being virtual demigods for all eternity, beginning with a rule over the restored and reformed earth within the immediate future. By 1967 God would impose the millennium upon the earth, and those who converted early, before the truth of the message became self-evident, and thus helped to bring about the inevitable, would occupy the most favored positions in the divine hegemony. Converts gave particular stress to this advantage of conversion in their proselytization: "those who get in early," one member often put it, "will be in on the ground floor of something big."

Religious seekership emerges, then, as a further portion of the path through the maze of life contingencies that leads to DP conversion. It is a floundering among religious alternatives, an openness to a variety of frequently esoteric religious views, combined with failure to embrace the specific ideology and fellowship of some set of believers.[10] This seekership functioned to provide the minimal points of ideological congruence that made these people further available for DP conversion.

Notes

1. Cf. Ralph Turner, "The Quest for Universals in Sociological Research," *American Sociological Review,* Vol. XVIII (December 1953), pp. 604-611; Howard S. Becker, *Outsiders* (New York: The Free Press of Glencoe, Inc., 1963), esp. pp. 22-25; and Neil J. Smelser, *Theory of Collective Behavior* (New York: The Free Press of Glencoe, Inc., 1963), pp. 12-21.
Portions of Chaps. 3 and 4 were previously published in the *American Sociological Review,* Vol. XXX (December 1965), pp. 862-875, in collaboration with Rodney Stark.
2. Peter Berger has provided us with a delightful characterization of the reconstructive functions of such tales. See his *Invitation to Sociology* (New York: Doubleday & Company, Inc., 1963), Chap. 3.
3. See, for example, Chap. 8, the cases of Stein and Santini [in the original volume].
4. It is currently fashionable to reduce this last to more mundane, "real" causes. This may be possible. However, it is not necessary here to prejudge the phenomenology.

5. It perhaps needs to be noted that this discussion is confined to isolating the elements of the conversion sequence. Extended analysis would have to give attention to the factors that *in turn* bring each conversion condition into existence—that is, to develop a theory for each of the elements, specifying the conditions under which they develop. On the form that this would likely take see Ralph Turner's discussion of "the intrusive factor," *op. cit.*, pp. 609-611.

6. Some readers might conclude that the supernatural entities and teleological postulates already constrict the range of possible clientele to a tiny proportion of the American population. Although a majority are probably excluded, it should also be pointed out that a minority of many millions does espouse these postulates. See Charles Y. Glock and Rodney Stark, *Religion and Society in Tension* (Chicago: Rand McNally & Co., 1965), Chaps. 3, 5 and 8.

7. See, for example, H. G. Brown, "The Appeal of Communist Ideology," *American Journal of Economics and Sociology*, Vol. II (November 1943), pp. 161-174; Gabriel Almond, *The Appeals of Communism* (Princeton: Princeton University Press, 1954).

8. See, for example, Eric Hoffer, *The True Believer* (New York: New American Library of World Literature, Inc., 1958), p. 10.

9. Cf. Herbert Blumer, "Collective Behavior," in Joseph B. Gittler, ed., *Review of Sociology* (New York: John Wiley & Sons, Inc., 1957), pp. 147-148.

10. Further suggestive materials on seekers and seeking may be found in H. T. Dohrman, *California Cult* (Boston: Beacon Press, 1958); Leon Festinger, Henry Riecken, and Stanley Schachter, *When Prophecy Fails* (Minneapolis: University of Minnesota Press, 1956); Sanctus De Santis, *Religious Conversion* (London: Routledge & Kegan Paul, Ltd., 1927), esp. pp. 260-261; H. Taylor Buckner, *Deviant-Group Organizations,* unpublished master's thesis, University of California, Berkeley (1964), Chap. 2. For discussion of a generically similar phenomenon in a quite different context, see Edgar H. Schein, *Coercive Persuasion* (New York: W. W. Norton & Company, Inc., 1961), pp. 120-136, 270-277.

22.

Jeffery M. Paige

POLITICAL ORIENTATION AND RIOT PARTICIPATION

The concept of political efficacy has been widely used to explain radical as well as conventional political participation. Indices of political efficacy (Campbell *et al.,* 1954: 187-188; Milbraith, 1965: 156-157) usually combined items expressing feelings of political powerlessness and ignorance with items expressing distrust of existing political arrangements and suspicion about government intentions. Individuals with strong subjective feelings of efficacy have been found to be more likely to vote, to take an interest in political campaigns and to participate in party activities (Mil-

From Jeffery M. Paige, "Political Orientation and Riot Participation." *American Sociological Review* 36, October 1971, pp. 810-820, with permission of the publisher.

braith, 1965). Alienated or apathetic individuals who lack such feelings of efficacy are less inclined to participate in all forms of conventional politics and are said to be particularly susceptible to radical or revolutionary appeals (Bell, 1964; Kornhauser, 1959; Lipset, 1960; Ransford, 1968). Both Almond and Verba (1965) and Gamson (1968), however, have argued that radical or revolutionary politics cannot be understood as a result of general feelings of alienation or apathy as indicated by a low score on an index of political efficacy. They suggest instead that radical political action depends on a combination of a strong sense of personal political competence combined with a deep distrust of the political system. This distinction between feelings of political competence and distrust is lost in an overall index of political efficacy. The present study is an attempt to examine the value of this distinction in understanding one form of radical political action—participation in the Newark riot of 1967.

The essence of the Almond and Verba and Gamson argument lies in their distinction between trust involving the administrative activities of the government and trust involving the political activities of concerned interest groups. Almond and Verba distinguish between "input" and "output" affect. The political input process refers to the activities of interest groups and individuals presenting demands to government; the output process refers to the decisions made and actions taken by the government and its administrative agencies. Gamson suggests that it might be useful to reserve the term "efficacy" for beliefs about the input process and to use "trust" to refer to beliefs about outputs. Politically efficacious individuals will feel that they can influence government functioning, are well informed about politics and are active politically. Those who are trusting will believe that the government is basically acting in their interests, whether or not they participate in the political input process. These two components of political beliefs may of course be empirically correlated—those who are ill informed or opposed to government outputs will frequently be apathetic or uninvolved politically. Nevertheless, Almond and Verba, and Gamson, argue that the combination of a sense of political efficacy and distrust of existing government is a critical determinant of radical political action. Almond and Verba use this line of argument in explaining the prominence of revolutionary ideology in the political culture of Mexico. Gamson suggests that the optimum condition for political mobiliza-

tion is a combination of high efficacy and low trust, "a belief that influence is both possible and necessary" (Gamson, 1968: 48). This fact poses difficulties for political organizers who must carefully balance the advantages of some small victory which might increase both efficacy and trust, against a small defeat which will have the opposite effect on both trust and efficacy. Particularly in the early stages of a radical movement, it may be useful to convince potential constituents that they cannot put their faith in the authorities by engineering a few small defeats. The organizer can then exploit the distrust to gain support for his movement.

The difference between the views of Almond and Verba and Gamson and more traditional perspectives on political efficacy (Campbell et al., 1954; Campbell et al., 1960; Milbraith, 1965) is a critical one for understanding the meaning of collective violence. If a simple dichotomy is made between the politically efficacious and the politically apathetic and alienated, then extremist tactics can be attributed to withdrawal from political life, or to ignorance of the true intentions of government. Collective violence and other forms of extremist politics can then be attributed to ignorance, despair, authoritarianism or some other personal failing which is not directly related to the behavior of political authorities. Such a theoretical perspective implies an excessively charitable view of authorities since it assumes that the more that is known about the government the more it will be trusted. Such a correlation, of course, depends on the government. The Almond and Verba and Gamson view establishes knowledge and interest in the government as a prerequisite for political participation but ties the exact form of the participation to beliefs about the intentions of the regime. Extremist political tactics, like other forms of politics, require

	Trust	
	High	**Low**
High	Allegiant Responsive/ noncoercive Democratic	Dissident Unresponsive/ noncoercive Unstable
Low	Subordinate Unresponsive/ noncoercive Traditional	Alienated Unresponsive/ coercive Totalitarian

Efficacy labels the vertical axis.

Chart 1. Relationship of Trust and Efficacy to Political Orientation, Behavior of Regime, and Nature of Political System.

interest in government but, unlike conventional forms, imply that the government is fundamentally untrustworthy.

The relationship between efficacy, trust and political participation depends not only on the characteristics of the group but on the relationship between the group and the political system. A knowledgeable citizenry with an unresponsive regime is likely to turn to radical or violent tactics, while the same level of knowledge in a responsive system would lead to loyalty and conventional political action. The relationships between citizen attitudes and regime behavior are summarized in Chart 1. This diagram shows four possible combinations of trust and efficacy assuming each variable can take simply a high and a low value. Each cell indicates the

dominant political orientation of a group with such a combination of trust and efficacy, the behavior of a regime which would most likely be associated with such attitudes, and the nature of the political system in which such attitudes and behavior would be found. In a situation in which both efficacy and trust are high, the predominant political orientation will be allegiance. Those who feel both that the government will be run in their interests and that they can influence it when necessary will be active supporters of the existing political structure. The high efficacy suggests that this group will be politically active but their actions will not be directed toward radical change. This kind of political orientation depends on a regime which is responsive to the demands of the allegiant groups. Decreased responsiveness to their demands would lower the level of trust. If such responsiveness is maintained, little force will be required to maintain the authority of the regime. Such attitudes and behavior are approximated for some, but certainly not all, interest groups in functioning democratic political systems.

The low efficacy, low trust situation produces an alienated orientation which would lead to withdrawal from any active political participation. Despite the fact that this group regards the existing political structure as unfair, their low levels of political interest and information will prevent them from supporting even radical political movements. The alienated orientation will develop in situations in which the government is unresponsive and maintains its power largely through coercive force. The result is a resentful population which has learned that political activities are both dangerous and unprofitable. This situation is typical of totalitarian political systems.

The low efficacy, high trust situation also suggests a passive adjustment, although in this case the population believes that the government is basically run in their best interests. Demands are seldom presented by interest groups so that responsiveness is not an important issue in such systems. The ruler maintains an image of beneficent paternalism which, because of the low levels of political interest on the part of his subjects, may or may not be an accurate reflection of his actual behavior. Unless the ruler reveals himself to be unconcerned with the people's welfare through some particularly flagrant act or fails to meet the minimal demands of the population, there will be little need for active coercion to support his authority. Such a situation exists in traditional societies with hereditary rulers.

The political orientation associated with paternalism might be called subordinate, since it leads to a loyal, unquestioning faith in the existing political structure.

These three situations share one important property—they are all relatively stable politically. Any of these three situations can and has persisted without apparent change for substantial periods of time. Western democratic societies which remain responsive to most interest groups have managed to retain essentially the same political structure for several generations. The same is true of totalitarian states when they are supported by sufficiently large and loyal internal security forces. The traditional societies which depend on an implicit faith in the concern of the ruling classes for the welfare of the people are actually the most stable of the three.

The remaining cell in Chart 1, those with low trust in the existing government but high political efficacy is, unlike the other three, inherently unstable. If the government is regarded as untrustworthy and there is a feeling that something can and should be done about it, radical actions aimed at changing the system are likely to result. The more extreme the distrust, the more radical the response. Thus this cell defines a revolutionary situation. Withdrawal of trust is not in itself sufficient to create such a situation since it can lead to withdrawal from politics. What is critical is a combination of high efficacy and low trust. This active dissatisfaction with the political structure might be called a dissident political orientation. It will occur when an essentially unresponsive regime is faced with a politically aware population and for some reason does not or cannot rely on effective military coercion. This situation is unstable since it will usually lead to either repression or increased responsiveness on the part of the government. If the repression is successful, there will be a move to the alienated, totalitarian situation. If the government becomes more responsive to the revolutionary group, the society may move in the direction of greater democracy. There will not, in general, be a return from a dissident to a subordinate situation directly. The myth of the paternalistic ruler will not be readily restored after a revolutionary situation, although extended repression might have this result.

If riot participation can be viewed as a form of revolutionary activity, then it might be expected that riot participants would be overrepresented among the dissident—those high on efficacy and low on trust. The other three groups in Chart 1 would be less likely to participate in a riot but for different reasons. Both the allegiant and the subordinate groups support the existing political arrangements and would be unlikely to join a mass movement aimed at attacking them. The alienated have withdrawn from political life and would be likely to remain uninvolved during a riot. The alienated group is critical for the general line of argument presented here. The conventional view of political efficacy suggests the alienated groups are the base of support for extremist movements and that extremist and conventional politics are at opposite ends of the efficacy dimension. Such a view neglects the political component of extremism in favor of emphasizing its irrational qualities. The alternate view suggested by Almond and Verba and Gamson treats political radicalism as a response to an unresponsive and untrustworthy regime by politically sophisticated activists.

While the high-efficacy, low-trust group should be most likely to participate in revolutionary activities, those high on efficacy but higher on trust will be likely to engage in less extreme forms of political activity. Those low on political efficacy, whether subordinated or alienated, will be unlikely to participate in politics, whatever the form. Within the high efficacy group, then, the exact form of political participation depends on the amount of trust in the government. Gamson (1968) has distinguished three techniques which partisan groups can use to influence authorities: persuasion, inducements, and constraints. Persuasion involves attempts to change the orientations of the authorities by presenting new facts and arguments. The use of inducements is based on some added advantage to the authorities ranging from promised election support to outright bribery. Constraints add some disadvantage to the situation of the authorities and can range from political retaliation to physical violence. Gamson argues that each of these techniques is associated with a particular level of trust in the authorities. Those who are extremely high on trust, who think that even in the absence of influence the authorities will almost always act in their best interests, would be most likely to use persuasion. Those who feel neutral and believe that the chances of the authorities acting in their behalf are about even would be more likely to use inducements. Finally, groups which believe that there is little or no possibility that the authorities will act in their behalf have little to lose and will rely on constraints. This relationship between trust and political tactics should exist for the high efficacy subjects. Not only should it be possible to distinguish low and high efficacy groups on rates of political participation generally, but also to further specify what forms the political participation will take within the high efficacy group.

The success of the predictions based on political trust and efficacy depends on the relationships of rioting to other forms of political behavior. If there is no political component in rioting, then none of these predictions will be supported.

Conclusions

There was strong support in the survey data for predictions drawn from the relationship between trust and efficacy suggested by Almond and Verba, and Gamson. Rioters were most often found among the dissident—those high on political information and low on trust in the government. They were much less likely to be found among the alienated (low information, low trust), the subordinate (low information, high trust), or the allegiant (high information and high trust). Among the high-information subjects there was a clear tendency for respondents to shift from inducements to severe constraints as trust in the government decreased. In general, there is evidence that rioting can profitably be considered a form of disorganized political protest engaged in by those who have become highly distrustful of existing political institutions.

23.

Alejandro Portes

POLITICAL PRIMITIVISM, DIFFERENTIAL SOCIALIZATION, AND LOWER-CLASS LEFTIST RADICALISM

One of the dominant theories in the study of lower-class politics envisions the tendency of these groups toward political extremism, not as a result of economic interests, but of certain psychological and interpersonal features inhering in their

From Alejandro Portes, "Political Primitivism, Differential Socialization, and Lower-Class Leftist Radicalism," *ASR*, Vol. 36, October 1971, pp. 820-35. Reprinted by permission of the American Sociological Association and the author.

The data on which this paper is based were collected under a grant from the Midwestern Universities Consortium for International Activities (MUCIA). The statistical analysis was partially supported by the Graduate Research Board of the University of Illinois. I wish to thank Professors Archibald O. Haller, Donald J. Treiman, William H. Sewell, and Morris Janowitz for their most helpful comments and observations. Responsibility for the entire content of the paper rests, however, with the writer.

structural situation. The theory, as presented by Lipset (1963: Ch. 4), argues that lower-class experiences are not conducive to the levels of knowledge, tolerance, and political information necessary for understanding the rules of democratic compromise.

Lipset equates democracy or democratic attitudes with complex rationality and extremism with simplistic irrationality. Leftist extremism is perceived not as a function of lower-class interests but of lower-class ignorance. It is argued that the rules of mutual respect of rights on which democracy rests are a sophisticated elaboration. Developing them, understanding them, and living by them are privileges of the educated, the ones who have risen above the primitive stages where sheer force runs supreme. The poor, the working classes, are, for the most part, also the ignorant and, so runs the argument, the least capable of understanding democracy.

Leftist radicalism among the working classes is thus conceptualized as the simplistic political response of those who know no better. The elements of force and totalitarian authority intrinsic to it, far from alienating these groups, are appealing to their primitive understanding of social reality: "Rather than being a source of strain, the intransigent and intolerant aspects of communist ideology attract members from that large stratum with low incomes, low-status occupations, and low education, which in modern industrial societies has meant largely the working class" (Lipset, 1963:90).

Lipset's arguments have been reinforced by the writings of Fromm (1963), Hoffer (1966), Kornhauser (1960), and others sometimes collectively identified as the "mass society school" (Gusfield, 1962). These authors have understood extremism as a consequence of an increasing lack of integrative bonds between individuals and the general social structure. Isolation, uprootedness, the anxieties of meaningless existence generate collective flights into the security of the totalitarian movement. The paternalistic appeal of the "leader" functions to comfort followers who at last find the peace of protection and belonging.

Formally, the argument is applicable to different social classes and to radicalism of the right as well as of the left. In Fromm's (1963) well-known essay, it was, for example, employed to account for the massive lower-middle-class support of the Nazi movement in Germany. Within the lower classes, however, social isolation and uprootedness have been viewed as leading predominantly to radicalism of the left.

Lower-class individuals have been characterized as especially susceptible to the appeals of extremist movements because of their greater lack of integrative bonds to the existing social order. The powerful are generally not socially isolated. Among the powerless, the absence of stable, primary relationships and of gratifying links with intermediate structures creates the greatest receptivity to totalitarian movements: "The greatest number of people available to mass movements will be found in those sections of society that have the fewest ties to the social order, for those who have the fewest opportunities to participate in the formal and informal life of the community have the weakest commitments to existing institutions. The working classes have the weakest ties to the social order, not only because they receive the smallest benefits from it but also because they have the fewest opportunities to participate in it" (Kornhauser, 1960: 212). As in Lipset's theory, "mass society theory" regards lower-class leftist radicalism less as a consequence of a rational calculus of economic means and ends than as the product of the particular psychological make-up associated with this socioeconomic situation.

These theories generally characterize the politics of the lower classes as a form of political primitivism whose etiology lies in low education, lack of information and media exposure, and social isolation, and whose main consequences are found in enhanced receptivity to leftist radical movements. As summarized by Lipset: "Low-status groups are also less apt to participate in formal organizations, read fewer magazines and books regularly, (and) possess less information on public affairs . . . these characteristics reflect the extent to which the lower strata are *isolated* from the activities of democratic society—an isolation which prevents them from acquiring the sophisticated view of the political structure which makes understandable and necessary the norms of tolerance" (Lipset, 1963: 102-108).

This statement suggests the following general hypothesis: *The more uneducated, uninformed, non-participant, and socially isolated lower-class individuals are, the stronger their tendencies toward leftist radicalism.* The goal of this paper is to examine this hypothesis empirically in the context of a developing country. For this purpose, data collected in four lower-class slums of Santiago, Chile, will be employed.

Method

Following most theoretical accounts, leftist radicalism is defined in this study as an endorsement of revolution and revolutionary violence as legitimate means to bring about the downfall of a social order perceived as exploitative, and its substitution by one more "just" toward the poor.

The empirical study of leftist radicalism has been made difficult by the relative absence of militant extremist movements in developed countries, which allow democratic freedom of expression, and the illegality of such movements in developing nations, where official suspicion and fear of reprisals prevent eliciting these attitudes through conventional methods of survey research. Chile, up to the present, has been the exception among developing countries in preserving a political system flexible enough to accommodate a broad ideological spectrum. This includes an alliance of extreme left parties powerful enough to win the presidential election of 1970. Legality of the extreme left Communist and Socialist parties and relative freedom of expression provided a unique opportunity, in the months before this election, to study radicalism of the left with research tools which, in other places,

would have yielded at best liberal or moderately leftist orientations.

The lower classes concentrate within the Chilean capital of Santiago in a vast ring of peripheral slum settlements occupying approximately half of the physical area of the city and amounting to 25 to 30% of its population (Rosenbluth, 1962; Abrams, 1965; Turner, 1968). Absence of adequate sampling frames prevented drawing a statistically representative sample of the entire peripheral slum population. For this reason, the study was conducted in four settlements, each deemed to be typical of one of the main types of slums to be found in Santiago's lower-class periphery: spontaneous settlements, squatter invasions, decaying housing projects, and government resettlement areas (Rosenbluth, 1962; ECLA, 1965; Portes, 1969).

Within each area, a 10% simple random sample of dwelling units was drawn on the basis of maps provided by the Chilean Housing Corporation (CORVI).[1] In each dwelling, the family head was interviewed. Sixteen percent of the original sample had to be replaced because of sampling errors. There were only two refusals, or less than 1% of the sample. Total sample size was 382.

Comparison of the frequency distributions of this sample on demographic and socioeconomic variables with those obtained by larger and/or more representative studies of the Santiago slum population (CORHABIT, 1969; CELAP, 1967) yielded close similarities suggesting the potential generalizability of present results to this larger universe. This evidence, as well as descriptions of the main types of slums in the Chilean lower-class periphery, is presented in detail elsewhere (Portes, 1970).

Most previous studies of radicalism of the left have operationalized this variable through preferences for the communist and/or other extreme left parties (Lipset, 1963; Soares, 1965; Kornhauser, 1960; Germani, 1966). Following their lead, the first indicator of leftist radicalism in this study is the respondent's statement of which political party he trusted most. This variable, labelled Party Preferences, is dichotomized into: (1) *Leftist*—Preferences for the Communist Party, Socialist Party, or FRAP—the communist-socialist alliance (coded highest) and (2) *Non-Leftist*—Preferences for the Christian Democratic, Radical, or National parties or no political preferences. Thirty-nine percent of respondents voiced leftist party preferences. The bulk of non-leftist preferences was composed of Christian Democrats (31%) and those expressing no particular political preference (24%).

There is an objection, however, to this measure. In Chile, as in many other countries, the Communist and Socialist parties played a crucial role in developing radical political consciousness in the working classes; yet, today, new extremist groups, following the Castro-Guevara traditions, regard these parties as representatives of an institutionalized left incapable of effective revolutionary action. Both parties, especially the Communist, are regarded as previously revolutionary movements now oriented to the representation of lower-class interests within the established democratic framework. This implies the need of measuring leftist radicalism in terms more general than leftist party preferences.[2]

A second measure was, therefore, constructed. This is a unit-weighted index of seven items selected from a pool of 25. This pool included questions concerning the United States and imperialism, Cuba as a revolutionary example, and the internal use of violence as a means of overthrowing the existing social order in favor of the poor. Twelve items were discarded because

of their weak or erratic correlations with the others. The thirteen remaining items were factor analyzed through the principal components method. Equating the first factor with the theoretical dimension under consideration (leftist radicalism), those items having low loadings (< .50) in the first factor or higher loadings on secondary ones were excluded. The others were combined into a single index by taking the simple sum of their standardized scores. The resulting Leftist Radicalism Index (LRI) is composed of seven items. Translation from Spanish of the actual questions employed, frequency distribution of responses, loadings on the first principal components factor, and item-to-total minus self-correlation for each item are presented in Table 1 [not reprinted here]. Evidence of reliability and convergent validity is presented elsewhere (Portes, 1970). For all items, leftist radical responses were coded highest.

Both indicators of leftist radicalism are clearly tentative and subject to considerable error. Each, however, approaches the general dimension from a different perspective: specific party preferences in one case, general political orientations in the other. Zero-order correlation between these measures, .362 (p < .01), though positive and statistically significant, is not high, indicating the absence of overlap, or common elements.

Results

A. Education and mass-media exposure

Among lower-class individuals, Lipset's (1963) theory explicitly predicts that higher levels of radical leftism will be associated with low levels of education and absence of information about current events through sufficient exposure to the mass media. This first hypothesis can, therefore, be stated as follows: *The lower the education and mass-media exposure of lower-class individuals, the stronger their tendencies toward leftist radicalism.* Education is measured in these data through years of formal school completed and ranges from "no education" (0 years) to "two years of college or more." Mass-media exposure is operationalized through two variables: (1) reported frequency of newspaper reading; (2) reported frequency of radio listening. In both cases four closed response categories were provided: "frequently" (coded highest), "occasionally," "almost never," and "never."

The correlation of education with leftist party preferences is —.02 (n.s.) and with the leftist radicalism index (LRI), —.01 (n.s.). Correlation of frequency of newspaper reading with leftist party preferences is —.02 (n.s.) and with LRI, .06 (n.s.). Correlations of frequency of radio listening with the same dependent variables are —.02 (n.s.) and .07 (n.s.), respectively.

These results support the conclusion of no linear association between education and leftist radicalism. However, when the data are examined in tabular form, it is found, contrary to the hypothesis, that middle educational levels show the highest proportion of leftist radicalism and low-education categories show the *least* amount of radicalism, as if the relationship were curvilinear. These findings do not provide grounds, however, for an alternative theory since tabular associations are well below statistical significance.

Summary and conclusion

This paper has employed data from a sample of Chilean lower-class slum dwellers to test several theories concerning determinants of leftist radicalism. No support is found for hypotheses defining

lower-class radicalism as the product of the political primitivism caused by lack of education, lack of mass media exposure and participation, and personal isolation from primary relationships. The consistent absence of fit between theory and empirical results leads to an examination of the assumptions underlying this set of hypotheses. Leftist radicalism is viewed by these theories as an abnormal or deviant development constituting, in essence, a simplistic emotional reaction to personal frustrations and solitude. An alternative image of this political ideology suggests that its emergence may follow normal processes of attitude development through differential exposure and influence of significant others. The tenets of leftist radical ideology, being non-self-evident, require a period of intellectual apprenticeship during the individual's past socialization. This alternative view is tested through three indicators of differential political socialization. Results lend support to the hypothesis.

Other investigations of lower-class leftist radicalism have arrived at similar conclusions. Fried's (1967) careful study of communism among rural migrants to Northern Italian cities finds this tendency due to the well developed communist system of channeling migrants toward active participation in the proper politically socializing groups. Occupations are found in factories where workers, foremen, and union stewards are communists. Housing is available mostly in "red" neighborhoods. Non-communist migrants are promptly socialized by the combined pressure of formal and informal association during work and leisure. Nelson (1969) appropriately notes that the label "communist" could be easily substituted in Fried's description by that of any other political party.

Similarly, differential exposure mechanisms, rather than ignorance or isolation, are found by Petras and Zeitlin (1968) to be crucial determinants of leftist radicalism among Chilean peasants. A strong association is reported between closeness of peasant areas to leftist radical mining communities and peasant support of communist and socialist candidates during elections.

Results of these and other studies in support of differential political socialization as the main determinant of leftist radicalism cannot, however, be overgeneralized. As stated above, when structural conditions in a society have favored emergence of powerful extreme left parties, as in Italy and Chile, ensuing development of radical leftist orientations in individuals may easily follow the normal patterns of attitude development through differential socialization. When extreme left movements are a well-established part of the political landscape, support of these movements by lower-class individuals may well be a natural and, in fact, most rational course of action.

When structural circumstances, on the other hand, have not favored the growth of leftist radical organizations rendering existing ones weak in numbers and alien to the main currents of national concern, the etiology of individual leftist radicalism may follow the abnormal, reactive course outlined by Lipset, Kornhauser, and others. National circumstances of this nature—exemplified by the relatively calm situations of the United States and other Western European countries at the time most theories of mass society and working-class authoritarianism were being written—may force existing extreme left organizations to recruit among the most ignorant, most desperately isolated lower-class groups, in accordance with the causal account provided by these theories.

Causal explanations of the emergence of leftist radicalism, like other political attitudes, seem thus conditioned by the broader structural circumstances and general political framework in which development of individual orientations takes place. Different societal conditions may result in qualitatively different etiologies of apparently identical political beliefs; contingent on them, the label "leftist radicalism" may conceal significantly different attitudinal phenomena.

Finally, the alternative account of lower-class radicalism offered here is useful in pointing out the qualitative difference between the etiology of individual political attitudes and that of major political movements. Dramatic theories of reactive formations in lower-class members often seem to extrapolate naively from the history of revolutions and extremist movements to individual histories. It is a form of ecological fallacy to assume that structural tensions giving rise to leftist radical movements must be reflected or re-created in each and all of its followers. The alternative explanatory path via differential socialization may provide, in many instances, a more accurate explanation of individual political extremism once the societal processes that led to the emergence and consolidation of the radical movement in the first place are satisfactorily understood.

Notes

1. Cooperation of CORVI officials is hereby gratefully acknowledged.

2. To be noted, however, is that neither the Communist nor the Socialist Party ever renounced its intention of carrying out a revolution in Chile. The Chilean Socialist Party is commonly regarded as more leftist than the Communist. Throughout the last decade both parties (especially the former) militantly supported the Cuban Revolution, and Socialist leaders had serious difficulties keeping party members from abandoning conventional politics for guerrilla warfare. FRAP commitment to electoral politics could thus be seen less as a matter of prin-

ciple than of pragmatic strategy, dictated by its numerical strength and military weakness. FRAP's triumph in 1970, while not necessarily implying that extreme left parties will be able to carry out their revolutionary programs, amply confirmed their view

of elections as the shortest route to political power. On the social bases and situation of extreme-left parties in Chile, see Zeitlin (1968); on the results of the 1970 election, Sanders (1970).

24.

Robert Frank Weiss

DEFECTION FROM SOCIAL MOVEMENTS AND SUBSEQUENT RECRUITMENT TO NEW MOVEMENTS

Social movements recruit members and lose some of them. Adherents defect in small numbers or *en masse*, in organized groups, or without organization. It can scarcely be doubted that when alternative movements are already available, or can be newly formed, some defectors will tend to join them.[1] The dependent variables with which this paper is concerned are the strength of the tendency to join a new movement following defection, and the choice of a particular social movement. The determinants of such new recruitment considered here are the social variables which produced the original defection together with certain social characteristics of the alternative movements. This paper will not concern itself with individual personality traits which may conceivably predispose some individuals to the indiscriminate joining of social movements. The present analysis may thus be characterized as stimulus-response (S-R), in that it seeks to relate the behavior (R) of the defector to certain

aspects of his social environment (S). Such an approach shares some of the assumptions of social institutional and historical materialist approaches, and may be contrasted with the response-response approach found in *The True Believer* or *The Authoritarian Personality*,[2] in which joining social movements (R) is regarded as largely dependent upon individual personality traits (R).

The S-R analysis conducted here is based on extrapolation from simple learnings laws and Hullian learning theory.[3] This theory has been developed primarily to predict the actions of individual subjects in highly controlled experimental situations. The theory has, nevertheless, been extended, with a considerable measure of success, into more complex areas.[4] The explanatory power of learning-theory stems, in part, from two sources. First, Hullian theory includes a number of principles which may be combined in a determinate manner. Principles which may seem relatively trivial when taken singly become powerful explanatory tools when the manner of their interaction can be specified. Secondly, Hullian theory is quantitative, with the usual advantages that attend scientific quantification.

Four processes underlying defection and new recruitment may be enumerated at

From Robert Frank Weiss, "Defection from Social Movements and Subsequent Recruitment to New Movements," *Sociometry*, Vol. 26, March 1963, pp. 1-20. Reprinted by permission of the American Sociological Association.

This investigation was supported, in part, by grant M-4523 from the National Institute of Mental Health, U.S. Public Health Service.

this point and discussed later. They are (*a*) *simple stimulus generalization*, related to the similarity and availablity of social movements; (*b*) *extinction*, related to the concept of non-reward; (*c*) *displacement* (owing to inhibition by approach-avoidance conflict), a more complex form of stimulus generalization related to the concepts of similarity and punitive social sanctions, and (*d*) *counterconditioning*, related to multiple participation and reward. A discussion of these four processes in defection and re-recruitment forms the next section of the paper. These four processes do not necessarily represent any kind of an exhaustive classification. The purpose of the theory is to explain and predict defection and re-recruitment, and only such distinctions as appear useful in this theoretical context have been made. It is clear that such terms as "similarity of social movements" and "non-reward" will require further elucidation. The next section will also clarify the meaning of these terms at a verbal level, while the final section will briefly discuss the problems (and possible solutions) involved in their measurement.

Some major boundary conditions

Before passing on to these topics it seems necessary to briefly note some of the phenomena specifically excluded from a detailed consideration. The theory is primarily concerned with people who join a movement and make a commitment to it. One group of people thus excluded from detailed analysis are those complying under duress. Such people may generally be expected to defect when the threat is mitigated, and revert to their former institutional allegiances. Thus, Baron Rosenberg reluctantly allied himself with the Hussite revolutionaries, when he felt himself menaced by the revolutionary armies of Prague and Tabor, reasserting his loyalty to the Emperor Sigismund and the Church at the first safe opportunity.[5] Similarly excluded from detailed consideration is the purely opportunistic association with social movements. The opportunist remains with the successful social movement—the "November revolutionaries" remained in the Stalin apparatus long after Old Bolsheviks had quit in disgust or been purged. When the movement founders, the opportunists leap to the nearest or most profitable refuge— thus the opportunist Kuomintang leader Wang Ching-wei concluded his career as a Japanese puppet.[6] The theory developed here is also best suited to those circumstances in which defection does not take place in organized factions. To the extent that defection is organized, additional analysis would probably be necessary to do any justice to the data. Actually, relatively unorganized defection is considerably more common than might be expected. Anabaptists defected *en masse* (but without organization) when John of Leyden's regime collapsed, and a steady stream of worker-Bolsheviks tore up their party cards during the NEP.[7] When defection does take place in organized groups or factions the principles elucidated here probably would provide a *partial* explanation.

Simple stimulus generalization

The effects of learning in one situation transfer to other situations; the less similar the situation the less transfer occurs. Thus, in a simple learning situation, a response may be conditioned to a particular stimulus (e.g., a 1000 cycle tone), and the strength of the tendency to make the conditioned response may then be assessed when the stimulus is the original tone, a somewhat dissimiliar tone (say, 900

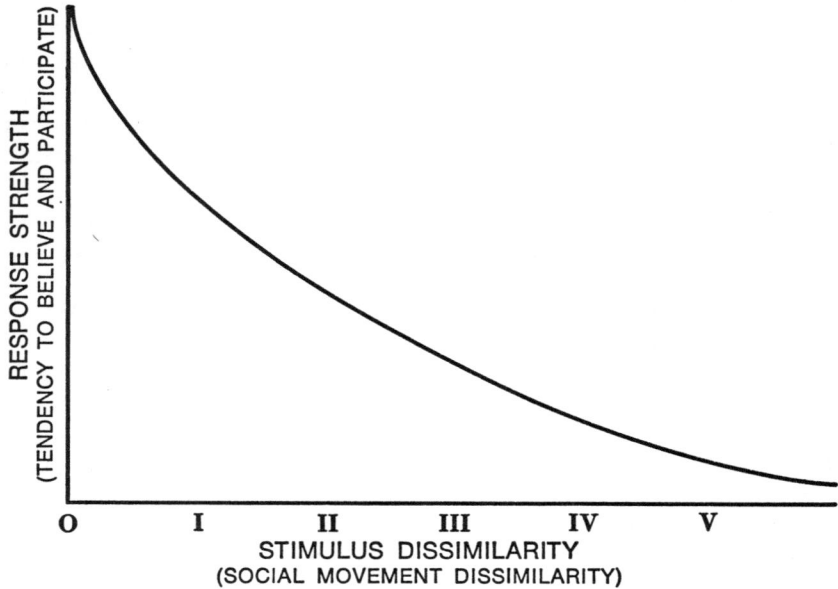

Simple Stimulus Generalization. Point O represents the stimulus (social movement) to which the response (tendency to believe and participate) was originally conditioned. Points I-V represent stimuli (social movements) which are progressively more dissimilar to the original stimulus (social movement).

Figure 1

cycles), a more dissimilar tone, etc. Figure 1 shows the results which have been obtained in numerous learning studies: in the absence of the original stimulus, the individual will tend to respond (with lesser strength) to similar stimuli.

Now let us consider the situation in which a social movement becomes unavailable to some or all of its members. One way in which this has happened is through emigration of members. Under such circumstances the stimulus complex to which the person's loyalties are attached is no longer available. Extended to this situation, the principle of stimulus generalization implies that such people would tend to transfer their loyalties to the available movement most nearly similar to the one

they formerly belonged to. A re-examination of Figure 1, using "social movement dissimilarity" as the independent variable and "tendency to believe and participate" as the dependent variable, shows this process more clearly. If several movements are available, the strongest tendency will be to believe and participate in the most immediately similar movement. The tendency to believe and participate in alternative movements decreases as similarity to the old movement decreases. Thus when several alternative movements are available, the movements which are most similar to the old movement will be joined in the greatest numbers, and the others in decreasing numbers. When there is only one alternative movement to be joined, the strength of the tendency to join at all will depend on the similarity to the old movement. An illustration of this kind of situation is afforded by the immigration to the United States, during the early part of this century, of members of European Social Democratic movements. When they joined any movement at all, they tended distinctly to join the foreign language federations of the Socialist Party. Thus, a member of the Social Democracy of the Kingdom of Poland and Lithuania (SDKPL) would join a Polish or Lithuanian language local of the Socialist Party of the U.S.A.[8]

A second way in which the movement may become unavailable to the individual is the collapse or destruction of the movement. Not infrequently, the forces which bring about the destruction or collapse of a social movement do *not* operate directly on the majority of its members.[9] Colonial administrators in Melanesia have typically reacted to cargo cult movements among the natives by jailing or exiling the leaders of the movement. The remaining members have sometimes been unable to replace these leaders (often limited to a prophet and a single organizer) and the movement has collapsed.[10] The apparent continuity of membership in successive cargo movements in some areas of Melanesia is probably due, in part, to generalization of habits of belief and participation from a given movement to its successor.

Extinction

Extinction of Both Belief and Participation. When people are continuously non-rewarded for both belief and participation, we would expect them to lose both their opinions and their tendency to participate, and consequently to defect. There would be no greater susceptibility to alternative

social movements than other people have. Indeed, since the effects of extinction generalize to similar stimuli, there would actually be somewhat greater resistance to recruitment to similar movements than would be found in people who had not been movement members. If a new recruitment did take place, it would most likely be to the old movement (spontaneous recovery).

Differential Extinction of Belief or Participation. When reward for participation is terminated, but the members continue to be rewarded for belief, they will lose the habit of participation, but retain their beliefs. It seems likely that such people would be extremely difficult to recruit for a new movement. In addition to the generalization of the extinction of participation to similar movements, the defector retains the ideology of his old movement—and this ideology may conflict in some regards with that of a new movement. An increase in motivation can increase the strength of the participation response so that the defector may once again be willing to participate. In such an instance, the defector would be more likely to rejoin his old movement (since he retains its beliefs, and participation is still most strongly conditioned to the old movement).

When reward for belief is terminated, but the members continue to be rewarded for participation, defection is not likely, since loss of belief does not necessarily imply the acquisition of new convictions incompatible with continued participation. What is to be expected, rather, is degeneration (if these conditions affect many members) into social clubism or opportunist manipulation, depending on the member's position in the movement. Those highly placed in the movement will become opportunist manipulators, while rank-and-file members will find themselves members of a club, rather than a movement. Repeated examples may be drawn from the history of reformist political parties.

Displacement
(due to inhibition by conflict)

In simple stimulus generalization the person is prevented from responding to the original stimulus because it is absent. In displacement, as discussed here, the person is prevented from responding to the original stimulus because there is a conflicting response of avoidance, based on punishment and sustained (for a time) by fear. An experimental method of producing such a conflict might involve training a rat to run down an alley for food, and then, on one trial, giving him an electric shock instead of food. The result of such a procedure is usually referred to as approach-avoidance conflict.

Punishment for Both Participation and Belief. (a) Where punishment is not sufficient to raise the avoidance gradient above the gradient of participation and belief at any point, then both participation and belief continue. Thus, small difficulties do not lead to displacement when belief and participation are relatively strong.

(b) When punitive sanctions are so severe that the gradient of avoidance is always higher than the gradient of participation and belief, then there will be no displacement. Members will defect and will be distinctly unrecruitable for the old movement or similar movements. The Canton Commune incident in the Chinese Revolution of 1925-27 represents an example of this process.[11] In the course of this revolution, the General Labor Union had seized power in Canton. The Chinese Communist Party, following a Stalin-dictated policy of close alliance with the Kuomintang, induced the workers to welcome Chiang Kai-shek's forces, and even to lay down their arms. A general massacre of the workers, accompanied by tortures, followed. Some time later the Communists, following a new turn in their opportunist line, attempted to stir the Cantonese to a second rising. There was no response. The Cantonese workers looked on in indifference while a handful of predominantly non-Cantonese Communists were easily defeated by the Kuomintang forces. It would be absurd to suggest that the principle described above represents a full explanation of the failure of the abortive Communist rising known as the Canton Commune. Many leaders and militants had been killed, and were hence not available for the second rising. More importantly, the workers' organizations had been destroyed or transformed into instruments of Kuomintang control. But in order to do justice to the remarkable *indifference* of the workers at the time of the Canton Commune (as contrasted with the first rising) a principle such as that introduced here seems essential.

(c) When punishment produces crossing gradients, as in Figure 3 [not reprinted here], the *strongest* displaced response will occur to movements which have an intermediate degree of similarity to the original one. Defection to more or less dissimilar movements is still possible, but the tendency is to choose the movement located at the point of strongest displacement.

(d) The tendency to join a new movement is weaker for defectors whose participation and belief in the original movement is blocked by approach-avoidance conflict than it is for people whose participation has been prevented by the unavailability of the original movement. That is to say, simple stimulus generalization leads to a greater tendency to join than displacement does, all other things (including the range of new movements available) equal. As shown in Figure 3, the movements of intermediate similarity (chosen in displacement) do not arouse as much generalized tendency to believe and participate as does the movement of greatest similarity (chosen by those who are prevented from participation by the absence of the original movement).

Punishment for Participation Only.

(a) When punishment for participation (but not for belief) has been so severe that the gradient of avoidance is always higher than the gradient of participation, there will be a tendency to withdraw from participation in the movement, while maintaining belief. This kind of social phenomenon is characteristic of certain traditionalist dictatorships (e.g. the Horthy and Salazar regimes) which suppress organized opposition, but are relatively unconcerned with private expression of belief.

(b) When punitive sanctions for participation produce crossing gradients (in the manner of Figure 3), there will be a displacement of participation (membership) and maintenance of belief. One clear example is afforded by the loss of the Menshevik mass support to the Bolsheviks, between February and October, 1917. The continuation of the war (supported by the Menshevik leaders, the increasing incidence of industrial lockouts (which the Menshevik leaders did not prevent), etc. represented severe punishments to the Menshevik workers, and the smaller number of Menshevik soldiers and sailors. The actions of the Menshevik leadership did not correspond to the beliefs of their mass membership. The Menshevik mass membership displaced their allegiance to the Bolsheviks, retaining their beliefs (which were in accord with Bolshevik ideas). [12]

(c) If the motivation underlying belief and participation increases, it will be possible for increasingly dissimilar movements to attract some of the defectors (in the manner of Figure 5 [not reprinted here]), while, at the same time, there is an intensification of the original belief. This appears to be a characteristic schismatic phenomenon—the pure doctrine, held with greater fervor, in a new sect or splinter party. This kind of phenomenon acquires a particular significance when movements of an intermediate degree of similarity to the original movement are not available to the defector.

Punishment for Belief Alone. Suppression of social movements by agencies of the established order involves, primarily, an effort to weaken or eliminate participation in the movement. A more totalitarian and demanding state or church may also seek to suppress deviant beliefs through punishment, while a less scrupulous authority may not trouble itself to differentiate between belief and participation, even where this is possible. Where punishment is resorted to on behalf of the established order, participation is the first target and belief is the second. It would not ordinarily be expected, therefore, to find the authorities neglecting punishment of participation while practicing punishment of belief. However, social movements have their own internal social control systems, which, in hierarchically structured movements, may be employed by the leaders in order to change the beliefs of the members, without, if possible, impairing participation. Punishment for belief, but not for participation, was therefore employed in the Anabaptist movement when John of Leyden promoted himself from prophet to messiah. [13] More familiar examples may be drawn from successive shifts in party line in various Communist parties.

(a) When punitive sanctions directed against belief (but not against participation) have been so severe that the gradient of avoidance is always higher than the gradient of belief, there will be a tendency to lose belief while maintaining participation. While new beliefs may be learned through internal propaganda, or the old beliefs may recover in time (as fear is gradually extinguished), permanent loss of belief together with retention of organizational loyalty does not appear to be an uncommon phenomenon.

(b) When punishment for belief produces crossing gradients of belief and avoidance (in the manner of Figure 3) there will be a displacement of belief and a maintenance of participation. This could conceivably lead directly to a relatively uniform change of belief among members. However, in the more likely case that punishment is unequally applied or initial strength of belief differs among members, a more likely possibility is the formation of factions within the movement. The Yugoslav Communist Party was instructed by the Comintern in 1935 to switch from its current beliefs (e.g., no cooperation with the Social Democrats, self-determination for the non-Serbian minorities) to Popular Front beliefs (e.g., cooperation with all anti-fascists, a strong united Yugoslav state). Yugoslav Communists were assailed and reprimanded for their beliefs. The short-term consequence of this was dissension in the Yugoslav central committee (Comintern quip: "Two Yugoslavs—three factions") and, it appears, consequent dissension in the rest of the Party. Until the repression was intensified, some members retained their old beliefs, while others displaced their beliefs in the direction of those advocated by the Comintern.[14]

The conditions required for making counterconditioning predictable in the laboratory are so stringent as to make it very doubtful whether the analysis can be properly carried beyond the description given above. If, however, three conditions are reasonably well satisfied, it may be possible to hazard some tentative predictions. Two conditions refer to the prediction of a particular choice: (1) the member is confronted with the two alternatives simultaneously; (2) the member may make the decision on an ideological basis or on any basis other than a conscious calculation of the rewards he has derived from belief or participation. The third condition refers to the background of decisions leading up to the particular choice to be predicted: once having chosen a course of action (such as between attending a Church or Party function held at the same time on a particular day) circumstances have compelled the member to adhere to that choice until the course of action is completed.

If these conditions are satisfied, a number of interesting relations may be tentatively expected. Any useful discussion of the principles of learning theory which permits the derivation of these relations would require considerably more space than would be appropriate for this paper. Since an exposition of learning theory can be found elsewhere[15] (though in terms appropriate for controlled experiments with non-articulate organisms, rather than the present social phenomena), only the specific predictions will be given here. The first two of these are fairly obvious from common sense, the others much less so.

(a) The greater the magnitude of the rewards typically derived from belief and participation in one movement, the greater will be the tendency to choose that movement.

(b) The greater the number of occasions on which the member has been rewarded for belief and participation in one movement the greater will be the tendency to choose that movement.

(c) The effects of motivation and magnitude of reward are independent, except when the strength of belief and participation in both movements is weak. If the strength of belief and participation in both movements is not weak, and motivation increases, there will be no effect on the tendency to choose the movement from which the member derived the greater magnitude of reward. If the strength of belief and participation in both movements is weak, and motivation *increases,* there will be a *decreased* tendency to choose the movement from which the member derived the greater magnitude of reward.

(d) If motivation increases, and the number of occasions on which the member has been rewarded for belief and participation is the same for both movements, the increase in motivation will have no effect on choice (all other things equal).

(e) If motivation increases, and the number of occasions on which the member has been rewarded for belief and participation is greater for one movement than for the other, the tendency to choose the more frequently rewarded alternative will increase.

(f) Information which supports a belief tends to have the same effects as a reward for espousing that belief.[16]

Counterconditioning is sometimes so effective that belief and participation in the original movement are completely replaced by belief and participation in the new movement. The original habits of belief and participation are not lost, but are merely overridden by the greater strength of the new beliefs and actions. If reward for the new beliefs and participation is terminated, extinction may weaken the tendency to belief and participate in the new movement to the point where the tendency to believe and participate in the

original movement is able to compete successfully with allegiance to the new movement. Such a sequence of complete counterconditioning followed by extinction of the new response is probably involved in the return to childhood religion shown by some defectors.

Measurement problems

Similarity of social movements

In simple learning situations, similarity of stimuli is generally varied along a physical continuum (brightness, loudness, pitch, etc.). Physical similarity is of lesser importance in the case of similarity of social movements. Here similarity is verbally mediated. Labeling physically similar stimuli with different words can lead to acquired distinctiveness, and labeling physically different stimuli with the same word can lead to acquired similarity.[17] This kind of mediated generalization has also been studied under laboratory conditions, but accurate prediction depends on knowledge of the verbal responses involved in the particular situation. Moreover, generalization in the defection situation may very well take place along more than one continuum of similarity. Such diverse continua as, say, radicalism-conservatism, and friendliness-impersonality might be involved. A rather good solution to the problem may be found in the statistical technique known as multi-dimensional scaling. In this method, subjects are asked to judge pairs of stimuli (e.g., names of social movements) with regard to their similarity. The subjects are asked only "how similar are these two," the criteria of similarity *not* being specified in advance. The multi-dimensional scaling extracts from these judgments the dimensions along which the subjects do their judging, though the subjects may be unable to verbalize these underlying dimensions themselves. The movements are thus arrayed along a dimension and the distances between them are known. (It remains for the researcher to give the dimensions a name, but the name is irrelevant to prediction in this case, the distances between movements being adequate for this.) If there is only one underlying dimension, prediction is obvious. If there is more than one underlying dimension, it is possible to estimate the generalization along each dimension separately. If the estimates of generalization along several dimensions do not agree in predicting the movement most likely to be chosen, it is possible to estimate the prominence of each dimension (amount of variance explained) and to arrive thereby at the probability of the subject's responding in terms of any given dimension alone. If any one dimension is distinctly more prominent than the remaining dimensions combined (a not unlikely outcome), it would again be possible to treat the results as if there were only a single dimension along which generalization took place.

While an adequate technique for the measurement of social movement similarity exists, the problem of when to apply the technique remains. It is possible that the events leading to defection, as well as experiences following recruitment to a new movement, could lead to changes in the defector's evaluation of the similarity of different movements. Ultimately, this remains a question to be answered by research, though the dimensional structure of perception is likely to be quite resistant to change.

Reward and punishment

It is difficult to determine adequately the manner in which rewards or punish-ments have impinged on members of social movements from historical records or from contemporary studies of social movement structure. Estimates of the numbers and magnitude of rewards or punishments may be obtained by several conventional methods. Among these would be questionnaires administered to the defectors as well as to members and ex-members of the movement who might be informed on the experiences of the defector. It would be possible to identify different dimensions of reward through factor analysis or multidimensional scaling. Probably such an elaborate form of analysis would be unnecessary. The major reason for identifying dimensions of reward would be to relate them to differences in the motivations of the defectors. However, laboratory studies of simple learning phenomena indicate that a given reward has the same effect when motivation is high as it does when motivation is low.[18] As previously indicated, information which supports a belief tends to have the same functional properties as a reward for holding that belief. The results in this situation agree with the results from simple learning experiments in indicating that the effects of belief-supporting information ("reward") on the strength of a belief are independent of level of motivation.[19]

Summary

A theoretical analysis of recruitment to social movements, following defection from a movement, was developed. The theory was concerned both with the strength of the tendency to join a new movement, and choice of a particular social movement. The determinants of re-recruitment considered by the theory were limited to the social variables which produced the original defection and certain characteristics of the social environment at the time of re-recruitment. A social-institutional and learning-theory approach was utilized, and the effect of individual personality traits was therefore excluded from consideration.

Four social causes of defection affecting subsequent recruitment were identified: (a) the movement becomes unavailable to the member, (b) the strength of belief or participation is decreased by non-reward, (c) the net strength of belief or participation is decreased by punitive social sanctions, and (d) the strength of belief and participation in an alternative movement is increased until defection from the original movement takes place. Four psychological processes were systematically related to each of these four social causes of defection: (a) simple stimulus generalization, (b) extinction, (c) displacement owing to approach-avoidance conflict, and (d) counter-conditioning (corresponding to social causes a, b, c, and d respectively). Prediction (actually, post-diction, since historical illustrations were used) depends on which process is involved, whether both belief and participation are equally affected, and the social conditions at the time of re-recruitment (especially the characteristics of the new movement). For example, when the movement becomes unavailable to the member (e.g., through emigration) simple stimulus generalization leads to recruitment into the available movement most nearly similar to the original movement. However, when punishment for belief and participation in a social movement causes defection, displacement through approach-avoidance conflict leads to recruitment into a social movement of moderate similarity to the original movement, *not* to the most nearly similar movement available. Moreover, displacement yields a weaker tendency to join a new movement than does stimulus generalization.

In the course of the analysis of re-recruitment, certain aspects of such phenomena as faction-formation and defection were also discussed. For example, when social movement members continue to be rewarded for participation, but reward for belief is terminated, the consequent extinction of belief leads not to defection, but to degeneration into social clubism or opportunist manipulation, depending on the members' position in the movement. Those highly placed in the movement become opportunist manipulators, while rank-and-file members find themselves to be members of a social club rather than a movement.

A brief discussion of measurement problems involved in such concepts as "similarity of social movements" was included in the paper. Illustrations of the processes involved were drawn from a variety of movements and incidents including the Canton Commune, Melanesian cargo cult movements, Bolshevik re-recruitment of Menshevik defectors, and forced recruitment in the Hussite revolution.

Notes

1. For example, Arthur G. Neal, *The Interchangeability of Social Movements,* Unpublished Master's Thesis, Ohio State University, 1956; Rudolph Heberle, *From Democracy to Nazism,* Baton Rouge, Louisiana: Louisiana State University Press, 1945.

2. Eric Hoffer, *The True Believer,* New York: Mentor Books, 1958; Theodore W. Adorno, Else Frenkel-Brunswick, Daniel J. Levinson and R. Nevitt Sanford, *The Authoritarian Personality,* New York: Harper, 1950.

3. See, for example, Clark L. Hull, *A Behavior System,* New Haven: Yale University Press, 1952; Neal E. Miller and John Dollard, *Social Learning and Imitation,* New Haven: Yale University Press, 1941; and Kenneth W. Spence, *Behavior Theory and Conditioning,* New Haven: Yale University Press, 1956.

4. For example, John Dollard and Neal E. Miller, *Personality and Psychotherapy,* New York: McGraw-Hill, 1950; Miller and Dollard, *op. cit.*

5. Frederick G. Heymann, *John Zizka and the Hussite Revolution,* Princeton: Princeton University Press, 1955. In order to make the subject matter under discussion clear, a number of illustrative examples are given throughout the paper. Illustration, of course, is not proof. However, consideration of well-chosen examples may facilitate constructive criticism, this analysis itself having been developed with concrete instances taken into account, rather than being illustrated after the analysis.

6. See, for example, Harold R. Isaacs, *The Tragedy of the Chinese Revolution,* Stanford, California: Stanford University Press, 1951.

7. Norman Cohn, *The Pursuit of the Millenium,* Fairlawn, New Jersey: Essential Books, 1957; Isaac Deutscher, *The Prophet Unarmed,* New York: Oxford University Press, 1959.

8. Theodore Draper, *The Roots of American Communism,* New York: Viking, 1957. The defection of foreign language locals from the Russian Empire areas (e.g., Russian, Finnish, Lettish, Ukrainian) to the new Communist parties, following the October revolution, appears to represent a striking example of mediated generalization.

9. New affiliations following defections induced by punitive social sanctions or termination of reward will be discussed later.

10. Peter Worsley, *The Trumpet Shall Sound,* London: MacGibbon and Kee, 1957.

11. See Isaacs, *op. cit.*

12. Leon Trotsky, *The History of the Russian Revolution,* Ann Arbor, Michigan: University of Michigan Press, 1957.

13. Cohn, *op. cit.*

14. For example, Fitzroy Maclean, *Disputed Barricade,* London: Jonathan Cape, 1957.

15. Spence, *op. cit.,* especially pp. 199-220, 237-244.

16. Robert Frank Weiss, Harve E. Rawson, and Benjamin Pasamanick, "Argument Strength, Delay of Argument and Anxiety in the 'Conditioning' and 'Selective Learning' of Attitudes," *Journal of Abnormal and Social Psychology,* in press; Weiss, "Persuasion and the Acquisition of Attitudes: Models from Conditioning and Selective Learning," *Psychological Reports,* 11 (Dec., 1962), pp. 710-732.

17. For example, Miller and Dollard, *op. cit.*

18. Robert Frank Weiss, "Deprivation and Reward Magnitude Effects on Speed Throughout the Goal Gradient," *Journal of Experimental Psychology,* 60 (Dec., 1960), pp. 384-390; William F. Reynolds and W. B. Pavlik, "Running Speed as a Function of Deprivation Period and Reward Magnitude," *Journal of Comparative and Physiological Psychology,* 53 (Dec., 1960), pp. 615-618.

19. Weiss, Rawson and Pasamanick, *op. cit.*

25.

Nan Lin

THE McINTIRE MARCH:
A STUDY OF RECRUITMENT AND COMMITMENT

There are few empirical studies of mass demonstrations. Our knowledge of social movements is based almost entirely on historical or case studies.[1] Furthermore, many interesting discussions focus on the origins rather than on the persistent structure and process of social movements.[2] Available data from the few existing studies of demonstrations are incomplete and unsatisfactory because they were gathered before or after, rather than during, the demonstration; and/or they are not based on representative respondents.[3]

The problem is twofold: (1) how to devise a sampling procedure that yields a representative sample of the participants, and (2) how to conduct successful interviews during the course of a mass demonstra-

From Nan Lin, "The McIntire March: A Study of Recruitment and Commitment." *Public Opinion Quarterly* 38, Winter 1974-1975, pp. 562-73, with permission of the publisher.

An earlier version of this article was presented at the Annual Meeting of the American Sociological Association, Denver, Colorado, in August-September, 1971.

tion. The only study that comes close to fulfilling both requirements was conducted by Barker *et al.* in London.[4] In that study, the researchers attempted to draw a sample of the demonstrators in a march against the war in Vietnam while the march was taking place.

The study reported here was an attempt to draw a representative sample from participants in a particular mass demonstration as the event unfolded and to study three aspects of it: (1) the recruitment of its participants from the population; (2) the communication process associated with the mobilization of the participants; and (3) the process by which participants became committed to the demonstration.

The demonstration

The mass demonstration selected for this study was the March for Victory held in Washington, D.C., on October 3, 1970, and led by the Reverend Carl McIntire.

Reverend McIntire, the fundamentalist right-wing pastor of the Bible Presbyterian Church in Collingswood, New Jersey, is president of Shelton College in Cape May, New Jersey. He disseminates his beliefs and opinions through two specialized mass channels: the radio program "Twentieth Century Reformation Hour," carried by 600 stations; and his weekly newsletter, the *Christian Beacon.* McIntire is known for his vigorous campaign against communism, theological liberalism, and protest marches and movements.

In a direct response to the Peace Moratorium held in Washington, D.C., on November 15, 1969, McIntire called for the first March for Victory on April 4, 1970. Although he forecast and claimed a turnout of 100,000 people at that event, the police estimated a gathering of only 10,000.

Again demanding total victory in Viet-

nam, McIntire held a press conference on April 9 and outlined a second March for Victory to be held on October 3, 1970, in Washington, D.C. He claimed that the turnout for the first march could have been two million people if the mass media had disseminated the news months earlier, or "even two weeks ago," instead of only four days before the march.

Then, on July 15, 1970, McIntire made a dramatic move by inviting Vice President Nguyen Cao Ky of South Vietnam to participate and speak at the second March for Victory. To the surprise of many, including the government officials of both the United States and South Vietnam, Ky announced on September 3 his acceptance of the invitation. However, pressure was exerted on Ky to change his plans and despite McIntire's personal visit to Ky in Saigon in mid-September, Ky eventually "postponed" his visit.

These dramatic events were reported at great length by the major mass media in the United States throughout the month of September. In fact, the second March for Victory received more national attention than any other right-wing movement or demonstration in recent American history.

Several leftist groups had planned massive counter-demonstrations against Ky's presence. Although Ky's absence diminished the impetus of counter-demonstrations, some left-wing groups made plans to celebrate his absence at Rock Creek Park, about a mile from the monument grounds where the rally of the March for Victory was to take place. Still others intended to counter-demonstrate at the monument grounds.[5]

Methodology and data

Personal interviews were conducted with a sample of participants at the march and at the counter-demonstrations starting immediately after the march columns reached the monument grounds for the rally.

The sampling method used was spatial sampling.[6] Since the population of participants was undefinable, no random sample of the participants could be made. However, since the physical space for the rally was finite (after the march down Pennsylvania Avenue the crowd conveniently formed between the speaker's platform and the Washington Monument), systematic sampling of the participants over the space became possible.

The fifteen interviewers were graduate and advanced undergraduate students trained intensively for two weeks in the sampling and interviewing techniques and familiarized with the interview schedule. Simulated interviews, each taking an average of ten minutes, were conducted within the group throughout the period. The interviewer would start the interview by saying, "Hello, we are doing a survey of the march participants. We want to get accurate information about the march rather than have distorted descriptions being passed around. May I ask you a few questions?" As he finished this statement, the interviewer was instructed to nod slightly and look into the eyes of the potential respondent. This nonverbal hinting technique proved effective in inducing the potential respondent to respond by nodding his head too.

Although McIntire predicted 500,000 marchers, the police estimated that between 15,000 and 20,000 participated. A total of 316 persons were approached by the interviewers and only 45 refused to be interviewed or failed to complete the interview.[7] An analysis of the respondents (demonstrators) and of the refusers showed no statistically significant difference (X^2 at .05 level) between the two groups on age, sex, race, or relative distance from the speaker's platform.

Eight respondents were disqualified either because they were there for a purpose other than demonstrating (e.g., FBI agents, reporters) or because they gave apparently inconsistent responses. Their responses were excluded from subsequent analyses and discussions.

Recruitment of participants

It has been suggested that a social movement does not attract participants uniformly from all segments of the population.[8] Pinard and others have found that those who join a social movement during its early stages tend to be from the middle socioeconomic strata; the more intensive participants tend to be from the lower socioeconomic strata.[9] Compared to census data for the U.S. population, the McIntire demonstrators tended to come from the middle-aged, more educated, more professional, politically right-wing, and Protestant sectors. Certainly, they were not socially or economically disadvantaged.

Participation in such political demonstrations is far from accidental. The behavioral commitment represents a manifestation of past social and psychological involvement in the generalized beliefs of the movement. The demonstrators were pessimistic about the outcome of the war in Vietnam if current U.S. policy was not changed. Fifty-one per cent of them had previously participated in similar demonstrations and rallies. Thirty-two per cent felt that the United States would be "defeated."

Almost three-quarters of the demonstrators (71 per cent) had traveled from outside Washington, D.C., Maryland, and Virginia to join the march. A significant portion of them (35 per cent) came from Pennsylvania and New Jersey, where McIntire's personal influence was strongest.

Still, a large number—36 per cent—came from other states.

The communication process

Most researchers in social movements agree that interpersonal relationships constitute a most crucial process in the study of social movements.[10] Yet, as pointed out by Pinard[11] and Orum,[12] empirical studies in social movements have to a great extent ignored this process. They suggest that convergence of the research traditions of social movements and innovation diffusion may result in fruitful developments. In this study, we intensively investigated the communication process associated with mobilization of the participants in the demonstration.

Two components of the communication process involved in mobilizing participants may be identified: (1) information is disseminated and diffused to the participants and (2) participants relay the information to others. The initial dissemination and diffusion process may be studied through an examination of two variables: (1) the source of the initial awareness about the demonstration or counter-demonstration, and (2) the length of such awareness.

In our study, the date of initial awareness was operationalized by the question, "When did you first hear about the march?" Our data (shown in Table 1) reveal that the median date of the demonstrators' initial awareness as of the march was 180 days before it took place. The overwhelming majority (73 per cent) heard about it either from McIntire personally, over his radio program, or through the specialized media such as the *Christian Beacon*.

Most influential in the demonstrators' decision to attend the march were egocentricity (self-conviction) and direct contact with McIntire or his radio program. That

external sources of influence were infrequently mentioned was mainly a function of the participants' strong predispositions.

These data confirm findings in mass communication and diffusion studies that interpersonal influence and conviction rather than the mass media play the important role of influencing people's decisions. The British data also showed the ineffectiveness of the mass media in influencing demonstration participants (only 16 per cent were so influenced to participate).[13]

A structural model of the participation commitment process

While the foregoing data offer a descriptive view of the characteristics of the

TABLE 1
The Communication Process

Variable	Demon-strators (N = 201)
Source of initial awareness of March[a]	
Prior McIntire gatherings	11%
McIntire's radio program	48
Specialized media (newsletter, leaflet, church, other rally)	14
Personal (family, friend)	11
Mass media (TV, newspaper, not radio)	9
Other (unspecified)	7
Source of influence to attend March	
Prior McIntire gatherings	13
McIntire's radio program	15
Specialized media	3
Personal (friends, etc.)	7
Mass media	5
Personal conviction or curiosity	53
Other (fun, weather)	6
Number of persons (outside own family) talked to about March	
None	14
From one to five	18
Six or more	66
Unspecified	2

[a] The median date of initial awareness of the March was 180 days.

participants and the communication process in the demonstration, the dynamic process by which a participant becomes committed to the demonstration may be conceptualized in terms of a number of temporally related stages. The participation commitment process may be said to begin when the respondent is informed by a source about the demonstration (source of initial awareness); that, in turn, affects the earliness of initial awareness (date of initial awareness); and it may be finally reflected in the extent of information and opinion relaying.

The purpose of this analysis, then, was to attempt to construct a model that would detect the dynamic process of participation commitment. The process of participation commitment, as the phenomenon to be explained in the model, was indexed by: (1) proximity to the original source in the initial awareness,[14] (2) the earliness of demonstration awareness, and (3) the extent of information relaying about the demonstration.

The potential antecedent variables selected included: (1) two demographic variables (age and education), (2) two social network variables (religious activism and previous commitment to similar demonstrations), (3) a political variable (pessimistic outlook on the Vietnam war)[15] and (4) a spatial variable (proximity to the demonstration and McIntire headquarters).[16] A model showing the initial construct of the commitment process is presented in Figure 1.

It was expected that certain types of participants—those who were older, less educated, more active in church, more pessimistic in war outlook, had to travel a greater distance, and had been in previous, similar demonstrations—would exhibit a greater extent of commitment (becoming aware earlier and through sources closer to McIntire, and relaying that awareness more extensively).

The data revealed the following:

(1) Respondents who used an information source close to McIntire tended to be older, more religiously active, and to have previously participated in similar demonstrations. These three factors indicate that becoming aware of the demonstration through a source close to its originator is a function of proximity to the originator in

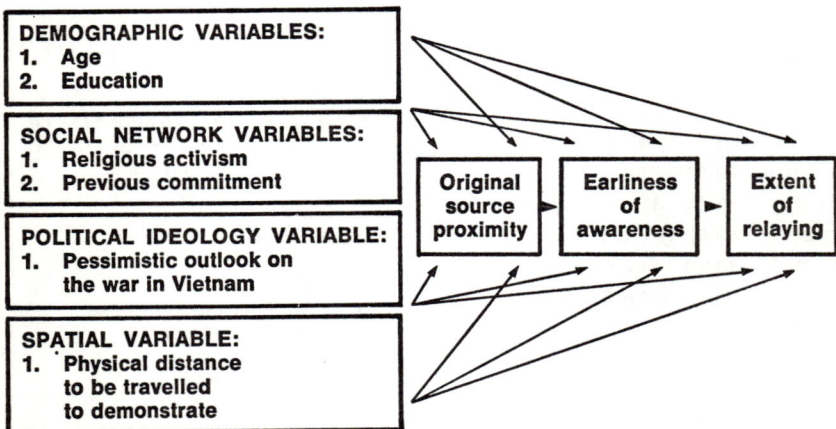

Figure 1. The Initial Model of the Commitment Process

previous activities. As mentioned earlier, the main thrust of McIntire's movement was religious. Thus, those active in his religious movement should be expected to to become aware of the demonstration through either McIntire or his associates in religious gatherings sponsored by the movement. A similar explanation can apply to the relationship between previous commitment to similar demonstrations and becoming aware of the March for Victory through a source close to McIntire. The fact that McIntire had a regular radio program eliminated any effect of physical distance on the knowers' gathering information from a source close to the originator of the demonstration. The data, in addition, showed that concern about the outcome of the war did not play any significant role in the respondents' receiving the information.

(2) Four factors significantly affected the relative earliness of awareness of the demonstration. Most important was the original source proximity. The early knowers tended to be informed by sources closer to the originator. Again, religious activism was significant in respondents' early aware-

ness. While physical distance did not affect the source of the respondents' initial awareness of the demonstration, it did influence its timing. The closer a person was to the site of the demonstration or the movement's headquarters, the earlier he was likely to become aware of the demonstration. Finally, the less-educated respondents tended to be early knowers.

(3) Three factors significantly affected the extent to which a respondent relayed information about the demonstration to others. As expected, those who heard about the demonstration earlier showed more relaying activities, as did the more religiously active respondents. Interestingly, physical distance also showed a positive affect on relaying: those further from the site of the demonstration and the movement's headquarters tended to relay information more often. Apparently to overcome the obstacle of greater distance in participating in the demonstration, a person needed more reinforcement, support, and, possibly, companions in his commitment.

The simplified and finalized model is shown in Figure 2.[17]

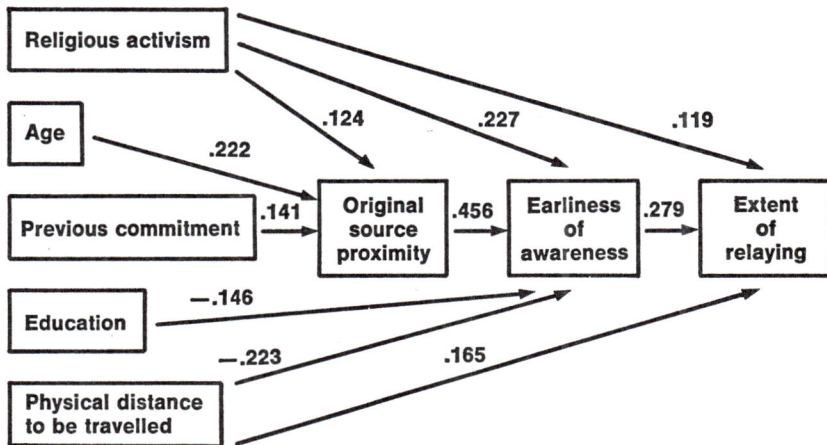

Figure 2. The Final Model of the Commitment Process
(For the intercorrelations among the independent variables, see Table 2)

Analysis of the participation commitment process thus shows that differential extent of participation commitment—as indexed by the original source proximity, relative earliness of awareness, and the extent of relaying—was affected by the extent of a person's involvement in the movement prior to the demonstration; a greater involvement in the movement—as indexed by relative religious activism and previous participation in similar demonstrations—induced hearing about the demonstration earlier and from a source closer to the originator of the movement and the demonstration. It also induced more extensive relaying—another indication of commitment.

On the other hand, concern about the war's outcome had no effect on differential extents of participation commitment. The evidence is rather conclusive that active participation in a demonstration results more from previous behavior in similar activities than from commitment to the explicitly salient ideology of the particular demonstration.

Summary and discussion

The data show that participants in the McIntire-led March for Victory did not come from the lower socioeconomic strata of the population. A substantial number of them had previous experience in similar activities. Most became aware of the demonstration through McIntire or his specialized media, committed themselves to the activity without any further external influence, and relayed the information to others.

Regressional and path analysis substantiated the effect of previous commitment to the movement on the demonstrators' active participation in the dynamic process of commitment. Those who were active church members or had participated in similar demonstrations before were informed early by McIntire or sources closely associated with him, and they engaged in extensive relaying activities. Political ideology relative to the war in Vietnam, although the dominant theme in the march, played an insignificant role in triggering active participation commitment.

It may be argued that the generalizability of the findings may be limited due to the unique nature of the demonstration. For one thing, the movement had a charismatic leader with a substantial and consistent following over a long period of time. This may not be the case in other movements. Also, the demonstration studied mobilized participants whose ideological commitment was "displaced"—from a religious to a political one. Other demonstrations may draw participants who share no beliefs other than the ones at issue in the demonstration.

However, the data clearly show the importance and effectiveness of a charismatic leader in the mobilization process for a demonstration and in the transformation of followers' commitment from one form of ideology to another, even though the followers' conviction in the latter is at best equivocal. Furthermore, the study design clearly demonstrates the feasibility and viability of studying social demonstrations as they actually unfold. Comparisons with available data from the British study encourage this conclusion.[18] This study should contribute a methodological path for future studies of demonstrations, thereby providing the mechanism necessary for a cumulative knowledge about many social manifestations of public opinion.

Notes

1. J. Hollaran, P. Elliott, and G.Murdock, *Demonstrations and Communication: A Case Study,* Middlesex, England, Penguin Books, 1970; J. Lof-

land and R. Stark, "Becoming a World Saver: A Theory of Conversion to a Deviant Perspective," *American Sociological Review,* Vol. 30, 1965, pp. 862-875; J. L. Simons, "On Maintaining Deviant Belief Systems: A Case Study," *Social Problems,* Vol. 11, 1964, pp. 250-256; J. W. Vander Zanden, "The Non-Violent Resistance Movement Against Segregation," *American Journal of Sociology* 68, 1963, pp. 544-550.

2. J. C. Davis, "Toward a Theory of Revolution," *American Sociological Review,* Vol. 27, 1962, pp. 5-18; J. A. Geschwender, "Explorations in the Theory of Social Movements and Revolutions," *Social Forces,* Vol. 47, 1968, pp. 127-135.

3. N. E. Devletoglou, "Responsibility and Demonstrations—A Case Study," *Public Opinion Quarterly,* Vol. 30, 1966, pp. 285-289; M. Pinard, J. Kirk, and D. Von Eschen, "Processes of Recruitment in the Sit-In Movement," *Public Opinion Quarterly,* Vol. 33, 1969, pp. 355-369.

4. P. Barker, H. Taylor, E. de Kadt, and E. Hopper, "Portrait of a Protest," *New Society,* October 31, 1968, pp. 631-634.

5. There were two groups of counter-demonstrators. The one that met at Rock Creek Park was estimated at about 500 by the police. The other, present at the monument grounds, was a small band of less than 100. A sample of 62 counter-demonstrators was taken. Because of the small number, data relative to the counter-demonstrators are not presented here. However, comparisons between this counter-demonstration group and the British anti-war march data showed striking similarities in terms of the distributions of age, education, sex, and political ideology characteristics.

6. The author wishes to thank James C. Coleman for suggesting this sampling technique.

7. The fifteen trained and conservatively dressed interviewers lined up before the speaker's platform facing the audience. They spaced themselves evenly to reach both ends of the high platform. As soon as the march columns arrived and began to form a crowd in front of the speaker's stand, each interviewer began interviewing the person closest to him. From there, moving away from the platform, the interviewer attempted to interview the next person alternately to his right or left at every tenth step he walked. If he encountered a refusal, the interviewer was to record the distance from the platform and to identify the refuser by approximate age, race, and sex. Then he would attempt to interview the person in the other direction (right or left) facing him—if he was not in the midst of an apparent group. If he was in the midst of a group, he would proceed ten more steps before interviewing the next person. When the interviewer reached the end of the crowd he would turn to his right or left (alternately) and walk five steps, then walk back in toward the speaker's platform continuing his sampling and interviewing.

8. J. Gusfield, "The Study of Social Movements," *International Encyclopedia of the Social Sciences,* New York, Crowell, Collier and MacMillan, pp. 445-452.

9. Pinard *et al. op. cit.*

10. J. Gusfield, *op. cit.;* M. Pinard, "Mass Society and Political Movements: A New Formulation," *American Journal of Sociology,* 73, pp. 682-690, 1968.

11. Pinard, *ibid.*

12. A. M. Orum, "On Participation in Political Movements: A Critical Appraisal of Some Old Theories and Modest Proposals for a New One," Denver, Colorado. Annual Meeting of the American Sociological Association, 1971.

13. Barker *et al., op. cit.*

14. This was scaled by the source closeness to McIntire: (1) previous McIntire gatherings, (2) McIntire's radio program, (3) specialized media, (4) other personal sources, and (5) mass media (see Table 1).

15. The variable was sealed on a continuum from extreme pessimism (United States would be defeated) to extreme optimism (United States would be victorious).

16. Other variables considered but excluded from analysis included occupation (too many unscalable categories such as housewife or student) and income (35 percent of the respondents were either supported by others or did not provide that information). Education was found to be highly correlated with income $(r = .356)$ (after deletion of the "illegal" categories). Thus, it was felt that the socioeconomic status was approximately but appropriately tapped by the educational level.

17. The ordinary least-squares estimates are computed for the remaining independent variables. It has been argued (K. C. Land, "Identification, Parameter Estimation, and Hypothesis Testing in Recursive Sociological Models," in A. S. Goldberger and O. D. Duncan, eds., *Structural Equation Models in the Social Sciences,* New York, Seminar Press, 1973) that such estimates are more efficient than the dependence analysis (R. Boudon, "A Method of Linear Causal Analysis: Dependence Analysis," *American Sociological Review,* Vol. 30, 1965, pp. 365-374). Estimates from the dependence variable showed very similar coefficients for the abbreviated model.

18. Barker *et al., op. cit.*

26.

Benjamin D. Singer

MASS MEDIA AND COMMUNICATION PROCESSES IN THE DETROIT RIOT OF 1967

A great deal has been written in recent years about mass media contributions to urban disturbances. Oberschall has suggested preparticipants in Watts used television to monitor locations for looting and police activity in specific areas[1]; Conot has asserted television coverage helped stimulate potential looters as well as providing locations[2]; various sources have suggested media coverage, particularly television, was important in helping to create a riot culture as well as stimulating the spread of disturbances.[3] Other sources have addressed themselves to the role of interpersonal sources in spreading "the message" of a disturbance.[4]

If, indeed, the mass media, particularly television, provide directions for participating in riots and serve to change the viewer's frame of reference toward riots, making these more acceptable over time through sheer repetition, then they perhaps exert such effects in two ways: (1) between cities, by demonstrating "how" in advance and building expectations that "our city will be next," or "our turn hasn't come yet," etc., and (2) within cities, helping to enlarge a disturbance in progress.

From Benjamin D. Singer, "Mass Media and Communication Processes in the Detroit Riot of 1967." *Public Opinion Quarterly* 34, Summer 1968, pp. 236-45, with permission of the author and publisher.

The study on which this article is based was supported by Public Health Service Grant No. 1 R12 MH-9254-01 and by a research grant provided by the Canada Council. The author would like to acknowledge the valuable suggestions of Dr. James A. Geschwender.

In spite of the interest in this area (and without denying the underlying problems and grievances of the Negro communities involved), very little has been done empirically to gauge the relevance of communication factors in urban riots. Most statements have been polemical in nature, or observations by journalists; or, as in the case of the Kerner Report, have tried to measure what was presented on television, rather than viewers' reactions. The present analysis focuses on the media and communications behavior of a group of persons arrested during the 1967 Detroit riot. The paper describes their past exposure to riots on television and the process by which they were informed of the Detroit riot prior to their alleged participation.

Between July 31 and August 4, 1967, interviews were conducted in the jails, internment locations, and prisons in Detroit and outlying areas where persons charged with participating in the Detroit riot were being held. The essentially open-ended interview guide concerned itself with socioeconomic characteristics of the respondent, attitudes toward civil rights, Negro leadership and riots, and "communication" variables—types of mass media exposure and interpersonal communication patterns. The interviewers were Negro males, most with college degrees and some form of interviewing or similar experience. The sample consisted of 499 Negro males who had been distributed in the order of their arrival to detention facilities depending upon available space.

The 499 interviews represented approximately a ten per cent sample of arrested Negro males, who made up the overwhelming majority of those arrested. The distribution of charges levied against the sample closely approximates that of charges against all males arrested, which is an important test of the representativeness of the sample.[5]

Television, other research has indicated, is the most important mass medium for black America.[6] In our sample, television ranked ahead of newspapers and radio as a medium for finding out about riots in other cities. It is perhaps the most likely way in which individuals acquire their knowledge of leaders, particularly the nationally known militants. The overwhelming majority (approximately 75 per cent) were able to report specific riots they had witnessed on television.

If television is implicated in the disturbances, and particularly the intercity spread, we might ask how it functions in this regard. The kind of stimulus value carried by televised riot sequences depends first on the perceived content; it is, in fact, not the *objective* content as revealed by various content counts but rather the *viewer's definition of the situation* which is critical. We attempted to assess this by asking those arrested, "What were most of the people doing in these race riots (seen on television)?"

Examination of Table 1 reveals that respondents reported approximately 50 per cent of the time viewing violent acts, including police brutality, arson, throwing rocks, fighting, screaming, killing, shooting, etc. Looting was mentioned only 21 per cent of the time. Thus, the opportunity for material gain was perceived less than half as often as actions presumably more charged with affective content. Respondents characterized past disturbances shown on television as involving violence more often than any other phenomenon; this is particularly significant when compared with the small number (5 per cent) who recalled presumably legitimate attempts by authorities to control crowds.

While there will inevitably be debate concerning the meaning of this finding, we can focus upon its manifest appearance and ask whether the perception of violence, as opposed to property offenses, increases the identification of the viewer with the participants on the screen; we can ask whether the perception of violence suggests a greater intensity and excitement

TABLE 1

Perceptions of What People Were Doing in Televised Riot Sequences

Perception	Percentage of Responses
Violent acts against persons	49.8%
Looting	21.1
Property destruction	6.5
People running, standing, milling	10.2
Arrests, crowd control	5.2
Peaceful demonstrations, other responses	7.2
Total (some respondents gave more than one answer)	100.0% (650)

TABLE 2

Reaction to Televised Riots

Respondent's Reaction	Percentage of Responses
Disapproval, sadness, disgust or opposed to televising of riots	48.9%
Feels whites responsible, resentment at authorities or community, happy with rioting	26.1
Indifference or ambivalence	12.3
Intellectualizes about cause or prevention of riots	3.1
Has never seen TV riots, don't know, and other	9.8
Total	100.2% (499)

for the potential participant; and we can ask whether the sight of violence, as opposed to e.g., property crimes, operates more to change norms in the direction of acceptance of riots as justified. While no answer at this point can be definitive, Table 2 provides information concerning the feelings that our respondents reported experiencing while viewing televised riots.

As shown in Table 2, over one quarter felt anger at whites or police or were happy with the attacks shown as directed at whites or white authorities; 49 per cent indicated varying degrees of disturbance at the sight or suggested riots ought not to be televised; only 12 per cent indicated sheer indifference or ambivalence to televised riots. Thus, respondents do appear to indicate a high degree of emotional involvement with television sequences of this nature. This may be more important than the Kerner Commission's report that less than five per cent of scenes broadcast on racial problems or riots for three days before and three days after a riot in a given city were of "actual mob action, or people looting, sniping, setting fires or being injured or killed."[7] Television needs to be re-examined with regard to what people perceived and were affected by.

Communication processes in the Detroit riot

The preceding section dealt with past television exposure. Presumably such exposure is a factor in what has been described as "riot culture." It would contribute to intercity spread. However, of major importance is the process by which knowledge about the Detroit disturbance was communicated to those charged with participating. First, a brief description of the setting and sequence of the disturbance will be presented.

At 3:45 a.m. on Sunday, July 23,

Detroit police conducted a raid on a drinking and gambling club on Twelfth Street which was operating after legal closing time, arresting some 82 persons. Approximately two hundred spectators watched the proceedings, some of whom voiced indignation at the raid. A few minutes after 5 a.m., an empty bottle crashed into one of the police car windows, to be followed by other missiles. Meanwhile, word spread that the police were using excessive force; a few hours later the crowds had swelled to thousands and window smashing and looting began.[8] At 8 a.m. several radio stations first reported the disturbance[9] and the first television report of it was carried at 2 p.m. According to one news director, "At least one radio station transmitted a voice report of a 'race riot' to its network, which in turn aired it across the country. Some of these early radio reports left the impression that the scene was worse than it really was during the early hours. The reports apparently had less inflammatory effect than they might have because of the relatively small radio audience early Sunday."[10]

The first television announcement was made by CKLW-TV at 2 p.m. "Violence broke out in west side Detroit early this morning when police raided a west side blind pig. A police lieutenant was hit with a rock, and one man was stabbed, as hundreds brawled for five hours." Another station, WXYZ-TV, falsely reported a policeman had been killed and WWJ-TV was reported to have alarmed thousands of persons by falsely reporting an anonymous phone tip to the effect that the rioters were spreading to the suburbs.[11] With time, the TV reports grew more detailed and by 7:30 p.m., CKLW-TV was reporting on shooting, blazing fires, rioters stoning firemen, etc.

When a disturbance begins in a given

city, it is enlarged through communication of two kinds: the interpersonal network—a very highly developed network of communications within the black community which operates on a word-of-mouth basis; and the local mass media, initially the broadcast variety. The potential participant is informed by someone else who may know of the disturbance firsthand or because someone else told him or because the mass media informed him; or the participant may have direct or mass media knowledge about the riot. The scheme, in part empirically derived, for categorizing knowledge about the riot, is set forth below:

I. Direct Experience
   1. On the scene
   2. Heard noise from house or other location or saw activity
II. Interpersonal Network
   1. Another individual told him in person
   2. Another individual telephoned him
III. Mass Media
   1. Radio
   2. Television
   *3. Newspapers
   *4. Publicly distributed or placed handbills

The interpersonal network may merely be later links in a chain that begins with either direct experience or the mass media. We do not know how the "other individual" happened to hear of the disturbance; furthermore, various combinations of the three knowledge routes are possible. Since the overwhelming majority of those who were participants in the Detroit disturbance were not present at the assumed precipitating incident (the raid on the blind pig), they heard about the riot through one of several means: direct experience, interpersonal communication, or the mass media. We are now going to

* Neither newspapers nor handbills were mentioned by those in our sample.

TABLE 3

Channels through Which Those Arrested Found Out about Detroit Riot

Channel	Percentage of Responses
Direct experience	26.9%
Interpersonal: Phone	8.8
Interpersonal: Person	39.0
Radio	16.5
Television	9.0
Total	100.2%
	(491)

examine the data concerning the method or medium by which respondents heard of the riot, the message (what they heard), and the relationship between the specific medium and the kind of message heard.

How respondents found out about the riot

As Table 3 indicates, the leading channel of information for those arrested was interpersonal communication, with 48 per cent finding out from another person. Following this, 27 per cent found out through some form of direct experience—through being present at the riot scene or hearing the commotion or seeing it from some distance. Broadcasting (mass media) informed another 26 per cent. As indicated earlier, our data do not reveal where the secondary source (interpersonal) re-

TABLE 4

Relationship between Source of Information and whether Arrestee Informs Another Person of Riot

Channel	Percentage Informing Another
Television	51%
Radio	54
Phone	51
Person	37
At scene	28
Total	39%
	(499)

ceived his information, but we must assume that the first stage of the process by which the word "got out" in the community was either direct experience or broadcast media, which were nearly equal as a source (27 per cent and 26 per cent respectively). The way in which the news

TABLE 5
Content of Riot Messages Reported

Message	Percentage of Responses
Riot (general)[a]	17.2%
Riot on 12th Street[b]	52.1
Police actions[c]	5.0
Looting, stealing	15.0
Arson	15.6
Streets blockaded	2.0
Curfew	5.0
Blind Pig raided	5.4
Ideological statement[d]	2.2
No response	1.4
Total (some respondents gave more than one answer)	120.9% (604)

[a] "Riot (general)" is a simple statement that a riot or civil disturbance was in progress, without indicating a location.
[b] "Riot on 12th" includes all statements indicating a location.
[c] "Police action" includes activities by the National Guard; the message usually indicated arrests, shooting, or police brutality.
[d] Ideological statements are those with a further message, often of a polemical nature, such as "Detroit police picking on Negroes again," "The riot has finally come to Detroit," etc.

first entered the Negro community is treated as the primary source—and the two channels would be either mass media or direct experience of an individual; from there, interpersonal channels take over with great effect. Table 4 provides data suggesting that the broadcast media were the most important primary source by which the information entered the black community.

The majority of individuals who found out about the riot through broadcast media or telephone then told another person; only 37 per cent of those who heard about the riot from another person told another; and finally, the smallest proportion, 28 per cent of those who were at the scene, then told another. In general, this suggests that the most powerful sources for spreading the news of the riot were the broadcast media if the communication behavior of those arrested was typical of other members of the black community.

What respondents heard: the message

Table 5 indicates the relative frequency with which different messages were heard. The news that the police had, perhaps unjustly or brutally, raided a blind pig was

TABLE 6
Messages by Different Media

Message	Radio	Television	Telephone	Person
Riot (general)	11.0%	11.9%	21.8%	18.7%
Riot on Twelfth St.	32.1	2.0	45.5	44.4
Police actions	3.6	10.2	3.6	2.1
Looting, stealing	16.5	18.6	10.9	11.2
Arson	14.7	10.2	12.7	12.4
Street blockaded	1.8	0.0	1.8	2.1
Curfew	8.3	11.9	1.8	2.9
Blind Pig raid	7.3	11.9	0.0	3.3
Ideological statement	0.9	1.7	0.0	2.9
No response	3.7	1.7	1.8	0.0
Total	100.0%	100.0%	100.0%	100.0%
N (Messages)	109	59	55	241

reported by only 5 per cent of the respondents, and thus it may not have been in general an important motivational element in causing individuals to enter the riot scene; that there were fires and looting were more frequently mentioned. The fact that police were on the scene taking repressive action was mentioned only 5 per cent of the time, as was the fact that a curfew had been established.

We can assert, then, if the characteristics of the message reported to us influence the decision to go to the scene, that merely knowledge of a disturbance and its location are sufficient to initiate this action for the majority of individuals arrested, with the general riot statement being next most frequent and the messages concerning looting (presumably an opportunity statement) and arson following in importance.

Each channel or medium has characteristics of its own which may be responsible for the kind of message presented, or, on the other hand, the content of the message as "received" by the audience. Table 6 indicates the content of the message by the source or medium. Although the message in all cases most often referred in general terms to the riot or its location, looting was mentioned more frequently by broadcast media than on any other channel. In addition, the possibly emotion-charged report of the precipitating incident, the blind pig raid, was also mentioned more often by the broadcast media. On the other hand, these media more often mentioned the curfew that had been imposed; this was a subject more rarely mentioned during interpersonal transmission of news.

Although the cells are small, the data are suggestive. The message in the case of all channels most often refers to the riot location. Interpersonal channels more often than mass media specify the location

of the rioting. The broadcast media, on the other hand, focus more on control measures (police taking repressive measures, the establishment of the curfew), on the precipitating incident (the blind pig raid), and on the looting which is occurring.

In any case, the data suggest that the population was already primed as a result of personal experiences in the ghetto and televised prior riots and other media presentations. The focus on the blind pig raid by broadcast media, the curfew warnings and statements about the presence of police did not seem significant, not nearly as much as knowing the location of the "action."

Conclusion

This paper has addressed itself to an area which has not received much research attention—the role of communication factors in riots. The present findings suggest that different media perform different functions. Television appears particularly important at the interurban level, as the most frequently mentioned means by which individuals learned of past riots. A substantial proportion of individuals reported violent aspects of past televised riots (in contradistinction to the implications of the Kerner Commission's findings) and were angry or disturbed by what they had seen; and it seems likely that this affective aspect, along with routine "instructions" on how a riot is conducted *when it arrives*, contributed substantially to the riot readiness of a large number of individuals.

A great deal of emphasis, most of it speculative, has been placed on the diffuse function of television in spreading a disturbance, but it is valuable to distinguish between television as an interurban and an intraurban force. In Detroit, television's pictorial qualities were not particularly important. When a disturbance finally begins in the individual's city, the precipitating incident and its affective connotations appear to be relatively unimportant components of the transmitted message. Just the knowledge that "there's a riot on," and its location, are sufficient to set the final stage for possible participation. At this point in time, interpersonal communication and broadcast media, particularly radio, transmit the message, which need not be elaborate or emotional but merely need inform individuals of the beginning of the riot and its location.

Notes

1. Anthony Oberschall, "The Los Angeles Riot of August, 1965," *Social Problems,* Vol. 15, 1968, pp. 322-341.

2. See Robert Conot, *Rivers of Blood, Years of Darkness,* New York, Bantam, 1967, pp. 97, 226, and 244 concerning the role of the mass media in the Watts disturbance of 1965.

3. The "technological" aspect of riot culture is penetratingly analyzed by Lee Rainwater in "Open Letter on White Justice and the Riots," *Trans-Action,* Vol. 4, No. 9, September 1967, p. 27. Among the

many statements critical of the mass media's role, see Drew Pearson and Jack Anderson, "The Almighty Eye," *New York Post,* April 17, 1968, and Allen C. Brawnfeld, "Television and the Big City Riots," *The American Legion Magazine,* Vol. 82, December 1967, pp. 6-8.

4. Concerning interpersonal means of communication, Fred Powledge has asserted: "We know that riots occur, by and large, after sudden relatively minor confrontations with persons of authority—the cops. We know that word of these confrontations is often magnified and carried by rumor at high speed through the Negro community. There is probably a better system of internal communications in the ghetto than in the National Guard. During the early hours of a riot, it functions like lightning, "What We Failed to Learn" *New Leader,* August 14, 1967, p. 5.

5. For further details on the methodology, see B. D. Singer, R. W. Osborn, J. A. Geschwender, *Black Rioters,* Lexington, Mass.: D. C. Heath, forthcoming, ch. 1.

6. Bradley S. Greenberg and Joseph R. Dominick, *Communication among the Urban Poor: Television Usage, Attitudes, and Functions for Low-Income and Middle-Class Teenagers,* Lansing, Michigan State University, Department of Communication, 1968.

7. *Report of the National Advisory Commission on Civil Disorders,* New York Bantam, 1968, p. 369.

8. *Ibid.,* p. 48.

9. Personal correspondence to Benjamin D. Singer from Robert J. McBride, WJBK-TV, Detroit, March 20, 1968.

10. *Ibid.*

11. *Newsweek,* August 14, 1967, p. 78.

IV. Organizational and Institutional Characteristics Related to Collective Behavior and Social Movements: Mid-Range Theory and Research

Introduction

Although there has been some work published on the relationship between organizational characteristics and elementary collective behavior, most of the work utilizing this level of analysis has been directed toward understanding social movement organization. Part IV includes material addressing the relationship between organizational characteristics and crowd behavior, but is primarily directed toward the nature and evolution of social movement organization, the relationship between social movement organization and formal organizational patterns, and how movement organization affects and is affected by the general process of social change.

The approach to the study of social movement organization employed by Zald and Ash (27) is an important link between formal organizational analysis and the study of collective behavior. The authors challenge the traditional notion that when social movements are extended over time they tend to become more bureaucratized, and hence more conservative in both goals and actions. Instead, they argue that, as a social movement evolves, various organizational forms are possible, depending on the configuration of certain internal and external factors, such as leadership, type of goals, and the social environment in which the movement exists.

In support of Zald and Ash, Myers (28) shows that civil disobedience groups tend to become more radical over time. In his study of the British Committee of 100, an anti-Viet Nam War protest group, Myers found two primary factors that account for this trend. First, civil disobedience groups are usually outgrowths of larger, more conservative movements, and although they have the same goals as the larger movement, they develop in opposition to its conservative tactics, and therefore attract the most dissatisfied members of the original movement. Second, because such groups employ illegal or quasilegal tactics, the risk of arrest and imprisonment will tend to weed out individuals with major outside responsibilities such as a job or family. Therefore, as the movement is extended over time, only the most radical individuals remain. In addition, once group members have been arrested or imprisoned, they tend to feel they have less to lose and hence become even more adamant in advocating radical organization and means of achieving their goals.

Gerlach's (29) article helps place Myer's observations within the framework of the study of all radical social movements. In analyzing the organization of revolutionary movements, this author found three major dimensions of organizational structure which he describes as segmentary, polycephalous, and reticulate. Revolutionary movements are *segmentary* in that they are composed of a wide range of diverse groups which tend to grow and divide into separate "cells." They are *polycephalous* to the extent that they lack central leadership and control. Instead, many participants compete for leadership roles, both within the movement as a whole, and within each segment. And finally, the organization of revolutionary movements can be described as *reticulate* in that the diverse groups which constitute the movement are organized into a network through various forms of communication, overlapping membership, joint activities and the sharing of common objectives. Gerlach addresses the processes inherent in each dimension of movement organization, thus providing a framework for interpreting the events described by Myers, as well as for further study of the general nature of revolutionary movements.

Whatever their form, social movements, by definition, develop some organizational structure in order to achieve their goals, and much attention has been focused on the relationship of movement organization to formal social organization. In addressing this issue, Swanson (30) develops an analogy between the processes inherent in formal organizations and those common to social movements. This author argues that a social movement organization is analogous to a formal organization to the extent that there is a legitimated procedure through which participants can affect group actions, and one or more "spheres of action" exist to which the procedure can be applied. The author also points out that in analyzing behavior in collectivities it is necessary to keep in mind that the participants, like persons in formal organizational contexts, have dual status: In one sense they attempt to use the group for their private purposes, but at the same time they must remain sensitive to the requirements of maintaining the collective, and are thereby required to act as its agent.

While Swanson approaches the study of collective behavior by focusing on the similarities between formal organizations and collectivities, Pfautz (31) argues that collective behavior can be more clearly conceptualized not in relation to formal groups or organizations but as "near groups," which are characterized by the relative permanence of diffuse role definition, limited cohesion, instability, and shifting membership expectations. Utilizing this framework in re-examining data collected on youth gangs in New York City, he sets forth a rationale for viewing youth gangs as "expressive social movements," concluding that such a perspective allows for greater understanding of how youths come to participate in the culture of the gang.

In addition to identifying the organizational structures and processes that have developed in collectivities, it is also important to determine the nature and sources of change in such organizations. Mohr's work (32) contributes to an understanding of this topic by focusing on the general determinants of change and innovation in organizational structures, as well as on environmental characteristics that promote and inhibit change. This author argues that a number of factors must be taken into consideration when attempting to predict new organizational patterns, such as the willingness of group members to change their behavior, the size of the organization and its available resources, the organizational norms related to change, and the rate of change in the environment of which the organization is a part.

The development of, and changes in, various forms of social organization should not be interpreted as a linear movement away from the dynamic processes inherent in the collectivity to the more routinized forms of social exchange that take place in the institutional setting. In his analysis of the general process of social change, Eisenstadt (33) argues that change is made inevitable by the general movement *toward* more routinized forms of inter-action. In analyzing change in various institutions throughout history, the author concludes, in part, that formalized social systems tend to create "anti-systems" or groups whose aspirations, orientations, and premises differ from those of the predominating social structure. Although institutions are, to a great extent, able to maintain their boundaries through various means of relieving the pressure to change, the potential for conflict and subsequent change emerges from the very processes that influence the development of organizational stability.

Because it serves as a fundamental element in the ongoing process of social change, collective behavior is instrumental in understanding the form social reorganization takes during periods of societal transition. Jonassen (34), for example, shows how social movements can serve to ease the process of change in developing countries. Utilizing a variety of historical data, this author argues that, as a traditional agrarian society develops into a modern industrial society, the social relationships formally determined by family, tribe, caste or religious group tend to give way, and individuals are freed from the dictates, customs, and mores of these groups. Although this process may result in an increase in personal freedom, individuals often experience feelings of *alienation* during these transitional periods. The necessities of general psychological support and social control must be replaced by other systems, and Jonassen views the voluntary association as one of the primary means by which societies in transition develop new psychological and social support systems.

But just as voluntary associations have the potential for easing the transition to modern society, Jonassen notes that they also have the potential for creating social unrest during these periods. Of course, this is true of all forms of human interaction. In any social situation, the *intention* of human association may not be realized, and totally unintended or unforeseen results may be created. In this instance, the intended outcome of voluntary asso-ciation is to alleviate social disorganization and achieve political stability. However, by bringing together the disaffected, and solidifying and intensify-ing hostilities, the movement can just as easily contribute to political instability and revolution. Although it is important to identify the specific functions of social movements in societies undergoing major periods of transition, social movements persist even in the most advanced industrial societies, and for this reason their "function" might be thought of more generally as *mediating* transition in an ever changing society.

Because social movements are at the center of the process of change in society, it is also important to understand the processes that take place within these collectivities, and the relation of these processes to the larger society. What little we know about the internal dynamics of social movements can largely be attributed to case studies, such as Broyles' (35) analysis of the activities of the John Birch Society. Drawing upon journalistic reports, fieldwork and extensive informal interviews with members of this society and those who oppose it, Broyles describes the organization, leadership and nature of the ideological beliefs that have developed, arguing that these characteristics form the basis for understanding the nature of the interaction that has evolved within the organization, and between Birch Society proponents and opponents.

In addition to providing the basis for understanding the nature and structure of social movement organizations, the middle-range level of analytic thought has also been utilized in addressing the relationship of formal institutions and organizations to incidences of crowd behavior that take place within the institutional framework. Denzin (36) presents a general framework for organizing the findings of a number of studies of collective behavior in total institutions such as prisons and mental hospitals. The author concludes that the central foci for understanding collective behavior in total institutions are identical to the characteristics that have been pinpointed as the bases for understanding collective behavior in institutions in civil society; that is, the nature and extent of the division of labor, how the channels of communication operate, and the general normative structure of the institution. Denzin shows how each of these generic variables affects the other, and how each has implications for understanding crowd behavior in the institutional setting.

Included are a number of studies utilizing mid-level analysis that have focused on riot behavior. Using the riot as the primary analytic unit, Firestone (37) provides a framework for understanding the riot process by addressing the underlying sources and conditions, as well as the precipitating events that lead to riot behavior. This author delineates several stages of the riot process, each characterized by an increasing level of violence and counterviolence. The careful descriptions presented here form a sound basis for understanding group dynamics in the riot process and provide a sound basis for future research in the area.

In addition to the nature of the riot process itself, it is important to understand the mid-level forces that contribute to riot participation. Warren (38) focuses on the characteristics of neighborhoods important in understanding riot participation, such as the extent of social interaction, reference group orientation, and values. This author formulates a typology of neighborhoods based on the nature and extent of social organization within the neighborhood, the extent to which the neighborhood is viewed as a positive reference group, and the relation of the neighborhood to the larger community. Warren concludes that an understanding of the dynamics of the neighborhood is a prerequisite to predicting riot behavior.

The final article in Part IV provides insight into a dimension of collective behavior rarely studied: the relationship between riot behavior and the attitudes and perceptions of social control organizations. Quarantelli et al. (39) present police department perceptions of four civil disturbances in American cities during the summer of 1969. Through interviews with key departmental personnel, the authors add to our knowledge of how organizational perceptions of riot participants and processes impact on behavior which is vital for a clear understanding of this aspect of collective behavior.

27.

Mayer N. Zald and Roberta Ash

SOCIAL MOVEMENT ORGANIZATIONS: GROWTH, DECAY AND CHANGE

Social movements manifest themselves, in part, through a wide range of organizations. These organizations are subject to a range of internal and external pressures which affect their viability, their internal structure and processes, and their ultimate success in attaining goals.

The dominant line of approach to the sociological study of the transformation of social movement organizations (hereafter referred to as MOs) has been the institutionalization and goal displacement model of organizational transformation. This model, which stems from Weber[1] and Michels,[2] takes the following line of analysis: As an MO attains an economic and social base in the society, as the original charismatic leadership is replaced, a bureaucratic structure emerges and a general accommodation to the society occurs.[3] The participants in this structure have a stake in preserving the organization, regardless of its ability to attain goals. Analytically there are three types of changes involved in

From Mayer N. Zald and Roberta Ash, "Social Movement Growth, Decay and Change," *Social Forces* 44, May 1964, pp. 327-41. Reprinted by permission of The University of North Carolina Press and the authors.

This paper is a revised version of a paper originally read at the annual meeting of the Institute for Social Research, Chicago, May 1964. It grew out of courses taught jointly by the senior author with David Street and, at an earlier time, Arthur Stinchcombe. It also grew out of a study of change in the Young Men's Christian Association of Metropolitan Chicago supported by the National Institutes of Health (GM-10777) USPHS. We have benefited greatly from critical readings by Mike Muench, Norman Miller, Joseph Gusfield, Eugene Weinstein and Thomas Smith.

this process; empirically they are often fused. The three types of change are goal transformation, a shift to organizational maintenance, and oligarchization.

Goal transformation may take several forms, including the diffusion of goals, in which a pragmatic leadership replaces unattainable goals with diffuse goals, so that the organization can pursue a broader range of targets.[4] However, according to the Weber-Michels model, whatever the form of goal transformation, it is always in the direction of greater conservatism (the accommodation or organization goals to the dominant societal consensus).

Organizational maintenance is a special form of goal transformation, in which the primary activity of the organization becomes the maintenance of membership, funds, and other requirements of organizational existence. It too is accompanied by conservatism, for the original goals must be accommodated to societal norms in order to avoid conflicts that could threaten the organization's viability.

Oligarchization may be defined as the concentration of power, in the Weberian sense, in the hands of a minority of the organization's members. (For our purposes, bureaucratization is that form of oligarchization which stresses a hierarchy of offices and prescribed rules for conducting affairs.) Of course, some MOs begin with a relatively oligarchical structure and de-oligarchization may occur. But the Michels part of the model treats mainly of the movement from democratic decision structures—a situation of dispersed power, to centralization and oligarchy. (This process is typically evaluated as morally wrong and as a prelude to member apathy and organizational conservatism.)

This line of sociological analysis has a distinguished place in the literature—if only for its imaginative concepts—goal displacement, iron law of oligarchy, routinization of charisma, and the like. Nevertheless, as a statement on the transformation of (social) movement organizations it is incomplete. There are a variety of other transformation processes that take place including coalitions with other organizations, organizational disappearances, factional splits, increased rather than decreased radicalism, and the like. And in fact, the Weber-Michels model[5] can be subsumed under a more general approach to movement organizations which specifies the condition under which alternative transformation processes take place.

An essay in theoretical synthesis, here we attempt to specify some of the major factors influencing the direction of change of MOs and to provide illustrative propositions. Each section contains several of these, but only a few propositions and predictions that summarize and sharpen the argument will be listed and set off.

We follow the general sociological approach to organizations most explicitly stated by Selznick and often called organizational or institutional analysis.[6] The approach can be applied to any kind of association or organization, not just those with bureaucratic structures. Briefly, large scale organizations are seen as a collection of groups harnessed together by incentives of various kinds to pursue relatively explicit goals. Both the ends and means of subgroups may conflict with those established by the authoritative elements in the organization; there may be conflict over the distribution of power and rewards within the organization. Organizations exist in a changing environment to which they must adapt. Adaptation to the environment may itself require changes in goals and in the internal arrangement of the organization. This view of organizations treats goals as problematic, and as changing in response to both internal and external pressures. It is especially useful for the study of MOs precisely because it focuses on conflict, environmental forces, and the ebb and flow of organizational viability.[7]

Our first task is to define the analytic characteristics of movement organizations —how does an MO differ from other complex or formal organizations? A social movement is a purposive and collective attempt of a number of people to change individuals or societal institutions and structures. Although the organizations through which social movements can manifest themselves may have bureaucratic features, analytically they differ from "full-blown" bureaucratic organizations in two ways. First, they have goals aimed at changing the society and its members; they wish to restructure society or individuals, not to provide it or them with a regular service (as is typical of bureaucracies). For example, proselytizing and usually messianic religious groups, melioristic political organizations, and conspiratorial parties are movement organizations by our definition. Goals aimed at change subject movement organizations to vicissitudes which many other types of organization avoid. For instance, if the society changes in the direction of the MO's goals, the organization's reason for being no longer exists. On the other hand, its goals of change may incur great hostility and repressive action in the society.

Second (and related to the goals of change), MOs are characterized by an incentive structure in which purposive incentives predominate.[8] While some short-run material incentives may be used, the dominant incentives offered are purposive, with solidary incentives playing a secondary role. Organizations which rely on purposive incentives often have the problem of maintaining membership commitment and participation, for the values represented by the MO's goals must be deeply held in order for the organization to command time and loyalty in the face of the competition of work and the demands of family and friends.[9]

As we have noted the Weber-Michels model predicts changes in goals (conservatism and organizational maintenance) and in structure (oligarchization). Although we will comment on the latter aspect of organizational change, we focus more on the transformation of and the interplay of goals and structure. On this point we challenge the Weber-Michels model by limiting its predictions to certain types of MOs, and by suggesting conditions under which alternatives are possible.

In this paper we first discuss the relation of movement organizations to the environment in which they exist—both the society at large and more narrowly the social movement of which they are a manifestation. The ebb and flow of sentiments, the results of success and failure in attaining goals, and the problems of coordination and cooperation among movement organizations are treated. The purpose of the first section is to show how the transformation of MOs is conditioned or determined by factors outside of itself. The second, briefer, section focuses to a greater extent on internal processes related to goals and commitment. There we discuss two topics, the causes of factionalism and schismogenesis and the relation of leadership to organizational transformation.

Environment and organization

The environment of MO's consists of two major segments. One segment is the broader social movement, which consists of potential supporters—members and financial backers and other movement organizations. The people who identify with the movement represent the potential support base for the organization. The other major segment of the environment is the society in which the social movement exists. The larger society may contain the target structures or norms which the movement organization wishes to change; but even in cases where the MO's goal is to change individuals, members or not, the larger society affects the MO because the attitudes and norms of the larger society affect the readiness of movement sympathizers to become members, and the readiness of members to participate fully.

There are at least three interrelated aspects of the environment of MOs which critically affect both their growth and transformation. Changing conditions in the society increase or decrease the potential support base of an MO; there is an ebb and flow of supporting sentiments. Second, the society may change in the direction of organizational goals, or events may clearly indicate that goals will not be attained; the possibilities of success or failure sharply influence member and potential member sentiments and attachments. Third, MOs exist in an environment with other organizations aimed at rather similar goals. Similarity of goals causes an uneasy alliance but also creates the conditions for inter-organizational competition.

The ebb and flow of sentiments

Any MO is dependent on the readiness for mobilization of potential supporters. This readiness is dependent on the ebb and flow of sentiments toward an organization, which in turn is a function of at least two major variables: (1) the extent to which there are large numbers of people who feel the MO's goals and means are in harmony with their own; and (2) the extent to which groups and organizations in the larger society feel neutral toward, reject, or accept the legitimacy and value of the social movement and its organizational manifestations. The attitudes in the larger society toward the movement and the MO condition the readiness of potential supporters to become actual supporters.

The difference between the ebb and flow of sentiment for a *social movement* and for a given MO has important consequences for organizational growth. Under some conditions there may be a strong sentiment base—at the same time that there is strong hostility to a particular organization in the society. "Front" organizations are attempts to capitalize on such a situation. The dimensions are partially independent. The ideal condition for organizational growth is obviously a strong sentiment base with low societal hostility towards the movement or its MOs. Periods of great religious revival are characterized by this condition. On the other hand, the more interesting case may be when there is a weak sentiment base and no or low societal interest. A petulant stance and organizational decline as in the Woman's Christian Temperance Union may be the consequence.[10]

The processes of change predicted by the Weber-Michels model are thus affected by the organization's relations to its environment. Organizational maintenance and other forms of goal transformation are the outcomes of a struggle to maintain membership in the face of changes in the larger society. The changes in the society that threaten the MO's viability may be either favorable (the goal is achieved and the MO seems to lose its *raison d'etre*) or unfavorable (widespread hostility arises).

However, the ebb and flow of sentiments does not affect organizational transforma-

tion at equal rates in all MOs. Two dimensions of movement organization mediate the extent to which MOs are affected by the ebb and flow of sentiments: (1) the extent of membership requirements, both initial and continuing, and (2) the extent to which operative goals are oriented to change of member or individual behavior rather than oriented to societal change. These two dimensions are related to the defining characteristics and recurring problematic foci of MOs stated earlier. Variability in them means that MOs can take a broad variety of organizational forms.

1. Membership requirements. The "inclusive" organization requires minimum levels of initial commitment—a pledge of general support without specific duties, a short indoctrination period or none at all. On the other hand, the "exclusive" organization is likely to hold the new recruit in a long "novitiate" period, to require the recruit to subject himself to organization discipline and orders, and to draw from those having the heaviest initial commitments. When such an organization also **has** societal goals of changing society it may be called a vanguard party.

Inclusive and exclusive MOs differ not only in recruitment procedures and requirements, but they also differ in the amount of participation required. The inclusive MO typically requires little activity from its members—they can belong to other organizations and groups unselfconsciously, and their behavior is not as permeated by organization goals, policies, and tactics. On the other hand, the exclusive organization not only requires that a greater amount of energy and time be spent in movement affairs, but it more extensively permeates all sections of the members' life, including activities with nonmembers. Any single MO may have attributes of both the inclusive and the exclusive organization; even the inclusive movement must have some central cadre.

The ebb and flow of sentiments in the society more markedly affect the inclusive than the exclusive organization. For example, membership figures compiled by Mike Muench indicate that the Socialist party had a more rapid decline in membership than the Socialist Workers' party during the McCarthy era, and a more rapid rise following the Irish peril. This, despite the fact that the SWP's ideology was more left-wing and more subject to charges of un-Americanism.[11] (The Communist party had an exclusive orientation and declined greatly, but it was under heavier and more direct attack than the other two.)

The inclusive MO's membership declines and rises faster than that of the exclusive's because competing values and attitudes are more readily mobilized in the inclusive organization. While members of both organizations may have similar goals, the members of inclusive organizations are more likely to be subjected to conflicts in the face of threats or in the face of competing social movements that appeal to other values. Their allegiances to other groups and values lead them to rather switch than fight.

2. Changing individual and member behavior versus changing society.[12] In many ways, as has often been noted, the religious sect and the vanguard party have much in common and, in our terms, are both exclusive organizations. The separation from other roles or positions, the total allegiance and discipline, the messianic vision are parallel phenomena. But a key distinction is their strategy for attaining fundamental goals: What are they trying to accomplish in the here and now? Some MOs, especially those with religious affiliations, have as operative goals the changing of individuals.[13] As such, they

may be less threatening to dominant values and other institutions. At least to the extent that operative goals are restricted to membership proselytization and are not relevant to control of institutional centers, to political action or to central societal norms counter pressures are less likely to be brought to bear on them. Furthermore, the commitment of members in this type of movement organization is less dependent on the external success of the organization. Commitment is based to a greater extent on solidary and/or expressive incentives than on purposive incentives.

Of course, the growth of religious sects is related to the ebb and flow of sentiment in the society. But it is possible that once recruits are gained the organization can maintain its members. First, focusing on member change, the sect may threaten the society less, calling forth fewer punishments for belonging. (In a theocratic state, however, the religious sect would be a direct challenge to the larger society.) Second, if the sect is not milleniastic, it is not subject to the problems of success and failure in the environment. Therefore, the rate of attrition is likely to be a function of the life careers of members rather than of wide swings in societal attitudes affecting members. Third, the organization that attempts to change individuals, especially its own members, is less constrained by the definitions of reality of the broader society.

Proposition 1: The size of the organizational potential support base, the amount of societal interest in the social movement and its MOs, and the direction of that interest (favorable, neutral, or hostile) directly affect the ability of the organization to survive and/or grow.

Proposition 2: The more insulated an organization is by exclusive membership requirements and goals aimed at changing individuals, the less susceptible it is to pressures for organizational maintenance or general goal transformation.

Inter-Organizational Competition: The Press to Left and Right. Thus far our discussion of the ebb and flow of sentiment has been presented as if within a social movement there was consensus on goals and tactics. However, there may be many definitions of proper goals and tactics and these may shift over time. Competition among MOs for support requires them to be responsive to these differences and to shifts in sentiment towards goals and tactics. It is our thesis that these shifts are a major determinant of the transformation of organizational goals.

The major thrust of the iron law of oligarchy deals with the internal bureaucratization of MOs; officials gain a vested interest in maintaining their positions and in having a stable and nonconflictful relation to the society. In the process of accommodating to the society, the goals of the MO become watered down. Over time, the prediction runs, MOs shift to moderate goals or even to goals of maintaining the status quo. But the competition for support among movement organizations leads to shifts in goals which may be towards the center, but *which may also be towards the extremes.*

In *An Economic Theory of Democracy,*[14] Anthony Downs argues that in a two-party, issue oriented political system, there are strong pressures to make the difference between parties minimal. If the parties are relatively well-balanced, movement away from the center of the distribution of attitudes by one party means loss of votes to the other party and, therefore, loss of the election. The competition is for election, not directly for long range goals. Only if there are large pools of abstaining and alienated voters at the extremes, does a movement away from the center promise greater support than a movement towards the center. The notion of the distribution

of sentiments in social movements permits an analysis similar to that of Downs.

This analysis uses as its example the case of the Civil Rights movement. Consider the situation before the Supreme Court's school desegregation ruling in 1954. The goals and tactics of the Urban League and the NAACP were in agreement with most active supporters of the movement. However, the number of actives was relatively small, and there were large segments of the potential supporters who were not active at all—college and high school students, working class Negroes, in both the north and south, and the clergy. After 1954 and especially after the Montgomery bus strike in 1958, the sentiment base of the movement changed—there was an increased readiness for mobilization of potential adherents, adherents expected more rapid change in a wider range of areas, and tactics acceptable to adherents became more militant. Furthermore, new or previously marginal organizations, such as CORE and SNCC, began to compete for the support of the enlarged potential support base. As a response both to the new opportunities for change presented by the society *and* the competition from other organizations, the stance of such organizations as the NAACP and the Urban League became more radical. *Failure* to respond to these pressures would have led to either a smaller relative support base and/or a less prominent role in the leadership of the Civil Rights movement.

This analysis is, of course, too simple. It ignores cleavages within movements; for instance, in the case of the Civil Rights movement differences in sentiment can be found between financial backers and between members of the same organizations, between class groups and generations. Furthermore, it ignores the polarization processes whereby the growth of intense attitudes on the left generates a large number of people with intense attitudes on the right. Lastly, it ignores the very complex problem of the competition and interaction of organizations with different primary goals that draw from the same pool of supporters—for instance, SANE, NAACP, and ACLU. Nevertheless, the essential point is clear.

Proposition 3: Goal and tactic transformation of a MO is directly tied to the ebb and flow of sentiments within a social movement. The interorganizational competition for support leads to a transformation of goals and tactics.

Failure and success in achieving goals[15]

The first problem of MOs is to gain support. But, an MO, like any organization, must have a payoff to its supporters. Aside from the joys of participation, its major payoff is in the nature of a promise; its goals or at least some of them must appear to have a reasonable chance of attainment. In a sense, the perfectly stable MO which avoided problems of organizational transformation, goal displacement, and the like, would be one which over time always seemed to be getting closer to its goal without quite attaining it.

A MO succeeds when its objective is attained; a MO is becalmed when, after achieving some growth and stability, its goals are still relevant to the society but its chances of success have become dim; a MO fails when the society has decisively rejected the goals of the organization and the MO as an instrument is discredited. Although the sources of the change in MO status differ in the three cases, in all three cases incentives to participate decline and the survival of the organization is threatened. Survival depends, partially, on the ability of the MO to muster solidary, material, or secondary goal incentives.

Success. There are various kinds of movement success. At the very least, one must distinguish between the actual attainment of goals and the assumption of power assumed to be a prerequisite to attaining goals. The analysis of the transformation of the MO ends when it or the movement it represents accedes to power; at that point, analytic concepts applicable to party structure and governmental bureaucracy become more relevant. The operating dilemmas of MOs that have assumed power have been well described by S. M. Lipset and others.[16]

But what happens when the goals of the MO are actually reached; what happens when a law is enacted, a disease is eradicated (for instance, women get suffrage, the threat of infantile paralysis is drastically reduced), or social conditions change, thus eliminating the ostensible purpose of the organization? Two major outcomes are possible: New goals can be established maintaining the organization or the MO can go out of existence.

The establishment of new goals to perpetuate the organization is more likely to occur if: (1) The MO has its own member and fund raising support base. (2) There are solidary or short-run material incentives that bind members to each other or to the organization. In order to continue obtaining such rewards, the members support a new goal. It must be noted that lacking such support, the organization leaders cannot maintain the organization. It is not the existence of a bureaucratic structure and office holders per se that guarantees continuance, if the rank and file or the contributors do not share the desire to continue the organization.

In some cases, however, the solidary and material incentives alone become sufficient to hold the allegiance of some of the members. This is the extreme case of a shift to organizational maintenance. Such an organization can hardly be classified as a part of a social movement, since it has abandoned both defining characteristics—purposive incentives and change goals. The remains of the Townsend movement represent such an ex-MO. The New Deal and old-age pensions cut away much of its programs and goals. But its solidary incentives, minimal membership requirements, and material resources from the sale of geriatric products allowed it to maintain itself, albeit at a minimum level of functioning.[17]

Several propositions about the relation of organizational change to success follow:

Proposition 4: MOs created by other organizations are more likely to go out of existence following success than MOs with their own linkages in individual supporters.

Proposition 5: MOs with relatively specific goals are more likely to vanish following success than organizations with broad general goals.

Proposition 6: MOs which aim to change individuals and employ solidary incentives are less likely to vanish than are MOs with goals aimed at changing society and employing mainly purposive incentives.

Proposition 7: Inclusive organizations are likely to fade away faster than exclusive organizations: the latter are more likely to take on new goals. (These predictions apply to the failing as well as to the successful MO.)

The Movement Becalmed. Many MOs do not represent either successes or failures. They have been able to build and maintain a support base; they have waged campaigns which have influenced the course of events; and they have gained some positions of power. In short, they have created or found a niche for themselves in the organizational world but their growth has slowed down or ceased. Members do not expect attainment of goals in

the near future, and the emotional fervor of the movement is subdued. As in the case of the successful organization, it is the existence of extra-purposive incentives which is a fundamental condition for maintaining the organization.

However, the goals of the MO are still somewhat relevant to society. Thus, the organization is able to maintain purposive commitment and avoids losing all of its purposively oriented members to competing causes.

It is such a becalmed movement that is most susceptible to processes predicted by the Weber-Michels model. (1) The lack of any major successes produces periodic bouts of apathy among the members. Membership is maintained, but attrition takes place over time and no new blood is attracted. (2) Leadership becomes complacent, resting on its control of material incentives. The leader's control over access to such material rewards increases their power, perhaps to the point of oligarchization. (3) The leaders become more conservative, because the pursuit of the MOs initially more radical goals might endanger the organizations' occupation of secure niches by provoking societal and, perhaps, members' hostility, consequently endangering the power of the leaders and their access to material rewards.

Proposition 8: A becalmed movement is most likely to follow the Weber-Michels model because its dependence on and control of material incentives allows oligarchization and conservatism to take place.

Failure. Where the successful organization loses members because it has nothing more to do, the failing MO loses members because they no longer believe their goals can be achieved with that instrument. The leadership cadre may attempt to redefine goals and to define external reality as favorable to the organization; nevertheless, members are usually not fully shielded from societal reality and have independent checks on the possibility of attaining goals.

A MO may also fail because its legitimacy as an instrument may be discredited. Discreditation may happen rapidly or may take several years. Central to the discreditation process is the MO's inability to maintain *legitimacy* even in the eyes of its supporters. Discreditation comes because of organizational tactics employed in the pursuit of goals. For instance, many moderate organizations have lost support when they appeared to accept support from extremist groups. The consequences of failure are not discussed by scholars using the Weber-Michels model.

One consequence of the failure of a MO is the search for new instruments. Where the member leaving a successful movement may either search for new goals and social movements or lapse into quiescence, different alternatives seem to be open to members leaving the failing organization: Either they search for a more radical means to achieve their goals within the movement, decrease the importance of their goals, or change the focus of discontent. A Mertonian analysis of anomie might be relevant to this point.

Interaction among movement organizations

Under some conditions the tactics of a MO in attempting to succeed or avoid failure involve it in direct interaction and coordination with other organizations from the same social movement. Above we discussed competition among MOs, but our analysis did not focus on direct interaction and exchange. Here, in our last topic under the heading of the relation of MOs to their environment, we treat of mergers and other aspects of inter-MO relations. Such relations could be treated as an organizational outcome. But we are chiefly concerned with how interaction affects member commitment and ultimately the goals of the involved organizations.

We distinguish three types of interaction: cooperation, coalition and merger. Typically, cooperation between MOs is limited. Except during full scale revolutions or total movement activities, MOs do not engage in a complex division of labor. It occurs primarily in situations where special competencies are required for legislative lobbying or legal work, and a simple symbiotic relationship may develop that does not lead to transformation in either organization.

More interesting are the creation of coalitions and mergers,[18] for here the interaction may lead to new organizational identities, changes in the membership base, and changes in goals.[19] The coalition pools resources and coordinates plans, while keeping distinct organizational identities. It will take place if it promises greater facilities, financial aid, or attainment of goals. Thus coalitions are more likely when MOs appear to be close to the goal than at other times, for then the costs of investing in the coalition seem small in comparison with the potential benefits.

Some coalitions resemble mergers in that only one organization retains an identity. However, within the MO the old MOs retain identities and allegiances. Such coalition-mergers are most likely to take place when there is one indivisible position or reward at stake; e.g., one governor or president can be elected, one law is required.

Each organization then may have a distinct role in the overall plan of attack. The coalesced organization is ruled through a committee or umbrella organization. Such an organization may be riven by factional positional jockeying if the leadership is not fully committed to the coalition. Further-more, not all MOs are equally capable of mergers or coalitions. The level of out-group distrust and the unlikelihood of shared perspectives makes it difficult for an exclusive MO to participate in mergers or coalitions.

A merger or coalition leads to a search for a common denominator to which both parties can agree. The more conservative party to the merger finds itself with more radical goals and vice versa. The goals of the more conservative party can remain nearly the same only if both organizations are trying to persuade a broader and even more conservative public.[20]

A true merger leads to the suppression of previous organizational identities. Be-cause of the likelihood that the basic stance of the MOs involved will change, a true merger does not necessarily broaden the support base for its program. The more conservative members of the con-servative partner and the more radical members of the radical partner may find that the goals (or tactics) of the newly formed organization are no longer con-genial. Both extremes drop away. Further-more, now only one organization speaks for the movement, whereas before several voices clamored for change. The merging of movement organizations may make the movement appear smaller from the out-side.

Since true mergers may have such po-tentially drastic effects on the support base, it is possible that they only occur when the leadership of one or both MOs feel their cause is lost, there is growing apathy, or the like. Then the merger ap-pears as a way of preserving some vestige of vitality.[21]

Proposition 9: Inclusive MOs are more likely than exclusive MOs to participate in coalitions and mergers.

Proposition 10: Coalitions are most likely to occur if the coalition is more likely to achieve goals or lead to a lärger resource base—when success is close or when one indivisible goal or position is at stake.

Internal processes and organizational transformation

All of the topics discussed in the previous section have dealt with the effects of external events or problems on the growth and change of movement orga-nizations. However, external events are not the only causes of change. Emerging bureaucratic structures, internal ideologi-cal factions, leadership styles, and other essentially internal factors also cause or-ganizational transformation. Here we fo-cus on MO factions and on leadership changes.

When discussing external factors the task of separating dependent from inde-pendent variables was relatively simple. The effects of the environment are medi-ated through membership recruitment, re-quirements, and incentives, or through the organizational structure, and ultimately affect goals. But here we deal with the influence of internal variables on each other; the cause and effect sequences cease to be analytically (much less empirically) distinct; vicious circles as well as casual chains are possible. Consequently we can no longer so clearly distinguish goals as our dependent variable. However, we still offer alternatives to the Weber-Michels model and point to a broader range of organiza-tional outcomes.

Factions and splits

Schismogenesis and factionalization has received but little attention from sociolo-gists.[22] A faction is an identifiable subgroup opposed to other subgroups, a split occurs when a faction leaves a MO. There are two major internal preconditions for splits and the development of factions, heterogeneity of social base and the doctrinal basis of authority.

The role of heterogeneity in creating conditions for organizational splitting needs little discussion. Richard Niebuhr's discussion of the role of class and ethnic factors in denominationalism remains the classic statement of the need for internal homogeneity in a MO with no ultimate and accepted internal authority.[23] Consciousness of kind and the solidary incentives gained from homogeneity lead to the development of schisms.

What is true for religious sects and denominations is also true for political MOs. The early history of the American Communist party as described by Theodore Draper, was marked by fights based on disputes between the left and the right and connected to the European (particularly, Dutch, Lettish, and German) versus American base of the party.[24] In this case, factions within the party were only finally suppressed by the use of the great external authority and legitimacy of the true revolutionaries, the Bolsheviks.

Factions and schisms occur not only because of the heterogeneity of a MO's support base, but also because of concern with doctrinal purity. MOs concerned with questions of ultimate ideological truth and with theoretical matters are more likely to split than MOs linked to bread and butter issues. It is not concern with ideology per se that is central to this proposition, but rather that ideological concerns lead to questioning the bases of organizational authority and the behavior of the leadership. Miller has argued that the difference between Catholic sects which remained in the church and those which left depended on the acceptance of the ultimate authority of the Word as revealed in the Bible, and interpreted by the Fathers of the Church, versus the word of contemporary church authorities: the Montanists of second century Phrygia and the Feeneyites of twentieth century Boston both rested their authority on the former and left the church, whereas St. Francis bowed to the latter.[25]

Unless the nonreligious movement organization possesses the prestige of success and material incentives, as did the Bolsheviks in relation to the American Communist party, the bases for authority are difficult to establish. In this respect, the inclusive organization with its looser criteria of affiliation and of doctrinal orthodoxy is more split-resistant than the exclusive organization. The inclusive organization retains its factions while the exclusive organization spews them forth. Given internal dissension, it may be that the inclusive organization retains its support base, but is crippled in its capacity for concerted action. Splitting, of course, leads to a decrease in membership in the original movement organization. For a short period of time, at least, it leads to higher internal consistency and consensus. As such, it may also transform organizational goals away from a conservative or organizational maintenance position, for the remaining remnant is not encumbered by the need to compromise.

Proposition 11: The less the short-run chances of attaining goals, the more solidary incentives act to separate the organization into homogeneous subgroups—ethnic, class, and generational.[26] As a corollary, to the extent that a becalmed or failing MO is heterogeneous and must rely heavily on solidary incentives, the more likely it is to be beset by factionalism.

Proposition 12: The more the ideology of the MO leads to a questioning of the bases of authority the greater the likelihood of factions and splitting.

Proposition 13: Exclusive organizations are more likely than inclusive organizations to be beset by schisms.

Leadership and movement transformation

Initially we suggested that the Weber-Michels model is a sub-case of a more general set of concepts explaining MO transformation. Using such concepts as the ebb and flow of sentiments, potential and actual support base, membership requirements, incentives, and goals, we have attempted to explain a number of organizational processes. In simplified terms, the Weber-Michels model predicts changes in organizations stemming from changes in leadership positions and leadership behavior; it also predicts what organizational changes lead to changes in organizational behavior. If our more general approach is to be of value, it must be able to deal with the same problems.

Analysis of leadership phenomena is an even more crucial aspect of the study of MO than of other large scale organizations. Because the situation of the MO is unstable, because the organization has few material incentives under its control, and because of the nonroutinized nature of its tasks the success or failure of the MO can be highly dependent on the qualities and commitment of the leadership cadre and the tactics they use.[27] Three aspects of leader-organization relations are discussed —the organizational transformation following the demise of a founding father, the factors affecting the commitment of leaders to goals, and the consequences for the organization of differences in leadership style.

The Replacement of Charisma. Following the death of a charismatic leader, several changes in MOs can be expected.

But the more bureaucratized the MO the less the replacement of a leader causes organizational transformation. Three kinds of change are likely in the less bureaucratized MOs.

First, there is likely to be a decline in membership and in audience as those drop away whose commitment was more to the man than to the organizational goal and sentiment base. Furthermore, we would expect the outer circle of those who were weakly committed to drop away first.

Secondly, the death of a charismatic leader can lead to factionalization. The divergent tendencies of subgroups and the power struggles of lieutenants may have only been suppressed by the authority of the leader. His "word" now becomes one ideological base for intra-organization debate as the factions seek their place in the distribution of reward and the definition of goals and tactics.[28]

Finally, there occurs the professionalization of the executive core and the increased attempts to rationalize the administrative structure of the organization that is heir to the charismatic leader's own organization. The routinization of charisma is not only an institutionalization and rationalization of the goals and guiding myths of the organization but also a change in the incentive base of the organization—from gratifications related to the mythic stature of the leader and the opportunity to participate with him to the gratifications afforded by the performance of ritual and participation in a moral cause. Rationalization also produces a routinization of material incentives.[29]

Proposition 14: Routinization of charisma is likely to conservatize the dominant core of the movement organization while simultaneously producing increasingly radical splinter groups.

Goal Commitment of Leaders. More relevant to the Michels argument than the problems discussed above are the organizational changes attendant on officers' increased attachment to their offices and perquisites. While attachment to office may lead leaders to be more interested in organizational maintenance than pursuit of goals, organizational maintenance seems to displace radical goals following the creation of a bureaucratic structure only under three prerequisite conditions: (1) A base of support independent of membership sentiment; in labor unions the payroll checkoff insures a constant flow of funds and permits the leadership to remain in office and to replace the original goals of the MO (the union) by the goal of clinging to their own relatively lucrative offices. (2) The commitment of leaders (and followers) to other goals—to social position, to a stable life, to a family (as Jesus Christ recognized); leadership concern with the maximization of non-MO goals is a major cause of decline in intensity in any organization.[30] (3) The co-optation of leaders by other groups with subsequent transformation of goals; co-optation is the most extreme result of what Gusfield terms "articulating leadership." The growth of "statesmanship" in labor unions is one example of articulating leadership producing changes in goals and tactics of a MO.[31]

However, none of these three conditions is in itself sufficient to produce a long range change in goals or tactics. A necessary precondition for leaders to become concerned with organizational maintenance is a change in member sentiment—a growing lack of interest.

Under some conditions, however, a decline in member interest may actually allow a movement to grow more radical. As members permit other concerns to tempt them away from the MO, they insist less on their right to participate in decision making. The decision-making apparatus of the organization thus falls into the

hands of the persons with the greatest commitment to the movement goals. In some cases, these persons may actually form a cadre of professional organizers. As the MO becomes oligarchical, contrary to Michels, it may become *more* rather than less radical in its goals.[32]

Proposition 15: If a leadership cadre is committed to radical goals to a greater extent than the membership-at-large, member apathy and oligarchical tendencies lead to greater rather than less radicalism.

Leadership Style. Gusfield distinguishes between the articulation function of leaders and the mobilizing function.[33] In brief, mobilization refers to reaffirming the goals and values of the organization and building member commitment to the goals, while articulation means linking the organization and its tactics to those of other organizations and to the larger society. There is an almost inherent dualism and conflict between these roles, for mobilization requires a heightening of the ideological uniqueness of the MO and the absolute quality of its goals, while articulation often requires the uniqueness of the organization to be toned down and an adoption of the tactics of compromise. In the simple interpretation of the Weber-Michels model mobilization is followed by articulating leadership. But, as Gusfield has shown in the case of the WCTU, no such simple progression holds—indeed, demands from the membership required Frances Willard, an articulating leader, to use a more mobilizing leadership style. And at a much later date, when organizational needs changed, more articulation followed the retirement of a mobilizing leader.

Not only is the notion of a simple and inevitable progression from mobilizing to articulating a false notion of leadership transformation, but different kinds of

MOs make different demands on leaders. For instance, the exclusive organization is restricted in its possibilities of articulation.

Proposition 16: An exclusive organization is almost certain to have a leadership which focuses on mobilizing membership for tasks, while the inclusive organization is readier to accept an articulating leadership style.

Proposition 17: The MO oriented to individual change is likely to have a leadership focused on mobilizing sentiments, not articulating with the larger society. Organizations oriented to changing the larger society are more likely to require both styles of leadership, depending on the stage of their struggle.

Conclusions: The relation of goals and structure

While there is often an association between growing institutionalization and bureaucratization *and* conservatism, there is no evidence that this is a *necessary* association. Instead it is a function of the cases examined and the frame of reference with which scholars have approached the study of social movement organization. In particular, many of the studies of movement organization have been conducted out of a "metaphysical pathos" of the social democratic left.[34] Left-leaning scholars have noted that the radical organizations of their youth have changed their goals and structure. The concepts they employed or which "caught on" both summarized the movements' trend *and* implied the emotional evaluation of the trend. In this paper we have attempted to work out of a relatively neutral frame of reference to account for organizational transformation. Furthermore, we have used a fairly general approach and set of concepts which, we think, allows us to examine the transformation of any MO whatsoever.

To briefly recapitulate, we have ex-amined the impact of a number of internal and external processes on the transformation of MOs. By examining the ebb and flow of sentiments and incentives available to organizations and interrelating these with the structural requirements for membership and the nature of organizational goals, two crucial analytic factors, we have made predictions about how different movement organizations will grow and decline and in what direction their goals will change. We have paid less attention to the internal authority structure, although it would be relatively easy to incorporate such analysis into our framework. We see one of the main advantages of our approach as raising to the center of sociological analysis a number of phenomena that have only rarely been at the center. For instance, the problems of mergers, of factions and schisms, of alternating leadership styles, and of inter-organizational competition all deserve greater attention than they have been given.

Our focus has been on organizational change, and we have examined the sequence from the environment and sentiment base to goals *and* structure rather than from goals *to* structure. But, the organizational leadership's commitment to a set of goals may also influence the structure. In some cases, goal commitment can act as a deterrent to the process of bureaucratization. To implement the more radical goals, an appropriate structure can be imposed on the organization: Members must invest more time and effort, sometimes to the point of professionalization; members are recruited from groups that have low commitment to a family or a career; workers are paid little and are frequently transferred to prevent attachment to the material rewards of office, and to prevent the creation of local support or empire building; the MO has a localized branch or even a cell structure with frequent meetings. In short, the militant MO is given a quasi-exclusive structure not only to implement goals, but also to maintain them in the face of pressures to become more conservative. The organization of CORE and SNCC illustrate some of these structural devices against goal displacement.

In focusing on change of organization we may have introduced our own metaphysical pathos; we have not looked at the other side of the coin, organizational stability, although the conditions are often the obverse of those discussed for change. However, some differences would enter in. For instance, Gusfield has discussed the problem of generations in the WCTU.[35] There, the circulation of elites in an organization is related to the rate of growth and the organization's relation to the larger social movement as well as to internal structural and constitutional conditions. As a general problem, the problem of stability can be encompassed within our framework.

We have proposed some general hypotheses specifying conditions of membership, goal type, success and failure, environmental conditions, and leadership that determine the extent and nature of the change of organizational goals. We have illustrated our propositions, but illustration is not proof. What is now needed is a systematic testing of the positions, using large numbers of historical and contemporary case studies—in short, a comparative analysis of social movement organizations.

Notes

1. H. J. Gerth, and C. W. Mills (eds.), *From Max Weber: Essays in Sociology* (New York: Oxford University Press, 1946), pp. 297-301.

2. Robert Michels, *Political Parties* (Glencoe, Ill.: The Free Press, 1949).

3. F. Stuart Chapin and John Tsouderos, "The Formalizations," *Social Forces,* 34 (May 1956), pp. 342-344.

4. Mayer N. Zald and Patricia Denton, "From Evangelism to General Service: On the Transformation of the YMCA," *Administrative Science Quarterly,* 8 (June 1963), pp. 214-234.

5. Although Michels' iron law of oligarchy was originally applied to political parties of the left, while Weber's routinization of charisma referred to a more general process, both deal with the adaptation and subsequent accommodation of social movements to the society. We treat them as one general line of analysis. Weber stresses the process of rationalization of organizational structure to a greater extent than does Michels. For any single organization, Weber is more concerned with internal processes than is Michels, who focuses more on goals.

6. Philip Selznick, "Foundations of the Theory of Organizations," *American Sociological Review,* 13 (February 1948), pp. 23-35.

7. In academic courses, the study of social movements for a long time has been the province of collective behavior courses. The sociological approach to organizations utilized here helps to bridge the gap between organizational analysis and collective behavior. Essentially, this paper deals with a particular type of complex organization, the social movement organization. Although many textbooks on collective behavior deal with the organization of social movements none that we know of use organizational analysis to systematically account for the transformation of movement organizations. See Neil Smelser, *A Theory of Collective Behavior,* in Ralph R. Turner and Lewis M. Killian (eds.), *Collective Behavior* (Englewood Cliffs, N.J.: Prentice-Hall, 1959), and Kurt Lang and Gladys Lang, *Collective Dynamics* (New York: Thomas Y. Crowell Co., 1961).

C. Wendell King uses a combination of a natural history approach and organizational analysis in accounting for the transformation of movement organization. *Social Movements in the United States* (New York: Random House, 1956), pp. 39-57. Maurice Duverger presents material on the growth and organization of political parties that is in part applicable to social movement organizations. *Political Parties* (London: Methuen and Co.; New York: John Wiley & Sons, 1954).

8. The notions of incentive structure used in this work are based on those of Peter B. Clark and James Q. Wilson, "Incentive System: A Theory of Organization," *Administrative Science Quarterly,* 6 (June 1961), pp. 129-166. Briefly, three major types of incentives can be offered by organizations to harness individuals to organizational tasks—material (money and goods) incentives, solidary incentives (prestige, respect, friendship), and purposive incentives (value fulfillment). Although any organization may be able to offer all three, different types of organization have more of one than the others to offer.

9. Of course, if members devalue material incentives or have independent access to them and if organizational goals represent central life interests of members, gaining and maintaining membership

commitment represents less of an organizational problem.

In a very different context V. I. Lenin recognized that the central problem of movement organization is gaining and maintaining commitment. Where most people think of organizational structure as pyramidal, Lenin described structure in terms of concentric circles of lessening commitment and participation. See V. I. Lenin, *What Is To Be Done?* (New York: International Publisher, 1929). Arthur Stinchcombe first drew our attention to this point.

10. The effect of attitudes of the larger society towards social movements on members' ideology, self-perception, and on organizational tactics and structure has been discussed by Ralph K. Turner in "Collective Behavior and Conflict, New Theoretical Frameworks," *Sociological Quarterly* (April 1964), p. 126.

11. Mike Muench, "The American Socialist Movement: Organization and Adaptation," unpublished paper, Chicago, 1961. The figures presented by Muench are estimates from official publications.

12. Our distinction follows that of Lang and Lang, *op. cit.*, p. 488, who, following Sighele, distinguish between "inward and outward" movement organizations.

13. In the case of the temperance movement both the movement and its MO's had both goals at different points in time. See Joseph Gusfield, *Symbolic Crusade: Status Politics and the Temperance Movement* (Urbana: University of Illinois Press, 1963).

14. Anthony Downs, *An Economic Theory of Democracy* (New York: Harper & Bros., 1957), esp. chap. 8, pp. 115-127.

15. Success or failure in goal attainment affects the ebb and flow of sentiment toward the social movement and its organizations. We treat the topic separately because (1) it represents a determinant of the ebb and flow of sentiment, not just a dependent consequence; (2) success or failure may be the result of organizational activity, whereas we have been treating the ebb and flow of sentiment as to a great extent being a resultant of the conditions in the larger society; (3) success or failure may question the validity of a given organization regardless of the sentiment for the social movement, and (4) because we have a lot to say about it.

16. S. M. Lipset *et al., Agrarian Socialism* (Berkeley: University of California Press, 1950). The organization in power is limited by its coalition dependencies—its links to other organizations; it is limited by the range of variables outside of its control, such as the general state of world economy; it is limited by lack of experience and competence, by its dependency on the holdover office holders; and whereas incentives were earlier of a purposive and idealistic sort, now material incentives become the rules of the day—the organization loses its romantic idealism.

17. Sheldon Messinger, "Organizational Transformation: A Case Study of a Declining Social Movement," *American Sociological Review,* 20 (February 1955), pp. 3-10.

18. For a general discussion of alliances among political parties see Duverger, *op. cit.,* pp. 281-351.

19. By and large, mergers and coalitions require ideological compatibility. Although extremist parties from both sides may work for the overthrow of the government (as in the Weimar Republic, for instance), they do not engage in planned coordinated attack. They do not support the center against the other extreme, and they independently work against the established government. For the role of ideological compatibility in coalitions see William Gamson, "Coalition Formation at Presidential Nominating Conventions," *American Journal of Sociology,* 68 (September 1962), pp. 157-172.

20. Following Osgood and Tannenbaum one might even argue that the merged movement will be perceived as more extreme than it really is. They hypothesize that if an associative bond is perceived between two objects of evaluation, the object that was originally more neutrally viewed will gain a more extreme evaluation while the extremely viewed object will lose very little of its polarized evaluation. C. Osgood, and P. Tannenbaum, "The Principle of Congruity in the Prediction of Attitude Change," *Psychological Review* (1955), pp. 62, 42-55.

21. These problems have arisen in the recent attempt to merge two MO's oriented to military disarmament, SANE and United World Federalists. These two organizations have differed in that the UWF has had historical attachments to the upper class, to Quakers, and to proper institutional types. It has been more educative and persuasive in technique. SANE has had a nervous, more alienated, liberal base, and has used heavier handed propaganda techniques. The proposed merger has been sharply questioned by members.

22. Norman Miller, "Formal Organization and Schismogenesis," unpublished paper, Chicago, 1963. See also a most neglected minor classic by Walter Firey, "Informal Organization and the Theory of the Schism," *American Sociological Review,* 13 (February 1948), pp. 15-24. For a history of the American Socialist experience that focuses on its proneness to factions and splits see Daniel Bell, "The Background and Development of Marxian Socialism in the United States," in *Socialism and American Life* (eds.), Donald D. Egbert and Stow Persons (Princeton: Princeton University Press, 1952).

23. Helmut Richard Niebuhr, *The Social Sources of Denominationalism* (New York: Henry Holt & Co., 1929).

24. Theodore Draper, *The Roots of American Communism* (New York: Viking Press, 1957). There were also factions within these groups.

25. Miller, *op. cit.*

26. It may be that the relation of splitting and developing factions to chances of attaining goals is curvilinear rather than linear. As movement orga-

nizations approach gaining power, latent conflicts over means, ends, and the future distribution of power, which have been suppressed in the general battle, rise to the fore.

27. Herbert Blumer, "Social Movements," in A. M. Lee (ed.), *Principles of Sociology* (New York: Barnes & Noble, 1955), pp. 99-220.

28. See the discussion of succession in S. M. Lipset, "The Political Process in Trade Unions," *Political Man* (New York: Doubleday & Co., 1960), pp. 412-416.

29. Analogously, such processes may take place in student and other highly age-graded movements. The graduation of the founding generation parallels the death of the charismatic leader. See Charles Goldsmith, "The Student Peace Union," unpublished paper, University of Chicago, 1965.

30. Alvin W. Gouldner, "Attitudes of Progressive Trade Union Leaders," *American Journal of Sociology*, 52 (March 1947), pp. 389-392.

31. Joseph Gusfield, "Functional Areas of Leadership in Social Movements" in A. W. Gouldner and R. de Charms (eds.), *Studies in Leadership* (rev. ed.), forthcoming.

32. A current example of oligarchization attended by radicalization is the growth of the Berkeley Free Speech Movement which appears to have begun as a representative coalition of campus groups but developed into a mass movement coordinated by an oligarchical executive committee. The committee was composed of leaders with the strongest commitment to "radical" mass tactics (and also apparently, the most concerned with the ultimate issues of alienation rather than the immediate issue of free speech).

33. Gusfield, *loc. cit.*

34. Alvin Gouldner, "Metaphysical Pathos and the Study of Bureaucracy," *American Political Science Review*, 49 (June 1955), pp. 496-507.

35. Joseph Gusfield, "The Problems of Generations in an Organizational Structure," *Social Forces*, 35 (May 1957).

28.

Frank E. Myers

CIVIL DISOBEDIENCE AND ORGANIZATIONAL CHANGE: THE BRITISH COMMITTEE OF 100

The recent rise in America and Britain of civil disobedience and nonviolent resistance as techniques of protest constitutes a challenge not only to the traditional framework of democratic debate but also to our understanding of how social protest movements grow and change. The Student Nonviolent Coordinating Committee in America and the Committee of 100 in Britain, in the ten years since their founding, have developed more radical tactics, more revolutionary goals, and more anarchic rather than more bureaucratic orga-

From Frank E. Myers, "Civil Disobedience and Organizational Change: The British Committee of 100," *Political Science Quarterly* 86, March 1971, pp. 92-112. Reprinted by permission of the publisher, *Political Science Quarterly*.

nization. Such a pattern runs counter to accepted theories of organizational development that, stated in a simplified way: (1) as organizations persist through time, leadership tends to become characterized less by close and egalitarian relations with followers and more by remoteness and the absence of accountability; (2) the organizational structure changes as a bureaucratic staff develops and the organization tends to become marked by an internal hierarchy of officials, by rules, constitutions, and bylaws, and by more definite conditions of membership; and (3) the tactics and goals are transformed, as leaders grow accustomed to the arts of negotiation and compromise and as they gain a stake in maintaining their newly won place in the larger social order, in the direction of opportunism and relative conservatism.[1]

Two factors always present in the case of civil disobedience groups operating in a democratic setting cause them to deviate from this model. First, civil disobedience groups are normally factions which compete with other more conservative protest organizations seeking similar goals. Second, members of civil disobedience groups face the possibility of arrest with consequent jail sentences and fines. This conditions both the composition and behavior of civil disobedience groups in ways not experienced by other protest groups in democratic systems.

These are my conclusions after a detailed study of the internal history of the Committee of 100.[2] I had provisionally adopted the standard model for the analysis of the Committee's development, but careful examination of the minutes and accompanying memoranda of Committee meetings, supplemented by interviews with Committee members and close observers, gradually revealed that the Committee did not conform to it. At first, this appeared to be simply a freakish phenomenon explainable by factors unique to this particular organization. Subsequent study of the Student Nonviolent Coordinating Committee and the Congress of Racial Equality in the United States, however, suggested the hypothesis that the Committee was not an anomaly, as we shall see, but a type of organization for which the standard model is not applicable.

Factional origins of the committee

The Committee of 100 was founded in 1960, the rebellious offspring of the Campaign for Nuclear Disarmament (CND) and the Direct Action Committee against Nuclear War (DAC).[3] CND was formed in 1958 as a moral protest against a defense policy based on nuclear deterrence. The objective of CND—to force by mass demonstrations a change in Labour party foreign policy—was called into question, however, when Labour lost the general election of 1959. CND began to split into two groups, one of which argued that the new political situation required CND to develop a sophisticated set of proposals for nuclear disarmament and, by working quietly through constituency parties and trade unions rather than relying on mass demonstrations, to try to persuade Labour leaders to adopt it. Opponents of this tendency agreed that CND reliance upon traditional forms of protest had failed, but advocated a more radical alternative—civil disobedience as practiced by the DAC.

DAC had been formed in 1957 as a pacifist group pledged to civil disobedience. Until the formation of CND, however, DAC activities had gone unnoticed by the public. After 1958, DAC gained great attention from the press and public, thereby giving some credence to arguments for the efficacy of illegal action. But DAC was always a small coterie. In the atmosphere of urgency created by international events in the spring of 1960 (the U-2 and RB-47 incidents and the collapse of the Paris summit talks), a young American named Ralph Schoenman wrote a letter to Bertrand Russell proposing a mass civil disobedience campaign and he found the CND president in a receptive mood.

Russell and Schoenman set out to combine the mass support of the CND with the capacity for sensational civil disobedience of the DAC. The initial plan was to obtain pledges from at least 2000 people to participate in a mass civil disobedience demonstration. Letters were sent out over Russell's signature to certain celebrities known to be sympathetic to CND asking for their participation in the demonstration and in the permanent Committee of

100 which was being formed to plan the protest campaign. When news of the Committee was leaked to the public, CND chairman Canon L. John Collins repudiated the plan and attacked Russell. Russell's subsequent resignation as president of CND and the establishment of the Committee completed the schism of the unilateralist movement.

Tactics

Since there was apparent agreement on objectives with CND, attention focused on the tactics of the Committee of 100 as its distinguishing feature. These were to publicize the unilateralist cause by soliciting the support of well known individuals and to stage demonstrations characterized by nominal violations of the law. The effectiveness of these demonstrations in directing public attention to the arguments against British nuclear defense policy depended on the Committee's ability to obtain large numbers of participants and to select targets of protest that were unambiguously relevant to the issues. These were, in short, the tactics of a single-issue protest campaign.

In its first phase, the Committee was successful in carrying them out. Famous Britons, particularly in the world of the arts and literature, lent their names and active support. The first demonstration staged by the Committee conformed precisely to its stated tactics. The target of protest was the Ministry of Defense in Whitehall, a point of military significance and well known to the general public. It was a mass demonstration; approximately 1200 of the more than 2000 who had pledged themselves to commit civil disobedience actually sat down and blocked the street in front of the Ministry. Another group of 3000 people marched through the streets of London in support of the demon-

stration. Moreover, the protest was timed to coincide with a relevant and, from the Committee's point of view, objectionable event—the arrival of a United States depot ship carrying missiles to the Polaris submarine base in Holy Loch. Finally, adequate publicity was assured because the protest was illegal, although no one was arrested.

Subsequent Committee demonstrations followed this general pattern. After an occupation of Parliament Square on April 29, 1961, at which 826 persons were arrested, public attention was concentrated on the Committee, whose activities became the talk of the day. To maintain the acquired momentum, the Committee decided to concentrate on a giant demonstration in September in London's Trafalgar Square. This demonstration was publicized throughout the summer of 1961 as an illegal sit-down scheduled for Sunday, September 17. The police, invoking their powers to prevent violations of the law prohibiting obstruction of the Square, arrested in advance 31 leaders of the Committee. On September 12, the 31, refusing to be bound over to keep the peace, were sentenced to jail.

The Committee announced that plans for the demonstration were unaltered. Indeed the trial of Russell and the others served to publicize the protest, and the result equalled the highest hopes of Committee leaders. More than 1300 persons were arrested, among them actors, scientists, a prospective Tory candidate for Parliament, a book publisher, writers, a trade union organizer, along with students and members of pacifist groups.

It might have seemed that this success would confirm in the minds of Committee leaders the validity of their adopted tactics. In fact, the demonstration began a process that was to transform the tactics of the Committee and to make it a much

more radical organization than its founders had either planned or desired. The very
success of the September 17 demonstration had placed the Committee in an awk-
ward position for future protests. The
turnout had been so large that the Committee could not hope to equal it in the
near future, and any demonstration with
fewer participants would be interpreted as
a sign of weakness. Many Committee
members, particularly the well known
ones, felt that with this demonstration and
arrest they had done their duty for the
cause of unilateralism. This notion was
reinforced by the manner of some of the
arrests; in certain instances the London
police performed their functions brutally
and succeeded in intimidating the protesters, who had not expected such treatment. The less radical—and perhaps less
committed—dropped out of the Committee. Not wanting the membership to fall
below 100, Michael Randle, the secretary,
appealed in a letter to supporters for
applications for membership to fill the
vacancies created by the arrests. In September and October 1961, the Committee
acquired 42 new members.[4]

This turnover in membership was more
profound than the numbers involved would
indicate. Apart from the first meeting on
October 22, 1960, until September 1961,
no meeting had been attended by even half
of the total membership, which ranged between 102 and 109. For many of the
celebrities whom the Committee founders
had been so anxious to attract, membership in the Committee was purely nominal.[5] Of the 53 persons who attended that
first meeting of the Committee, only 18
were present at any meetings after the September 17 sit-down. Thus, with the exception of a few regulars, the demonstration had led to the establishment of a new
Committee. These regulars were the direct
descendants of DAC. Since they had gen-

erally joined the Committee before the
September shake-up, they were regarded
as "old timers" by the 51 newcomers. This
attitude was reinforced by two factors:
first, the former DAC people were generally more experienced than were the new
members in organizing protest campaigns,
and second, many of the new members
were very young.

The increased voice of the former DAC
members within the Committee hastened
trends toward the radicalization of tactics,
reflected in the choice of the site for the
Committee's next protest. It was not to be
one mass sit-down in London or some
other population center, but a series of sit-
downs at several NATO air bases on December 9, 1961. Moreover, in contrast to
the openness toward the police that had
characterized previous Committee demonstrations, an atmosphere of conspiracy
settled over the preparations. Ostensibly,
the demonstration was to resemble earlier
symbolic protests by the DAC at North
Pickenham and Finningley. For the activities at the Wethersfield NATO base, however, the Committee developed a secret
plan to have "a number of trained people"
break away from the bulk of demonstrators and enter the base where they would
lie down in front of planes and other
equipment in order to hinder actual military operations.[6]

The Wethersfield demonstration was a
disaster for the Committee. Only 5000 to
6000 demonstrators participated. Fear of
arrest for violating the Official Secrets Act
kept many away. Committee publicity had
focused on the Wethersfield sit-down, calling for 50,000 demonstrators, and the decline in numbers as compared to the
12,000 who participated in the September
17 sit-down appeared to be a sign that the
Committee was losing its appeal.[7] The
demonstration, moreover, had been poorly
planned and organized. Briefing meetings

had started late and were conducted without agenda. The problem of transporting participants to Wethersfield, a remote base, proved insurmountable. Busses had been chartered, but the bus company refused to let them out after police warned that they might be used as part of a plan to violate the Official Secrets Act, and no emergency transportation plan had been prepared. When they arrived at the base, moreover, Committee leaders found that, contrary to expectations, there were no gaps through which protesters could enter in the barbed wire surrounding the base.

The poor planning was related to the influx of new members into the Committee in September 1961. Young new members had gained influence in planning Committee activities; indeed, a small group of teenagers came to dominate the working group. As members of the Committee resigned or were jailed, they were replaced "in what would seem to be a fairly random way from other names of potential substitutes taken off a list more or less in rotation." Thus, people on the Committee and its working group were chosen for their availability, rather than for the representativeness of their supporters or for their own skills. Generally, they were young people chosen "partly because these have fewer responsibilities and have more spare time, and also because chronic lack of funds in the initial stages ruled out the engagement of professional staff." The planning of the Wethersfield demonstration was carried out, therefore, at meetings packed with outsiders, chaired by inexperienced and ineffectual chairmen, cluttered with irrelevant speeches—meetings which regularly, as one member observed, "degenerated into utter chaos."[8]

The subsequent history of the Committee's tactics reflects the influence of the changing membership. Although demonstrations similar to those already described continued to be held, their by now routine nature displeased the Committee. It turned to the consideration of more radical measures, including political strikes in defense industries. The Committee began to distribute literature and to make speeches at factory gates,[9] but it recognized that it would be years, at best, before large numbers of workers could be persuaded to close down defense industries for political reasons. Beyond agitation and propaganda, little could be done. In the fall of 1962, the Committee considered embarking on a "troops against the bomb" campaign, the ultimate objective of which was "incitement of troops to sedition."[10] The campaign would attempt to confront "troops with the ultimate logical step they should take if they oppose nuclear war preparations" and "to develop an attitude among servicemen which might prove definitive at a moment of acute crisis when orders were issued to push the final button."[11] The plan was felt to support also eventual industrial action, since a political strike of defense industries would probably result in the calling out of troops who would, hopefully, under the Committee's influence, refuse to perform their tasks.

Conclusion

This analysis of the Committee of 100 pinpoints the overwhelming significance to a protest group of adopting civil disobedience. Such a tactic sets into motion a series of processes that tend, in this and similar cases, to produce similar lines of development:

(1) Groups adopting illegal actions as explicit tactics normally originate as factions of larger protest organizations. The faction forms in opposition to the tendency of the parent organization, which has relied on traditional tactics, to become

conservative and oligarchical, a characteristic of most large organizations with pyramidal structures. Factional groups using illegal tactics tend to draw supporters from dissatisfied and more radical elements of the parent organization.

This analysis points to the parallels between the Committee of 100 and such American organizations as the Student Nonviolent Coordinating Committee and the Congress of Racial Equality. While neither American group was, in a strict sense, a faction of the National Association for the Advancement of Colored People, both groups developed in the early 1960s as challenges to the NAACP. They tended to attract civil rights activists who were disenchanted with the methods of the NAACP, even though all three organizations had the same ostensible aim, racial equality.[12]

(2) Groups employing illegal tactics tend, with the passage of time, to draw younger rather than older persons into positions of leadership. The leadership, moreover, tends to become more rather than less dedicated to the radical implications of the groups' goals and tactics. The extreme demands on the loyalties of the most active members—odd hours, frequent trips to protest sites, some of which may be remote from urban centers, long meetings, and especially the threat and fact of repeated arrests, arraignments, and jail sentences—are normally too demanding for members with families and the need for regular incomes. Those members who do not have family responsibilities and who do not require steady employment tend to assume an ever greater share of the groups' leadership tasks. And among members with such obligations, only those most dedicated to the aims of the groups will continue to serve as leaders. One would expect this to be generally true in organizations in which leadership is accompanied by distinct material disadvantage.

(3) Groups employing civil disobedience are likely, at least in the eyes of their followers, to fall below expectations in achieving their aims. In part, the sense of failure exists because the expectations of the members are often unrealistically high. Committee members, for example, expected a striking reversal in the attitudes of both the political leadership and the general public within a period of months, or at most a few years. The recognition that such a change is not taking place occurs some time after the groups have been functioning and marks a watershed in the movement. The tactic of limited civil disobedience is likely to be criticized, usually from a radical perspective. Rather than emulate the evolution of the parent organizations, the civil disobedience groups are prone to move in a revolutionary direction. This change involves both goals and tactics. Goals tend to "expand," explicitly encompassing ever broader areas of public policy than those originally considered by the groups. The goal expansion accompanies changes in tactics, which may occur in one of two ways. The groups may turn away from civil disobedience to some form of violence; or (as in the case of the Committee) the groups may reject the conception of civil disobedience as a publicity maneuver and attempt to use nonviolent tactics to coerce the government into a change of policy.

In the case of the Committee, a reconsideration of tactics came after the recognition of the failure of the Wethersfield demonstration in December 1961. During the next few months the Committee began to adopt an increasingly radical self-definition. In the case of SNCC, the recognition of failure to achieve objectives came in

1962, and SNCC began to shift its primary interest from sit-ins to voter registration in Lowndes County, Alabama. The act of registering black voters in Alabama, and subsequently elsewhere, was not only a much more revolutionary challenge to the social system in that context, but was also treated much more severely by law enforcement agents than were sit-ins.[13]

A similar radicalization marked the development of the Congress of Racial Equality, which in 1960-61 relied primarily on the tactic of nonviolent civil disobedience and espoused a liberal doctrine of racial integration similar to that of the NAACP. But the experience of being arrested tended to weed out the more moderate white and black leaders of CORE, and by 1963 nonviolence as an ideal and as a tactic was declining within the organization. CORE eventually dropped all emphasis on nonviolence as well as the immediate goal of integration as it changed its focus to organizing the black community in northern ghettos.[14]

The relatively narrow question of the effectiveness of civil disobedience groups in achieving their objectives is difficult to determine, for they operate more or less in conjunction with other groups having similar goals. In some cases, as in that of SNCC in its early years, they can be very effective. They may heighten the sense of urgency around the protest and even improve the bargaining position of their more moderate allies.[15] But effectiveness of this sort is more likely in cases of bread-and-butter politics, where specific concessions can be demanded and given. On issues such as defense policy, civil disobedience must affect the public at large. Leaders of CND generally felt that the sensational tactics of the Committee hindered the process of persuading Labour party leaders who might have tended to support uni-

lateral nuclear disarmament. Moreover, while the Committee did contribute greatly to forcing public discussion of defense policy, its precise effect was ambiguous. No sudden and dramatic shift in public opinion occurred, and many Britons doubtless were alienated by Committee activities. British attitudes to defense policy, as well as government policy itself, did change significantly, however, in the years after 1960, and the Committee's contribution must be reckoned in any assessment of that process.

But a broader question concerns the implications of these observations for the prospect of democracy in organizations and in nations. Theories about the tendency toward oligarchical control and goal displacement have been viewed as profoundly pessimistic and have been received as a challenge by social democrats. But having discovered a type of organization in which revolutionary fire does not diminish and in which bureaucratic self-interest is not likely to follow upon spontaneous participation and open decision-making, should we then celebrate a new democratic form? Some who have advocated civil disobedience and nonviolent action have argued just this—that not only are such tactics effective in bringing about peaceful social change, but that they may contain as well the seeds of a purer democracy. But an evolution from civil disobedience designed to persuade to civil disobedience designed to coerce does not necessarily augur well for democracy, pure or impure.

Notes

1. The literature in this area is voluminous, but a sampling of relevant interpretations, applications, and critiques may be found in Robert Michels, *Political Parties: A Sociological Study of the Oligarchical Tendencies of Modern Democracy* (New York, 1962); Seymour M. Lipset, Martin A. Trow, and James S. Coleman, *Union Democracy: The In-*

ternal Politics of the International Typographical Union (New York, 1962); Rudolf Heberle, Social Movements: An Introduction to Political Sociology (New York, 1951); Mayer N. Zald and Roberta Ash, "Social Movement Organizations: Growth, Decay and Change," Social Forces, XLIV (1966), pp. 327-41; Robert T. Golembiewski, William A. Welsh, and William J. Crotty, A Methodological Primer for Political Scientists (Chicago, 1969), pp. 356-88; Sheldon Messinger, "Organizational Transformation: A Case Study of a Declining Social Movement," American Sociological Review, XX (1955), pp. 3-10; and John D. May, "Democracy, Organization, Michels," American Political Science Review, LIX (1965), pp. 417-29.

2. Frank E. Myers, "British Peace Politics: The Campaign for Nuclear Disarmament and the Committee of 100, 1957-1962" (Unpublished Ph.D. dissertation, Columbia University, 1965).

3. Full length accounts of the history of the unilateralist movement may be found in Christopher Driver, The Disarmers (London, 1964) and Frank Parkin, Middle Class Radicalism: The Social Bases of the British Campaign for Nuclear Disarmament (New York, 1968).

4. Michael Randle, "Letter to Committee of 100 Supporters," Sept. 8, 1961 (unpublished circular); "Minutes," Sept. 30, 1961 and Oct. 28, 1961 (unpublished circular).

5. Committee of 100 minutes give attendance at meetings and total membership only between Oct. 22, 1960 and Jan. 28, 1962, and even membership figures are not always given. After Jan. 28, 1962, the Committee dissolved into local groups, and figures for membership and attendance are not available. Minutes of meetings give the following attendance and membership figures:

Date of Meeting	Attendance	Total Committee Membership
Oct. 22, 1960	53	—
Nov. 26, 1960	44	102
Jan. 21, 1961	48	103
Mar. 12, 1961	48	106
Mar. 26, 1961	29	—
May 7, 1961	42	109
May 27, 1961	39	106
Aug. 4, 1961	31	—
Aug. 18, 1961	22	—
Sept. 9, 1961	48	—
Sept. 30, 1961	35	—
Oct. 28, 1961	62	—
Nov. 26, 1961	55	—

Ten of the best known Committee members who attended the founding meeting on Oct. 22, 1960 never returned. These were Doris Lessing, Alex Comfort, Bernard Kops, James Corbett, Shelagh Delaney, John Osborne, Heather Richardson, Lindsay Anderson, Reg Butler, and Bertrand Russell. In Russell's case, failure to attend meetings did not indicate lack

of interest since he continued to communicate by telephone and mail and through his secretary Ralph Schoenman. Some of the Committee's most distinguished members—such as Augustus John, Sir Herbert Read, John Braine, Lord Boyd-Orr, and John Berger—never attended any meetings at all.

6. Committee of 100, "Letter to Marshalls" by Terry Chandler, Nov. 27, 1961 (unpublished). Further details of the demonstration were revealed in the trial which followed. See especially the opinion of Lord Reid in Chandler and Others v. Director of Public Prosecutions, House of Lords [1962], 3 ALL E. R. p. 142.

7. Committee of 100, "Minutes," Dec. 17, 1961, contain a full post mortem on the Wethersfield demonstration. See also George Clark, Second Wind (London: CND, 1963), p. 12 ff.

8. Committee of 100, "Minutes," Dec. 17, 1961, memorandum from Geoffrey Frampton. See also Peter Cadogan's memorandum, "After December 9th," included in the same minutes.

9. Committee of 100, "Report of Industrial Sub-Committee," Mar. 31, 1962 (mimeograph circular). In May 1962, Bertrand Russell called for industrial action as a means of compelling the government to alter its policies; see Bertrand Russell, Bertrand Russell's May Day Message—1962 (London: Committee of 100, n.d.).

10. London Committee of 100, "Minutes," Sept. 29-30, 1962.

11. Committee of 100, "Report of a Sub-Committee of the London Committee of 100 and National Committee of 100 Planning Committee on: Troops Against the Bomb" (mimeograph circular, n.d.). Committee records do not reveal the extent to which such plans actually were put into effect, but in the spring of 1963, the Air Force sentenced two RAF technicians to prison for attempting to form an anti-bomb group within the service. In the same period, disciplinary action was taken against several other men for voicing anti-bomb views while in the military service. See The Guardian (Manchester and London), Mar. 8, 11, 16; Apr. 11; and May 1, 1963 for stories on advocacy of nuclear disarmament by members of the armed services.

12. Louis E. Lomax has argued that "the current Negro revolt is more than a revolt against the white world. It is also a revolt of the Negro masses against their own leadership and goals"; Lomax, The Negro Revolt (New York, 1962), p. 79. The difficult relations between the NAACP and CORE before the latter's first sit-in are described graphically by Inge Powell Bell, who reports that "A fairly large proportion of CORE members had been recruited out of the NAACP Youth Council"; Bell, CORE and the Strategy of Nonviolence (New York, 1968), p. 97. Benjamin Muse, The American Negro Revolution: From Nonviolence to Black Power, 1963-1967 (Bloomington, Ind., 1968), gives a factual account of the transformation of the ideology and political objectives of the organizations participating in the black

revolution. For SNCC, the best source still is Howard Zinn, *SNCC: The New Abolitionists* (Boston, 1964).

13. Stokely Carmichael and Charles V. Hamilton, *Black Power: The Politics of Liberation in America* (New York, 1967), pp. 98-120.

14. Bell, pp. 165-93, gives a detailed description of these developments in CORE.

15. Jack L. Walker, "The Functions of Disunity: Negro Leadership in a Southern City," *Journal of Negro Education,* XXXII (1963), pp. 227-36.

29.

Luther P. Gerlach

MOVEMENTS OF REVOLUTIONARY CHANGE

We have been concerned for some time about how movements are structured and how they work to transform individuals and produce social change. In other publications, including two films (Gerlach, 1968, 1970a), a book (Gerlach and Hine, 1970b), and various articles (Gerlach and Hine, 1970a, Gerlach, 1970b, Hine and Gerlach, 1969), we have examined movement structure and function according to five factors:

(1) movement *organization*
(2) means of *recruitment*
(3) the process by which movements enculturate and *commit* new participants
(4) movement *ideology*
(5) movement perception of and response to *opposition*

In this paper we shall focus only on the factor of movement organization, described as "segmentary, polycephalous, and reticulate."

(a) *Segmentary:* a movement is composed of a range of diverse groups, or cells, which grow and die, divide and fuse, proliferate and contract.

(b) *Polycephalous:* this movement organization does not have a central command or decision-making structure; rather it has many leaders or rivals for leadership, not only within the movement as a whole, but within each movement cell.

(c) *Reticulate:* these diverse groups do not constitute simply an amorphous collection; rather, they are organized into a network, or reticulate structure through cross-cutting links, "traveling evangelists" or spokesmen, overlapping participation, joint activities, and the sharing of common objectives and opposition.

Segmentation process

Observation of the segmentary nature of movement organization suggests four basic ways in which cells split, merge, or proliferate:

(1) Movements characteristically include in the ideology a concept of personal power. In religious movements, this involves beliefs concerning the direct access of God from whom power is derived. In the black power movement, this concept is expressed in terms of "doing your own thing." Each individual as well as each small group is credited with and encouraged to "do his own thing" and to take initiative in acting to promote movement goals he considers im-

Excerpts from "Movements of Revolutionary Change: Some Structural Characteristics," by Luther P. Gerlach and reprinted from *American Behavioral Scientist* Vol. 14, No. 6 (July/August 1971) pp. 812-36 by permission of the publisher, Sage Publications, Inc., and the author.

portant. This results in organizational splits over ideological or methodological approach and stimulates the gathering of new recruits to support each new venture.

(2) Preexisting socioeconomic cleavages, factionalisms, and personal conflicts are carried over into the movement and increase the so-called "fissiparous," or splitting nature, of the movement organization.

(3) Movement members, especially those with leadership capabilities, compete for a broad range of economic, political, social, and psychological rewards. For example, black power leaders are continually vying with one another for funds which whites contribute through fear, guilt, or a genuine desire for social change. Similarly, Pentecostal evangelists compete for the honor of leading a large revival and ecology spokesmen contend for media and student attention. This personal competition leads to continual splitting of cells, realignment of followers, and intensified efforts to recruit new participants and broaden bases of support.

(4) Segmentation of movement organization occurs over ideological differences. As we have pointed out in other papers, a truly committed movement participant experiences an intensity of involvement over ideological differences that the ordinary person feels only for events which threaten his immediate well-being, his family, or home. For instance, we indicated above how differences in opinion about the "system" and its ability to change are a basis for significant organizational fission in the ecology movement.

Decentralization and polycephalous structure

Leadership in the movements we have studied, in Weberian terms, is charismatic more than bureaucratic. Power and authority tend to be distributed among several of the most able and dedicated members of a group, of which one is recognized as *primus inter pares*, the "first among equals." This is similar to the pattern of leadership in various African,

Asian, and Middle Eastern societies which anthropologists have characteristically called segmentary and *acephalous*. The term acephalous, or "headless," indicates the strong bias which scholars have had against such noncentralized organization. If the tribal organization has many leaders, Western observers call it headless. We prefer the term polycephalous. A typical leader in a polycephalous tribe or in a movement achieves his status by building a personal following and displaying abilities and characteristics pertinent to situational needs and the expectations of his adherents and potential recruits. He must prove and continue to demonstrate his worth to maintain his position.

In his study of segmentary lineage systems, Sahlins (1961) points out that leadership in such systems is often situation specific and hence ephemeral. A man who proves himself as a war leader over a confederation of segments fighting a common foe is not necessarily able to work as a leader of this confederation or of its components in peace.

This situational aspect of leadership is characteristic of the movements we have studied, especially black power. Those qualities which enhance the leader's reputation in some types of militant and action-oriented operations may not be pertinent to assure maintenance of leadership under different conditions. A person may secure leadership over a group or collection of groups by his ability to "sock it to Whitey," or mobilize and lead a short-run militant operation and obtain concessions from the establishment. But he may not have the ability to lead these groups in the more routine consolidation of gains, and hence might fade, at least for a time, into the background while persons with more pertinent organizational skills assume control.

Even where leaders have both charisma-tic-action and bureaucratic-administrative capabilities most will find it difficult to employ both at one time. Administering the ordinary activities of many of the black power groups often implies working to some degree with whites, taking their advice and funds (often with some strings attached or implied) and reducing overt manifestations of militancy. This leads other blacks to brand such leaders as Uncle Toms and accuse them of being coopted by the system. Similarly, some environmental activists wind up working with government or industry and exper-ience similar problems of identity. Of course, a few gifted individuals will ac-tually thrive in such situations, and switch back and forth from administrative to militant role, playing one off against the other with deceptive ease.

Although certain particularly charisma-tic and able leaders, such as Stokely Carmichael, H. Rap Brown, Dick Greg-ory, Eldridge Cleaver for black power, or Paul Ehrlich for ecology activism, or David Wilkerson for Pentecostalism, may be highly revered and widely influential at any moment, the newest convert to the movement can perceive them more as "soul brothers" than as "commanders of the faithful." Each has organizational power only over his own segment of the movement, and this only for a limited time. To outsiders, such men often appear to be the key individuals without whom the movement would grind to a halt. But not one of them could be called the leader of the movement as a whole, because:

(1) They quite clearly disagree upon such crucial matters as the goals of the move-ment and the means by which these goals should be achieved.
(2) Not one of these leaders has a roster, or even knows about all of the groups which consider themselves participants in the movement.
(3) They can make no decisions which are bind-ing upon all or even a majority of the par-ticipants in the movement.
(4) This is most frustrating for representatives of the established order: none of these lead-ers has regulatory powers over the move-ment. In the case of black power, city officials are often upset when well-known leaders whom they assume to have incited a riot, cannot control it, even when they are obviously working tirelessly to do so. Offi-cials then conclude either that the leader is not sincere in his efforts to stop the riots or that it got out of hand and beyond his original orders. In one riot in Miami in 1968, city and state officials called in a well-known black power leader, who had been speaking in the area, to plead for an end to the violence. Local black leaders said afterwards that they felt this only made the situation worse. The assumption that local groups were under his control angered them. In the environmental issues estab-lished authorities frequently want the ecol-ogy protesters to centralize, hire a lawyer to represent them, and negotiate.
(5) Another manifestation of the polycepha-lous, segmentary nature of the movement is that there is no such thing as a card-carrying member of the movement. That is, there are no objective requirements to qual-ify a person as a movement member, al-though some groups do have such member-ship requirements. Participants in the movement share a common history and experience and recognize each other through bonds of objectively perceived commitment. This means that there is no leader who can determine objectively who is or is not a member of the movement, let alone direct, regulate, or speak for the movement as a whole.

Reticulation

The decentralized, segmentary, organi-zational structure of a movement owes its cohesion to linkages among the autono-mous cells. Through these linkages the various cells intermesh to form a network which, following Mayer (1966), we regard as essentially "unbounded." That is, the network ramifies extensively throughout society and there are no well-defined limits to such extension. We identify five types of such linkages:

(1) Lines of kinship, friendship, and other forms of close association between individual members of different local groups. Often a single individual will be an active participant in more than one group as well. Even after an organizational split over some issue, previous ties of friendship tend to form loose linkages between the resulting splinter groups. Such ties form the basis for potential cooperative action in the face of future large-scale opposition.

(2) Personal, kinship, or social ties between leaders and other participants in autonomous cells form networks that sometimes extend beyond the local community and tie together independent groups in distant cities. Such ties are extended and facilitated by telephone and letter. Circulating newsletters play such a role in Pentecostal and ecology movements.

(3) Every movement has its traveling evangelists who criss-cross the country as living links in the reticulate network. Abernathy, McKissick, Cleaver, and others are only the better known of hundreds of black power spokesmen whose influence spread beyond their own local groups. For participatory ecology we can mention such noted eco-evangelists as Paul Ehrlich and Barry Commoner. When such an evangelist-organizer comes to town, members of many different local segments bury the hatchet temporarily to hear him speak and often act in concert under his ad hoc leadership in a specific activity such as a demonstration or march. Ordinary movement participants can also travel along the movement network. For example, a university student and ecology activist from Minneapolis traveled along such an ecology network up and down the West Coast. Everywhere his ecology contacts gave him housing and food, shared ideas about ecology and change with him, and sent him on to new contacts in his next stopping-off place. As he traveled, he disseminated his growing in-formation, like Johnny Appleseed, sowing seeds to bear tomorrow's fruit.

(4) Closely related to the rally or the revival meeting of the traveling evangelist are the more permanent cross-cutting activities of the areawide, regional or national "in-gathering." One example of the regional and national in-gathering for black power was the Poor People's March. Another, somewhat earlier example, was the open housing demonstration of Father Groppi and the "Commandos" in Milwaukee. For the ecology movement the April 1970 Teach-Ins not only helped to bring ecology and related counterculture groups together, but also generated new awareness and poured it out across the land.

As the local committees of such area, regional, and national associations continue and become more permanent organizations, they become roughly analogous to the age sets in polycephalous African societies which cut across loyalties to the lineage segments (Eisenstadt, 1959).

(5) A crucial cross-cutting linkage providing movement unity are those basic beliefs which are shared by all segments of the movement, no matter how disparate their views on other matters. All movement ideologies are split in the sense that there are a few basic themes and an infinite variety of interpretations and emphases. The variety of interpretation is the ideological basis for fusion, enabling members of warring factions to conceptualize themselves as participants in a single movement or revolution. Sometimes these unifying tenets spread as powerful integrating concepts, such as the concepts of ecosystem, interdependence, limited resource base, spaceship earth, no-growth economy. Sometimes such concepts become slogans which transcend initial meaning and epitomize the movement. The term "ecology" is one example of this. Black power gives us a splendid instance of the condensation of ideology into battle cry and unifying slogans: Black Power, Black is Beautiful, Racism is Whitey's hang up, Green Power through Black Power, and the like. The concepts of ecology, system, interdependence, limited resource base, spaceship earth, have interpenetrated the ecology movement. Such statements express the

core beliefs which make possible the system of intercell leadership exchange, temporary coalition on specific actions, a flow of financial and other material resources through nonbureaucratic channels, and an often surprising presentation of a united front in the face of external opposition. They are comparable to the common ancestor or common religious concepts of the Arabs, Nuer, or Tiv, and Somali peoples, who unified on this basis when necessary.

Extramovement linkages

This movement structure articulates and gains strength from various significant extramovement linkages. We can identify two such linkages to groups, organizations, and persons in the established order, and linkages to other movements. Here, again, those links ramify in an essentially unbounded, expanding web. For example, participants in the black power movement will have various white or black friends, associates, and other contacts who are not involved in the movement. These relationships may have been established through or quite independently of black power activities. A participant in any one movement cell may prevail upon his extramovement friends and associates to aid him in ways which directly or indirectly help the movement locally or nationally. Through their relationship with any one participant, or cell, nonparticipants may be influenced to support the movement by word or deed. In turn, many such nonparticipants will use their own networks of friends, relatives, or associates either directly or indirectly to help them provide such support. As an example of these extramovement linkages, we can note that personal associations of varying intensity among several dynamic black militant spokesmen and various white churchmen, community leaders, students, and university faculty members in one urban center

provided the primary and initial channels through which these black leaders were able to obtain financial and political support to establish a unique and controversial community center in one city where we conducted research.

As is well known, Students for a Democratic Society (SDS) often seeks to join in common cause with militant black power groups. In part they do this because black power activities so often zero in on the gap between the noble ideals expressed in the "American Dream" and the harsher manifestations of real life in the United States. Thus, black power causes provided SDS with ideological motive and justification for implementation of confrontation tactics. In a similar fashion the radical segments of the Ecology movement overlap with various SDS groups and counterculture groups providing the latter with a useful ideological club—racism, pollution, and the Vietnam War. All are considered caused by the same evils inherent in the established order. Yet white radicals also warn that the established order wishes to use the seemingly safe ecology issue to deflect interest from antiwar and antiracism activities. Some activists, seeking to remake established church structure and purpose, are also becoming involved in the ecology movement. In a very few cases Pentecostals are also involved in ecology, black power, and antiwar concerns.

As yet we do not note significant overlap between black power and ecology. Our survey of *Muhammad Speaks*, the Black Muslim newspaper, indicates that Black Muslims suspect the concept of zero population growth as a device of genocide. Black militants can also argue that ecology represents a white establishment cop-out from issues of racism and war. But there is some basis of mutual interaction, represented in the statement that blacks suffer more from urban pollution than anyone else.

Summary

Social movements are characteristically *segmentary*; that is, composed of many groups of varying sizes and scope. And they are *polycephalous*; that is, their varied groups have many competing leaders. Popular opinion has it that such organization is at best inefficient—at worst it is no organization at all, but an amorphous collectivity. But the diverse cells which and the many leaders who compose a movement in fact weave together to form a network or *reticulate* structure. In short, movements are well described as segmentary, polycephalous, and reticulate.

Segmentation and proliferation of groups within a movement occur because of a belief in personal access to power, because of preexisting social cleavages, because of personal competition, and because of ideological differences.

Leadership is ephemeral and weakly developed above a local group level just as organized activity above this level is ephemeral. As in polycephalous, segmentary societies, leaders "build a name" and establish a following on the basis of personal qualities and skills and personally established social links and bonds. In spite of these centrifugal characteristics, these varying groups manifest sufficient cohesion and ideological unity to be perceived as a large-scale movement. Such cohesion is obtained through a range of integrating, cross-cutting links, bonds, and operations, including ties between members and group leaders, by the activities of traveling evangelists or spokesmen, large-scale demonstrations and "ingatherings," sharing of basic ideological themes, and collective perception of, and action against, a common opposition.

Such organization is adaptive in implementing social change and helping the movement survive. It makes the movement difficult to suppress; it affords maximum penetration of and recruitment from different socio-economic and subcultural groups; it maximizes adaptive variation through diversity; it contributes to system reliability through redundancy, duplication, and overlap; and, finally, it encourages social innovation and problem-solving. Such organization appears to generate countermovement intelligence activity of a segmentary, polycephalous nature.

30.

Guy E. Swanson

AN ORGANIZATIONAL ANALYSIS OF COLLECTIVITIES

Collectivities as corporate actors

The root idea is that every collectivity is in some measure a corporate actor. A collectivity has a life and character of its own apart from the lives and characters of its members. And then we will contrast a collectivity with a social aggregate, saying that a collectivity, but not an aggregate, is a corporate entity, and that its corporate existence is contained (1) in a legitimated procedure through which participants can undertake collective actions and (2) in a legitimated sphere of action to which this procedure may be applied—a sphere of jurisdiction. When the use of this legitimated procedure is relatively self-conscious, we are likely to talk not merely of collective action, but of the making and implementing of collective decisions.

Within a collectivity there may well be more than one sphere of jurisdiction and more than one set of procedures by which collective action is formulated and carried out. The most fundamental of these is the collectivity's constitutional system. It is distinguished from the others by three criteria: (1) It alone applies to actions of the collectivity as a whole and to actions of members when they relate to one another as members of the whole. (2) It specifies original and independent powers of control that can legitimately be exercised over actions of the collectivity. And (3) within the collectivity, there is no higher authority

From Guy E. Swanson, "An Organizational Analysis of Collectivities," *American Sociological Review* 36, August 1971, pp. 607-24, with permission of the publisher and author.

to which appeal can be made. As a corporate actor, every collectivity *consists in* a constitutional system. My typology is a classification of constitutional systems.

The word "constitutional" would lead us astray were it taken to mean a differentiated apparatus of government. That is not my intention. There is no such apparatus in a friendship, but a friendship, like any other collectivity, consists in procedures and rules for taking collective action and in a special area over which these procedures may legitimately be applied. So also in the very simplest of societies. Ethnographers speak of these societies as lacking government. Collective action does occur, but only by informal means. Nonetheless these societies have a constitutional order. Action is legitimately taken only in accordance with legitimated procedures, and the populations and spheres of action to which these procedures legitimately apply will mark the operational boundaries of these societies. On the other hand, in more complex groups, it is often a convenience to use governmental structure as the operational definition of the constitutional order.

A classification of constitutional systems

The principles for classifying constitutions have remained much the same since Aristotle (1943, Books 4, 5, 6). Certain main considerations are embodied in the marginal entries of Chart 1, beginning with a distinction between the authority of agents and the authority of constituent bodies. This distinction, like all of the others in the margins of Chart 1, is rooted in the very conception of a collectivity.[1] [Chart 1 not reprinted here.]

The participants in a collectivity have a dual status. All of them try to use the collective relationship for their private— their special—interests. But, at the same time, they find that to use the collectivity they must maintain it and hence must serve as its agents: they must be sensitive to its requirements and must support its interests. In the first capacity, these participants are constituent bodies. In the second, they are agents. Constitutional systems vary in the formal recognition they provide for this distinction. The variations that I have had to take into account in my own research are contained in the remaining marginal entries of Chart 1.

As indicated in the Key to this Chart, the entries indexed by Roman numerals refer to five steps in a process that (1) begins with the setting of a collectivity's sphere of jurisdiction, (2) proceeds to the making of specific choices on matters that fall within that sphere, and (3) concludes with the supervision of acts that implement any choice that is made.

This series of steps covers familiar ground. Social scientists have repeatedly found it useful to itemize the stages in action that lie between the general orientations of an actor and the point at which he comes to implement his choices (Parsons and Smelser, 1956; Swanson, 1970). Constitutional systems vary in the number of these stages for which they have relevance and in the authority they afford to constituent bodies or to agents from one stage to another. In Chart 1, these differences in authority are indicated by the capital letters within each row and each column. The letter "A" stands for the absence in a constitutional system of a provision for authority over a particular stage; the letter "B" for authority granted to

anyone who is a member of the collectivity; and the letter "C" for authority granted to those who hold a specified office.[2]

The meaning of these distinctions becomes clear when we examine the constitutional systems entered in the cells of Chart 1. (Moving from the top of the figure down and from left to right, we note that the systems increase in the complexity of their structure.[3])

(1) Individuated heteronomy

The simplest constitutional system in this series is the one I have called heteronomous and individuated. This is the entry that first appears in the row and column labeled I.B.

In samples drawn for my own research, I have found that a substantial proportion of primitive societies and of families known to university undergraduates are organized as individuated heteronomies. (The exact percentages are recorded in Table 1.) [Table 1 not reprinted here.] Here is a description I wrote of individuated heteronomy as found in primitive societies (Swanson, 1969):

. . . There is a "rule of law" in the sense that many norms exist which govern people's rights and obligations once their interaction begins. There is lacking a continuing organizational apparatus for making decisions or a political apparatus having a specified membership. There exists, instead, the appreciation by participants that they are more closely linked by kinship or territorial proximity to some of their fellows than to others. When in need of collaborators, they call first upon these "neighbors" for help. There may be no normative rule specifying that such requests should be honored. There are, however, strong pressures upon "neighbors" to assist if they are later to mobilize assistance for themselves and there are, once assistance is contemplated, norms governing the establishment and operation of these *ad hoc* relationships. The ethnographer is likely to report such things as the following:

There are no means of making binding decisions or of enforcing decisions that are made. The people are highly individualistic, perhaps irascibly so.

And here is a description I wrote to guide the coding of families as cases of individuated heteronomy (for the sake of clarity, I include some prefatory instructions that applied to the coding of other types of family as well):

Every family is a group and almost every group has a way of going about its business—a way of carrying out its activities—a kind of "standard operating procedure." This procedure may not ever be verbalized among the members of a family, but every family has one. There may be occasions, even frequent or important occasions, on which the group deviates from its standard procedure, but the group tends to return to it again and again as "home-base."
In some families, both parents are viewed as having joint responsibility for deciding what the group will or will not do. There are differences, however, in the extent to which parents must consult with each other before they announce their position on an issue and before it is carried out.
[Individuated heteronomy] In this family, it is harder to see the existence of standard procedures for the conduct of business. Often things are done, or not done, pretty much as the moment dictates. The parents may or may not consult with each other before coming to a decision or before setting out on some course of action. If either dislikes what the other is doing, his main recourse is to block his partner or to withhold resources (e.g., money, time, encouragement) that are necessary for the support of his partner's activities. Similarly, he will often find that, rather than consultation or discussion, the principal means to get his partner to take some action is to make the resources available to the partner, earmarking them specifically for the purpose he intends.

Notice that these descriptions are phrased in terms of the constitutional form actually in practice in these collectivities. It is my rule, in coding, to classify by actual social relations. These are usually congruent with people's norms on consti-

tutional matters, but there can be discrepancies. For example, it has been shown that families having a schizophrenic member should often be coded one way according to their constitutional practice and another according to the norms that their members profess (Lidz et al., 1965).
How is the pattern of individuated heteronomy defined in Chart 1? It is indeed a limited constitutional system. The members of the collectivity are equally empowered to serve as its agents, but the only point at which they are authorized so to act is in declaring that some social relationship is, or is not, a matter of public interest and that collective norms should be taken into account by persons engaging in such relations (or that no such norms are relevant). Looking across row IB, we see that the powers of constituent bodies are organized and limited in the same way. All members are equally recognized as constituent bodies and, as such, are authorized to express and take into account their private interests in relating to their fellows, this being normatively limited only by their simultaneous role as agents of the collectivity. But no one is empowered to make a choice on behalf of the collectivity itself or to support or implement such a choice.

(2) Commensal heteronomy

Just below individuated heteronomy in Chart 1 is a type of constitutional system called commensal heteronomy. Here, as in all constitutional systems, there is a legitimated sphere of jurisdiction and a set of legitimated procedures for collective action. The additional feature is a structural arrangement for generating and identifying a collective sentiment.
In some societies, all small in population and localized in residence, the whole people, or the men, or all adults, will gather

informally, once a day, to gossip, socialize, and debate. There is a customary place for such gatherings: beside the sea, around the well or community fireplace, in the plaza or ceremonial lodge. There is no agenda, no machinery for making decisions, and no apparatus for the people's acting jointly to carry out a collective task or to authorize some participants to represent or enforce the common view. There is an informal "leader" whose position depends upon the respect his abilities warrant. He periodically summarizes the drift of the discussion and continues to do so over whatever period of hours, days, or weeks it continues; this until there is no substantial dissent form his report. As the ethnographers are likely to say, it seems that these societies are governed, not by authorities or conscious decisions but by opinion and tradition.

Here is the description of commensal heteronomy that I employ in my current study of family structure:

In this family, "decision-making" is too strong a word for the parents' standard way of doing business. Rather, they talk over problems, and talk around them, until a kind of common view emerges. This view is then the basis for action.

What is entailed in saying that routinized occasions for discussion and, in primitive societies and many other groups, the role of leader-summarizer represent structural differentiations beyond the constitutional arrangements found in individuated heteronomy? First, there is the establishment of a procedure not found under individuated heteronomy, the development of rules for the proper conduct of this new activity, and the setting aside of resources and facilities (e.g., special times and places) to sustain it. Second, there is the fact that this new procedure consists in a mechanism by which the group can

authoritatively conduct and monitor an activity carried out informally under individuated heteronomy, people have some sense of social sentiment and know that certain procedures and behaviors have general social approval whereas others do not. Commensal heteronomy involves collective authorization for a mechanism by means of which sentiment and approval can be authoritatively determined. When this mechanism is employed, the "findings" obtained supersede determinations obtained through other procedures. Third, the new procedure is linked to other collective activities. It is an extension of procedures available to the group for the taking of collective action and, when it is employed, it can produce a reaffirmation or change of participants' rights and duties as members of this group. Fourth, it is probable that the appearance of a formal procedure for determining the common sentiment entails a complementary tendency to formalize the spheres of life in the group that are to be considered private rather than common.

Chart 1 gives us the bare bones required for a definition of commensal heteronomy. It is a constitutional system in which authority is lodged in the generality of a collectivity's membership and that authority extends to their setting the boundaries of the collectivity's jurisdiction and extends to their formal determination of the collectivity's choice or preference from among alternatives. It does not extend further.

(3) Commensalism

In some groups one additional development has occurred. They have attained a means for enforcement of at least some authoritatively established collective sentiments, thus transforming some sentiments into decisions. As shown in Chart 1, commensalism is like commensal heteronomy in that all or a large proportion of the members of the group participate as equals in the authoritative determination of public sentiments. Leadership is also of the sort found in collective heteronomy. The new feature is the differentiation of a decision from other collective sentiment. This is embodied in a procedure for judging whether enforcement will be encouraged and for the designating of all or some members of the group to act as its agents. In the typical case, this procedure involves the attainment of consensus or of a close approximation to it. Here is how I describe commensalism in the code for my study of families:

In this family, both parents have to talk about the problem and agree upon a solution before they announce their decision to the family and/or before they begin to carry it out.

Note that enforcement of collective sentiment will in fact occur under commensal heteronomy as well. People will act toward their fellows in terms of that sentiment. The difference is that, in commensalism, enforcement is explicitly authorized by the group. A person who then enforces collective sentiment is formally an agent of the group as a whole and not merely a private person.

If we examine a sample of societies having a commensalist system, we will find that these societies differ in the extent to which an administrative apparatus has been developed to implement the choices that are arrived at, and sanctioned, through constitutional arrangements. There may be no such apparatus or, as in the case of ancient Athens or medieval Venice, both having commensal constitutions, there may be an elaborate and important administrative system. Similar variations in

administrative development will be found within each type of constitutional system lying below commensalism, or to its right, in Chart 1. By definition, the authority exercised by administrative structures derives from the constitutional system, the latter being the original and independent authority.

Among the constitutional systems in Chart 1, commensal systems and communal heteronomies have in common a) the possibility of undertaking collective action and b) the need to achieve consensus among participants, or near consensus, before anything can be done. The other constitutional systems in Chart 1 require less in the way of consensus. They avoid it by putting collective action in the hands of one man or a small group of men or by employing a principle of majority rule. These considerations led me to a prediction and tabulation mentioned earlier in this paper. I predicted that families organized as commensal systems would be able to function well only if their members had exceptionally close and supportive relationships and that, in consequence, there would be greater pressures in these families than in others for members to anticipate and serve one another's needs. I assumed that, by contrast, individuated heteronomies would generate the least pressure for supportive behavior, because they lack a basis for defining and pursuing any purpose and because their members are generally oriented to personal rather than to common ends. As already indicated, this is the result obtained in my current study of families.

(4) Heterarchy

The distinctive point about heterarchy is that the collectivity consists of units that have considerable autonomy in their internal affairs, the collectivity's choices being made and implemented by those units jointly or by meetings of their representatives. This is what we ordinarily mean by federalist democracy.

It may seem wrong, in Chart 1, to conceive of the authority of these units over the collectivity as residing in an office that they hold, but that seems to be their situation. Consider, for example, the Winnebago Indians who had a federal government in tribal affairs, the several clans being the members of the tribal collectivity. Clans were represented on the tribal council not because of their autonomy but because each was regarded as being legitimately a member of the tribal collectivity as a whole, and the tribe was defined as the union of these clans formed for the conduct of their joint enterprises. The authority of each clan in tribal affairs was derived from its being accepted as a member of the tribe by all of the other clans acting jointly. This state of affairs corresponds closely to the customary meaning of an office (Gould and Kolb, 1964, 474-475):

. . . a status and role which is well defined, authoritatively sanctioned, and recognized as being separable from the persons occupying and performing it.
. . . a status created and sanctioned by authority. Thus a person occupying such a status must act only within the limits authoritatively set in rules, laws, or administrative regulations.

In sum, the role of the constituent bodies in a federal system is not merely an expression of the powers they autonomously control but of authorization by the total collectivity. In a federal system, this office of constituent bodies is vested not in the participants generally but in those subsidiary units whose members are recognized as constituting distinctive corporate entities—the entities, but not their component members directly, being authorized to participate in making decisions for the collectivity as a whole and authorized to exercise considerable independence in the conduct of their internal affairs.

It is possible for a small group as well as a large one to be organized on heterarchic lines. Many families, for example, have this form of constitution. These families are distinguished from those operating under commensalism by their assumption that each member is a special unit having great autonomy and special interests, and by their practice of using some criterion other than complete agreement among the members in determining a collective choice, for example, the criterion of a majority vote. Here is the operational definition of heterarchy that I have been using in my own research on families:

In this family, both parents often consult with each other about what the family will do. If they consult with each other, they will reach agreement on a solution before they announce their decision to the family. However, each parent alone also has the right to decide upon a course of action, announce his decision to the family, and even begin carrying it out without first consulting his partner. Each parent always has the right of review over any action which has been initiated by the other parent without prior consultation. This means that, if he wishes, he may question the action of his partner and may hold up the implementation of this action until they have consulted together and reached an agreement about the final course of action.

Heterarchy, like commensalism, may be accompanied by a highly developed administrative structure that is subordinated to its constitutional apparatus, or it may have no such structure at all. In any case, it involves a complex set of differentiations: the public interest is separated from the private and the two are articulated with one another; implementation is separated from policy making and both are related to the structure of common and of special interests; the existence of an apparatus for the making of collective decisions implies the differentiation of social interdependence, common sentiment, and agency.

(5) Simple centralism. Types a and b

Beginning here, we deal with constitutional systems having a governor. A governor is an individual, or small group, having important discretionary powers as an executive on behalf of the collectivity as a whole. A king, a president, or a primitive chief is commonly a figure of this sort. So is a council of state if it serves as the collectivity's chief executive. A governor has powers of general supervision over the implementation of the collectivity's choices.

Governorship is clearly a special office and an office as an agent of the collectivity. Collective resources are set aside for the support of this role, and some procedure is specified for legitimate access to it. Within the sphere defined for the role, legitimate decisions by the office-holder supersede all others.

Constitutional systems having a governor differ in the extent to which the governor has to share his powers with constituent bodies. The distinctive feature of simple centralism is that the governor has to share with constituent bodies the determination as to which matters fall within the collectivity's jurisdiction. This power of constituent bodies may reside generally within the membership of the collectivity. On the other hand, the constituent bodies may be organized jointly into a special, corporate office—a parliament, for example—for the purpose of exercising this particular authority. The presence or

absence of such a special office among constituent bodies is the basis for distinguishing the two types of simple centralism, Types a and b, in Chart 1.

This type of power of constituent bodies was explicitly recognized in medieval times as power in *jurisdictio*, and medieval thinkers understood that it consisted in the power to determine which questions and objects were properly the subject of collective authority and which were not. Because taxes, financial aid, military service, and other forms of service were seen as provisional grants of private resources for public purposes, the right to assent to such grants, or to withhold assent, was commonly defined as a right of constituent bodies in matters of jurisdiction. So were the admission of new members to the roster of constituent bodies, the interpretation of the customary law, the making of decisions concerning the legitimacy of a governor's accession, and questions of war and peace.

As indicated in Table 1, families as well as societies are frequently organized in the pattern of simple centralism.[4] Here is the description I used to code families:

In this family, one parent is seen by all as being the "head" of the family. Although that parent does make the final decision, each parent has a special sphere of responsibility and competence. Thus, if one parent is finally the "governor" of the family, the other has a legitimate role as his counselor. This counselor's advice will nearly always be sought and taken into consideration before a final outcome is decided by the governor. The counselor expects to be consulted on important family matters and generally is.

(6) Unitary centralism

In unitary centralism, the governor is not officially limited by having to share authority with constituent bodies. He may consult other people, but that is not required in principle. Once again, I draw upon my work on families for an illustrative operational definition:

In this family, one parent is, without question, the head of the family. This governor has the final word in deciding what action the group shall take and how it shall be taken. There is no established or regular counseling procedure in this family. The other parent sees himself as playing a subordinate role to the governor in family affairs and does not expect to be called upon for advice, although this advice may be sought by the governor on occasion.

In the samples tabulated in Table 1, unitary centralism is relatively frequent among primitive societies and relatively infrequent in societies in early modern Europe or among the families with which American undergraduates are familiar. It was very common as the form of constitution for ancient empires.

Of all the constitutional systems given in Chart 1, simple centralism and unitary centralism provide the cases in which a governor has most power relative to the power of constituent bodies. That observation was the basis for my performing the tabulation given in Chart 3. It occurred to me that the boasting and personal display that Slater and Slater (1965) take to be indications of narcissism might sometimes be indications of ingratiation. As Jones (1964) makes clear, ingratiation often includes efforts to call favorable attention to oneself in relations with one's superiors. It seemed possible that constitutional systems having the sharpest distinctions between superiors and subordinates might likewise be associated with high levels of boasting and display. That is what we find in Chart 3.[5]

(7) Limited centralism. Types a and b

In the two remaining forms of centralism—limited centralism and balanced centralism—constituent bodies have a constitutional role in sharing with a governor the supervision of action based upon the collectivity's choices. In limited centralism, constituent bodies do not share the powers of general supervision, but they do share in supervision over policies as these are applied to specified parts of the population. This can be illustrated in early modern Europe. In several countries a governor, or a governor and a parliament, might make the laws, but the local implementation of at least some important sectors of legislation would rest largely with local groups having a considerable autonomy in their internal operations. The population might be organized into regions, for example, the freemen or nobles of each region being empowered to implement the laws on crime or commerce. The governor would have supervision over their work but would be forced by constitutional provisions to employ these local bodies as his officers and to honor their exercise of considerable discretion within the guidelines established in law. In some European societies, organized as city-states under a governor, the guilds had this kind of authority over the application of the law to their own members.

A distinction is drawn in Chart 1 between limited centralist systems in which constituent bodies share with the governor the determination of the collectivity's sphere of jurisdiction (Limited centralism, Type b) and those in which they do not (Limited centralism, Type a). In the 16th and 17th centuries, England would have been an instance of Type b and Prussia of Type a.

Limited centralism entails an internal heterogeneity of interests and of power over the application, but not the determination, of policies. This pattern is rare in modern American families. Even in samples of societies, it is not until we approach modern times that this form of constitution appears with appreciable frequency.

(8) Balanced centralism

In balanced systems, constituent bodies have a formal share with a governor in all five stages of a collectivity's operations. These systems are especially distinguished from other types of centralism by the fact that constituent bodies share with a governor in the general supervision of action on the collectivity's choices. Thus constituent bodies may name, or share in the naming, of some or all major officials under the governor, these officials then being responsible in some measure to these autonomous bodies as well as to the governor. Or constituent bodies may jointly develop and fund programs, the implementation of which is then assigned by them to the governor or to certain of his officials. Or constituent bodies may establish an officialdom of their own that parallels the one that is directly under the governor, the two sets of officials being required to concur in the administration of the state.

The constitutional system of the United States has this combination of features. The President is a governor, but the several states have important areas of independent and original jurisdiction and their representatives in the Congress not only pass laws (with the President's signature or with his unstated assent), but their agreement must be sought in his appointments of Federal judges, high officers of the armed forces, diplomatic representatives, and officers of his cabinet and officers of the major Federal agencies. Moreover, these representatives of the states must concur before a declaration of war can be issued or a treaty concluded.

They can devise and promote programs over a wide range of concerns; they can give or withdraw financial support for programs of their own or those of the President; and they have the power to impeach a President.

This form of constitution is not common. It occurs in a few primitive societies. It is also found in some societies in early modern Europe, and in a small percentage of families known to American undergraduates.[6]

Organizational analysis and functional analysis

I have suggested to this point that the analysis of collectivities contained in Chart 1 is highly general and generic, being rooted in defining characteristics of all collectivities. I have also shown that this analysis concerns constitutional rather than administrative features of collectivities and have suggested that it is a powerful tool for the explanation of some kinds of dependent variance. An additional point deserves attention. This analysis of collectivities is organizational rather than interactional or functional. I want to clarify what that means in order to place this form of analysis in relation to others and to specify its potential role in systems of explanation.

All three types of sociological analysis have as their point of reference the life and character of a collectivity. All provide some treatment of structures and processes, of stability and dynamics, of causes and effects, of forms and functions, and of form and substance. These similarities have obscured an essential point at which they differ. An interactional analysis examines collectivities from the point of view of their constituent bodies, a functional analysis from the point of view of their agents, and an organizational analysis from the view of constituent bodies, and of agents, in their status as structuring units.[7]

In interactional analyses, a collectivity is seen as a state of interdependence among constituent bodies. The independence of those bodies from one another and from the collectivity is stressed. The collectivity is conceived as a network of social relations that is created by constituent bodies to enable them to exchange utilities with one another. Each constituent body seeks to serve its own requirements through this network, and the network's existence is pictured as depending upon the continuing need of constituent bodies for the benefits they get from participation in it. Examples of such interactional analyses are found in the work of Homans (1961) and of many conflict and coalition theorists (Coser, 1956; Caplow, 1969).

As has often been noted, functional analyses emphasize the fact that constituent bodies have a common interest in maintaining their relations with one another. In functional analyses, the collectivity is conceived as expressive of that common interest—as a corporate enterprise—and participants in the collectivity are treated in their status as agents of the collective relationship: as its supporters and maintainers. The most general and salient features of their activities are therefore given in the very definition of agency and collectivity. These prove to be the same features that are itemized in Parsons' well-known list of "system functions" (Parsons, 1966).

Agency means that ". . . one person (agent) is dealing with another (third party) on behalf of still another (principal)" (Llewellyn, 1930:483). In the present case, agents of the collectivity (which is their "principal") take into account whatever directives or guidelines their principal provides (Parsons' "latency" function),

and they use these guidelines as the basis for their actions toward third parties and other objects (Parsons' "adaptive" function).

The agents of concern here are different from others by virtue of their serving a collectivity, hence by their being empowered to employ certain of its resources and facilities for their work. Those resources and facilities include activities of members of the collectivity. To employ such activities, an agent must sanction their activities, positively or negatively, as may be required, and must coordinate and evaluate their work. Thus, to implement collective guidelines, agents of a collectivity are authorized to direct the activities of their fellows in such a way that the corporate relationship is strengthened (Parsons' function of "goal gratification") and, to that end, agents are authorized to coordinate and evaluate members' relations with one another (Parsons' "integrative" function).

The chief point about an organizational analysis is that a collectivity is examined from the point of view of the units whose relations define its existence, units which, in that sense, bear a formative or structuring relationship to it. The focus is on the joint control over the collectivity by constituent bodies and agents, all exercising rights and fulfilling obligations, their joint activities constituting the choices and actions of the collectivity as a corporate body.

From the perspective of the structuring units, a collectivity is a corporate instrumentality through which these units are able jointly to relate to objects. Seen in this way, a collectivity combines features that are emphasized in interactional analyses with features stressed in functional analyses. As in interactional analyses, the collective relationship is a kind of tool. On the other hand, it is designed to enable its participants to undertake some joint endeavors and not merely to satisfy their own needs. As in functional analyses, the participants' interest are kept in view, but their common undertaking is more than the maintenance of their relationship. Rather it is an effort jointly—corporately —to act upon an external situation. This last point is the one highlighted in Parsons' (1960:17) conception of organization:

As a formal analytical point of reference, *primacy of orientation to the attainment of a specific goal* is used as the defining characteristic of an organization. . . .

The attainment of a goal is defined as a *relation* between a system . . . and the relevant parts of the external situation in which it acts or operates. This relation can be conceived as the maximization, relative to the relevant conditions such as costs and obstacles, of some category of *output* of the system to objects or systems in the external situation. . . .

The "contract" that underlies the corporate relationship may be tacit or explicit. It specifies the objects with reference to which the collectivity is an appropriate instrumentality, the extent to which relations to those objects can be pursued by means of that instrumentality, the control over the use and work of that instrumentality by the structuring units, and the responsibilities to the collectivity that these units assume. Certain main differentiations are of special interest when a collectivity is conceived to be a corporate instrumentality. These will be differentiations having to do with the specification of the aspects of instrumental activity for which this corporate relationship was undertaken (Parsons and Smelser, 1956:139; Smelser, 1963: Chap. 2; Swanson, 1970).

The characteristics of a collectivity as a corporate instrumentality are recorded in the marginal entries of Chart 1, where the structuring units are termed constituent bodies and agents; the objects for collective action are referred to as the collectivity's jurisdiction. The extent to which instrumental relations to objects can be pursued by means of the collectivity is specified in the sequence of headings indexed by Roman numerals (moving from top to bottom and from left to right), and the control over the use and work of the collectivity by constituent bodies and by agents is specified in the entries in the cells.

Interactional, functional, and organizational analyses complement each other, and not merely in the sense that they are analytically distinct. They direct our attention to empirical conditions that vary with considerable independence of one another. Primitive societies, for example, have a much lower level of functional differentiation than did most societies in early modern Europe, but one finds in samples from each universe of societies almost the full array of constitutional systems contained in Chart 1. Societies are more likely than families to exhibit functional differentiation, but families as well as societies vary widely in the form of their constitutional system. Buck and Jacobson (1968) and Abrahamson (1969) have recently shown that there are only low to modest correlations between indices of a society's interactional, functional and organizational elaboration, their samples of societies being taken from the universe of modern nations and from that of preindustrial societies.

The place of organizational analysis

Whether an organizational analysis is what we want depends upon the observations we are trying to explain. In general, an organizational analysis is in order if we want to understand a collectivity to be operating as a corporate whole: making choices and implementing those choices and bringing all of its action and its component subdivisions into conformity with its constitutional system (Swanson, 1959). An organizational analysis is also required if we want to relate the operations of a collectivity as a corporate whole to its most immediate environments: to culture, to the personalities of the human individuals who participate in it, and to the system of social ecology in which all are involved.[8] When these relationships are the kind that we want to examine, we need some typology of the organization of collectivities that enables us to treat collectivities as a whole and to study correlates of variations in their overall organization. That is the kind of problem that led me to develop this typology of constitutional systems.

Like other social psychologists of a sociological persuasion, I have been forced to relate personalities, collectivities, and culture, attributing to each a large measure of independence while considering all as interdependent. I will close with some illustrations from my own research on problems of this sort. Each problem requires us to understand a relationship between culture and personality as that relationship is generated, or mediated, by the overall organization of a collectivity.

Consider first the extent to which the members of a society will find present and available in the very organization and operations of that society the ultimate values around which its life is organized. Weber (1963) and Troeltsch (1931) are thinking of differences along this dimension when they observe that Protestantism, especially Zwinglian and Calvinist Protestantism, denies that God's own essence as a person—his personal characteristics—can be found in any created or historical things, these "things" to include the

choices, declarations, rituals, and structure of the visible church and the acts or elements of the sacraments. From that perspective, the ultimately valuable is experienced as less immediately available to men than it is within a Catholic conception.

In a study (Swanson, 1967) occasioned by an interest in this differential availability of values, I tried to specify the conditions under which some form of Protestantism would come to be accepted in a society as contrasted with the conditions under which Catholicism would be retained. My procedure depended upon my conceiving of societies as constitutional systems.

I argued as follows. The personal essence of the divine consists of purposes, judgment, choice, and the like that are extraneous to individuals, yet in constant relationship with them. In the perspective of natural science, and as Durkheim (1947b) observed, experiences of such transcendent personal characteristics are to be found in men's experiences of a society, and of a society—not as a social aggregate, but as a corporate entity—that takes action and that may even make and implement decisions. I proposed that corporate purposes and choices would be more likely to be experienced as present and compelling in the acts of those societies in which the constitutional system—the collective apparatus for making authoritative choices—provided a legitimate role for corporate interests and traditions of component groups and individuals in the society. In societies having such a constitutional structure, I predicted the retention of Catholicism. In societies in which the constitutional apparatus made a legitimate place for special as well as common interests in the formulation of authoritative action, I predicted the acceptance of Protestant views. (These are the distinctions indexed by the letters "e," "f," and "g" in Table 1 and mentioned toward the beginning of this paper.) The rationale for these predictions is already published and need not concern us here.

When these ideas were operationalized through a typology of societies, and then tested against the historical accounts for 41 European societies in the period 1480 through 1685, there emerged relationships of an impressive size. As of 1480, all of these societies seemed to have polities of the sort I associated with a Catholic view. Between that time and their final acceptance or rejection of the Reformation, several of these societies adopted a form of polity that I had anticipated would be congenial to a Protestant world view. Those that did accepted the Reformation.

These promising results suggested that yet another problem might be ripe for solution (Swanson, 1968, 1969). Theory and evidence have been pointing for some time to the possibility that rules of descent—matriliny, patriliny, bilaterality, and the others—symbolize the relations between a society as a corporate parent on the one hand, and, on the other, the members of that society in their status as its children. My first thoughts on this subject were inspired by the important role of female figures in Catholic doctrine—the Virgin, the Mother of God, the Church which is our Mother and the Bride of Christ as well as His Mystical Body. I contrasted Catholic doctrine in these matters with the absence of female figures in Protestant doctrine and the presence there of powerful male and paternal figures. I wondered whether one might discover, among societies at lower levels of functional differentiation, an association between matriliny and the presence of the constitutional systems that I had found associated with Catholicism in 16th century Europe, and also an associa-

tion between patriliny and the kind of constitutional systems associated with the acceptance of Protestantism at the time of the Reformation. And could my typology of constitutional systems be elaborated to specify the conditions under which, in simpler societies, one would find a bilateral rule of descent?

I elaborated these ideas and made them operational for a population of primitive and ancient societies. (The index letters "h," "i," and "j" in Table 1 guide us to most of the groupings employed.) Coders who were unacquainted with my theory were trained to read ethnographic accounts and to classify societies according to their constitutional systems. Codes for descent were available from Murdock's Ethnographic Atlas (Murdock, 1967). As stated near the beginning of this paper, the results were strongly in the predicted direction.

My work on the Reformation was also the source of a renewed interest in the study by Child et al. (1958) on need achievement in folk tales. McClelland (1961) argues that need achievement is a principal component, if not the major component, of the Protestant ethic. It occurred to me that collectivities having the types of constitutional systems associated with Protestantism might also exhibit high scores of need achievement, and, having already classified the constitutional systems of many societies in the sample used by Child et al., I made the tabulation reported in Table 1, discovering the significant association contained in that table.[9]

"Bringing men back in"

We need in sociological analyses to explicate the links between collectivities and the actors who create and use and serve them. I propose that organizational analysis in the sense developed here can help to effect that restoration without our abandoning what is distinctive about social facts and without discarding the important advances made under one or another of the "functionalisms" developed in this century.[10] That seems to me one immediate possibility in the construction of general theory in sociology.[11]

Notes

1. The typology is also unrelated, or only loosely related, to many standard indices of complexity in collectivities and to other independent variables commonly used by sociologists. Thus, in my present study of families, I find that a family's classification in Chart 1 is unrelated, or only slightly related, to its size, to the occupation, education, or income of the father, to the family's religious preference, the size of the community in which it resides, the degree to which the breadwinner's job is bureaucratized, the marital status of the parents, or the parents' race or their ethnic background.

2. Certain concepts that I have used in earlier analyses can be related systematically to the marginal entries in Chart 1. My discussion of jurisdiction seems to refer to the activities indicated by Roman numeral I, whereas my use of the notion of gubernaculum refers most explicitly to activities indicated by Roman numerals II through V. A distinction between participating units as elements and as parts is represented in the capital letters in column I: units have more the status of elements as we move from A to B to C, and they have more the status of parts as we move in the opposite direction. A distinction between a collectivity's organization as an association and its organization as a social system is indicated by the capital letters associated with the remaining columns: the collectivity having more the status of an association as we move from A to B to C, and more the status of a social system as we move in the opposite direction. (For earlier uses of these concepts and the emergence of the formulations in Chart I, see Swanson 1967, 1968, 1969, and 1971a.)

3. The sequence of activities indicated by Roman numerals I through V seems to meet strict criteria for an evolutionary series: a) each step later in the sequence contains and presupposes all of those that precede it and contains one new attribute in addition; b) each step entails a differentiation in structure of activities present but undifferentiated in the preceding step; c) each step provides a collectivity with an increased capacity to act as a collectivity. It seems, moreover, that collectivities actually develop the capacity for these five activities in the order specified by the Roman numerals, this observation being based

on studies of the growth of informal groups (Swanson, 1970) and studies of the development of whole societies (Swanson, 1971b; Parsons, 1966). On the other hand, there is no significant evidence that the three criteria for an evolutionary sequence are met by the emergence in a society of the arrangements designated by the capital letters in the margins of Chart 1, and there is a great deal of evidence for the importance in the appearance of those phenomena of struggles for power and of the formation of a series of coalitions, this series moving toward a system of coalitions that is sufficiently stable to govern. Whatever the findings of future research, it seems clear that the institutionalization of the constitutional arrangements designated by the letters B and C in the rows and columns of Chart 1 does represent an evolutionary change in the important if limited sense described by Sahlins and Service (1960) under the rubric of "general evolution."

4. In earlier analyses I included feudalism among these constitutional systems. It is not included in Chart I because it consists in a special form of union among societal collectivities, each collectivity retaining its separate identity and each being separately organized as Simple Centralism, Type b.

In a feudal structure, a member of one collectivity can equally and legitimately be a member of another that has an overlapping sphere of jurisdiction, these collectivities not being parts of some more embracive organization. Thus a vassal might be related to each of two lords and have the protection of both and also the right, with each, to share in legislative and judicial activities. The vassal would presumably have agreed to support both lords with arms, economic aid, and counsel. The only definite limit on his relationship with either might come at the point at which one lord was the opponent of the other.

Feudalism has another aspect of great importance. Vassals can, in principle and in fact, have vassals of their own who are not, in turn, related to their lord's lord. Thus a vassal, in order to fulfill his obligations to his lord, might have to mobilize his own vassals and get them to fulfill their obligations to him. In this situation, one and the same man would be vassal of his lord, lord of his own vassals, and would perform a managerial function of mobilizing men and resources in the service of this superior.

Historians associate feudalism with a breakdown of ancient imperial society: a kind of organizational regression from which new systems were finally born. An analysis of the feudal system indicates, however, that it was far more differentiated than most, perhaps all, of the constitutional systems that preceded it, the "regression" consisting only in the scope and distinctiveness of the spheres of jurisdiction to which this new constitutional relationship applied.

5. A different meaning of boasting and display is found in primitive societies that have an economy based upon raiding or upon the conquest and exploitation of new territory, their own lands being abandoned as new land is secured. In these societies,

economic advance as well as social position is dependent upon the exploits of warriors who attack as an aggregation of individuals rather than as an organized army, and much attention is given to individuals for their personal prowess, skill, and courage. There is often an explicit rating system for this purpose (*e.g.*, counting coup). All such societies noted in Chart 3 are high on the Slaters' index of narcissism. When these societies are added to the ones productive of ingratiation, chi-square is 13.08 (computed by the maximum likelihood method: $df = 2$; $p = < .01$; $C = .51$).

6. It should not be thought that, as we move downward or to the right in Chart 1, we encounter constitutional orders that are certain to generate or harness more physical energy than those above them or to the left (Sahlins and Service, 1960). The only point one can safely make is that "higher" levels in this figure have an existing capacity to take account of certain conditions, for example the powers of independent local groups. If other things are equal, this capacity gives them a greater range of situations to which they can make a rapid and coherent response. The fact is, however, that other critical things are often anything but equal. Provision for the special concerns of rather autonomous groups is often a sign of divisiveness in a population and of corresponding weakness of their corporate life and effort. Indeed, in the primitive and ancient worlds, it is the societies having a unitary centralist system that are generally the most powerful in population and resources. They are also the most likely to have a complex administrative and functional development. Unitary centralism affords the greatest possibility of mobilizing by formal means whatever resources there are and of applying them to a collective task. On the other hand, when societies become integrated under the principle of nationhood—a principle that still is poorly understood—then forms of constitution more complex than unitary centralism begin to proliferate and societies having these higher forms are substantially more likely to be in the van of administrative and functional advance and to prove most effective in the development and use of physical energy.

7. I find it more precise in conceptual and operational definitions to conceive of this process as one in which people or subsidiary collectivities are empowered to serve as agents and do whatever "acting" is done. The idea of a "social system" of functions as an actor seems to me a metaphor that hinders both explanation and empirical research. By abandoning this metaphor and adopting the formulation I suggest, we also give the "system functions" a more precise and, to me, a more understandable onto-

logical status than they sometimes have had. Parsons himself has made an important advance in clarifying and objectifying these functions, in his recent distinctions among them, according to the environment toward which action is directed (Parsons, 1966, Chapter 2).

8. Persons as well as collectivities can be analyzed in interactional, functional, and organizational terms. For an effort to analyze some of the systematic links between personal and collective organization in the rise of collectivities, see Swanson, 1970.

9. It is not certain, however, that this association is produced by the factors that lead to a relationship between the typology of constitutional systems and the spread of Protestantism. There is an association that approaches statistical significance between the complexity of political development of societies in this sample (political development being coded by Murdock [1967]) and scores on need achievement. Moreover, it is a peculiarity of this sample that it contains few societies that are politically complex and that also have the form of constitution that tends to be associated with Catholicism, namely simple centralism. As a result, an interpretation of the finding in Chart 2 should be held in abeyance until it can be checked in a sample of primitive societies containing a good representation of simple centralist systems.

10. The distinctions given in this paper help us to place the several versions of functionalism now extant (Demerath and Peterson, 1968). Thus the functionalism of Radcliffe-Brown (1952) or Merton (1963) consists simply in the assertion that, for actors, the expected consequences of action can constitute a force for the continuation of that action and of the structures through which it is performed. Such a premise is useful in some phases of many analyses, and Stinchcombe (1968:57-148) has formalized the logic that it entails. Malinowski's (1939) brand of functionalism treats the formation of special collectivities, or of objectives of collectivities, in response to the needs of their constituent participants, and thus is most germane in an interactional analysis. This is essentially the position of Homans (1961) as well. Parsons' (1966) and Durkheim's (1947a) functionalism is elaborated in the direction of the most general phases or aspects of an agent's several concurrent operations as agent. Nagel (1961) has tried to explicate the formal properties of this particular version.

11. Gouldner's (1959) consideration of the connections between Mertonian functionalism and processes of reciprocity has many similarities to the approach sketched in this paper.

31.

Harold W. Pfautz

NEAR-GROUP THEORY AND COLLECTIVE BEHAVIOR: A CRITICAL REFORMULATION

In commenting on the discontinuities between empirical research and systematic theorizing which seem to plague our discipline, Merton makes a plea for "codification" as a corrective procedure.[1] This process involves the conceptual assimilation of data from diverse empirical contexts in order to arrive at more inclusive theoretical propositions. It is the general thesis of this paper that the conceptual recasting of data from a single piece of research provides another useful attack on this problem.[2]

Our taking-off point is the fascinating study of adolescent delinquent gangs and gang warfare in New York City made by Yablonsky, who interprets his findings in terms of what he has called "near-group theory."[3] In our opinion, however, the findings can be more productively and cogently organized in the general theoretical tradition of "collective behavior" and in terms of the concept of "social movement" in particular. Such a recasting of Yablonsky's observations obviates the introduction of the "near-group" neologism, widens the theoretical relevance of the data at stake, and, in addition, points up collective factors in the etiology of such gangs and their violent behavior. In addition, we will also suggest how this restructuring of Yablonsky's

From Harold W. Pfautz, "Near-Group Theory and Collective Behavior: A Critical Reformulation," *Social Problems*, 9:2 (Fall 1961), pp. 167-74. Reprinted by permission of the Society for the Study of Social Problems and the author.

findings provides additional insight into the "conflict" pattern of delinquency described by Cloward and Ohlin.[4]

Delinquent gangs as near-groups

On the basis of four years of intensive observation using a variety of field-study techniques, Yablonsky concludes that the image presented by both the mass media and professional sociologists of these adolescent delinquent gangs as "true-groups" is fundamentally incorrect. Rather, they are "near-groups," and their much publicized *rumbles* are "not the meeting of two structured teen-aged armies meeting on a battlefield to act out a defined situation," but "a case of two near-groups in action."[5] Near-group theory is summarized as follows:

. . . mid-way on the group-mob continuum are collectivities which are neither groups nor mobs. These are structures prevalent enough in a social system to command attention in their own right as constructs for sociological analysis. Near-groups are characterized by some of the following factors: (1) diffuse role definition, (2) limited cohesion, (3) impermanence, (4) minimal consensus of norms, (5) shifting membership expectations. These factors characterize the near-group's 'normal' structure.

True groups may manifest near-group structure under stress, in transition, or when temporarily disorganized; however, at these times they are moving toward or away from their normative, permanent structure. The near-group manifests its homeostasis in accord with the factors indicated. It never fully becomes a group or a mob.[6]

Further, Yablonsky proposes:

. . . The measure of organization or disorganization of an inclusive social system may possibly be assessed by the prevalence of near-group collectivities in its midst. The delinquent gang may be only one type of near-group in American society.[7]

Given the amorphous structure, disturbed leadership, shifting membership and other characteristics of near-groups, the primary function of such phenomena is "unclear" according to Yablonsky. However, in the case of gangs as near-groups, their prime function is "to provide a channel to act out hostility and aggression to satisfy the continuing and momentary needs of its members."[8] For the less disturbed and the less involved members, gang membership is seen as "a convenient temporary escape from the dull and rigid requirements of a difficult and demanding society."[9] In the final analysis Yablonsky views these gangs primarily in psychological terms: their lack of structure as well as their violent behavior emanate from the emotionally disturbed character and "limited social ability" of their members.[10]

While Yablonsky has made an interesting, significant, and undoubtedly valid discovery concerning the structure of these gangs, we cannot agree that the concepts discussed in the sociological literature on crowds and mobs do "not seem to adequately describe and properly abstract the underlying characteristics of the delinquent gang."[11] Quite the opposite, by eschewing the literature on collective behavior Yablonsky unnecessarily complicates the theoretical situation by introducing such neologisms as "near-group" and the invidious "true group." He also reveals a basic misunderstanding of certain fundamental sociological postulates which blinds him to the operation of collective factors in the nature, causes, and functions of the adolescent violent gang.

Collective behavior and near-group theory

Collective behavior comprises the area of sociological interest which deals with relatively ephemeral, unstructured, and spontaneous instances of social interaction—e.g., crowds, mobs, publics, fads, social movements—in contrast to the more permanent and structured forms of group life which comprise the area of social organization.[12] Although Yablonsky is correct in his formulation of a "group-mob continuum," he is incorrect in his assumption that the theoretical distinction at stake is that between non-groups (mobs) and "true groups." The criteria of differentiation which inform the continuum are, rather, the degree of organization and, correlatively, the degree of persistence through time of the interaction.

Moreover, the sociological division of labor between the study of collective behavior and the study of social organization (which constitute the poles of the continuum) is neither static nor merely classificatory. Theoretically, the continuum adumbrates a basic sociological postulate: out of collective behavior grows social organization. In this inheres the theoretical significance of the formulation, for the study of concrete instances of collective behavior provides an empirical basis for insights into the nature and course of social change and the development of organized human groups and institutions.

Finally, in so far as collective behavior involves more or less spontaneous attempts on the part of large numbers of unorganized individuals to act together in the absence of an adequately functioning social structure and set of normative definitions, it is not only a mechanism by which a new social order arises but also an index of social disorganization. When traditional institutional forms break down, various types of collective behavior are likely to occur.

With these remarks in mind, it is clear that Yablonsky is also superficially correct in locating his gangs as "near-groups" mid-way on the mob-group continuum. Again, however, his theoretical rationale is defective. More logically and cogently, the mid-point on the *collective behavior— social organization* continuum is occupied by "social movements" as a type of human grouping. Unlike the more elementary groupings such as crowds and publics, social movements exhibit continuity beyond the concrete interacting situation because they develop a "culture" in the sense of a set of "ideas, theories, doctrines, values, and strategic and tactical principles"; on the other hand, social movements are something less than organized groups because they lack a fully developed and functionally effective social structure.[13] A chain of command and a set of normative definitions are only in the process of developing and are thus incapable of controlling effectively the activities of the members.

The formal sociological status of social movements is that of *social collectives* which, as Heberle points out, while containing organized groups are not themselves organized.[14] They consist of a "core-group" which is the center and locus of structural developments plus an amorphous "extension" which is comprised of a congeries of other organized and quasi-organized groups as well as of unattached individuals.[15] Indeed, from an internal point of view, the career of a social movement is the record of the attempt on the part of the leaders and the most involved members in the core-group to control and to structure the activities of those located in the extension.

Finally, it should be noted that the most general precondition for the rise of a social movement as a collective enterprise to bring about changes in the values and social structure of a society is the existence of a degree of social unrest. Significant numbers of individuals must be sufficiently detached from and dissatisfied with the functioning of the prevailing social order to be willing and able to act in a direct fashion, outside of the established norms and social organizations, to achieve their aims.

The parallels between Yablonsky's so-called "near-group" theory and the theoretical apparatus of "collective behavior" are so exact as to require no further comment. It remains, however, to apply the latter frame of reference to his observations concerning the adolescent delinquent gangs and gang wars in New York City.

Delinquent gangs as adolescent expressive movements

In his analysis of social movements, Blumer singles out for special comment a type which he calls "expressive." Such movements:

. . . do not seek to change the institutions of the social order or its objective character. The tension and unrest out of which they emerge are not focused upon some objective social change which the movements seek collectively to achieve. Instead, they are released in some type of expressive behavior. . . .[16]

If the analysis of the gangs observed by Yablonsky is recast in terms of the expressive movement concept, not only can all of his factual and theoretical statements be assimilated but additional insights into collective elements in the situation are provided.

The gang as a social collective

Yablonsky's observations concerning the structure of these adolescent gangs clearly indicate that we are dealing with a social collective, consisting of a core-group and an amorphous extension. In this connection, he speaks of three characteristic levels of membership organization: at the center is a group of youths, "always working to keep the gang together and in action, always drafting, plotting, and talking of gang warfare."[17] The other levels comprise the extension and involve decreasing degrees of identity with the leaders and more committed members of the core-group and less frequent participation in gang activities.

Most of the other characteristics of these gangs described by Yablonsky flow from this basic structural feature: e.g., decreasing gradient of cohesiveness as one moves from the core-group to the extension; and a minimum of consensus with respect to normative expectations, definition of membership, role definitions, and goals of the group. Correlatively, the membership is characteristically shifting. And, under such conditions, leadership is apt to be "self-appointed" and the internal social structure "shifting and personalized."[18]

Collective factors in the origin and function of the gangs

In his recognition that the violent adolescent gangs observed are fundamentally different from those which provided the empirical bases for the formulations of Thrasher and Whyte, Yablonsky is on solid theoretical ground.[19] However, in his emphasis on the gang as "a convenient

and malleable structure quickly adaptable to the needs of emotionally disturbed youth" who lack an effective degree of interpersonal competence, Yablonsky fails to appreciate that the gangs and gang wars also constitute collective attempts to solve the problems faced by a particular segment of adolescents in a particular social situation.[20]

In fact, Yablonsky's observations refer primarily to the activities of lower class youths in disorganized slum areas which give rise to a type of delinquent "subculture" whose basic dimensions have more recently been clarified by the work of Cloward and Ohlin. The latter regard slum areas as disorganized when they lack the prerequisites for the emergence of stable systems of social relations. They describe the forces making for such disorganization as involving:

. . . high rates of vertical and geographical mobility, massive housing projects in which 'site Tenants' are not accorded priority in occupancy, so that traditional residents are dispersed and 'strangers' re-assembled; and changing land use, as in the case of residential areas that are encroached upon by the expansion of adjacent commercial and industrial areas.[21]

The pace of social change is so rapid that community organizations fail to develop or adequately to function; "transiency and instability become the over-riding features of social life."[22]

Cloward and Ohlin infer that the above combination of factors leads to an inability of the community to provide its adolescent members access either to legitimate or to illegitimate means of attaining internalized success goals.[23] This double frustration, coupled with the inherent weakness of social controls in such a situation, produces tendencies to violence. The final result is the emergence of a *conflict* in contrast to a *criminal* delinquent

subculture. Whereas the former is epitomized by "the manipulation of violence,"[24] the latter is characterized by
more or less rational and conventionalized
criminal activities:

> In summary, severe limitations on both con-
> ventional and criminal opportunity intensify
> frustrations and position discontent. Discon-
> tent is heightened further under conditions in
> which social control is relaxed, for the area
> lacking integration between age-levels of of-
> fender and between carriers of conventional
> and criminal values cannot generate pressures
> to contain frustrations among the young. These
> are the circumstances, we suggest, in which
> adolescents turn to violence in search of status.
> Violence comes to be ascendant, in short,
> under conditions of relative detachment from
> all institutionalized systems of opportunity and
> social control.[25]

Quite in contrast to Yablonsky's psychological interpretation in terms of the
limited social abilities of these adolescents,
Cloward and Ohlin explicitly recognize the
collective nature of both the causes and the
character of adolescent gang violence.
Moreover, in their discussion of the
criminal delinquent subculture, they provide an insightful clue to what is the
unique motif of the "bopping" gang by
differentiating between "instrumental"
and "expressive" stealing. Where criminal
learning environments and opportunity
structures are absent (as is the case in
disorganized urban slum areas), they
hypothesize that stealing "may simply be
an *expressive* act in defiance of conventional value."[26] We propose, in turn, that
the seemingly senseless violence that
characterizes the activities of these youth-
ful gangs should be similarly interpreted.

The violent behavior is *expressive* rather
than symbolic; it is not simply or even
primarily the way to "rep" and the badge
of "guts" and "heart." Rather it is the
only and the most elementary way in which

these youths can act together in the face of
the social unrest which is indigenous to
their social environment.

Parenthetically, on the adult level,
Lipset's distinction between "class" and
"status" politics and their differential
consequences for collective political action
provides a suggestive analogue: In the case
of the latter, Lipset emphasizes that
clear-cut goals, involving economic and
political reforms, are lacking:

> Where there are status anxieties, there is
> little or nothing which a government can do. It
> is not surprising, therefore, that political move-
> ments which have successfully appealed to
> status resentments have been *irrational* in
> character.[27]

Mutatis mutandis, adolescents who are
deprived of access both to legitimate and
to illegitimate means for achieving their
internalized success goals attempt collectively to adapt by participating in an
expressive social movement—an adolescent rebellion without a cause.

The violent adolescent gang as
an expressive movement

Yablonsky is, of course, correct in his
observation that there is a lack of consensus among the members of these gangs
regarding objectives and goals. But this is
not because "such collective behavior is
individualistic and flows from emotional
disturbance."[28] To be sure, some of these
adolescents are emotionally disturbed and
this may be true of a disproportionate
number of core-group members. It is to be
doubted, however, that the majority of the
participants in these delinquent gang activities have such a clinical status. The
lack of shared objectives is more simply a
characteristic of the type of collectivity
involved: expressive movements are not

goal oriented; they are not going any-where; they do not seek specific reforms.

Cloward and Ohlin are also correct in their identification of the disorganized urban slum as the "cause" of the violent delinquent gang as well as in their identification of the organized urban slum as the "cause" of the criminal pattern of delinquency. Yet, a question can be raised concerning the cogency of their "subcul-tural" interpretation of the conflict pat-tern—i.e., the violent adolescent gang.

There is no doubt as to the rich content of the criminal delinquent subculture with its age-graded associational structure and proliferation of criminal techniques.[29] On the other hand, beyond a *vocabulary of motives*, the "culture" of violence is *com-paratively* undeveloped.[30] While it makes sense to speak of criminal learning and criminal skills, Yablonsky's recorded in-terviews make clear that there is little "technique" to violence:

Everyone was pushin' and I pulled out my knife. I saw this face—I never seen it before, so I stabbed it.

He was laying on the ground lookin' up at us. Everyone was kicking, punching, stabbing. I kicked him on the jaw or someplace; then I kicked him in the stomach. That was the least I could do was kick 'im.[31]

This is not to say that the core-group of an expressive movement has no social structure or that such movements do not develop a culture.[32] Given, however, the inherently *ad hoc* and incidental quality of lower class urban street-life and the transi-tional, anomalous nature of adolescent status, structural and cultural develop-ments are often likely to have the mini-mum of viability and functional signifi-cance.[33] Thus, while the gang members may refer to themselves in terms of a

"T.O."—"war counselors," "chiefs," etc. —these statuses are apt to be more conno-tative than denotative, more expressive than functional. They in no sense consti-tute "careers." And Yablonsky's observa-tions concerning the participant's varying estimates of the size of his gang further buttresses the expressive quality of such structural and cultural developments.[34]

The concept of stable role-models and the implication of a complex and highly functional status system are belied by the inherent dynamism of violence: the rela-tive prestige and power of the individual participants as well as of rival gangs are necessarily subject to constant testing and revalidation, providing only momentary solutions to status discontent. Further, no concept in the vocabulary of motives of the adolescent delinquent gang member is more poignant than that of "turf." Not only is habitat the minimum basis for so-cial interaction and organization but, in the disorganized slum area in which tran-siency and physical mobility are the rule, it takes on a mythical quality which is characteristic of social movement ideolo-gies.[35] Lacking the tools to carve out for themselves a place in social space, these rootless adolescents seek collectively by violence to define a place in physical space, the last refuge of society and of self.

Summary and conclusions

To view the violent adolescent gang as an expressive social movement is to sug-gest that its nature and consequences for both the individual and the community turn primarily on its associational charac-teristics rather than on the psychic struc-ture of its members or on the content of its culture. Theoretically, it is the psychic dividends of factually participating in a collective act rather than the achievement of status in a social organization that is primarily at stake for the individual. Again, just as the psychic cohesion of the sectarian religious movement thrives on its "war with the mores," so, too, the incidental mobilization of collective behavior in the gang war is functionally more important than the social structure of the core-group and the culture of the movement for the integration of the participants and the continuity of the social collective.

Such a perspective allows us to understand not only why adolescents in disorganized urban slum areas are so readily co-opted into the collective violence of the *rumble* but also why (in contrast to those involved in the criminal and retreatist sub-cultures), it may be relatively easier for the participants in this "Children's Crusade" to negotiate "a shift in reference groups identification from the delinquent group to that of law-abiding, lower class society."[36] For, just because a social movement is an incomplete and highly vulnerable social system, membership and participation do not involve either the degree of commitment or involvement that is characteristic of delinquent subcultural patterns.[37]

The violent delinquent gang has been considered as an expressive social movement representing the attempt on the part of adolescents living in disorganized, lower-class urban slums to act together in the face of social unrest. Practically, such a view suggests that neither therapy nor the *ad hoc* accolade of the street gang worker attack the problem at its roots. Only by providing community contexts which are so organized as to make it clear to adolescents that society has a place for them as adolescents and a meaningful future for them as adults will such social eruptions and their attendant collective violence disappear from the urban scene.[38]

Finally, the progress of sociological theory and research depends not only on our ability to correct for the projections of "autistic observers" as Yablonsky suggests.[39] It also depends on our scholarly obligation to recognize the relevance of existing theoretic traditions, exemplified by Cloward's and Ohlin's imaginative use of the formulations of Durkheim and Merton in their analysis. Clearly, autistic conceptualizations can be as dysfunctional as autistic observations.

Notes

1. Robert K. Merton, *Social Theory and Social Structure,* revised ed., Glencoe, Ill.: The Free Press, 1957, p. 101.
2. Merton sees the reconstruction of data primarily as a by-product of "conceptual clarification," which functions "to make explicit the character of data subsumed under a concept." See *ibid.,* pp. 89-93.
3. Lewis Yablonsky, "The Delinquent Gang as a Near-Group," *Social Problems,* 7 (Fall, 1959), pp. 108-117.
4. Richard A. Cloward and Lloyd E. Ohlin, *Delinquency and Opportunity,* Glencoe Ill.: The Free Press, 1960.
5. Yablonsky, *op. cit.,* p. 110.
6. *Ibid.,* p. 109.
7. *Ibid.,* p. 117.
8. *Ibid.,* p. 115.
9. *Ibid.,* p. 116.
10. *Ibid.,* p. 115.
11. *Ibid.,* p. 108.
12. For some classic formulations of the field of collective behavior, see: Herbert Blumer, "Collective Behavior," in Alfred M. Lee (ed.), *Principles of Sociology,* New York: Barnes and Noble, Inc., 1953, pp. 167-222; Robert E. Park and Ernest W. Burgess, *Introduction to the Science of Sociology,* rev'd. ed., Chicago: University of Chicago Press, 1924, pp. 865-934; and Ralph H. Turner and Lewis M. Killian, *Collective Behavior,* Englewood Cliffs, N.J.: Prentice-Hall, Inc., 1947.
13. Rudolf Heberle, *Social Movements,* New York: Prentice-Hall, Inc., 1951, p. 23.
14. *Ibid.,* p. 8.
15. See, for example, Arendt's distinction between "party members" and "sympathizers" in her discussion of the organization of totalitarian movements. Hannah Arendt, *The Origins of Totalitarianism,* New York: Meridian Books, Inc., 1958, pp. 364-365.
16. Blumer, *op. cit.,* p. 214.

17. Yablonsky, *op. cit.,* p. 113.

18. *Ibid.,* p. 116.

19. Both Thrasher and Whyte view the delinquent gang as an organized social group. See Frederick M. Thrasher, *The Gang,* Chicago: University of Chicago Press, 1936; and William Foote Whyte, *Street Corner Society,* Chicago: University of Chicago Press, 1943.

20. Yablonsky, *op. cit.,* p. 115.

21. Cloward and Ohlin, *op. cit.,* p. 172.

22. *Ibid.*

23. The authors make clear that the internalized success goals are oriented to improvement in economic position without change in life style (i.e., middle-class membership) in the case of the members of delinquent gangs. See *Ibid.,* pp. 94-97.

24. *Ibid.,* p. 175.

25. *Ibid.,* pp. 177-178.

26. *Ibid.,* p. 170, *emphasis added.*

27. S. M. Lipset, "The Sources of 'The Radical Right,'" in *The New American Right,* Daniel Bell (ed.), New York: Criterion Books, 1955, p. 168, *emphasis added.*

28. Yablonsky, *op. cit.,* p. 115.

29. The *retreatist* sub-culture mentioned by Cloward and Ohlin (especially in its "beatnik" and "drug-addict" expressions) is also well developed in content.

30. For developments of the vocabulary of motives concept, see Kenneth Burke, *Permanence and Change,* New York: New Republic, 1936, pp. 30-53. Donald R. Cressey, *Other People's Money,* Glencoe, Ill.: The Free Press, 1953, pp. 93-138. Hans Gerth and C. Wright Mills, *Character and Social Structure,* New York: Harcourt, Brace and Company, 1953, pp. 112-129.

31. Yablonsky, *op. cit.,* pp. 111-112.

32. Expressive movements can have careers, are subject to routinization, and can become institutionalized. Thus, it is not impossible that a "conflict sub-culture" can develop, that Yablonsky's observations refer to an early stage, that Cloward's and Ohlin's formulation refer to a later stage, and that the present formulation is relevant for a theory of the origin of "conflict-oriented" delinquent gangs. I am indebted to James F. Short, Jr., for this suggestive possibility. However, the prospects of institutionalizing *conflict* among lower class adolescents living in disorganized slum areas would seem to be at a minimum on sheerly sociological grounds.

33. Short is impressed by what he has termed the "aleatory" factor in delinquent behavior episodes— i.e., those aspects "which are beyond either understanding or, potentially, prediction." Such a formulation only emphasizes the contingent, episodic, and non-routinized nature of this "collective behavior." See, James F. Short, Jr., "Street Corner Groups and Patterns of Delinquency, A Progress Report from NIMH Grant M-3301," University of Chicago, Department of Sociology, March 1, 1961, mimeo. pp. 9-12.

34. Yablonsky, *op. cit.,* p. 110.

35. Georges Sorel, *Reflections on Violence,* trans. by T. E. Hulme and J. Roth, Glencoe, Ill.: The Free Press, 1950, p. 48.

36. Richard A. Cloward and Lloyd E. Ohlin, "Types of Delinquent Subcultures," New York: New York School of Social Work, December, 1958, mimeo. p. 38.

37. This also helps to explain the differences in resistance to change exhibited by the three types of delinquent behavior discussed by Cloward and Ohlin, who interpret the differences in terms of their external and internal cultural integration. See, Cloward and Ohlin, *Delinquency and Opportunity, op. cit.,* p. 192.

38. See Paul Goodman, *Growing.Up Absurd,* New York: Random House, 1960, and Martin R. Haskell, "Toward a Reference Group Theory of Juvenile Delinquency," *Social Problems,* 8 (Winter, 1960-61), pp. 220-230.

39. Yablonsky, *op. cit.,* p. 112.

32.

Lawrence B. Mohr

DETERMINANTS OF INNOVATION
IN ORGANIZATIONS

The present study is an attempt to identify the determinants of innovation in public agencies, i.e., the degree to which they adopt and emphasize programs that depart from traditional concerns. Innovation is suggested to be the function of an interaction among the motivation to innovate, the strength of obstacles against innovation, and the availability of resources for overcoming such obstacles.

The significance of the research can be viewed in terms of Hyneman's observation nearly twenty years ago that bureaucratic agencies ". . . may fail to take the initiative and supply the leadership that is required of them in view of their relation to particular sectors of public affairs. . . ."[1] His concern was the responsiveness of the public sector not only to expressed wants but to public wants that may go unexpressed, or be only weakly expressed, and whose utility is much more easily recognized by the informed bureaucratic official than by the ordinary citizen.[2]

From Lawrence B. Mohr, "Determinants of Innovation in Organizations," *American Political Science Review* 63, March 1969, pp. 111-26, with permission of the author and publisher.

I wish to express my gratitude for valuable advice and comments from Robert Friedman, Irwin Rosenstock, Philip Converse, Ferrel Heady, M. Kent Jennings, Robert Northrop, and John Romani. Many of the ideas were sharpened and elaborated in discussions during the preparation of "Innovation in State and Local Bureaucracies," by R. S. Friedman, L. B. Mohr and R. M. Northrop, a paper presented at the annual meeting of the American Political Science Association, New York, 1966. The research reported here was supported by the Public Health Service, Research Grant No. CH 00044 from the Division of Community Health Services.

While the results and conclusions to be reported appear to be largely valid for organizations in general, the empirical focus will be local departments of public health which, as a class, have had a rather dramatic succession of opportunities to respond to new public problems over the past twenty-five years. A brief introductory paragraph will orient the reader to the applied setting.

By the early 1940's—the end of the "traditional" period in public health programming from the viewpoint of this study—the American Public Health Association had defined the task of the local health department essentially in terms of a basic set of six services: vital statistics, basic sanitation, communicable disease control, laboratory services, maternal and child health services, and health education.[3] Since the middle 1940's, infectious diseases (which these services were designed to combat) have declined radically as a health problem. In the last two decades, the professional leadership has increasingly called upon local health departments to turn their attention to the control of chronic diseases, the prevention of accidents, the provision of mental health services, the control of the quality of water and air, to dental health needs and to a host of additional non-traditional concerns. Many local public health organizations have responded to these newer concerns as advancing technology has provided ways of meeting them. However, it appears that while some departments have indeed reacted innovatively, a great many others continue to pursue the traditional objectives, if not exclusively, then certainly with primary emphasis.

The study group for the present research included all full-time local health departments in Illinois, Michigan, New York, Ohio, and Ontario, serving a jurisdiction no greater than 600,000 in population, whose chief executive—the local health officer—had occupied his current position during the entire period of 1960-1964. This group comprised 94 agencies. Since one health officer refused to participate in the study, ninety-three elements were provided for analysis. The data were collected primarily by interviews with the local health officers during the summer of 1965.

I. The concept of innovation

Because the term innovation has been employed so widely and ambiguously, it is essential to specify at the outset how the concept will be used and how it is related to other usages. Innovation will be defined here as *the successful introduction into an applied situation of means or ends that are new to that situation.* Alternative and generally more inclusive definitions have been offered in the past.[4] For example, there has been a frequent tendency to combine the idea of adoption or adaptiveness with the idea of invention; occasionally, the term "innovative" has been assigned to mean exclusively what is more generally called "inventive" or "creative."

It seems important at the present stage of research and theory to separate the idea of invention from the idea of innovation. Invention implies bringing something new into being; innovation implies bringing something new into use.[5] In the organizational world this distinction is particularly important, for we are interested at times in whether an organization can create something new for its own use or for exploitation by others, and at other times in whether an organization can successfully adopt goals or processes or policies that are new in the sense of being departures from its own tradition.

There appears to be a good deal of agreement now on some of the factors that most enhance inventiveness or creativity in organizations, including the availability of individuals capable of producing new ideas[6] and the development of an organizational pattern that maximizes flexibility and opens lines of communication.[7] Unfortunately, less unanimity can be reported on the correlates of organizational innovation. There has been much more empirical research in this area, but it consists of scattered projects representing different disciplines, motivated by different considerations, and employing a strikingly heterogeneous selection of independent variables.

If any one group of variables may be said to stand out among all others as empirically determined correlates of innovation, it is the group of interrelated factors indicating size, wealth, or the available of resources. Mansfield,[8] Mytinger,[9] Hage and Aiken,[10] Eisenstadt,[11] and Rogers[12] all conclude that organizational size and wealth are among the strongest predictors of innovation in the sense of readiness to adopt new patterns of behavior. Other organizational characteristics have also been identified as predictors of innovation in this sense, including informality, complexity, and decentralization in organizational structure,[13] breadth of organizational goals, and absence of dominance by a single professional ideology.[14]

In addition to the organization itself, the environment of the organization appears to be extremely important in two ways. An organization may be more likely to innovate when its environment is rapidly changing than when it is steady. In this sense, "environment" includes such factors as market conditions, technological changes, clientele needs and demands, and the labor market. Burns and Stalker count this variable heavily as determining whether or not the firms they studied adopted new, more organic management techniques.[15] In addition, innovation should also be more likely when the *social* environment to which an organization (or an individual) belongs has norms that favor change than when its norms do not favor change. In this regard, Rogers reports research in which fairly strong correlations were found between innovation and the norms of the relevant community, placed on a dimension from "traditional" to "modern."[16]

Each of the foregoing correlates of innovation must be viewed as an attribute of a collectivity—an organization. To complete the list, numerous variables measured at the individual level have also been found to relate to the type of innovative change of interest to us here. It would appear from a review of the literature that chief among these are the attitudes of an individual toward change, or any ideology he may have that would influence a specific type of innovation. Such factors were found to be important by Blau, Fliegel, Rogers and Eisenstadt.[17] In addition, the "cosmopoliteness"[18] of an individual is reported to be a significant correlate of innovation by Mytinger and by Rogers.[19] Blau found both the competence of an individual and his material and status interests to be associated with innovation.[20] A positive professional orientation was found by Rogers to be associated with innovation, as was opinion leadership status within a relevant communications network.[21]

It seems fairly clear, then, that the determinants of invention and the determinants of innovation in organizations are not identical. Inventiveness seems to be affected most by individual creativity and by the degree of hierarchical informality in organizational structure. Innovation, on the other hand, has been linked to size, wealth, environment, ideology, motivation, competence, professionalism, non-professionalism, decentralization, opinion leadership, and still other variables. Because of this difference, it appears highly desirable to distinguish innovation from invention in research.

If the preceding discussion is considered in light of the definition of innovation offered above, it is clear that we have been elaborating upon the word "introduction" and upon the sense of the phrase "new to that situation." We have, in other words, emphasized that innovation is meant to exclude creativity *per se* and to include the notion of adopting something nontraditional whether it was invented within or outside of the organization concerned.

The term "successful," like "introduction," has important implications for the measurement of innovation. The successful introduction of some new method or goal implies its acceptance by the individual or group that constitutes the human element in a pertinent applied situation. If a health department tentatively introduces a new program, action of the department to increase emphasis on the program over time continues to be innovative behavior until the change has been completely accepted by organizational personnel, the public or other relevant groups. Such action is no longer innovative, of course, when the idea has become part of the organization's tradition.

The same point has been made in connection with innovation by individuals, but is especially significant in organizational behavior, where we have long recognized and been concerned with the phenomenon of resistance to change.[22] It is important to note that both organizations and individuals may adopt a practice and then discontinue it for one reason or another or maintain it only on a token level. Rogers reports some studies in which discontinuance rates were found to be quite high.[23] It may help us to gain insight into innovation, therefore, if we do not restrict ourselves to its usual operational definition, the simple adoption of new practices, but include also a definition that allows for increased emphasis upon non-traditional programs recently introduced.[24] For this reason and others to be noted subsequently, two basic working measures of innovation will be employed in the analysis. One is the total number of non-traditional services adopted by the department. The other is the total number of personnel units (measured in man-years or the equivalent in dollars) that were added in all non-traditional program areas during the five-year period 1960-1964. This latter view of innovation will be labeled "progressive programming."

The term "new" appears almost invariably and as a matter of course in definitions of innovation, but it has an implication that should not be taken for granted. Innovation is difficult because it involves doing something new. The introduction of innovative practices into a social setting implies actions that entail a certain amount of uncertainty, risk, or hazard. This, then, suggests one significant factor that may help to explain innovation, i.e., there are certain obstacles or deterrents to innovation that may be more or less operative in any given case.[25] These are, first, the cost of such things as materials, time, or skills, and second, the

power of human forces and fears, individual and social, that may be arrayed against the introduction of new means or ends. The latter category may include the power of tradition and social values, the power of individuals and groups who may be threatened by an innovation, and the power of one's concern for his own safety, security, and self-esteem, as well as the security of people who are important to him. The more staunchly these forces are arrayed against a particular innovation, the more difficult will it be for that innovation to take place, other things being equal. Furthermore, when one thinks of "newness" in these terms, it is not the absolute or objective sense of the word that counts, but rather the relative newness of an idea to a given role or set of roles, for it is in that context that obstacles to innovation will frequently arise. Thus, the innovations we will consider here are not necessarily new to the professional leadership in the field of public health, but they are indeed innovations for the local community, the organization, or the small clique of fellow health officers or local physicians.

Although obstacles may generally be expected to inhibit innovation, previous studies indicate that other factors may stimulate or enhance it. One individual or organization will usually have greater motivation than another to adopt a new idea. In addition, one may have greater resources than another, including not only the money and skills to overcome obstacles of expense, but also resources such as a position of authority, a charismatic effect, the support of prestigious individuals and self-confidence to overcome obstacles presented in terms of human forces.

On the basis of the foregoing considerations, the following three-dimensional hypothesis is specified: *Innovation is directly related to the motivation to innovate, inversely related to the strength of obstacles to innovation, and directly related to the availability of resources for overcoming such obstacles.*

It is thus possible to specify in more general terms why some of the many independent variables covered by previous studies were related to innovation; each indicated either a relative absence of obstacles or a relative presence of motivation or resources. Environmental changes and demands, for example, frequently constitute an important source of motivation, as do material and status interests and certain relevant ideologies. "Traditional" community norms, personal attitudes generally unfavorable to change, worker resistance to change, narrow organizational goals, lack of information, mechanistic decision structures—all of these are examples of obstacles to innovation. Competence and wealth are significant resources for innovation.

IV. Conclusions

This research began with a concern for the responsiveness of public agencies to changes in the general problems they were designed to meet. We did not study the whole of this question but rather attacked one essential facet, the ability of such organizations to adopt and emphasize programs that depart from traditional behavior. On the other hand, our focus goes somewhat beyond the problem of responsiveness in that it is relevant to questions of organizational innovation in general, whether justified by environmental changes or prompted by any of a host of other possible stimuli.

It was initially proposed that extent of innovation is a negative function of obstacles and a positive function of the motivation to innovate and the availability of relevant resources. The data collected from 93 local public health organizations supported this proposition, although, as operationalized, the relationships were weak in some cases. The variable emerging as by far the most powerful predictor of innovation was "size," but we concluded that this relationship cannot be considered theoretically complete. Rather, size should be expected to predict innovativeness only insofar as it implies the presence of motivation, obstacles, and resources. In the present case, organizational size proved to be an excellent indicator of the relevant resources available to local health departments for the adoption of a large number of non-traditional programs.

The analysis of the data yielded several additional conclusions that would seem to merit further test and elaboration:

a. In attempting to derive accurate predictions of behavior from attitudes or beliefs, such as ideologies, the belief itself should be qualified by the intensity with which it is held and one may well expect the belief-behavior relationship to be qualified by one or more contingent conditions.

b. With regard to many kinds of innovation in public organizations, the relationships among community size, organizational size and extent of innovation form a developmental sequence. Larger communities generally require larger service organizations, and it is the resources of the larger organization that lead to innovation. Thus, large organizations in small communities may be expected to adopt many innovations: small organizations in large communities will adopt few.

c. A great deal of innovation in organizations, especially large or successful ones, is "slack" innovation. After solution of immediate problems, the quest for prestige rather than the quest for organizational effectiveness or corporate profit motivates the adoption of most new programs and technologies.

d. Once the diffusion of innovations has progressed far enough to include late adopters, organizational size and wealth will have no bearing upon the relative emphasis accorded to innovative as opposed to traditional activities.

e. Lastly, and perhaps most importantly for theoretical development, innovation is viewed as a multiplicative function of the motivation to innovate and the balance between the obstacles and resources bearing upon innovation.

Notes

1. Charles S. Hyneman, *Bureaucracy in a Democracy* (New York: Harper and Brothers, 1950), p. 26.

2. For a much more recent treatment of bureaucratic innovation and public responsiveness, see Herbert A. Simon, "The Changing Theory and Changing Practice of Public Administration," in Ithiel de Sola Pool (ed.), *Contemporary Political Science: Toward Empirical Theory* (New York: McGraw-Hill Book Co., 1967), pp. 86-120. "The 'power' to innovate," says Simon (p. 106), ". . . is probably the principal power of the bureaucracy in the realm of policy and value."

3. Haven Emerson, *Local Health Units for the Nation: A Report* (New York: The Commonwealth Fund, 1945), p. 2.

4. See Victor A. Thompson, "Bureaucracy and Innovation," *Administrative Science Quarterly,* 10 (June, 1965), p. 2; Everett M. Rogers, *Diffusion of Innovation* (New York: Free Press of Glencoe, 1962), p. 308; James Q. Wilson, "Innovation in Organization: Notes Toward A Theory," in James D. Thompson (ed.), *Approaches to Organizational Design* (Pittsburgh: Univ. of Pittsburgh Press, 1966), p. 196; Homer G. Barnett, *Innovation* (New York: McGraw-Hill Book Co., 1953), p. 7.

5. The same general distinction has been made by others. *Cf.,* Rogers, *op. cit.,* pp. 195-196, and Simon, *op. cit.,* p. 107.

6. See Gary A. Steiner (ed.), *The Creative Organization* (Chicago: The University of Chicago Press, 1965), pp. 16-18.

7. Harold Guetzkow, "The Creative Person in Organizations," in Steiner, *op. cit.,* pp. 35-45; Tom Burns and G. M. Stalker, *The Management of Innovation* (London: Tavistock Publications, 1961), pp. 85-86, 89, 121-122; Thompson, *op. cit.,* p. 12.

8. Edwin Mansfield, "The Speed of Response of Firms to New Techniques," *Quarterly Journal of Economics* (May, 1963), pp. 293-304.

9. Robert E. Mytinger, *Innovations in Public Health* (unpublished doctoral dissertation, Univ. of California at Los Angeles, 1965), p. 212.

10. Jerald Hage and Michael Aiken, "Program Change and Organizational Properties: A Compara-

tive Analysis," *American Journal of Sociology,* 72 (March, 1967), pp. 516-517.

11. Samuel N. Eisenstadt, *The Political Systems of Empires* (New York: The Free Press of Glencoe, 1963), pp. 27, 33-112.

12. Rogers, *op. cit.,* pp. 40, 285-292.

13. Hage and Aiken, *op. cit.,* pp. 503-519.

14. Mayer N. Zald and Patricia Denton, "From Evangelism to General Service: The Transformation of the YMCA," *Administrative Science Quarterly,* VIII, No. 2 (September, 1963), p. 234.

15. Burns and Stalker, *op. cit.,* p. 96.

16. Rogers, *op. cit.,* pp. 285-292.

17. Peter M. Blau, *The Dynamics of Bureaucracy* (2d ed. rev.; Chicago: Univ. of Chicago Press, 1963), p. 246; Rogers, *loc. cit.;* Frederick C. Fliegel, "A Multiple Correlation Analysis of Factors Associated with Adoption of Farm Practices," *Rural Sociology,* 21 (September-December, 1956), pp. 288-289, 291; Everett M. Rogers, "A Conceptual Variable Analysis of Technological Change," *Rural Sociology,* 23 (June, 1958), pp. 139-140, 143-145; Eisenstadt, *loc. cit.*

18. Robert K. Merton, *Social Theory and Social Structure* (Glencoe: The Free Press, 1949 and 1957), pp. 387-420; Alvin W. Gouldner, "Cosmopolitans and Locals: Toward an Analysis of Latent Social Roles," *Administrative Science Quarterly,* 11 (December, 1957), pp. 281-306, and (March, 1958), pp. 444-480.

19. Mytinger, *op. cit.,* p. 195; Rogers, *Diffusion of Innovation, op. cit.,* pp. 285-292.

20. Blau, *op. cit.,* p. 246.

21. Rogers, *loc. cit.*

22. See Harold J. Leavitt, "Applied Organizational Change in Industry: Structural, Technical, and Human Approaches," *Handbook of Organizations,* ed. James B. March (Chicago: Rand McNally & Company, 1965), pp. 1144-1170, for a valuable summary and critique.

23. Rogers, *Diffusion of Innovation, op. cit.,* pp. 88-93.

24. See the introductory paragraphs, above, for examples of traditional and non-traditional programs. The primary sources for determining the precise composition of the two lists were "An Official Declaration of Attitude of the American Public Health Association on Desirable Standard Minimum Functions and Suitable Organization of Health Activities," *American Journal of Public Health,* 30 (September, 1940), pp. 1099-1106; and Harry S. Mustard, *Government in Public Health* (New York: The Commonwealth Fund, 1945), pp. 128, 140-182.

25. *Cf.,* Mytinger's discussion of "barriers" to innovation. Robert E. Mytinger, "Barriers to Adoption of New Programs as Perceived by Local Health Officers," *Public Health Reports,* 82 (February, 1967), pp. 108-114.

33.

S. N. Eisenstadt

INSTITUTIONALIZATION AND CHANGE

This paper illustrates the combination of systematic institutional analysis with the analysis of change, showing that the explication of change is inherent in the systematic analysis of concrete societies or parts thereof.

Claims have long been made that structural or "structural-functional" analysis, with its stress on systems, equilibrium, common values and boundary-maintenance, not only neglects problems of change, but is analytically incapable of dealing with them. In response, many sociologists have recently asserted that not only is there no necessary contradiction between structural analysis and the analysis of change, but that on the contrary the two are basically compatible.

As formulated, for instance, by Moore, the argument is that every society (or social system) is inherently predisposed to change because of basic problems to which there is no overall continuous solution.[1] These problems include uncertainties of socialization, perennial scarcity of resources relative to individual aspirations, and contrasting types of social orientation or principles of social organization (e.g.,

Gemeinschaft vs. *Gesellschaft*) within the society. While this general view has been accepted to some extent, it has given rise to the contrary claim that it is couched in terms too general to explain the specific directions of change in any concrete society, that such specificity is beyond the province of "structural" analysis, and that such analysis can explain any concrete change only by reference either to very general and hence inadequate causes, or to forces external to the system.[2]

These difficulties can be at least partially overcome by recognizing that the general "predilections" to change inherent in any social system become "concretized" or "specified" through the process of institutionalization. Our major point is that the institutionalization of any social system—be it political, economic or a system of social stratification or of any collectivity or role—creates in its wake the possibilities for change. The process of institutionalization is the organization of a societally prescribed system of differentiated behavior oriented to the solution of certain problems inherent in a major area of social life.[3]

The organization of such systems of behavior involves the creation and definition of norms to regulate the major units of social behavior and organization, criteria according to which the flow of resources is regulated between such units, and sanctions to ensure that such norms are upheld. All these involve the maintenance of the specific boundaries of the system, i.e., the maintenance of the units that constitute it, of its relations with outside

From S. N. Eisenstadt, "Institutionalization and Change," *ASR*, Vol. 29, April 1964, pp. 235-47. Reprinted by permission of the Americn Sociological Association and the author.

This paper was written in 1962-63 when the author was Carnegie Visiting Professor of Political Science at M.I.T. I am indebted to Professor R. N. Bellah for detailed comments on earlier versions of this paper. Parts of this paper were presented at the Fifth International Congress of Sociology, Washington, D.C., in September 1962.

systems, and of the norms that delineate its specific characteristics.

And yet the very attempt to institutionalize any such system creates in its wake the possibility for change. These are possibilities not only for general, unspecified change but for more specific changes, which develop not randomly but in relatively specific directions, to a large extent set by the very process of institutionalization. Hence a systematic structural analysis is a prerequisite for an adequate analysis of change.[4]

II

We shall illustrate this general point by analyzing the process of institutionalization in one type of political and one type of religious system, drawing on recent work on the social and political structure of the historical centralized bureaucratic Empires, i.e., the Sassanid, Roman, Byzantine, Chinese, Caliphate and Ottoman Empires and the European states in the period of absolutism,[5] and on the development of religious institutions within them.[6]

The majority of these Empires developed from (a) patrimonial empires such as Egypt or the Sassanid Empire; (b) dualistic nomadic-sedentary empires (necessarily sharing many characteristics with the patrimonial ones); (c) feudal systems, such as the European absolutist states; or (d) city-states (the Roman and Hellenistic Empires). Despite the great variety in historical and cultural settings, we may designate some common features in the first stages of establishment of such politics.

The Empires were first established through interaction between the political goals of the rulers who established them, and the broader conditions prevailing in their respective social structures. The initiative for the establishment of these polities came, in all cases, from the rulers—emperors, kings or members of a patrician ruling elite (like the more active and dynamic element of the patrician elite in Republican Rome). These rulers came, in most cases, from established patrician, patrimonial, tribal or feudal families. Some were usurpers, coming from lower-class families, who attempted to establish new dynasties or to conquer new territories, and some were conquerors who attempted to establish their rule over various territories.

In most cases such rulers arose in periods of strife and turmoil during dismemberment of the existing political system or during acute strife within it. Usually their aim was to reestablish peace and order. They did not, however, attempt to restore the old order in its entirety, although for propagandist reasons they sometimes upheld such restoration as political ideology or slogan. They sought to establish a more centralized, unified polity in which they could monopolize and set the political goals, without being bound by traditional aristocratic, tribal or patrician groups. Even the conquerors—as in the Roman, Islamic or Spanish American Empires—had some vision of distinctly political goals and attempted to transmit it to at least part of the conquered population. These aims were very often oriented against, and opposed by, various social and political groups. However great the turmoil, unrest and internal strife, some groups always either benefited from it (or hoped to do so) or aimed to reestablish the "old" order in which they held positions of power and influence.

To implement their aims against aristocratic patrician forces, the rulers found allies, active or passive, among the strata whose interests were opposed to those of the aristocratic groups and who could benefit from weakening the aristocracy and establishing a more unified polity. These allies were, basically, of two kinds. The first were the more active (mostly urban) economic, cultural and professional groups who, by origin or by social interest and orientation, or both, were opposed to the traditional aristocratic groups. The second were the larger, politically and socially more passive strata, including especially peasants and also lower urban groups who could benefit, even if indirectly, by the weakening of the aristocratic forces.

To implement their aims the Emperors attempted to establish a relatively centralized administration and to mobilize the resources needed for the neutralization, weakening or destruction of their enemies.

III

The successful institutionalization of the organizations through which the rulers could realize their aims was thus dependent first on the emergence of political entrepreneurs, the Emperors and their immediate entourage, who had the vision and ability to create new political entities.

Second, it depended on the existence, within the broader society, of certain specific conditions. Briefly, the most important of these conditions was the development, in all major institutional spheres, of a certain level of differentiation, i.e., the development of specific collectivities and roles in the major institutional spheres, such that the activities and resources of large parts of the population were freed from ascriptive (kinship, lineage, aristocratic) commitments and thus could be made available to the rulers.

These different social groups were willing to provide resources and support mostly because they perceived these Emperors as the best available choice among the various existing possibilities (as compared to more traditional aristocratic pretenders or to a state of continuous disorder). They may have identified themselves to various degrees with the goals and symbols of the Emperors; they may have hoped that the Emperors would help them attain some of their own goals, and in maintaining their values, establish norms and organizations to help regulate some of their internal problems, or they may have seen these Emperors as the least evil among the available choices.

To the degree that both sets of conditions developed in a given society, the possibility that a new imperial political system would be institutionalized was relatively great.

These conditions developed, for instance, though in varying degrees, in China from the beginning of the Han dynasty, in Byzantium and the Roman Empire in their formative stages, and in the Caliphates at the initial stages of their development.

In the Greek City States, on the other hand, while the broader social conditions did develop, there arose no group of leaders or entrepreneuers capable of forging a new polity. In other historical cases—e.g., those of Charlemagne or Genghis Khan—such leaders did arise but the broader social conditions were lacking.[7]

IV

But even when such conditions were propitious, and the new political leaders could obtain enough support, such support was of varying quality and intensity.

Several basic attitudes of the major strata toward the premises of the political systems of these Empires and toward the rulers' primary aims can be distinguished. The first attitude, evinced chiefly by the aristocracy, was one of opposition to the premises of the political systems. The second, passivity, was manifested mainly by the peasantry and sometimes also by other groups interested only in maintaining their limited local autonomy and their immediate economic interests.

The third attitude, found mostly in the bureaucracy, in some urban groups and in part of the professional and cultural elite, consisted of basic identification with the premises of the political system and willingness to fight for their interests within the framework of existing political institutions. The fourth attitude, developed mainly by the more differentiated urban groups and by the professional and intellectual elite, favored changes in the scope of the political system.

These attitudes often overlapped in concrete instances, and the attitudes of each group and stratum varied in different societies and periods. Moreover, the attitudes of any one group were never homogeneous and stable, and they could change according to the conditions or the demands made by the rulers. The concrete constellations of these various political attitudes of the major social groups greatly influenced the extent of their political participation.

V

Out of the interaction between these goals of the rulers on the one hand, and the broader social conditions and the varied attitudes of the various social strata on the other, the specific characteristics of these Empires became institutionalized.

Whatever the differences between the aims of various rulers and whatever the attitudes of the various groups, once the major contours of the Empires were institutionalized, various organizations developed within them—mostly through the efforts of the rulers—to implement policies designed to maintain the specific external and internal boundaries of the system, that is, its specific institutional contours and characteristics.

The most important characteristic of these Empires was the coexistence, within the same political institutions, of traditional, undifferentiated political activities, orientations and organizations with more differentiated, specifically *political* goals. Or in more general terms, the autonomy of the political as a distinct institutional sphere was limited. Autonomy of the political sphere was manifest first in the tendency toward political centralization, second, in the development by the rulers of autonomous political goals and third, in the relatively high organizational autonomy of executive and administrative organs and activities.

But the differentiation of political activities, organizations and goals was, in these political systems, limited by several important factors. First, the rulers were usually legitimated in terms of basically traditional-religious values, even where they stressed their own ultimate monopoly of such values. Second, the subject's political role was not fully distinguished from other basic societal roles—such as, for instance, membership in local communities; it was often embedded in local groups, and the citizen or subject did not exercise any direct political rights through a system of voting or franchise. Third, many traditional ascriptive units, such as aristocratic lineages or territorial communities, performed crucial political functions and served as units of political representation. As a consequence, the scope of political activity and participation

was far narrower than in most contemporary political systems.

Let us briefly analyze the policies of the
rulers. First, they were interested in the
limited promotion of free resources and
in freeing them from commitments to traditional aristocratic groups. Second, the
rulers wished to control these resources,
to commit them, as it were, to their own
use. Third, they tended to pursue various goals—e.g., military expansion—that
could, in themselves, have exhausted
many of the available free resources.

Perhaps the most interesting example of
these policies is the rulers' attempts to
create and maintain an independent free
peasantry with small-holdings and to
restrict the big landowners' encroachments on these small-holdings, in order to
assure both the peasants' independence
and the provision of resources to the
rulers.

Of special importance too was the
establishment of colonies and settlements
of peasant soldiers, to make certain that
the state would have sufficient military
man power. These colonies were not
necessarily state-owned: they were closely
associated with more complicated economic measures and policies, like various
types of taxation. The policy of establishing such colonies evolved particularly in
societies whose problems of frontier defense were of paramount importance. In
Byzantium one purpose of the famous
system of themes, supposedly evolved by
the Emperor Heraclius (A.D. 610-641),
was to provide adequate manpower for
frontier garrisons. This was achieved by
starting colonies of free peasants from
which soldiers were involuntarily recruited. A similar pattern was established in
the Sassanid Empire by Khousru the
Great. The T'ang Emperors of China also
organized the peasant militia on similar
lines. [8]

VI

But the initial institutionalization of
these political systems did not, in itself,
assure their continuity. The very process of
institutionalizing these Empires created
new problems—mainly because maintaining the conditions necessary for these
institutions became a more or less continuous concern of the rulers, so that special
policies, activities and organizations had
to be set up to ensure their perpetuation.
Because the rulers had to pursue continuously certain policies oriented against
some social groups and in favor of others,
the contradictions among their various
goals and in the attitudes of various groups
to the basic premises of the system were
evoked, and the negative orientations of
certain groups were intensified. Though
not always consciously grasped by the
rulers, these contradictions were nevertheless implicit in their structural positions,
in the problems and exigencies with which
they dealt, and in the concrete policies
they employed to solve these problems.

These internal contradictions developed
in almost all the major institutional
spheres, but perhaps especially in the
sphere of legitimation and stratification.
As we have seen, the rulers often attempted to limit the aristocracy's power
and to create new status groups such as the
free peasantry, a non-aristocratic officialdom, and so on. But these attempts faced
several obstacles. Regardless of the number of new titles created or of the degree to
which new or lower strata were encouraged, the symbols of status used by
the rulers were usually very similar to those
borne by the landed, hereditary aristocracy or by some religious elites. To create
an entirely new secular and "rational"
legitimation based on universalistic social
principles was either beyond their capacities or against their basic political interest,

or both. To do so would necessarily have enlarged the sphere of political participation and consequently increased the influence of various strata in the political institutions. The rulers therefore were usually unable to transcend the symbols of stratification and legitimation represented by the very strata whose influence they wanted to limit.

Thus the ability of the rulers to appeal to the lower strata of the population was obviously limited. Even more important, because of the emphasis on the superiority and worth of aristocratic symbols and values, many middle or new strata and groups tended to identify with them and consequently to "aristocratize" themselves.

Contradictions in the rulers' policies and goals developed in another direction as well. However tradition-bound the ruling elite may have been, its policies required the creation and propagation of more flexible "free" resources in various institutional fields, and the propagation of free resources gave rise to or promoted many religious, intellectual and legal groups whose value orientations differed from the traditional ones. Although in many societies all these groups were weak and succumbed to the influence of more conservative groups, in other cases—as in Europe—they developed into relatively independent centers of power, whose opposition to the rulers was only stimulated by the latter's conservative policies.

Similar contradictions also existed in the military, economic, and cultural spheres. Thus, for example, the growing needs of the Sassanid and Byzantine Empires in the last centuries of their respective Empires, for military manpower and economic resources, caused them to weaken the independent peasantry through mobilization and taxation, and to increase the power of the landed aristocracy. These policies undermined the very bases of their Empires. [9]

VII

But contradictions in the activities of the rulers and in the attitudes of the various strata did not constitute the only important foci of potential change in these political systems. Of no less importance was the possibility that the very organs created to implement the goals and policies of the rulers could develop goals and activities opposed to the basic premises of these political systems. The most important problem of this kind arose from the tendency of members of the bureaucratic administration to develop autonomous political orientations and activities.

First, the power that these bureaucracies acquired in societies in which there were usually but few "constitutional" limits on power and in which access to power was relatively limited, put the members of the bureaucracy in an especially privileged position. Second, the great emphasis, in these societies, on ascriptive symbols of status, necessarily "tempted" the members of the bureaucracy to use their power to acquire such symbols or to convert their positions into ascriptive, often hereditary status symbols. Third, the relatively low level of economic development and social differentiation permitted only limited development of special professional roles and only inadequate remuneration for them. The fact that in most of these societies the sale of offices was a very common expedient fully attests to this.

As a result of these conditions, members of the bureaucracies often tended to distort many of the customary or explicit rules and to divert many services to their own benefit or to that of some social groups with whom they were identified, and they tended to be both alienated from other groups in the society and oppressive toward them. In other words, they displaced the goal of service to the rulers and the various social strata, emphasizing goals of self-interest and aggrandizement instead.

On the other hand, the relative weakness of many political groups, and the great dependence of the bureaucracy on the rulers, often weakened and undermined the relative autonomy of the bureaucracy and brought about its total subjugation to the rulers. The latter could divert all the activities of the bureaucracy to their own exclusive use and prevent it from upholding any general rules for providing services to other strata in the society.

Thus the bureaucratic administration in these societies could, potentially, develop political orientations which were to some extent opposed to the basic premises of these polities and which generated changes that could not be contained within the institutional framework of the polity.

VIII

In these ways the very process of institutionalizing the political systems of these Empires created the possibility of change—change that could be absorbed within the institutional structures as well as change that undermined them.

The concrete reasons for these changes were usually series of events closely related to the various contradictions described above, the impingement of external events (such as wars, invasions, or fluctuations of trade routes), or interaction between internal and external processes.

In more concrete terms, the main factors generating processes of change in these Empires were (a) the continuous

needs of the rulers for different types of resources and especially their great dependence on various "flexible" resources; (b) the rulers' attempts to maintain their own positions of control, in terms of both traditional legitimation and effective political control over the more flexible forces in the society; (c) the development in most of these societies, of what has been called *Primat der Aussenpolitik*[10] and the consequent great sensitivity of the internal structure of these societies to various external pressures and to international political and economic developments; (d) the development of various autonomous orientations and goals among the major strata and their respective demands on the rulers. These changes were more intensive so far as the rulers emphasized very "expensive" goals that exhausted the available economic and manpower resources, or different strata developed strong, autonomous political orientations.

In such situations, the rulers' tendency to maintain strong control over the more differentiated strata could become predominant, thus increasing the power of traditional forces and orientations and sharpening the conflicts between the traditional and the more flexible, differentiated strata, so that the latter were destroyed or alienated from the rulers. The excessive demands of the rulers in such situations, the growing public expenditures and the consequent increase of taxation and inflation, if not checked, often struck hardest at those groups whose economic organization was based on more flexible resources.

At such times, a continuous flux of foreign elements—mercenaries, hirelings and personal helpers of the rulers—often invaded the centers of the realms. With the depletion of the native strata and the growing external and internal exigencies, they succeeded in infiltrating some of the most important political posts (such as those of eunuchs, military commandments and viziers) and finally in totally usurping the ultimate power. Foreign merchants sometimes played a similar role, as in Byzantium or the Ottoman Empire, where they gradually succeeded in monopolizing all the tradeposts abandoned by the depleted indigenous merchants.

Where, as in Europe, these economically and socially more active strata were not depleted, they became alienated from the rulers, their policies and the political institutions of the society, becoming hotbeds of revolt and change.

Such developments usually intensified the great sensitivity of the rulers and the society to various external economic and political changes (in trade routes or in international price movements, or through the intrusion of foreign elements). Usually, some combination of external and internal pressures and exigencies precipitated changes in the political systems of these Empires. Hence, the greater the intensity of these internal contradictions and the greater the pressure of external exigencies that could not be dealt with by internal forces, the more quickly changes accumulated in these societies.[11]

IX

Some salient features of these changes were: First, interaction between internal and external events was greatly dependent on the special systemic characteristics of these political systems. While naturally enough many external events, such as invasions, were entirely beyond the control of any given Empire, each polity constituted part of a relatively "international" environment. Because of its basically expansionist goals and its great dependence on free economic resources, each Empire was especially sensitive to various specific developments in its broader environment. Moreover, external events and influences could very easily become closely interwoven with many of the internal problems of these Empires.

Second, while some such exigencies and problems are common to all political systems, their *specific* nature depends on the structure of the institutional system. Thus, the special sensitivity of the centralized bureaucratic Empires to such exigencies and pressures and to international economic fluctuations was rooted first, in their rulers' great emphasis on military and expansionist goals and second, in their need for various "free" resources, the availability of which depended on the international economic situation.

Similarly, while all political systems are influenced by and dependent on the efficiency and political loyalty of their administrative personnel, these Empires were especially sensitive to the possibility that the bureaucracy might become "aristocratized," "parasitic," and inflated. This sensitivity was due first to the fact that the bureaucracy was the ruler's main instrument for implementing his goals and overcoming his political opponents, and second, to the constant danger that the free resources so necessary for the implementation of his goals might be depleted by the encroachments of various aristocratic or traditional groups and by the aristocratic tendencies of the bureaucracy.

These specific sensitivities also determined the location of the foci from which the impetus to change developed. Such foci tended to develop, in these political systems, mainly though certainly not only, in two basic spheres. One was that of economic and social organization. The level of differentiation of this sphere and the nature of its internal, autonomous organization was crucial to the development of different levels of resources on the one hand and different levels of political demand on the other.

The other sphere was that of values, or "culture." This sphere encompassed the legitimation of the system and of the ruler and, because the active cultural elites regulated many aspects of communication in the society, it greatly influenced the level of demands made on the central political institutions. While in many cases cultural values kept the level of such demands within the confines of the system, in other cases, as in the Islamic or European countries, values became a very important focus of charismatic innovations that might easily have undermined the existing system and created entirely new perceptions of the political sphere among many social groups.

Both economic organization and special cultural values strongly influenced the specific sensibilities of these systems and the generation of change within them. And when the two developed simultaneously, in the direction of either increasing or diminishing differentiation, their impact on the destiny of these political systems was of crucial importance.

Finally, the directions of change and the outcomes of the processes of change were to a very large extent set by the nature of the institutional systems of these Empires and by their internal problems. The range of political systems that arose on the ruins, as it were, of these Empires was relatively limited. Short of total disorganization, they could either "recede" into some type of relatively uncentralized patrimonial or feudal system (but not, for instance, into a city-state or a primitive system) or become a relatively more differentiated oligarchic

modern system (but not a mass democracy or a "canton-democracy").

X

The preceding analysis has drawn on illustrations only from the political sphere. But the same problems of institutionalization are found in any other major social sphere. We shall briefly illustrate this by analyzing the problems of institutionalization of religions and religious organizations in the Empires analyzed above.[12]

The religions that developed within the confines of these Empires were among the major world religious systems: the Mazdean religion in Iran, Confucianism, Taoism and Buddhism in China and India, Islam, Eastern Christianity in Byzantium, Catholicism in Europe and Spanish America and, later in Europe, Protestantism. These religions were usually developed through the activities of great religious innovators—either outstanding individuals or small groups of intense religious devotees—who attempted to create new cults and doctrines, and to spread and establish them in their respective societies.

Despite the great variety among these religions, they share important characteristics in some aspects of their value orientations, especially in their orientations to social reality.

The first such aspect is the breadth of the "group referent" of these religions; in most cases it was wider than any ascriptive or territorial group in these Empires. The basic religious group referents were the total society as the bearer of religious values, the specific religious community, and such wider potential religious collectivities as "all believers" or "all mankind."

The second major characteristic of these religious value orientations is their emphasis on individual moral or religious activism, stressing the devotee's commitment to certain religiously prescribed tenets and lines of action and to the endeavor to implement them in social life.

Third, each of these value systems developed relatively independent ideological systems, attempting to organize and evaluate, in terms of ultimate values, the social reality in which they grew up, to shape the world in terms of religious values and purposes, and to convert others to the same endeavor. The commitments imposed by these ideological systems were not simply embedded in ritual and religious acts but implied the development of more specific social or political activities.

All of these orientations denote the detachment of religious orientations from basic ascriptive symbols and communities. They were developed mainly in the centers of religious activity by the more active religious leaders and innovators. Among the broader strata the differentiation of religious activities and organizations was much more limited. Nevertheless these orientations did develop to some extent, constituting the basis for the potential willingness of these groups to join the new religions and for the possibility of their institutionalization.

From the interaction of the major religious orientations with the religious leaders' concrete goals and with the broader social and religious conditions prevalent in the society, as well as from the more specific relations with the rulers and other groups, developed the specific institutional characteristics of these religions, their organization into churches, orders and sects or the more diffuse organizational patterns characteristic of China.

But in all these Empires, the distinctiveness of the religious sphere was limited. On the one hand, there were many specialized religious organizations, such as temples, religious "foundations," priestly associations, sects, churches, and monastic orders, many of which were organized in a bureaucratic manner, and, in conjunction with these, many specialized religious roles—priests, preachers, monks, and occupants of different positions in ecclesiastical organizations and hierarchies. On the other hand, however, the worshipping community was, to a very large extent, either identical with local groups or closely related to them. Only within the various sects and monastic orders did a special type of religious community develop.

Neither the institutionalization nor the continuity of these religious systems was assured. The religious leaders who aimed to establish and institutionalize them within their respective societies faced several basic problems. The most general problem stemmed from the existence of relatively free-floating cultural and religious orientations and activities which were not embedded in ascriptive units. To maintain their place in the cultural order, religious organizations had to shape and direct these resources. They not only had to ensure the loyalty and adherence of their members, but they also had to compete for economic resources, manpower, allegiance and support, both with other religious groups and with other social spheres, especially the political and economic ones.

Thus, the leaders of these religions were faced with the internal problems of formulating and formalizing their creeds and traditions so as to articulate and organize them on a relatively differentiated cultural level, and also with the necessity of regulating and channelling the diverse dynamic orientations and elements that could develop within them.

In connection with these internal problems several policies and patterns of activity were developed by the religious elites and organizations in these societies. Perhaps the most important of these was the very extensive formalization and codification of religious traditions, as manifested in the codification of sacred books, in the development of schools devoted to interpretation of the texts, in the growth of special educational organizations for the spread of religious knowledge and in the elaboration of comprehensive ideologies.

The religious leaders also faced more concrete organizational and external problems. Because they depended, in all their endeavors, on both the rulers and the broader strata in the society, they developed several basic aims. The first was to gain full official recognition and protection from the State as the established religion or, at least as a secondary but recognized and protected one. The second aim was to maintain independence and autonomy in the performance of the major religious functions, especially in internal government, organization of activities, and recruitment of members. This meant relative autonomy in the propagation of the creed and the maintenance of shrines, temples, and educational institutions, as well as independent determination and transmission of the major religious values and dogma. The demands for autonomy were directed mainly against the rulers and the bureaucracy who, as we have seen earlier, usually aspired to control the activities of the religious elite and to incorporate them into the general framework of their administrative activities.

The third major political objective of the

religious elite, closely related to the first, was to preserve and extend the material bases (i.e., property) of the religious groups and institutions and to enhance their general social positions. A fourth objective, at least for some members of the religious elite, was to obtain positions of political and administrative influence.

XI

Whatever the success of the religious leaders in achieving these aims, the very institutionalization of these religions within the framework of their respective societies and polities could create continuous tension and give rise to several new problems.

The religious organizations needed the protection and help of the political institutions to establish and maintain their positions, organizations, and property, just as the political institutions needed the basic legitimation and support that could be provided only by the religious elite. This mutual dependence of relatively autonomous spheres could easily create many tensions, since each aimed to control the structural positions of the other and thus provide for its own needs. But whatever the scope of such conflicts and tensions, some *modus vivendi* was usually established, constituting a basic aspect of the institutionalization of these religions.

Thus in all of the societies studied, the religious elite upheld both the traditional legitimation of the rulers and supported, in principle, at least some of their political orientations and policies, despite the numerous conflicts over concrete issues arising between themselves and the political elite. Moreover, in most of the societies studied, the political participation of religious groups was, at least for certain periods of time, contained well within the basic framework of bureaucratic policy and institutions. In such cases these groups furthered the development of legitimate political struggle and contributed in this way to the continuity of the regime. The Mazdean Church in Persia, the Byzantine Church, and especially the Confucians and Buddhists in the Chinese Empire actively participated in politics and cooperated with the rulers. Thus they contributed, directly or indirectly, to the continuity of these systems. At the same time, the State provided important protection for the religious organizations.

But whatever the concrete *modus vivendi* between the rulers and any given religious elite or organization, in almost none of these societies—with the partial exception of Confucianism in China—did such mutual accommodation persist throughout the life of the Empire or of the religious organizations.

The very institutionalization of any such *modus vivendi* created the possibility for change both within the religions themselves and in their relations with other institutional spheres. The process of institutionalizing these religions and the necessity for continuous maintenance through varied policies and accommodations could easily enhance the contradictions inherent in the orientations of the religious leaders.

These contradictions were of several, often overlapping, kinds. One was between a "conservative" orientation that accepted the existing social order and the place of religion within it, on the one hand, and, on the other hand, a more radical orientation aiming to extend the autonomy of religious orientations and activities. Another was between an "otherworldly" emphasis stressing the perfection of purely religious attitudes and activities,

and a more active, this-worldly orientation aiming at the transformation of the world.

Such contradictions were rooted in the relative autonomy and independent historical origins of the religious sphere, in its continuous interaction with the political sphere and in the nature of its value orientations. All these characteristics could serve as foci of crystallization for new religious groups—sects, groups of devotees, or "free-lance" religious intellectuals upholding one or another of these orientations in its purity as against the more "compromise-ridden" activities of the established religious leaders and organizations. The religious elites, in the course of working out and implementing their various *modi vivendi* with the rulers, and in attempting to maintain their own interests, tended to alienate some of the religiously active elements as well as some of the broader strata.

Moreover, the relatively complex organizations of these religions, and the great importance of a formal written tradition and its exegesis, were fertile ground for the rise of various sectarian movements and orders. The possibility of sectarian development was also enhanced by the fact that in many of these societies several religious bodies and organizations competed with one another for predominance.

Hence within all these religions there developed many processes of change, which created new forms of religious organization. Some of these could be contained within the established religious framework, while others completely undermined it.

The same factors frequently also predisposed some of the religious groups and elites to develop more extreme political orientations and to participate—as in

China, Persia, or Byzantium—in radical political and social movements, such as peasant uprisings, urban movements, and conspiracies. Cooperation between popular movements and leaders of religious secret societies was a common characteristic of rebellions in China and to some extent Byzantium and of peasant uprisings in France.

In still other cases—or in the same societies under changing circumstances—these religious organizations could also influence processes of change in the political system by instigating or furthering the withdrawal of active social and political support from the ruling elites. In this way they undermined the political frameworks of the Empires and indirectly also the bases of the *modus vivendi* between political and religious institutions.

The exact strength and direction of these processes of change depended greatly on the basic value orientations and institutional characteristics of the religions and on the nature of their struggles and accommodations with the rulers and other centers of power in the society.

But the direction of these changes was not random, nor were these changes limitless. Organizationally, religious institutions could either undergo what might be called the "ossification" and "indrawing" of existing churches, as in the case of the Eastern Church after the fall of the Byzantine Em . . . sects and more independent religious activities, be transformed into less homogeneous and monolithic, more differentiated structures, as was the case in Western Christianity, especially in Protestantism, and to a lesser extent in early and "middle" Islam. The effect of these changes on religious orientations is either to enhance the tendency towards "other-worldliness," social passivity, withdrawal and mysticism, or to encourage more active and differentiated this-worldly activity.[13]

XII

The preceding analysis of the processes of change in the centralized Empires and in the major religions that developed within them is intended to illustrate the ways in which the institutionalization of a political, a religious, or any other social system in itself creates the potentialities and directions of change.[14]

The institutionalization of any social system means that certain norms, sanctions and organizations must be set up, and that policies through which these norms can be upheld and applied to a relatively large and complex variety of social situations must be implemented. These things are done by people who are placed in or attempt to achieve strategic positions and who aspire to certain goals. The new norms regulate the provision of various resources from other parts of the society to these power positions and to the new organizations, some of the relations among the different groups in the society, and the obligations of the occupants of these positions toward various groups in the society.

While the occupants of these positions naturally attempt to set up norms in accord with their own values, goals and interests, they also define certain norms shared by a number of groups. Very often they legitimize these norms by values that are purportedly shared, to some extent, by a large part of the society and symbolized by themselves. Hence, such values tend to be binding on the rulers themselves.

But whatever the success of such attempts to establish common norms and legitimize them in terms of common values and symbols, these norms are probably never fully accepted by the entire society. Most groups within any society or collectivity tend to exhibit some autonomy in terms of their attitudes toward any such institutionalization, and they vary greatly in the extent of their willingness or ability to provide the resources demanded by the system. While for very long periods of time a great majority of the members of a given society may be to some degree identified with the values and norms of the system and willing to provide it with the resources it needs, other tendencies also develop. Some groups—like the aristocracy in the case of the Empires discussed above—may be greatly opposed to the very premises of the institutionalization of a given system, may share its values only to a very small extent, and may accept these norms only as the least among evils and as binding on them only in a very limited sense.

Others may share these values and accept the norms to a greater degree but, like the cultural and economic elites or sects, may look on themselves as the more appropriate repositories of these same values, may oppose the concrete level at which the norms are institutionalized by the elite in power, and may attempt to interpret them in different ways. Others again may develop new interpretations of existing values and strive for a change in the very bases of the institutional order. Hence any institutional system is never fully "homogeneous," that is, fully accepted or accepted to the same degree by all those participating in it, and these different orientations all may become foci of conflict and of potential institutional change.

Even more important, from the point of view of our analysis, is that whatever the initial attitudes of any given group to the basic premises of the institutional system, these may greatly change after the initial

institutionalization of the system. Any institutionalization necessarily entails efforts to maintain the boundaries of the system, through continuous attempts to mobilize resources from different groups and individuals, and to maintain the legitimacy of the values, symbols and norms of the system. But continuous implementation of these policies may affect the positions of different groups in the society, giving rise to continuous shifts in the balance of power among them and in their orientations to the existing institutional system and its values.

Moreover, the institutionalization of any system usually creates new collectivities and organizations, such as the bureaucratic organizations in the centralized Empires. These organizations necessarily develop needs, interests, and orientations of their own which may impinge on various other groups and institutional spheres.

Similarly, changes in the balance of forces within the system also facilitate the development and "maturation" of certain inherent tendencies in the structure and orientation of key groups and elites, as in the tendencies of some religious groups to develop and establish wider universalistic orientations and membership units, which may then develop beyond the basic premises of the system.

These processes may be intensified by the systemic relations between any given institutional framework or sphere and other spheres within the society. Whatever the degree of integration of the "total" society, systemic relations between, e.g., the political and the economic, or the political and the kinship systems, are inherent in any on-going society. But as has been so often pointed out, the basic or predominant orientations and norms regulating each of these institutions differ to some extent. For example, family and kinship units tend to emphasize particularistic, diffuse, and ascriptive orientations while economic units emphasize universalism and achievement.[15]

These different institutional spheres, represented by the structurally patterned activities of occupants of the major positions within them, attempt to maintain their autonomy and tend to make contradictory demands on different groups to provide them with the necessary resources. Each may look for support from different groups in the society, thus exacerbating potential conflicts among the various groups, changing their relative strengths and possibly undermining the premises of a given institutional system.

These contradictions, conflicts and shifts in the balance of power may lead to the depletion of the resources needed to maintain a given system or give rise to the crystallization of new foci of resources and orientations which may in turn seek to create a new institutional system.

Events leading to different processes of change, as has been pointed out before, also affect the relations between any given institutional system and its external environment. Each institutional system is especially sensitive, in terms of dependence on resources and maintenance of its own boundaries, to certain aspects of its relations with its environment.

XIII

Thus we conclude that the institutionalization of a system creates the possibility that "anti-systems," or groups with negative orientations toward its premises, will develop within it. While the nature and strength of such anti-systems may vary, as between different institutional (i.e., religious, political) systems and between different types within each, and while they may often remain latent for very long periods of time, they also constitute important foci of change, under propitious conditions.

The existence of such contradictions or conflicts among the different institutional spheres and among different groups does not, of course, preclude the possibility that the system will maintain its boundaries more or less continuously, through a hierarchy of norms and accommodation or partial insulation of different subsystems, and that a definite order and stable relations among the system's parts will persist. But the possibility of conflict and potential change is always present, rooted in the very process of institutionalization, and the direction and occurrence of change depend heavily on the nature of this process.

Just as the predilection for change is necessarily built into any institutional system, so the direction and scope of change are not random but depend, as we have shown in discussing the processes of change in the Empires and in the great religions, on the nature of the system generating the change, on its values, norms and organizations, on the various internal forces operating within it and on the external forces to which it is especially sensitive because of its systemic properties. These various forces naturally differ between religious and political institutions and among different societies, but sensitivity to these forces and the tendency to change are inherent in all of them.

The analysis presented above does not pretend to solve all the problems in analyzing social change; we have not discussed the mechanisms of change, nor the relations between changes at different institutional levels of a given society. But at least we have indicated that for conceptual tools adequate to the analysis of change we need not necessarily go beyond systematic sociological analysis; rather, a full explication of systematic sociological concepts can provide a fruitful initial step for the analysis of change.

Notes

1. See Wilbert E. Moore, "A Reconsideration of Theories of Social Change," *American Sociological Review*, 25 (December 1960), pp. 810-818, and Kingsley Davis, "The Myth of Functional Analysis as a Special Method in Sociology and Anthropology," *American Sociological Review*, 26 (December, 1959), pp. 752-772.

2. See, for instance, Ronald Philip Dore, "Function and Cause," *American Sociological Review*, 26 (December 1961), pp. 843-853; Kenneth E. Bock, "Evolution, Function and Change," *American Sociological Review*, 28 (April 1963), pp. 229-237.

3. Following Alvin W. Gouldner and Helen P. Gouldner, *Modern Sociology, An Introduction to the Study of Human Interaction*, New York: Harcourt, Brace, 1963, p. 484; see also Harry M. Johnson, *Sociology, A Systematic Introduction*, New York: Harcourt, Brace, 1960, chapter 2; Talcott Parsons, *The Social System*, Glencoe, Ill.: The Free Press, 1951, chapters 2 and 5.

4. Some parallel indications can be found in Thomas F. O'Dea, "Sociological Dilemmas, Five Paradoxes of Institutionalization," in Eduard A. Tiryakin (ed.), *Sociological Theory, Values and Sociocultural Change, Essays in Honor of Pitirim A. Sorokin*, New York: The Free Press of Glencoe, 1963, pp. 71-91; see also Neil J. Smelser, *Theory of Collective Behavior*, New York: The Free Press of Glencoe, 1963, especially chapters 2 and 3.

5. See Samuel N. Eisenstadt, *The Political Systems of Empires*, New York: The Free Press of Glencoe, 1963, and "The Causes of Disintegration and Fall of Empires—Sociological and Historical Analyses," *Diogenes*, 34 (Summer 1961), pp. 82-158.

6. See Shmuel N. Eisenstadt, "Religious Organizations and Political Process in Centralized Empires," *The Journal of Asian Studies*, 21 (May 1962), pp. 271-294, and *The Political Systems of Empires, op. cit.*

7. For a fuller exposition of this statement, see Eisenstadt, *The Political Systems of Empires.*

8. *Ibid.*, chapter 7.

9. *Ibid.*, chapter 12.

10. This term has been often used by F. Altheim in his studies of Roman and Sassanid history; see, for instance, F. Altheim, *Gesicht von Abend und Morgen*, Frankfurt: Fischer Verlag, 1955, passim.

11. See Eisenstadt, *The Political Systems of Empires*, chapters 7 and 10.

12. See Eisenstadt, "Religious Organizations and Political Process," *op. cit.*

13. *Ibid.*

14. The same basic considerations are applied to role analysis in Shmuel N. Eisenstadt, Dov Weintraub and Nina Toren, "Analysis of Role Change," Jerusalem: The Hebrew University, Department of Sociology, Technical Note No. 7.

15. See Alvin W. Gouldner, "Reciprocity and Autonomy in Functional Theory," in Llewellyn Gross (ed.), *Symposium on Sociological Theory*, Evanston, Ill.: Row Peterson, 1959, pp. 241-271, and Gideon Sjoberg, "Contradictory Functional Requirements and Social Systems," *The Journal of Conflict Resolution*, 4 (June 1960), pp. 198-258.

34.

Christian T. Jonassen

FUNCTIONS OF VOLUNTARY ASSOCIATIONS IN DEVELOPING NATIONS

Max Weber's essay, *The Protestant Ethic and the Spirit of Capitalism*, started a discussion which has captured the interest and stimulated efforts of scholars for many decades (Sombart, 1902; Weber, 1930; Brentano, 1916; Tawney, 1926; Fanfani, 1930; Warner, 1930; Troeltsch, 1931; Jonassen, 1947; Ashton, 1948; Samuelson, 1957; Smelser, 1959). As an explanation of relationships between religion and a specific form of economic system, the Weber-initiated dialogue poses an antithesis to Marx's position that "relations of production" determine the superstructure of ideas. While often regarded as germane largely for the sociology of knowledge, this long intellectual research effort and discussion is also instructive for the light it throws on the social, cultural, economic, and psychological factors which were involved in European development. This literature plus that which concerns currently developing countries in Asia and Africa (Wilson and Wilson, 1945; Van der Kroef, 1956; Singer, 1956; Lerner, 1958; Hauser, 1959; Kahl, 1959; Kennedy, 1962; Jonassen, 1947; Jonassen, 1973; Eisenstadt, 1966; Inkeles, 1966; Weiner, 1966; Myrdal, 1968; Meadows and Miz-

rucki, 1969; Rogers and Stenning, 1969) enable us to make some generalizations about the nature of development and the factors which create obstacles to, or facilitate, the process. These sources demonstrate that development involves elemental processes of great complexity and scope and that those who would move from a traditional to a modern society must: relate themselves differently to the environment, shifting from an organic to an inorganic energy base; they must alter their ontology, accepting a different conitive base for their relief system; they must reorganize their social structure, enlarging its scale and complexity; they must adopt new values, forsaking old ones or integrating them somehow with the new values; indeed, they must psychologically refashion traditional man and his energizing and motivational system. The all-encompassing task of development requires the involvement of all sectors of society and different types of social units. This paper examines the nature and position of voluntary associations in the historic process of modernization and development.

Voluntary organizations in development

Characteristically, as a society evolves from a traditional to a modern type, the functions and social relationships that were determined by family, caste, tribe, or religious body are progressively freed from the dictates of the customs and mores of these groups. The result is greater perso-

From Christian T. Jonassen, "Functions of Voluntary Associations in Developing Nations." *Rural Sociology* 39, Winter 1974, pp. 529-535, with permission of the publisher.

This article originated as a working paper for a seminar at the Third World Congress for Rural Sociology, Baton Rouge, Louisiana, August 1972. It was revised and presented at the Annual Meeting of the American Sociological Association, August 1973.

nal freedom; however, if this freedom is not to be bought at the price of anomie and alienation, the instrumentalities of social control, motivation, and psychological support must be replaced with other support and control systems. Voluntary associations enable many of these vital functions to be performed outside the traditional institutions. Characteristics of voluntary associations may also be adopted by traditional institutions as, for example, in the United States where religious, political, and educational functions are performed largely by groups that have many features of voluntary associations. Even the family, especially that part of it which is outside of the family of orientation, has been largely voluntarized (Sussman and Burchinal, 1962).

America, in its developmental stage, turned to voluntary associations to solve most problems. This was noted early by Alexis de Tocqueville. He observed in 1831 that Americans of all ages, all conditions, and all dispositions constantly formed associations and that "wherever at the head of some new undertaking you see the government in France, or a man of rank in England, in the United States you will be sure to find an association" (de Tocqueville, 1946: 106). Many others have suggested that the tendency to form associations is a peculiar American trait, but observers of the situation in modern towns of Africa (Banton, 1956; Clement, 1956) found that "the most striking characteristics of these modern towns is the very large number and variety of voluntary associations. These include a host of new political, religious, recreational, and occupational associations" (Little, 1957: 581-582).

The rapid increase and importance of voluntary associations in business, industry, labor, science, and religion were also present in England in its period of rapid economic development in the late eighteenth and early nineteenth centuries (Smelser, 1959; Warner, 1930). Historical and present events thus suggest that voluntary associations evolve as coping responses to the problems and challenges of development.

Development is a process of social change which involves cultural and social systems as well as personality systems; because only individuals can respond to stimuli, evaluate, and act, what occurs in cultural and social systems is reciprocally related to events in the personality system. An analysis of the voluminous historical and current research on development in various parts of the world reveals that these motivations and habituations seem to be necessary for development—a sense of responsibility, method, and discipline in lifestyles; rational work as a calling; and rational pursuit of duty in the interest of a higher value, such as God, the state, the class, or the tribe. Where development occurs, there is encouragement of systematic pursuit of economic values and the cultivation of worldly asceticism. The impact of new values is apparent not only in the individual psychology of motivation and behavior, but also in the evolving social structure because the ethical and value systems provide for support, legitimization, and encouragement of the formation of certain institutions and structural forms that are essential for the economic development of modern society (Jonassen, 1963; Jonassen, 1973).

Much field research as well as laboratory investigation has determined that cognitive, attitudinal, and behavioral changes are not achieved through a one-way process where the person is merely a target for environmental stimuli and mass communication. In the Sherifs' apt phrase, "Man is both an agent and a target of social change"; attitudinal change is, therefore, most efficiently and permanently achieved when the individual is an active participant with others (Lazarsfeld, Berelson, and Gaudet, 1948; Hyman and Sheatsley, 1964; McGuire, 1969; Klapper, 1960; Sherif and Sherif, 1969). In a series of experiments the Sherifs showed that "attitudes formed during interaction as reference groups take shape and function in problem situations permitting numerous possible modes of reaching highly appealing goals" (Sherif and Sherif, 1969: 477). Shannon and Shannon (1968: 69-70), applying Sutherland's "differential association theory" to the assimilation of migrants to the city, found that:

Assimilation is more likely to take place if interaction is intense. Migrants engaging in primary groups interacting with members of the larger society are more likely to be assimilated than those who have had only contacts of a secondary group nature.

Based on research of the modernization process among workers and peasants in six developing countries, Inkeles (1966: 138-141) concluded that these changes were required for modernization: the transformation of the nature of man; a change of spirit with new ways of thinking, feeling, and acting; and a readiness for new experience and an openness to innovation. Studies of the acceptance of innovation in Africa, South America, and the United States have shown that it is most acceptable when it is introduced by example and precepts in face-to-face groups where the credentials of the innovator are known and where the consequences of its acceptance can be checked by personal observation and experience (Little, 1957; Banton, 1956; Rogers and Stenning, 1969). These conditions are facilitated in voluntary associations of peers in a community

where results can be checked and demonstrated.

Lerner (1958) found in studies of developing countries of the Middle East that an impediment to development was the "constructive self," the inability of traditional man to imagine himself in other than his traditional roles or of holding opinions over a large number of issues that arise in places other than his immediate environment. A similar impediment was noted by Inkeles (1966: 141). That participation in voluntary associations as an actor or participant observer facilitates the restructuring of the self-image of individuals in a developing country has been demonstrated by McClelland's results in India (McClelland, 1966: 31-36).

Restructuring of the self-image is closely related to the problems of participation. Development requires the mobilization of actors in economic and civic affairs, but traditional man has habitually regarded public matters as the activity of rulers, priests, and other elites and none of his business (Lerner, 1958; Banfield, 1958). New role definitions depend on a new self-image which further encourages participation and the cultivation of skills in the many facets of activity necessary in development. Through participation in voluntary associations a person can learn that it is proper and effective for him also to have opinions on a great variety of matters and for him to participate in decision making.

Development requires belief in the calculability of the world and confidence that man can master nature and events by planning and following a rational, deliberate pursuit of goals (Hauser, 1959; Lerner, 1958; Kahl, 1969; Smith and Inkeles, 1966; Kluckhohn and Strodtbeck, 1961). Success in the achievement of goals of voluntary associations pursued according to rational, orderly, and scientific procedures can demonstrate the efficacy of such procedures. For example, the Cooperative Extension program in the United States, by using voluntary organizations as transmission belts and demonstration units for scientific information, has been enormously successful in raising agricultural productivity in this country. Such activity might also demonstrate another idea crucial for development; namely, the belief that rewards will be according to competence and contribution, and not according to ascribed positions or to the fortuitous whims of elites, fate, spirits, and luck.

Colonial masters monopolized leadership and neglected training of native specialists in economic, social, and political affairs. When they departed, they left these countries bereft of leaders and specialists in industry, commerce, and education. This leadership void was apparent in former French possessions, such as Viet Nam, Laos, and Cambodia, and in Dutch Indonesia. Research in Nigeria indicates that voluntary associations can be effective settings for the recruitment and training of leaders in the processes of democratic participation and decision making (Bogdan, 1969: 239-240).

Hauser (1959) and others see the cultural, racial, economic, and linguistic *pluralism* of many developing nations as being great impediments to development because development requires an increase in scale of economic, cultural, and political units (Wilson and Wilson, 1945; Eisenstadt, 1966; Weiner, 1966). Voluntary associations can be instrumental in increasing structural scale by building a national consciousness and freeing man from the constraints, blinders, and myopia produced by local parochialism and narrow loyalties to family, clan, or village as shown by Little (1957) and Bogdan (1969) in Africa and McClelland (1966) in India. Voluntary associations can thus function as vital ganglia for the evolution of ever-widening loyalties and networks of social and economic relationships so essential for development and nation-building.

In conclusion

I have taken a positive view of the role of local organizations in development. There is, however, a need to end with a word of caution. The positive possibilities and achievements of local organizations in the process of development are great, but we should also be aware that intended results will not automatically be realized; indeed, voluntary associations because they are such powerful social instrumentalities can produce results not intended by their creators. Though they can contribute to political stability and alleviate social disorganization, they may, by bringing together the disaffected, solidify and intensify hostilities and contribute to instability and a revolutionary situation. While local organizations can promote modern roles, attitudes, and aspirations, they may also raise expectations beyond the possibility of achievement, thus creating severe dissatisfaction. Another possibility is what Jean Rouch has called "super-tribalization," a virtual resuscitation of the tribal system (Little, 1957) which inhibits growth of civic loyalty or responsibility for the individuals' towns of residence (Busia, 1950) and for their developing nation. A rejection of everything Western may also develop as a reaction and defense of a group's self-esteem under pressure of the developing consciousness and knowledge of developed countries.

There is great unanimity among students of development that development requires the very transformation of traditional man—the playing of new social roles, the generating of new values, habits, and ways of thinking, and the alteration of social structures and relationships. Research on man's motivations and cognitive processes shows that such alterations take place most efficiently and permanently when the actor is involved in the interaction process in a social setting, where all elements and environmental stimuli in-

volved become variables in the interaction process. Evidence from research conducted in developed countries, as well as data from developing nations of Africa, South America, and Asia, supports the conclusion that voluntary associations are the type of social systems which meet these requirements and have a record of success in facilitating the social, cultural, and psychological processes involved in development.

35.

J. Allen Broyles

THE JOHN BIRCH SOCIETY: A MOVEMENT OF SOCIAL PROTEST OF THE RADICAL RIGHT[1]

In this paper a social-psychological analysis is undertaken of the organization, ideology, and activities of the John Birch Society, one of the major organizations described in current journalistic literature as "radical right" or as "right-wing extremist."

Among the proliferation of groups within this general movement it is by far the most rationally organized. It has a well defined top leadership position (Robert Welch); a small, less well defined "kitchen cabinet" of administrative assistants and advisors; a Council, the functions of which are "to lend prestige to the Society, to offer advice to Robert Welch, and to select his eventual successor;" a sizeable office staff

(about 44 full-time workers at the "home office" in Belmont, Massachusetts); a large group of organizers (roughly 30 paid, and 100 volunteer, "coordinators") who organize and supervise approximately 60,000 local members (who are gathered into chapters of from ten to twenty. members located in nearly all the states, but concentrated in Southern California, Texas, and the Mid-West). Its most important organizational publication (the monthly *Bulletin*) is geared directly to members to provide them with current interpretation of national and world issues and events and with suggested individual and local chapter agenda.

Activities of members of the Birch Society are motivated by the conviction that most of the leaders of our major economic, religious, educational, and political institutions are willing or unwitting Communist agents. The activities of the Society, directed largely through the

From J. Allen Broyles, "The John Birch Society: A Movement of Social Protest of the Radical Right," *Journal of Social Issues* 19-2, April 1963, pp. 51-62; reprinted in J. Allen Broyles *The John Birch, Anatomy of a Protest,* Beacon Press, 1964, rev. paperback, 1966.

monthly *Bulletin*, are designed to expose, dramatize, and if possible thwart what they perceive to be instances of Communist subversion within these major institutions, both locally and nationally.

The Society, organized in late 1958, came to public prominence in the Spring of 1961 as awareness of its fairly widespread organizational accomplishments and of the more extreme opinions of its founder, Robert Welch, were brought to public attention by the press.

Research approach

My overall research plan blended an examination of bibliographical resources with a field study. Many of the publications of the John Birch Society were examined with particular reference to the content as well as the formal aspects of the framework of the ideology as exhibited in its presentation. Field research was undertaken in a number of cities across the country. Using a mail questionnaire, a preliminary survey[2] was made of a number of cities which journalistic reports had identified as centers of activity of local chapters of the Birch Society. The cities selected by these criteria were Gloucester, Little Rock, El Paso, Dallas, Los Angeles, San Diego, Santa Barbara, Phoenix, and Wichita.[3] Spending an average of a week in each city during early 1962, I interviewed observers within the cities to determine more specifically the activities in which Birch Society members had participated. I interviewed those perceived as active participants in local Birch Society controversies on both sides. The procedure of asking each interviewee involved in the conflict to identify the leaders of both sides served to "legitimize" for each of the opposing groups my interviews with the other side. Surprisingly enough, Birch Society members were fairly willing to be interviewed and greatly appreciated a chance to be heard, even by one they suspected to be on the fringe of the "other" side.

The first half of the interview, which in its entirety lasted an average of two hours, was more or less open-ended. With a Birch Society member or Birch-like person, this part of the interview opened with his analysis of why we have this "upsurge of conservatism," continued with his attempt to sharpen how and why he came to join in this movement, and concluded with his report of the activities and motivation of local or national Birch Society opponents. With a Birch Society opponent or "observer," this first part of the interview opened with his description of the local activities and conflicts in which local Birch Society members had participated, continued with an attempt to sharpen how and why people were attracted to the Birch Society, and concluded with his estimate of the motivation of local Birch Society members and leaders. The second half of the interview consisted in the administration of a questionnaire drawn from the Dogmatism and Opinionation Scales of Rokeach (7 and 8) and from the standard F Scale and F Scale reversals discussed by Christie (2). It was administered when the person being interviewed was clearly identified as an active participant in local controversy involving the Birch Society, and when the setting was such that the questionnaire could be administered.

A review of conclusions drawn from the study

The following general conclusions and interpretations were derived from an evaluation of the research data collected in the study.

1. The Birch Society functions as a "fundamentalist reaction" to its social set-

ting. As in many other periods of history we find this era involving the American social system in greatly accelerated alteration and realignment of its social, economic and political institutions. In the midst of such changes there have often arisen protests from those seeking or dispossessed of positions of influence or of cherished values. When such protests urge a return to idealized institutional structures and arrangements, values, and beliefs of the immediate or distant past, they may be characterized as conservative or radical right. Parsons identifies a tendency toward political extremism under conditions such as these. Thus in the case of the present radical right-wing movement, it may be appropriately labeled a "fundamentalist reaction" (6, p. 119-20).

2. The top leadership of the Society is charismatic. The criteria of charismatic leadership elaborated by Weber[4] deal with the recognition of charismatic authority, the necessity "success" of charismatic leadership, the "staff" of disciples, the refusal to exploit charisma financially or to engage in mundane economic activity, and the radical reorientation of followers. The nontraditional and nonrational charismatic authority of Welch is accepted by most of his followers to a fairly high degree. So are the other four criteria with the exception of the modifications necessitated by the inclusion of a rational-bureaucratic staff.

The conclusion that Welch's leadership is charismatic also serves to illuminate one of the appeals of the Society. Our social system setting could be described in Weberian terms as undergoing a transformation of traditionally legitimated institutional structures, arrangements, and values through the accelerating intrusion of rationally legitimated values and bureaucratic institutional structures. These structures are being further "sharpened"

by continued application of rationally legitimated analysis and criticism. This process has uprooted many older elites. Predictably, many among these older elites have not as yet acknowledged either the legitimacy of rational-bureaucratic leadership or its capability of dealing with the overshadowing threat of Communism. In a setting where defenders of traditionally legitimated institutions and values see themselves being by-passed, where they look with distrust upon rational-bureaucratic leadership, and where they look with fear toward Communism, an anti-Communist charismatic leader who is, by definition, largely impervious to the thrusts of suspect rationality, has considerable social-psychological appeal.

3. The organizational-leadership structure of the Society is an unstable mixture of both charismatic and rational-bureaucratic elements. This "mixture," which is a distinctive feature of Welch's "staff" and the major qualification of his charismatic leadership, has both strengths and weaknesses. The major strength of this paid rational-bureaucratic staff (administrative assistants, office staff, and coordinators) is its ability to multiply the efforts of Welch with a fairly high rate of efficiency. Its major weakness for the Society is the alternative to "loyalty" toward the charismatic leadership of Welch which it presents for these crucial staff members. The latter have the alternative and implicit criteria of rationality and functional utility. Thus, if Welch is perceived to be abandoning norms of rationality (however narrowly conceived) by members of his rational-bureaucratic staff or, if they perceive the organizational structure of the Society to be faltering in its functional utility, these individuals can feel legitimated in their withdrawal from the Society.

In addition, it was noted that the

rational-bureaucratic leadership labors under the strains of trying to direct chapter leaders superior to them in social status, as well as having to possess, or at least to exhibit, a loyalty and an emotionalism toward the "cause" and toward Welch, and of trying to control and channel the emotional fervor of those attracted to or aroused by Welch and his Society.

I would predict that the future of the Society depends upon the nature of the probable shifts in the relative strength of the inherently unstable combination of charismatic and rational-bureaucratic structures of leadership. If the Society resumes its growth, the rational-bureaucratic structure will tend to increase both numerically and in its strength. If the Society continues to shrink, and if financial resources are consequently lost, the rational-bureaucratic leaders will dissipate leaving the charismatic leadership standing alone.

4. In its charismatic fervor, in the stringency and ultimate sanctions claimed for its ideological beliefs, and in its determination to destroy Communism, the Birch Society is classified, within the typology of Yinger (10, pp. 142-55), as an *aggressive* sect.

The future of this organizational stance depends upon the turn of the ideology. Yinger maintains that an aggressive stance cannot long be maintained by a sect against such strong opposition as the Society has provoked within both liberal and conservative camps (10, p. 153). Therefore it seems reasonable to predict that if members withdraw seeking what they hope might be more "successful" radical right-wing leadership, the rational-bureaucratic leadership will follow, leaving Welch and his most faithful followers engaged in "ritualistic aggression."[5]

By "ritualistic aggression" is meant that, in the face of such determined op-

position the leaders and members of the Society will probably give up hope for success in their ideological goals and will "just go through the motions" in their defense of their ideology and in pursuit of their activities of social protest. As the opposition senses this abandonment of hope by Welch and his followers, we can expect their concern with the Society to decline. Ritualistic aggression could serve two functions. It would allow leaders and members of the Society to retain both a sense of remaining true to their convictions and of "doing something" about them. Secondly, it would be less threatening to those who opposed what was being said or done, so as to arouse no more than token, or similarly ritualistic opposition in them. This token opposition would, in turn, give the ritually aggressive Birchers further confirmation that they were "getting the job done."

5. The activity and ideology of social protest represents the major appeal of the Society. The leaders and members interviewed responded to the secondary appeals of the "push" of the social system setting and to the "pull" of the social-psychological "solutions" offered by the Society for the crises and strains of this setting, to the charismatic leadership of Welch, to the hierarchical organization of the Society, and to the reference group attraction of socially superior Council members and chapter leaders as well as peers.[6] But none of these appeals appears to have been primary. *The major appeal for the members and leaders interviewed appears to be the ideology and related activity which are intended to expose, protest, and if possible, destroy Communism wherever the leaders or members of the Society perceive it.*

6. The ideology of the Society is substantively and formally logic-tight and, characteristically, those who affirm it are

highly closed-minded. The substantive ideological framework is characterized as logic-tight because, despite the internal logical consistency of their cluster of interpreting concepts, there is no provision made by its adherents for an analysis of the validity of these concepts.

Within the formal ideological and psychological aspects of this framework, one finds that both a characteristically closed-minded perception of "other"[7] and a closed-minded inability to separate data relevant to a situation from the source so classified,[8] contribute to the rigid and invulnerable character of the total ideology for the leaders and members of the Society interviewed.

7. Within the troubled setting of the American social system their ideology provided the social-psychological appeals of certainty, understanding, and of direction; a sense of self-righteousness for being on the "right" side in "the central conflict of our era"; and a sense of superiority over those on the "wrong" side. Furthermore, the ideological redefinition of the sources of frustration avoids displacement and "justifies" direct aggression toward otherwise invulnerable objects of frustration.

8. As a fundamentalist reaction, the Society fails to serve its manifest function and none of its latent functions appear to be constructive; in fact some are latently dysfunctional even for its own existence.

The analysis of the direction in which the Society's organizational structure may move, its aggressive stance, and its dysfunctionality as a fundamentalist reaction are of course contingent upon the maintenance of what can be described, at best, as the tentative stability of the international setting of our social system. In short, significant losses in either military or nonmilitary competition with Soviet Russia could thrust the Birch Society, or some fellow anti-Communist organization with a similar conspiratorial view, into a strong position politically.

9. The conflict in which the Society engages as it pursues its ideology and activity of social protest is characteristically noncommunal. Because the present *Journal* issue deals with other radical-right groups within the American social system, an important issue to be considered concerns the modes of conflict in which each group characteristically engages. Therefore we shall turn to a somewhat more extended discussion of the characteristic Birch Society mode of conflict.

Social conflict can be defined as follows: social conflict involves the existence of two or more parties who perceive themselves to be in opposition as they try overtly either to gain their own goals or oppose those of the other's through communal or noncommunal modes involving direct or indirect[9] contact, and by exercise of rational argument and/or political or armed force. It should be noted that pro- and anti-Birch Society persons or groups who do oppose one another, do not always come into conflict with one another.

There are four major characteristics of the conflicts which most typically arise between the members and leaders of the Birch Society and those whom they choose or who select them as opponents. They have to do with the tone, the intent, the "progress," and the "resolution" of the conflict. They all spring from the fact that the conflict tends to be non-communal;[10] that is, the conflicting parties do not perceive one another to be pursuing legitimate goals or utilizing legitimate means.[11] As one party perceives the other to be seeking such illegitimate goals through equally illegitimate means, in the expression of an ideological belief—or analysis—or in undertaking relevant action, conflict is initiated.

A. Tone of the conflict

Since each party sees the other as destroying valued legitimate goals and pursuing, in their place, illegitimate goals by illegitimate means, neither party feels obligated to use what it holds to be legitimate institutionalized means in contending with the other. Therefore, the parties often move into conflict with one another, using means which they themselves hold to be illegitimate. Thus the character of their attacks upon the other confirms each in their initial perceptions of the other as outside the bounds of legitimate goals and means. As a consequence the tone of the conflict becomes acrimonious at its onset.

B. Intent of the conflict

Each party perceives the other as so far beyond the pale of legitimacy, in their pursuit of mutually exclusive goals, that little hope is entertained that the other will "see the light" and reverse his position. It follows that the intent of the conflict is propagandistic and is not designed to resolve points of disagreement between the conflicting parties, but to seek allies from the uncommitted public. For the public must be "alerted" and mobilized against the "evil" and "error" of the other party and in support of the "goodness" and "truth" of the first party. The intent of the conflict, therefore, is to convince the public, not the opposing party.

C. The "progress" of the conflict

The progress of communal conflict, in which there is agreement upon legitimate goals and means and in which each party perceives the other as abiding by them, sharply contrasts with the progress of a noncommunal conflict. Communal conflict tends to start with just a few issues and at a fairly low level of intensity; then to get somewhat acrimonious as the conflict and the issues in question build up; and finally, as the parties proceed to resolve their points of disagreement, to reduce the intensity of the tone and the number of issues at stake in the conflict. The progress of the issues and tone of communal conflict can be conceptualized as two vertical and parallel bell-shaped curves in union at both the bottom, as conflict is initiated, and at the top, as the conflict is resolved.

In contrast, the "progress" of issues and tone of noncommunal conflict can be conceptualized as an inverted pyramid with no top. Conflict starts as one party perceives the other as revealing its "actual" and illegitimate goals and either begins or quickly becomes and remains at a highly acrimonious tone. Since there is no intent to resolve issues, they tend to increase at a geometric rate and consist only of propagandistic charges and countercharges as each party seeks allies from the uncommitted public. Allies so attracted are urged to accept the "complete package," interpreting the opposite party as wholly illegitimate in its goals and means and the chosen party as wholly legitimate in its goals and means. The recruitment of allies in this manner tends to set the stage for future non-communal conflict within a given community, involving an ever-broadening base of participation. The tone of the conflict begins and remains at almost the same highly acrimonious level. Logically (in terms of the "logic" of the conflicting parties), the perception of the other, by each party, as totally evil in his choice of goals and means would lead to assassination or warfare.[12] But, with rare exceptions, the participants in the non-communal conflicts which were observed between the members of the Birch Society and their opponents are socially adjusted to the degree of having internalized the norms of conflict acceptable within American society. The highest pitch of conflict condoned by the norms of our society, and likewise by our law enforcement agencies, is that commonly observed near the close of a long and bitterly contested political campaign. This is the tone with which internal noncommunal conflict within this country, throughout most of its history and at the present time, begins and remains.

D. The "resolution" of the conflict

There is no resolution of noncommunal conflict in the traditional sense of a negotiation of differences thereby allowing the conflicting parties to resume a working relationship. For parties who perceive themselves to be in noncommunal conflict, the development of a working relationship would be interpreted as appeasement. But there is, nevertheless, a "resolution" of a sort for non-communal conflict. This "resolution" comes about as the active participants are literally overcome by the emotional strain involved in conflict carried on in a highly acrimonious tone; and because the participants are literally overcome by the sheer weight and complexity of the geometric growth of propagandistic charges and counter-charges purported to be issues. Yet there is little real confrontation of the issues. Thus the conflict is "resolved" by being abandoned. The parties involved withdraw for a time to recoup their energies, to congratulate themselves for their "victory," and to prepare

for a new major, noncommunal conflict. During the interim between major conflicts, the illusion of maintaining a continual battle for the truly legitimate goals and means can be maintained by the less demanding pursuit of conflict through "ritualistic" aggression. Members of the Birch Society, for example, always can fall back to the ritualized conflict over Earl Warren and spend their time signing one another's petitions for his impeachment.

In summary, noncommunal conflict between members of the Birch Society and their opponents is characterized by the following: first, the conflict is initiated on and remains on a highly acrimonious tone; second, the intent of the conflict is propagandistic and is not designed to resolve issues of difference between the parties but rather to attract allies from the uncommitted public; third, as the conflict progresses, it broadens rather than narrows; and finally, the conflict is "resolved" only as it falls of its own weight.

Notes

1. This is a summary of methods and findings for a dissertation submitted in partial fulfillment of the requirements for the degree of Doctor of Philosophy in the Department of Sociology and Social Ethics of Boston University Graduate School, June 1963. Grateful acknowledgment is made to Dr. Paul Deats, Dean Walter Muelder, and Dr. Robert Chin for their guidance and criticism of this study.
2. In this preliminary survey information was gathered from educational and religious leaders with whom members of the Boston University Graduate School Faculty or the author were personally acquainted. These respondents, in response to specific questions, described the leaders, members, and activities of the Society in their locality. They were also asked to assess the reaction of local educational, religious, political, and journalistic leaders and to describe the impact of the Society upon the tone of the life of the community.
3. Other cities considered in the course of the preliminary survey were Indianapolis, Cincinnati, Atlanta, Houston, Tucson, Chicago, Macon, Ga., Billings, Mont., and Cody, Wyo.
4. The pure types of legitimation of authority are traditional, rational-legal, and charismatic. They

may be differentiated by the relationship between the leader and follower. This relationship is bounded in the first two types by norms of tradition and rationality respectively, which are accepted as legitimate by both leaders and followers. Charismatic authority may draw upon some of these same norms but it is, in its pure type, explicitly independent of them. Charismatic authority is dependent upon neither adherence to a common tradition nor common rationality but, rather, faith in and loyalty toward the leader. See Weber, pp. 328 ff. for a fuller definition of these three pure types of legitimation of authority.

5. The author finds the roots of this concept of "ritualistic aggression" in the work of Merton (5, pp. 140 ff.), and Campbell and Pettigrew (1, p. 68).

6. The members and leaders interviewed do not appear to fall into any distinctive sociological groupings. This observation is relevant at this point because such sociological groupings, in themselves, often function as appeals within a social movement.

7. Robert Chin identifies a universal mode of "chain" of classification of "other" which is inferred from the "links" of belief system, intention, action, and consequences as interpreted and as anticipated. A closed-minded person is characterized by his willingness to infer from slight evidence in one link all the other links and by the rigidity of the classification to which he comes thereby (personal communication).

8. This is the major differentiation between those of an open or closed-mind identified by Rokeach (7, pp. 55-70).

9. By indirect contact is meant that which does not involve an actual confrontation of the opposing parties or their representatives. It is exemplified as each party tries to convince a third party, such as an elected representative or an uncommitted public, of the legitimacy of its own and/or the illegitimacy of the other's goals and/or means.

10. Lewis Coser describes communal conflict as occurring when conflicting parties are and remain within the context of the common acceptance of basic ends or values. Noncommunal conflict occurs when this context is not present (4, pp. 73-76).

11. With reference to the paradigm used by Merton related to adaptation to culture goals and institutionalized means, each side perceives itself to be in conformity with the legitimate culture goals, and perceives the other as rebelling against both legitimate goals and means and as substituting in their place illegitimate culture goals and institutionalized means. The paradigm in question is to be found in Merton, p. 140.

12. And to the mentally unbalanced, this incitement sometimes leads to such violence. There are numerous individual attempts at such violence, represented by the account of the man who recently drove up into the steps of the Department of Justice with a "bomb" in his car demanding the impeachment of Warren and Kennedy. This man was never identified as a member of the Birch Society but he had obviously been exposed to the fairly standard radical right-wing ideology expounded by the Society. A "ritualized" preparation for warfare is represented by the latter-day "Minutemen."

36.

Norman K. Denzin

COLLECTIVE BEHAVIOR IN TOTAL INSTITUTIONS: THE CASE OF THE MENTAL HOSPITAL AND PRISON[1]

The study of collective behavior within the mental hospital and other similar total institutions has long been a recurring problem to the sociologist.[2] Instances of

From Norman K. Denzin, "Collective Behavior in Total Institutions: The Case of the Mental Hospital and the Prison," *Social Problems*, 15:3 (Winter 1968), pp. 535-65. Reprinted by permission of The Society of Social Problems and the author.

collective behavior among mental patients, for example, have been observed under such diverse conditions as: (1) lack of staff consensus over ward and patient policy;[3] (2) turnover of patient and staff leaders;[4] (3) breakdown of communication between patients and staff;[5] (4) patient dissatisfaction with ward policy;[6] and (5) failure of staff to enforce previously sanctioned ward policy.[7]

When replication studies have been undertaken, in an attempt to validate earlier findings, little or no support has been found.[8] As Caudill has noted:

Collective disturbances—when the majority of patients on a ward become upset at once—provide a strategic situation for the collaboration of social science and psychiatry, although such situations are not as yet *too well understood.*[9]

Similarly, as Wulbert has recently stated:

Most analyses of collective behavior in mental hospitals speculate on, rather than demonstrate, the association of variables.[10]

This apparent complexity of findings is not confined to studies of collective behavior in the mental hospital. In the prison, collective behavior has been observed under such conditions as: (1) excessive prison crowding and size; (2) unwise sentencing and parole practices; (3) enforced inmate idleness; (4) inadequate official staffing; (5) the presence of substandard personnel;[11] and (6) excessive prisoner abuse.[12] In his brief summary which deals in part with the prison riot literature, Schrag notes, in line with Wulbert's conclusion, that:

. . . the various theories mentioned have serious logical and empirical defects. Indeed none of them appears to meet even the minimal standards for balance, boundaries, claims and congruence.[13]

In short, one must conclude that this area of investigation has been characterized by a lack of continuity, organization, and theory construction.

The present paper attempts to provide a preliminary framework for organizing previous studies of collective behavior among inmates in mental hospitals and prisons.

The mental hospital

Roland Wulbert, in a recent article, attempted to set forth the rudiments of a conceptual framework which would integrate findings from the previous researches cited above. It is to this article that we first turn.[14]

The essence of Wulbert's theory is as follows—First, patients in mental hospitals are alienated from their public status as patients. Second, as a consequence of this alienation, patients attempt to deny their presence in the hospital by placing themselves in a "timeless" state. Third, customs are developed which define the stay in the hospital as a trip away from home—a trip to a place which they "are only passing through." Fourth, when the element of time is forced upon them by the release of other patients, or by staff turnover, they become disturbed because this forces them to publicly recognize their patient status. Fifth, when they do become disturbed, their behavior takes the form of a "mass action," or undifferentiated collective behavior. As a consequence of this lack of focus, their disturbance is turned either inward or toward other patients. To turn to or against staff members would publicly acknowledge their adherence to the inmate status. Thus, the collective behavior takes the unorganized form of suicide attempts and assaults against other patients. Sixth, and last, patients are reluctant to reestablish leaders and order in the social system because to do so forces them to accept the fact that time has passed.[15]

Wulbert states that this lack of inmate pride, or low identification with the inmate role, differentiates mental patients from inmates in other institutions, in the prison for example, where: "inmate pride runs high, customs communicating the worth of inmates and organized, externally aggressive behavior are associated."[16]

While Wulbert's attempt at theory construction is noteworthy in that it is virtually the first such proposal to appear, it suffers from the basic limitation that a number of its assumptions are not supported by previous studies of behavior among mental patients, in either periods of crises, or during their daily rounds of activity.

Various studies indicate that the assumption of alienation from the patient role is not as prevalent as stated by Wulbert.[17] Of particular relevance is the Smith and Thrasher finding that five of the nine patient role types identified actively accepted the role of patient and attempted to facilitate the hospital staff in their treatment. Similar findings are also given by the other authors cited above.

Wulbert's assumption that collective behavior among mental patients takes the form of a mass undirected action is also not entirely supported by previous research. The Miller study quite vividly demonstrates that the collective behavior observed was group oriented and directed.[18] The adolescents focused on a salient social object—ward norms—and together set out to change these norms. The scarification crisis studied by Strauss et al. is another example of a collective attempt by patients to change some aspect of the ward.[19] In this case, the patients were simply bored and dissatisfied with ward policy and were looking for an effective way to express this dissatisfaction.

The assumption that when disturbed, patients do *not* turn to or against staff members, is also not supported by previous research. Stanton and Schwartz suggest that, to the contrary, patients actively directed their disturbances against staff members. The most frequent act was

a complaint about ward service.[20] The Strauss study similarly supports this argument. In addition to harming themselves, the Strauss patients also "pestered" and complained to staff members.[21]

The last assumption of Wulbert's which can be tested by existing research is that of low inmate interaction. Wulbert states:

Low inmate pride is manifest in low rates of interaction, alienation from other inmates, attachment to outsiders and absence of attempts to raise inmate rank or proclaim its superiority.[22]

Goffman's research suggests that patients *do*, in fact, develop elaborate and conjointly sustained mechanisms to "beat" the formal hospital system.[23] He notes, for example, the existence of a patient transportation system which is used to convey illicit forms of patient communication as well as denied social objects.[24] The implication is, of course, that patients do actively join together to aid one another during their course of hospitalization. The assumption of low rates of patient interaction is simply not supported.

Taken together, the investigations just cited indicate that the inmate pride theory is conceptually and empirically inadequate as an explanation of the behavior of mental hospital inmates during either periods of collective behavior or during their day to day encounters in the hospital.

A proposed framework: the civil society perspective

It appears that the explanation of inmate behavior during periods of collective behavior lies elsewhere. It is our position that the conceptual framework employed by Turner and Killian for the explanation of collective behavior among persons in civil society *is also applicable* within a total institutional setting.[25] Turner and Killian note that any human social organization is based on three interdependent factors: a division of labor, a normative order, and a network of communication.[26] Change in any one of these salient features of an organization leads to changes in the others. Collective behavior is then seen as arising out of those situations where the social order becomes unstructured (e.g., where change occurs in the norms, channels of communication, and/or the division of labor).[27]

Application of this framework to the study of the *mental hospital* sensitizes the observer to the normative system (both formal and informal) of the hospital, to its division of labor (both staff and inmate), and to its channels of communication (again on both the staff and inmate levels). Changes in the salient features of a hospital's normative system as exemplified by a reordering of goal priority (e.g., treatment versus custody or research versus treatment) would thus lead to changes in the division of labor, or different types of professional and non-professional personnel would be required to implement the goals and this would in turn lead to changes in the channels of communication among staff and between staff and patients. While it is not possible to make definitive statements about *what* the division of labor, channels of communication, and normative system of *all* mental hospitals are, it does appear, as Goffman, Smith and Thrasher, and Strauss *et al.* have noted, that as a *type* of social organization the mental hospital does have unique organizational features.[28] Normatively, these include the use of power mechanisms that *socialize* the patient into doing what is to be done, rather than *coercing* him.[29] The goal priority system of the American mental hospital appears to

be dichotomized into primary and secondary goals. Primary goals consist of minimal care for patients, socialization of patients, community protection, and treatment. Secondary goals consist of such matters as experimental therapy programs, detailed research investigations, training and education of staff members and students, and community education programs. The typical custodial hospital described by Belknap clearly conforms to the primary goal model, while Chestnut Lodge described by Stanton and Schwartz fits the latter type.[30]

The division of labor among mental hospital personnel appears also to be a distinctive variety. At the top of the hierarchy is, of course, the hospital administrator, followed by the chief psychiatrist and the psychiatry staff. Below this level then follows nursing service, social work, and nutrition and housekeeping staffs. The line of authority, formally, is quite clear; psychiatrists at the top with non-professional and lesser trained medical specialties at the bottom. Below the pyramid are, of course, the patients. This hierarchical model, of course, varies depending on the goal priority system of the hospital with therapeutic communities being more democratic while custodial settings follow the more autocratic mode. Channels of communication also follow the hierarchical model with information flowing from the top down and only infrequently from the bottom up. Psychiatrists communicate to nurses who give directives to aides and attendants who then translate these orders into patient care and supervision.

While we could further specify the actual dynamics of the typical organization of the mental hospital, it is important to note that the Turner and Killian framework directs the observer to these *three* classics of variables when analyzing instances of normal and collective behavior among inmates.[31] Viewed from this framework, the instances of collective behavior previously observed in the mental hospital are readily classifiable and understood. In each example reported, one segment of the social organization on a ward changed, creating a momentarily undefined situation for the patients and staff. Failure or inability to correct this change resulted in the collective behavior disturbances observed.

Changes in division of labor

The Caudill study indicates, for example, how uncertainty concerning the ward division of labor precipitated a breakdown in established channels of communication which in turn led to a redefinition of the salient norms which guided both patient and staff behavior.[32] Caudill notes that in the months preceding the collective disturbance:

. . . the senior staff members were engaged in trying to define their own roles, determining therapeutic policy and in finding ways to formalize the routine of the hospital so that these would serve to implement therapeutic goals.[33]

He goes on to note that:

this unsettled state among the staff was reflected in the patients—in a lack of certainty as to what were correct and permitted actions.[34]

The above illustrates how an inability to arrive at consensual definitions about a division of labor (e.g., confusion over the role of psychiatrists) leads to unclarity concerning norms and rules of conduct. In the Caudill study, the above situation led to a blocking of communication both within and between staff and patients. The consequent output was an extended period

of patient disturbance which lasted some two weeks.

Similar processes occurred in the Wulbert, and the Stanton and Schwartz studies.[35] In the Wulbert investigation, the ward division of labor was broken down following the turnover of key staff and patient leaders. This turnover led to situational uncertainty among patients concerning choice of leaders, which in turn precipitated an attempt at redefinition of the ward norms. Similarly, in the suicide epidemic reported by Stotland and Kobler we observe an instance of collective behavior arising out of uncertainty on the part of both staff and patients concerning proper treatment policy, the role of the therapist and the nurse, and the impact the family was to have upon patient care.[36] In this case, a breakdown in consensus concerning both the normative structure and the hospital division of labor led to a collapse in communication channels between patient and staff. This disruption of the hospital social order was manifested initially in staff dissensus, then in patient suicide attempts, and, finally, in the closing of the hospital. Had the hospital staff been able to reestablish the old social basis of the hospital it is likely that the prolonged period of collective behavior observed would not have occurred.

Changes in communication channels

The Strauss *et al.* paper demonstrates how the existence of a subversive network of communication among patients can lead to a breakdown in formal channels of staff-patient communication, eventually leading to collective behavior among both staff and patients.[37] The authors noted that a change in the age structure of the patient population in the hospital placed the staff in a situation which they were ill-

equipped to handle. A sudden influx of
adolescents onto the wards caught the staff
off-guard and soon the adolescents:

. . . developed cliques; they fought; they often
"got into trouble" out of boredom. They hung
signs ("Help! Help!") out of the window, and
they pestered and taunted the personnel.[38]

The authors go on to note that the adolescents:

developed excellent channels of communication, so that the staff could scarcely hope to
manage each adolescent separately.[39]

The collective behavior which resulted
from this situation was referred to by the
authors as the "scarification crisis" and
lasted some several weeks. In this example
a countervailing system of communication
was developed which subverted the formal
hierarchical communication network of the
hospital.

Changes in the normative system

The ability of changes in the normative
structures of a ward to precipitate collective disturbances is illustrated by the Miller study.[40] In this situation the failure of
staff members to enforce previously sanctioned norms concerning appropriate patient conduct created an unstructured situation for the patients. This situation was
allowed to continue and soon the patients
joined in a collective effort to redefine the
ward norms. Miller notes:

The leader of the group exhibitionistically
became sexually involved with an 18-year-old
girl. Normally this would have led to a withdrawal of privileges, as a mark of disapproval.
. . . But in this instance, for only three or four
days was there any restriction of the patient's
freedom. . . .

Because of the short duration of punishment and the severity of the delinquent be-

havior, the group felt that his action had
been condoned.[41] Miller goes on to say:

The group began to use the age-old principle
of "divide and rule."[42] Soon the staff was faced
with a group of "unmanageable" adolescents
and the collective disturbance lasted until
patient leaders were removed from the ward
setting.

These observations lead us to the position that such variables as the passage of
time, patient-staff turnover, and low inmate pride, taken alone, are insufficient as
explanations of collective behavior in the
mental hospital. A more comprehensive
framework must consider the complex
inter-relationships between the division of
labor, normative standards, and channels
of communication on the ward. Changes
in any one of these key variables set the
stage for changes in the other dimensions
of the social organization of the ward. If
these changes are not carefully directed,
and if a stable social order is not rapidly
replaced, a social situation can develop
which precipitates the types of collective
behavior observed by earlier investigators
in the mental hospital.

Collective behavior in the prison

While the systematic analysis of instances of collective behavior within the
prison have been just as infrequent as
those within the mental hospital, we now
apply the framework just outlined to the
case of the prison. Keeping in mind that
the Turner-Killian approach is basically
sensitizing in its focus, it is still possible to
delineate the basic structural features of
the prison as a form of social organization.

In his useful analysis of the social organization of the prison, McCleery notes that
structurally the traditional prison is based
on an autocratic power and communication network.[43] At the top of the system is

the warden followed by his chief lieutenants who transmit orders to prison guards and other more minor administrative and custodial officials. The organization of the prison is such that there are two basic groups of persons—the authorities on the one hand and the inmates on the other. Normatively, the prison is organized around the principle that the inmate is a societal reject who must either be permanently secluded from that society or made over into a responsible social person. A basically derogatory value system develops which views the inmate as an "unworthy" person who may cause trouble and a person who is always to be watched and never trusted.

While these features are seldom if ever entirely observed in any given prison, they do serve to place in perspective the instances of collective behavior studied in this type of total institution.

Perhaps the most outstanding analysis of prison riots is that of Hartung and Floch.[44] In their discussion, which attempts to account for the outbreak of prison riots during the years 1952-1953, Hartung and Floch argue that special characteristics of the maximum security prison led to the riots observed during this period. Of particular relevance, they note, are the following variables: (1) the total institution flavor of the prison which breaks down all elements of inmate self-government; (2) the tendency of the prison to co-mingle several different types of prisoners; (3) the failure to replace elements of inmate self-government; and (4) the tendency to treat each prisoner individually.[45] These elements represented a radical departure from traditional forms of prison organization and, as such, forced staff and prisoners as well to adjust to a totally new form of *social organization*. Channels of communication were now directed in different directions; normative

standards took on a new flavor; the prisoner was now a person to be individually treated and the policy of instituting individual treatment programs destroyed all forms of inmate cohesion and solidarity. In the face of this situation, Hartung and Floch argue that it was not surprising that so many riots occurred during this two-year period.[46]

In the light of the framework we have outlined it can be argued that the riots represented the collective effort of inmates in a variety of prisons to redefine their social situation in the face of what were to them unacceptable and uninterpretable circumstances.

Sykes's discussion of the New Jersey maximum security prison similarly fits our framework.[47]

As he notes:

. . . the prison suffers from a number of structural flaws which create strong pressures in the direction of what we have chosen to call the corruption of authority . . . the result is a partial transfer of power or control from the captors to the captives.[48]

Given this tendency for the division of labor within the prison to be "corrupted" or redefined, Sykes notes:

The social system of the prison finally reaches a point where the inmates have established their own unofficial version of control. The custodians have withdrawn to the walls to concentrate on their most obvious task, the prevention of escapes.[49]

However, this illicit form of inmate self-government contains the seeds of its own destruction and:

at this point the social system of the prison begins to swing toward the moment of explosion.[50]

Sykes's discussion clearly fits the framework we have been outlining. The crucial element of a division of labor within the prison breaks down, staff members withdraw into their own groupings, and soon subversive channels of communication have been established. Concomitant with this process is the full-blown development of an inmate and staff set of values which are at once at odds with each other. The staff focuses all attention on preventing escapes and inmates focus attention on the construction of their own form of government. In each case the formal goals and values of the prison are subverted; the stable features of its social organization become redefined and soon the ground is laid for the types of riots observed by both Sykes and by Hartung and Floch.

McCleery's discussion of the riots in the Oahu Prison prior to 1947 and the Central Prison riots in North Carolina in 1953 similarly support the Turner-Killian model.[51] In these two instances attempts were made by prison officials to move from a traditional form of social organization to a more modern, equalitarian system which placed the inmate in a new normative perspective. McCleery observed efforts by liberal prison officials to seize control and revolutionize policy. The new officials attempted to create "open" and informal interaction patterns between themselves and the inmates. Unaccustomed to this mode of control, inmates and staff withdrew into their own groupings and began to conspire against the formal authority. Simultaneous with these events were efforts by the traditional prison officials to turn back the wheels of change and return to the earlier forms of control. These pressures resulted in a period of social disorganization among inmates and staff. Old cons turned against new cons and the traditional role of the guard was undercut by the new guard. The inmate hierarchy system was soon destroyed with leaders now emerging who supported the individual-

istic guidance programs of the new administration. Soon the monolithic control system of the system collapsed and violence and disorder ran rampant in the yards of the institutions. Staff members quit in disgust, inmates battled collectively against one another, and at one point:

. . . a mass outbreak was avoided by posting machine guns on the roof and transferring leaders of the younger group to another prison. Inmate society approached a condition of anarchy in which physical force was the only recognized authority.[52]

This period of rioting and violence was followed by the:

collapse of the customary patterns of communication.[53]

Stability returned only after policy issues were renegotiated with inmates and after staff members themselves came to a consensus regarding the role of inmate and official within the institution itself.

Thus we observe again the collapse of a salient feature in the social organization of the prison. When communication channels became blocked, riots appeared in full-blown force.

Collective behavior in total institutions: a comparison with civil society

The present discussion has attempted to indicate the relevance of the Turner-Killian framework for the study of collective behavior within total institutions. It is clear, however, that this model has limitations based in part on the unique nature of life within the walls of the prison and the mental hospital.

As Goffman has cogently noted, life within the total institution is characterized by:

. . . a place of residence and work where a large number of like-situated individuals, cut off from the wider society for an appreciable period of time, together lead an enclosed, formally administered round of life.[54]

He goes on to amplify these points by arguing that:

. . . the central feature of total institutions can be described as a breakdown of the barriers ordinarily separating these three features of life (e.g., sleeping, playing and work). First, all aspects of life are conducted in the same place. . . . Second, each phase of the member's daily activity is carried out in the company of a large batch of others. . . . Third, all phases of the day's activities are tightly scheduled.[55]

These characteristics alone are sufficient to make any comparisons between behavior within total institutions and that in civil society quite different. We have observed, for example, that the types of collective behavior in the mental hospital and the prison in virtually no case took the forms of social movements, mass behavior, public opinion behavior, or *strict* crowd-like behavior. Rather, the behavior observed was representative of efforts by groups of inmates to redefine collectively their present social situations. Inmate groupings consisted of persons well-acquainted with one another, all of whom shared common values and all possessed with the consensual agreement to collectively change some feature of the institutional setting.

In effect, then, we do not observe in the total institutions the emergence of these other forms of collective behavior. It seems a plausible hypothesis that this is the case fundamentally because of the very institutional features described by Goffman. Like-situated persons cut off from larger society are forced to band together, to submerge individual differences and orientations if they choose to collectively change features of their social order.[56] The short-lived, spontaneous, emotional, and indi-

vidualistic features of elementary crowd-like behavior are typically not present. Similarly, the complex features of social movements are not present.

We also observe institutional variations in modes of social control. In the prison and the hospital, *social control mechanisms* are rapid, often quite brutal—as in the prison—and in nearly every case are not based on the rules and laws of civil society. Total institutions create their own civil and moral orders which are often at wide variance with those of the larger society. It is, therefore, not uncommon to see more punitive forms of social justice wrought, as well as to observe collective behavior attempts which are relatively much more short-lived than those in the larger society.

This observation must be tempered, however, with the fact that collective behavior within mental hospitals is different from that within prisons. We typically do not observe mob threats of brutality and long periods of isolation of inmates in the mental hospital. This is, in part, due to the unique total institutional flavor of the mental hospital. Here, as Goffman notes, the institutional attempt is to strip the self of the inmate and to reshape a new social object that conforms with the moral order of the setting. In the prison, the attempt is frequently quite different. A clear violation of the legal code is evident for the inmate, and social and moral considerations regarding the self are often of less importance. Therefore, the prison guard or official has at his disposal methods of control which vary from firearms to threats of isolation and confinement. In the mental hospital threats of brutality frequently derive from treatment sources—such as electric shock therapy and surgery. These are forms of *individual* control mechanisms and *not* forms of *group control* per se. This fact alone may account for the variations in staff responses to inmate collective behavior.

On another level, we observe variations between the two institutional settings in terms of the *type* and *nature* of the collective behavior. It appears that riots and crowd-like behavior in prisons involve complex negotiations between and among inmates. An inmate division of authority evolves with prestigious elites governing the affair while less prestigious prisoners are delegated to other functions. As Clemmer has noted, the prison riot is caused usually by a long series of "abuses" which, over a period of time, are brought to the attention of the inmate body by leaders.

Occasionally a riot will be planned and staged. More often than not, however, it is spontaneous and the leaders that arise do so spontaneously.[57]

This development of a leadership structure which adjudicates and negotiates with officials appears not to be present in the mental hospital. While the evidence is at most inconclusive on this point we as yet lack adequate descriptions of mental hospital life to identify types of inmates in the manner of the prisoner literature. To what extent "big shots," "politicians," "rats," "wolves," "fags," "merchants," "peddlers," "toughs," and other such roles are present in the mental hospital is not known. Therefore, it is difficult to identify the actual substantive nature of collective behavior instances in the mental hospital.

Similarly, to what extent collective behavior instances in mental hospitals and prisons represent merely *episodic* occurrences as opposed to quite routinized affairs is unknown. It is Sykes's position that they are not episodic in the prison.[58] To what degree we can regard these forms of institutions in a continual process of collective behavior is conjecture at this point. It is clear following Blumer, however, that collective behavior in the total institution

parallels that in civil society to the extent that:

it is concerned with large group activity that comes into being and develops along the lines that are not laid out by preestablished social definitions. Such activity and the organization of people which it presupposes are formed or forged to meet undefined or unstructured situations.[59]

We do then observe certain salient similarities between collective behavior within the walls of institutions and that in the broader domains of civil society. It is important to remember, however, as Blumer notes, that as modern society moves steadily toward "large-scale organizations," instances of collective behavior within such organizations will become more and more prevalent.[60] We have only to note the Berkeley riots of 1965, the airplane strikes of 1966 and the National Farmer's Organization in 1967 to support our notion that instances of collective behavior are moving in modern society from single, isolated non-institutional areas to the domain of the modern bureaucratic organization. Such observations alone should be sufficient to document the need for systematic analyses of collective behavior within the walls of the total institution.

Summary

In summary, then, it appears that: (1) There are wide variations in the substantive nature of collective behavior instances in the prison and the mental hospital; and (2) there are wide differences between instances of collective behavior in civil society and in the total institution. These observations raise the question: how relevant is the Turner-Killian framework for the study of collective behavior in the total institution? Our conclusion is that it is quite relevant—to the extent that it sensitizes the observer to a class of variables which generically, at least, point to the main issues involved in this form of social behavior. From this point, however, the framework loses utility, for we *must specify in each* institutional setting what the parameters of the division of labor, channels of communication, and normative order are. To merely point to these three variables is insufficient. We need then a complex and detailed series of investigations which specify similarities and differences *across* mental hospital and prison settings. We also need *more precise investigations which delineate the differences and similarities between collective behavior within and external to the walls of the total institution.* We need to know more about the actual components of the collective behavior episodes observed in these settings and we need to know whether the form of such behavior in the total institution is due to the uniqueness of the setting or to variables as yet unidentified.

We have attempted to present the preliminary elements of a conceptual framework which would account for and explain instances of collective behavior among inmates located within the total institutions of the mental hospital and the prison. An attempt was made to integrate findings from previous investigations and it is our contention that while this framework is at most preliminary, it does provide a set of more than heuristic concepts which, if systematically explored in future investigations, could lead to a profitable theory of collective behavior as it occurs within the walls of total institutions.

Notes

1. This is a revision of a paper presented to the 62nd Annual Meeting of the American Sociological Association and the Society for the Study of Social Problems, San Francisco, California, August 27-31, 1967. It was financed, in part, by the Iowa Mental Health Authority and by National Institute of Mental Health Grant #HM-8303-0351. I am grateful for the comments and suggestions provided by Daniel Glaser, George J. McCall, Carl J. Couch, and Richard P. Boyle.

2. We take this to be one of the general problems to which Anselm Strauss *et al.*, have directed their efforts. See their "The Hospital and its Negotiated Order," in Eliot Freidson, editor, *The Hospital in Modern Society,* New York: Free Press, 1963, pp. 147-169. See also William Caudill, "Social Processes in a Collective Disturbance on a Psychiatric Ward," in Milton Greenblatt, Daniel J. Levinson and Richard H. Williams, editors, *The Patient and the Mental Hospital,* Glencoe, Ill.: Free Press, 1957, pp. 438-471.

3. Alfred H. Stanton and Morris S. Schwartz, *The Mental Hospital,* New York: Basic Books, 1954, pp. 342-365; Anselm Strauss *et al., Psychiatric Ideologies and Institutions,* New York: Free Press, 1964, pp. 316-348; Ezra Stotland and Arthur L. Kobler, *Life and Death of a Mental Hospital,* Seattle: U. of Washington, 1965, esp. pp. 121-212.

4. D. H. Miller, "The Etiology of an Outbreak of Delinquency in a Group of Hospitalized Adolescents," in Greenblatt *et al., op. cit.,* pp. 427-437.

5. Caudill, *op. cit.*

6. *Ibid.;* also Miller, *op. cit.;* and Stanton and Schwartz, *op. cit.*

7. Miller, *op. cit.*

8. Anthony F. C. Wallace and Harold A. Rashkis, "The Relation of Staff Consensus to Patient Disturbance on Mental Hospital Wards," *American Sociological Review,* 24 (December, 1959), pp. 829-835.

9. Caudill, *op. cit.,* p. 438.

10. Roland Wulbert, "Inmate Pride in Total Institutions," *American Journal of Sociology,* 71 (July, 1965), p. 1.

11. See the following for a summary of the prison collective behavior literature: Clarence Schrag, "Some Foundations for a Theory of Correction," in Donald R. Cressey, editor, *The Prison: Studies in Institutional Organization and Change,* New York: Holt, 1961, pp. 309-358; Richard H. McCleery, "The Governmental Process and Informal Social Control," also by McCleery, "Authoritarianism and the Belief System of Incorrigibles," both in Cressey, *Ibid.,* pp. 149-188 and 260-308; *Prison Riots and Disturbances,* New York: American Prison Association, 1953; "Aftermath of Riot," *The Prison Journal,* 34 (1954), entire issue; Austin H. MacCormick, "Behind the Prison Riots," *Annals of the American Academy of Political and Social Science,* 293 (1954), pp. 17-27; Vernon Fox, *Violence Behind Bars,* New York: Vantage, 1956; P. McGraw and W. McGraw, *Assignment: Prison Riots,* New York: Holt, 1954; *Theoretical Studies in Social Organization of the Prison,* New York: Social Science Research Council 1960, especially the papers by McCleery, Sykes and Messinger, and Cloward; *Prison Riots and Disturbances,*

New York: American Prison Association, 1953; Frank T. Flynn, "Behind the Prison Riots," *The Social Service Review* 27 (March, 1953), pp. 73-86.

12. Donald Clemmer, *The Prison Community,* New York: Holt, 1940, p. 148.

13. Schrag, *op. cit.,* p. 521.

14. Wulbert, *op. cit.,* p. 9.

15. *Ibid.*

16. *Ibid.*

17. See Jean Harmon Thrasher, "The Role-Set and Socialization of the Psychiatric Patient," unpublished doctoral dissertation, U. of North Carolina, 1961; Harvey L. Smith and Jean Thrasher, "Roles, Cliques and Sanctions: Dimensions of Patient Society," *International Journal of Social Psychiatry,* 9 (Summer, 1963), pp. 184-191; Daniel J. Levinson and Eugene B. Gallagher, *Patienthood in the Mental Hospital,* Boston: Houghton Mifflin, 1964, pp. 34-35, 219-234; Strauss *et al.,* Norman A. Polansky, Robert B. White and Stuart C. Miller, "Determinants of the Role-Image of the Patient in a Psychiatric Hospital," in Greenblatt *et al., op. cit.,* pp. 380-401; Strauss *et al., op. cit.,* pp. 100-150; and Stanton and Schwartz, *op. cit.*

18. Miller, *op. cit.,* pp. 429-433; Stanton and Schwartz, *op. cit.,* similarly note group participation in the collective behavior they observed. This is also the case in the Caudill study.

19. Strauss *et al., op. cit.*

20. Stanton and Schwartz, *op. cit.* See also Miller's findings. Miller, *op. cit.,* pp. 432-433.

21. Strauss *et al., op. cit.*

22. Wulbert, *op. cit.,* p. 7.

23. Erving Goffman, "The Underlife of a Public Institution: A Study of Ways of Making Out in a Mental Hospital," in his *Asylums,* Garden City, N.Y.: Anchor, 1961, pp. 171-320.

24. *Ibid.,* pp. 254-274.

25. Ralph H. Turner and Lewis M. Killian, *Collective Behavior,* Englewood Cliffs, N.J.: Prentice-Hall, 1957, pp. 20-39.

26. *Ibid.*

27. Actually it is problematic how structured any social situation ever is. The recent statements by Strauss *et al., op. cit.,* suggest that interaction within even the most formal social organization is often based on moment to moment plans of action which are negotiated by the relevant parties. Erving Goffman's *Behavior in Public Places,* New York: Free Press, 1963, implies such a position also.

28. Goffman, *op. cit;* Smith and Thrasher, *op. cit.;* Strauss *et al., op. cit.*

29. See our unpublished paper, Stephen P. Spitzer and Norman K. Denzin, "The American Mental Hospital as a Social Organization."

30. Ivan Belknap, *Human Problems of a State Mental Hospital,* New York: McGraw-Hill, 1956; Stanton and Schwartz, *op. cit.*

31. See Herbert Blumer, "What is Wrong with Social Theory," *American Sociological Review* 19 (February, 1954); pp. 3-10, where concepts as sensitizing devices are discussed. Our position is that the Turner-Killian framework is largely sensitizing in its implications. It is therefore of only minimal usefulness to specify in an a priori fashion the specific dimensions of the concept(s) under analysis. To paraphrase Blumer, "we go to specific social settings, identify the presence of theoretically relevant concepts and then go to other settings to assess the effect of those settings upon the concepts under consideration." This is what we propose to be the proper line of inquiry concerning the Turner-Killian framework.

32. Caudill, *op. cit.*

33. *Ibid.,* p. 440.

34. *Ibid.*

35. Wulbert, *op. cit.;* Stanton and Schwartz, *op. cit.*

36. Stotland and Kobler, *op. cit.*

37. Strauss *et al., op. cit.*

38. *Ibid.,* p. 317.

39. *Ibid.*

40. Miller, *op. cit.*

41. *Ibid.,* p. 432.

42. *Ibid.*

43. McCleery, *Theoretical Studies in Social Organization of the Prison, op. cit.*

44. See Frank E. Hartung and Maurice Floch, "A Social-Psychological Analysis of Prison Riots," in Turner and Killian, *Collective Behavior,* pp. 24-28.

45. *Ibid.*

46. *Ibid.*

47. Graham M. Sykes, *The Society of Captives: A Study of a Maximum Security Prison,* Princeton, N.J.: Princeton U., 1958, esp. pp. 109-129.

48. *Ibid.,* p. 127.

49. *Ibid.*

50. *Ibid.,* p. 129.

51. McCleery, *op. cit.*

52. *Ibid.,* p. 73.

53. *Ibid.*

54. Goffman, *op. cit.,* p. xiii.

55. *Ibid.,* p. 6.

56. This was suggested to me by Daniel Glaser.

57. Clemmer, *op. cit.*

58. Sykes, *op. cit.,* p. 110.

59. Herbert Blumer, "Collective Behavior," in Joseph B. Gittler, editor, *Review of Sociology,* New York: Wiley, 1957, p. 130.

60. *Ibid.,* p. 131.

37.

Joseph M. Firestone

A THEORY OF RIOT PROCESS

The state of theorizing about the riot process is not as developed as the theory of underlying conditions. The reason for this is that the few major theoretical efforts of social scientists interested in generality have been directed toward the study of social conflict, revolution, or collective behavior rather than toward the particular area of riot occurrences. There exists, thus, general theory about underlying conditions and about collective behavior as a class of concrete events but development of a concept of what the riot process itself is like has lagged behind.

We hope, in this paper, to contribute to the growth of knowledge about the riot process by offering a new theoretical framework for the study of the immediate precipitants and over time process characteristics of riots and by presenting, along with the framework, a loose "translation" of it in mathematical terms.

A central problem to be addressed here may be called the competitive explanation orientation to theorizing about riots. In a previous study (Firestone, 1972a), an examination of hypotheses advanced to account for the onset and development of riots revealed the essentially unintegrated and implicitly (sometimes explicitly) competitive character of theorizing about riots. Competition among theories is a desirable and natural characteristic of the scientific process, and it has been argued that such competition is a necessary condition for the growth of knowledge. But the existence of competitive explanations also presents the challenge of potential synthesis, because it raises the question of whether explanations are necessarily competitive or are complementary when viewed from the perspective of a broader theoretical approach. Once again, the field of riot theory currently presents us with the problem of unintegrated competitive explanations. The theoretical framework to be advanced presents a possible synthesis of diverse explanations.

A transactional orientation

In a brief review of some of the theoretical issues surrounding the riot process, we have noted (Firestone, 1972a) the still chaotic state of theory in this field and the diverse set of hypotheses being put forward as relevant to an explanation of the riot process. Table 1 organizes these issues in terms of distinctions between the precipitating event and the riot process, and within the riot process category between within-group interaction factors and factors relating to external interaction between contending social actors.

Excerpt from "Theory of the Riot Process," by Joseph M. Firestone is reprinted from *American Behavioral Scientist* Vol. 15, No. 6 (July/August 1972) pp. 859-82 by permission of the publisher, Sage Publications, Inc., and the author.

Author's Note: This paper is a much abbreviated version of a study entitled "The Causes of Urban Riots: A New Approach and a Causal Model." The longer study deals with both theory of underlying conditions and theory of the riot process. Support for the original version was provided by the Lemberg Center for the Study of Violence, Brandeis University. Special thanks are due to John P. Spiegel, Director, and Dr. Ralph Lewis, Director of Research of the Lemberg Center for their criticism of earlier drafts.

TABLE 1

Hypotheses on the Causes of Riots

| | Riot Process | |
Precipitating Event	Internal Crowd Characteristics	Interaction Among Contending Parties
1. Police brutality (Kerner, 1968)	1. Contagion of affect and behavior (Le Bon, 1952)	1. Escalatory interaction between citizens and civil authorities (Spiegel, 1969a, 1971; Marx, 1970; Spilerman, 1970)
2. Random events aroused by hot weather	2. Carnival spirit (Banfield, 1970: ch. 9)	
3. Night-time street-crowding	3. Emergent norms in a directionless crowd (Milgram and Toch, 1969)	
4. Rumors		
5. Focusing of a generalized belief embodying latent hostility of rioters to the society (Smelser, 1963; Spiegel, 1969a, 1971)		

A number of points relating to Table 1 are worth noting. First, the hypotheses generally reflect a view of riots which locates their *immediate source,* as well as much of the reason for their emergent dynamics, primarily in the actions of dissidents. In making this claim, we do not imply that riot explanations do not take due account of *underlying conditions* which may justify or explain dissident protest from this broader viewpoint. But, in speaking to the characteristics of the riot subsystem itself, many theorists, as indicated by the hypotheses and their sources in Table 1, seem to view dissidents:

(a) as those who begin riots in reaction to an external stimulus such as police brutality, hot weather, street-crowding, and so on; and

(b) as those among whom the riot process develops through contagion, the occurrence of a carnival spirit, and the development of emergent norms.

This view of riots is one-sided in that it does not consider what, for example, the effect of hot weather, rumors, street confrontations, or the focusing of a general-

ized belief is on police brutality. Or further, whether such factors as contagion, the carnival spirit, or emergent norms affect the functioning of the dominant group as its members move toward interaction with dissidents in a riot context.[1]

The hypothesis of escalatory interaction with authorities does introduce a transactional point of view to the analysis of riots, and the writings of Marx (1970), Spilerman (1970), Spiegel (1971, 1969b, 1969c), Nieburg (1969), and Nardin (1971), which essentially adopt such a point of view, also suggest our point of the one-sided character of much previous theorizing in the riot process. In any event, our own approach to the riot process will be a transactional one and will attempt to be integrative relative to the hypotheses of Table 1, many of which, as stated earlier, have been viewed as implicitly competing.

Spiegel's stage theory of the riot process: a basis for a new framework

The most developed conceptualization of riot dynamics is Spiegel's (1969a) stage or phase theory of the riot process. We have called attention (Firestone, 1972a) to the disagreement between Spiegel's stage concept, and the Kerner Commission's (1968) feeling that there were no typical riots. We further pointed to the need for integration and nonstage dynamic views of riots with more static explanatory hypotheses such as those of Table 1. Though Spiegel's theory is a stage theory, closer examination of it will suggest the concepts and interrelations we will need to take account of in our framework, while at the same time illuminating how both stage and nonstage assumptions about dynamic interrelations relate to the framework.

This will be done through an examination of the interrelations among actors and variables implicit in the stage theory, in abstraction from its phase structure.

Figure 1 presents Spiegel's theory. The relation of the theory to underlying conditions of riots is described by the notion of "concrete manifestation of a hostile belief." Hostile beliefs are attitudinal predispositions. Incidents resulting in situational orientations reflecting these attitudes can, in the presence of inadequate social control, be precipitating events for a riot. From this point, Spiegel's description specifies the interaction of dissident activities with continued official under- and over-

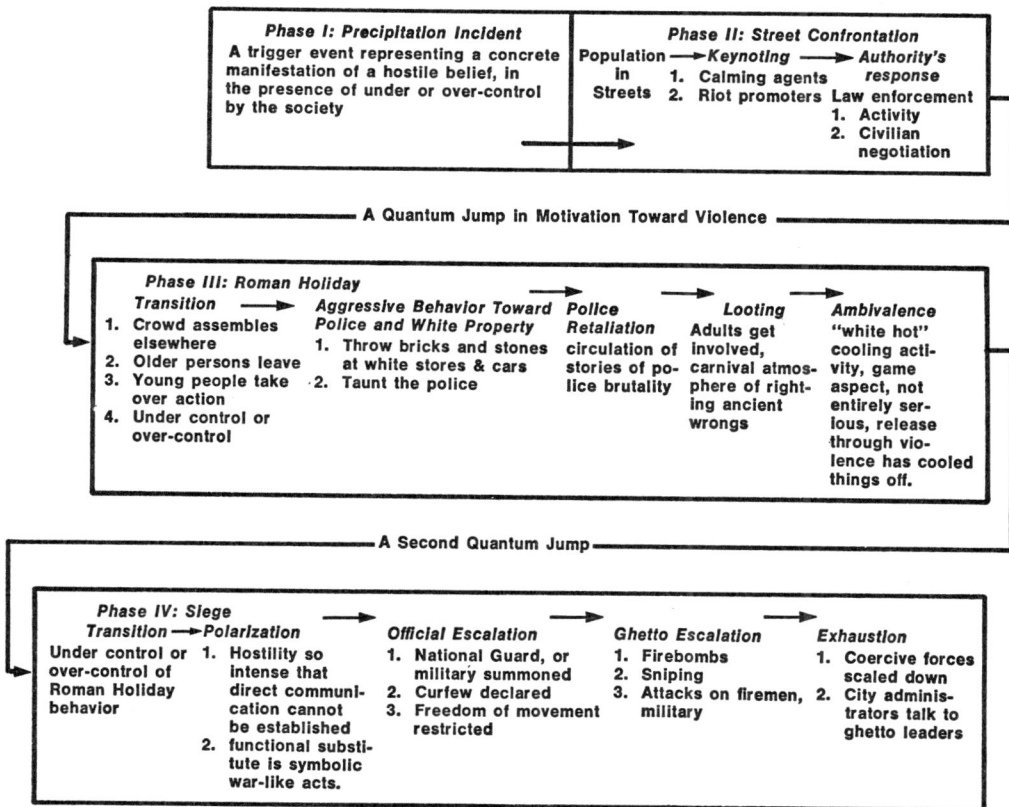

Figure 1. Spiegel's Theory

control as the key to continued progress of the riot to higher stages. The picture presented is one of a balance of interacting forces, some tending to escalate, and others to dampen the riot. Over- and under-control by authorities are never precisely defined, and this is a major difficulty in the scheme. But the interaction of situational and psychological aspects of riots is usefully described or hinted at, and we will attempt to develop this aspect of Spiegel's formulation for present purposes.

Psychological motivations in phase 1 are based on the notion that hostility toward the adversary is caused by grievances of the social actor which arise from the actor's perception of "extraordinary" behavior by the adversary, "beyond the pale of accepted norms." This formulation raises the immediate question of further psychological response to the sense of grievance by those in the riot situation and relates to the current dispute over whether rioters have rational or irrational motives.

One possible type of response to grievance is arousal of motivation directly associated with violence. The aggression incentive in Fanon's (1963) sense and in the sense specified by the frustration-aggression hypothesis (compare Gurr, 1970) is one such motive. Smelser's (1963) concept of anxiety identifies another. That is, the release of anger, induced by frustration, or of anxiety, induced by threat, is dependent upon the use of violence. Violence is valued in itself, as a consummatory behavior (see Birch and Veroff, 1966: ch. 1), on this account, and is a nonrational motivation.

A second type of response to grievance and to the precipitating event is to think in terms of the riot as an opportunity for social protest, to call attention to, and to seek redress for, one's grievances. Skolnick (1969) and Nardin (1971), among others, have called attention to the possible prevalence of this rational motive for riots.

Spiegel's theory does not explicitly call attention to this distinction between types of motives for violence, but elsewhere (1971: 79-80) he does recognize it, and in the statement of the theory he implicitly associates under-control with the rational protest view and over-control with the anger or aggressive response view (Spiegel, 1969a: 334-335):

In the condition of undercontrol, law enforcement personnel are insufficiently active. The dissident group, noting the weakness of the authorities, seizes the opportunity to express its hostility. The in-activity [sic] of the police functions as an invitation to act out long-suppressed feelings, free of the social consequences of illegal behavior. In the condition of over-control, police, state troopers, or the National Guard are brought in too early, and make unnecessary arrests with unnecessary brutality.

In other communities over-control is instituted almost from the onset of the disturbance. Police and state troopers are rushed to the scene and begin to manhandle everyone in sight. Since the action is out of proportion to the event, it generates an intense reaction.

If we accept the notion that the precipitating event arouses feelings of grievance and hostility followed either by arousal of motivation which has violence as its goal (aggression, anxiety, dominance strivings, and the like) or by arousal of motivation relative to which violence is instrumental behavior (the protest or the riot for profit view), or both in a mix of some sort, we can much more easily interpret the interaction between authorities and dissidents described in phases II, III, and IV of the theory.

Phase II, the street confrontation phase, identifies the interaction of "calming agents," "riot promoters," law enforcement officials, and possibly civil authorities. We can theorize that "calming agents" attempt to appeal to the "strategic" aspect of riot ideology and to call attention to the ineffectiveness of the particular riot occurrence as protest, or perhaps even to condemn all riots as ineffective because of their destructive effect on the community. This is essentially also the appeal of civilian authorities should they choose to negotiate with rioters at this stage. By offering concessions at an early stage of the riot, civilian authorities can underline the view that large-scale violence is not necessary, that the protest motive for riots has already been satisfied.

Riot promoters probably present a mixed appeal in their keynoting activities. At the rational level, their speeches articulate a protest justification for the riots, but the style of their advocacy, and the content of some of their arguments undoubtedly contain aggressive cues whose function is to "whip up" those gathered, to arouse their aggressive incentive.

Law enforcement activity has an extremely delicate role to play at this point. Under-control may belie the arguments of calming agents, because the relative absence of police or a minimum show of strength may support the rational aspect of the arguments of riot promoters, and may cause people to conclude that they indeed have a good opportunity for violent protest in the under-controlled situation. On the other hand, too great a show of force, including initiation of large-scale police violence, may, as Spiegel says, cause an intense reaction—in our terms, cause the utilitarian aspects of the riot situation, including the cost-reward calculation implicit in the rational view, to be eclipsed by the arousal, in response to police violence, of moral indignation (Lupsha, 1971) and with it the aggressive incentive system. Punishment of the police and of the dominant society becomes the primary goal and not the expression of protest.

Thus, the street confrontation (phase II) may be looked upon as a phase in which rational and aggressive motivation for violence vie for supremacy, depending upon the interaction of the contending parties. In contrast, the Roman Holiday phase seems to be characterized by violent behavior as consummation, rather than instrument. This is why the carnival atmosphere prevails during encounters with the police and later when the looting starts. This also explains why a quantum jump divides phases II and III. Motivation in phase II is ambivalent, the possibility of withdrawal from the confrontation still may be attractive; in short, the aggressive incentive is not yet dominant. But in phase III, the aggressive incentive is dominant, is fed by police retaliation and by rumors of police behavior, and results in the carnival or "king-for-a-day" atmosphere, the "rioting for fun" aspect remarked on by some observers.

But then the fun begins to end. Violence, as any form of consummatory behavior (see Birch and Veroff, 1966), tends to wear thin with time. Release has been achieved. "White hat" and ghetto leader cooling activity begins to be effective as the rational aspect of the riot asserts itself once again. If the purpose was protest, it has been had in full measure. The moral aspects of continued violence begin to weigh heavily, and the opportunity for a negotiated settlement, at least from the ghetto standpont, again exists. At this point, under-control will not hurt the situation (a view not shared by Spiegel, 1969a: 337), for grievances have been expressed both from the standpoint of protest, and from the standpoint of those who want to "even the score." But over-control of Roman Holiday behavior can introduce threat into the situation, can further frustrate those who need to express anger, and can propel the riot into siege (phase IV). The ghetto is divided into three kinds of people: those who perceive that the safest place for them is home; those whose intense anger impels them to violence upon the persons of those representing the dominant group; and those for whom the riot has never been merely protest, but rather a means of unmasking the true, ruthless, dehumanized nature of the dominant society, and who continue therefore to act to provoke further escalation, until exhaustion comes.

This interpretation of Spiegel's phase theory of the riot process departs from his own formulation at a number of points which are clear from comparison of Figure 3 with my account. However, its purpose is to illustrate that the phase structure of the riot can, at least loosely, be interpreted in terms of the ebb and flow of aggressive and rational incentives for violence, and in terms of the complex interaction effects of motivational change with police, city government, and ghetto efforts to either dampen or arouse violence. It is not even necessary to accept the phase structure of the theory in order to accept its main general propositions. *Hence, the phase description can be looked upon primarily as an illustration of the general interrelations sketched, rather than as an explicit claim that certain feedback relations produce stable correlations among variables during specified time periods* (though, of course, the latter claim is what distinguishes a stage or phase theory from the type of view expressed by the Kerner Commission).

In any event, the propositions which can be abstracted from our interpretation of Spiegel's framework, neglecting its stage implications are:

(1) Grievances crystallized by the precipitating incident give rise to both instrumental and consummatory strivings toward violence.

An important element in this process is within-group keynoting.

(2) Negotiations tends to dampen both types of motivation, but, once the aggressive incentive is fully engaged, offers of negotiations will not dampen aggression until release of frustration or anxiety through aggressive behavior has occurred.

(3) Therefore the effectiveness of negotiation early in the riot process depends on the mix of aggressive and rational incentives resulting from the precipitating incident.

(4) Suppressive activity tends to dampen rational motivation toward violence at the cost of increased resentment, and to arouse aggressive motivation. The latter relation, however, is curvilinear. If suppression is weighty enough, aggressive motivation, too, is dampened, but also at the cost of continuing resentment which feeds back to the underlying conditions of violence.

(5) There will be turning points in a riot, when instrumental and consummatory, protest and aggressive, motivations are reasonably satisfied. In a sense, the riot is where it was before the precipitating incident occurred. Its continuance depends upon whether conciliation or suppressive tactics again crystallize grievance; if they do, the possibilities inherent in propositions 2-4 again present themselves.

(6) Escalation of a riot through peaks of rational and aggressive motivation to turning points, to new peaks of motivation, can develop to the point where aggressive motivation has, fed by fear and mistrust, reached such heights that direct communication is impossible. All that has *value* in the motivational sense is aggressive consummatory behavior and the search for dominance.

(7) Once the peak of conflict in 6 is reached, and aggressive incentives are acted out in mutual exchange of conflict and violent transactions, exhaustion becomes the dominant factor. Aggressive needs are satisfied. Negotiations can again take place.

Here we must consider three important issues raised earlier in our discussion. First, how do stage and nonstage theories relate to the propositions as stated?

Nonstage or continuous theories assume that contiguous time intervals of the riot process do not exhibit unchanging or slowly changing values of the state variables of the process. The state variables as identified by the propositions are aggressive and rational motivations for violence or for its dampening, conciliatory, and aggressive activity by the dominant group, conciliatory (negotiation, "cooling," "calming") and aggressive activity by the dissident group. Therefore a nonstage theory would have to postulate, simply, continuous change in these with change in time. On the other hand, Spiegel's stage theory postulates that one can identify time periods in which instrumental and consummatory motivation levels remain where they had been as a result of the precipitating incident. These change as a function of conciliatory and aggressive behavior by the parties to the conflict, and suddenly the growth of aggressive motivation accelerates, instrumental motivation is dampened, and the new stage of the Roman Holiday is reached. Once again, there is relative stability of motivation and interaction pattern between dissidents and authorities, until new initiatives involving over-control again result in a new and stable pattern of interaction until exhaustion is reached.

The propositions stated by us, of course, say nothing about the rate of change of values of the state variables with change in time, or very much about their feedback relations. They do not state hypothesized sequential relations among variables, however, which will be of use to us later. As for choosing between stage and nonstage theories of riots, we, again, see no necessity for this. Obviously, Spiegel's stage theory does not detail a necessary progression of riot phases for every riot. Violence can be dampened in any one of the four

phases according to this theory. Moreover, it seems clear that phases of the riot could be short-circuited in any given instance by events which immediately created a Roman Holiday and skipped Street Confrontation or which jumped directly from Precipitating Incident to Siege, given strong enough responses by the authorities and a strong will to resist by dissidents.

But the issue is not really whether particular riots follow the stage theory precisely, or even whether a good many do not. The stage theory will still be useful if many riots do, given certain conditions, conform to the pattern of progression sketched. And nonstage theories will be useful if riots in some cities correspond to the continuous change patterns they postulate. The probability, in fact, is that a number of stage and nonstage theories will all prove useful in the analysis of riot process, for human behavior is not so uniform that one chain of events, like the continual progression of planets around the sun, will again and again recur.

Second, how do some of the other hypotheses adduced to explain the riot process relate to our framework?

Police brutality, rumors, and hostile beliefs obviously easily fit into the precipitating event notion as formulated. Escalatory interaction is a major aspect of the framework. The carnival notion relates to the release of frustration through aggressive behavior and to the Roman Holiday phase. Contagion may be found in the keynoting process and in the rumors of brutality passed in the Roman Holiday stage. Emergent norms we may view as crystallized by the outcome of the keynoting phase and as part of the process of crystallizing motivation.

Hot weather and street-crowding are not related directly to the scheme. But both states can be considered deprivations which are socially correctable (air conditioners?), and they therefore may relate to the hostile belief notion in a loose way. In any event, it seems clear that a process model of riots like Spiegel's can resolve some of the chaos besetting riot theory, by relating to one another, through a dynamic model, the various factors mentioned as important to the riot process.

Last, we must raise the question of transactional analysis. As stated, the model does not present a complete view of the dominant group actor in the riot process. The activities of law enforcement personnel and city officials, where these are directed toward the dissidents, are taken account of in the model. But the transactional view is incomplete, in that it neglects counterparts of Precipitating Event, Keynoting, and Roman Holiday activities within the dominant group. Since the dominant group may not be out in the streets to the same degree as the dissidents, their keynoting activities may be less visible. But in another place, Spiegel (1971) has called attention to the role of the media in "labeling" riot situations for the dominant community, surely an aspect of keynoting. Strategic conferences among police and civil authorities during riots may serve to exacerbate polarization in the community by defining the situation for these representatives of the dominant social group in a way that demands an aggressive response from them. Defining a riot situation as a task involving reestablishment of "law and order" is greatly different from defining the situation as one of "resolving" or "managing" violent conflict. The images and roles called up by the two levels differ. The psychological motives—in one case, aggression, dominance, moral indignation; in the other, a problem-solving motivation—also differ.

In general, we think the internal processes of dominant group mobilization affecting its use of violence in riot situations is much the same as that of dissident groups' internal processes. Consequently, we emphasize that propositions 1 to 6 above apply to the dominant group as well as to the dissident group. There is for the dominant group also a precipitating incident which engages it in the riot process. Keynoting determines instrumental or consummatory motivation ("let us get back to normal" versus "let us teach those rioters a lesson" views). Attempts by dissident group members to defuse the riots may not be supported by the police or the city administration, because by this time the latter want to dominate, and not defuse, the riot. How the dominant group reacts to attempts by ghetto groups to "cool down" the riot also depends on the mix of aggressive and rational incentives in that group. Aggressive activity by dissident group members serves to dampen the rational motivation of the dominant group toward managing riot violence, though initial aggressive activity has aroused the problem-solving motive in the first place. Moreover, continued aggressive activity by the dissident group tends to feed the dominant group's aggressive orientation. Again, the relation here is curvilinear in principle. But the dissident group cannot, at least in the American urban context, bring enough force to bear to suppress the dominant group.

We will not go on with an interpretation of remaining propositions as seen from the standpoint of the dominant group, as the reasonableness of applying the propositions to both sides of the transaction process is apparent. The result of our discussion of Spiegel's stage theory of riots is a somewhat more abstract formulation of six propositions meant to highlight the mix of rational and nonrational elements present in urban riots, the interaction of these psychological elements with elements of within- and between-group interaction. Essentially, the pattern of causation sketched is one of an extremely sensitive, goal-directed system subject to environmental constraints and human influence, driven at one moment toward peaks of violence, and at the next toward a return to normalcy, in response to changes in the environmental constraints or in human purposes.

Notes

1. The interaction referred to here is broader than interaction of authorities and dissidents. The dominant community remains in interaction with dissidents even during riots. Dominant group businesses are closed. Curfews, depending on how widespread they are, may affect dominant group members. The press is in direct contact with the riot, of course, and the community is in contact with the press through the various media.

38.

Donald I. Warren

NEIGHBORHOOD STRUCTURE AND RIOT BEHAVIOR IN DETROIT: SOME EXPLORATORY FINDINGS

The recent spate of studies and surveys[1] in cities which have experienced major civil disorders have stressed either the individual attributes of rioters[2] or the process of collective behavior in rioting.[3] These studies show a lack of concern with the social structure of urban ghettoes.[4]

Moreover, the preoccupation of such research has been with delineating the level of riot participation. In contrast, the Kerner report points out: "In all but six of the 24 disorders [studied by the Kerner Commission], Negro private citizens were active on the streets attempting to restore order primarily by means of persuasion."[5]

From Donald I. Warren, "Neighborhood Structure and Riot Behavior in Detroit: Some Exploratory Findings," *Social Problems,* 16:4 (Spring, 1969), pp. 464-84. Reprinted by permission The Society for the Study of Social Problems and the author.

Furthermore:

In a Detroit survey of riot-area residents over the age of 15, some 14 percent stated that they had been active as counter-rioters. . . . The typical counter-rioter . . . was an active supporter of existing social institutions. . . . As the riot alternately waxed and waned, one area of the ghetto remained insulated. . . . When the riot broke out, the residents, through the block clubs, were able to organize quickly. Youngsters, agreeing to stay in the neighborhood, participated in detouring traffic. . . . In some areas residents organized rifle squads to protect firefighters.

These patterns of behavior suggest a need to examine in greater detail the social organization of the black ghetto. Such an opportunity is present in Detroit because of extensive data collected prior to the July, 1967 disorder and by a post-riot survey done in August, 1967. Our focus in

TABLE 1
A Typology of Neighborhoods Based on Social Organization and Reference Orientation

	Typology	Informal and Formal Organization	Orientation to Larger Community
Neighborhood is a positive reference group	INTEGRATED	+	+
	PAROCHIAL	+	−
	DIFFUSE	−	−
Neighborhood is not a positive reference group	STEPPING-STONE	+	+
	TRANSITORY	−	+
	ANOMIC	−	−

the present paper, therefore, is less on the individual rioter than on his social milieu—in particular, his immediate neighborhood.[6] Ecological correlations[7] provide a convenient method for discovering the forms of social control which promote or restrain riot activity.

The significance of the local neighborhood

Evidence of the important role played by the area of residence reveals the neighborhood to be a potentially key social unit[8]—a cohesive center for social interaction. The influence of neighborhoods involves the "structural effects" of selection and socialization of residential clusterings[9] as well as the formal and informal social participation patterns organized on a geographic basis.[10] Neighborhoods as reference groups[11] or integrating mechanisms[12] for social mobility represent small units roughly corresponding to a "walking distance" social milieu.

Aside from defining the proper size or the exclusiveness of a "neighborhood effect,"[13] it is important to focus on the concept of social control and examine the structural elements of neighborhoods which are conducive to given social processes. Neighborhoods may (or may not) support the values and goals of other social institutions such as the family, and the

economic and political structures of society as a whole. Two kinds of influences may be distinguished: those directly related to the individual's attitude toward social interaction with neighbors, and those related to the institutional structure of a neighborhood. An individual may be willing to alter his behavior or to engage in joint social action with his neighbors, but may find no available means to do so. For purposes of the present discussion, we are giving priority to this latter problem in order to move toward understanding alienation and civil disorder in urban ghettoes.

Types of neighborhoods and consequences of particular settings

In Table 1 we have suggested a typology of neighborhoods using criteria of social organization and reference orientation.[14] It is possible to attribute to each of the six varieties some potential for the effective or ineffective enforcement of prevailing values, or the creation of new values or social goals. Those neighborhoods in which there is a positive attitude and identification reflect reference orientations that may be sources of both integration and alienation.

The Integrated neighborhood individuals are bound to one another by frequent face-to-face contacts and/or extensive membership in formal organizations. The norms and attitudes of these persons support the values of the larger community and there are behavioral indicators of such support, such as voting in elections and initiating contact with the political members of the community.

The Parochial neighborhood is characterized by an extensive amount of face-to-face contact with neighbors but an absence of values or behavioral ties to the larger community. A typical example of such areas is the public housing project which is both physically and organizationally separated from the rest of the black or white community. In the settings where a positive identification with the neighborhood exists, structural weaknesses may occur as a result of deviant values or ineffective social control for conforming values. In the Parochial neighborhood this problem is likely to be a serious one. For example, a lack of ties to the larger community may cause "definitions of the situation" to emerge which do not take into account events impinging from the larger community. Neighborhood organizations which define problems in localized ways may be unable to link up with other groups to carry out social goals sought by large portions of a community. Moreover, the separate and isolated subculture of the neighborhood may exacerbate conflicts with the values and goals of the larger society. This may produce greater estrangement from such values as well as withdrawal from participation in voting or other areas of the larger community's functioning.

In the Diffuse neighborhood social participation is not extensive. Even a person's activity in formal organizations may not substitute for face-to-face "neighboring." Because of the lack of flexibility in social communication, the Diffuse

neighborhood may develop both an active elite and an active formal organizational network which do not necessarily reflect the values of persons in the area. Such a situation might produce intra-neighborhood conflict or result in the inability of new social goals or values to be effectively carried out by the existing network of organizations in the area.[15] The Diffuse neighborhood may face the danger of developing a common set of values without the means to implement them. Thus, even if a program of neighborhood improvement could be accomplished without the aid of larger social institutions, it may fail due to lack of communication and organization. Common values and local identity act as sources for social alienation by reinforcing a sense of powerlessness and potential withdrawal from efforts at social change.

The Stepping-stone neighborhood as defined by Litwak and Fellin[16] is one in which individuals have learned ways to become involved rapidly or in which the neighborhood has the social institutions to involve newcomers quickly. Their value orientation and ultimate identity may lie with a future status or neighborhood, or they may be willing to give up their current locale if job or other commitments necessitate a move. The Stepping-stone neighborhood provides for effective operation of socialization mechanisms and the possible resources of higher-status leaders. What is likely to occur, however, is that conflicts may arise in given areas of goal striving between the needs of the local neighborhood and the values of the larger society. In addition, when value conflicts exist in an area, contact in organizations may aggravate them and hasten the movement out of local organizations of persons already oriented to such a transition.[17] Such conflicts may cause high personnel turnover in organizations. However, if effective mechanisms exist for speeding the integration of newcomers, this problem may not be a serious one.

Residents of *the Transitory neighborhood* fail to participate and identify with the local community. Any neighborhood structure is absent except as persons may deliberately avoid participation or involvements which might interfere with other values or status destinations. Anticipatory socialization and other processes often prevent neighborhood integration from becoming effective or extensive. The Transitory neighborhood has potential for social deviance because of the absence of social control mechanisms. As Litwak *et al.* have pointed out,[18] this might be particularly desirable for upwardly-mobile families who do not want their values undermined by contact with those neighbors who do not share their outlook. Thus the Transitory neighborhood, viewed as a temporary way station by upwardly-mobile persons, may deprive the remaining population of the benefit of elite leadership to carry out social goals.

The Anomic neighborhood, which is a more generally defined situation of urban disorganization, represents the absence of both social organization and social identity with a neighborhood. In this setting individuals are atomized. Attributes of the "mass society" concept are evident. Estrangement from the values of a larger community manifests itself in non-voting and indifference to the goals of a larger community, be they racial, class, or societal. The Anomic neighborhood would be unlikely to influence or change its residents' values or enforce existing values. The very absence of social organization might itself suggest the emergence of values defined as deviant by the larger community. However, the more reasonable hypothesis is that residents of the Anomic neighborhood engage in passive behavior and cannot identify a cause of their alienation.

Pertinence of neighborhood typology for the black ghetto

One of our central theses is that the role of the local neighborhood is more significant in a black ghetto than in white communities. This argument rests on the following assumptions and empirical generalizations:

1. Ghettoization compresses the arena of social interaction of blacks.
   a. This leads to heightened status conflicts between ghetto inhabitants.
   b. This limits institutional alternatives (which are available to whites) to achieve social goals and enforce social values.
2. Ghettoization enforces isolation from the larger society and community.
   a. This heightens the role of the neighborhood as an arena for value definition and social control.
   b. Where socioeconomic status is homogeneous, neighborhoods will become particularly isolated from the values and structures of the ghetto as a whole and the outer community. Deviant subcultures and social withdrawal may be alternative consequences.
   c. Where neighborhoods are heterogeneous in status, neighborhood interaction may heighten conflict and lead to withdrawal of some elements and alienation from outer community values by others.[19]

As starting points for considering the role of neighborhoods in black ghettoes, these assumptions and generalizations suggest that the typology we have constructed may show a statistical distribution in the ghetto that is different from that in the white community. While we cannot validate such a hypothesis, we can strongly suggest, from what we know of ghettoization, that particular kinds of neighborhoods may be prevalent in the ghetto. These would be the Parochial, the

Stepping-stone, and the Transitory. The attributes of these neighborhoods seem to reflect processes that are more pronounced in the ghetto than elsewhere. Socioeconomic status may determine neighborhood setting to some extent—but ghettoization gives rise to additional consequences and determinants.

Data utilization and methodology

Our concern here is to discover relationships between neighborhood types and riot behavior. Pre-riot data were available from two studies done in 1963 and 1964 in a number of Detroit neighborhoods where rioting later occurred or where a high proportion of persons surveyed later indicated riot participation. These early studies permitted an *ex post facto* test of propositions about neighborhoods.

The major portion of analysis, however, is based on a post-riot survey conducted in August, 1967 in the two zones in Detroit where major riot activity took place in July, 1967. This study was carried out using a block sample and personal interviews of blacks. The post-riot survey yielded 417 respondents and contained questions which provided indicators analogous or identical to questions in the two earlier studies.[20]

The pre-riot basis for definition of neighborhood was the elementary school district. Its relatively small size, high degree of physical homogeneity, and built-in provision for shared interests in the given school met most of the criteria considered in defining neighborhood. In the 1963 study, directed by Litwak and Meyer,[21] mothers of fifth and sixth grade children from 18 elementary school districts were interviewed. A sample of 593 Negroes in eight (of the 18) districts was obtained by analyzing only all-Negro neighborhoods. Of these eight, four

proved to be centers of riot activity, and four experienced virtually no riot activity. The same eight elementary school neighborhoods in the 1964 study yielded a sample of 260 respondents.

In order to match the concept of neighborhood employed in the pre-riot studies, the post-riot survey sample population was grouped according to their location in 19 elementary school districts. Six of these 19 neighborhoods overlapped with the 1963-64 areas studied. Although the sampling procedures differed somewhat, the use of the elementary school neighborhood as a basis permitted reasonable and valid comparisons over time.

Summary and conclusions

Reviewing our overall findings, the following relationships are implied by the data:

1. *Integrated neighborhood*—associated with counter-riot behavior, particularly when using white institutional ties.
2. *Parochial neighborhood*—characterizes the non-riot areas using the 1963-64 studies.
3. *Diffuse neighborhood*—characterizes the riot neighborhoods when 1963-64 data are used, the withdrawal areas when using the post-riot correlations.
4. *Stepping-stone neighborhood*—associated with the non-riot neighborhoods in 1963-64, some support for this type defining counter-riot areas using the post-riot data.
5. *Transitory neighborhood*—characterizes the riot areas using post-riot data, particularly if measures of linkage to the larger Negro, not white, community are employed.
6. *Anomic neighborhood*—characterizes the withdrawal and riot neighborhoods using post-riot data.

In a study done immediately after the 1967 Detroit riot, we have analyzed data from 19 neighborhoods in Detroit using the elementary school district as the unit of analysis. We also employed data from studies which were done three and four years prior to the July, 1967 riot. Although both the sampling procedures and the limited overlap in operational measures restricted the validity of our implied longitudinal analysis, our primary purpose was to relate our findings to our typology of six neighborhoods. With a degree of success we found relationships which suggest that riot, counter-riot, and withdrawal behaviors of individuals correlated with particular, carefully defined, types of neighborhood settings.

The essential inquiry was: "Given certain criteria of social participation and value orientations in a neighborhood, what forms of behavior are likely to emerge from these varied milieus?" The answers, in terms of the black ghetto, have important implications for social organization at middle levels of power—i.e., individual effort can become effective through informal and formal neighborhood-based activities.

We found that neighborhoods that experienced high riot activity were lacking in extensive informal social interaction. Moreover, while there was no strong reference orientation to the neighborhood where riot behavior was extensive, there was fairly extensive involvement with the larger community.

Where counter-riot activity took place, neighboring was extensive and linkage to the larger community was present, but more in terms of white than black centers of power. Here the Stepping-stone neighborhood type, where weak local reference-group ties exist, was suggested—particularly when the estrangement from Negro leaders and parents was taken into account.

The withdrawal from riot behavior was much more appropriate to the model of the alienated urban dweller. In neighborhoods with a high degree of withdrawal from the riot, informal social ties and both attitudinal and behavioral linkage to the larger white and black communities were lacking.

The data appear to imply further that estrangement from white institutions increased in the relatively short interval spanned in this analysis. The period between the 1963-64 and the 1967 studies reflects important shifts, particularly in riot neighborhoods. However, the immediate post-riot setting may have exaggerated these differences.

Whatever attitudinal shifts have occurred, the basic questions addressed in our analysis concern the structural underpinnings for enforcing values. We have suggested that neighborhoods vary greatly in this capacity. The mobilization of both riot and counter-riot activism required forms of social organization. In the majority of instances, riot and counter-riot areas more closely match one another than they do the withdrawal areas, despite the low correlation between riot and counter-riot indices themselves. We may conclude that neighborhood units are useful starting points for defining social organization in the black ghetto.

Given the relative absence of alternative mechanisms and structures in an essentially segregated urban environment, it is particularly important to note the potential for social action found in the immediate residential area. Were this unit to be employed as a focus of amelioration by both indigenous groups and external agencies, a more effective basis for implementing and evaluating programs would be provided. The neighborhood offers a visible yardstick of progress in social welfare and social change. Too often the ghetto is viewed monolithically when it is frequently as alienating and amorphous a concept to its inhabitants as is the "White Power Structure."

Certainly the data we have analyzed are more suggestive than definitive, since weaknesses exist in some of the measures used. However, the failure of social scientists, particularly sociologists, to attend to the varieties and functions of *middle-level* social structures in urban settings is a more salient criticism, for this failing ought to be redressed. Studies of the family, on the one hand, and community-wide power structures on the other may well overlook the linkage between the bottom and the top in community organization.

The present effort to draw a social-structural analysis of riot behavior has been useful if it stimulates further efforts to define the context of the ghetto dwellers' existence. Analysis and social action related to the black ghetto must go beyond the concern with the ghetto's sporadic, albeit dramatic, outbursts.

Notes

1. Among the most pertinent studies are those of the 1965 Watts riot, by Raymond J. Murphy and James M. Watson, "The Structure of Discontent," Institute of Government and Public Affairs, UCLA, 1967; and a survey conducted by Nathan Caplan for the Detroit Urban League and discussed in the Report of the National Advisory Commission on Civil Disorders, 1968. Studies of the Detroit riot are: "The Detroit Riot," U.S. Department of Labor, Manpower Administration, March, 1968; Sheldon Lachman and Benjamin Singer, *The Detroit Riot of July, 1967,* Detroit Behavior Research Institute, Detroit, 1968; C. Darrow and P. Lowinger, "The Detroit Uprising: A Psychosocial Study," Department of Psychiatry of Wayne State University School of Medicine and the Lafayette Clinic, paper presented at the Meeting of the American Academy of Psychoanalysis in New York, December, 1967. See also Angus Campbell and Howard Schuman, editors, Supplemental Studies for the National Advisory Commission on Civil Disorders, 1968. See in particular Robert M. Fogelson and Robert B. Hill, "Who Riots? A Study of Participation in the 1967 Riots," pp. 221-248.

2. See Report of the National Advisory Commission . . . *op. cit.,* chap. 2, footnotes 111-143, pp. 171-178; and Fogelson and Hill, *op. cit.,* pp. 229-248; Murphy and Watson, *op. cit.,* passim; Nathan Caplan and Jeffrey M. Paige, "A Study of Ghetto

Rioters," *Scientific American,* 219 (Aug., 1968), pp. 15-21; and Jay Schulman, "Ghetto Residence, Political Alienation, and Riot Orientation," in L. Masotti and D. R. Bowen, editors, *Riots and Rebellion,* Beverly Hills, Calif.: Sage Publications, 1968.

3. Stanley Lieberson and Arnold R. Silverman, "The Precipitants and Underlying Conditions of Race Riots," *American Sociological Review,* 30 (Dec., 1965), pp. 887-898; Allen D. Grimshaw, "Urban Racial Violence in the United States: Changing Ecological Consideration," *American Journal of Sociology,* 66 (1960), pp. 109-119; Milton Bloombaum, "The Conditions Underlying Race Riots as Portrayed by Multidimensional Scalogram Analysis: A Reanalysis of Lieberson and Silverman's Data," *American Sociological Review,* 33 (Feb., 1968), pp. 76-91; National Institute of Mental Health, *Toward an Understanding of Mass Violence,* August, 1967, pp. 3-30; Kurt Lang, "Racial Disturbances as Anomic Movements," paper given at the 62nd Annual Meeting, American Sociological Association, San Francisco, 1967; Allen D. Grimshaw, "Civil Disturbance, Racial Revolt, Class Assault: Three Views of Urban Violence," paper presented at the American Association for the Advancement of Science, New York City, 1967.

4. Aside from considering social structure in terms of socioeconomic position of individuals, no analysis of the recent riots has treated social structure as an independent variable. An article which treats the support for violence in terms of the concepts of isolation and alienation uses individual attitudinal data to define such variables. See H. Edward Ransford, "Isolation, Powerlessness, and Violence: A Study of Attitudes and Participation in the Watts Riot," *American Journal of Sociology,* 72 (Mar., 1968), pp. 581-591. A study of riot support in Bedford-Stuyvesant in 1964 points to higher social participation in formal organizations as a correlate of support for rioting. See J. R. Feasin, "Social Sources of Support for Violence in a Negro Ghetto," *Social Problems,* 15 (Spring, 1968), pp. 432-441.

5. All quotations here are from the Report of the National Advisory Commission . . . , *op. cit.,* pp. 127, 129, 96, and 92 respectively. The study by Anthony Obershall points out that one-third to one-half of the Negroes in Watts sympathized with the rioters. The question he fails to ask is, "How do we account for their attitudinal rather than behavioral support for the riot?" See "The Los Angeles Riot of 1965," *Social Problems,* 15 (Winter, 1968), pp. 322-331.

6. The significance of local neighborhood in riot behavior is indirectly suggested in several riot studies. In their Watts study Watson and Murphy point out that "measures of life style (area of residence and condition of home) show more consistent trends than the individual socioeconomic measure when related to discontent." "Structure of Discontent," *op. cit.,* p. 77.

7. See the classic article by W. S. Robinson, "Ecological Correlations and the Behavior of Indi-

viduals," *American Sociological Review*, 15 (June, 1950), pp. 351-357. In the ecological correlation the variables are percentages, descriptive properties of groups, and not descriptive properties of individuals. While it is theoretically possible for the two (individual and ecological correlations) to be equal, the conditions under which this can happen are far removed from those ordinarily encountered in data. For a fuller analysis of the relationship between geographical units and the data derived from such analysis see Otis D. Duncan, *Statistical Geography*, Glencoe, Ill.: Free Press, 1961.

8. See for example W. Bell and M. D. Best, "Urban Neighborhoods and Informal Social Relations," *American Journal of Sociology*, 42 (Jan., 1957), pp. 391-398; Scott Greer, "Urbanism Reconsidered: A Comparative Study of Local Areas in a Metropolis," *American Sociological Review*, 21 (Feb., 1956), pp. 19-25; T. Caplow and R. Forman, "Neighborhood Interaction in a Homogeneous Community," *American Sociological Review*, 15 (June, 1950), pp. 357-366; M. B. Sussman, editor, *Community Structure and Analysis*, New York: Crowell, 1959, pp. 61-92.

9. Peter Blau, "Structural Effects," *American Sociological Review*, 25 (April, 1960), pp. 178-199. For a careful and rigorous application of this approach to neighborhood influence see Shimon Spiro, "Effects of Neighborhood Characteristics on Participation in Voluntary Associations," dissertation unpublished, University of Michigan, 1968.

10. M. Axelrod, "Urban Structure and Social-Participation," *American Sociological Review*, 21 (Feb., 1956), pp. 13-18; M. Deutsch and M. F. Collins, *Interracial Housing*, Minneapolis: U. of Minnesota, 1951; Leon Festinger *et al.*, *Social Pressures and Informal Groups: A Study of Human Factors in Housing*, New York: Harper, 1950; J. Smith *et al.*, "Local Intimacy in a Middle-Sized City," *American Journal of Sociology*, 60 (Nov., 1954), pp. 276-283.

11. Eugene Litwak, "Reference Group Theory, Bureaucratic Careers, and Neighborhood Cohesion," *Sociometry*, 23 (Mar., 1960), pp. 72-84; Phillip A. Fellin, "A Study of the Effects of Reference Group Orientations and Bureaucratic Careers on Neighborhood Cohesion," unpublished doctoral dissertation, 1963, University of Michigan, chap. 8, pp. 131-145.

12. E. Litwak, "Voluntary Associations and Neighborhood Cohesion," *American Sociological Review*, 26 (April, 1961), pp. 258-271; Phillip Fellin and E. Litwak, "Neighborhood Cohesion Under Conditions of Mobility," *American Sociological Review*, 28 (June, 1963), pp. 364-376.

13. E. Litwak, H. Meyer, and D. Warren, Relationship Between School-Community Coordinating Procedures and Reading Achievement, *Final Report*, Project No. 5-0355, U.S. Department of Health, Education and Welfare, Office of Education, 1960, p. 124.

14. There are two logical possibilities for neighborhoods not included in Table 1. There is a situation where there is a plus-plus with a positive reference group, and a plus-minus where the orientation is negative. In the first situation we would have to imagine persons living in an area, being attached to it, but remaining totally uninvolved and having no social interaction with neighbors. Only temporarily could such a situation prevail, since either a lack of attachment to the neighborhood would develop or the continuation of a positive orientation would lead to social interaction. In the second situation we would have to conjure up a setting in which no positive orientation prevails, yet extensive informal and/or formal social interaction and participation occurs. In other words, social interaction would occur focused on neighborhood values and goals but still the orientation to the neighborhood would be negative. Both situations seem improbable.

15. This is analogous to the distinctions made by Litwak between the advantages of bureaucratic forms of organization versus primary groups. E. Litwak, "Bureaucratic Structures and Primary Groups," *American Journal of Sociology*, 73 (Jan., 1968), pp. 468-481.

16. Fellin and Litwak, "Neighborhood Cohesion Under Conditions of Mobility," *op. cit.*

17. In discussing the role of voluntary associations Litwak states that "where individuals are negatively oriented toward their neighbors, the longer their residence, the more likely they are to realize the differences and the more likely they are to seek to dissociate from their neighbors. In this case they may use voluntary associations as a bridge out of the neighborhood." Litwak, "Voluntary Associations and Neighborhood Cohesion," *op. cit.*, p. 268.

18. See Litwak, Meyer, and Warren, Relationship Between School-Community . . ., *Final Report, op. cit.*, Part II, pp. 79-181.

19. Several unpublished papers by the author deal with both the theoretical and applied implications of ghetto social structure at the middle level of social organization. A research grant focused on such analysis is now underway: Grant #MH 16403, "Social Structural Processes in the Ghetto."

20. Because of ongoing work on neighborhood structure in Detroit, the 1967 riot afforded a unique opportunity to test some assumptions about three consequences of neighborhood structure: 1) passive alienation—the sense of distance and impotence of individuals from the larger social institutions of their society leading to withdrawal from such participation; 2) active alienation—rejection of the institutionalized means of social influence in favor of extremist solutions and goals; and 3) traditionalism—supporting values which are antithetical to social change under conditions that make given social forms inappropriate. These three outcomes might be labeled as withdrawal, left-wing, and right-wing alienation. Because the operation of these processes was to be measured by voting patterns, the occurrence of rioting in the Detroit ghetto did not lend itself to this analysis. However, the development of

certain patterns of individual behavior during the rioting suggested a rather close analogue to the three outcomes. First, the rioter was engaging in behavior which, although not necessarily politically motivated, reflected anti-status quo values. The fact that about as many persons reported themselves to be counter-rioters—i.e., persons who took action to support the police and fire department or to "stop the riot"—indicates behavior supportive of the status quo. This can be related to traditionalism. Finally, the fact that many persons left their neighborhoods during the riot or stayed in their homes reflects a withdrawal associated with passive alienation. For further consideration of these forms of alienation see Donald I. Warren, "Faculty Research Fellowship Report: An Analysis of School Millage Voting and Neighborhood Alienation in 18 Detroit School Districts," Wayne State University, unpublished paper, 1967.

21. The data gathered in 1963 and 1964 related to 18 elementary schools and neighborhoods—12 inner-city and six outer-city. Of these eight were substantially or entirely Negro neighborhoods. Analyses using these areas exclude the white respondents, who formed small minorities. The study was directed by Eugene Litwak and Henry Meyer and dealt with school-community relations and the administrative style of schools. Neighborhoods were not randomly sampled but picked in accordance with matching criteria to schools where special programs were underway. No peculiarity of selection can be traced to neighborhood social structure *per se.*

39.

E. L. Quarantelli, J. Rick Ponting, and John Fitzpatrick

POLICE DEPARTMENT PERCEPTIONS OF THE OCCURRENCE OF CIVIL DISTURBANCES[1]

This paper reports on a part of a larger study of four different civil disturbances that occurred in the summer of 1969 in four large American cities with a substantial non-white population. Each riot centered around a confrontation between some black "ghetto" inhabitants and predominantly white-manned social control agencies such as the police and the National Guard. The disorders ranged from relatively minor to relatively major incidents as measured by number of participants, and by degree of looting, fires and casualties involved, although none were close to the massive disturbances that occurred in Watts, Detroit, or Washington (as reported, e.g., in Conot, 1968; Locke, 1969; and Gilbert, 1968).

Methods

Typically, when students of collective behavior deal with riots, they attempt to synthesize all accounts and perspectives into one overall picture of "what really happened," i.e., a "true" description of the event. The very possibility of doing this has recently been challenged by researchers associated with the Lemberg Center for the Study of Violence. Kapsis and his associates (1970) argue that the traditional or unidimensional methodological approach conveys a false sense of authenticity by attempting to synthesize divergent strands of what happens during a civil dis-

From E. L. Quarantelli, J. Rick Ponting, and John Fitzpatrick, "Police Department Perceptions of the Occurrence of Civil Disturbances." *Sociology and Social Research* 59, October 1974, pp. 30-38, with permission of the publisher.

The research in this paper was supported in part by PHS Grant 5 R01 MH-15399-04 from the Center for Studies of Mental Health and Social Problems, Applied Research Branch, National Institute of Mental Health. A version of this paper was presented at the Annual Meeting of the Southern Sociological Society in Atlanta, Georgia, on April 19, 1974.

turbance. Furthermore, the strain towards descriptive consistency inherent in the unidimensional approach to reporting is seen as underemphasizing the very essence of a civil disturbance, which is a series of group conflict encounters. Using a riot in Richmond, California, as an example, these researchers suggest that a more valid approach would be multi-dimensional, with a separate depiction of the phenomena as perceived by the different groups involved. We would also add that most efforts to describe and to analyze riots, to the extent that perceptual differences are taken into account, do so from an individual rather than group or organizational point of view.

Our larger study took the multidimensional approach, with the object of presenting the varying perceptions and divergent accounts of the disorders as seen from the perspective of social control agencies, the multiplicity of black organizations and the different mass media groups involved. Other parts of this larger study are detailed elsewhere (Fitzpatrick, Ponting and Quarantelli, 1973); in this paper we confine ourselves to a report of the perceptions of civil disturbances by the social control agencies, primarily the police forces, in the communities in which the disorders occurred. With rare exceptions (e.g., Dynes, Ross and Quarantelli, 1972), accounts of disturbances are seldom presented from the viewpoint of the police as we attempt here. Almost as infrequent is the use of an organizational rather than a social psychological perspective of the parties involved in a riot.[2]

Three sets of data were used to build a composite organizational perspective of the social control agencies in the four disturbances.

1. In 1968 teams from the Disaster Research Center (DRC) studied a number of public agencies in these four cities as well as others in an attempt to gather baseline data on organizational and community expectations and planning for civil emergencies (see Dynes and Quarantelli, 1973, for initial reports on these studies). Data from this research were gathered through over 100 views some six to nine months prior to the outbreak of any of the disturbances we studied. This data provided material on previously held organizational perceptions of when and where racial hostilities would emerge, "troublesome" people and groups within given cities and projected techniques for suppressing civil hostilities.

2. About 50 tape recorded interviews were obtained by DRC teams a few days to several weeks after the disorders. The bulk of these interviews were with high-ranking officials from the police and fire departments of the affected cities, county sheriff organizations, and National Guard units from their respective states. They provided rich descriptive details of organizational perceptions at the times of the riots.

3. Concurrent with the interviewing, several dozen documents were obtained from the different social control agencies. These documents included intra-organizational memoranda, after-action reports, organizational logs, arrest records and plans and handbooks of operational procedures. Such material particularly helped to establish chronologies of the disturbances as well as rationales for particular courses of action undertaken.

Findings

Our examination of the data suggests that the findings can be subsumed under five general statements. In what follows, after each general statement we provide an analysis about the organizational perception involved, and conclude with a brief discussion about what might underlie the social control agency perspective.

1. *Social control agencies view disturbances as emanating from one fairly specific event rather than from a series of sequential happenings.*

The tendency is to see one fairly specific event as being "responsible" for the disturbance. Thus, the shooting and death of a black male, the attempted arrest of an "agitator" after police intervention in a fight and shooting into the doorway of a church, were all seen as the direct precipitant of the emergence of crowd and riot behavior in the different disturbances studied. A fairly direct cause and effect relationship tends to be posited between a relatively clearly identifiable action and later illegal activities which necessitated the response of the social control agencies.

This organizational perception is of interest for two reasons. First, the ensuing collective behavior did not immediately follow from the specified event. In all cases, there was a considerable time span, in two instances extending over half a day, between the event and the appearance of clear cut riot behavior. Second, quite similar if not almost identical events were noted as having occurred numerous times in the past without any noticeable consequences. In the city in which the greatest disorder occurred, police department records and interviews indicated at least four different incidents happened in the days prior to the outbreak of the disturbance which overtly appeared to be equally potential "precipitating events" but which were not followed by any disorders. What seems to be overlooked in the organizational perception is what Turner and Killian have called keynoting behavior, that is, activities which present some type of positive suggestions in an ambivalent situation which encourage the development of subsequent actions (1972: 89).

Social control agencies are usually mobilized or brought into a situation by some specific happening. Our analysis suggests that there is a tendency to let that happening dominate the initial actions that are undertaken and to overlook the possible dynamics of the situation. Thus, in one of our case studies, the police viewed the disorders as an outburst that was a product of a shooting and generally ignored such keynoting behaviors as persons calling for action on the part of the group that had gathered at and around the site of the incident. In another of our cases, the focus was on the shooting into the church and far less on the activities associated with the arrest of a black woman attempting to prevent her two sons from being taken into custody. Interestingly, the police riot plans of the two cities involved did emphasize the importance of locating, isolating, and arresting potential "leaders" of disturbances. But this prescription was not heeded. Limitation of the keynoting process to prevent the development of riotous behavior was recognized in organizational plans, but not in the field operations of social control agents.

Some of the reasons for such a limited focus seem clear enough. Situations which later develop into disturbances are often initially responded to by small numbers of social control agents. A few persons can only do so much. Also, in many cases the actual event which mobilizes the organization, such as a shooting, requires the attention of the responding officers to specific details such as the collection of evidence, the identification of witnesses and so on. Thus there is a general diversion away from possible keynoters or keynoting behavior. Furthermore, many keynoting actions in themselves are not necessarily criminal acts, whereas behavior likely to catch police attention initially is more likely to be illegal. Thus, the restricted focus on the specific event which mobilizes them tends to lead police to overlook the dynamics of the situation in which they are operating. In the vast majority of instances in which the police normally act, it is probably true that the specific situation (e.g., a murder, a traffic violation, etc.) will not continue to develop, but this is not so in potential disturbance situations.

2. *Social control agencies view disturbance-generating events as the results of individual actions rather than as the consequences of social conditions.*

Social control personnel were aware of both the poor living conditions and the grievances being expressed about them within the black communities, especially the ghetto areas. Respondent after respondent alluded to such conditions as widespread unemployment, inadequate housing, insufficient recreational facilities, poor educational opportunities and insufficient channels of communication with city agencies. That blacks voiced complaints about these and related matters was also readily admitted.

However, while social control personnel acknowledged the existence of the aforementioned conditions and associated voicing of grievances, there was a tendency to downplay their importance, especially as being significant factors in the outbreak of the disturbances. The dominant tendency was towards personalizing the circumstances leading to the disturbances. That is, riots were seen primarily as the product of malcontent, easily misled or troublemaking individuals. In this perception, neither current conditions within the black community nor their historical antecedents were viewed as important contribut-

ing factors in the rioting. In Gary Marx's phrase, the riots were seen as "issueless" (1970).

In essence, the organized perception is not that social conditions occasion riots, but that people do, by choice. Such a conception is consistent with Rossi's findings with reference to police attitudes towards the causes of civil disorders (1968: 110). This is a point of view, for example, different from that expressed in the Kerner report (1968). In that analysis, stress was given to the centuries of neglect and discrimination by whites against blacks and to the general and inadequate response, both public and private, to problems within the black community, whether housing, education, unemployment, or whatever. Research by social scientists has tended to support these notions, while in addition suggesting other variables as involved in the disturbances such as the close contact of people, rumors, milling, emergent norms and the convergence of large numbers of people at a location, to mention just a few (e.g., Hundley, 1969).

What academicians or investigative committees suggest as the "causes" of civil disturbances versus what social control agents and organizations perceive may be a moot point for some purposes. To use an overworked social psychological proposition, "situations defined as real are real insofar as their consequences are concerned." It is patently clear that to the extent that civil disturbances are seen as the result of the activities of individual participants, emanating from one rather than from a series of happenings or out of the background of the black community history and conditions, then social control tactics will, in part, mirror this view. The analysis of control tactics and strategy in each of the cases studied partially bears out this thesis of a relationship between the strategy used and the social control agency perception of the disturbances. For example, in the case of the most intense disturbance, the control strategy used was definitely that of a show-of-force. This case also illustrates the harshest definition of the riot and the rioters. Thus, there was personal blame rhetoric about "subversiveness" and "revolutionaries," conspiracy themes, rumors (checked out consistently by the police) of militants coming to town to keep things in turmoil, the definition of the disturbance as a meaningless one, and seeing it as triggered by the shooting event and not by preferential police treatment of the assailant as blacks charged. In another case, on the other hand, the containment strategy mirrored a more moderate perception of those participating in the disturbance. Here, themes of conspiracy were far less common, personalization of blame occurred, but in more moderate tones, (e.g., "agitators, militants") and the initiation of the riot was seen as something in which police officers had a part.

Nevertheless, in this and in the other cases also, conditions within the black neighborhoods were generally overlooked as possible causative factors in the disturbances. This is understandable for the police as other groups in American society (including social scientists if one looks at their explanations of police behavior, as discussed in Galliher, 1971) tend to explain social behavior in terms of the makeup of individuals. Answers for social problems especially are sought not in the social structure but within the participants in the system. *Who* is to blame, not *what* is responsible is the general question asked. The police in looking at civil disturbances reflect this general American view of the world and reality.

3. *Social control agencies see individual actions in disturbances as being relatively unorganized and unplanned.*

Superficially, it might appear that social control organizations saw planning and organization in the disturbances. This theme was certainly voiced. Pre-planning for a riot was visualized in some instances with organized elements seen as being involved from the very onset of the process. This view particularly prevailed in one case where certain black groups were said to have met over a three-week period to agitate the black community over a black-white altercation incident. In two of the other case studies, some social control personnel saw organization emerging after the initiation of the disorders. That is, certain groups were seen as working at some "semblance of organization" and "there were people that after this thing (i.e., the disorder) was off the ground, that managed to try and keep it going."

However, the idea of pre-planning or organization of the disturbance was not one that prevailed across-the-board. While this point of view was expressed, it was frequently denied or not supported in the remarks and observations of other officials in the same social control agencies. While some even saw nation-wide conspiracy and usually couched such statements in highly dramatic terms, most respondents simply did not see the actions of riot participants, which were interpreted as individual rather than collective actions, as something that was the result of organized criminal conspiracy.

The denial of any organization or planning in the disturbance was even more strongly expressed by higher officials in the social control agencies, and also particularly by specialized personnel, such as members of police intelligence units. Many such respondents openly scoffed at reports of organization and planning.

They often noted that they had heard rumors about "outside agitators" coming into the local community and frequently checked on these kinds of stories, but seldom found they had any validity whatsoever. This point is neatly illustrated in the major disorder where the highest officials, members of the intelligence squad and the official report all explicitly denied any organization or planning in the riot whereas some individual line officers in interviews claimed just the opposite.

At the agency or organizational level, it is even clearer that little validity was given to notions of planning of the disorders. The social control agencies we studied on the whole were not receptive to such a perception of the situation. They had reached the same conclusion as had the Kerner report that "the Commission has found no evidence that all or any of the disorders or the incidents that led to them were planned or directed by any organization or group, international, national or local" (1968: 202).

There were times during and after the disturbances when some of the social control agencies did issue statements through representatives that sounded as if conspiracy notions were being supported. However, such remarks about planning and organization of disorders seemed almost ritualistic statements of a public relations nature voiced for the consumption of the organization's assumed audience rather than because agency officials voicing them believed them to be true.

In fact, this observation may be an indicator of what is involved in this seeming discrepancy between individual and group perceptions of the situation, and what was sometimes expressed for public consumption. It has been suggested with regard to other social phenomena that there sometimes exists a general belief about a situation which, however, participants disavow as applying to themselves. For example, there is a widespread belief that college and university students find higher education impersonal, uninteresting and nonrelevant, but surveys indicate that while most students believe that this is true in general, they find their own personal educational experiences satisfying and rewarding (Lipset, 1972). At a different level, studies show that Americans believe life in recent years has become worse, more problematic and difficult, but they themselves have few individual complaints and assert that they and their families are doing relatively well. Similarly, many social control personnel project a widespread belief about conspiratorial planning in disturbances, although they do not personally hold such a view. Thus, when faced with the need for a public explanation, some social control personnel rather than indicating what appears to be a very deviant position, make statements along expected lines, which it is thought might be applicable elsewhere. Police departments, as do most other groups, are not above engaging in organizational rhetoric; their public statements about their views of social reality are not always to be taken literally or at face value.

4. *Social control agencies perceive disturbances as stemming from the involvement of certain types of persons.*

There is a strong tendency to label or typologize participants in civil disturbances. The types specified, their number and their degree of explication differed in each of our case studies. Nevertheless, about six basic riot-related "roles" tend to be identified. As might be expected from a common sense typology, the categories are neither mutually exclusive nor based on a single principle of differentiation. The labels applied are our own.

(1) The *agitator* role was most clearly distinguished in all of the four case studies with its content being most consistently and concisely defined. Essentially it was applied to young males using affectively charged exhortations to direct violent actions. Such persons were seen as operating primarily before the actual emergence of disturbances and were not perceived as taking direct actions themselves.

(2) The *enactor* role was also clearly distinguished to all four case studies. It was generally attributed to mostly pre-teen and teen-aged youngsters who were seen as "fertile ground for the agitators." Their activities were primarily seen as consisting of roaming the streets in small groups, hurling missiles and verbal assaults at social control personnel and engaging in firebombing, looting and destroying property.

(3) The *sustainer* role was not as clearly delineated as the two previous roles but seemed generally to refer to persons who, when a disturbance was underway, attempted to keep it going. A variety of motives were attributed for such behavior, ranging from personal to ideological reasons. No particular age or sex category was singled out as engaging in this role.

(4) The *supportive* role was seen as being played by persons who provided either explicit or implicit support for the developing disturbance. This behavior is viewed as essentially of a passive nature, almost that of a bystander at the scene, but nevertheless encouraging agitators, enactors, and sustainers just by their very presence. Females were generally perceived as filling this role more than males, with all ages being possibly involved but with a predominance of middle-aged persons or older.

(5) The *non-participant* role has reference primarily to the local black population not taking part in the disorders. The vast bulk of local black ghetto residents are classified in this way, with constant reiteration of the theme that in black communities "95 to 98 per cent are just as law abiding as anyone else." Their actions in the disturbances consist of avoiding any seeming support (even of the passive nature) of the more active participants.

(6) Finally there is the *counterrioter* role (for a discussion of the concept, see Anderson, Dynes, and Quarantelli, 1974). Counterrioters are perceived as individuals actively working to prevent a disturbance, or if one has started, attempting to bring it to a halt. Altruistic as well as opportunistic motives are attributed to counterrioters. They are most often seen as representatives of traditional Negro organizations, although in some cases young, local black males are perceived as playing the role.

Perhaps equally as important as the use of a typology is that the social control agencies implicitly seem to attribute the emergence of disturbances partly to the interplay of the varying roles. The differentiated mass of black persons in their communities is linked to a pattern of riot dynamics. This is not unexpected. It has long been noted that undifferentiated perceptions are characteristics of groups with little contact with one another whereas social control agencies and ghetto area interactions are extensive and intensive. Furthermore, of necessity there is a "popular sociology" of dramatic events. Faced with disturbances, it is hardly surprising that social control agencies attempt to account for them in some way and draw elements of the explanation from the social class, occupational and subcultural backgrounds of their organizational members.

The implicit riot dynamics model involved in social control agency perceptions of disturbances appears to be somewhat as follows. The world is seen in relatively concrete terms. Thus a disturbance is directly associated with a specific event (e.g., a shooting) to which in retrospect it can be chronologically linked. The event itself is seen as primarily involving people. In *Gestalt* terms, the figure rather than the ground stands out. Thus, the people involved in the initial event are seen as crucial in what may develop. The confusion and uncertainty associated with the situation in the initial stages clearly argues against any collective planning of the event. More important, social control agency personnel do not perceive an undifferentiated mass of people responding to the event. Rather they see some persons (i.e., the agitators) trying to initiate disorderly actions, others (i.e., the enactors) willing to carry out advocated actions, still others (i.e., the sustainers) wanting to continue any ongoing order-disorders, with still more (i.e., the supporters) willing to encourage in a passive way any developing disturbance. On the other hand, most theoretically potential recruits (i.e., the non-participants) stay away as much as possible from the event and there are even a few (i.e., the counter-rioters) who actively oppose illegal activities.

Disturbances occur when certain kinds of people (i.e., those playing the first four social roles mentioned) get more heavily involved in the situation than other certain kinds of people (i.e., those playing the last two roles listed). In essence, social control agencies see the source of disturbances in the participants themselves, as to an extent they also see the absence of disorders stemming from the personal characteristics of ghetto residents. Rather oversimplified and overstated but still capturing the basic perceptual idea involved, disturbances are seen as occurring when the "bad guys" dominate the situation rather than the "good guys."

5. *Social control agencies visualize themselves as blameless for disturbances.*

Social control agencies do assign responsibility or blame for disorders or riots. But it is placed on other than their own organizations or personnel. Thus, even in the one case where the disturbance was seen as resulting from the police attempt to arrest someone defined as an "agitator," our respondents saw "troublemakers" and black militants as the major source of the initiation of the disturbance, even though "the militants didn't get the participation of the real black community." In general, there is a strong tendency to assign responsibility or blame for the disturbances on a relative handful of "agitators" along with a somewhat larger number of "enactors," "sustainers," and "supporters." Rossi and his colleagues in their study of police in the ghetto suggest a similar theme. They note that "while individual policemen differed considerably in their ascription of responsibility for the problems they face (normal police work as well as civil disorders), most tended to see disorders as a result essentially of lawless, negligent, belligerent, and criminal uprising of some elements of the Negro community." (1968: 110).

This point of view is essentially consistent with what has been called the "riff-raff theory of riot participation." Fogelson and Hill note that it involves three closely related themes:

First, that only an infinitesimal fraction of the black population actively participated in the riots. Second, that the rioters, far from being representative of the Negro community, were principally the riff-raff—the unattached, juvenile, unskilled, unemployed, uprooted, criminal—and outside agitators. Indeed many public figures have insisted that outside agitators, especially left-wing radicals and black nationalists, incited the riff-raff and thereby provoked the rioting. And third, that the overwhelming majority of the Negro population—the law abiding and respectable 98 or 99 percent who did not join in the rioting—unequivocally opposed and deplored the riots (1968:222).

Drabek and Quarantelli (1967) in a study of three disasters in American society indicate that there is a tendency to seek the cause of non-natural disastrous events in a *who* rather than a what. This process is no less true in civil disturbances, as mass media accounts, official police reports and the records of post-disturbance investigative commissions and groups will readily testify. The major difference in their treatment of the issue is the matter of who is to blame, that is, social control agents or their opposition, be it blacks, students, or whatever.

Social science research into civil disturbances often utilizes a synthesis approach; that is, draws on material from all sides and attempts to construct a dispassionate one "true" account. The result is to move even further away from the scapegoating process found in the accounts of participants or organizations close to the disturbance. There are many advantages to the synthesis approach, but it does tend to discount the possible significance of the fact that contending groups in disturbances do blame one another, and perhaps more important, obscures the fact that organizations act on the basis of such perceptions, although other factors are also operative in determining group actions.

In our four studies, the dominant perception among our social control agencies was that some part of the black community was at fault with regard to the disturbances. To use an analogy that was implied in many remarks and observations, the disturbances were often viewed as if

they were a mass "mugging." On the other hand, there are the focuses "forces of evil," the "subversives," the "hate-brained people" and those relatively small segments of the black community which initiate and support the rioting for a variety of reasons. On the other hand, there are hapless and innocent bystanders, the passing motorists, blameless businessmen and merchants, and so on who are violated and attacked by "riff-raff" elements, unless or until social control agencies step in to curtail them.

Viewed this way, it is understandable why social control agencies disavow any responsibility for disturbances. From their point of view, far from being a possible source of disorders, they are trying to prevent them. In many ways social control personnel transfer to the unusual collective actions of racial disturbances their view of fighting individual everyday crimes. As already pointed out, perceptions of reality are often mirrored in related actions. The nominalistic view of the disturbances presented by our respondents finds its action corollary in the tactics and strategies of their agencies. Be it a show-of-force or containment strategy, the basic orientation is the same: the removal of "deviant" individuals from the disturbance scene thereby preventing or quashing the development of disturbances. This tends to be the view taken with respect to ordinary crime. Even massive civil disturbances are perceived in a parallel fashion.

Conclusion

In some respects the results of this study are not unexpected. The major finding that social control agencies perceive certain numerically small "bad elements" in the black community as responsible for the disturbance is in line with the frequently expressed "riff-raff" riot theory attributed to law enforcement organizations in American cities. Others of our findings, such as that social control organizations see disorders as being unorganized and unplanned, are not consistent with other also widely expressed views on how the police, for example, tend to view mass racial disturbances. But perhaps more important than specific findings was that we obtained some data on a group seldom directly studied and that we did it from their perspective, a seldom used research stance. If, as we indicated earlier, a synthesis approach to disturbances, crowds and other kinds of collective behavior is on questionable methodological grounds, a whole series of studies using the multiple

perspectives of all parties involved is badly needed. This paper is an attempt to move in that direction.

Notes

1. The term "civil disturbance" is used interchangeably in this paper with such terms as "riot" and "civil disorder" so as to avoid the political implications that any one of these labels might otherwise imply, as discussed by Grimshaw (1968).

2. Organizations as such, of course, can not perceive. However, we use the aggregate of perceptions as provided by high organizational officials as well as the perspective set forth in official organizational documents to delineate an overall organizational perception of the situation. The problem here is the usual one of attributing processes and activities to a supra-individual entity when most concepts available have originally been derived from the behavior of individuals.

V. The City and Nation as Primary Unit of Analysis: Macro-level Characteristics Related to Collective Behavior and Social Movements

Introduction

Recent work in collective behavior at the macro-level focuses on two primary topics: the identification of various social, economic and political factors that influence collective action in cities and nations, and the specification of comprehensive models and perspectives useful in organizing observations. Back's (40) work begins this part of the volume and is exemplary of such all encompassing perspectives. In arguing for a re-examination of the biological model of social change which has long been in disrepute, the author shows how the unidirectional interpretation of biological change set forth by the early Darwinists has been replaced by a more problematic interpretation of evolution that has yet to be seriously examined by those in the social sciences. Back develops an analogy between biological processes and change within social systems based on current interpretation of biological theory. He points out that both biological organisms and societies are organized in such a manner so as to preserve their existence and identity, and maintain relative stability, while at the same time allowing for change in some of their elements. Within this perspective, those actions which fall under the rubric of collective behavior are viewed as natural processes of evolutionary change as the social system, like the biological organism, struggles for existence in an often hostile, ever changing environment.

Although such overall perspectives are useful in systematizing information and relating seemingly disparate sets of observations, theory building requires prediction, and prediction requires a specification of observational units. Davies' article (41), focusing on revolutionary activities, is a step in this direction. This author attempts to develop a general framework for predicting revolution, while challenging the traditional notion that revolutions are the result of a progressive degradation of some segment of the population. To the contrary, Davies argues, revolutions are most likely to occur when a prolonged period of economic and social prosperity is followed by a period of sharp reversal. From this perspective, the absolute state of social and economic conditions is not as important as the blockage of "progress" coupled with the expectation that the social structure will be unable to satisfy the essential demands of persons in the society in the near future.

Breton and Breton (42) develop an economic theory of social movements, and in doing so support Davies' claim that political and social unrest is most likely to occur when a long period of economic development is followed by a sharp decline in the fulfillment of social and economic expectations. The authors expand and clarify this notion by focusing on the processes that explain *why* unrest is most likely to occur during these periods. An analogy is developed that relates economic theory of the firm in the marketplace to the individual in collective behavior situations. Economic theory asserts that the demand for products creates opportunities for entrepreneurial endeavors aimed at profit. The authors argue that in the same manner the demand for social change, sparked by a decrease in the economic system's ability to fulfill basic expectations, creates opportunities for "social profit," such as power, prestige, and control of resources which "social entrepreneurs" will take advantage of by "supplying" social movements.

Parvin (43) lends empirical support to the work of Davies and the Bretons by focusing on the societal level processes that motivate individuals to participate in radical political activity. Central to Parvin's analysis is the notion that one of the primary forces that accounts for political unrest, as well as a wide range of other human behaviors, is the desire to avoid economic deprivation. Thus, when an absolute or relative decline in the flow of economic necessities occurs, individuals may, in attempting to avoid a decline in their personal status, advocate political change. In testing this theory, Parvin defines the elementary properties of "economic well-being" such as relative and absolute income levels, and the nature of economic expectations, and then tests each component for its relative importance in predicting political unrest in a nation. In doing so, the author found an "optimum rate of economic growth" associated with political stability in capitalist countries. Economic processes inherent in very fast growth rates, such as the need for increased personal savings in order to supply the demand for capital, drawn from more immediate expectations and demands, and if extended over time, may lead to economic dissatisfaction. On the other hand, a very slow growth rate has its own set of problems such as the potential for high unemployment, which may also contribute to general political unrest. Parvin concludes that political stability is best achieved through controlled economic growth that minimizes the negative effects of very fast and very slow growth rates. It should be noted that the "Optimum rate of growth" is not yet known, and although useful as a barometer for measuring economic fluctuations, it is rarely, if ever, realized. Nonetheless, recent economic analyses, such as those presented in this volume, have pointed to the important role of economic factors in understanding the underlying forces shaping collective behavior at the national level.

Of course, economic factors are not alone in their effect on political unrest in nations. Various social factors have also been cited as important predictors of social unrest, although not always in ways one might expect. The work of Cooper (44), for example, has shown that once other factors are controlled statistically, the extent of political representativeness does not, as some have argued, produce political stability, but actually increases the chances for political unrest. Both politically representative and politically nonrepresentative countries have experienced political unrest and revolution, and a specification of the conditions under which political turmoil occurs in each of these circumstances is an important area for further research.

In addition to the major economic and social changes that have taken place in the last 50 years, massive technological changes have also led to the development of new forms of collective behavior. One of the most significant technologically based changes has been the diffusion of various means of mass communication. In analyzing the relationship between the diffusion rates of newspapers, films, radio and television between 1900 and 1960, De Fleur (45) lays the groundwork for future research on the causes and consequences of the adaptation of new means of communication. Although this author speculates about the relationship between the diffusion process he describes and various social, economic and political changes in the society, he notes that his work is preliminary in so far as diffusion concepts have to be identified in terms directly related to social action to be of general theoretical value. That is, it is necessary to define the diffusion process on the individual level before statements about the process of adaptation can be justified. The identification of individual and group processes related to the adaptation of new means of communication, as well as the effect of such changes, remains an important area for future research.

The remaining articles in Part V analyze the racial disturbances that occurred in American cities during the late 1960s. Two central issues have emerged from research in this area: First, what is the most appropriate operational definition of "riot behavior," and second, what characteristics of the urban environment are important in predicting the locations where riots will take place.

The measurement controversy has centered around whether it is best to simply account for the *occurrence* of riots, or to measure the *severity* of each occurrence. Although this issue has generally been resolved in favor of measuring severity, no clear agreement has emerged as to what criteria constitute adequate measures. Each of the articles presented here is concerned with characteristics of cities important in predicting the severity of riot behavior. However, each researcher argues for a different form of measurement, pointing to the general lack of agreement concerning the measurement of various behaviors both in collective behavior and in social science generally. Consensus with respect to operational definitions is essential for scientific development because even measurement techniques that appear similar often produce substantially different correlations and correspondingly different conclusions when related to other variables.

A comparison of the work of Morgan and Clark (46) and Spilerman (47) is a good illustration of this problem. Both articles attempt to pinpoint the correlates of the severity of racial disturbances in 42 U.S. cities, 23 of which had experienced some form of racial disorder in 1967. Morgan and Clark report that the size of the city and dissatisfaction with housing inequality between Blacks and Whites are the best predictors of the severity of racial disturbances. They interpret these findings as an indication of an underlying level of frustration experienced by Black urban residents.

In contrast, Spilerman finds no evidence to support the contention that the severity of urban riot events is related to the level of frustration experienced by Black ghetto residents. Presenting data on 322 riots in major U.S. cities in 1967 and 1968, this author first formulates a rationale for redefining the measure of riot severity used by Morgan and Clark. In addition to questioning the validity of certain items used in their measure of riot severity, Spilerman also points out that severity can often be confounded by history: Prior racial disturbances may lead to an increase or decrease in riot severity, depending on the reaction of social control agencies to the first event and general post-riot perceptions of the situation on the part of the participants.

In analyzing particular aspects of urban social organization likely to be related to the severity of riots, Spilerman attempts to determine how riot behavior is conditioned by the way cities are structured socially and politically, and by the pervasiveness of the deprivation experienced by Blacks in the urban setting. Unlike Morgan and Clark however, Spilerman finds no evidence to support the conclusion that riot severity is a function of social and economic deprivation. Spilerman, pointing out that most riots took place in a very restricted time span, speculates that the severity, as well as the occurrence of riots, can be attributed to national phenomenon, such as the wide availability of television. He argues that such factors may have contributed in a fundamental way to Black solidarity which transcended the boundaries of individual communities, and led to an intensification of riot activity.

The final article in Part V also focuses on the measurement of riot severity. Wanderer (48) argues that the best way to measure the severity of riots is to develop a Guttman scale based on certain critical events that usually take place in sequence during a riot. *Guttman Scaling* is a means of analyzing the underlying characteristics of three or more variables to determine if each is measuring some single underlying characteristic. Although there are a number of techniques available in the social sciences for doing this, Guttman scales are unique in that the items used in the measure can be ordered by their *degree of difficulty*. That is, if a city scores positively on the most difficult item, it can be reasonably assumed, within a given margin of error, that certain other events of a less difficult nature have also occurred. For example, Wanderer reports that those cities experiencing sniping during a riot usually experienced looting, interference with firemen, and vandalism. In this instance, sniping is the most difficult item, and in those cities where sniping took place the other events were usually present and had begun prior to the sniping. Wanderer develops a series of items that he orders in such a way so that the vast majority of cities that have experienced the second most severe indication of riot severity had also experienced the first, and those that had experienced the third most serious indicator had also experienced the second and first, and so forth. In this way this author shows that events constituting civil disorders have a relatively predictable sequence that corresponds to riot severity, and that substantial differences exist between the strength and substance of the correlates of this measure when compared to the correlates of riot occurrence.

This level of analysis is subject to a problem of interpretation that should be noted. The processes affecting the behavior of cities or nations in an overall sense are not necessarily identical to those affecting individual behavior, and caution must be exercised in generalizing research findings from this level of analysis to the individual or micro-level. For example, in a study of political stability, we might find that as the proportion of unemployed persons in a specified geographic area increases, the chances for political instability also increase. Such findings are often interpreted to mean that being unemployed leads to radical political activity, and hence political instability. While this may be true, such a statement cannot be supported with macro-level data. Such interpretations, often referred to as *ecological fallacies,* are erroneous in that while it may be true that those *geographic areas* (i.e., cities, nations, etc.) with higher proportions of unemployed persons are more likely to face political instability than those with less unemployment, it may be that *employed* persons living in areas where the unemployment rate is particularly high are the most likely to participate in radical political activity. In order to link individuals to political unrest (or any other form of collective behavior) it is necessary to collect and analyze data on the individual level. So long as interpretations are limited to the unit of analysis under consideration this problem does not occur.

40.

Kurt W. Back

BIOLOGICAL MODELS OF SOCIAL CHANGE

The analogy of society as an organism is old, attractive, and disreputable. It has been used to justify existing schemes of hierarchical structures, sometimes with telling effect if legend is to be believed. According to Livy, Menenius Agrippa, a patrician, settled an incipient revolt by the plebeians by telling them a story about the usefulness of the stomach. Although the stomach apparently does not do any work but gets all the food which the other parts of the body make a great effort to obtain, a strike against the stomach by the rest of the body is obviously self-defeating. Hence, the necessity for an analogous group in society or, as we may say today, a leisure class. Similar facile applications have reoccurred, using new insights into the biological process. Thus when organic evolution showed itself to be a workable theory, Social Darwinism tried to adapt this theory to explain the current social and economic system. Again the data on biological organisms were used to justify an existing state of affairs, and the deficiencies of this approach soon became apparent. In the development of scientific sociology, grand developmental theories treating society like an organism have become extremely suspect.

Even with all these setbacks, the idea of a social unit as a kind of organism dies slowly. Common language, from the "body politic" to "heads of state," bears witness to man's inclination to find organic traits in societies. Over the years these have ranged from the analogy comparing human life to the life of a culture to theories explaining the structure of small groups in terms of the psychoanalytic organization of the psyche. There is, after all, an intuitive similarity between the organization of the human body and the kinds of organizations men create. And so, undaunted by the failures of the human-social analogy through time, new theorists try afresh in each epoch.

With the revived interest in large scale models of social change and development, this approach has also come in for renewed criticism. Robert Nisbet (1970) has given some of the most incisive critiques; his structures against developmentalism can be grouped into two headings: (1) in general, there is more permanence than change; therefore any model should account more for stability than for change, especially the even rarer, abrupt changes. (2) Changes in society do not occur in a vacuum—depending only on intrinsic features—but in history, and they cannot be understood without reference to historical events. In this sense changes are unique and cannot be fitted into a general developmental scheme. Nisbet shows the challenges of any analogy between organisms and society which have to be overcome in any serious effort. The difficulties rest on the great obvious differences between organisms and societies. The shapes of organic configurations and

From Kurt W. Back, "Biological Models of Social Change," *ASR,* Vol. 36, August 1971, pp. 660-67. Reprinted by permission of The American Sociological Association and the author.

Paper presented at the meetings of the Southern Sociological Society in Atlanta, Georgia, April 9-11, 1970.

societies are determined by particular circumstances. An organism owes many of its peculiar characteristics to its particular survival situation. And societies are formed in great part by historical accidents, and, looking at them, one finds that they look very different. If we take societies as a whole, we can consider only such a small number that each exception must be dealt with separately, and most of the theory will look like ad hoc reasoning. On the other hand, the wealth of detailed information on living organisms and the abundance of animal species have made possible detailed biological theories. Thus the stress on history in discussing social systems as compared to biological systems rests largely on the larger size and smaller number of social systems. However, the same difficulty with intrinsic theories which Nisbet discusses plagues also theories of organisms, if we substitute biographical for historical idiosyncracies. Thus the disengagement theory of aging (Cummings and Henry, 1961) has been criticized as depending overly on intrinsic factors while overlooking influences of personal history analogous to Nisbet's strictures on developmentalism (Lowenthal and Boler, 1963; Maddox, 1965). The usual effort of the analogists has been to assimilate societies to the biological theories of the development of species and individuals and to fit in a selected few examples of social change. Thus in Western history the unique occurrences of the fall of the Roman Empire and the French Revolution have led to the expectation of regularity in falls of empires and courses of revolutions.

Any model which purports to display general features of development must be able to face Nisbet's two strictures. It must attempt to show similarities in mechanism beyond historical accidents and account for persistence as well as for change.

If the study of biological organisms can help in understanding society, it has to go beyond the accidents of biological and social conformation. Both societies and organisms are organized in such a way that they are self-maintaining, they react to preserve their organizations, and they maintain a certain stability or identity while changing some of their parts. These are characteristics which all living systems have in common, which make them "open systems." Allport (1960) states four conditions for an open system. They are input and output of matter and energy, maintenance of steady states, increase in complexity, and active interaction with the environment. Thus any living organism or complex of organisms can be considered to be an open system.

The first two conditions relate to the maintenance of the system; last two, however, make change part of the definition of the system. This seeming contradiction—that the nature of systems is both preservation and change—makes it possible to describe both stability and change. The biologist has distinguished mechanisms, some of which maintain equilibrium under changing conditions, some of which create change in the system, and some of which are indicators of breakdown of adaptation. Study of the essential characteristics of these processes can help the sociologist in understanding stability and change in social systems.

There are several ways in which the model of the biological open system can be related to models of society. One distinction is between material and formal relationships. The former refers to the fact that man is a physiological organism and a separate species which has to obey the general laws of biology. Thus Duncan's (1964) paper on ecology treats population processes from the point of view of a species living in an ecosystem. Work of social psychologists in sociobiology (cf. Shapiro and Crider, 1969) has shown the importance of physiological processes in social interaction. The other mode of extension, which we shall be using here, is the formal mode; here the emphasis is on the equivalence of processes which occur in all living systems, biological as well as social. We shall pursue here a theoretical, logical analysis of the importance of biological concepts in understanding social change and equilibrium, not an application of the biological characteristics of man to social processes.

The formal approach has been used productively by the general system theorists (Bertalanffy, 1968; Buckley, 1967; Miller, 1965). However, in the main they have been working on the principles which characterize *all* system processes, starting with such concepts as information, communication, organization, or decision. This approach has lost some of its power by being too general, by the difficulty to translate these general concepts into specifics. We shall here attempt to overcome this obstacle by concentrating not on general system characteristics but on distinct processes which have been identified in biological systems and show their explanation in social systems. Presumably other concepts are more conveniently identified first in social systems and may help in understanding biological events; concepts which come to mind are stratification, organization, or power. In this paper we shall attempt to understand the functioning of six processes which have been studied in detail in biological organisms and determine their meaning in social systems.

The types of transaction

The six processes which biologists have used in characterizing living systems (Quarton, 1967) are commonly identified in biological organisms as perception, learning, maturation or growth, immunity, heredity, and evolution. These processes differ according to four characteristics: the manner in which organisms process information, the time span over which they operate, the feedback mechanisms they employ, and the source of their motive power.

A. Interaction process

One of the conditions which distinguishes living systems is their use of communication and transmission of information instead of the transport of matter and energy. The basic feature of the communication process is the translation of available facts into a composite code which can be stored and transmitted easily. The form of the code and its storage depend on the particular transmitting system used. The code carries the information, which can be retrieved at a later time. However, the original input and output may be quite different from each other. The retranslation from the code will depend on the context, the conditions under which retrieval occurs. The retrieved information will be decoded and become a new body of facts influenced by the new situation. These facts may be coded again if new transmission is needed. The newly coded information may be the same in spite of a change by the organism during adaptation to the current situation. Thus coded information will be constant over time, but the interpretation will determine whether transmission occurs at all. For instance, in the case of genetics, the coded information is called genotype, or basic state, and the interpretation, phenotype, or seeming state. The genotype persists over time, depending on the viability of the phenotype.

In looking at biological systems, we find three ways of dealing with information. One is the processing of information and acting on it directly by the system. An example of this would be the reflex arc. A second way is the storage of information for use at a later time, for instance, use of memory. The third is the alternation of the above two systems—one phase which interacts with the environment and the other which transmits the information. This is the mechanism of genetics which implies growth, decline, and death of the single organism.

There are several ways in which organisms can use these three information-processing mechanisms in their interaction with the environment. In identifying these processes in organisms, we find two kinds of mechanisms for each of the ways of dealing with information, and the six resulting combinations are those previously mentioned as being characteristics of living systems. For the direct reaction we have perception and evolution. For memory we have learning and immunity. For genetics we have maturation, or growth, and heredity.

B. Time span

The second of the four characteristics used to describe the processes by which the organism establishes its dynamic equilibrium is that of the time dimension. The processes are, from shortest to longest duration: perception, learning, maturation, immunity, heredity, and evolution. The first three—perception, learning and maturation—refer to the life-span of one organism; the last two—heredity and evolution—refer to the continuity between organisms. The immunity mechanism is a peculiar development of higher organisms. It consists of the creation of specific proteins which become defenses against invasion by foreign bodies; its ability to conduct the defenses is partly genetically determined, and partly formed through encounter with particular invaders. After one experience the protein keeps the shape adapted to this invasion and in a way learns to recognize the specific danger. The immunity process is thus a specific learning ability to defend the integrity of the organism and to maintain its boundaries. It may apply to individuals as well as to the whole species and is thus intermediate in time span.

We shall not look for direct analogies to these processes in societies. At this point we may only take notice of the importance of the time range of these processes and how different durations lead to quite different types of maintenance processes.

The time span is the most easily noticeable characteristic, and the differences have been discussed usually under the heading of the cultural and biological evolution. Thus, Campbell (1965) has contrasted two pairs in our scheme, perception and learning, on one side and heredity and evolution on the other, to demonstrate that biological principles do not lead necessarily to a theory of unilinear progress. He then shows how elective retention can operate on shorter and longer time spans.

C. Feedback

One of the most discussed features of living systems is the feedback mechanism which is the third characteristic given above (Watzlawick et al., 1967). Some part of the output of a transmission is channeled back toward the input to the same transmission, creating in this way a kind of loop. Feedback can be of two types, positive and negative. In positive feedback the new input increases the outside stimulation and therefore makes the reaction stronger. Negative feedback counteracts the ongoing transaction . . . (i.e., evolution) the system will establish a gradual drift to a new adaptive mode.

In the internally motivated transactions the situation is the opposite. Maturation or growth of one individual has positive feedback and no specified equilibrium; this is compensated for by the equilibrium positions of heredity-connecting generations. Thus the alternation principle is maintained by the system itself. This contrast results then in a wave-like pattern: growth and decay over the short range (i.e., maturation) and repetition of the pattern (i.e., heredity) over the long range.

Learning has a different position. We have distinguished two types of learning: cognitive learning or memory processes, and immunity which is learning of identity. In both cases there is a question how far internal or external motives prove to be present, or whether there is selection or instruction. Learning in any case is the most "living" of all the processes discussed. It determines the individuality of the organism and society, its peculiar abilities and its identity. Basically it is probably an equilibrium-producing transaction, but it can easily upset the equilibrium; cognitive learning may lead to strengthened activity, and in the long range immunity process, the transaction may lead to over-rejection and upset of equilibrium with the environment.

For memory, the figure shows three pairs of processes of information transmission. One set (perception and evolution) regulates the adaptation to environment; the system will either immediately react to a disturbance of its equilibrium, or over the long range will change its whole equilibrium condition. The second pair of processes (growth and heredity) is the mechanism of internal development corresponding to the alternation of phenotypi-

cal configuration and the coded genotype. The transcription will result in cumulative change, adapting the particular phenotype to the life situation of the organism. The stability of the message itself is guaranteed through a longer-range process which reduces the basic message and transmits it.

Finally there are the learning processes which are both active and passive. They are ambiguous as well in whether they establish an equilibrium or destroy it, and are, in the main, what Allport meant by activities in active interaction with the environment which keep the system open.

Catastrophic changes and system boundaries

The regular workings of living systems are carried on by the forenamed six processes. In these cases, the systems work in a stable manner and show adaptation to the environment. However, in addition to this slow kind of change, we find some abrupt, creative, or catastrophic kinds of change which occur when the processes function differently from the normal situation. For instance, positive feedback occurring in perception will lead to the organism's seeking more and more intense stimulation and experiences. Further, if perception is internally stimulated, then the organism is subject to illusory-wrong information about its environment and may act in a nonadaptive manner. These experiences may produce strong emotions in an individual leading to abrupt personal changes. The conditions for peak experiences in the individual are the reversal of normal conditions of short-term stimulation of the organisms, making their reactions destitute of equilibrium and adjustment but reaching new states with potentially deep effect.

A similar effect can occur in the long-range transactions which maintain equilibrium. Under some conditions coding is defective and does not create the equilibrium and adjustment of the original gene-pool. Mutation of genes produces changes which are not framed in relation to the environment, but which upset the state through positive feedback, increasing quickly some tendency which may have no relation to the current surroundings. These spontaneous changes are frequently detrimental, but they provide an important avenue for completely novel ventures.

The fact that a comprehensive system theory has to provide for maintenance of equilibrium and gradual adaptation and catastrophic change has led to many difficulties in sociological system theories. Functional theories, such as Parsons', stress the maintenance of equilibrium, while conflict theories from Marx on have concentrated on revolution, i.e., catastrophic change. It is necessary to specify the functioning and breakdown of each type of mechanism to be able to study the conditions under which each kind of stability and change occurs.

Catastrophic changes lead to major changes, sometimes making the original unit unrecognizable. This brings up the question of the definition of the system, of its limits and boundaries. Admittedly, the definition of the system and its boundary is a difficult problem for systems analysis. The definition of a system is to some degree arbitrary, a decision of the investigator, and to some degree derived from measurable distinctions between what is included in and what is excluded from the system. Here, the biologist has the advantage over the sociologist; organisms are generally well defined. But even with biological systems the boundaries are not always obvious, the single organism is in effect an abstraction (Back, 1971) as it functions only within an ecological context; controversy on the point where an embryo is an independent organism also points to the ambiguity of the definition.

In compensation the sociologist has his own advantage, namely one of the most effective measures distinguishing membership within the system. In effect, there are two ways to determine the boundaries of a social system: one through identification of the members themselves, the other through other indicators, such as internal similarity or networks. All of these measures can be used to determine whether an abrupt dislocation produced change in the same system or destroyed the system completely.

An example of this problem is the definition of region as social units. The question whether the "South" has persisted as a meaningful system can be answered partly by the affective meaning of "Southerner" as identification, and it is also possible through a series of demographic, economic, and ecological measures (Winsborough, 1965). Contrast between these two positions has persisted since Odum (1936), and is represented in two articles in a recent issue of this *Review* (McKinney and Boueque, 1971; Gastil, 1971).

General principles of change in living systems

We have tried to organize the modes of a system's transactions with its environment. In doing so, we have used the individual organism as a model, because on this level the mechanisms are distinct and have been studied in detail. This feature has led sometimes to the erroneous organic analogy with society which has brought this whole procedure into disrepute. In this paper we have attempted to avoid this pitfall and have identified some general principles which may be applicable to systems in general, both organic and social, and can be tested on each level. In particular, we introduce four dimensions whose combination could lead to some general principles. They are time span, mode of information processing, feedback, and sources of motive power. We can now state some principles, based on the interaction of these four dimensions on the organic level, which are relevant to social change.

1. Maintenance of internal equilibrium is one of the functions of every system. Equilibrium is maintained in two ways. At any time there is one ideal equilibrium point (set point) which the system tries to maintain: one of the important mechanisms here is negative feedback. Minor deviations are corrected and compensated for quickly. If the situation persists and stress occurs, the system can change completely through cumulative effects, and a new equilibrium condition, a new set point, may be reached. Thus different mechanisms will exist for immediate re-establishment of equilibrium, and there are those which allow for long-term drift. There will also be mechanisms for the balance of internal conditions. Within the system itself there will be mechanisms for rhythmical growth and those which assure that their rhythm will have a stable base line.

Thus work groups will maintain a constant output using sanctions on those group members who produce below the normal level as well as on those who produce above it. Change of productivity will occur only when a new group norm is set, and this level is again used as a standard to be enforced. A similar analysis can be made of other normative behavior; the concept of quasi-stationary equilibrium has been employed to distinguish temporary and long-range changes (Lewin, 1947).

2. Besides maintenance of equilibrium, a system has mechanisms for maintaining identity. It has some mechanisms which maintain boundaries and those which reject intrusions even if they pass the boundaries. The specific definition of hostile intrusions will depend on the experience of the system, but the system is so organized that some definition will be reached. In terms of societies, ethnocentrism is not inborn, but the tendency to obtain some social identity and to defend it is.

The processes by which identity of a social system is defended can be better understood by considering their structural analogy to immunity processes. The ambiguity of immunity with regard to time span is duplicated by these defenses. Social identity is maintained by cultural tradition, but its expression is learned fresh by each member of the society through his own experiences inside and outside the system. Language is one of the mechanisms of maintaining social identity. The tenacity of clinging to languages and conflicts over the adoption of another language is a process closely analogous to maintenance of immunity (Fishman, 1966; Deutsch, 1953). We can also trace the beneficial effects for maintaining cohesion and in-group functions as well as potentially harmful results, such as overreaction (analogous to allergy) and rejection of new ideas (analogous to transplant rejection).

3. The previous point has alerted us to the importance of learning processes. Identity learning is so important that it frequently has separate mechanisms, but cognitive learning is also as important for stability and change. Both types of learning are intrinsically neutral about stability and change and can have effects in each direction. They are the mechanisms which lead to the understanding of the particular system and to general differentiation, the

anti-entropy states of open systems. Thus development of . . . and therefore keeps the resultant output on an even keel. In general, interest has centered on negative feedback, as this is the mechanism through which equilibrium or balance is maintained. However, positive feedback may have equal importance. This process works against stability, but it can result in increased power of the transaction, and on an individual level, in emotion and excitement. As it is a one-sided incremental process, it cannot go on unchecked. Therefore, it has been considered to be pathological, as the vicious circle. Unchecked growth due to hormonal imbalance in the individual organism can be compared on the interpersonal level with the pathological conditions leading to schizophrenia (Bateson, 1956) or with Richardson's (1960) theory of arms races. Rapoport (1968) has noted that the same process may be beneficial and lead, say, to better understanding and disarmament. There is no term, however, denoting this beneficial effect. We may classify the six processes listed above according to their affinity for negative or positive feedback.

Perception, learning, and heredity seem to be mainly dependent on negative feedback; they are the equilibrium-maintaining processes. The organism's perceptual apparatus has developed to give it a stable view of its surroundings, giving constancy to an ever changing world of phenomena. The same may be said of learning and memory over a somewhat longer time span. Similarly the mechanisms of heredity insure the stability of transmission of the organism's characteristics to its offspring. On the other hand, maturation and evolution as mechanisms of change are especially open to positive feedback. Maturation of a single organism typically implies growth which depends on positive feedback; if the organs which are changing work well, they will be more and more stimulated and will keep growing and functioning even more as time passes. What is true for the growth of the individual is true for evolution between generations. Success in adaptation will encourage more survivors to breed, and drift in a certain direction will become established as continuous. In this way new species are formed.

Immunity is ambiguous with regard to feedback as well as to time. It is self-limiting, restricting itself to eliminating noxious intruders, but positive feedback occurs frequently and leads to the generalization of immunity and frequently to exaggeration or allergies. Again, the boundary-maintaining function is sometimes ambiguous.

Conclusion

The use of biological models via the general systems approach leads to new perspectives on social stability and change. Systems analysis has two aspects. One tries to show the general principles to which all systems, both organic and social, conform. The other characterizes the applicability and expressions of the systems at each level. The principles enumerated here define specific social processes derived from the biological level. They remain hypotheses to be tested at the social level. They give guidelines to further investigation as well as a framework for integrating much existing knowledge.

41.

James C. Davies

TOWARD A THEORY OF REVOLUTION

In exhorting proletarians of all nations to unite in revolution, because they had nothing to lose but their chains, Marx and Engels most succinctly presented that theory of revolution which is recognized as their brain child. But this most famed thesis, that progressive degradation of the industrial working class would finally reach the point of despair and inevitable revolt, is not the only one that Marx fathered. In at least one essay he gave life to a quite antithetical idea. He described, as a precondition of widespread unrest, not progressive degradation of the proletariat but rather an improvement in workers' economic condition which did not keep pace with the growing welfare of capitalists and therefore produced social tension.

A noticeable increase in wages presupposes a rapid growth of productive capital. The rapid growth of productive capital brings about an equally rapid growth of wealth, luxury, social wants, social enjoyments. Thus, although the enjoyments of the workers have risen, the social satisfaction that they give has fallen in comparison with the increased enjoyments of the capitalist, which are inaccessible to the worker, in comparison with the state of development of society in general. Our desires and pleasures spring from society: we measure them, there-

From James C. Davies, "Toward a Theory of Revolution," *ASR*, Vol. 27, June 1962, pp. 5-19. Reprinted by permission of The American Sociological Association and the author.

Several people have made perceptive suggestions and generous comments on an earlier version of this paper. I wish particularly to thank Seymour Martin Lipset, Lucian W. Pye, John H. Schaar, Paul Seabury, and Dwight Waldo.

fore, by society and not by the objects which serve for their satisfaction. Because they are of a social nature, they are of a relative nature.[1]

Marx's qualification here of his more frequent belief that degradation produces revolution is expressed as the main thesis by de Tocqueville in his study of the French Revolution. After a long review of economic and social decline in the seventeenth century and dynamic growth in the eighteenth, de Tocqueville concludes:

So it would appear that the French found their condition the more unsupportable in proportion to its improvement.... Revolutions are not always brought about by a gradual decline from bad to worse. Nations that have endured patiently and almost unconsciously the most overwhelming oppression often burst into rebellion against the yoke the moment it begins to grow lighter. The regime which is destroyed by a revolution is almost always an improvement on its immediate predecessor.... Evils which are patiently endured when they seem inevitable become intolerable when once the idea of escape from them is suggested.[2]

On the basis of de Tocqueville and Marx, we can choose one of these ideas or the other, which makes it hard to decide just when revolutions are more likely to occur—when there has been social and economic progress or when there has been regress. It appears that both ideas have explanatory and possibly predictive value, if they are juxtaposed and put in the proper time sequence.

Revolutions are more likely to occur when a prolonged period of objective economic and social development is followed by a short period of sharp reversal.[3] The all-important effect on the minds of people in a particular society is to produce, during the former period, an expectation of continued ability to satisfy needs—which continue to rise—and, during the latter, a mental state of anxiety and frustration when manifest reality breaks away from anticipated reality. The actual state of socio-economic development is less significant than the expectation that past progress, now blocked, can and must continue in the future.

Political stability and instability are ultimately dependent on a state of mind, a mood, in a society. Satisfied or apathetic people who are poor in goods, status, and power can remain politically quiet and their opposites can revolt, just as, correlatively and more probably, dissatisfied poor can revolt and satisfied rich oppose revolution. It is the dissatisfied state of mind rather than the tangible provision of "adequate" or "inadequate" supplies of food, equality, or liberty which produces

the revolution. In actuality, there must be a joining of forces between dissatisfied, frustrated people who differ in their degree of objective, tangible welfare and status. Well-fed, well-educated, high-status individuals who rebel in the face of apathy among the objectively deprived can accomplish at most a coup d'état. The objectively deprived, when faced with solid opposition of people of wealth, status, and power, will be smashed in their rebellion as were peasants and Anabaptists by German noblemen in 1525 and East Germans by the Communist élite in 1953.

Before appraising this general notion in light of a series of revolutions, a word is in order as to why revolutions ordinarily do not occur when a society is generally impoverished—when, as de Tocqueville put it, evils that seem inevitable are patiently endured. They are endured in the extreme case because the physical and mental energies of people are totally employed in the process of merely staying alive. The Min-

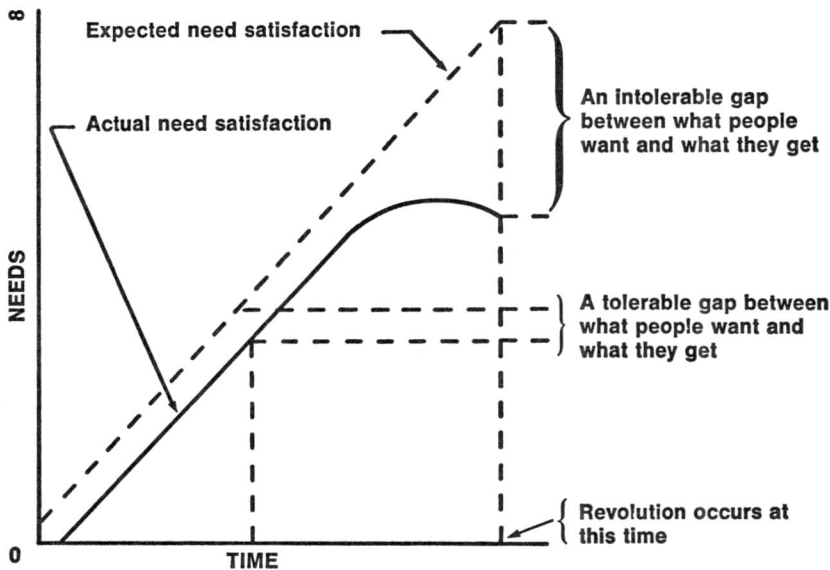

Figure 1. Need Satisfaction and Revolution

nesota starvation studies conducted during World War II[4] indicate clearly the constant pre-occupation of very hungry individuals with fantasies and thoughts of food. In extremis, as the Minnesota research poignantly demonstrates, the individual withdraws into a life of his own, withdraws from society, withdraws from any significant kind of activity unrelated to staying alive. Reports of behavior in Nazi concentration camps indicate the same preoccupation.[5] In less extreme and barbarous circumstances, where minimal survival is possible but little more, the preoccupation of individuals with staying alive is only mitigated. Social action takes place for the most part on a local, face-to-face basis. In such circumstances the family is a—perhaps the major—solidary unit[6] and even the local community exists primarily to the extent families need to act together to secure their separate survival. Such was life on the American frontier in the sixteenth through nineteenth centuries. In very much attentuated form, but with a substantial degree of social isolation persisting, such evidently is rural life even today. This is clearly related to a relatively low level of political participation in elections.[7] As Zawadzki and Lazarsfeld have indicated,[8] preoccupation with physical survival, even in industrial areas, is a force strongly militating against the establishment of the community-sense and consensus on joint political action which are necessary to induce a revolutionary state of mind. Far from making people into revolutionaries, enduring poverty makes for concern with one's solitary self or solitary family at best and resignation or mute despair at worst. When it is a choice between losing their chains or their lives, people will mostly choose to keep their chains, a fact which Marx seems to have overlooked.[9]

It is when the chains have been loosened somewhat, so that they can be cast off without a high probability of losing life, that people are put in a condition of proto-rebelliousness. I use the term proto-rebelliousness because the mood of discontent may be dissipated before a violent outbreak occurs. The causes for such dissipation may be natural or social (including economic and political). A bad crop year that threatens a return to chronic hunger may be succeeded by a year of natural abundance. Recovery from sharp economic dislocation may take the steam from the boiler of rebellion.[10] The slow, grudging grant of reforms, which has been the political history of England since at least the Industrial Revolution, may effectively and continuously prevent the degree of frustration that produces revolt.

A revolutionary state of mind requires the continued, even habitual but dynamic expectation of greater opportunity to satisfy basic needs, which may range from merely physical (food, clothing, shelter, health, and safety from bodily harm) to social (the affectional ties of family and friends) to the need for equal dignity and justice. But the necessary additional ingredient is a persistent, unrelenting threat to the satisfaction of these needs: not a threat which actually returns people to a state of sheer survival but which puts them in the mental state where they believe they will not be able to satisfy one or more basic needs. Although physical deprivation in some degree may be threatened on the eve of all revolutions, it need not be the prime factor, as it surely was not in the American Revolution of 1775. The crucial factor is the vague or specific fear that ground gained over a long period of time will be quickly lost. This fear does not generate if there is continued opportunity to satisfy continually emerging needs; it generates when the existing government suppresses or is blamed for suppressing such opportunity.

Some conclusions

The notion that revolutions need both a period of rising expectations and a succeeding period in which they are frustrated qualifies substantially the main Marxian notion that revolutions occur after progressive degradation and the de Tocqueville notion that they occur when conditions are improving. By putting de Tocqueville before Marx but without abandoning either theory, we are better able to plot the antecedents of at least the disturbances here described.

Half of the general, if not common, sense of this revised notion lies in the utter improbability of a revolution occurring in a society where there is the continued, unimpeded opportunity to satisfy new needs, new hopes, new expectations. Would Dorr's rebellion have become such if the established electorate and government had readily acceded to the suffrage demands of the unpropertied? Would the Russian Revolution have taken place if the Tsarist autocracy had, quite out of character, truly granted the popular demands for constitutional democracy in 1905? Would the Cairo riots of January, 1952 and the subsequent coup actually have occurred if Britain had departed from Egypt and if the Egyptian monarchy had established an equitable tax system and in other ways alleviated the poverty of urban masses and the shame of the military?

The other half of the sense of the notion has to do with the improbability of revolution taking place where there has been no hope, no period in which expectations have risen. Such a stability of expectations presupposes a static state of human aspirations that sometimes exists but is rare. Stability of expectations is not a stable social condition. Such was the case of American Indians (at least from our perspective) and perhaps Africans before white men with Bibles, guns, and other goods interrupted the stability of African society. Egypt was in such a condition, vis-à-vis modern aspirations, before Europe became interested in building a canal. Such stasis was the case in Nazi concentration camps, where conformism reached the point of inmates cooperating with guards even when the inmates were told to lie down so that they could be shot.[11] But in the latter case there was a society with externally induced complete despair, and even in these camps there were occasional rebellions of sheer desperation. It is of course true that in a society less regimented than concentration camps, the rise of expectations can be frustrated successfully, thereby defeating rebellion just as the satisfaction of expectations does. This, however, requires the uninhibited exercise of brute force as it was used in suppressing the Hungarian rebellion of 1956. Failing the continued ability and persistent will of a ruling power to use such force, there appears to be no sure way to avoid revolution short of an effective, affirmative, and continuous response on the part of established governments to the almost continuously emerging needs of the governed.

To be predictive, my notion requires the assessment of the state of mind—or more precisely, the mood—of a people. This is always difficult, even by techniques of systematic public opinion analysis. Respondents interviewed in a country with a repressive government are not likely to be responsive. But there has been considerable progress in gathering first-hand data about the state of mind of peoples in politically unstable circumstances. One instance of this involved interviewing in West Berlin, during and after the 1948 blockade, as reported by Buchanan and Cantril. They were able to ascertain, however crudely, the sense of security that people in Berlin felt. There was a significant increase in security after the blockade.[12]

Another instance comes out of the Middle Eastern study conducted by the Columbia University Bureau of Applied Social Research and reported by Lerner.[13] By directly asking respondents whether they were happy or unhappy with the way things had turned out in their life, the interviewers turned up data indicating marked differences in the frequency of a sense of unhappiness between countries and between "traditional," "transitional," and "modern" individuals in these countries.[14] There is no technical reason why such comparisons could not be made chronologically as well as they have been geographically.

Other than interview data are available with which we can, from past experience, make reasonable inferences about the mood of a people. It was surely the sense for the relevance of such data that led Thomas Masaryk before the first World War to gather facts about peasant uprisings and industrial strikes and about the writings and actions of the intelligentsia in nineteenth-century Russia. In the present report, I have used not only such data—in the collection of which other social scientists have been less assiduous than Masaryk—but also such indexes as comparative size of vote as between Rhode Island and the United States, employment, exports, and cost of living. Some such indexes, like strikes and cost of living, may be rather closely related to the mood of a people; others, like value of exports, are much cruder indications. Lest we shy away from the gathering of crude

data, we should bear in mind that Durkheim developed his remarkable insights into modern society in large part by his analysis of suicide rates. He was unable to rely on the interviewing technique. We need not always ask people whether they are grievously frustrated by their government; their actions can tell us as well and sometimes better.

In his *Anatomy of Revolution,* Crane Brinkton describes "some tentative uniformities" that he discovered in the Puritan, American, French, and Russian revolutions.[15] The uniformities were: an economically advancing society, class antagonism, desertion of intellectuals, inefficient government, a ruling class that has lost self-confidence, financial failure of government, and the inept use of force against rebels. All but the last two of these are long-range phenomena that lend themselves to studies over extended time periods. The first two lend themselves to statistical analysis. If they serve the purpose, techniques of content analysis could be used to ascertain trends in alienation of intellectuals. Less rigorous methods would perhaps serve better to ascertain the effectiveness of government and the self-confidence of rulers. Because tensions and frustrations are present at all times in every society, what is most seriously needed are data that cover an extended time period in a particular society, so that one can say there is evidence that tension is greater or less than it was N years or months previously.

We need also to know how long is a long cycle of rising expectations and how long is a brief cycle of frustration. We noted a brief period of frustration in Russia after the 1881 assassination of Alexander II and a longer period after the 1904 beginning of the Russo-Japanese War. Why did not the revolution occur at either of these times rather than in 1917? Had expectations before these two times not risen high enough? Had the subsequent decline not been sufficiently sharp and deep? Measuring techniques have not yet been devised to answer these questions. But their unavailability now does not forecast their eternal inaccessibility. Physicists devised useful temperature scales long before they came as close to absolute zero as they have recently in laboratory conditions. The far more complex problems of scaling in social science inescapably are harder to solve.

We therefore are still not at the point of being able to predict revolution, but the closer we can get to data indicating by inference the prevailing mood in a society, the closer we will be to understanding the change from gratification to frustration in people's minds. That is the part of the anatomy, we are forever being told with truth and futility, in which wars and revolutions always start. We should eventually be able to escape the embarrassment that may have come to Lenin six weeks after he made the statement in Switzerland, in January, 1917, that he doubted whether "we, the old [will] live to see the decisive battles of the coming revolution."[16]

Notes

1. The *Communist Manifesto* of 1848 evidently antedates the opposing idea by about a year. See Edmund Wilson, *To the Finland Station* (Anchor Books edition), New York: Doubleday & Co. (n.d.), p. 157; Lewis S. Feuer, *Karl Marx and Friedrich Engels: Basic Writing on Politics and Philosophy*, N.Y.: Doubleday & Co., Inc., 1959, p. 1. The above quotation is from Karl Marx and Friedrich Engels, "Wage Labour and Capital," *Selected Works in Two Volumes*, Moscow: Foreign Languages Publishing House, 1955, vol. 1, p. 94.

2. A. de Tocqueville, *The Old Regime and the French Revolution* (trans. by John Bonner), N.Y.: Harper & Bros., 1856, p. 214. The Stuart Gilbert translation, Garden City: Doubleday & Co., Inc., 1955, pp. 176-177, gives a somewhat less pungent version of the same comment. *L'Ancien regime* was first published in 1856.

3. Revolutions are here defined as violent civil disturbances that cause the displacement of one ruling group by another that has a broader popular basis for support.

4. The full report is Ancel Keys *et al., The Biology of Human Starvation*, Minneapolis: University of Minnesota Press, 1950. See J. Brozek, "Semi-starvation and Nutritional Rehabilitation," *Journal of Clinical Nutrition*, 1 (January, 1953), pp. 107-118 for a brief analysis.

5. E. A. Cohen, *Human Behavior in the Concentration Camp*, New York: W. W. Norton & Co., 1953, pp. 123-125, 131-140.

6. For community life in such poverty, in Mezzogiorno Italy, see E. C. Banfield, *The Moral Basis of a Backward Society*, Glencoe, Ill.: The Free Press, 1958. The author emphasizes that the nuclear family is a solidary, consensual, moral unit (see p. 85) but even within it, consensus appears to break down, in outbreaks of pure, individual amorality—notably between parents and children (see p. 117).

7. See Angus Campbell *et al., The American Voter*, New York: John Wiley & Sons, 1960, Chap. 15, "Agrarian Political Behavior."

8. B. Zawadzki and P. F. Lazarsfeld, "The Psychological Consequences of Unemployment," *Journal of Social Psychology*, 6 (May, 1935), pp. 224-251.

9. A remarkable and awesome exception to this phenomenon occurred occasionally in some Nazi concentration camps, e.g., in a Buchenwald revolt against capricious rule by criminal prisoners. During this revolt, one hundred criminal prisoners were killed by political prisoners. See Cohen, *op. cit.*, p. 200.

10. See W. W. Rostow, "Business Cycles, Harvests, and Politics: 1790-1850," *Journal of Economic History*, 1 (November, 1941), pp. 206-221 for the relation between economic fluctuation and the activities of the Chartists in the 1830s and 1840s.

11. Eugen Kogon, *The Theory and Practice of Hell*, New York: Farrar, Straus & Co., 1950, pp. 284-286.

12. W. Buchanan, "Mass Communication in Reverse," *International Social Science Bulletin*, 5 (1953), pp. 577-583, at p. 578. The full study is W. Buchanan and H. Cantril, *How Nations See Each Other*, Urbana: University of Illinois Press, 1953, esp. pp. 85-90.

13. Daniel Lerner, *The Passing of Traditional Society*, Glencoe, Ill.: Free Press, 1958.

14. *Ibid.*, pp. 101-103. See also F. P. Kilpatrick & H. Cantril, "Self-Anchoring Scaling, A Measure of Individuals' Unique Reality Words," *Journal of Individual Psychology*, 16 (November, 1960), pp. 158-173.

15. See the revised edition of 1952 as reprinted by Vintage Books, Inc., 1957, pp. 264-275.

16. Quoted in E. H. Carr, *A History of Soviet Russia*, vol. 1, *The Bolshevik Revolution: 1917-23*, London: Macmillan, 1950, p. 69.

42.

Albert Breton and Raymond Breton

AN ECONOMIC THEORY OF SOCIAL MOVEMENTS

Introduction

Social movements do not make their appearance at random; instead they tend to emerge in relatively well-defined circumstances and to be accompanied by identifiable socioeconomic factors. Consequently, in the present paper, we develop a hypothesis about the origin of social movements based on these "facts." To that end, the paper is divided into three parts: the first elaborates a theory of the demand for social change or, more specifically, a theory about why the demand for change manifests itself in social movements. This first part, in turn, is subdivided into two sections examining: first, some structural components of the environment in which social movements originate and discussing, second, the definitions and assumptions of the proposed theory as well as its essential mechanisms. The second part introduces the concept of the supply of social movements and examines how this supply is related to the demand for social change.[1] This discussion, incidentally, sheds some new light on the question of social change itself. This is briefly discussed in Section III.

I. The demand for social change

If a small number of individuals choose to participate in one or more activities of a social and political character, these decisions should probably be analyzed predominantly in terms of factors related to the persons making the decisions; if, however, the number of individuals making the same or similar decisions is large, the environment in which the persons operate should also be examined. Since the social and political activities catalogued as social movements usually involve a relatively large number of individuals, it follows from the strategy just outlined that we should examine the environment in which these activities take place as well as the individuals engaging in them. It turns out that we can specify an important structural character of the environment which is sufficient to induce individuals to participate in activities aimed at inducing social change. We examine it immediately.

The environment

Given that the constituent components of the social structure are highly interdependent, it is usually possible to characterize the environment by one carefully selected index. In the present study we use the rate of change in the level of social (national and regional) income or product for that purpose.[2] We assume that when the rate of growth in social income falls

From Albert Breton and Raymond Breton, "An Economic Theory of Social Movements." *American Economic Review* 59, May 1969, pp. 198-205, with permission of the publisher.

This paper (or some earlier version of it) has greatly benefited from the comments of Yoram Barzel, James Coleman, Harry Johnson, Douglass North, Maurice Pinard, Arthur Stinchcombe, Pierre Trudeau, Gordon Tullock, and Mason Wade. We thank them and also assure them that they stand exonated of its shortcomings and of any charges that may be levied against it.

from a previously sustained high rate of growth to a lower one by a "significant" magnitude and for a "significant" period of time, the environment will act as a constraining factor on the plans and expectations of individuals. What will constitute a significant reduction in the rate of growth and what will be the critical length over which this fall will be maintained for the social environment to be constraining will certainly vary from place to place and from time to time, but one would expect that the reduction in the rate of growth for an economy growing at 4 percent per annum would have to be at least 2 percentage points, and the time period over which the reduction should persist would have to be of at least two or three years. These, however, are empirical questions that should finally be settled on empirical grounds.

The hypothesis

Since we will not be preoccupied with aggregation problems, it is immaterial whether we conduct our analysis in terms of the behavior of one individual or in terms of that of a group; consequently we will speak indifferently of one or the other, assuming that it is always possible to sum individuals into groups whenever that is necessary.

Consider, therefore, a typical group of individuals: at any point in time they will hold more or less definite plans about the future profile of their income and career plans. They can imagine that the time-shape of these flows and paths is such that their income and career prospects will point upwards for ten or more years and then level off, or that they will keep on increasing until they retire, or that they will have any of a number of possible contours. We assume that these individuals have more or less definite ideas about the factors which determine the size and behavior of these paths and furthermore that they classify these factors into personal factors such as experience, education, ability, aggressiveness and into environmental factors such as technology, the level of aggregate demand, the state of the balance of payments, and other similar factors which they assume to be outside of their control.

Individuals will have a tendency to weight heavily the environmental factors when comparing themselves with more successful individuals and personal factors when the opposite comparison is made. For example, individuals who experience a certain success relative to others will usually make reference to virtues (such as love of risk, initiative, hard work, courage, perseverance) and to vices (such as laziness, indolence, lack of initiative, unimaginativeness) in explaining their "success" and the "failure" of others. On the other hand, individuals experiencing failure relative to others will usually explain it in terms of bad luck, fatalism, their unfair exploitation by others and other environmental factors. [3]

The three foregoing assumptions relate to the individuals themselves and to the judgments they make about the determinants of their income and career history. The following assumptions relate to conditions which are outside the individuals. To be specific, we now assume that there exists an "objective" relationship defined in terms of "real" factors and "real" forces which are taken to be the "true" determinants of the income streams and of the career paths of individuals. It is therefore possible, given this set of assumptions, to analyze the difference between the imagined and the real weights given to each factor in the determination of income and to ascertain the extent to which the individuals hold "correct" opinions about themselves and the state of the world.

Now a protracted reduction in the rate of growth of economic activity will, by definition, manifest itself through environmental factors and since it is reasonable to postulate, in line with the third assumption made above, that the changes in the contribution of personal factors to changes in the behavior of incomes and career paths are either zero or known to the individuals, it follows that changes in their situation will lead them to look to changes in the environment for an explanation of what is happening to them.

To summarize, we have assumed the existence of individuals who hold opinions about the size and time-shape of their income streams and career paths and about the factors determining them. We have also assumed that these opinions can be correct or incorrect when appraised against an objective benchmark; if individuals find that their opinions are incorrect, they will change them, though this does not imply that those they will adopt will be correct ones: they may simply change the weights given to personal and environmental factors so as to minimize the damage to their self-image.

II. The supply of social movements

In this part we start by assuming, in strict analogy with the economic theory of the firm and of markets which asserts that the demand for products creates opportunities for profits which entrepreneurs, after a more or less prolonged period of time, will want to make the best of, that the demand for social change creates opportunities for social profit which social entrepreneurs will want to reap and in so doing will "supply" or provide social movements to those who want them. Before examining this hypothesis any further

we must pause to define the concepts of social profits and of social entrepreneurs which have just been introduced.

Social profits are in the nature of a flow of rewards which accrue to the social entrepreneurs and to their partners as long as the "product" which they sell is purchased. Social profits have both monetary and nonmonetary dimensions: the monetary dimension can be measured in terms of a flow of command over real resources which is made available to the entrepreneurs as a result of their activities. When social movements have reached their peak, this monetary flow of rewards can be sizable and for a given social entrepreneur often much higher than his alternative worth. This excess may be a quasi-rent to some specific quality which he possesses, but it may also be a transitory monopoly profit reflecting the disequilibrium of the market. If the latter explanation is correct, the appearance of new social entrepreneurs entering as competitors will wipe the profits away; if the first explanation is valid, that is, the flow of monetary rewards is in the nature of a quasi-rent, we should expect some new entrepreneurs to be unsuccessful in their effort to attract the profits to them. The nonmonetary dimension of social profits is more in the nature of prestige and power. The efforts of social entrepreneurs to get their names in the mass media is an indication that for many of them this dimension of profits is a very important one.

We have also used the concept of social entrepreneurs. We use it in analogy with that of industrial and commercial entrepreneurs—concepts which can be found in economic theory and in the literature of the role of the entrepreneurs in economic growth. While the latter are busy promoting and developing industrial and commercial enterprises, the former devote their energies to social and political endeavors. At any point in time a society has a total stock of actual and potential entrepreneurs of the three types, who may be more or less good substitutes for each other. The allocation of this stock between the three types will depend first on the profitability of alternative occupations, a dimension which will depend in turn on the distribution of the demands of society for the products and services of the various entrepreneurs; if the three types of entrepreneurs are not perfect substitutes for one another, the distribution will also depend on their comparative advantages in meeting these demands. This allocation will also depend on the relative level of communication, information, and especially organizational costs; if the relative costs of organizing a social movement are *ceteris paribus* lower than the costs of promoting a business, more entrepreneurs will engage in the first of these two activities.

Let us suppose that as a result of a reduction in the rate of growth of social income some individuals in society have begun to revise the image of their environment and of the factors responsible for the alteration in their income, consumption, portfolio and career plans; they are, as it were, groping for a new *weltanschauung* or a new ideology.[4] It is the social entrepreneurs' role to furnish them with one, which should be simple enough to be capable of wide diffusion and still complex enough to have the appearance of a *weltanschauung* or ideology.[5] These will therefore generally be grounded in such difficult areas as money, race, morality, the place of the individual and/or of the government in society, and others of this nature. The social entrepreneur electing to emphasize the place and role of money in the economy, for example, will link all the troubles of the world to the behavior of the central bank, or to the stock of money, or to the level of interest rates. He will be identified

with such movements as Social Credit and Thirty-Dollars every Tuesday, while the social entrepreneur who selects race as the factor responsible for the consequences of the constraining environment will be an anti-Semitic, or anti-American, or anti-Negro, and try to show that these groups are responsible for the difficulties felt by individuals. Another will blame the communists for all the troubles and difficulties of individuals, and he will be identified with the John Birch Society, for example; another one, still, will set out to show that big business is the culprit and he will sell a socialist ideology or *weltanschauung*. Depending on his background, his aptitudes, his knowledge and a host of other factors, lumped under the heading of comparative advantage, each entrepreneur will elect one factor (or maybe more than one for a new synthesis!) which he believes or at least wants others to believe is the prime cause of the difficulties through which some members of society are passing. The success of each social entrepreneur in selling his particular product will depend on the response which it receives; this in turn will depend on whether the individuals who are assumed to be in the process of changing the weights they had given to the personal and to the environmental factors in explaining their own altered personal situation elect to listen to one entrepreneur more than to another and to adopt a particular point of view. This choice in turn will be conditioned by the desire of individuals to minimize the damage to their self-image or self-esteem.

Before examining the types of behavior supplied by social entrepreneurs in addition to ideologies, we would like to state a number of testable implications of the above hypothesis which are either implied or contained in the foregoing discussion. A first such implication is that all social movements are accompanied by an ideology; that is, by a simplified (if not simplistic) explanation of the sources of trouble and difficulty facing individuals as a result of a reduction in the rate of growth of social income. A second, and one that should be obvious from the discussion of Section I, is that individuals with a high ratio of debt to income should have a higher propensity, *ceteris paribus,* to join social movements than others. A third is that a social movement will generally not appear in isolation; instead many movements will be observable at the same time. An exception to this could occur in the case of small reductions in the rate of growth of income generating only a weak demand for social change and in consequence only a small social profit capable of attracting and sustaining only one or very few social entrepreneurs. When the reductions are pronounced, many social entrepreneurs will wish to partake in the profits, so that many social movements will be supplied. Since in many instances small reductions in the rate of growth may not give rise to social movements of any significance, we would expect our general proposition to hold most of the time. A fourth implication is that the entrepreneurs leading the various social movements will be in strong competition with one another even when they are advocating substantially the same thing, and they will, therefore, spend considerable time arguing that other social entrepreneurs are wrong. This phenomenon, of course, will be much stronger when social movements are on the wane. Last, social entrepreneurs will devote a large part of their efforts in "differentiating their product" from that of competitors.

III. The process of social change

In the introduction we mentioned that the theory of social movements developed in this paper had implications for the question of social change. We discuss this question here because it is an essential part of the theory outlined above.

The demand for change can manifest itself in at least three different ways: First, through social action of a magical character. In such instances, environmental changes are attributed to the actions of a supernatural being who must be persuaded or influenced to change the course of events. Second, through economic and/or political action by means of organizations and procedures set up for the purpose of instigating certain specific changes or change in general. And, third, through action of an economic and/or political character, but within the existing institutional structures, rules and procedures. This is essentially a mechanism characterizing democracy. The first two expressions of demand for social change are usually referred to as social movements, but it is obvious that the third expression could also be called a social movement.

Whatever kind of change is in demand, there are likely to be social entrepreneurs who will attempt to satisfy this demand, as we have argued above. The next question pertains to the conditions under which one type of action rather than another will be provided. When will social entrepreneurs be the leaders of existing institutions and when will they be initiating new associations or attempting to create new organizations? There are two ways in which the manifestations of the demand for change differ which are important in relation to this question. First, the location of the sources of control over the environment differs and, second, the extent to which this source of control is deemed manipulable also differs. A supernatural being can be seen as intractable or as responsive to expressions of deference and supplication of various sorts. Similarly, if the control over a situation is considered as being in the hands of certain individuals or groups, then the possibility of influencing these powerful individuals or of penetrating their organizational structure will give rise to actions of a representative nature: support for a given political party or for a certain party platform, pressure on labor, government, business or religious leaders. But if people find their leaders and institutions unresponsive to their problems, they will follow the leadership that develops marginally to the existing institutions.[6] They will support the new party that a political entrepreneur is creating; they will support political reform associations whose purpose it is to shake the government out of its lethargy; they will join manifestations of all sorts. Similarly, there will be social actions aimed at the social groups identified—rightly or wrongly—as being in control of the unresponsive institutions.

We are not advancing the scapegoat interpretation of social movements. On the contrary, we are arguing that people who are under the constraints of a protracted growth rate and who impute the cause of this to environmental factors will try to hit at those groups and institutions which are seen as either responsible for the situation or as responsible for doing something about it or both, and new movements will be supported when existing structures remain apathetic or, of course, hostile. For instance, a new political party is not likely to appear if the leadership of at least one of the existing parties is not tightly controlled by "conservative" groups (i.e., by groups unresponsive to the demand for change), thus allowing new issues and new policies to be introduced into the party platform. However, there may be groups who become the targets of social dissatisfaction but who cannot really do anything about it since they do not have any insti-

tutional power. Ethnic minorities and immigrant groups are frequently in that situation. Because of this, they appear as being treated as scapegoats, but in reality there is not really a "transfer" of aggressive tendencies on them; they are seen as part of the cause of the state of affairs, but they are not in a position to bring about a solution. In this sense, hostility against certain groups may be rational, but it is unlikely to be productive of any socially profitable change.

Because of the speed at which social and political institutions function, the reduction in the rate of income growth is likely to witness a number of social movements, even if political leaders are very responsive. It takes time to bring about effective solutions, especially to long-neglected problems. This is particularly the case when problems have been neglected because the elite did not have the resources to cope with them or simply did not know what to do about them. During periods of protracted reduced growth, then, both institutionally instigated changes and social movements are likely to occur; but the amount and strength of the social movements depend largely upon the responsiveness of the political and social elite.

Conclusion

The hypothesis formulated above appears to be consistent, at least in the large, with what is known of the history of social movements in Canada, in the United States, and in Europe during the first part of the twentieth century.[7] In particular, it helps to understand the appearance of the civil rights movement in the United States, of separatism in French Canada, of aggressive anti-Americanism in English Canada and of Welsh and Scottish nationalism in the United Kingdom during the current[8] protracted reduction in the rate of growth of these economies. A more systematic and refined treatment of data will not, we hope, have to wait too long.

Notes

1. For other approaches to the formulation of the theory of social movements, see N. J. Smelser, *Theory of Collective Behavior* (Free Press of Glencoe, 1963), esp. Chaps. 1 to 3; R. Heberle, *Social Movements* (Appleton-Century-Crofts, 1951); W. Kornhauser, *The Politics of Mass Society* (Free Press, 1959) and J. C. Davies, "Towards a Theory of Revolution," *Amer. Soc. Rev.*, 1962, pp. 5-19.

2. This is done to simplify and to give operational power to the theory. However, any factor or set of factors that created a "significant" difference between individual aspirations and "reality" would serve our purpose as well.

3. The particular specification of weights sketched in the text is essential for the empirical analysis of who joins and who does not join social movements.

4. This term is used in the precise sense given it by A. Downs, *An Economic Theory of Democracy* (Harper & Row, 1957).

5. Social entrepreneurs sell *weltanschauungs;* in this way they resemble entrepreneurs selling advertisements, so that the characteristics of the *weltanschauungs* should in many ways resemble advertising messages. For a description and analysis of the latter, see H. G. Johnson, "Advertising in Today's Economy," in *The Canadian Quandary* (McGraw-Hill, 1963), pp. 269-84.

6. In "One-Party Dominance and Third Parties," *Canadian J. of Econ. and Polit. Sci.*, Aug., 1967, M. Pinard has presented a complete model related to this point.

7. This history has been briefly sketched for Canada by the writers in "Le Séparatisme," *Cité Libre,* Apr., 1962.

8. The exact dates vary from country to country, but they are all rather easily identified.

43.

Manoucher Parvin

ECONOMIC DETERMINANTS OF POLITICAL UNREST

Introduction

It is reasonable to assume that some degree of latent political unrest exists in all societies at all times. However, not until substantial pressures for economic and political changes have risen to a threshold level is such latent unrest qualitatively transformed into manifest political unrest in the forms of political demonstrations and civil disobedience. Thus, the critical threshold of violence is transgressed when-

ever a significant number of individuals have grown sufficiently dissatisfied and frustrated with existing economic or political conditions that the promotion of the breakdown of law and order is preferred to their preservation (Nieburg, 1962).

In recent years, social scientists have subjected the relatively uncharted area of internal political unrest to further scholarly exploration, despite certain theoretical and methodological difficulties (Eckstein, 1964). Although most of these studies have been qualitative in nature (Eckstein, 1964; Rosenau, 1964; Sorokin, 1937; Brinton, 1969; Lasswell and Kaplan, 1950; Wright, 1964), some quantitative studies have arisen (Richardson, 1960a, 1960b; Tanter, 1966; Rummel, 1966,

"Economic Determinants of Political Unrest: An Econometric Approach," by Manoucher Parvin is reprinted from *The Journal of Conflict Resolution,* Vol. XVII, No. 2 (June 1973), pp. 271-96 by permission of the publisher, Sage Publications, Inc., and the author.

1963; Deutsch, 1961). Several writers have tried to enumerate and explain factors which contribute to manifest political unrest. The Feierabends (1966) outline a psychological theory of political instability, which they explain as resulting from situations of unrelieved, socially experienced frustration.

The element of social frustration is also dealt with by Karl W. Deutsch (1961) in terms of adequate political and economic capability to compensate the rising needs and expectations accompanying the increasing social mobilization of national populations in developing countries. Gurr (1968a) constructs a model in which the level of violence is explained by a number of psychological and social factors, showing elsewhere (Gurr, 1968b) that the level of "strife varies directly in magnitude with the intensity of relative deprivation." Furthermore, in a more recent work concerning the sources of rebellion in Western societies (Gurr, 1970) he concludes that internal strife in recent years could be explained by the range and intensity of collective discontent, combined with the strength of normative and utilitarian justifications for rebellion among discontented groups and balance of social control between contending groups. In addition, Grinshaw (1970) concludes that superordinate/subordinate relationships based on social categories are inherently unstable and that social violence is likely to occur when accommodative structures lose their viability.

Weinert (1966), studying the level of violence in Colombia, concludes that violence does not result from sociopolitical frustration, but that it is a common phenomenon in developing countries, and it reflects a feudal, premodern conflict generated by modernization. Williamson (1965), on the other hand, suggests that outbursts of violence in rural Colombia are related to the level of literacy, the quality of leadership, and the access to sanctioned channels for expression of discontent in that country. In addition, Mitchell (1969) offers a location theory of violence in a case study of the Huk rebellion in the Phillippines.

The important characteristics of the aforementioned specifically related, but by no means exhaustive, recent studies and those of the past are the following:

(1) Etiologically, the causes of political unrest are ascribed in recent studies to one or more sociopsychological traits or political factors, interspersed occasionally with insights taken from the discipline of economics.
(2) Methodologically, when the approach is quantitative, the studies focus on special cases where primarily specific factors associated with a special situation or locality are considered as explanatory variables of political unrest.
(3) Historically, the approach to the economic explanation of political unrest has been exclusively descriptive or analytical when considered by the classic political economists and political sociologists due to the unavailability of an advanced quantitative method and sufficient data.

This study is thus a preliminary attempt to bridge a few gaps by focusing mainly on the economic explanation of political unrest, by considering universal, in contrast to particular, factors or local situations, and finally by adopting a modern quantitative approach for the testing of the proposed formal theory.

Economic determinants of political unrest

Stationary economic determinants

A category of material and service *necessities* constitutes a primary prerequisite of human biological existence. Furthermore, over and above these biological *necessities,* certain categories of commodities defined as socioeconomic *needs* comprise the prerequisites of group-specific socioeconomic membership. It should be noted that the members of an economic class may be sociologically differentiated, while members of a group within a class possess certain common sociological characteristics such as professional, ethnic, racial, and so on. The biological necessities and group-specific economic needs together constitute the commodity flow requirements for the maintenance of an ongoing level of the biosocial consumption process in a national social unit.

It is assumed that some members of an income class or group within a class would react unfavorably to any threat to, or the actual decrease in, the ongoing commodity flow to that class or group. In addition, it is assumed that an unfavorable relative change in income—in contrast to the aforementioned absolute one—may generate similar negative reactions or resistance between classes or among groups within the same class. Furthermore, it is assumed that the nature and the extent of the politically manifested reactions, and the associated likelihood of their occurrence, depend on the degree of change, real or imagined, potential or manifest, and the level and scope of individual and group consciousness concerning the change itself and its implications. Thus, violent protests of labor unions associated with relative or absolute change in income and food riots, past and present, in various countries, are examples of extreme reactions induced by the diminution, respectively, of needs and of necessities flow.

It is important to note that the struggle to maintain the flow of necessities and needs does not follow the sequential order of importance for members of a national unit—i.e., even if some members of a national unit receive one or both, others may receive none. Thus, even in national units as prosperous as the United States, the struggle for biological existence is an everyday reality for certain individuals and families.

Temporal economic determinants

Some members of one or more groups may at one moment in time have *expectations* concerning flow which are beyond necessities and needs. Such expectations are, over time, transformed into *demands*. Demand is defined herein as constituting words uttered and actions undertaken for the purpose of inducing change leading to the realization of expectations. Thus, demand implies an explicit request for change in the ongoing processes of production or distribution of commodities in a quantitative or qualitative sense. Two major categories of demand for change are recognized. First, specific-interest demand by an individual or a group, and second, general-interest demand for change. In the individual demand for change, or "ego-focused image of change" (Hirshman, 1964), the individual is only concerned with private gain, implying an increase in consumption above the average increase accrued to the members of a group to which he belongs. This category of demand can be fulfilled only if individual upward class movement is possible. The lack of sufficient provisions for interclass economic mobility, especially for those individuals with relatively superior abilities, and achievement motivation, may lead at first to individually experienced rising frustration. In the case of group specific-interest demand for change or "group-focused image of change" (Hirshman, 1964), the individuals conceive of and desire the economic change which affects equally all members of the group with which they identify. However, technological progress in production, as well as consumption, inducing evolutionary transformation of economic structure and function, may reduce the relative or absolute economic significance of a certain group, thus rendering impossible the realization of even a modest expectation of maintenance of relative group income position. In addition, legislation or executive order—such as those affecting the tax structure, tariffs, and allocation of resources for welfare and public goods—may have similar, nonuniformly distributed results causing a change in the structure of income distribution. Accordingly, technologically induced income growth, government economic policies, and the economic effects of other nonuniformly distributed forces (e.g., natural or social), may give rise to (or attenuate) the net group-experienced frustration. Finally, it should be noted that the two specific-interest demands for change—ego and group—may not be complementary or compatible but contradictory, and thus their simultaneous existence may serve as obstacles to change itself (Hirshman, 1964) and give rise to increasing frustration.

The general-interest demand for economic change can be subdivided into two categories: national and international demand for change. In the first case, individuals from various groups demand changes which affect the entire citizenry of a national unit uniformly or not, and in the second case, some citizens of a national unit demand certain economic changes which affect a part or the whole membership of another national unit. The growing demand for the abatement of environmental pollution constitutes an example of national demand for change requiring reallocation of resources on a national level. However, this demand is gradually becoming an international demand for change. The continuation of the economic aspect of apartheid policy in the Republic of South Africa has served as a frustration-generating source in other countries, leading to a demand for the redistribution of income and power in that country by the citizens of others. Moreover, it should be noted that a specific demand by an individual may grow into a group-specific demand, and further into a national or international demand for change, depending on the nature and universality of the demand, and on the mode and intensity of communication. The aforementioned demands for change have generally grown out of small units—whether social or geographic—to larger units. Thus, some of today's specific demands for change could become tomorrow's universal demands for change. Notice that, in the above and what follows, it is the present value of expected future flow that is considered by the decision-maker, whether an individual or a larger social unit.

The nature of economically induced frustrations

Absolute or relative change in the flow of commodities to an individual or group is generally associated with change in social status. This does not imply that all demands for change have economic roots or consequences. But the above classification of stationary and temporal commodity flow in terms of necessities, needs, and demands implies the latent possibility of various forms of frustration experienced by individuals, groups, or other social units. For instance, a decrease in the flow of necessities implies biologically experienced frustration on the part of individuals directly affected, while a decrease (relative or absolute) in the flow of needs implies psychosocially experienced frustration. Furthermore, the lack of realization of specific-interest demand—ego or group demand—may lead, respectively, to psychologically or socially experienced frustration, while the failure to attain general-interest demand may lead to intellectually as well as spiritually felt frustration. These experienced forms of frustration are frequently interdependent—i.e., one form may cause others; biologically experienced frustration may, for instance, lead to psychosocially felt frustration. Accordingly, some of the discontent and frustration experienced in various forms by an individual or group is found to have economic roots.

Thus, the stationary and temporal economic factors—necessities, needs, and demands—together represent and are the measure of a complex entity of existing or expected economic well-being or deprivation. The desire for economic well-being or the avoidance of economic deprivation compels or induces numerous human actions, including political actions, considered or classified as constructive or destructive, normal or abnormal, legitimate or illegitimate (Gurr, 1970). Hence, we proceed by stating the following nonrestrictive hypothesis. Economic well-being (or deprivation) is a fundamental motive of political action in general and manifest political unrest in particular. It should be noted that this hypothesis claims neither the primacy nor the exclusivity of economic factors as determinants of political unrest; it merely asserts their importance. The main task of this paper, then, is to break down the complex entity of economic well-being into its elementary component parts, test them for relevance and significance, and measure their strength and effect direction as explanatory factors of political unrest.

Econometric approach

The adopted methodology is one of multivariate statistical analysis. It is not, however, our concern here to investigate the scientific merits or demerits of this form of approach in the social sciences. We proceed by the analytical study of a set of universal economic factors hypothesized as explanatory variables of political unrest, the formulation of an appropriate mathematical (stochastic) model containing such variables, the construction of indices, and, finally, the empirical analysis of the model leading to a test of various hypotheses proposed here and elsewhere (Gurr, 1968b; Weinert, 1966; Williamson, 1965). The choice of elements of the set of explanatory variables entering the political unrest model is formally based on a priori and theoretical considerations. More specifically, however, in the choice of independent variables of the model, the following criteria are considered—proceeding from the general to particular characteristics.

(1) *The independent variables* of the model are economic and universal factors. The specific, local, or noneconomic factors, such as geographical peculiarities are excluded, while universal economic magnitudes such as per capita income (as a measure of the absolute level of welfare or deprivation), inequality in income distribution (as a measure of relative welfare or deprivation), the rate of income growth (as a measure of the rate of the realization of general-interest demand), economic mobility (as a measure of the rate of realization of individual specific-interest demand), and communication and urbanization (as indices for measuring the intensity of convergence of demand forces in social and geographic terms) are included. Such factors are universal economic indicators from a spatial and temporal point of view unbounded by historical, cultural, and system specificities.

(2) *The variables of the model* are universal in another sense. They seem to be relevant and significant in various

social units, ranging from the individual to communities and national units. Broadly speaking, they appear to exhibit the same properties spatially and temporally, and influence the behavior of social units from micro and macro in the same direction. Accordingly, the problem of induction from part to whole and interaction between various units is avoided, since our interest lies only with the net effect. However, since the main purpose of the study of the investigation of the relevance and significance of universal economic factors —in the most general sense—influencing the political unrest, the national is formally specified as the appropriate social unit for the quantitative analysis of the data. Yet the universality of the variables considered in this model implies their applicability to the study of smaller social units, such as groups or communities differentiated ethnically, racially, or geographically within the same national unit. It should be noted that some extremely important local factors may not be relevant, let alone significant, in cross-national studies. Finally, it may easily be recognized that one or more of the aforementioned three criteria (economic nature, universality of the factors, and the quantitative approach to the question) represent—though not necessarily simultaneously—a major departure from previous approaches to the question of the causes of political unrest. We are not interested in the study of the causes of political unrest manifested by a special case of political upheaval, but in the general underlying economic forces which may loom behind the seemingly local or specific factors.

(3) *The conclusions of other investigators* in this field are utilized in the model as explanatory factors if such inclusions have been considered appropriate and feasible. The above criteria and the following analysis indicate that such inclu-

sions or exclusions of variables are neither arbitrary nor automatic.

Duality

It appears that each universal economic factor considered has a complex effect on political unrest. Thus, such effects attributed to a single factor are not undirectional—i.e., some influence political unrest positively and some negatively, some directly and some indirectly. The dual nature of such factors is a source of methodological difficulty when the approach to the problem is exclusively descriptive or analytical. Given the complex nature of the forces, how is the direction of the sum total or net effect of a particular factor on the political unrest determined? How are the strengths of such an influence and the associated likelihoods measured? Some writers have maintained that the process of economic development may affect political unrest adversely (Deutsch, 1961; Weinert, 1966). But such processes make possible the partial fulfillment of existing and rising expectations, thereby leaving only some, instead of all, new or old demands unattained. Accordingly, the quantitative approach can yield the measurement of the net effect of political unrest of a many-sided process of economic development and growth. The problem of duality is further explored in the following sections as each explanatory factor is discussed.

Dependent variable

Manifest political unrest—denoted by "V"—the dependent variable, may be defined for operational considerations as the absolute number of deaths resulting from domestic group violence per 1,000,000 population (Russett, 1964). The choice of this indicator is made on the basis that it directly and unambiguously measures the immediate end-product of riots, coups, political assassinations, and rebellions, while excluding deaths by murder and execution. Inasmuch as the reported data are reliable, the number of people killed as a result of domestic group violence is deemed to be a dependable index of political unrest above the threshold of violence. Other indicators of political unrest can also be used where the index may be more suitable for the specific purpose at hand (Russett, 1964; Gurr, 1970).

Independent variables

Per capita income

Per capita income—denoted by "Y"—is assumed to be the measure of absolute level of existing economic well-being (or deprivation) among the residents of a given country. It is thus a measure of the necessities and needs flow and is partly indicative of the past expectations fulfilled. Furthermore, from an individual's point of view, the opportunity cost of violence is likely to vary directly with his income. This means that those individuals who have little to lose are more inclined to engage in violent activities than those who are materially better off. It should be noted, however, that this factor has a dual nature since an increase in per capita income is generally accompanied by a rise in the level of industrialization, causing associated psychosocially experienced frustrations as well as an increase in environmental pollution leading to biologically experienced frustration. It should also be noted that the level of per capita income provides information concerning neither the relative percentage of national product devoted to private consumption nor its mode of distribution. Nevertheless, this factor is expected to have a net effect upon, and thus partially explain, the level of political unrest. The present hypothesis is that, all effects considered, per capita income and political unrest are inversely related.

Income distribution

The coexistence of extreme affluence and deprivation, as observed in many societies, gives rise to political unrest for any level of per capita income. Thus, the index of inequality in income distribution, which is a measure of relative well-being or deprivation, denoted by "A," is assumed to be a determining factor of "V." The larger the inequality in income distribution, the greater the intensity of ego- and group-specific interest demand for change —hence, the latent political unrest. The inequality in income distribution is measured by the ratio of the area between the Lorentz curve and the diagonal representing full equality to the area under the diagonal. The larger the ratio, the greater is the index of income inequality (Kuznets, 1963). We postulate that the degree of envy and frustration experienced by low-income individuals is directly related to the index of income inequality within a given society.

$$V = f_2(A) \text{ ceteris paribus}$$

$$\text{and } \frac{\partial V}{\partial A} > 0$$

where A is the index of inequality in income distribution.

Thus, in terms of partial elasticities, we postulate that a percentage change in the index of inequality is associated with a percentage change, in the same direction, of the level of violence—i.e.,

$$\frac{\partial(\log V)}{\partial(\log A)} > 0$$

But to assume that such a postulated relationship holds for all levels of income inequality implies that a uniform distribution of income minimizes political unrest as far as the effect of this particular factor is concerned. This is, of course, a doubtful proposition, since any substantial change toward egalitarian society will lead to political unrest and violence by higher-income groups and individuals. It is therefore more reasonable to assume that an optimum level of income inequality exists for any level of per capita income. Subsequently, beyond this optimum level, the net effect of further redistribution of income toward more or less equality may imply increasing, not decreasing, political unrest. Recognizing the existence of duality, our original hypothesis concerning the relationship between inequality in income distribution and political unrest, is, then, conditioned by the fact that existing income inequalities are well below the optimum level of income distribution. Thus, redistribution of income toward less inequality will, in sum, decrease the level of political unrest.

Income growth

The percentage growth rate of per capita income, "G," is assumed to have important social and political implications since it can be interpreted as a measure of a society's ability to meet the growing demands of its members. It is therefore a measure of the rate of realization of general as well as group-specific interest demands. Alternatively, from the individual's point of view, this factor may be considered as a rate of fulfillment of short- and long-run expectations. Thus, the potential level of welfare imagined feasible in a life cycle is associated with the magnitude of "G" over time. This fact also contributes to the opportunity cost of violence

as viewed by groups or individuals. The higher the rate of income growth, the greater the present value of the future income flow, and the greater the employment level at the present. Thus, the greater is the potential cost of violence from the individual's point of view. Conversely, the lower the rate of growth, the smaller the present value of future income and thus the smaller the potential cost of violence. In the first instance, an individual or group has a future to think of and in the second instance "nothing to lose but the chains." Hence, it appears that political unrest and the rate of income growth are inversely related. But it is important to recognize that a high rate of income growth is generally associated with technological change in production, which necessitates change in consumption technology, the break-up of certain stabilizing cultural traditions, job dislocation, and the subsequent disruption of sociopolitical order in the short run. The above stabilizing and destabilizing forces caused by income growth may, to a certain degree, neutralize each other in the process. However, our hypothesis concerning the income level implies the attenuating effects of a sustained income growth on the level of political unrest.

Socioeconomic mobility

Another factor determining "V" is the degree of socioeconomic mobility in a given society, which is the measure of the rate of realization of individual specific-interest demand. The extent to which an individual is allowed to achieve his own aspirations relative to his ability is mainly determined by the accepted norms of socioeconomic mobility and social provisions available for the effective furtherance of personal ambitions. Since the educational level attained determines to a large degree the socioeconomic position of an individual in many societies, then to the extent that educational means are available to members of a society for their personal advancement, socioeconomic mobility is enhanced. Here the opposite effects manifest themselves in two important forms.

(1) The politicoeconomic mobility of some individuals may create insecurities for others who hold privileged and unique positions.
(2) Increased mobility creates further demands which may remain unattained giving rise to more frustration.

The above analysis suggests an optimum level of mobility insofar as political stability is concerned. The study and testing of such a hypothesis is, however, beyond the scope of this paper. Thus, the inverse relationship between economic mobility and political unrest is postulated in conjunction with the net effect and not only with the primary effect and subject to historical and contemporary socioeconomic realities. In the final analysis, the data will resolve the issue of the direction of the net effect; no amount of argument can substitute for quantitative analysis in such cases.

Modes of communication

Every stage of economic development is associated with a given mode or modes of communication and the extent of their utilization. Communication as a socioeconomic phenomenon is a factor in the formation of expectations and their transformation into demands. Furthermore, as a social prism, it contributes to the diffusion of such demands, thus increasing its scope while simultaneously, as a social lens, it serves to focus the demanding forces, giving rise to their level of intensity. For instance, as people are brought into contact with the living habits of others, "the revolution of rising expectations" and demand are set in motion, potentially inducing the evolution of rising dissatisfaction. Furthermore, the communication media may focus the attention of the individuals, groups, or general public on conflicts and inconsistencies within a government (Lerner, 1963; Schiller, 1969). Frustrations which may translate themselves into political unrest are most likely to occur when the rate of rising expectations, "E," leading to the intensification of specific- or general-interest demands, is greater than the possible rate of fulfillment of such demands given by the rate of growth, "G." In some cases, the individuals' imagination quickly outdistances societal achievement (Lerner, 1963).

However, the communication media can also provide entertainment and soothing propaganda, which may have an attenuating effect on "V" through the inverse process of decreasing the level of or fragmenting expectations and demands.

The number of radios per capita, "R," is selected as an index of communication on the basis that the ownership and use of a radio receiver does not require any literacy or, relatively speaking, a high purchase cost (Russett, 1964). Furthermore, in most countries, a receiver can be tuned to external as well as internal transmitters.

Urbanization

Finally, urbanization, "U," fundamentally an economic phenomenon, is used as a measure of the geoeconomic expectation demand integrative factor. There are some socioeconomic forces which indicate a direct relationship between "V" and "U," and some which point to an inverse one. It is not the purpose of this paper to make an extensive analysis of such complex factors, but let us point out a few important consequences.

On the one hand,

(1) urbanization and population concentration —caused generally by economic progress and industrialization—beyond a certain limit increases the tension between the members of a community due to a number of complex causes beyond the scope of this study;
(2) unemployment is usually a socioeconomic problem magnifying the gap between poor and rich; and
(3) inequality in income distribution is readily observed and the cost of anti-government propaganda, agitation, and organizational activity is reduced, increasing the rate of formation of new expectations, their transformation into new demands, and finally resulting in increased political unrest.

On the other hand,

(1) the cost of control and propaganda by government (per person) is reduced; and
(2) generally speaking, the degree of urbanization reflects a given degree of exposure to modernity by a given segment of the population which is affected. Modernization has certain economic benefits which are desired.

Theoretical results are suggestive but fail in general to provide exact procedures for the specification of the model—i.e., the determination of the functional form which relates the variables of the model once they are singled out. Because, in principle, an infinite number of specifications is possible (even for a two-variable model), it is neither necessary nor desirable to specify the model in advance and treat it as an immutable theoretical construct. For the task at hand, however, only two widely used functional forms in econometrics are considered—the most simple and plausible specifications from a theoretical point of view. Perhaps a greater

correlation coefficient could have been obtained by further "curve fitting," but this has not been our purpose. The linear function has two important properties— namely, the property of proportionality, indicating that the result of the action of each separate factor is proportional to its value, and the property of independence, implying that the total result of an action is equal to the sum of the results of the action of separate factors. But the first property does not appear useful, relevant, or realistic for the problem at hand since it implies, for instance, that each fixed change in the level of urbanization causes a corresponding fixed change in political unrest or stability, as the case may be, irrespective of the initial magnitude of the variables. Consequently, it was recognized that a model which relates the corresponding percentage changes in the variables may be more realistic.

Data and regression results

We have used cross-sectional, cross-national data from 26 countries of different regions where data have been available, reliable, and complete. The magnitude of variables of the model are averages of several years, representing a single point. The main advantages of using cross-sectional data in this particular case are as follows:

(1) The greater range of variation in the economic variables among countries of different regions, coupled with a lesser degree of interaction between independent (explanatory) variables, makes possible a more reliable determination of the regression coefficients than does the time series data. In addition, since the countries are at various stages of socioeconomic development, they may be thought to represent points on a path that a typical country would follow in a hypothetical process of instantaneous

growth to an advanced economy (Chenery, 1960).

(2) The data actually available are mainly cross-sectional, and, since they have been collected recently, they may be more accurate than time series data.

(3) Representing the average value of several years as one point has the benefit of averaging out a large portion of the transient or random fluctuations of the variable.

(4) Generally, achievement claims by governments may be more exaggerated for a short period than for a long stretch of time, especially when later administrations are ready to correct the inflated claims of their predecessors. This constitutes another advantage of representing each point by the average magnitude of several years instead of an instantaneous value at one moment in time.

(5) Finally, despite the aforementioned advantages of using cross-sectional data in this particular case, it must also be pointed out that, due to the scarcity of time series data in general, other approaches are not readily available.

Although there exist some differences in the statistical accuracy of the information available for various countries (Russett, 1964), there are four reasons why we have not tried to improve or correct the available data by certain arbitrary means:

(1) Large variations in the actual magnitudes of variables lessens the significance of such errors.

(2) It is not certain that the manipulation of data based on an a priori rule would lead to its improvement.

(3) In general, it is not possible to find the exact means by which data are actually obtained and processed in each particular case.

(4) The purpose of this paper is not to contribute to the methodology of the usage of data in econometric models.

Finally, it should be pointed out that, assuming the validity of the range and associated probabilities of errors as stated in the data source reference, the results obtained and conclusions reached in this paper could only be marginally affected.

Summary and conclusion

In general, our empirical analysis strongly supports the a priori assumptions postulated and the theoretical results obtained in this study.

The model explains a large portion of the variation in the level of political unrest, using certain universal explanatory economic factors. Specific or local factors—such as location, ethnic, racial, and religious differences—could also be included and tested in more complicated time series or cross-sectional models. Here, however, we have been interested in universal factors—hence, the analysis of cross-national data.

(1) *The results obtained* in this paper suggest that concrete economic conditions must be improved in order to reduce political unrest. Note that the material "composition" of the gross national product—and not merely its associated monetary magnitude—may also be a determining factor of violence, although it is not investigated or tested here. For example, would two countries equivalent in income level, but one with a greater production and ownership of private guns and the other with a greater construction and use of playgrounds, exhibit the same level of violence? A corollary of the above is the division of income into public and private sectors, which may be a contributing factor to political stability or instability.

(2) *Income growth makes feasible* the realization of a number of current expectations and demands and creates an optimistic time structure concerning the future flow of additional benefits from the viewpoint of an individual or of larger social

units. According to the regression results, it appears that, in economic and social terms, the benefits of a sustained income growth are greater than its cost. However, our conclusion here refers to the range of growth rates observed in the world today.

Increasing the income growth rate requires increased savings and necessitates a higher rate of social transformation, inflicting greater hardships on various social units and society as a whole. In fact, it is rather obvious that, beyond a threshold level, a higher income growth rate would increase violence rather than decrease it. Thus, as far as political stability is concerned, there exists an optimum rate of income growth. This optimum growth rate may be different for different countries or may vary for the same country over time. We have not attempted here to determine an average optimum rate for one or more countries.

(3) *Consistent with the conclusion* of other writers discussed previously, the weighted regression results in this study indicate that income inequality is a contributor to political unrest. However, it should be noted that the *level* of per capita income, the absolute level of economic well-being, is a more influential factor than the extent of income inequality, or the relative economic well-being. At least from an economic point of view, this conclusion should modify the emphasis on relative deprivation theories of political unrest. It is reasonable to speculate here that income inequality *among* countries may also give rise to political unrest. This observation and its logical implications have comprised perhaps one major reason besides political interests and humanitarian considerations for various proposals concerning a certain degree of income redistribution among nations. The present model, however, does not test the validity of the hypothesis that income inequality among nations may be a contributing factor to political unrest within, or friction among, nations. Furthermore, no attempt is made here to determine the optimum level of income inequality.

(4) *Socioeconomic mobility,* measured by the extent of the availability of educational opportunity, affects political unrest in the predicted direction. Apparently the stabilizing effects of socioeconomic mobility overcome the previously stated possible destabilizing consequences for the present socioeconomic structure of the countries in the sample.

(5) *The fact that socioeconomic mobility* and the income growth rate are stronger explanatory factors than is relative deprivation in explaining the level of violence permits us to formulate the following tentative principle. Ceteris paribus, the impact of deprivation on political unrest is of a lesser importance than the rate of its dissolution; hope for a better day evidenced by favorable change makes an intolerable condition tolerable, while hopelessness due to persistent stagnation may make an otherwise tolerable situation intolerable.

(6) *In our theoretical discussion,* we hypothesized that mass communication could affect the level of political unrest one way or the other, depending on the level of expectations, "E," and the extent to which these are fulfilled, "G." This indicates that, generally, formation of the rate of expectations and their transformation to demands, "E," is greater than the rate of fulfillment, "G," or that the rate of rising dissatisfactions is greater than the rate of their compensating remedies in the countries considered.

Conclusions (4) and (5) together permit us to formulate the following tentative yet important principles: The more the facts of a social condition are known by the people, the greater will be the likelihood that they will learn to dislike it more (or appreciate it less), and, conversely, the less people know about the facts of a social condition, the greater will be the likelihood that they will dislike it less (or appreciate it more). Furthermore, economic resources allocated to censorship and to the production and distribution of misinformation by the governments, past and present, of various countries supports the above principle. In addition, this principle suggests that an increase in knowledge concerning the facts of a social condition and the associated heightened consciousness of sufficient members of a social unit is necessary for the formulation of demands and for the implementation of any social transformation. Thus, heightened social consciousness leads to dissatisfaction and, if not heeded, to political violence. This finding will hold true as long as heaven on earth remains unattainable and man remains curious and imaginative and has preferences.

(7) *An important general conclusion* concerning the variables possessing a dual nature and exerting a dual effect on political unrest is the following: In some cases, opposing forces are almost neutralized, leaving the variable in question with small "net" explanatory power, while in others, one set of forces becomes the dominating one. From a methodological point of view, the necessity of empirical research in such cases is unquestionable and imperative. No other method seems capable of assessing or predicting the net effect of such variables on political unrest. However, for some explanatory variables such as income growth rate, political unrest is not a monotonically dependent variable for all ranges of independent variables. Thus most present theories of political violence which are based on this or that factor(s), be it economics or otherwise, are at most piecewise explanations. In such theories, only an arbitrary range or direction of one or more explanatory factors is taken into account. We have concluded here that the change in the magnitude or direction of a single factor may result in an increase or decrease of the political violence depending on the initial level of the factor under consideration and the existing historical epoch.

With the generation of data from more countries and the increasing availability of data concerning other indicators, further work in this area becomes possible. These results should be considered a first step and, at best, a first approximation.

44.

Mark N. Cooper

A REINTERPRETATION OF THE CAUSES OF TURMOIL: THE EFFECTS OF CULTURE AND MODERNITY

Turmoil, the form of civil violence defined by Gurr (1970b: 131) as "relatively spontaneous, unorganized strife with substantial popular participation," has proven more difficult to explain and predict, in the statistical sense, than the other two forms of civil strife—internal war and conspiracy.[1] While numerous studies have succeeded in explaining turmoil relatively well within certain groups of nations (see Gurr, 1970b; Feierabend et al., 1970; Bwy, 1968; Midlarsky and Tanter, 1967), none has succeeded in explaining it across the universe of nations. We believe that the reason explanation is improved by dealing with specific groups of nations is that the causes of turmoil and the perception of turmoil itself vary from one group of nations to another. In attempting to predict across all nations, these differences are overlooked.

In this paper, the model of civil violence proposed by Ted Robert Gurr (1972a) is used as a base on which a comprehensive explanation of turmoil is built. Two variables will be added to Gurr's model. The universe of nations will be divided, first, into cultural groups, and then into groups based on the level of modernity, and the model applied within groups. Finally, a small number of variables which appears to be the salient cause of turmoil in each

group of nations will be isolated and proposed as a basis for further study.

Theoretical background

Grouping nations

The difference between turmoil and the other two forms of civil strife can be reduced to differences in three characteristics: degree of organization; clarity of goals; and extent of citizen participation. The idea of spontaneity is central to the first two characteristics. Because turmoil tends to be spontaneous, it tends to be disorganized and not to have clearly defined goals. For instance, Gurr (1972a) calls turmoil "unstructured, mass strife," while he calls conspiracy "planned strife," and internal war "focused strife."[2]

The third characteristic—extent of citizen participation—clearly distinguishes turmoil from conspiracy, but does not distinguish between turmoil and internal war. That is, both turmoil and internal war have large-scale participation, while conspiracy tends to have small-scale participation. It is the spontaneous aspect of turmoil with which we will be most concerned.

Gurr's (1972a: 204) conclusion about turmoil, in view of its spontaneity, is: "The most likely substantive interpretation of the relatively low predictability of turmoil, however, is that much turmoil is a response to a variety of locally incident deprivations and social conditions of the sort not represented in this study."

"A Reinterpretation of the Causes of Turmoil: The Effects of Culture and Modernity," by Mark N. Cooper is reprinted from *Comparative Political Studies*, Vol. 7, No. 3 (October 1974), pp. 267-91 by permission of the publisher, Sage Publications, Inc., and the author.

The fact that turmoil can be viewed as 'situationally determined, unstructured, mass behavior,' suggests that theories of collective behavior are possible sources of explanations of turmoil. The type of collective behavior which is most like turmoil is what Smelser terms the "hostile outburst." The hostile outburst can be viewed as an attempt by participants to redefine a situation which has become intolerable.

Viewing turmoil in this way, at least part of the difficulty which has been encountered in explaining turmoil would appear to lie in the fact that the definition of situations which are intolerable, and the responses to such situations which are acceptable, vary widely from culture to culture and individual to individual. As Smelser (1963: 45) notes, "Before we classify any event or situation as a source of strain, we must assess that event or situation with reference to cultural and personal expectations."[3] With the nation-state as the unit of analysis, it is not possible to determine or control for personal expectations, but cultural and societal factors which affect expectations can be taken into account.

The aspects of culture in which we are most interested are the values and norms which govern behavior. Shibutani (1965: 62) refers to these as vocabularies of motives: "One of the most important aspects of the culture of any group is its vocabulary of motives. Much of what a man does depends upon his intentions, and in each culture a somewhat different set of intentions is regarded as the natural ground of conduct."

Behavior, then, even spontaneous, unstructured behavior, generally remains within and is bounded by what is culturally acceptable. Because culture determines, in part, the definitions of situations and prescribes acceptable responses to these situa-tions, it provides a useful framework for the explanation of turmoil. That is, while turmoil events are similar across cultures, the impetus toward, and definition of, these events may vary widely from culture to culture.

A particular aspect of culture which makes it a useful framework for the explanation of turmoil is the effect that culture has on interpersonal communications. Shibutani argues that, in order for collective, violent behavior to occur, there must be a certain level and type of communication present, a process that can be called the 'collectivization of discontent.' By collectivization of discontent, we mean that, in order for collective, violent behavior to occur, individuals must come to share a definition of a situation as irritating or intolerable, and they must feel social support for their violent behavior. Shibutani (1965: 318), speaking of ethnic conflict, says:

Under ordinary circumstances an angry individual is not likely to attack a member of an ethnic minority or, for that matter, anyone else. Such assaults become possible only when large numbers of people are sufficiently aroused to engage in violence or at least condone it. Thus, in explaining inter-ethnic tension and conflict, one must ask how individual frustrations become shared so that they provide a basis for concerted action. In unsettled times, large numbers of people experience frustration but they must be able to communicate with one another before sufficient consensus develops to mount a concerted attack upon unpopular people.

The process of the collectivization of discontent is determined, in large part, by cultural norms which define the pattern of communication in a society. Differences in culture may result in differences in the process of the collectivization of discontent. In trying to explain turmoil across all nations, this underlying difference is overlooked and the explanation of turmoil is confounded.

One way of taking culture into account and controlling for differences is to aggregate nations into relatively homogeneous culture groups. In this way, we hold culture constant within groups, and we can examine the causes of turmoil within groups, relatively free of the confounding effects of culture. At the same time, we can compare the causes of turmoil between the different cultural groups.[4]

A second major factor that provides a useful framework for the explanation of turmoil, and one which can be treated much like culture, is modernity. The Feierabends (1972: 43) define modernity as follows:

The notion of modernity denotes a very complex set of social phenomena. It includes the aspirations and capacity in a society to produce and consume a very wide range of goods and services. It includes high development in science, technology, and education, and high attainment of scores of specialized skills. It includes, moreover, new structures of social organization and participation, new sets of aspirations, attitudes, and ideologies.

Modernity, by affecting aspirations, attitudes, and ideologies, clearly affects the norms and expectations governing behavior. Similarly, by affecting structures of social organization and participation, modernity affects the communication network in society (see Southall, 1959; Lerner, 1958). Thus, like culture, modernity should provide a useful framework for the explanation of turmoil.

Additional variables

A similar argument applies to the two variables which we propose to add to the Gurr model. Since the hostile outburst is dependent upon a broadly shared defini-tion of a situation as intolerable, structural features of the society which are conducive to such a definition should be included in causal model of turmoil. Similarly, structural features which are conducive to the collectivization of discontent should also be included.

While there are many factors which might be considered, we feel that the crucial factors are those which pertain to the way the demands of large numbers of people are handled in society.

As a cause of turmoil, the failure to meet the demands of large numbers of people fits very well into both the expectation-achievement argument utilized by Gurr and the more general argument proposed by Tilly and Snyder (1972). Their argument focuses on conflicting claims to scarce resources as the cause of turmoil. Tilly and Snyder (1972: 526) conclude: "Collective violence, then, tends to occur when one group lays claim to a set of resources, and at least one other group resists that claim."

Implicit in the idea of conflicting claims to scarce resources is the idea that both sides cannot carry out their claims. It is in the failure to achieve claims that frustration and the potential for turmoil lie.

Two key areas in the demand structure are, according to Almond and Coleman (1960), "interest articulation" and "interest aggregation." Interest articulation involves the formulation and the statement of citizen demands for presentation to the government, while interest aggregation involves the ways in which demands are received by the government. Almond and Coleman define three types of groups which articulate demands in society: associational, nonassociational, and institutional groups. Associational groups are organizations such as labor unions, chambers of commerce, and the like. Nonassociational groups are religious, ethnic, language- or kinship-based groups, while institutional groups are organizations such as the military, major churches, major bureaucracies, and so on.

Associational groups, as defined by Almond and Coleman, tend to be made up of individuals with diverse characteristics.[5] That is, while individuals associate on the basis of a particular characteristic (e.g., occupation), their other characteristics tend to diverge. Of course, the other characteristics show some degree of nonrandom variation, but the important point is that individuals in associational groups tend to be more diverse than individuals in nonassociational or institutional groups. In these latter groups, the characteristics of individuals (language, religion, race, education, occupation) tend to be less diverse and to reinforce one another.

A second important difference between associational groups and nonassociational or institutional groups is that associational groups are formulated for the specific purpose of articulating interests. They do so formally and are integrated into the system for handling demands. Nonassociational or institutional groups are often not formed for the express purpose of articulating interest, and, when they do so, they do so informally and irregularly.

On the basis of these two differences, Almond and Coleman conclude that interest articulation via associational groups is conducive to stability in society, while interest articulation via nonassociational or institutional groups is conducive to instability. Dahrendorf (1959) has made a similar argument as part of his general theory of conflict, and it is his discussion that we will outline in detail.

It is important to note at the outset that Dahrendorf (1959: 213) uses interchangeably conflict group and class, and conflict and class conflict.

If, in a given society, there are fifty associations we should expect to find a hundred classes, or conflict groups in the sense of the present study. In fact, of course, this extreme scattering of conflicts and conflict groups is rarely the case. Empirical evidence shows that different conflicts may be, and often are, superimposed in given historical societies, so that the multitude of possible conflict fronts is reduced to a few dominant conflicts. I suggest that this phenomenon has considerable bearing on the degree of intensity and violence of empirical conflict.

Dahrendorf (1959: 239) goes on to describe the nature of the relationship between superimposition of conflict fronts and conflict.

The intensity of class conflict decreases to the extent that class conflicts in different associations are dissociated (not superimposed). The intensity of class conflict decreases to the extent that different group conflicts in the same society are dissociated (and not superimposed).

Since associational groups are characterized by dissociation of interests, while nonassociational and institutional groups are characterized by superimposition of interests, it follows that associational group interest articulation would lead to less intense conflict than nonassociational or institutional group interest articulation.

Dahrendorf (1959: 239) goes on to state that "the violence of conflict decreases to the extent that class conflict is effectively regulated."

It is our argument that because associational groups are formal, recognized mechanisms for interest articulation, they facilitate conflict regulation and are conducive to less violent conflict. Dahrendorf (1959: 225-26) identifies three characteristics that are necessary for conflict regulation to take place:

First, for effective conflict regulation to be possible, both parties have to recognize the necessity and reality of the conflict situation, and in this sense, the fundamental justice of the cause of the opponent. . . . A second prerequisite of effective conflict regulation is the organization of interest groups. . . . Thirdly, in order for effective regulation to be possible, the opposing parties in social conflict have to agree on certain formal rules of the game that provide the framework for their relations.

It is the first and third factors which associational groups possess to a greater degree than the other two types of groups. Because associational groups are made up of more diverse members, these members are likely to have different interests. They are more likely to line up on different sides of different issues—i.e., to be on different sides of conflict fronts. Hence, they are more likely to acknowledge the justice of opposition. They are also more likely to acknowledge the necessity and benefit of adhering to the rules of the game. Moreover, because associational groups are formal, recognized mechanisms for interest articulation, they are specifically subject to the rules of conflict regulation. These rules involve,

Such procedural norms as are binding for the contestants without prejudicing the outcome of the contest. Normally, they would include stipulations as to where and how to meet, how to proceed, how to reach decisions, what sanctions to apply in case of non-compliance and when and how to change the rules themselves [Dahrendorf, 1959: 226].

The classic example is collective bargaining in labor disputes.

Thus, associational groups are conducive to less intense and less violent conflict than either nonassociational or institutional groups. Following our earlier argument, they would be conducive to less turmoil.

Turning to interest aggregation, a similar argument can be made. Without proper interest aggregation, demand flows and responses cannot proceed smoothly.

Demands become blocked, and, as was argued above, the failure to achieve demands leads to frustration. This situation is conducive to turmoil.

Dahrendorf has argued that there are two crucial determinants of conflict in this regard, the possibility and necessity of realizing interests collectively. We are concerned, here, with the necessity of collectively realizing interests.[6] Dahrendorf (1967: 20) states, "Class conflict is that form of contest which becomes necessary if large numbers of individuals cannot realize their interests by individual endeavor."

It is in situations where demands are not properly handled by the government that individual interests become blocked and individuals resort to conflict. It is at this point that the earlier social-psychological argument converges with Dahrendorf's structural argument. Demand structures (i.e., the structure of interest articulation and aggregation) by blocking interests, and throwing together, in the case of nonassociational and institutional groups, individuals with very similar, reinforcing interests, can create not only discontent, but the conditions which facilitate the collectivization of discontent.

Almond and Coleman identify other areas in the demand process that may cause instability. In fact, our discussion of interest aggregation is, perhaps, a half step beyond theirs. However, we believe that the articulation and aggregation stages, as we have described them, are the most important points, and we will attempt to take them into account in the model.

Methodological considerations

The Gurr model of turmoil[7]

Gurr's causal model of civil strife includes two types of variables: 'causal variables' and 'mediating variables.' The three causal variables are all measures of deprivation.

Persisting Deprivation (Perd) is defined as long-term deprivation of either a political or social-economic nature. This is operationalized by measuring political, economic, and social discrimination, potential separatism, dependence on foreign capital, religious cleavages, and lack of educational opportunity.

Economic Deprivation (Ecd) and Political Deprivation (Pold) are defined as politics or conditions which cause short-term deprivation. Indicators of these concepts include inflation, trends in trade value, growth rate of GNP, restrictions on participation, and an evaluation of the number of people affected by adverse conditions.

The remaining five variables are what Gurr terms mediating variables, because they are social conditions which intervene between deprivation and collective violence. Coercive Potential (Coerp) is a measure of the size and loyalty of the military. Institutionalization (Inst) attempts to gauge the strength and stability of institutions in society. This is measured by political party stability, labor union membership, and government expenditure as a percentage of gross domestic product. Past Levels of Strife (Passt) is a measure that attempts to gauge the justification for strife and the societal experience and strife. Facilitation (Facil) is conceived of as those elements which aid the initiators of strife. These include geographic factors, foreign money for the initiators of strife, and Communist Party membership. The Legitimacy variable (Legit) attempts to gauge the degree to which people feel that the directives of the government are worthy of obedience. This is operationalized by evaluating the origin of national institutions and the occurrence of the most recent reforms.

The dependent variable for this analysis is turmoil. As defined by Gurr, it includes demonstrations, political strikes, riots, political clashes, and localized rebellions. Each strife event over a five-year period (1961-1965) was scored as to pervasiveness, duration, and intensity and the scores were summed into a magnitude of turmoil score for each nation.

The cultural dimension

In creating the cultural grouping of nations, we would like to achieve a homogeneity of norms governing behavior within groups. In the study of violence, using macro-cross-national data, there have generally been three criteria used to divide nations into culture groups. Gurr (1963; Gurr and Ruttenberg, 1971) uses sociocultural groupings based on the Russett scheme (1964). Nesvold (1969) uses politicocultural groupings based on the Almond and Coleman (1960) scheme. We have opted for a third procedure, a slightly modified version of the geocultural groupings in Banks and Textor (1963). The three schemes emphasize, respectively, structure, politics, and geography.

The geocultural criteria achieves the greatest homogeneity of norms governing behavior. To be sure, there is still a great deal of variance in norms governing behavior that remains within groups, but within the limits of the very simple strategy used here, the geocultural groupings are, we believe, the most efficient.

The modernity dimension

For the modernity dimension, we chose the categorizations used by the Feierabends (1972). They create a modernity index which takes into account eight criteria (GNP, Caloric Intake, Telephones, Physicians, Newspapers, Radios, Literacy, and Urbanization) and provide a comprehensive means for classifying nations. There are three categories—modern, transitional, and traditional—and the vast majority of those nations left unclassified by the Feierabends (primarily sub-Saharan Africa) was assigned to the traditional category.

Additional variables: interest articulation configuration and representativeness

We have concluded on theoretical grounds that the greater the level of interest articulation via associational groups, and the lower the level of interest articulation via nonassociational and institutional groups, the less turmoil there should be in a society.

For measures of interest aggregation, we used the Banks and Textor variable entitled "representativeness." Representativeness is easily tied to our earlier discussion of interest aggregation. Dahrendorf (1967: 20) states, for instance,

If, for example, one group monopolizes the distribution of chances for participation over a lengthy period of time, then even individuals with widely divergent interests are compelled to join forces and try their strength by collective action. This then is how classes in the sense of inclusive social and political conflict come about.

It is precisely in nonrepresentative situations that groups monopolize chances for participation, presentation of demands, and meeting of demands.

It is important to note an argument that runs counter to this. Relative deprivation theory suggests that the proliferation of demands in representative government may lead to turmoil because reality cannot keep pace with expectations. Similarly, Tilly and Snyder (1972) have argued that violent political activity varies directly with nonviolent political activity. In fact, these arguments are not necessarily in contra-

diction with Dahrendorf's general analysis of conflict or, for that matter, with the general democratic formulation. Turmoil is not an intense, or violent form of conflict, compared to the other forms of civil violence. In fact, Dahrendorf has argued that democratic governments maintain themselves by restricting conflict to its less intense forms. Lipset (1959: 91) has made a similar argument,

Inherent, however, in all democratic systems is the constant threat that the conflict among different groups which are the life blood of the system may crystallize to the point where societal disintegration is threatened. Hence, conditions which serve to moderate the intensity of partisan battle, in addition to effectiveness, are among the requisites for a democratic system.

We have used a four-point scale from the Banks and Textor study ranging from nonpolyarchic (1), to polyarchic (4).[8] To be sure, more sensitive interval measures of representativeness than the Banks and Textor measure exist for many nations. However, no one study includes the number of nations under study here. Each study operationalizes its measures in a different way, which makes combination of measures problematic (see Lipset, 1959; Cutright, 1963a, 1965b; Neubaur, 1967; Almond, 1969; De Shweinitz, 1970). Therefore, we have chosen the simpler, more comprehensive measure. Moreover, in using the Banks and Textor study, we remain in the same time frame as Gurr.

Problems of sample size

Dividing a sample of 114 nations into five culture groups and three modernity groups creates a major problem in terms of sample size. Using ten variables in samples as small as fifteen creates a question as to the stability of coefficients. The standard error of estimate increases rapidly as n decreases, and as the number of variables increases, relative to the degrees of freedom, coefficients are almost always inflated.

This problem is often present in macro-cross-national research, where the nation-state is the unit of analysis. Due to the limited number of nations, traditional means of solving this problem (increasing the sample size) are not possible. However, even our small sample consists of close to eighty percent of the universe of nations. Therefore, from the point of view of sampling error, coefficients may cautiously be interpreted as reasonable estimates of the population parameters. In fact, certain of the clusters exhaust the specific types of nations, so that, in a strict sense, there is no sampling error.

Ultimately, one solution to this problem is to reduce the number of variables. This is, in one sense, the purpose of this paper. We are arguing that culture and modernity establish the framework for turmoil behavior. For each group of nations, we hope to trim down to a few variables which are salient in that cluster. The sensitivity of coefficients makes this trimming tentative and only replication on different sets of data can build confidence in our belief that we have located the salient causes of turmoil in each cluster.

The model and the data

Since this is a first step toward creating parsimonious models of turmoil for each cluster, and because we are severely limited in regard to degrees of freedom, we have treated all relationships as linear and additive. We have regressed all variables at one time, rather than impose a stage-wise order, as the theory suggests. In this way, the amount of variance which each of the dependent variables accounts for is determined solely by the strength of its

TABLE 1

Comparison of Models and Groupings of Nations[a]

| | Gurr Groupings | | | Cooper Groupings | |
| | Gurr Model | | Gurr Model | Cooper Model | |
	R^{2b}	n	R^2	R^2	n
All Nations	28	(114)	28	34	(114)
Cultural Groups					
Western	66	(21)	51	73	(29)
Latin American	62	(24)	73	78	(22)
Middle Eastern	60	(21)	60	63	(15)
Asian	36	(17)	50	83	(19)
African	64	(23)	56	61	(19)
Average	57.6			73.6	
Modernity Groups					
Modern (High)	49	(37)	67	76	(22)
Transitional (Medium)	30	(39)	69	71	(39)
Traditional (Low)	45	(38)	36	43	(53)
Average	41.2		57.3	63.3	

[a] The Gurr model includes the following variables: Economic Deprivation, Political Deprivation, Persisting Deprivation, Past Strife, Facilitation, Institutionalization, Coercive Potential, and Legitimacy. The Cooper model adds Interest Articulation Configuration, and Representativeness to the Gurr model.
[b] Decimals cleared by multiplying through by 100.

relationship to the dependent variable and its multicollinearity with other independent variables. After selecting out those variables which appear most promising, we will be in a better position to investigate nonlinearity, nonadditivity, and the interaction between the groupings and the variables.

Results

The discussion of the results will be divided into three sections: (1) The effects of grouping, (2) the effects of the additional variables, and (3) comparisons between groups and selection of parsimonious models for each group.

The effects of grouping

The overall effects of grouping the nations is to improve prediction considerably. These effects were demonstrated by Gurr (1969) earlier and have been reaffirmed (see Table 1).

There is no consistent or striking difference between our cultural groupings and Gurr's. Our groupings increase the R^2s in the Latin American and Asian clusters, but the R^2s decrease in the Western and African clusters. It is important to note that the increase in R^2s does not come at the expense of a decrease in n size. However, the decrease in R^2s are associated with increases in n size.

Variations in grouping on the modernity dimension appear to have a major impact on the level of explanation.[9] We have increased the R^2s by an average of 15.9 percentage points by using our groupings as opposed to Gurr's. A rather striking result is the fact that in our middle category, 39% more of the variance is accounted for than Gurr's middle category

(with n's equal). The difference between Gurr's classification and ours can be crudely summarized by saying that we have taken fifteen nations from his middle category and placed them in our low category, and fifteen nations from his high category and placed them in our middle category. Because we have achieved a high level of explanation in the high and middle categories, we will focus our attention on the low category. Specifically, we will focus on the nature of nations which seem to lie between the low and middle categories, for it is in shuffling these that the level of explanation in the middle category increases and the level of explanation in the low category declines. From a theoretical point of view, it is in these countries that we would expect to find norms in the greatest state of flux. We suggest that there may be a large difference between those nations which have just begun the transition and strictly traditional or fully transitional nations. By including these nations in the low category, we may have defined that category too broadly. That is, we may have failed to achieve the homogeneity of norms we were seeking.

In this regard, the argument has been made (Smelser, 1963; Shibutari, 1965; Turner and Killian, 1957) that the fluctuations of norms itself is an extremely irritating and intolerable situation—i.e., a situation typified by strain. We do, indeed, find that the fifteen 'problematic' nations which stand between categories have a mean turmoil score of 6.6, while the remaining 38 traditional nations have a mean turmoil score of 5.2. The 39 strictly transitional nations have a mean turmoil score of 5.1, and the modern nations have a mean turmoil score of 4.1. What this analysis suggests is that there may be two tiers within the traditional category, one which is strictly traditional, and one which is just beginning transition. Treating them separately would lead to a higher level of explanation. It would also, of course, compound the problem of n size.

Additional variables

Entering the two additional variables into the model increases the level of explanation, and makes it more uniform across clusters. The average increase in R^2 is 10.9 percentage points, but there are only two cases in which the increase is appreciable. In the Asian and Western clusters, which were two of the worst predicted by the Gurr model, we seem to have identified a cause of turmoil which the Gurr model did not take into account. The behavior of these two variables will be examined below, in conjunction with the other variables.

Selecting parsimonious models[10]

On the basis of partial r's we can make a series of statements that appear to have good theoretical support and can guide us in building parsimonious models for each cluster. Because n sizes are so small relative to the number of variables used, we stress again the tentative nature of these conclusions.

(a) In general, we find that there is no case in which turmoil is a result of only mediating variables. That is, in every cluster at least one form of deprivation is relatively important.[11]

(b) A more complex statement about deprivation can be made. In only the modern and Western clusters are both measures of short term deprivation (Pold, Ecd) of relatively little importance. Tentatively we can say that in these firmly established, ongoing societies, short-term downswings do not pose a serious threat to people's interests and do not elicit violent responses. Relative deprivation theory asserts that fluctuations in expectations, relative to reality are the producers of violence. Our findings, in accordance with this, suggests that in the modern and Western clusters, short-term swings do not affect the balance of expectations and reality. There would appear to be enough confidence in the system to overcome the effects of short-term deprivation.

(c) Institutionalization and interest articulation configuration will be considered together because they are conceptually and operationally akin, and exhibit similar behavior. We find that the variance which they account for tends to decrease as nations become more modern. While these variables are indirectly related to turmoil (both simple r's and beta weights), this relationship grows weaker as the clusters become more modern. Within the realm of relative deprivation theory, we can frame an explanation as follows: the poorer societies are the ones in which expectations far outdistance capabilities, especially those just beginning the transition.[12] In these cases, the way frustrations are mediated, the way people are integrated into society, takes on added importance. In terms of collective behavior theory, the strain is present, and the structural conduciveness for violence, or lack of it, becomes crucial (Smelser, 1963).

(d) Representativeness, as predicted by the Tilly argument and the relative deprivation arguments cited above, is directly related to turmoil. Every partial is positive, and four of the eight are significant at the .05 level.[13] Moreover, we note that, in the more representative clusters (with the exception of Asia), the partials are larger and the percentage of variance accounted for is also larger. In fact, representativeness and interest articulation configuration are the only variables whose partials do not change signs in any cluster.

(e) For the facilitation variable in the Asian, African, and traditional categories, the sign is opposite than predicted, and opposite than in the other categories (significant at the .05 level in the traditional category). There is a large gap between the mean facilitation scores for these categories and the others. A threshold effect may be at work here. Societies may require a specific level of organization before things such as monies for dissidents, and dissident party membership begin to become causes of turmoil. Moreover, these nations have extremely high inaccessibility scores. Inaccessibility, which may be almost a prerequisite for internal warfare, may have little effect on turmoil. In fact, turmoil usually requires concentrations of population and intensive communication (as suggested above).

(f) One very specific non-uniformity stands out. Past strife has a negative partial in the Latin American cluster (significant at the .05 level) while in several of the other clusters it is substantially positively related to turmoil (four of seven significant at the .05 level).

In light of these results, we can select a small set of variables in each cluster which may provide a relatively high level of explanation of turmoil. These models have been selected in a somewhat arbitrary fashion (the best four variables) but they do reflect the generalizations made above.

There is a similarity between the models across dimensions that is worthy of note. The Western model is reflected quite closely in the modern model, while the African cluster is reflected quite closely in the traditional model. If the level of explanation can be raised in the traditional category by dividing it into two tiers, as suggested above, it would be advisable to use this dimension as a basis for building an explanation of turmoil rather than the culture dimension. There are two reasons for this. First, the average n sizes would be larger, and second, modernity, as a context, could very well prove easier to deal with, both in terms of quantification

and in terms of division into its component parts.

These models are merely skeletal. We have discussed only a few substantive reasons why the particular models might operate in each cluster, and we have done so in a very general manner. The discussion of specific models is beyond the scope of this paper. Hopefully, by limiting the number of variables within each cluster, this task can be made easier.

Summary and conclusions

In this paper, we have attempted to improve the explanation of the type of civil violence generally identified as turmoil by treating it within the framework of general theories of collective behavior. Relying on the definition of turmoil as a collective attempt to redefine a situation which has become intolerable, we have divided nations into cultural groups and modernity groups within which we believe there is a general uniformity of norms and definitions regarding such situations.

While we have used the model of civil violence proposed by Ted Robert Gurr as our basic model, we have also proposed two additional variables (representativeness and interest articulation configuration) which we believe contribute greatly to the definition of a situation as intolerable, and which affect the patterns of response in those situations. Both the groupings and the additional variables improved the level explanations considerably. However, the reduction in sample size inherent in grouping and the reduction in degrees of freedom inherent in adding variables make any conclusions we draw tentative. Replications with different sets of data using similar techniques are necessary to build confidence in the conclusions we have drawn.

In general, we find that short-term deprivations become less and less a cause of turmoil as societies become more economically advanced and established. At the same time, we find that the means by which deprivations are mediated are more important in the societies that are economically less developed.

We have also found evidence for the fact that it is the societies which are just beginning the transition from a traditional to a modern society that are the most turmoil-ridden. This is at odds with an earlier theory (see Feierabend et al., 1972) which hypothesized that the peak of turmoil might occur in the middle of transition. We have proposed that the beginning transitional countries might be dealt with as a group by themselves.

The most striking finding is that, once we control for all other variables, we find that increasing turmoil is associated with increasing representativeness. This is at odds with the earlier "general democratic theory" (see Cutright, 1963a; Lipset 1959) which suggests the opposite. However, it is consistent with both Dahrendorf's (1959) and Tilly and Snyder's (1972) theories.

Intensive studies of individual nations and the characteristics which define the clusters of nations which are necessary to give better theoretical and substantive meaning to the statistical models have been briefly described in this paper. Ultimately, we must understand how contextual variables, such as culture and modernity actually bear upon the behavior of individuals, especially violent behavior, in order to understand the occurrence of turmoil.

Notes

1. Gurr (1972: 296) defines internal war as "large scale, organized, focussed strife," while conspiracy is defined as "intensively organized, relatively small scale civil strife." These dimensions of civil violence have been consistently defined in numerous factor and scalogram analyses (see Feierabend et al., 1972; Rummel, 1971; Nesvold, 1969; Tanter, 1966).

2. Rummel's (1972: 62) formulation is similar: "One can divide domestic conflict into three independent continua: a disorganized, spontaneous conflict behavior, a turmoil dimension: an overt organized conflict behavior, a revolutionary dimension: and a covert, organized conflict behavior, a subversive dimension. The second and third appear to represent organized conflict behavior, i.e., that is planned with definite objectives in mind."

3. Gurr (1969: 616) has stated a similar idea, "In other words, the cultural heritage of a nation may tell us more about the conditions to which discontented men are sensitive than information about its political or economic systems."

4. In essence, this means of grouping is an attempt to eliminate nuisance variance in the dependent variable (see Blalock, 1964).

5. Kornhauser (1959) calls this cross-cutting characteristics. Dahrendorf (1959) calls it dissociation.

6. The possibility pertains to coercion, which is already in the model.

7. For a complete description of the variables, see Gurr (1972a). For an extensive theoretical discussion of the variables, see Gurr (1970a).

8. Banks and Textor intend their typologies to be ordinal, so in performing mathematical operations upon them, and in using them in regression analysis, we have taken some liberties with the level of measurement assumption.

9. It should be pointed out that culture and development are, themselves, very poor predictors of turmoil, accounting for less than nine percent of the variance. This is a strong indication that there is an interaction between the groupings and at least some of the independent variables.

10. Blalock (1962) suggests that we not rely on beta weights or partials alone in deciding the relative importance of variables, but that we use additional means to verify our results. His argument is made in regard to creating specific models, and in regard to causal priority. Here we are not proposing any specific models, only that different ones exist. We are also making no assertions about causal priority.

11. In the transitional cluster, Perd accounts for six percent of the variance, but it is the third most important variable.

12. The Feierabends (1972) suggest that, in transitional nations, demands increase far more rapidly than capabilities, due to the spread of literacy and the media.

13. The meaning of significance for nonrandom samples is quite problematic. Levels of significance will be reported as a matter of course.

45.

Melvin L. De Fleur

MASS COMMUNICATION AND SOCIAL CHANGE

Excellent histories of each of our principal mass media have been available for some time. These have extensively documented the dates, contributions of individuals, invention of technical devices and other details which have played significant parts in the development of each major form of mass communication. Almost uniformly, these histories have been prepared by writers specialized in the study of some particular medium (journalists, students of the cinema, educators in broadcasting, etc.).[1] Sociologists and other social scientists have paid relatively little attention to the patterns of growth of the media in terms of their broader implications for the study of social change. Although themselves often intimately involved in the process by which new cultural traits become accepted into society, the mass media may be viewed in their own right as cultural innovations. In recent years, substantial advances have been made in understanding the processes by which new items of culture spread through a social system achieving widespread adoption by the members of its population. Such "diffusion studies" of the "adoption of innovation" promise to provide the foundation for the eventual development of an analytical, quantitative and empirically-based

theory of social change.[2] It is the intent of the present paper to clarify a number of concepts which will enter such a theory, to suggest points where they can be linked to broader sociological theory, and then to present data which illustrate the potential utility of the conceptual framework.

The illustrative sets of data are the *diffusion curves* which four major mass media of communication have followed during their respective periods of acceptance by American households. These curves are related to a background of classical studies of the adoption of innovation, and are compared with each other in terms of similarities and differences from one medium to another. The major social, political and economic events which appear to have influenced these quantitative growth patterns are brought out for each medium. While most studies of mass communication attempt to unravel ways in which the media influence society, the present analysis tries to bring out ways in which society has influenced the media.

Toward a clarification of basic terms and a convergence with more general theory

The terminology of the growing body of literature reporting on the diffusion of items through populations is characterized by a considerable lack of uniformity in the use of terms.[3] For this reason, more rigorous efforts need to be directed toward standardization of the *meaning* of concepts, and toward *consistency* in their use from one writer to another. Such stan-

Reprinted from *Social Forces,* Vol. 44 (March 1966). "Mass Communication and Social Change," by Melvin L. De Fleur. Copyright © 1966 The University of North Carolina Press.

The present article is an outgrowth of a paper presented at the annual meeting of the American Sociological Association, Montreal, Canada, 1964. The writer is indebted to Elaine C. El-Assal for her many contributions to both works.

dardization needs to be based upon definitional principles *which also underlie more general sociological theory* so that an emerging empirical theory of social change which rests in part upon contributions from the diffusion studies can eventually converge with broader conceptual schemes. Two obvious requirements along these lines are (1) that the variables to be included in an empirical theory of social change must be *measurable*, and (2) that theoretical concepts related to the diffusion process must be defined in such a way that their social action or behavioral *referents* are clear.

Elementary as they may seem, the two requirements noted above have not been adequately met in the past, and this has been a source of substantial confusion. For example, in the sociological literature, even the word "innovation" itself is used in a bewildering variety of ways. It sometimes means newly-invented items of *technology,* such as hybrid seed corn.[4] It also means the act of working out some new *deviant form of behavior* which will aid the individual in achieving a culturally approved goal (by illegitimate means).[5] For other writers, the term refers to a *cultural modification*, such as the development within a group of a new code of approved conduct.[6] For still others, it has meant the psychological and overt actions associated with the *acquisition* of some new procedure, belief, device, etc., including the reaching of a decision to adopt and also the overt act of adopting.[7] Other terms (invention, diffusion, etc.) used widely in research related to the study of innovation have shown equal degrees of confusion in definition and meaning.

The present discussion is not intended as a suggestion that such heterogeneous classes of events are unimportant objects of study. But when such a variety of referents are all denoted by the same

symbol, thought and communication are severely hampered. A standardized terminology has become an indispensable and urgent prerequisite for the further development of a systematic approach to social change *via* the quantitative study of diffusion and related phenomena.

A second urgent prerequisite is the linking of theoretical concepts from diffusion studies and the study of innovation to concepts from more general sociological theory. One of the reasons why this has not been done extensively in the past is undoubtedly explainable by the fact that sociologists have not yet developed very much in the way of validated general theory about which widespread consensus exists.

The work of Talcott Parsons, among contemporary American sociologists, makes a claim to being directed toward this goal. There is no complete agreement as to how well this goal is being reached by his particular efforts, but there is at least one aspect of Parsons' "theories of systems" that seems to provide linkage points for potential convergence with an empirical and analytical theory of social change.[8] This key aspect is Parsons' approach to the conceptualization of social action by treating it within three broad systems:

First, the orientation of action of *any one* given actor and its attendant motivational processes becomes a differentiated and integrated system. This system will be called the *personality,* and we will define it as the organized system of the orientation and motivation of action of one individual *actor.* Secondly, the action of a plurality of actors in a common situation is a process of interaction, the properties of which are to a definite but limited extent independent of any prior culture. This interaction also becomes differentiated and integrated and as such forms a social system. Personality and social system are very intimately related, but they are neither identical with one another nor explicable by one another; the social system is not a plurality of personalities. Finally, systems of culture have their own forms and problems of integration which are not reducible to those of either personality or social systems or both together.[9]

Even at the time the general theory of action was formulated, these divisions were neither new nor unique; they were simply introduced as focal points around which the details of the theory were then elaborated. But for present purposes, it can be shown that certain explanations and theories concerned with diffusion and innovation have been formulated at one or the other of these levels, and thus fall within (or are special cases of) one of the three systems of action in the sense implied above.

Illustrations are provided by the attempts of diffusion theorists to explain diffusion curves. For example, an early study by Pemberton showed that when plotted over time on a cumulative basis, the typical diffusion curve usually assumes an "S" shape. The finding that such curves frequently assume this particular form has been attributed by Rogers,[10] Sheppard,[11] and others to "interpersonal influence," that is to interactional mechanisms within the *social system*.[12] According to this approach to conceptualizing the diffusion of innovation, actors in a social system who have already adopted a particular item "expose" or otherwise influence those who have not. Adoption, under this view, is role interaction between a user of the item and one or more non-users which results in alterations of the roles of the latter in such a way that usage of the item becomes part of their roles. If one such actor influences (say) two others, who in turn influence two others, and so on, the curve of adoption will follow a cumulative binominal expansion, much as is the case in an unchecked infectious epidemic. Given sufficient time, the available roles in the system will be altered.

That is, saturation will be approached and the curve will tend to level off. The end result of this interactional process, which we can call the "epidemiological" theory of diffusion (and which we have oversimplified here), is the classic S-shaped diffusion curve, sometimes called the "logistic curve of adoption." This approach to the study of social change, through the analysis of the adoption of particular new combinations of culture traits and through interactional events within the social system, appears (when stated in the above terms) to be easily subsumable under the general theory of action as laid out by Parsons and his colleagues.

The data to be presented in the present paper have an important bearing upon the potential validity of the epidemiological theory of diffusion as a *general* model of the adoption of innovation. Such an explanation requires that the actors in the relevant social system be available to each other through time so that the required interactions can take place. If a diffusion curve is found which stretches over a century or so, so that early adopters are long dead before the later adopters acquire the item, then the observed process would not fit well with required underlying assumptions concerning stability in the system of action through time. Such a diffusion curve is in fact clearly in evidence for one of the mass media under study (newspapers).

This suggests that a more adequate explanation of this pattern must be sought within the *cultural* system of the society into which the new item was introduced. New items are adopted by members of groups, communities, or societies who have institutionalized ways of relating themselves to each other. The traditions, group values, social norms, level of technological accumulation and other variations in cultural conditions can serve as prerequisites to (or barriers to) social change. The rate of adoption or degree of penetration of a given new item will be significantly influenced by such factors. A substantial literature has accumulated with respect to this problem.[13]

Another widely used approach to the study of diffusion has focused attention more heavily upon events within the *personality* system. This is well illustrated in the work of Rogers, who defines the "adoption process" as, "the mental process through which an individual passes from the first learning about an innovation to final adoption."[14] The adoption process is broken down into five stages: *awareness, interest, evaluation, trial* and (permanent) *adoption.* Insofar as such actions may be thought of as contributing to the maintenance of the personality system, or as aiding the system in achieving some form of equilibrium, there appears to be no barrier whatever regarding convergence of this formulation with more general theory. In particular, the Parsons *et al.* treatise on "Personality as a System of Action" provides a sophisticated set of concepts and propositions which appear to be more than adequate for handling the "adoption process" as a special case of orientation, motivation and performance of a given actor.[15] In any case, this conceptualization sees the new item moving through a group or community as the result of the separate actions of individuals as they pass through their decision-making series. This approach also appears to be somewhat limited as a *general* model of the adoption process because it rests upon assumptions of systematic rationality and deliberated decisions on the part of all adopters. Perhaps more important, it tends to ignore events which occur in the other systems mentioned. Its articulation with such systems remains to be made clear.

These varied approaches to understanding the diffusion of innovations have resulted from the broad interdisciplinary attacks which have been made on this problem. The twin needs for conceptual standardization and for providing linkages with more general theory have become more and more urgent as the body of research reports has grown richer. It is toward these needs that the following attempt at conceptual clarification of basic terms is addressed. The definitions given below do not purport to be either new, sophisticated, or particularly unique; the concepts defined are elementary. The definitions attempt, however, to provide clear *action referents* for these simple terms (so as to permit convergence with theories of action), and to provide a reasonably standardized framework for approaching data concerning the spread of the mass media and for diffusion studies in general.

A *new item* will refer to some combination of culture traits, mechanical, symbolic, normative or other, which has not previously been widely incorporated into the cultural system of the relevant group or society. Such new items can come to the attention of the relevant group or society through borrowing or through invention.

Invention will refer to the *act* of forming some new combinations of culture traits, that is, some new item. This definition makes invention a behavior pattern of an actor rather than an element of mechanical or other technology.

Innovation will indicate some *change in patterns of conduct or action* related to some culture trait or item (combination of traits). Such a definition is anchored in potentially observable events and focuses upon patterned action rather than upon new devices, psychological processes, or stages in an individual's acquisition of new habits. Innovation (as change in patterns of action) *may* take place through the adoption of new items brought to the attention of the group or society, but it may also come about because of changing modes or conduct toward items which already exist as part of the established cultural system. Such a definition frees the study of innovation from being simply the study of the adoption of newly borrowed or invented things and broadens it to include behavioral, that is normative, reorientations toward items concerning which a group already has some action pattern. Innovation is thus an event in the cultural system of a group or society.

Obsolescence can be defined as the abandoning of formerly institutionalized modes of conduct related to some established item. Defined thus, obsolescence is a *special case of innovation*, that is a *special case of change* in patterns of action related to some culture trait or item (combination of traits).

Diffusion curve refers to a quantitative function describing the proportion or number of members of a group or society who have acquired a given new item or who have changed their action patterns with respect to it over some period of time. Obsolescence should show a kind of "reverse" diffusion curve. Its form should be opposite to the familiar S-shaped curve describing adoption. There should be a "curve of abandonment" for once-institutionalized behavior forms that are dropping out of the social or cultural system of a given group or society. Diffusion curves may or may not be reliable indices to the patterns of action which the members engage in with respect to the item. An actor may possess an item but not use it; use it but not possess it, etc. They do, however, reveal important data on the degree to which an item has been accepted, rejected or abandoned by a group or society.

Institutionalization will refer to the stabilizing of widespread patterns of action related to some cultural trait or combination of traits. In this sense institutionalization is the end product of innovation and represents *equilibrium* in a system rather than change. If behavior patterns related to a particular item have been institutionalized, it can be postulated that such an item fulfills some *functional need* in the social system in question. The diffusion curve for an item whose relevant behaviors have become institutionalized should show a distinct "leveling off" to a relatively long-term "plateau."

These six definitions (and the meanings given or implied for the several auxiliary terms contained within them), provide a simple conceptual framework for the comparative analysis of quantitative data on the patterns of innovation and obsolescence related to the media of mass communication as they have appeared in the American society.

In the sections which follow, the diffusion curves of each of the four major media (newspapers, movies, radio, and televi-

TABLE 1

The Growth of Daily Newspapers in the United States, 1850-1957

Year	Total Circulation of Daily Newspapers (Excluding Sunday)	Total Number of Households	Circulation per Household
1850	758,000	3,598,240	.21
1860	1,478,000	5,210,934	.28
1870	2,602,000	7,579,363	.34
1880	3,566,000	9,945,916	.36
1890	8,387,000	12,690,152	.66
1900	15,102,000	15,992,000	.94
1904	19,633,000	17,521,000	1.12
1909	24,212,000	19,734,000	1.23
1914	28,777,000	22,110,000	1.30
1919	33,029,000	23,873,000	1.38
1920	27,790,656	24,467,000	1.13
1925	33,739,369	27,540,000	1.22
1930	39,589,172	29,997,000	1.32
1935	38,155,540	31,892,000	1.20
1940	41,131,611	35,153,000	1.17
1945	48,384,188	37,503,000	1.29
1950	53,829,072	43,554,000	1.23
1955	56,147,359	47,788,000	1.17
1957	57,805,445	49,543,000	1.17

Sources:
U.S. Bureau of Census, *Historical Statistics of the United States, Colonial Times to 1957*, Series R-176 (Washington, D.C.: U.S. Government Printing Office, 1960), p. 500.
U.S. Bureau of Census, *Historical Statistics of the United States, Colonial Times to 1957*, Series R-169 (Washington, D.C.: U.S. Government Printing Office, 1960), p. 500.
U.S. Bureau of Census, *Historical Statistics of the United States, Colonial Times to 1957*, Series 255 (Washington, D.C.: U.S. Government Printing Office, 1960), p. 96.

sion) have been charted and these have been related to temporal patterns and to concomitant variations in social, economic or other cultural conditions in the society. The ways in which the suggested definitions given above can aid in understanding these quantitative patterns and can clarify patterns of development in one medium as related to another, are brought out.

Newspapers

Table 1 presents the basic data for newspapers in terms of circulation figures for daily papers over approximately a century. Data are also presented on the number of households in the United States during the same period. The household is used as a meaningful unit of adoption within the social system of the American society. The diffusion curve of daily newspapers *per household* is shown graphically in Figure 1. Obviously, this curve can be

only an approximation. Some newspapers are purchased by adoption units other than households. Nevertheless, the graph shows with some clarity the general pattern of the spread of the newspaper through the American population during more than a century. The most significant feature of this curve is that it resembles the classic S-shaped temporal diffusion pattern very well. (A smooth curve of logistic form has been drawn through the observed data.)

The history of journalism shows very clearly that the diffusion curve of the daily newspaper is closely related to the occurrence of such broad social and cultural changes as the spread of education, the development of press technology, the growth of cooperative newsgathering, news-distributing agencies, and the increasing urbanization of the American society. These significant concomitant trends have undoubtedly been of substan-

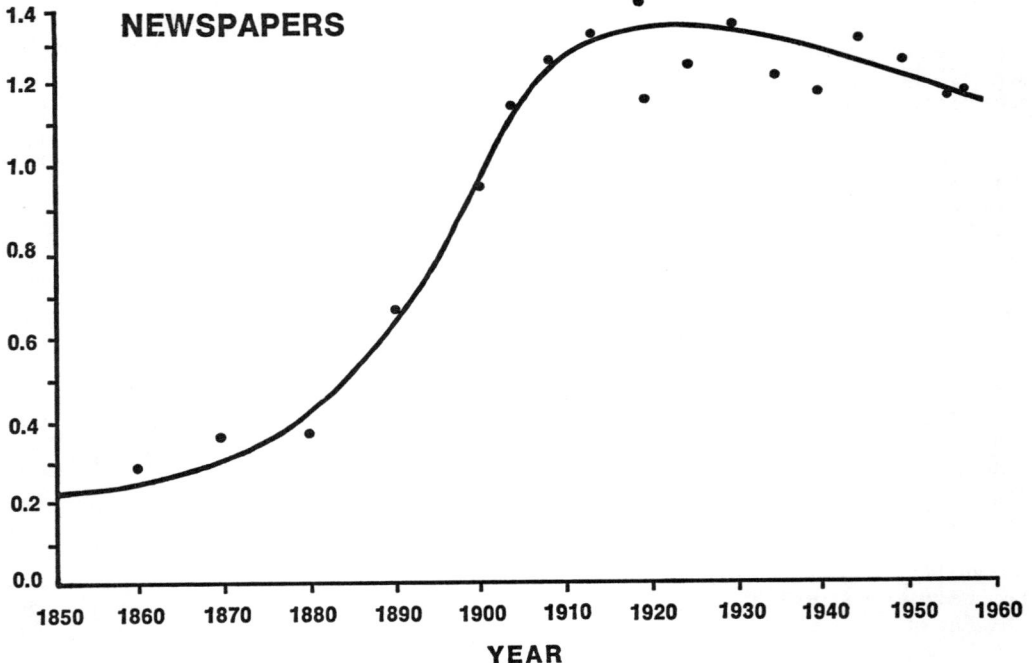

Figure 1. The Diffusion Curve for Newspapers: Number of Subscriptions to Daily Newspapers Per Household

tial importance as major influences on the shape of the diffusion curve for newspapers. The general curve in terms of its overall pattern seems to have been relatively unaffected by war, political change or even economic fluctuation (although these would undoubtedly be related to more minor variations in the actual circulation figures around the general pattern).

The period of most rapid growth was from about 1880 to about 1905. This corresponds very closely to the infamous episodes of "yellow journalism," when the great metropolitan newspaper empires of the late nineteenth century were locked in bitter competition for increased circulation. The spur which this vigorous promotion gave to circulation probably had a considerable influence on the adoption curve (although such an ex post facto interpretation would be difficult to demonstrate conclusively).

Interpersonal activities within the social system may have played some part in generating this diffusion curve. A given person perhaps influenced others to subscribe to a paper. But an explanatory theory based solely upon such considerations would appear to have severe limitations for this type of diffusion data. Furthermore, while the diffusion curve shown in Figure 1 indicates that the daily newspaper reached virtual saturation as a new item in the American society shortly after the turn of the century, subscriptions per household have *declined* somewhat since. It would be very difficult to account for this turn of events by appealing to interactional mechanisms within the social system, other than to suggest the unlikely possibility that individuals were exerting personal influence on each other to stop reading daily newspapers. A more likely interpretation is that the development of

additional media during the several decades of the 20th century has provided *functional alternatives within the cultural system*, which are making modest inroads in the degree to which the society satisfies its collective needs for communication content through the "consumption" of newspapers. However, the complex of various institutionalized social processes related to the use of the newspaper in our society have become so deeply established that it will undoubtedly be some time before these modest trends toward obsolescence become accelerated. Additional research is needed to bring out the influences responsible for this modest obsolescence.

The diffusion curve for newspapers actually reveals very little of the behavioral alterations which took place in our society because of their introduction. Subscribing is obviously only one of many forms of action that can be related to this particular item. Newspaper readership has been studied in considerable depth, and it is known to vary markedly from one segment of the population to another. Thus, the diffusion curve provides only a very inadequate index to *innovation* (as defined earlier), revealing only the fact that newspapers were purchased. Whether they were skimmed, read with care, used as a basis for forming political opinion, or merely used to wrap garbage cannot be determined from the curve. The development of an adequate understanding of the actual innovations in conduct related to such an item requires increasing attention to empirical research on *every aspect of newspaper usage* and related forms of action among those who consume them.[16]

Motion pictures

The motion picture had an early development and subsequent growth, which, in terms of historical detail, showed little correspondence to that of the newspaper. However, Table 2, showing average weekly movie attendance *per household*, indicates that motion pictures followed a rough

TABLE 2
The Growth of Weekly Motion Picture Attendance in the United States, 1922-1955

Year	Average Weekly Movie Attendance	Total Number of Households	Weekly Attendance per Household
1922	40,000,000	25,687,000	1.56
1923	43,000,000	26,298,000	1.64
1924	46,000,000	26,941,000	1.71
1925	46,000,000	27,540,000	1.67
1926	50,000,000	28,101,000	1.78
1927	57,000,000	28,632,000	1.99
1928	65,000,000	29,124,000	2.23
1929	80,000,000	29,582,000	2.70
1930	90,000,000	29,997,000	3.00
1931	75,000,000	30,272,000	2.48
1932	60,000,000	30,439,000	1.97
1933	60,000,000	30,802,000	1.95
1934	70,000,000	31,306,000	2.24
1935	80,000,000	31,892,000	2.51
1936	88,000,000	32,454,000	2.71
1937	88,000,000	33,088,000	2.66
1938	85,000,000	33,683,000	2.52
1939	85,000,000	34,409,000	2.47
1940	80,000,000	35,153,000	2.28
1941	85,000,000	35,929,000	2.37
1942	85,000,000	36,445,000	2.33
1943	85,000,000	36,833,000	2.31
1944	85,000,000	37,115,000	2.29
1945	85,000,000	37,503,000	2.27
1946	90,000,000	38,370,000	2.35
1947	90,000,000	39,107,000	2.30
1948	90,000,000	40,532,000	2.22
1949	70,000,000	42,182,000	1.66
1950	60,000,000	43,554,000	1.38
1951	54,000,000	44,656,000	1.21
1952	51,000,000	45,504,000	1.12
1953	46,000,000	46,334,000	.99
1954	49,000,000	46,893,000	1.04
1955	46,000,000	47,788,000	.96

Sources:
   U.S. Bureau of Census, *Historical Statistics of the United States, Colonial Times to 1957*, Series H. 522 (Washington, D.C.: U.S. Government Printing Office, 1960), p. 225.
   U.S. Bureau of Census, *Historical Statistics of the United States, Colonial Times to 1957*, Series A. 242-244 (Washington, D.C.: U.S. Government Printing Office, 1960), p. 15.

S-shaped curve of growth during much of their adoption period. Figure 2 presents the same data graphically.

The data show both considerable variability and what may appear as a substantial departure from the classical S-shaped curve. The latter is due primarily to the severe drop in weekly movie attendance per household which occurred in the postwar period. This drop had become so pronounced by 1955 that weekly attendance at motion picture theaters had been reduced to half of the peak which this medium had achieved before World War II. It should be noted that "weekly attendance" at a motion picture theater is a form of social action. For this reason, this diffusion curve reveals actual innovation (as defined) more accurately than a curve based upon the possession or acquisition of the motion picture as a technical item— as might be the case for a curve based, say, upon the number of motion picture theaters per household over a given span of time.

Because of this closer correspondence between diffusion curve and innovation, the S-shaped diffusion curve can be seen in this case to have a reverse counterpart, namely a pattern of *obsolescence,* by which certain forms of social action associated with movies, once deeply institutionalized, now are fading out of the American society.[17] If this trend continues, then periodic attendance at a motion picture theater may join the buffalo hunt, barn-raising, and the bare-knuckle boxing match as extinct forms of social activity. Such curves of obsolescence, and the factors associated with them have received far less research attention than adoption curves, although from a theoretical point of view they are equally important for the study of social change.

While it is true that attendance at public theaters is disappearing, the motion pic-

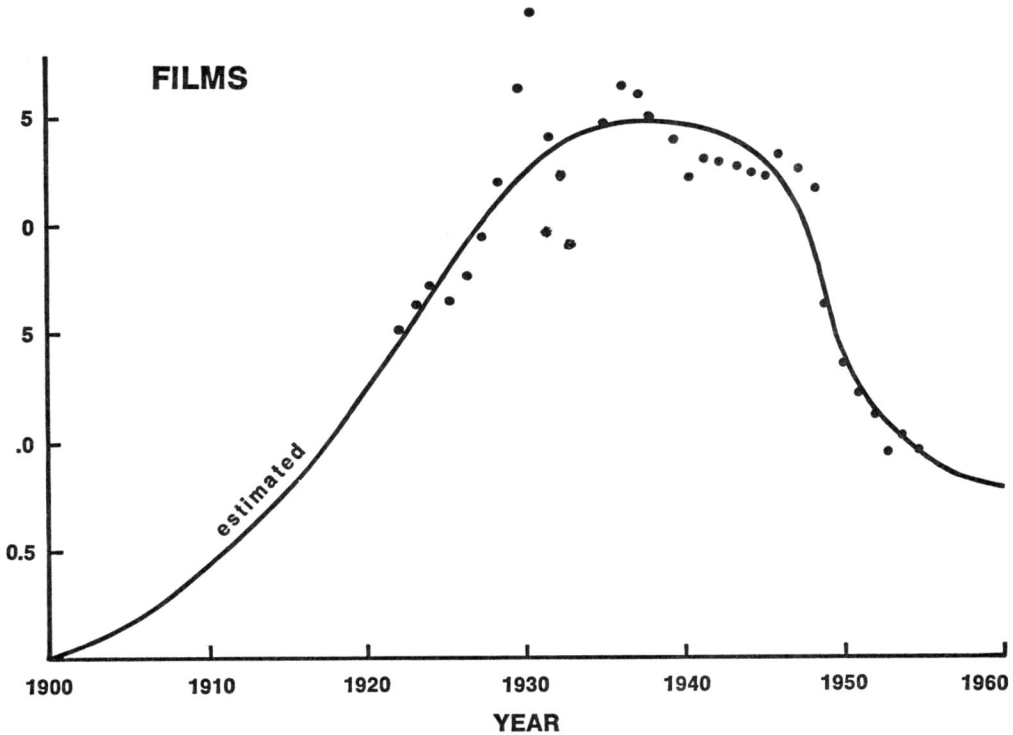

Figure 2. The Diffusion Curve for Films: Weekly Attendance at
Motion Pictures Per Household

ture as a technical item is not. Probably more people actually *see* movies now than ever before, but *via* their TV set. Thus, while the film and associated technical items (projector, screen, etc.) have not changed very much, there has been a great modification in associated forms of action. This situation provides an excellent example of innovation and obsolescence with respect to an item already established in the technological culture, an item which in itself has changed but little, but with respect to which substantial alterations in social action have occurred. A diffusion curve based upon social action data more faithfully reveals actual patterns of innovation.

The major fluctuations around the general pattern of per household movie attendance have been closely related to economic, political, and other cultural events within the larger society. Such attendance plunged sharply downward during the depression years (Figure 2) but recovered as war approached. World War II, which disrupted normal family activities in many ways, had a decidedly limiting effect on weekly movie attendance. The shape of this curve thus appears to be governed both by interactional events in the social systems and by trends in the cultural system.

The overall declining trend in motion picture attendance is obviously inversely correlated with the growth of the electronic media. Radio and television both appear to have made inroads on motion pictures. While it may be true that "movies are better than ever," they appear to be losing ground sharply as their pattern of obsolescence has developed. This trend, of course, raises the issue as to why the forms of action surrounding one medium remain as established institutions and those of another are threatened by oblivion. The answer would appear to lie in the social and psychological needs (in the functional sense) to which the medium relates itself, and in the types of concomitant cultural and technological changes which develop within the society. The American society is apparently "gratifying its needs" as a system in ways other than by going to the movies, and the time formerly devoted to this pastime is now being given over to other activities which serve as functional alternatives.

Radio

Radio's history has been brief, but in terms of set ownership it has become the most massive of our mass media. Table 3 shows that there are now more than three radio sets per household on the average in the United States. This adds up to nearly *180 million* sets!

Figure 3 shows graphically that radio in a brief life span achieved saturation adoption in a period of only about 40 years (1922-1962) as compared to about 75 years for newspapers. Movies also required about four decades to reach their peak.

An interesting feature of the S-shaped diffusion curve for radio is the plateau which occurred during the World War II period (see Figure 3). This, of course, was due to restrictions on the manufacture of radio receivers for the consumer market during the national emergency. However, the most striking feature of radio's adoption curve is the "recovery" that it made following the war years, even when faced with competition from television. Thus, radio's curve of diffusion was little influenced by either the Depression, which

TABLE 3

The Growth of Radio Set Ownership in the United States, 1922-1962

Year	Total Number of Sets	Total Number of Households	Sets per Household
1922	400,000	25,687,000	.016
1925	4,000,000	27,540,000	.145
1930	13,000,000	29,997,000	.433
1935	30,500,000	31,892,000	.956
1940	51,000,000	35,153,000	1.451
1945	56,000,000	37,503,000	1.493
1950	98,000,000	43,554,000	2.250
1955	135,000,000	47,788,000	2.825
1960	166,000,000	52,610,000	3.155
1962	176,000,000	54,652,000	3.220

Sources:
The World Almanac 1963 (New York: New York World-Telegram, 1963), p. 761.

U.S. Bureau of Census, *Historical Statistics of the United States, Colonial Times to 1957,* Series A 242-244 (Washington, D.C.: U.S. Government Printing Office, 1960), p. 15.

U.S. Bureau of Census, *Current Population Reports: Population Characteristics,* Series P-20, No. 106 (Washington, D.C.: U.S. Government Printing Office, 1951), p. 11.

U.S. Bureau of Census, *Current Population Reports: Population Characteristics,* Series P-20, No. 119 (Washington, D.C.: U.S. Government Printing Office, 1962), p. 4.

occurred shortly after it started to be adopted, or by the impact of wartime restrictions. But in spite of its spectacular numbers, radio in many ways has shown unmistakable patterns of obsolescence at least on the part of its mature adult audience. At one time, the behavior patterns of the American family with respect to the livingroom radio were deeply institutionalized. Radio listening occupied the evening hours of millions of people. But with the arrival of television, radio was forced out of the livingroom and out of the attentions of most families during the important evening period. In the face of the functional alternative offered by TV, which took over the fulfillment of needs which radio formerly served, the latter resorted to *alternative audiences* and *alternative needs* which could be appealed to at the beach, in the kitchen, or in the auto-

RADIO

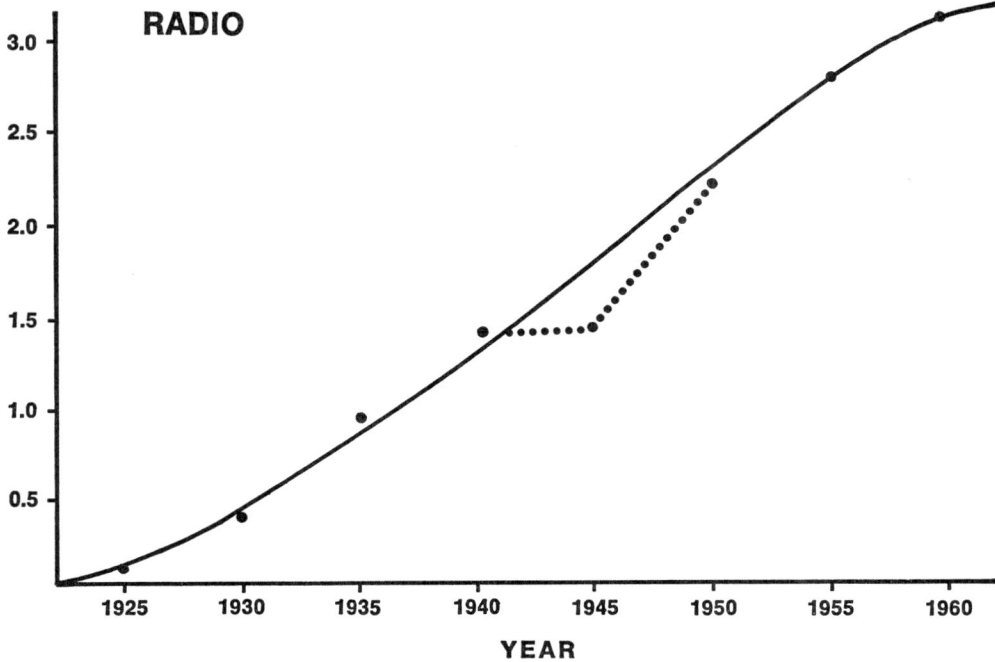

Figure 3. The Diffusion Curve for Radio: Number of Sets Owned Per Household

mobile. The current affluence of the American society has placed millions of transistorized sets in the hands of children and teenagers. Radio's programming has increasingly been tailored to appeal to this immature audience. The diffusion curve of radio, developed from set ownership, may be an accurate record of the acquisition of sets. However, such a curve provides no hint of the actual patterns of innovation and obsolescence that have occurred as forms of social action with respect to this item (which itself has changed but little, other than to become smaller and more portable).

The growth of radio, then, must be understood not only against a series of political and economic conditions which characterized the cultural system but against competitive functional alternatives, a shift to new technology (transistors), a successful shift to alternative audiences with different needs to fulfill, and broad changes in patterns of social action associated with receiving sets. Unlike movies, with their cumbersome public theaters, radio emerged as a medium capable of making far more flexible adjustments in the face of these changing conditions in the social and cultural systems than was the case with films. Finally, the patterns of innovation, institutionalization and obsolescence as forms of observable action which lie behind the diffusion curve of radio cannot be fully understood through attempts to explain

TABLE 4

The Growth of Television Set Ownership in the United States, 1946-1961

Year	Total Sets in Use	Total Number of Households	Sets per Household
1946	8,000	38,370,000	.0002
1947	250,000	39,107,000	.0064
1948	1,000,000	40,523,000	.0247
1949	4,000,000	42,182,000	.0948
1950	10,500,000	43,554,000	.2411
1951	15,750,000	44,656,000	.3527
1953	28,000,000	46,334,000	.6043
1957	47,200,000	49,543,000	.9527
1960	54,000,000	52,610,000	1.0264
1961	56,900,000	53,291,000	1.0677

Sources:
  U.S. Bureau of Census, *Historical Statistics of the United States, Colonial Times to 1957,* Series 242-244 (Washington, D.C.: U.S. Government Printing Office, 1960), p. 15.
  U.S. Bureau of Census, *Current Population Reports, Population Characteristics,* Series P-20, No. 106 (Washington, D.C.: U.S. Government Printing Office, 1961), p. 11.
  U.S. Bureau of Census, *Current Population Reports, Population Characteristics,* Series P-20, No. 119 (Washington, D.C.: U.S. Government Printing Office, 1962), p. 4.

such curves with "epidemiological" reasoning, or with the "adoption process" conceptualized solely in psychological terms. More complex models are needed, which take into account important variables from the personality *and* social systems, as well as the impact of functional alternatives or other conditions of the *cultural* system.

Television

Television's introduction into the American society was beset with difficulties. First, World War II stopped its technical development completely for several years. Then there was the postwar "freeze" on new station licenses imposed by the F.C.C. for the purpose of achieving a workable frequency allotment plan. In spite of these setbacks, television's growth has been extremely rapid. It can be contrasted with that of newspapers, which required three-

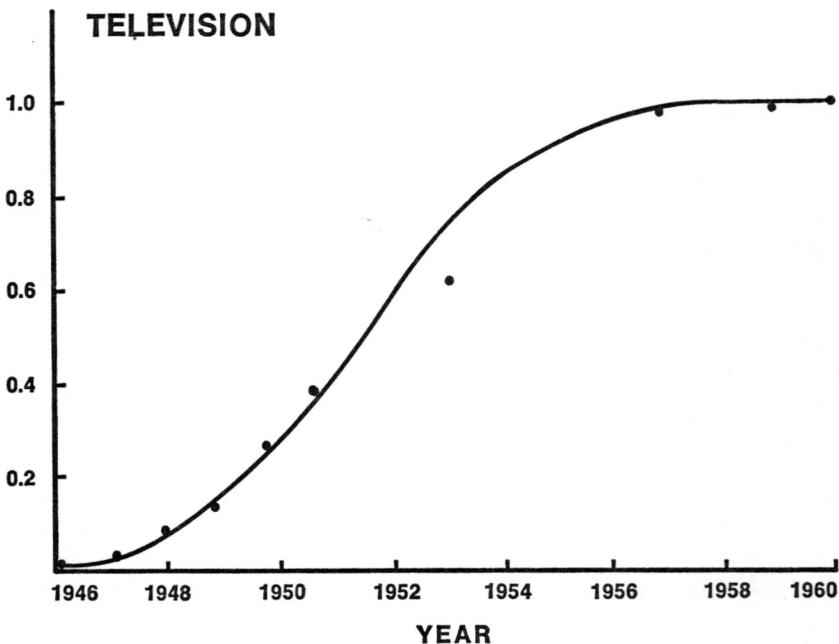

Figure 4. The Diffusion Curve for Television: Number of Sets Owned Per Household

quarters of a century to become a common household item. Television required only a decade to reach virtual saturation. Table 4 shows that there is now more than one TV set per household in the United States. The graph shown in Figure 4 indicates that TV's growth followed a somewhat accelerated S-shaped diffusion curve of the general classical pattern. It is little wonder that social scientists have not as yet been able to make definitive statements concerning television's impact on modern society or upon human personality.

The social and cultural conditions which facilitated the growth of television were several. The society had achieved a level of technology which permitted mass manufacture of receiving equipment at a price within the means of the ordinary citizen. Established cultural practices concerning broadcasting, including the role of the federal government and the relationship of news services to broadcasters, had already been institutionalized. A huge pool of entertainment talent was available from films, radio and the stage. The profit goal and its financial base (from advertising revenue) was copied from radio. Network programming had already been widely used and awaited only adequate electronic technology suitable for TV. The population had for more than two decades become accustomed to the moving picture image complete with sound. The set was also a natural baby sitter, aiding with a nagging problem in some families. Thus, television was a new item which "fit" remarkably well within the personality, social and cultural systems of the society to which it was presented. Finally, no political or economic upheaval prevented its rapid acquisition.

We need not assume that television is the final medium. It is still largely chained to the A.C. outlet by its power supply cord; it is chained to the transmitting station by

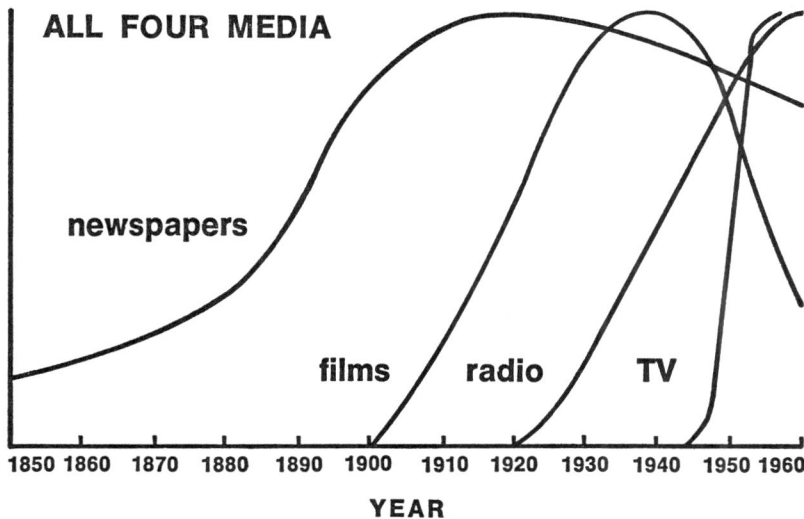

Figure 5. The Diffusion Curves for All Four Media with Ordinate Standardized

its frequency band; and it is in many ways chained to the cultural tastes of its mass audience who *still* prefer the "horse opera" to the Metropolitan Opera.[18] A more sophisticated medium would be one which permitted an almost unlimited range in program selection (in the form of tapes or records), an independent power supply, natural color, complete portability and high quality reproduction. Thus, a more sophisticated medium may combine the best qualities of stage, concert hall, movie theater, stereo records, books, and newspapers in a completely portable device. Our present television sets will probably one day appear as obsolescent as the crystal set.

By plotting the curves for each of the present media on a single graph in Figure 5 (with the units of each "standardized" so as to reach their peak at the same level on the ordinate axis), the general patterns of diffusion of each of these four cultural items can be compared. The long slow growth of newspapers stands out against the quick rise of television. In spite of these differences, each is a reasonable approximation of the classic S-shaped diffusion curve.

Conclusions

The study of the media within this broad perspective cannot reveal the nuances of interaction which occurred within individual households when decisions were made to adopt or not to adopt each medium as part of the family's routines. Such a perspective does show that the spread of the media occurred according to patterns followed by other invented items. The S-shaped curves for the radio receiving set, the daily newspaper, and household television appear to have followed the same general regularities in their spread through the population as such unrelated items as hybrid seed corn, instant coffee, hair spray, and oral contraceptives. Motion picture theaters, on the other hand, show signs that they are headed in the same directions as the kerosene lamp, the straight razor, and the buggy whip, and due largely to the same theoretical principles of social change.

The present discussion has suggested that the study of social change based upon examination of quantitative diffusion curves can have severe limitations. Such curves provide a beginning point for an analytic theory of social change. But when diffusion concepts are not defined in social action terms (as they need to be), it becomes clear that they can obscure drastic changes in behavior, revealing only the number of some technical item which has passed into the hands of a population. This by no means implies that the quantitative study of diffusion curves based upon item acquisition is not worthwhile. Such data are important in their own right, but the relationship between possession and usage may remain unclear.

The present discussion also suggests that the development of a quantitative, analytical, and empirical theory of social change based upon diffusion data will require a great deal of prerequisite effort directed toward conceptual clarification. Such clarification will depend in large part upon the standardization of the meaning of terms through the use of behavioral or action referents. Only by this means can students of social change build the foundation for the theoretical structures which will eventually link their efforts at explanation with a more general theory of social action. The definitions of diffusion concepts presented earlier in this paper have indicated some of the points where such linkages are possible.

As for the mass media themselves, viewing them within the perspectives of the present paper has perhaps revealed few startling or new insights into the factors which "caused" them to emerge and spread through society; nor does it permit new generalizations concerning their "effect" on the population which has altered their daily lives around them. It does, however, place them within a context of more general processes of social change and social action. This should aid in the formulation of hypotheses concerning their growth, saturation or decline. While such theoretical explorations tell us little of the ways in which the mass media influence society, they do help reveal some of the complex ways in which society has influenced the mass media.

Notes

1. See, for example, Frank Luther Mott, *American Journalism* (New York: The Macmillan Co., 1941); Henry L. Smith and Edwin Emery, *The Press in America* (Englewood Cliffs, N.J.: Prentice-Hall, 1954); Lewis Jacobs, *The Rise of the American Film* (New York: Harcourt, Brace & Co., 1939); Benjamin Hampton, *A History of the Movies* (New York: Corvici, Friede, 1931); Llewellyn White, *The American Radio* (Chicago: University of Chicago Press, 1947); Meyer Weinberg, *TV in America* (New York: Ballantine Books, 1962).

2. A number of such studies have been summarized in Everett M. Rogers, *Diffusion of Innovations* (New York: The Free Press of Glencoe, 1962).

3. For a summary of early diffusion studies in sociology see Melvin L. De Fleur and Otto N. Larsen, *The Flow of Information* (New York: Harper & Bros., 1958).

4. Bryce Ryan and Neal C. Gross, "The Diffusion of Hybrid Seed Corn in Two Iowa Communities," *Rural Sociology,* 8 (March 1943), pp. 15-24.

5. Robert K. Merton, *Social Theory and Social Structure* (Glencoe, Ill.: The Free Press, 1959), pp. 141-149.

6. An excellent example of this usage is contained in Richard Colvard, "Risk Capital Philanthropy: The Ideological Defense of Innovation," in George K. Zollschan and Walter Hirsch (eds.), *Explorations in Social Change* (Boston: Houghton Mif-

flin Co., 1964), pp. 728-48. The "risk capital" concept constitutes a new norm or code for philanthropic foundations.

7. The use of adjectives, verbs and nouns, e.g., "innovation," "to innovate," and "innovators" as derivatives of "innovation" implies this usage. See Herbert Menzel, "Innovation, Integration and Marginality: A Survey of Physicians," *American Sociological Review,* 25 (October 1960), pp. 704-13. See also Rogers, *op. cit.,* pp. 193-95.

8. By the term "analytical" is meant "based upon the study of elementary units." If traits are considered as elementary units of culture, then a study of the adoption of or diffusion of a particular trait, or a theory which approaches social change, within such a framework, can be said to be "analytical" in this sense.

9. Talcott Parsons *et al., Toward a General Theory of Action* (New York: Harper & Row, Harper Torchbooks, 1962), p. 7.

10. Rogers, *op. cit.,* p. 154.

11. David Sheppard, *A Survey Among Grassland Farmers* (London: Central Office of Information, Social Survey Number 274).

12. Many of the possible explanations behind such "diffusion curves" have been discussed in mathematical as well as behavioral terms in pioneering work by Stuart C. Dodd. See, for example, "Diffusion Is Predictable: Testing Probability Models for Laws of Interaction," *American Sociological Review,* 20 (August 1955), pp. 392-401.

13. For an excellent summary and broad interdisciplinary overview of this literature, see Elihu Katz, Martin L. Levin, and Herbert Hamilton, "Traditions of Research on the Diffusion of Innovation," *American Sociological Review,* 28 (April 1963), pp. 237-52.

14. Rogers, *op. cit.,* p. 76.

15. Parsons *et al., op. cit.,* pp. 111-58.

16. Studies of the social and psychological functions of the newspaper indicate that the daily paper satisfies many needs and is probably here to stay, at least for some time. See Bernard Berelson, "What Missing the Newspaper Means," in Paul Lazarsfeld and Frank Stanton (eds.), *Communication Research, 1948-1949* (New York: Harper & Bros., 1949). Also see Penn Kimball, "People Without Papers," *Public Opinion Quarterly,* 23 (Fall 1959), pp. 389-98.

17. See Eliot Freidson's excellent discussion of the way in which movie attendance is related to social interaction within primary groups. "Communication Research and the Concept of the Mass," *American Sociological Review,* 18 (June 1953), pp. 313-17.

18. Paul F. Lazarsfeld and Robert K. Merton, "Mass Communication, Popular Taste and Organized Social Action," in Lyman Bryson (ed.), *The Communication of Ideas* (New York: Harper & Bros., 1948), pp. 95-118.

46.

William R. Morgan and Terry N. Clark

THE CAUSES OF RACIAL DISORDERS: A GRIEVANCE-LEVEL EXPLANATION

Introduction

Several recent studies (Lieberson and Silverman, 1965; Bloombaum, 1968; Downes, 1968; Wanderer, 1969; and Spilerman, 1970, 1971) have correlated measures of racial disorders and structural characteristics of American cities. Their results generally support various deprivation-producing conditions; but as for which structural characteristics are crucial, the studies do not agree. One cause of this inconsistency may be the theoretical and empirical complexity of the link between structural preconditions and the actual manifestation of collective behavior episodes. A second possibility, argued by Spilerman, is that during the 1960's any local variations in structural conditions were greatly outweighed in their possible

From William R. Morgan and Terry Nichols Clark, "The Causes of Racial Disorders: A Grievance-Level Explanation," *ASR*, Vol. 38, October 1973, pp. 611-24. Reprinted by permission of the publisher, The American Sociological Association, and the authors.

A much earlier version of this paper was originally presented by the authors at the joint meeting of the Midwest-Ohio Valley Sociological Societies, Indianapolis, May, 1969. The authors are grateful to Karl Schuessler for comments on an earlier draft, to Elton Jackson, Jack Sawyer, and George Dowdall for helpful suggestions at various stages of the research, and to Carolyn Mullins for editorial assistance.

Clark's final contributions were made while he was Visiting Associate Professor at the Departments of Sociology and Political Science, and Institution for Social and Policy Studies, Yale University (Fall 1972) and at the Sorbonne (Paris V, Spring 1973). We are grateful for partial support from the National Science Foundation (GS-1904, GS-3162).

causal effects by a uniformly-perceived national climate of protest among blacks.

Spilerman's evidence (1970: 639-45) comes largely from analysis of community disorder proneness, i.e., community characteristics which best account for the fact that some cities have more disorders than others. His principal finding was that sixteen indicators of social disorganization, black deprivation, and responsiveness of the political structure could not explain variation in disorder proneness as well as the single variable of nonwhite population size. Although the sixteen variables (together with a dummy variable for southern region) explained 42% of the variance, the single variable nonwhite population with southern region explained slightly more: 47%. The sixteen variables entered into the regression equation after non-white population, explained only 4% more of the total variation. Spilerman rejected the possibility that nonwhite population might simply be a proxy for the other community characteristics on the ground that when included in the regression after the other sixteen variables, nonwhite population explained an additional 9% of the variation.

Because these sixteen community characteristics had no substantial effect on disorder proneness independent of nonwhite population size, he argued that they were not causal conditions; rather "they are the incidental characteristics of cities with large Negro populations" (Spilerman, 1970: 645). Spilerman essentially concluded that the more blacks in a city, most of whom perceived and supported a national climate of protest, the more able was the city's black community to mobilize a disorder, and hence the more likely was an occurrence of collective racial aggression.

Our data both expand and modify Spilerman's findings. Our argument is that variables other than nonwhite population size affect disorder potential. Furthermore, disorder frequency by contrast with disorder potential is governed by quite different dynamics. Our analysis was conducted on a set of cities drawn from the NORC Permanent Community Sample. Earlier work based on this sample used fifty-one cities, selected as a representative sample of places of residence of the American population. These ranged in population size from 50,000 to 750,000 (1960 census). Further details are reported elsewhere (Clark, 1971, 1972). The present paper used only forty-two of the fifty-one because nonwhite census data were unavailable for the nine cities with less than 1,000 nonwhites. The majority of eliminated cities were generally white suburban towns; not surprisingly, none had experienced racial disorders.[1] The data on racial disorders were obtained from the Lemberg Center for the Study of Violence and are exclusively for 1967. They show that disorders occurred in twenty-three of the forty-two cities in the sample.

The results are reported in three main sections. First is a factor analysis of the racial disorder variables. In conjunction with it we suggest reasons why community correlates of disorders vary with different disorder dimensions. Second is an analysis of the relationship Spilerman found between nonwhite population size and disorder frequency. Finally, using a grievance-level framework, we analyze the impact of specific community conditions on disorder severity.

The structure of racial disorders

Operating definitions of disorders

Spilerman used four criteria to define racial disorders: (1) occurrence during 1961-1968, (2) involvement of thirty or more individuals, (3) an act of Negro aggression rather than white aggression or interracial violence, and (4) "spontaneous" or unplanned origin. The last three criteria, while difficult to operationalize with precision, enabled him to define a fairly uniform set of disorders for constructing his dependent variable, the number of disorders. However, the very uniformity of these criteria necessarily reduces the range of variation in disorder activity and, correspondingly, possibilities of correlation with structural variables.

For our analysis, racial disorders were defined as (1) crowd behavior (the activities of four or more people acting in concert) (2) which represented episodes of racial tension. Racial tension was defined as aggressive behavior either by blacks against whites or whites against blacks, involving either damage to persons or property and/or defiance of civil authority.[2] By contrast with Spilerman's requirement of thirty persons, the minimum lower limit of four used in this definition avoids the risk of falsely eliminating an incident that has, say, only twenty-five participants but all other disorder characteristics. Furthermore, the risk of falsely including an incident is quite small; an incident involving as few as four participants would probably fail to meet the necessary behavioral criteria. As it turned out, all the disorders included here were reported to have at least fifty participants.

Our expanded definition combined with our restriction to 1967 disorders produces a data set different from Spilerman's (which spanned 1961-1968). The difference gave our analysis at least one major advantage. While any cross-section analysis is bound to specific historical conditions, correlations found within a single year may be less ambiguous than correlations that aggregate several years of disorders. Several general conditions during the 1960's could have affected the causal structure behind racial disorders. These include (1) the escalation of the Indo-China War and several political assassinations (both contributed to a national climate of violence and civil disobedience among both civilians and police); (2) the belief of many black citizens in the efficacy of racial disorders as political action (apparently this belief first swelled, then ebbed); (3) the increasing ability, with experience, of local and federal agencies to contain and prevent disorders; and (4) the change in national political leadership as it affected both white and black citizens.

In 1967 the probable net effect of these conditions was to heighten, at least within black communities, the perceived value of

racial disorders as social protest (cf. Tomlinson, 1968; Paige, 1971). A particularly strong social protest impetus undergirded black participation in that year. Therefore, one would expect grievance-producing community characteristics to be more important in 1967 than in other years.[3]

Despite the differences, our analysis and Spilerman's have one overriding similarity. Much riot research has focused only on "communal" riots (Janowitz, 1969) which occurred, for the most part, prior to World War II.[4] Other research (e.g., Lieberson and Silverman, 1965) has included both "communal" riots and the "commodity" riots of the 1960's. Both our analysis and Spilerman's focus only on the commodity riots.

Disorder variables

Nine separate disorder variables were used in this analysis—number of active participants, number of police at scene,

TABLE 1[a]

Variable[b]	Factor 1 Severity	Factor 2 Precipitation	Factor 3 Frequency	Communality
Arrests, Total	.85	−.12	−.02	.74
Duration, Days	.84	−.17	.15	.76
Injuries, Total	.84	−.15	.27	.79
Property Damage, Dollars	.83	.07	.02	.69
Militancy Index	.76	.20	.11	.64
Rioters, Total	.68	.50	.08	.71
Police at Scene, Total	.64	−.02	.31	.51
Precipitation Index	−.11	.94	−.06	.91
Disorder Frequency	.14	−.04	.97	.97
Percent of Total Variance Explained (Cumulative)	48%	62%	75%	

[a] Source of data for the racial disorder variables: Lemberg Center for the Study of Violence (1968a), Report of the National Advisory Commission on Civil Disorders (1968). Data on property damage, total rioters, and total police at scene were unavailable for five cities. Correlations with these measures were computed only for cities with complete data.

[b] In order to approximate conditions of normality and homogeneity of variance, disorder frequency was transformed by $\sqrt{x}$, and the other variables, by log $(x+1)$. The average intercorrelation of the seven severity variables was .56. Their average correlation with precipitation index was .06; with disorder frequency, .23.

number of arrests, duration (days), number of injuries, estimated property damage, a precipitation index, a militancy index, and the frequency of 1967 disorders. For the eight sampled cities with more than one disorder, the first eight variables were defined as applying only to the most severe disorder. In every case, consistent with the national trend, the most severe disorder was the first one (see the National Advisory Commission on Civil Disorders, 1968: 113).

These nine variables were subjected to an orthogonal factor analysis employing a principal component solution and varimax rotation (Table 1). The first three factors explained 75% of the total variance. The first factor, the disorder severity dimension, accounted for 48% of the variation and was defined by the seven variables measuring extent of participation and intensity of action (see boxed variables in Table 1). The second and third factors were each defined by a single variable, precipitation index and disorder frequency respectively.

Disorder precipitation conditions

The precipitation index shown in Table 1 was measured by a four-point scale of degree of instigation by blacks rather than by civil authorities or whites. Certainly there are many more dimensions to a precipitating event (the final incident before a disorder begins) than this "who started it" measure; but more sophisticated measures are generally unrealistic, given the available descriptions of most events. At the zero-point of black instigation, a group of whites attacked blacks, who in turn resisted (9% of the disorders studied); at the next level, black onlookers became enraged at police action against a fellow black who had been stopped for a minor infraction (35%); at the third level, the

leaders were unable to retain control of an organized black protest rally (9%); at the fourth level, a group of blacks initiated attacks on white property or persons in the apparent absence of an immediate issue (48%).[5]

Spilerman's definition of disorders would have excluded disorders at the first and third levels of instigation. (The black aggression criterion excluded instances of white aggression or interracial violence; the spontaneity criterion excluded disorders "which had their origins in civil rights demonstrations, in school settings, or in other activities which might provide a focus for contending groups" [Spilerman, 1970: 630]). His reason was that riots of these two types would differ either in basic nature or in frequency or severity from riots of the other two types. The fact that our precipitation index loaded on a factor independent of the severity and frequency variables suggests that these exclusions may have been unnecessary; in our data, all four types are undifferentiated on these variables. Of course, this noncorrelation could simply indicate a high degree of measurement error in our index. However, if we assume the accuracy of the measurement, then this variable's independence suggests substantively that the degree of immediate black instigation is *not* associated with either the number of blacks participating in disorders or the frequency of disorders.

Disorder frequency and severity

Spilerman limited his analysis to disorder frequency, contending that the "underlying level of frustration in the community" (1970: 630, nn. 38) was more likely to be captured by a measure of the number of outbreaks than by a measure of severity. His position is based on the assumption that disorder severity, in contrast to frequency, results largely from the response of social control agencies to the precipitating incident. This position is doubtful on two counts. First, the substantial number of disorders precipitated by routine police-citizen encounters contradicts the assertion that social control agencies are somehow less important for the outbreak of disorders than for their escalation. Second, disorder escalation, as represented by disorder severity variables, involves a joint spiraling process of widened civilian and police involvement. We grant that the higher levels of participation by blacks in some cities, as manifest in the more severe disorders of those cities, may have resulted partly from ineffective control strategies in those cities. However, without any evidence to the contrary, the alternative explanation—that a higher level of participation grew largely out of deeper and more widespread discontent—must remain at least equally plausible.

The results of the factor analysis document the association between disorder intensity (or violence) and level of participation. The three measures of participation (number of arrests, number of participants, and number of police) all load on the first factor together with four measures of disorder intensity (duration, number of injuries, estimated property damage, and militancy index). The militancy index is a four-point scale including (1) disorders involving only rock-throwing, window-breaking, and/or police taunting (in five cities), (2) those involving (1) plus looting (in four cities), (3) those involving (1) and (2) plus fire-bombing (in five cities), and (4) those involving (1), (2), and (3) plus alleged sniping (in nine cities).[6] Another indication of the correspondence between participation and disorder intensity is that in seven cities with 0-5 persons arrested, the median number of injuries was one; in

nine cities with six to fifty persons arrested, the median number of injuries was ten; in five cities with fifty-one to eight hundred, the median was fifteen; and in the two cities with over eight hundred, the median was six hundred.

The association between severity and participation is crucial. If a grievance-level model is to be proved satisfactory in explaining disorder severity (as will be done below), level of participation must first be presented as a more significant attribute of disorder severity than the more commonly perceived attribute, disorder intensity. *The more widespread the grievances among blacks, the greater the number of potential disorder supporters, and hence the more severe a disorder is likely to be, once it occurs.*

Also important in considering whether grievance-level variables would relate equally to disorder frequency and severity as dependent variables, this analysis suggests that the outbreak of a disorder in 1967 followed a far less uniform pattern than did subsequent escalation. Escalation, by definition, has always involved increased levels of participation; whereas, an outbreak only indicates some form of civil disobedience by a minimum number of blacks acting in concert. We argue that such outbreaks in the past, regardless of their frequency, may have had little or no community-wide significance. Substantial escalation, however, at least in 1967, seems to have coincided with widespread feelings of grievance among blacks.

Grievance level and disorder participation

The grievance-level model

Two different causal perspectives might explain variance in disorder escalation. Both are similar to those discussed more generally by Gamson (1968). One is based on the relative ability of local authorities to manage discontent among blacks. The city characteristics most relevant to this perspective are those that reflect the effectiveness of local government and other control agencies. The other perspective has to do with the degree of discontent among blacks insofar as this discontent would mobilize participation once a disorder was initiated. The relevant city characteristics here are those that affect racial discrimination and life style dissatisfaction among blacks. A full analysis integrating both perspectives is beyond the limits of this paper. Because more empirical indicators are presently available for the second rather than the first, we have chosen to concentrate on the second, a grievance-level approach.

Grievance level—or the "underlying level of frustration," to use Spilerman's term—is thus our principal theoretical link between the objective social conditions of cities and the subjective decision of individuals to participate in disorders (see Mattick, 1968, for a related discussion of grievances among blacks). The relationship between the two main components of the grievance level, experience of discrimination and life style dissatisfaction, is diagrammed below (see Figure 1) using conventional path notation to indicate

direct and indirect effects. Conditions that foster an unsatisfactory life style directly raise the grievance level, as do conditions that maintain racial discrimination. The direct effect of the former means that if certain cities had more blacks who were dissatisfied with their life style, the grievance level in that city would be higher even if the specific discrimination-producing conditions were constant across cities.

TABLE 3

Zero-Order Correlations with Disorder Severity of Selected City Variables[a]

Variable[b]	r
Racial Inequality[c]	
1. Percent housing substandard	.40
2. Percent males with low status jobs	−.48*
The "Central City Syndrome"	
3. Total population	.31
4. Residential segregation index	−.14
5. Population density	.42*
6. Increase in percent population nonwhite, 1950-60	.36
7. Percent population nonwhite	.11
8. Percent population foreign born	.35
9. Median age white males	.18
10. Percent whites college educated	−.40
Government Service Capability	
11. City budget expenditures per capita	.20
12. Urban renewal expenditures per capita	.20
13. Police per capita	.51*
14. Police salary level	.08

* $p < .05$, two-tailed test.
[a] Source of data for the 14 community structure variables: variables 1-3, 7-10, Census Tracts for SMSA's (U.S. Bureau of the Census, 1960); variable 4, Negroes in Cities (Taeuber and Taeuber, 1965); variables 5, 6, County City Data Book (U.S. Bureau of the Census, 1967); variables 11, 12, Finances of Municipalities (U.S. Bureau of the Census, 1962); variables 13, 14, The Municipal Yearbook (International City Manager's Association, 1967).
[b] Skewed variables were transformed as follows: variable 4 by x^2; variable 6 by $\sqrt{x+7}$; and variables, 5, 7, 9-14, by $\log_{10}x$.
[c] Both variables are in black minus white difference score form. Substandard housing consists of all occupied dwelling units rated in a condition other than 'sound.' Low-status employment consists of employed adult males working as service workers and nonfarm laborers.

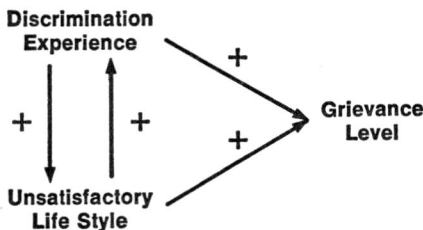

Figure 1. The Grievance-Level Model

Unsatisfactory life style conditions also have an indirect effect on grievance level through their effect on discrimination experience; they further raise the grievance level by making the experience of discrimination more difficult. This indirect effect implies that the less cushioned a person is by a satisfying life style, the more sensitive he will be to daily discrimination. Similarly, the indirect effect of discrimination conditions works by lowering the quality of life style experienced and thereby increasing the grievance level.

Because most available indicators pertained more to style than to discrimination conditions, the present test of the grievance-level model emphasizes conditions more relevant to the former than the latter. Consequently, the net effect of an unsatisfactory life style may be overestimated since the indirect effect of discrimination conditions is included in the estimate.

Determinants of life style

Three sets of community variables affect life style satisfaction among blacks: (1) amount of racial inequality, (2) the "central city syndrome," and (3) government service capability. The relevant variables and their zero-order correlations with disorder severity are presented in Table 3.

TABLE 4
Mean City Scores For Blacks and Whites On Housing and Job Status Variables[a]

	Blacks	Whites	Difference (B-W)
Percent in Substandard Housing	38.9%	6.6%	32.3%
Percent in Low Status Employment	37.7%	12.3%	25.4%

[a] Source of data: Table 3.

Racial inequality was measured using differences between blacks and whites in (1) proportion of occupied dwelling units in substandard condition,[7] and (2) proportion of employed males in low-status jobs.[8] The substantial mean differences between blacks and whites (see Table 4) make these variables good reflections of the prevalent inequalities in jobs and housing as they varied from city to city.

The "central city syndrome" here refers generally to changes experienced most strongly by older and larger American cities. Eight variables derived from the U.S. Census were used to measure this global quality of cities: (1) total population, (2) density (population per square mile), (3) index of residential segregation (Taeuber and Taeuber, 1965), (4) increase in percent of population nonwhite, 1950-1960, (5) percent population nonwhite, (6) percent population foreign born, (7) median age of white males, and (8) percent of white college educated. Downes (1968), the main proponent of the "central city" explanation, suggests this syndrome adversely affects the life style of the total citizenry, but especially that of blacks, for whom it is the most serious.

Government service capability refers to the ability of urban institutions to deliver desired services, particularly to blacks. Four variables from the 1967 Municipal Yearbook were used to measure this ability: (1) budget expenditures per capita, (2) urban renewal expenditures per capita, (3) police per capita, and (4) police salary level. The term roughly corresponds to the explanation offered by Lieberson and Silverman (1965) when they summarized the differences between riot and nonriot cities in their analysis of American race riots from 1913 to 1963. Obviously government service capability, like the central city syndrome, is a rather demanding label to place on these particular variables; we

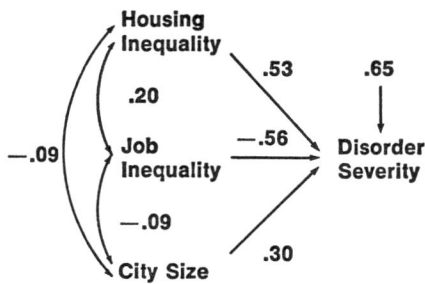

Figure 2. Path Diagram for Grievance-Level Model of Disorder Severity

introduce the terms simply to represent as clearly as possible the arguments of earlier writers.

Findings

The best three-variable regression model utilizing the above variables to explain variance in disorder severity proved to consist of the two inequality variables plus city size. This model is presented as a single stage path diagram whose exogenous variables are job inequality, housing inequality, and city size, and whose endogenous variable is disorder severity (Figure 2). Since our analysis is exploratory, we do not claim that this set of variables fits all the specifications for a formal system of structural equations. However, for variance explained, they are quite adequate.

The three variables together explained 58% of the variation in disorder severity (p < .01). No other variable, added singly to the model, increased the percent of variance explained by more than five points. Furthermore, no three of these variables produced a multiple correlation with disorder severity as high as did the two inequality variables. The two inequality variables without city size still explained 48% of the variance.

Housing and job inequality both had strong, direct effects on disorder severity; but unexpectedly they worked in opposite directions. Inequality in housing increased the severity of disorders while inequality in jobs decreased it.

Job Inequality. The unexpected negative effect of this variable necessitated a reinterpretation. Instead of generating active dissatisfaction among blacks, high rates of job inequality appeared to contribute to complacency (i.e., it suppressed rather than raised the grievance level). High job inequality in a city (indicating a more racially stratified occupational structure) could produce this complacency in at least two ways. First, a more stratified structure would reduce the opportunity for equal-status contacts with whites and thus the salience of white standard-of-living norms as referents for blacks. Second, a more racially stratified structure, presumably of long duration, would reduce occupational mobility expectations among blacks, and thus dissatisfaction with one's current job. These possibilities contradict our earlier working assumption that the use of whites as a reference group, and of the norm of equality as a basis for comparison, would operate for blacks in the same way across cities. This interpretation is supported by the fact that cities with more job inequality were often in the South, the region in which such effects should be expected to operate most effectively. The zero-order correlation of job inequality with a dummy variable for South was .61 (p < .01). (Further analysis of the relation of region to grievance level is reported below.)

Housing Inequality. The effect of this variable, as expected, was strong and direct. The underlying dynamic was presumably that blacks living in cities with more housing inequality were more likely dissatisfied with their life style; this situa-

TABLE 5
Reported Satisfaction of Blacks and Whites With Their Housing and Jobs, 1949-1969[a]

Year of Survey	Satisfied with Their Job[b]			Satisfied with Their Housing		
	Whites	Blacks	Differences	Whites	Blacks	Difference
1949	69%	55%	14%	67%	59%	8%
1963	90%	54%	36%	76%	43%	23%
1966	87%	69%	18%	77%	51%	26%
1969	88%	76%	12%	80%	50%	30%

[a] Source of columns 1, 2, 3, 5, and 6: Gallup Opinion Index (1969:8, 12).
[b] The wording of the question was: "On the whole would you say you are satisfied or dissatisfied with: The work you do? Your housing situation?"

tion should raise the grievance level in those cities. The critical issue here is why housing inequality had the expected positive effect on grievance level and disorder severity when job inequality did not. Perhaps it is that when blacks compare social reforms regarding housing and jobs, less has been accomplished with the former, relative to what was promised. Or it may simply be that the conception of an adequate life style for blacks is more tied to housing equality than to job equality.

Whatever the reason, independent survey evidence suggests that the different effects of housing and job inequality were not simply statistical artifacts. Table 5 reports the results of four national Gallup polls (taken between 1949 and 1969) concerning the satisfaction of blacks and whites with their jobs and housing. These attitudinal data reveal the pattern that we found. Over the twenty-year period, the proportion of blacks satisfied with their jobs increased 21 percent; while the proportion satisfied with their housing decreased 9 percent. By contrast, increasing proportions of whites were satisfied with both their jobs and housing (the overall increases being 19 and 13 points, respectively). Moreover, although whites were more satisfied than blacks on both situations, in the last poll the difference between whites and blacks in percent satis-

fied was two and one half times greater for housing than for jobs. In short, the striking overall trend is that while blacks in the 1960s became more satisfied with their jobs relative to whites, they became less satisfied with their housing.

Regional Variation. The possibility of regional influence on the job satisfaction variable deserves further investigation. Five of our twenty-three sample cities experiencing disorders were in the South. The zero-order correlation between a dummy variable for the South and disorder severity was an insignificant —.12, indicating that, at least for this sample, southern disorders were no more or less severe than those elsewhere. By contrast, the job and housing variables correlated .61 and .42, respectively, with the South. Apparently, in these southern cities the mitigating effect on grievance level of high job inequality counteracted the aggravating effect of high housing inequality; the result was a distribution of disorders similar to that for the cities outside the South.

Disorder Frequency. The final analysis turned again to disorder frequency as the dependent variable. Disorder frequency was regressed on the two inequality variables. Only 1% of the variation in frequency was explained by this analysis (compared with 48% for disorder severity).

This finding complements the earlier one that the size-related variables which explained disorder frequently could not explain much variation in disorder severity; the finding further supports the prior distinction between community conditions related to the dynamics of initial outbreak and those related to the dynamics of participation and escalation.

Conclusions

Community conditions made a significant difference in both the frequency and severity of 1967 disorders. Cities with a greater confrontation probability (with respect to number of blacks and number of police) had more frequent disorders. Cities with a higher grievance level among blacks (with respect to the two inequality measures) had higher rates of disorder participation and hence more severe disorders. In particular, a high degree of housing inequality raised the grievance level, while a high degree of job inequality tended to suppress it.

In our sample, as in Spilerman's, the number of blacks in a city did predict the frequency of disorders; but it did so less well than two other measures related to city size—total population and police force size. This overall city-size effect, and not the black population size effect as Spilerman argued, was explained simply by its ability to increase the probability of a disorder-creating confrontation between blacks and police.

Spilerman argued that a large black population increased the opportunity for mobilizing a disorder. At this point we go one step further, suggesting that mobilizing for a disorder involves social control agents as well as black civilians. In fact, as we observed in our analysis of precipitating events, the initial mobilization in some cities apparently came exclusively from the police.

Our findings support Spilerman's assertion that no community conditions besides the size factor are causally related to disorder frequency. But again, our interpretation must differ. Spilerman suggested that this nonrelationship was generated by a national climate of protest among blacks, which suppressed the effect of local conditions on disorder frequency. We suggest, instead, that the variable "disorder frequency" has even less utility than Spilerman implies. The "underlying level of frustrations" (Spilerman) or grievance level (our preferred concept) among blacks is not tapped by disorder frequency, as Spilerman contended, but by disorder severity. When community conditions inducing grievances were in fact examined for their effects on disorder severity, strong effects, independent of the size relationship, were found.

What generalizations can be drawn from our results? To what extent will our explanation hold for a different set of disorders, occurring in a different sample of cities? As in any research, the final answer will come from replications of our research. The current study, however, presents three pieces of affirmative evidence. First, despite our smaller sample of cities and disorders, we were able to replicate Spilerman's positive finding. Second, we showed that the range of disorder precipitants in our sample resembled that reported in the National Advisory Commission Report (1968). Third, the importance of the particular grievances studied was reinforced by data from four national surveys on changes in the relative satisfaction of blacks concerning jobs and housing over a twenty-year period.

While our findings have yet to be corroborated by others, two policy conclusions may be inferred. Those in a position to influence policies concerning black-white differences in jobs and (especially) housing should be conscious of the import of decisions in these areas compared to others. If significant differences between blacks and whites continue in these areas, grievances, and hence potential disruption, are more likely. To decrease these tensions, housing conditions for blacks should be improved.

Those concerned with organizing blacks can conclude from these findings that many grievances may be common to blacks in all American cities. Nevertheless clear discrepancies in job and housing patterns exist across cities, and these significantly affect the grievance level. These differences should be heeded, both in decisions regarding the selection of cities for organizational effort, and in the selection of grievances upon which to build an organization.

Notes

1. The cities excluded were Amarillo, Tex.; Bloomington, Minn.; Clifton, N.J.; Duluth, Minn.; Euclid, Ohio; Fullerton, Calif.; Irvington, N.J.; Manchester, N.H.; Warren, Mich.

2. A full working definition of the concepts used here is presented in the Lemberg Center's *Riot Data Review* (1968b: 2). The data used here were crosschecked against those in the *Report*, National Advisory Commission on Civil Disorders (1968). For 1967, the screening process and definition used by the Lemberg Center produced 218 incidents over 184 communities, as compared with the 164 in 128 communities reported by the Commission. The crosscheck resulted in our adding to the analyses one city not included in the Lemberg data.

3. By contrast, the second large wave of disorders in the spring of 1968 (precipitated by the assassination of Martin Luther King) more accurately fit Smelser's (1963) conceptualization of disorders as nonrational, "hostile outbursts."

4. Communal riots were usually struggles between residents of mixed black-white neighborhoods; these riots, then, did not occur in areas of clear racial domain. Commodity riots, by contrast, begin within the black community rather than at its periphery. They are commodity riots in the sense that the blacks' violence often centered on property (e.g., retail establishments), owned usually by outside white proprietors.

5. This distribution of precipitating events compares with the national distribution in 1967 of the twenty-four disorders classified as serious in the National Advisory Commission Report (1968). Of those disorders, 50% were precipitated by spontaneous protest against police action; 21% started after organized protest rallies; 21% started after police mobilization in response to rumors; 4% involved interracial violence, and 4% had no apparent instigating event. The range of precipitating conditions is similar in both samples of disorders, although the distribution within that range is somewhat different. The lower proportion of disorders reported by the Commission to be without any known precipitant may be related to that study's restriction to "serious" disorders only.

6. The scale is equivalent to Downes' (1968) Intensity Index and Wanderer's (1969) severity index except that the latter scaled the actions of both civil authorities and black civilians.

7. It appears that the definition of substandard housing, that is, dilapidated structures, varied greatly across cities and thus reflected conditions of local housing markets. The proportion of black dwelling units in substandard condition correlated across cities only .25 with the proportion of black dwelling units rented (p > .05), .12 with the proportion of black dwelling units having one or more persons per room, —.09 with the proportion of black dwelling units in a bulding with five or more dwelling units, and .25 with the proportion in a building more than twenty years old. Consequently, we used the substandard housing variable alone, on the assumption that it came closer to reflecting the extent of satisfactory housing than any other variable separately or in combination.

8. The proportion of employed black males in low-status jobs correlated across cities .65 (p < .01) with the proportion of black families earning under $3,000 annual income. However, the former was chosen for the regression analysis for its substantially lower correlation in difference score form with the other inequality measure, the proportion of families in substandard housing.

47.

Seymour Spilerman

STRUCTURAL CHARACTERISTICS OF CITIES AND SEVERITY OF RACIAL DISORDERS

The issue of disorder severity is conceptually a separate matter from accounting for the locations of disturbances. This distinction was recognized by Wanderer (1969), although the particular procedures he employed to analyze the severity of racial incidents which took place during 1967 have been criticized (Spilerman, 1970a). The rationale for distinguishing between the determinants of disorder location and the determinants of severity can be illustrated most compellingly with respect to the organization and training of social control forces: it may be impossible for the police to react with sufficient alacrity to prevent the occurrence of most "spontaneous"[1] collective outbursts (especially if an inclusive definition of disorder requiring a low level of violence is used); nevertheless, their manner of response may be an important determinant of the intensity to which an incident will escalate.[2]

A plausible argument also can be made to the effect that the variation across communities in severity of collective aggression will reflect differences among them in the degree of discontent experienced by their inhabitants. With respect to racial turmoil in the 1960s, it has been reported that the disturbance *locations* were unrelated to a number of objective indicators of Negro social and economic status or to their living conditions in a city (Spilerman 1960b; 1971). This lack of significance of the community characteristics was interpreted as evidence for a thesis that the frustrations which provoked ghetto residents during this period were nation-wide in impact and not rooted in circumstances peculiar to the stricken communities. Instead, an explanation was proposed which emphasized the wide availability of television and the role of network news programs in exposing Negroes uniformly to stimuli of a frustrating nature, and in propagating in all cities the same role models regarding how ghetto residents in some communities were responding to the deprivations endemic to Negro life in America.

However, an assessment that community conditions were altogether irrelevant to the riot process would constitute an overinterpretation of those empirical findings since the preceding studies examined only the determinants of disorder location (i.e., outbreak frequency in a city). It still may be the case that the frustrations felt by Negroes which derive from their local situations are salient to other aspects of the disturbance process. In this regard, there is certainly reason to expect com-

From Seymour Spilerman, "Structural Characteristics of Cities and the Severity of Racial Disorders," *ASR*, Vol. 41, October 1976, pp. 771-93. Reprinted by permission of the publisher, The American Sociological Association, and the author.

The research reported here was supported by funds granted to the Institute for Research on Poverty at the University of Wisconsin by the Office of Economic Opportunity, pursuant to provisions of the Economic Opportunity Act of 1964. An earlier version of this paper was presented at the national meetings of the American Sociological Association in Denver, Colorado, September, 1971. I wish to thank David Dickens for assistance with the statistical computations. The conclusions are the sole responsibility of the author.

461

munity differences to exist in the level of Negro discontent. The conditions under which they live vary enormously among cities, in absolute terms and relative to white circumstance. For instance, in 1960, the range in median Negro income was $1,880 to $9,079; relative to median white income the range was .30 to 1.19.[3] Disparities of such magnitude must mean that an individual's life chances, and a social group's ability to organize and effectively promote its collective interests, are conditioned in dramatically different ways from one community to the next. It is not unreasonable to expect corresponding variations to be present in the degree of frustration that is experienced by Negro residents in these cities.

There is precedent for proposing that the frustrations may come to be expressed in the *intensity* of a release, if not in the frequency of outbreak. Evidence from laboratory studies underscores the importance of the intensity variable. For example, Berkowitz (1965) reports that angered subjects send shocks of greater frequency *and duration* to stooges; Baron (1971) observed that anger arousal motivated shocks of high severity; and Zimbardo (1969) describes a laboratory study in which aggression was expressed in shock duration, even though frequency was permitted to vary. With respect to collective behavior in natural settings it also has been suggested that "the fury of the destructive reaction will vary with the indignity of the disappointment" (Milgram and Toch, 1969: 549 paraphrasing Dollard et al., 1939).

The argument as to why frustration may come to be expressed in severity of aggression, rather than in frequency, can be made in the following way. In our society, acts of collective violence are inhibited by deep-rooted mores as well as by a fear of apprehension and punishment. In fact,

despite the large number of racial disturbances during the 1960s, a disorder was actually a rare event in any given community. While some 170 cities (from among the 673 with 1960 populations exceeding 25,000) did experience some racial turmoil during 1961-68, fewer than ten cities witnessed more than five disturbances during that eight-year interval.[4] Viewed from this perspective, even during a decade of great urban unrest the inhibitions which normally deter hostile outbursts appear to have been overcome only infrequently in a particular community.

Breaching the barriers against collective violence may require a precipitant of immense significance. Indeed, 168 of the 341 racial disturbances can be associated with one of two extraordinary events: the massive Newark riot of 1967 (which received extensive television coverage) or the assassination of Martin Luther King. Once the inhibitions against violence have been overcome, however, it is conceivable that the severity of the resulting outburst will be conditioned by the frustrations which have accumulated among Negroes in the community from years of deprivation and powerlessness. As Smelser (1963: 259) has observed, "once hostile outbursts begin . . . they become a *sign* that a fissure has opened in the social order, and that the situation is now structurally conducive for the expression of hostility." With regard to disturbances during the 1960s, evidence in support of a relation between community-based deprivations and riot severity has been reported by several investigators, principally Downes (1968) and Morgan and Clark (1973). The latter (1973: 622) are most emphatic in their conclusion: "Cities with a higher grievance level among blacks . . . had higher rates of disorder participation and hence more severe disorders."

Two additional factors warrant consideration. First, apart from the relevance of the social and economic organization of a community, there is a possibility that an outbreak of violence will alter the expected intensity of a subsequent disorder in the same city. The most reasonable conjecture is that later disturbances would be less severe since the initial event would have stimulated police preparation and training in crowd control procedures.[5] Second, superimposed upon the foregoing processes, a time trend may exist in disorder severity. For instance, the disturbances subsequent to the assassination of Martin Luther King may have been unusually destructive and violent because of the intensity of bereavement among Negroes. Or, just as the police in a city which has experienced a disorder may be motivated to routinize their crowd control techniques, these tactics might become more widely diffused as other communities recognize that they may not be immune to racial turmoil. Thus, with the passage of time, the severity of even a *first* racial incident in a city might decline.

The above comments constitute a rationale for investigating the variation in disorder severity, and for doing so with reference to several categories of potential determinants: the social and economic situation of Negroes in a community, the preparation by social control forces, the prior disturbance history of the community, and the location in time of the incident. In the following section, preliminary to examining the correlates of severity for the disorders of the 1960s, we discuss the specification and measurement of this construct.

Measurement of disorder severity

The measurement of disorder severity raises several conceptual and methodological issues. One matter concerns the question of dimensionality. Wanderer (1968), Downes (1970) and Morgan and Clark (1973) all have treated severity as a unidimensional concept. Indeed, Wanderer reports that the 75 incidents which he analyzed form an eight-category Guttman scale.[6] In our considerably more extensive data set (322 incidents), information on aspects of disorder severity is not systematically available. However, the few intercorrelations which can be computed among the component indicators are large and suggest that a unidimensionality assumption is not unreasonable.[7] We will proceed here under this assumption; additional evidence to support unidimensionality will be presented in a later section.

A second issue concerns specification of the severity scale categories and selection of items appropriate to the construct. On this matter, we have three disagreements with Wanderer concerning strategy in scale construction. (1) The items he used are all qualitative and, hence, insensitive to the magnitude of an activity type. For instance, two successive items in his scale are "all of the above plus looting" and "all of the above plus sniping." An incident of brief duration, with a minor amount of looting and one or two snipers (who cause no injuries), would be scaled by Wanderer as more severe than a disorder lacking a sniper but having thousands of looters and vandals, engaged in running battles with the police for many hours, and resulting in numerous injuries and arrests. Intuitively, we prefer to consider the latter a more severe disturbance. (2) Wanderer's scale omits items which we believe should be major components of a disorder severity instrument: crowd size, number arrested, and number injured. (3) Two of his categories—"called National Guard" and "called state police"—confound an organizational response to rioting with the intensity of the stimulus. An implication of

TABLE 1
Riot Severity Scale

0. Low intensity—rock and bottle throwing, some fighting, little property damage. Crowd size < 125; arrests < 15; injuries < 8.

1. Rock and bottle throwing, fighting, looting, serious property damage, some arson. Crowd size 75-250; arrests 10-30; injuries 5-15.

2. Substantial violence, looting, arson, and property destruction. Crowd size 200-500; arrests 25-75; injuries 10-40.

3. High intensity—major violence, bloodshed and destruction. Crowd size > 400; arrests > 65; injuries > 35.

this latter point will be considered at the end of the present section.

Using data much the same as ours, Downes (1968; 1970) constructed a four-category ordinal scale which incorporates quantitative information on the extent of several kinds of riot activities.[8] We chose to use a somewhat more elaborate version of Downes' scale (Table 1), the main difference being that our instrument specifies numerical bounds at each scale level for crowd size, number of arrests, and number of injuries to supplement the descriptive information pertaining to severity. The bounds were specified to overlap one another because the component aspects of severity are not perfectly correlated. Some disturbances have large crowds but few injuries, while other incidents with relatively few participants may be exceedingly sanguinary and result in a great many injuries. In assessing severity, the coders were instructed to use the bounds as guides, in conjunction with the descriptive materials on a disorder, rather than to code in an inflexible manner.

A final issue concerns measurement properties of the severity scale. Whereas Downes utilized ordinal ranks in his computations, we chose to assign interval scores to the categories, in recognition of the fact that our knowledge about the scale levels exceeds rank order information. For instance, it was apparent to the coders that the disorders at each successively higher

rank were, on average, considerably more severe than ones in the preceding category. Interval values were assigned to the rank differences in the following manner: after classifying all incidents, each coder was instructed to consider the disparity between category 1 and category 0 disorders as equal to one unit of intensity, and then to estimate the severity difference between category 2 and category 0 disorders, and between category 3 and category 0 disorders. The values they assigned were very close and averaged to the scale scores 0, 1, 4, 12, corresponding to the ranks, 0, 1, 2, 3. These interval values define the dependent variable in the main analyses to be reported in this paper.

Our primary data sources were Lemberg Center (1968a; 1968b) and the New York Times Index. Newspaper accounts and the Civil Disorder Chronology (Congressional Quarterly, 1967) were consulted in reference to the pre-1967 disturbances, but information concerning those events was too sketchy to permit reliable classification in terms of severity. The incidents analyzed in this study, therefore, are limited to the period 1967-68. Three hundred and twenty-two events satisfied the minimal criteria of violence necessary for consideration as disorders (Spilerman, 1970b: 630) and were used in the analysis.[9]

Following the instructions outlined above, two coders, working independently, classified all incidents. Where information on some aspect of severity was missing,[10] they were instructed to assign the incident to a rank category on the basis of available data. Agreement between the coders was obtained in 96 percent of the disorders. In every instance of disagreement, a single rank difference was involved and the matter was resolved by averaging the two values.

To validate the resulting scale as a severity instrument, the component variables (number of arrests, number of injuries, and crowd size), the three-category severity classification employed in the Kerner Report (National Advisory Commission, 1968: 65) in conjunction with the 1967 disorders, and the composite indices described in this paper were intercorrelated using a pairwise-present calculation. The results are presented in Table 2 and reveal a substantial correspondence between our indices and the other measures of severity.

Inclusion of organizational response items in the severity scale

In the preceding section, we suggested that the inclusion of items such as "called state police" and "called National Guard"

in a severity scale would confound an organizational response to a disturbance with the intensity of the stimulus. This is an undesirable situation because the kind of external assistance which is provided to a city may be a function of its structure and demography, in addition to the severity of the incident. This contention is elaborated upon here.

The particular scale items cited above are among those used by Wanderer (1968: 197) to define severity levels. He considered "called National Guard" (item 6 in footnote 6) as indicating greater disorder severity than "called state police" (item 5). An alternate possibility, however, is that communities with particular structural and demographic features will tend to specialize in obtaining one or another form of outside assistance. In particular, for a given level of severity (as measured by the extent of violence), we suggest that large communities will be less likely than small places to receive state police aid. The reasons for this assertion are the following: (1) because of their sizable police forces, large cities are less likely to require external assistance of any sort; (2) in many states the state police have a primarily rural and small town jurisdiction; (3) con--

TABLE 2

Intercorrelations[a] among Severity Components and the Composite Scales

	Severity (0-12)	Arrests[b]	Injuries[b]	Crowd Size[c]	Kerner Index[d]
Severity Scale (0-3)	.893	.769	.754	.570	.597
Severity Scale (0-12)		.712	.741	.586	.676
Arrests			.684	.533	.489
Injuries				.566	.537
Crowd Size					.444
N[e]	322	294	258	209	145

[a] Pairwise present correlations were calculated.

[b] log (x + 1).

[c] Crowd size was coded 0, 1, 5, 18 in accordance with coder estimates of crowd size at each rank. We point out that these values are close to the ones which Abelson and Tukey (1959:228) recommend when information exceeds rank order knowledge and increasing intervals can be assumed.

[d] Kerner index was coded 0 to 2.

[e] Number of observations in correlations with the composite severity scales.

sidering the amount of assistance that would be necessary to effectively reinforce local police authorities in a large community when they cannot quell a disturbance, a substantial redeployment of state troopers, from many jurisdictions, would be required to provide sufficient manpower. For these reasons, when external assistance is requested by large cities we expect the National Guard to be mobilized, rather than the state police to be called.

An analogous difficulty regarding the inclusion of organizational response items in a severity scale involves the possibility of anticipatory deployment of external personnel. Following the assassination of Martin Luther King, for example, National Guard troops were dispatched to many cities *in the expectation* of violence and turmoil. Consequently, it is possible that the item "called National Guard,"

rather than having disorder severity as a pure stimulus, is contaminated instead by other considerations.[11]

To convey more concretely the import of the foregoing objections to the inclusion of organizational response items in a severity scale, dummy variables for "called National Guard" and "called state police" were regressed against our measure of disorder severity and against terms for city size, region, and time period.[12] The entries in column (1) of Table 3 are unstandardized regression coefficients corresponding to the dependent variable "called state police." The significant negative coefficient for city size indicates that, holding severity constant, large cities were, indeed, less likely to obtain assistance from the state police than were small communities. Use of the item "called state police" to define a severity level would therefore make small

TABLE 3
Regressions of Social Control Response Items on Severity, City Size, Region and Time Period

	Unstandardized Regression Coefficient[a]			
	Dependent Variable[b]			
	(1)		(2)	
Independent Variable	Called State Police		Called National Guard •	
Constant	.949**	(5.44)	.134	(0.95)
Severity[c]	.042**	(6.33)	.063**	(11.80)
City Size (log)	−.071**	(−4.94)	−.014	(−1.17)
South[d]	−.013	(−0.28)	.227**	(5.61)
t_2[e]	.118	(1.74)	−.062	(−1.11)
t_3[f] (Post-Martin Luther King-Assassination period	−.016	(−0.33)	.104**	(2.62)
t_4[g]	−.065	(−0.97)	−.061	(−1.12)
t_5[h]	−.041	(−0.61)	−.005	(−0.08)
R^2	.17		.37	
No. of observations	300		300	

* Significant at $p < .05$.
** Significant at $p < .01$.
[a] t-values are shown in parentheses.
[b] Dependent variable coded 1 if social control agent was called, 0 otherwise.
[c] Scale values are coded 0, 1, 4, 12.
[d] Coded 1 if southern city, 0 otherwise.
[e] Dummy term coded 1 if disorder occurred during August 1967–March, 1968, and coded zero otherwise. Deleted term is for January–July, 1967.
[f] Dummy term for April, 1968.
[g] Dummy term for May–July, 1968.
[h] Dummy term for August–December, 1968.

communities appear to have had more serious outbursts, and large cities less serious disorders, than is suggested by descriptive information on the amount of violence and by quantitative data on crowd size, number of arrests and number of injuries.

In the National Guard equation (column 2), the significant coefficient corresponding to the post-Martin Luther King-assassination period indicates that inclusion of this organizational response item in a severity scale would make the disturbances following the murder appear more turbulent than is warranted on the basis of our severity index. This finding supports the anticipatory deployment contention. With respect to the term for South, its significance in the regression suggests that, holding the extent of violence and other factors constant, a southern state was more likely than a northern one to provide this manner of law enforcement assistance to locales contending with hostile outbursts. In summary, we find that the social control items contained in Wanderer's severity scale are intimately related to other community characteristics. If used to measure severity, they will provide an inaccurate description of the amount of violence and destruction that actually transpired.

Reinforcement effects and time trend

The variables in this study which bear the greatest sociological significance are ones which refer to structural and demographic features of a community. The findings with respect to these factors can inform us about how the severity of hostile outbursts is conditioned by the way our cities are organized and governed and by the pervasiveness of the deprivations to which Negro residents are subjected. Most of the community characteristics that we

shall examine change only slowly during a brief time interval, such as the period covered by this study (1967-68); therefore, we will treat them as constant in time and employ cross-sectional procedures. What we shall be investigating, then, is the presence of a severity value that is community specific and relatively stable over time, both properties deriving from its conceptualization as a function of community demography and social organization.

Before addressing this issue, we discuss some *volatile* aspects of a community's severity value. This matter is of importance because we wish to acquire a comprehensive understanding of the determinants of severity and, also, because controls will be necessary for the responsible factors in order to obtain unbiased estimates of the community effects. One possible source of volatility relates to the presence of multiple disturbances in a city during the two-year interval; often they were at different levels of severity. While this may be simply a consequence of random variation about a community's "characteristic value," it also could reflect the influence of systematic factors. In particular, as we suggested in the introduction, a reinforcement process might operate whereby an outbreak of violence alters the expected severity of a subsequent disorder in the same city. This would happen, for instance, if the police were to increase their preparation in riot control procedures following an initial outburst (thereby lowering the expected severity of later disorders), or if insensitive police actions during the first incident were to leave a residue of bitterness and hostility in the black community (in which case the intensity of subsequent violence might be raised). In either case, the expected severity of a disturbance would be a function of the history of prior racial

TABLE 4

Disorder Severity by Ordinal Position of the Disturbance in a City and by Time Period, 1967-68

Period	First Disturbance in City[a]		Subsequent Disturbances in City	
	(1) Mean Severity[b]	Number of Disorders	(2) Mean Severity[b]	Number of Disorders
Jan.–July, 1967 (t_1)	.782	78	.913	46
Aug., 1967–March, 1968 (t_2)	.750	16	.825	20
April, 1968 (t_3)[c]	.510	51	1.270	37
May–July, 1968 (t_4)	1.000	13	.789	26
Aug.–Dec., 1968 (t_5)	.923	13	.659	22
N		171		151

[a] Includes only cities for which a first disorder occurred in 1967–1968.
[b] Untransformed scale values (0–3) were used to reduce the effect of very high severity scores. The pattern of results is unchanged but the effects more pronounced if transformed severity values (0–12) are used.
[c] Post-Martin Luther King-assassination period.

turmoil in the city. A second potential source of volatility relates to the presence of a time trend. Outbreaks of exceptionally severe disorders following the assassination of Martin Luther King would constitute an example of such temporal variation.

Evidence for both contentions can be found in Table 4. The entries in column (1) report mean severity rank by time period[13] for the first disturbance in a community; in column (2) analogous figures are presented for disturbances subsequent to the first one. These values suggest that disorder severity was a relatively stable phenomenon until the assassination of Martin Luther King. In the weeks following his murder, the severity of a first disorder in a city declined, while communities with a history of racial turmoil incurred a marked increase in intensity of violence. A reversal of this pattern is apparent in the final time periods: first disorders exhibit a severity increase while later outbreaks in a city show a decline.

Although these effects are striking and suggest the operation of both a time trend and different influences upon first and

later disorders in a city, the responsible mechanisms are not discernible from an inspection of Table 4. In order to unravel the determinants of the volatility in disorder severity, we resort to a regression formulation in which the processes outlined above are taken into account, and controls are also incorporated for community differences in disorder-*proneness*. Controls for the latter factor are necessary because cities with different characteristic severity values may differ as well in their proneness to incur disturbances, and this feature may be confounded with the aforementioned processes. In particular, communities with high severity potentials might tend to experience many disorders and therefore would probably undergo a first disturbance in an early time period. This situation would produce a spurious time trend unless the determinants of disorder-proneness are explicitly controlled.

The dependent variable in the regression was disorder severity, while the independent variables were dummy terms for time period, number of prior disorders in the city and South, plus a continuous term for nonwhite population size. The latter two variables were included because they have been cited as major determinants of community disorder-proneness (Spilerman, 1970b). One further point regarding model specification deserves comment. Many American cities incurred multiple disturbances during 1967-68. Since each of the incidents constitutes an observation in our analysis, there is a possibility that the residuals from the regression will be serially correlated. This would occur, for example, if certain community characteristics that are determinants of severity were omitted from the regression equation. The error terms for the disorders in a particular city would tend, then, to be either all high or all low, depending on the effect of the omitted factor. In either case the residuals would be correlated, and this will invalidate tests of hypotheses with respect to the regression coefficients (Kmenta, 1971: 281). However, an examination of the residuals (Appendix I) failed to reveal autocorrelated errors, and ordinary least squares was used.

The results reported in Table 5 provide evidence for each of the preceding contentions regarding the determinants of volatility in disorder severity. With respect to a temporal trend, the entries in column (1) reveal that the post-Martin Luther King-assassination disturbances in April, 1968, were unusually severe, net of the other variables in the equation. On our 12-unit scale, a disturbance at that point in time tended to be approximately one unit more severe than one in the reference interval (t_1). This effect appears to have spilled over into the early summer months of 1968; although owing, possibly, to the few incidents in that period, the coefficient for (t_5) is not statistically significant.

The two community characteristics that were included in the regression because of their known influence on disorder frequency (nonwhite population size and a

TABLE 5

Regressions of Disorder Severity[a] on Time Period, Number of Prior Disturbances, Nonwhite Population Size and Region

Independent Variable	Unstandardized Regression Coefficient[b]			
	(1)		(2)	
Constant	−6.698**	(−5.09)	−6.772**	(−4.85)
t_2	.033	(0.05)	.019	(0.03)
t_3[c]	.967*	(2.21)	.971*	(2.20)
t_4	1.034	(1.76)	.928	(1.60)
t_5	.311	(0.51)	.384	(0.62)
1 Prior Disorder[d]	−.275	(−0.60)		
2 Prior Disorders[d]	−1.668**	(−2.64)		
3 + Prior Disorders[d]	−2.657**	(−4.05)		
Number of Prior Disorders[d]			−.445**	(−3.74)
Nonwhite Population Size (log)	.892**	(6.25)	.890**	(6.16)
South	−1.146**	(−2.63)	−1.154**	(−2.62)
R^2	.149		.134	
No. of observations	300		300	

* Significant at $p < .05$.
** Significant at $p < .01$.
[a] Scale values of severity are coded 0, 1, 4, 12.
[b] t-values are in parentheses.
[c] Post-Martin Luther King-assassination period; see Table 4 for exact specification of the time period terms. Deleted term is t_1.
[d] During 1961–68.

dummy term for South) have effects on severity which are identical to the ones reported for them in the disorder-proneness study (Spilerman, 1970b: 643). Both severity and frequency vary directly with nonwhite population size (a large population provides the human resources for many disturbances and for severe ones). Also, severity and frequency both were substantially lower in the South; according to the specification of equation (1), the average severity of a disturbance in this region was more than one scale unit below that of a non-southern incident, net of the other factors. In the disorder-proneness study, we speculated that the regional difference might reflect lower expectations on the part of southern Negroes regarding the likely rate of improvement in their conditions (and, hence, less frustration from observing the actual rate of progress) and a greater fear of repression and retribution. This same explanation would account for disorders being less severe in the South since the salient point, again, is that there would be fewer potential riot participants in cities in this region.

Perhaps the most intriguing finding concerns the contribution from prior outbreaks. With the occurrence of each incident, the expected severity of a subsequent disorder in the same city declined. It is noteworthy that the contribution from one prior outbreak is not as large as the marginal contribution from two, or from three or more, prior outbreaks. I interpret this to mean that participant exhaustion may have had more to do with the decline in severity than did improved police preparation in response to previous racial turmoil in the city. Under the latter process, a first incident should have had the largest effect, with additional police training and preparation stimulated by subsequent disorders making progressively

smaller marginal contributions to the reduction in severity. However, the regression results reveal the reverse pattern, one that is more understandable in terms of an explanation which emphasizes cumulative exhaustion and growing disinterest on the part of potential participants to engaging in yet another disturbance. This interpretation is highly speculative, of course; presumably both processes operated in varying degrees, and a more detailed analysis than we are prepared to undertake here would be necessary to disentangle their separate effects. Nevertheless, irrespective of which interpretation one prefers, the empirical finding is quite clear: severity declined as a function of the number of prior outbreaks in a city. This is a very important point because other investigators (Downes, 1968; 1970; Morgan and Clark, 1973) have chosen to characterize each city by a single severity value corresponding to its most severe incident.[14]

Because of the tendency of the dummy terms for each higher number of prior disorders to show effects which decrease in an almost linear fashion, we can replace them by a single variable, the number of prior outbreaks in a city. The coefficients for this more concise model are presented in column (2) of Table 5 and differ only in minor ways from the parameters of the preceding equation. These variables will be the controls in our investigation of the impact of community structure and demography on disorder severity. Before undertaking that analysis, we turn to the question of the robustness of the regression results.

Sensitivity analysis

While we believe that the severity measure accurately depicts the magnitude of violence and destruction that transpired in particular disorders, it is nonetheless true that other researchers, employing alternative methods to assess severity, might have constructed different indices. It behooves us, therefore, to ascertain whether the results we have reported are an artifact of the particular coding scheme that was used or whether they are robust with regard to specification of the severity index. We address this issue in the present section.

One potential source of error relates to our assignment of interval scores to the rank differences. In order to ascertain the sensitivity of the findings to the particular values that were selected, the analysis summarized in Table 5 was repeated with alternate specifications of the rank differences. These results are presented in the form of *standardized* regression coeffi-

cients in columns (1) through (3) of Table 6.[15] Standardized coefficients are reported because they are more suitable for comparisons which involve different dependent variables than are unstandardized coefficients; the magnitude of the latter will vary with the choice of metric for the dependent variable.

With respect to number of prior disorders, nonwhite population size and South, the results appear *not* to be sensitive to the precise specification of the severity measure. In regard to these variables, our conclusions would not be changed if a moderately different severity index were substituted for ours. The results for the time period effects, however, do display sensitivity to the values assigned to the rank differences. In particular, if severity were measured on the 0-3 scale we

TABLE 6
Sensitivity of the Regression Results to Alternate Specifications of the Severity Measure

	Standardized Regression Coefficient						
	Dependent Variable						
Independent Variables	(1) Severity 0–3	(2) Severity 0–12	(3) Severity 0–25	(4) Crowd Size[a]	(5) Log Arrests	(6) Log Injuries	(7) Canonical Model[b]
t_2	.011	.002	.001	.063	.054	.071	.075†
t_3[c]	.049	.139*	.161**	.110	.118*	.156**	.127
t_4	.047	.095	.107	−.068	−.013	.136*	.035
t_5	.047	.038	.037	.024	−.009	.107	.049
Number of Prior Disorders[d]	−.293**	−.306**	−.300**	−.177*	−.233**	−.256**	−.206
Nonwhite Population Size (log)	.459**	.478**	.464**	.615**	.486**	.507**	.615
South	−.160**	−.153**	−.145**	−.191**	−.125*	−.157**	−.140
R^2	.12	.13	.13	.31	.15	.17	.37
No. of Observations	300	300	300	194	275	241	169

* Significant at p < .05.
** Significant at p < .01.
† Significance tests not available for individual coefficients in the canonical model.
[a] Alternate assignments of values to crowd size ranks produced comparable results.
[b] Values rescaled so that coefficient for nonwhite population size would be identical to value for this term in the crowd size equation. The entry in the R^2 row is the square of the canonical correlation coefficient.
[c] Post-Martin Luther King-assassination period.
[d] During 1961-68.

would conclude that the post-Martin Luther King-assassination disorders were not especially violent, while if it were measured on the 0-25 scale we would envision the events of this period as significantly more violent than we have reported with the 0-12 scale. While we believe that our instrument provides a more accurate representation of the severity levels than either of the alternatives, the time period effects should be seen as less well established than the other findings.

A second potential source of error relates to classification of the individual disturbances into severity categories, a task which was performed in accordance with the criteria described in Table 1. For a portion of the incidents we have available quantitative information on facets of severity—crowd size, number of arrests, number of injuries—and were able to replicate the analysis using these components as dependent variables. The results are presented in columns (4) through (6) of Table 5 and are consistent with the findings obtained with our composite index. Number of prior disturbances and the two determinants of disorder-proneness (nonwhite population size and South) show effects that are very similar to the ones already reported for them. With respect to the time period terms, t_3 is significant in two of the three equations and t_4 is significant in one equation. This provides supporting evidence for the contention that the post-assassination disorders were more severe than incidents in the other time periods. It should also be noted that the fact that these results parallel the ones obtained with the composite index means that the unidimensional conceptualization of severity is not obscuring relationships between components of this construct and the other factors.

Finally, a canonical correlation model was estimated taking as observations those disturbances for which we have data on all three severity components. The substantive perspective underlying use of this model here involves viewing severity as an unobserved construct for which we have available three indicators: crowd size, number of arrests and number of injuries. This formulation therefore utilizes information on the three severity facets simultaneously in forming the "dependent variable."[16] It is unlike our composite measure in that the weights assigned to the components combine them in a linear fashion, in that the weights are estimated by making use of their relationships to the "independent variables," and in that nonquantitative information on the incidents is not utilized. Despite these differences the coefficients of the independent variables in the canonical model are quite consistent with the preceding findings.[17] Although we lack significance tests for the individual variates, they are similar in sign and in magnitude to the coefficients obtained with the other formulations. We conclude that the results reported in Table 5 are not idiosyncratic of the severity and under different analytic procedures the same substantive assessment would have been reached.

Community-based deprivations and disorder severity

In the introductory section, we presented a rationale for investigating the impact of Negro living conditions in a community on the severity of its disorders. We indicated that while the kinds of discontent which derive from community-based deprivations have not been found to be related to the *frequency* of hostile outbursts, there are theoretical considerations and results from other empirical studies

(Wanderer, 1968; Downes, 1968; 1970; Morgan and Clark, 1973) which suggest that this may not be the case with disorder severity; that once a disturbance has begun, the frustrations which have accumulated among Negroes as a result of their circumstance in the community may well be expressed in the intensity of the aggression.

To the extent that the frustrations which provoked Negroes to riot during the 1960s were a consequence of local deprivations, we would expect the variation across cities in disorder severity to correspond to the variation in the indicators of the relevant deprivations, once other salient factors have been controlled. This raises the question of which conditions were responsible for the discontent expressed in the rioting. The presence of city differences in important determinants of Negro well-being is not a sufficient reason for concluding that a corresponding variation will exist in the frustration level of inhabitants in different ghettos. Many potential sources of discontent are only that—potential sources—until attention is called to them and they are invested with symbolic import and racial significance. (Examples are Negro-white disparities in various social areas, which form a basis for reference group explanations of frustration.) There are other community characteristics whose values in different cities are likely to induce corresponding variations in the level of discontent, irrespective of whether or not they become foci of attention. For instance, there probably is greater discontent where median Negro income is low than where it is high, because of the enormous importance of this factor for access to a variety of institutions and desirable life styles. However, this does not mean that the greater frustration in poor ghettos necessarily will

be articulated in severity of rioting; the disorders of the 1960s may have been reactions to entirely different provocations than community conditions.

Because we are not prepared to assert which inequities were especially galling to Negroes or whether they were oriented in this period to a particular reference group, our strategy will be to postulate a number of plausible ways by which frustration may derive from community conditions and then ascertain the relation between measures of the relevant factors and disorder severity. A detailed discussion of this procedure has been presented elsewhere (Spilerman, 1970b: 639-41); consequently, the argument only is summarized here and the reader is referred to the earlier report for details. In essence, we have selected community characteristics which can serve as indicators for a social disorganization explanation, for reference group explanations and for a thesis which associates the severity of rioting with an unresponsive municipal political structure.

Social disorganization

According to this perspective on the causes of collective aggression, individuals who are weakly integrated into their community, in the sense of having few associational ties or little personal identification with it, are less encumbered by the constraints which would dissuade others from participating in a destructive outburst. One formulation of this thesis refers to the disorienting effects of rapid population change. A locale which has experienced a substantial influx of new residents would have acquired many persons who are unacquainted with the institutionalized procedures for seeking redress of grievances; at the same time, these individuals would have little investment in solving problems in a manner which avoids rancor and conflict in the community (Coleman, 1957: 20-1). Frustration is not the animus here; rather, it is the absence of social links which normally permit informal control to be exercised and prevent disputes from polarizing and degenerating into hostility and violence. A second version of the social disorganization thesis stresses the negative association with community that is likely to characterize the attitudes of residents in the worst ghettos because of their continual exposure to crime, filth and dilapidated housing. As indicators of the first formulation, we used the census variables percent change in total population and percent change in nonwhite population.[18] As indicators of the second formulation, we employed the variables percent of nonwhites residing in dwellings constructed before 1950 and percent of nonwhites living in housing with substandard plumbing.

Political structure

During periods of rapid change in the status of a minority, such as occurred for Negroes during the 1960s, issues frequently arise which require the representation of its views in the municipal government. Also, if bitter disputes involving the group are to be resolved without confrontation and violence, there is a need for city officials to be oriented toward compromise and accommodation. While we lack performance measures on how racial disputes were processed in the many cities which experienced disorders during 1967-68, there is evidence that certain electoral procedures and political structures make for greater responsiveness to the sensitivities of diverse constituents, and we have measures of the presence of these arrangements. In particular, Lieberson and Sil-

verman (1965) and Wilson (1960: 25-7) have argued that a municipal government will be more representative of community composition when council members are elected from established districts, rather than at-large, and when the council districts are small; the rationale being that opportunity is thereby increased for a numerically small but geographically concentrated group to elect its own members. It has also been suggested (Coleman, 1957: 14-6; Alford and Scoble, 1965) that a mayor-council structure and partisan elections will enhance governmental responsiveness to the diverse and conflicting interests of a socially heterogeneous community. In our analysis we included dummy variables for presence of nonpartisan elections and for mayor-council government and continuous variables for population per councilman and proportion of the city council elected at-large.

Deprivation explanations

These approaches to explaining frustration may be classified according to whether or not the presence of a reference group is postulated. *Absolute* deprivation explanations attribute the inter-city variation in level of Negro discontent to community differences in social and economic opportunity for ghetto residents. The presumption here is that where many persons earn low incomes or are employed at unsatisfying tasks, discontent will be more widespread. Since it focuses upon the economically most disadvantaged population segment in a community, this is an instance of an underclass explanation of the sources of violence and aggression (Downes, 1968: 513-4). As indicators of the level of absolute deprivation of Negroes, the following variables were used: percent of nonwhite males employed in low status occupations (household workers, service

TABLE 7

Correlations between Disorder Severity and Aspects of Community Structure[a]

Community Attribute	(1) Zero-Order Correlation with Disorder Severity[b]	(2) Partial Correlation, Controlling for Region, Nonwhite Population, Temporal Effects and Number of Previous Disturbances[c]
Region and Nonwhite Population Size[d]		
South (Dummy)	−.062	−.151**[h]
Nonwhite Population (log x)	.270**	.339**[h]
Indicators of Social Disorganization[d]		
Percent Change in Total Population, 1950–60	−.093	−.016
Percent Change in Total Population, 1960–70	−.053	.008
Percent Change in Nonwhite Population, 1950–60	.048	.099
Percent Change in Nonwhite Population, 1960–70	.001	.035
Percent of Nonwhites Living in Housing Built before 1950	.083	−.014
Percent of Nonwhites Living in Housing with Substandard Plumbing	.130*	.018
Indicators of Absolute Deprivation[d]		
Percent of Nonwhite Males Employed in Traditionally Negro Occupations[f]	−.139*	−.084
Nonwhite Male Unemployment Rate, 1960	.068	.044
Nonwhite Male Unemployment Rate, 1970	.047	.027
Nonwhite Median Family Income	.060	.034
Nonwhite Median Education	.021	−.065
Indicators of Relative Deprivation[d]		
Percent of Nonwhite Males Employed in Traditionally Negro Occupations Divided by White Figure	−.105	−.049
Nonwhite Median Family Income Divided by White Income	.074	.063
Nonwhite Unemployment Rate Divided by White Rate, 1960	.028	.031
Nonwhite Unemployment Rate Divided by White Rate, 1970	−.016	.012
Nonwhite Median Education Divided by White Education	.109*	.005
Percent Nonwhite[g] ($\sqrt{x}$)	.148**	.033
Indicators of Political Structure[e]		
Population per Councilman	.175**	−.019
Percent of City Council Elected At-Large	−.089	−.040
Presence of Nonpartisan Elections	−.066	−.022
Presence of Mayor-Council Gov't.	.110*	.018

* Significant at $p < .05$.
** Significant at $p < .01$.
[a] Number of observations equals 300.
[b] Disorder Severity coded (0–12).
[c] Control variables specified by equation (2) of Table 5. A separate regression was run for each community characteristic, containing it and the controls.
[d] Source: U. S. Census of Population (1963; 1973).
[e] Source: Municipal Yearbook (1965).
[f] Service workers + household workers + laborers.
[g] See footnote 19 regarding inclusion of this variable with the indicators of relative deprivation.
[h] Controls are for other variables in equation (2) of Table 5.

workers, laborers); the nonwhite male unemployment rate; nonwhite median family income; and nonwhite median education.

Relative deprivation explanations posit the existence of a reference group or an objective standard against which individuals compare their status or their progress. The level of frustration for the underprivileged is usually specified as a function of the size of the gap between the two populations on relevant variables. One possible reference group for Negroes would be whites in the same community. To measure Negro circumstance relative to this group, the absolute deprivation indicators were divided by comparable indices of white living standards. Alternatively, in a highly segregated society such as ours, Negroes may have more familiarity with the stylized version of white family life which is depicted in situation shows on television and may compare their own circumstances to this portrayal. In the disorder-proneness study (Spilerman, 1970b: 640), it was argued that the indicators of *absolute* deprivation provide the appropriate measures for this relative deprivation thesis. Finally, these same community characteristics may be associated with yet additional explanations, which argue an expectational or a competition thesis.[19] While such complexities are discussed in the preceding report (Spilerman, 1970b: 639-41), they are not elaborated upon here since the empirical results will not require ascertaining which of these explanations is to be given greatest credence.

Significance of the community characteristics

In order to ascertain whether disorders tended to be more severe where the objective measures of Negro circumstance in a community indicate greater disadvantage, it is necessary to include in the analysis other major determinants of severity that are correlated with the community factors of interest (Blalock, 1964: 48). Controls were introduced for the variables listed in Table 5 (second model). The importance of adjusting for these effects can be motivated in the following way: because of the Negro revolt character of the disturbances in the 1960s, the term for Negro population size measures the availability of participants for large (and severe) disorders; holding this variable constant allows us to compare communities having different sized pools of potential participants. The term for South permits an additive regional adjustment in the relationship between the community variables and disorder severity; it is introduced in recognition of the very different cultural traditions of the geographic regions in race relations.[20] (We already have seen that the regional effect is to depress severity in the South.) In an analogous fashion, the controls for number of previous disturbances and for time period adjust for any obscuring effects arising from these volatile determinants of disorder severity.

In Table 7 we report zero-order correlations between each of the community characteristics and disorder severity (column 1) and partial correlations (column 2) controlling for the variables in Table 5. (The latter entries derive from 21 regressions, each containing the controls and a single deprivation indicator.) We see that while there are several significant zero-order effects, none remains significant once the control variables are entered into the equation. Again, these results are not an artifact of the particular interval values that were assigned to the severity ranks or of the manner in which the disturbances were categorized. The analysis was replicated taking as dependent variables the two alternate interval assignments and the

TABLE 8

Percent of Variance in Disorder Severity Accounted for by Different Variable Clusters

Variable Cluster[a]	(1) Percent of Total Variance Explained by Cluster and Controls[b]	(2) Percent of Total Variance Explained by Nonwhite Population When Entered After Cluster and Controls[b]	(3) Percent of Total Variance Explained by Cluster When Entered After Nonwhite Population and Other Controls[b]
Nonwhite Population[c]	13.4	—	—
Social Disorganization	6.0	9.5	1.8
Absolute Deprivation	4.2	10.6	1.4
Relative Deprivation	6.7	7.5	.8
Political Structure	6.4	7.2	.2

[a] See Table 7 for a description of the variables included in each cluster.
[b] In this table "controls" refer to all variables in Table 5, column 2, except nonwhite population.
[c] This cluster refers to the equation of Table 5, column 2.

three quantitative components of severity (crowd size, number of arrests, number of injuries). This exercise produced results that are virtually identical with the ones reported here.[21]

Another approach to evaluating the importance of the explanations which associate disorder severity with Negro deprivation in a community is to assess the joint contribution from each cluster of variables toward accounting for the unexplained variation in the dependent variable. The terms in each cluster listed in Table 7 were therefore entered into a regression equation containing the controls. These results are reported in Table 8. In no instance does a cluster add as much as two percentage points of explained variation to the 13.4 percent accounted for by the control variables (column 3); also, in every case, the added R^2 is insignificant at the .10 level, as judged by a conventional F-test.

We stress that this result is not a consequence of the deprivation indicators and nonwhite population size sharing the same variation.[22] In no case does the significance of the population term in a regression fail to reach the .01 level in the

presence of either a single deprivation measure or a variable cluster. Indeed, while none of the clusters, entered after the controls, increased the R^2 by as much as two percentage points (over the initial 13.4 points), the nonwhite population term alone, entered after the other controls and any cluster of deprivation indicators, adds a minimum of 7.2 percentage points to the explained variation (column 2).[23]

Our analysis therefore indicates that in the period of the 1960s, the severity of a disturbance had little basis in community organization or economic structure. Holding constant a measure of the size of the pool of potential participants and several determinants of the volatility in severity, it is *not* the case that an outbreak of racial violence tended to be more severe where Negro status is low (in absolute terms or relative to one of several reference groups), where community disorganization is extensive, or where the structure of the municipal government suggests it would be unresponsive to the interests of Negro constituents.[24] Instead, as we have reported with respect to the determinants of disorder-proneness (Spilerman, 1970b; 1971), the only stable community characteristics that are related to severity are nonwhite population size and a contextual term for South.

These results are at variance with the findings by Morgan and Clark (1973) who argue that disorder severity in the mid-1960s was a function of the grievance level of Negroes in a community. In particular, they report that severity was raised by racial inequality in housing conditions, but depressed by inequality in occupational status. We find their analysis less than persuasive[25] for the following reasons. (1) Their assertions are based on only 23 observations. This is a small sample, particularly for establishing a counterintuitive result such as the occupational effect. (2) They confounded disturbances of very different types. Although their explanatory variables were justified as indicators of Negro grievances in a community, the disorders they analyzed include incidents in which the aggression was perpetrated by whites, as well as instances of Negro aggression (Morgan and Clark, 1973: 612). It is unclear, however, what the rationale is for analyzing the severity of white-instigated violence in terms of Negro grievances; at a minimum, the relationship with severity would not be the same for the two types of disorders so they should not have been mixed. (3) Morgan and Clark failed to include proper controls for the size of the potential participant pool, which is necessary to ascertain the contribution from the grievance indicators net of city differences in available manpower for mounting a severe disturbance. They did incorporate a term for city size[26] but this is not the correct control for potential participants. Where rioting is principally by Negroes, adjustment should be made for the size of this population group (or its relevant age cohort); where the aggression is by whites, the size of that group should be controlled.

Conclusions

We have sought in this investigation to ascertain whether certain structural arrangements or demographic features of a community were responsible for especially severe disturbances during the 1960s. In previous studies (Spilerman, 1970b; 1971), we reported that the disturbance *locations* were unrelated to a number of objective indicators of Negro well-being in a locale. As a result, it was suggested that explanations of the causes of the riots must be sought in frustrations which carried nationwide salience, and the areal distribution of the incidents should be understood in terms of mechanisms which promoted geographic diffuseness in the impact of provocations. Our findings with respect to the determinants of disorder severity underscore that assessment. The severity of a disturbance, as well as its location, appears not to have been contingent upon Negro living conditions or their social or economic status in a community. Not surprising, it is also the case that the effects of the control variables— nonwhite population size and South—were much the same in the two studies: large ghetto populations provided the participants for frequent and for severe disturbances; also, net of this factor, a southern city tended to have fewer and less violent outbursts, possibly because Negroes in that region held lower expectations regarding improvements in their circumstances and were more fearful of retribution from participating in racial protest.

Taken together, these studies suggest that despite considerable differences in Negro circumstance from one city to the next, this consideration did not find expression in the two aspects of the disturbance process that we have examined. Although we would not claim that local conditions never influenced disorder-proneness or disorder severity, we do assert the absence of a systematic tendency for either of these facets of the racial turmoil to be associated with the extent of Negro deprivation in a community. This assessment is neither unreasonable nor counter-intuitive when viewed against other characteristics of the disturbances and against trends which were operative during the period. In particular, the incidents tended to cluster in time following a few dramatic events such as the massive Newark disorder in July, 1967, and the assassination of Martin Luther King in April, 1968. Also, the entire time interval during which disorders occurred in large numbers was itself concentrated within a few years in the mid-1960s. It is difficult to conceive of the kinds of developments in individual communities which could account for this sudden and practically simultaneous occurrence of hundreds of outbursts.

We also can enumerate trends which functioned to produce a geographically uniform pattern of behavior by Negroes. For one, black consciousness and black solidarity were real phenomena during the 1960s, having been stimulated by the imaginative and appealing tactics of civil rights activists in desegregating retail establishments in the South and placing Negroes on the voter rolls. For another, various civil rights bills were before Congress during much of the decade; these were salient to Negroes in all communities and would have served to heighten their racial awareness and racial identification. Yet, the factor I would stress as being responsible in a most essential way for the outbreaks having occurred in great numbers and for community conditions having been irrelevant to the disorder process is the wide availability of television and its network news structure.

By bringing scenes of civil rights marches, demonstrations and sit-ins into every ghetto, television contributed in a fundamental way to the creation of a black solidarity that would transcend the boundaries of community. Of more immediate relevance to the outbursts, the extensive media coverage accorded to many of the incidents, with the actions of participants depicted in full relief, served to familiarize Negroes elsewhere with the details of rioting and with the motivations of rioters. Observing the behavior of persons who face similar deprivations and must contend with the same discriminatory institutions as oneself—in short, individuals with whom the viewer could identify—provided a model of how he, too, might protest the indignities of his circumstance. By conveying the intensity and emotion of a confrontation, television provided an essential mechanism for riot contagion; also, as a result of its national network structure, the provocations which arose in diverse settings were made visible in the ghettos of every city.

The importance of television as a vehicle for the propagation of violent acts is not restricted to racial disorders. There is considerable evidence that skyjackings, prison riots, bomb threats and aggressive crimes of other sorts have been spread by television and the other mass media.[27] Indeed, a question which eventually will have to concern this nation is the determination of a policy to guide the reporting of destructive and potentially contagious events. However, the treacherous issue of media regulation is not a topic which need concern us here.

Notes

1. What is intended by this expression are disturbances which were not outgrowths from planned confrontations such as civil rights demonstrations. The precipitants of "spontaneous" disorders typically were the kind of incidents that occur frequently in American cities and are usually disposed of in routine

fashion (such as an arrest on a ghetto streetcorner) or unanticipated events of profound significance concerning which information was propagated by television (e.g., the assassination of Martin Luther King). Most of the racial disturbances during the 1960s had such origins.

2. There is a widespread belief that police tactics and manner of response to an incipient disturbance can restrain or exacerbate the intensity of the incident. For example, the International Association of Chiefs of Police (1963) recommends the following procedures for controlling hostile outbursts: extricate the leaders; cordon the area to prevent recruits to the mob from entering; fragment the crowd into small isolated groups; introduce plainclothesmen to inject competing slogans and raise divisive issues (Milgram and Toch 1969: 579). Also consult Smelser (1963: 261-8) for related comments.

3. Figures are from the 1960 Census of Population (U.S. Bureau of the Census, 1963) and pertain to the 413 communities in the contiguous United States with total population exceeding 25,000 and Negro population in excess of 1,000.

4. Figures in this paper which pertain to the *location* of racial disturbances during the 1960s were computed from the data set used in the author's earlier investigations (Spilerman 1960b; 1971). To be included in that data set, an incident had to involve at least 30 participants, be characterized by primarily Negro aggression, and be "spontaneous" in origin. For additional details on the definition and categorization of the disturbances, see Spilerman (1970b: 630).

5. One police innovation designed to reduce tension and quell turmoil involved the deployment of "youth patrols." In a number of cities, ghetto youth were encouraged to form police auxiliaries and patrol their neighborhoods at the onset of rioting. Knopf (1969), in an examination of the effectiveness of these groups in 12 instances of civil disorder, credits them with restraining the level of violence.

6. Wanderer's severity scale contains the following items: (0) No scale items; (1) Vandalism; (2) All of the above plus interference with firemen; (3) All of the above plus looting; (4) All of the above plus sniping; (5) All of the above plus called state police; (6) All of the above plus called National Guard; (7) All of the above plus law officer or civilian killed (Wanderer, 1968: 196-7).

7. The correlations among severity components are reported in Table 2, following the discussion of data characteristics.

8. Downes' severity scale consists of the following items: (0) Low intensity—rock and bottle throwing, window breaking, fighting; (1) Medium intensity—the above plus some looting and arson; (2) High intensity—the above plus much looting and arson, reports of sniping; (3) Very high intensity—the above plus widespread looting and arson, sniping (Downes, 1968: 519). Downes included an additional severity category for cities not experiencing a disorder, which

he ranked below "low intensity." It was properly (in our opinion) omitted in his second paper (Downes, 1970: 355-6).

9. Because the unit of observation here is the disturbance, not the potential riot site, community characteristics had to be collected only for cities which experienced racial turmoil. This permitted the inclusion of incidents which occurred in cities with populations less than 25,000. (These were omitted from the riot location studies because systematic information on small cities is absent in the Alford-Aiken data file, our primary source of data on the independent variables.) Forty-five incidents in small cities are contained in our figure of 322. Due to the large amount of missing data on characteristics of small communities, approximately half of these added disturbances subsequently were eliminated from the main analyses.

10. Data on number of arrests were available for 294 incidents; information on number of injuries was recorded for 258 disorders. Crowd size was reported less systematically: sometimes a range was specified; in other instances, statements were written such as "a crowd estimated to be larger than . . ." or "a small band of Negro youth." In 209 cases the coders were able to estimate approximate crowd size in terms of the following scale: (0) less than 100 participants; (1) 100-300 participants; (2) 300-700 participants; (3) more than 700 participants. Clearly, the very notion of "participation" is ill-defined, and this index should be recognized as subject to much error.

11. In fairness to Wanderer, it should be noted that the post-Martin Luther King-assassination period was not included in his study, which was restricted to disturbances during 1967.

12. There is a statistical problem in using a dichotomous dependent variable because the assumption of homoscedasticity is no longer valid. The least squares estimators of the regression coefficients still will be unbiased but their standard errors will be biased and inconsistent. One alternative is to use the two-stage method described by Goldberger (1964: 248-50). This procedure was applied here with the first stage predictions restricted to the ranges (.1, .9), (.06, .94) and (.03, .97), which has the effect of permitting observations at the end points of an interval to contribute, respectively 1.6, 2.1 and 3.0 times the weight of an observation at the midpoint. No difference in substantive findings arose from these manipulations. OLS results are presented in the text because the two-stage procedure provides slightly different parameter estimates depending on the first-stage range selected, and there is no rationale to guide a particular choice. Alternate methods such as probit and logit analysis are computationally cumbersome and unlikely to produce different results, given the stability of findings under the two-stage procedure.

13. The time periods were specified with two considerations in mind: to place roughly equal numbers of cities in each interval and to group dis-

orders in a way that would heighten the impact of substantive events. T_1 reflects primarily the many incidents which followed the major Newark disorder; t_2 is a residual category; t_3 contains the post-Martin Luther King-assassination disorders; t_4 and t_5 divide the summer of 1968 disturbances. The latter two periods are presented separately because of the different effect each has in the regression models (Table 5).

14. The procedure which Downes followed in assigning severity to cities is not evident from his articles. It was clarified in an exchange of letters with the author. We point out that despite the tendency to lower severity with each additional disorder, this assignment would associate high severity values with high multiple disorder cities. A city with many incidents simply has had more opportunity to incur a severe disturbance.

15. The regression coefficients in column (1) correspond to an assignment of the values 0, 1, 2, 3 to the dependent variable. In column (2), the scale values are the ones which were used in our composite severity index so the entries here are beta coefficients for the second model in Table 5. In column (3), the values 0, 1, 6, 25 were assigned to the severity ranks.

16. The canonical model does not distinguish between "dependent" and "independent" variables and simply forms the linear combinations in the two sets of variables which maximizes the correlation between them. For details on the procedure, see Van de Geer (1971, ch. 14). For the purpose of clarity in our substantive argument, we retained the traditional labels.

17. The canonical weights assigned to the severity components (dependent variables) were .68, .20 and .27, corresponding to crowd size, log (arrests) and log (injuries). Because of the greater importance of crowd size in the linear combination, the entries in column (7) of Table 6 were rescaled with reference to that equation.

18. Although we are examining events which occurred during 1967-68, the community characteristics were drawn largely from the 1960 Census of Population. Despite the fact that 1970 census data are a couple of years closer in time to the disturbances, the earlier census year is preferable because our hypotheses refer to the impact of conditions which have been in existence for some period of time. It is also the case that most of the community variables are stable in the sense that the correlation over cities between their 1960 and 1970 values is high. In a few instances, this is not the case; percentage change in total population, percentage change in nonwhite population, and the unemployment rates for the racial groups can be very different in successive census years. In these instances, both the 1960 and 1970 values of the variables were used in the analysis.

19. With regard to the latter theme, Lieberson and Silverman (1965) suggest that racial violence may be more common where Negro and white males earn proximate incomes, occupy similar occupational statuses and, generally, are interchangeable in the social and economic life of the community. According to this explanation, small racial disparities would be associated with a high level of tension. For convenience, the percent nonwhite variable, which also has been interpreted as an indicator of interracial competition (Blalock, 1957), is included in this cluster (Table 7).

20. We emphasize that the two variables, nonwhite population size and South, were introduced into the investigation of volatility in disorder severity for a different reason than they are entered here. Formally, they served as controls for community disorder-proneness. Had other variables been found to be determinants of disorder-proneness, nonwhite population size and South would still be added at this point for the reasons cited in the text.

21. In the five replications, there were two instances in which a community characteristic remained significant in the presence of the controls. Percent change in nonwhite population was significant when severity was coded 0-3; nonwhite median education was significant in the log (arrests) equation. Because significance in each case was barely attained at the level $p < .05$ and because there was no corroborating evidence from other variables in a cluster, these results are discounted in the discussion. In no instance was an entire cluster significant as judged by an F-test on the added R^2.

22. Only one of the 21 zero-order correlations between log (nonwhite population) and a deprivation indicator exceeds .5 in magnitude: r(log[nonwhite population], population/councilman) = .78.

23. In addition to the additive regressions reported in the text, we examined several interaction models to ascertain whether unusually severe disturbances tended to occur where there is both high deprivation and a large Negro population. In one formulation, log (nonwhite population) was added to an equation containing the other controls listed in Table 5 (equation 2) and the interaction term Dep x log (nonwhite population), where Dep represents a deprivation measure listed in Table 7. In every instance (21 equations), the interaction term dropped to insignificance ($p > .05$), while the population variable was significant at the .01 level. In a second formulation, the two variables Dep and Dep x log (nonwhite population) were added to an equation containing the controls. As judged by an F-test on the added R^2, in all but one instance these terms were insignificant at the .05 level. The sole case of a significant interaction involved the variable low nonwhite occupational status. Since the sign of this interaction was negative (counter to the postulated thesis) and since the other indicators of absolute deprivation were insignificant, we discount this finding. The interaction results were invariant across the three interval-level specifications of the dependent variable.

24. A parallel analysis also was carried out with a few variables which tap police organization and training. Although we lacked detailed data on police

preparation in riot control tactics in the various cities, information on a few police characteristics is reported in the Municipal Yearbook (1966). A presence/absence code was constructed for the following factors: existence of a special riot control unit: existence of a prepared plan for riot control: and use of dogs in riot control.

When these variables were entered subsequent to the controls, all were found to be statistically insignificant. (This finding is consistent with our suggestion that improved police preparation as a result of a disturbance may have had less to do with the severity decline than did participant exhaustion or lessened interest in further rioting.) Yet, the notion that police tactics and training have little impact on how quickly a disorder is contained is difficult to accept. Because our indicators are few in number and not particularly sensitive to the quality of police preparation, because they relate to police organization in the early 1960s before disorder control became a major issue, and because our primary interest here concerns the relation between severity and objective measures of Negro frustration in a community, these results are mentioned only *en passant*.

25. While this is not the place to review Morgan and Clark's analysis of the determinants of disorder *frequency*, because that topic is intermixed in their paper with the severity study, a few salient comments seem in order. (1) Their attempt to select among explanations according to the magnitudes of correlation coefficients (Morgan and Clark, 1973: 616-7) is in error. With N = 42 observations (cities), the zero-order correlations in their Table 2 are not statistically different from one another, nor are the partial correlation coefficients different. In other words, in their data set, there is no basis for preferring one variable to another on statistical grounds. Also, I would point out that Morgan and Clark neglect to include a term for South which, as I have reported, (Spilerman, 1971: 429) enhances the relation between disorder frequency and Negro population size. (2) Considering their reason for introducing city population size—to measure the "opportunities . . . for social contacts that could precipitate a disorder" (Morgan and Clark, 1973: 616)—they have used the wrong variable. The appropriate measure of disorder-precipitating contacts between whites and Negroes would be $Tp(1-p)$, where T equals city population size and p equals proportion Negro in the population. (3) The matter of mixing disorders of different types (discussed in the text) is also material to this analysis, particularly in regard to the meaning of the variable *Negro population size* in instances of white-instigated aggression.

26. In our data set, incidentally, this variable turns out to be a weaker predictor of riot severity than nonwhite population size. While our principal specification of the severity determinants (Table 5, equation 2) explains 13.4 percent of the variation in severity, if the nonwhite population term is replaced by log (city size) the R^2 value drops to 9.4 percent.

27. For references and additional discussion on this subject, see Spilerman (1975).

48.

Jules J. Wanderer[1]

AN INDEX OF RIOT SEVERITY AND SOME CORRELATES

This paper is divided into two sections. The first describes an Index of Riot Severity. The second reports the results of an examination of select social, economic, and demographic variables to ascertain which among them is correlated to riot severity as measured by the Index.

An index of riot severity

The Index is based upon the analysis of seventy-five riots and civil-criminal disorders reported to have taken place during the summer of 1967.[2] The analysis employed Guttman scaling techniques, and the derived Index is a Guttman-type scale. Information used in the construction of the scale was provided by mayors' offices at the request of a U.S. Senate subcommittee.[3] The subcommittee's request for information from cities experiencing major riots and civil-criminal disorders covered the years 1965-67. For each of these years the subcommittee tabulated the following kinds of information: date of disorder, the city in which it occurred, 1960 population, percentage Negro, number of civilians and law officers killed and injured, types of criminality (e.g., sniping, vandalism, arson, interference with firemen), the number of arrests, the number of convictions, police action, estimated financial losses, and a mayor's report of "triggering incident."

From Jules J. Wanderer, "An Index of Riot Severity and Some Correlates," *The American Journal of Sociology,* 74, March 1969, pp. 500-505. Reprinted by permission of the publisher, The University of Chicago Press, and the author.

The information selected for the construction of the Index was based upon the subcommittee's tabulations for 1967, from April 1 to September 8. While an index of riot severity might ideally incorporate information from diverse sources, the Index reported here includes only those items that could be directly ascertained from official mayors' reports to the Senate subcommittee.

The final scale includes the following seven items of riot severity: killing, calling of the National Guard, calling of the state police, sniping, looting, interference with firemen, and vandalism.[4] The Coefficient of Reproducibility of this Guttman scale of riot severity for seventy-five riots and seven items of severity is 92 per cent. Table 1 shows the obtained scale.

TABLE 1
Guttman Scale of Riot Severity

Scale Type	% Cities (N = 75)	Items Reported	Scale Errors
8	4	No scale items	2
7	19	"Vandalism"	10
6	13	All of the above + "interference with firemen"	3
5	16	All of the above + "looting"	3
4	13	All of the above + "sniping"	7
3	7	All of the above + "called State Police"	4
2	17	All of the above + "called National Guard"	11
1	11	All of the above + "law officer or civilian killed"	2
Total			42

Note. Coefficient = 1 − 42/515 = 92%.

TABLE 2
Cities by Scale Types

Scale type 8:	Scale type 5:	Scale type 2:
Louisville, Ky.	Birmingham, Ala.	Portland, Ore.
West Palm Beach, Fla.	Cincinnati, Ohio	South Bend, Ind.
Mount Clemons, Mich.	Buffalo, N.Y.	Providence, R.I.
	Dayton, Ohio	Tampa, Fla.
Scale type 7:	Mt. Vernon, N.Y.	Waterloo, Iowa
Fresno, Calif.	Passaic, N.Y.	San Francisco, Calif.
Kansas City, Mo.	Cincinnati, Ohio	Poughkeepsie, N.Y.
Omaha, Neb.	New York City, N.Y.	Phoenix, Ariz.
Montgomery, Ala.	Washington, D.C.	Nashville, Tenn.
New Britain, Conn.	Syracuse, N.Y.	Grand Rapids, Mich.
Houston, Tex.	Minneapolis, Minn.	Cambridge, Md.
Sacramento, Calif.	Toledo, Ohio	Tucson, Ariz.
Massillon, Ohio		San Francisco, Calif.
Rockford, Ill.	Scale type 4:	
Elgin, Ill.	San Bernardino, Calif	Scale type 1:
Kalamazoo, Mich.	Houston, Tex.	Milwaukee, Wis.
Albany, N.Y.	Peoria, Ill.	Rochester, N.Y.
Lima, Ohio	Waterbury, Conn.	Detroit, Mich.
Peekskill, N.Y.	Riviera Beach, Fla.	Pontiac, Mich.
	Chicago, Ill.	Cincinnati, Ohio
Scale type 6:	New York City, N.Y.	Newark, N.J.
Hamilton, Ohio	Englewood, N.J.	Plainfield, N.J.
Long Beach, Calif.	Boston, Mass.	Jackson, Miss.
Peterson, N.J.	New York City, N.Y.	
Erie, Pa.		
Wyandanch, N.Y.	Scale type 3:	
Hartford, Conn.	New Haven, Conn.	
Greensboro, N.C.	Saginaw, Mich.	
Erie, Pa.	Wichita, Kan.	
New York City, N.Y.	Wilmington, Del.	
Hattiesburg, Miss.	Flint, Mich.	

With one exception, the items included in the scale are in the same form as they appeared in the mayors' reports, that is, indications of the presence or absence of the event. The exception involves the alteration of a quantitatively defined variable, number of civilian and police deaths, so that it could be coded simply as a dichotomy: "no deaths" and "N-deaths."

Events were selected as items for the scale if they appeared to be logically linked or related to riot severity. To obtain a Guttman scale means, of course, that the items are located in a systematic and cumulative fashion along the unidimensional continuum of severity and that the continuum also locates cities on the severity scale.

Cities are organized into eight scale

types, or eight categories ordered on the severity dimension. Table 2 shows the cities that compose each scale type. The reader will note that each riot is treated as a unit.[5] The alternative is to treat each city as a unit, thus eliminating the repetition of those cities with two or more riots. As a consequence of adopting the riot as the unit in developing the Guttman scale, one city is included three times; three cities are included twice each; and one city is included four times.[6]

Some correlates: a comparison with other studies

Explanations of riots have followed from different lines of inquiry. Newspaper reports, personal accounts, and biographical statements have supplied us with a body of popular notions about riots, their causes, courses, and effects. Findings of technical studies have thrown additional light on the characteristics of large numbers of disorders.[7] In these studies, findings usually emerge from a comparison of riot with nonriot (control) cities.[8] In the discussion that follows, however, variables are examined in terms of their relationship to *riot severity,* not in terms of their relationship to the *presence* or *absence* of rioting.

Lieberson and Silverman studied seventy-six events classifiable as Negro-white race riots between 1913 and 1963. They found that when riot and control cities were compared, (1) percentage increase of Negro population was unrelated to the presence of riots, (2) racial composition did not distinguish between riot and control cities, and (3) housing measured in terms of higher or lower quality did not distinguish between riot and control cities.[9]

Percentage increase of nonwhites

Lieberson and Silverman found that percentage increase of Negroes did not differentiate between riot and control cities. They discovered "no sizable difference between riot and control cities in their percentage gains in Negro population during the decades."[10] For each of the cities in the scale reported here,[11] the percentage increase of non-whites in the total population of the riot city in the decade 1950-60 was computed.[12] The Spearman rank correlation coefficient, computed between the *scale types* ranked on severity and mean percentage non-white increase, was .833, significant beyond the .01 level.[13] It seems that while percentage increase of Negroes is unrelated to the presence or absence of a riot, the percentage increase of non-whites is significantly related to riot severity as measured

by the Index. Once a riot takes place, the greater the percentage increase of non-whites, the greater the severity of the riot.

Racial composition

Included in each mayor's report was information pertaining to the proportion of the city's population that was Negro. For each scale type the mean percentage of Negroes was computed. The rank order of scale-type mean percentages did not correlate significantly with the Index. A second step involved the elimination of southern cities and again computing scale-type mean percentages. The rank correlation was not significant. It appears that racial composition is neither related to the presence or absence of riots[14] nor to riot severity as measured by the Index.

Housing

Six variables relating to housing were examined to ascertain their relationship to riot severity: (1) percentage living in multi-family dwellings, (2) percentage living in newer than ten-year-old dwellings, (3) percentage in units with substandard plumbing, (4) percentage in housing with more than one person per room, and (5) percentage who owned their own homes.[15] For each scale type, the median percentage was computed for each of the six variables. Of the six variables, only one showed a statistically significant rank correlation between median percentage and riot severity. Measured by the Spearman rank correlation, riot severity and percentage living in newer than ten-year-old dwellings correlated —.86, significant beyond the .01 level. Once a riot occurs, the fewer non-whites in dwellings constructed in the decade 1950-60, the greater the severity of the riot. None of the other five housing variables showed any systematic variation by the Index of Riot Severity.

Economics of housing

Three additional housing variables were examined: (1) median non-white rent, (2) median value of non-white place of living, and (3) median percentage of non-white home owners.[16] For each of the variables, scale-type medians were computed and correlated with riot severity. None showed any relationship to severity.

Density

It is popularly believed that areas of high population density provide arenas for a variety of disruptive behavior. For each scale type the mean population density was computed.[17] The Spearman rank correlation coefficient between scale types and mean population density was .18, not significant at the .05 level. It may be concluded that intensity of riots and civil-criminal disorders as measured by the Index is not related to population density.

Larceny and assault

It may be thought that cities with traditions of violence and criminality lend themselves to the generation of more severe riots than cities without such a tradition. One measure of criminal tradition is indicated by the aggravated assault rate and the larceny rate of each city.[18] The mean aggravated assault rate for each scale type was computed and ranked. The rank correlation between riot intensity and mean aggravated assault rates as measured by the Spearman rank correlation is negligible.

In the same fashion, the mean larceny rate for each scale type and riot intensity were correlated. The Spearman rank correlation coefficient was .24, not significant at the .05 level.

Two measures of criminality are found to be unrelated to the severity of disorders as measured by the Index.

Police preparation

To what extent are the preparations of the police before the outbreak of disorders related to the subsequent intensity of the disorder? Eight types of information on police preparations were examined.[19] They include: (1) presence of inservice training for police, (2) riot training for police, (3) presence of an auxiliary police force, (4) riot training for the auxiliary police, (5) mutual aid arrangements with a neighboring law enforcement agency, (6) presence of a special riot unit on the police force, (7) presence of a special riot plan, and (8) use of dogs to control crowds of people.

Only two of the above variables showed a tendency to vary with riot severity, and just one correlated significantly. The correlation between riot severity and mean percentage of scale-type cities employing dogs was .56, not significant at the .05 level. The mean percentage of cities in each scale type that reported having a special riot plan was computed and correlated with riot severity. The Spearman rank correlation coefficient was .70, significant beyond the .05 level.[20]

Interpretation of the relationship between the variable police preparation and riot severity poses special difficulties. Previously discussed variables did not imply direct human involvement in anticipation of riots and civil-criminal disorders. Consequently a significant correlation between riot intensity and police preparation may be interpreted in different ways. The correlation may lend support to the assertion that the magnitude of the riot was accurately assessed by the police beforehand and that their preparations thus corresponded to the severity of the riot. On the other hand, a contradictory assertion suggests that police preparation is an example of the self-fulfilling prophecy and is a factor in the escalation of the riot.

The absence of a statistically significant correlation between police preparation and subsequent riot intensity may also be interpreted in the same fashion. Either the police overprepared, or an accurate assessment of the potential led to preparations that did, in fact, reduce the intensity of the disorders. A final interpretation suggests that adequate police preparation might even have prevented the start of the disorder.

Sniping

Janowitz distinguished between two patterns of riots in American cities, communal and commodity riots.[21] The latter are of recent vintage and characterized by widespread use of rifles and other arms among rioters. It can be seen that in the scale of riot severity reported here, thirty-six scale-type cities reported sniping (see Tables 1 and 2). There are scale errors; in fact, thirty-two cities reported sniping. Thus sniping appears as an event midway along the continuum of severity, occurring in less than 50 per cent of the riots and civil-criminal disorders reported to the Senate subcommittee.

Conclusion

It has been shown that while certain variables do not correlate with the presence or absence of riots in American cities, they do correlate with riot severity. Such variables are more influential in determining the severity of a riot, once it has begun, than they are in determining the outbreak of that riot.

The Index—a Guttman-type scale—suggests that the events that constitute riots and civil-criminal disorders are *not*

bizarre, non-patterned, or randomly generated.[22] On the contrary, employing the properties of Guttman scales, we may predict the sequence of events for levels of riot severity. The Index was developed from materials describing disorders occurring in 1967. Future riots and civil-criminal disorders may not be similarly constituted. Either the set of events or the sequence of events may be altered by social existential conditions.

Notes

1. I wish to acknowledge the assistance of Alfred J. Claassen, Hunter H. Durning, Patricia L. Gotchall, and Sigmund W. Krane, who prepared some of the materials used in the following analysis. Tables 1 and 2 were previously published in "1967 Riots: A Test of the Congruity of Events," *Social Problems,* XVI, No. 2 (Fall, 1968), pp. 193-98.

2. Reported by mayors in *Riots: Civil and Criminal Disorders* (Hearings before the Permanent Subcommittee on Investigation of the Committee on Government Operations, U.S. Senate, 90th Cong., 1st sess., November 1, 2, 3, and 6, 1967. Part 1. [Washington, D.C.: Government Printing Office, 1967]).

3. Of 137 cities contacted, 128 responded with reports for the years 1965-67.

4. These items are ordered from most to least severe, or from least to most frequently reported. One aspect of the scale as shown in Table 1 should be noted. Of the cities, 4 per cent did not report any of the items in the ordered sequence generated by the Guttman scale. Since the item defined as "not responding to any of the items" lacks sufficiently large marginals to be considered "scalable," it might be dropped from the scale. The inclusion of that item, however, does not inflate the Coefficient of Reproducibility; in fact, its inclusion deflates the Coefficient. In order to preserve the substantive character of the sequence of events, the item is included in the scale presented here.

5. This approach has been used widely. See Stanley Lieberson and Arnold R. Silverman, "Precipitants and Conditions of Race Riots," *American Sociological Review,* XXX (December, 1965), pp. 887-98; and Milton Bloombaum, "The Conditions Underlying Race Riots as Portrayed by Multidimensional Scalogram Analysis: A Re-analysis of Lieberson and Silverman's Data," *American Sociological Review,* XXXIII (February, 1968), pp. 76-91.

6. Cincinnati reported three disorders; Erie, Houston, and San Francisco reported two disorders; and New York City reported four.

7. Recent examples, to name just a few, include Peter M. Green and Ruth H. Cheney, "Urban Planning and Urban Revolt: A Case Study," *Progressive Architecture* (January, 1968), pp. 134-56; Anthony Oberschall, "The Los Angeles Riots of August 1965," *Social Problems,* XV (Winter, 1968), pp. 322-41; Tom Parmenter, "Breakdown of Law and Order," *Trans-action,* IV (September, 1967), pp. 13-22, which is but one of a series of papers in the same issue analyzing urban violence; Jerry Cohen and William S. Murphy, *Burn, Baby, Burn* (New York: E. P. Dutton & Co., 1966); Morris Janowitz, *Social Control of Escalated Riots* (Chicago: University of Chicago Center for Policy Study, 1968); Lieberson and Silverman, *op. cit.* (n. 5 above); Bloombaum, *op. cit.* (n. 5 above); and Irving Louis Horowitz and Martin Liebowitz, "Social Deviance and Political Marginality: Toward a Redefinition of the Relation between Sociology and Politics," *Social Problems,* XV (Winter, 1968), pp. 280-96.

8. Lieberson and Silverman, *op. cit.,* Bloombaum, *op. cit.*

9. These are only three of the variables that were examined by Lieberson and Silverman.

10. Lieberson and Silverman, *op. cit.,* p. 893.

11. Southern cities were omitted from the calculations.

12. Source of information is *United States Bureau of Census: County and City Data Book, 1967* (Washington, D.C.: Government Printing Office, 1967), pp. 464-572.

13. A description of Spearman rank correlation may be found in Sidney Siegel, *Nonparametric Statis-*

tics (New York: McGraw-Hill Book Co., 1956), pp. 202-11.

14. As reported in Lieberson and Silverman, *op. cit.* (n. 5 above), pp. 893-94.

15. Source of information on non-whites is *United States Bureau of the Census: Census of Housing* (Washington, D.C.: Government Printing Office, 1960), Table 8.

16. Source of information for variables (1) and (2) is *ibid.* Source of information for variable (3) is *United States Bureau of the Census: Census of Population* (Washington, D.C.: Government Printing Office, 1960), Table 78.

17. Source of information is *United States Bureau of Census: County and City Data Book, 1967* (n. 12 above), pp. 464-573.

18. Source of information is *Uniform Crime Reports—1966: Crime in the United States* (Washington, D.C.: Government Printing Office, 1967), pp. 170-85.

19. Source of information is *Municipal Yearbook, 1966.* (Chicago: International City Managers' Association, 1966), pp. 445-65.

20. After correction for ties.

21. Janowitz, *op. cit.* (n. 7 above), esp. pp. 9-13.

22. For a review and criticism of the tradition which interprets crowd behavior as bizarre and sociologically primitive, see Carl J. Couch, "Collective Behavior: An Examination of Some Stereotypes," *Social Problems,* XV (Winter, 1968), pp. 310-22; and Jules J. Wanderer, "1967 Riots: A Test of The Congruity of Events," *Social Problems* (Fall, 1968), pp. 193-98.

Master Bibliography

Abelson, Robert P., and John W. Tukeey
  1959 "Efficient Conversion of Non-Metric Information into Metric Information." *Proceedings American Statistical Association* (Social Science Section), pp. 226-230.

Aberle, D. F.
  1962 "A Note on Relative Deprivation Theory as Applied to Millenarian and Other Movements," pp. 209-214, in Sylvia Thrupp (ed.), *Millennial Dreams in Action: Essays in Comparative Studies in Society and History.* The Hague: Mouton.

Abraham, Mark
  1969 "Correlate of Political Complexity." *American Sociological Review* 34: 690-701.

Abram, Charles
  1965 *Squatter Settlements: The Problem and the Opportunity.* Report of the U.S. Agency for International Development. New York: Department of Housing and Urban Development.

Adams, J. S.
  1965 "Inequity in Social Exchange," pp. 267-299, in Berkowitz (ed.), *Advances in Experimental Social Psychology.* New York: Academic Press.

Agburn, William F., and O. D. Duncan
  1964 "City Size as a Sociological Variable," pp. 129-147, in E. W. Burgess and D. J. Bogue (eds.), *Contributions to Urban Sociology.* Chicago: Chicago University Press.

Alford, Robert R., and Harry M. Scolde
  1965 "Political and Socioeconomic Characteristics of American Cities," pp. 82-97, in *Municipal Yearbook.* Chicago: International City Manager's Association.

Alker, H. A., and Poppen, P. J.
  1973 "Personality and Ideology in University Students." *Journal of Personality* 41: 653-671.

Allport, F. H.
  1924 *Social Psychology.* Boston: Houghton.

Allport, G.
  1960 "The Open System in Personality Theory." *Journal of Abnormal and Social Psychology* 61: 301-311.

Almond, G. A.
   1969 "Political Development: Analytical and Normative Perspectives."
          Contemporary Political Studies 1: 447-470.
Almond, G. A., and J. S. Coleman
   1960 *The Politics of Developing Areas.* Princeton: Princeton University
          Press.
Anderson, W., B. J. Berger, M. Zelditch, and B. P. Cohen
   1969 "Reaction to Inequity." *Acta Sociologica* 12: 1-12.
Anderson, William, Russell R. Dynes, and E. L. Quarantelli
   1974 "Urban Counterrioters." *Society* 11: 50-55.
Aristotle
   1943 *Politics.* Benjamin Jowett, trans. New York: Modern Library.
Ashton, T. S.
   1948 *The Industrial Revolution.* London: Oxford University Press.
Back, K. W.
   1971 "Biological Models of Social Change." *American Sociological Review*
          36: 660-667.
   1971 "Epidemiology Versus Cartesian Dualism." *Social Science and*
          Medicine.
Banfield, E. C.
   1958 *The Moral Basis of a Backward Society.* Glencoe, Ill.: The Free Press.
   1970 *The Unheavenly City.* Boston: Little, Brown.
Banks, A. S.
   1970 "Modernization and Political Change: The Latin American and
          Amero-European Nations." *Contemporary Political Studies* 2: 405-
          418.
Banks, A. S., and R. B. Textor
   1963 *A Cross Polity Survey.* Cambridge, Mass.: MIT Press.
Banks, A. S., and P. M. Gregg
   1965 "Grouping Political Systems: Q-Factor Analysis of a Cross Polity
          Survey." *American Behavioral Scientist* 9.
Banton, Michael
   1956 "Adaptation and Integration in the Social Systems of Temne Immi-
          grants in Freetown." *Africa* 26: 354-368.
Baron, Robert A.
   1971 "Magnitude of Victim's Pains Cues and Level of Prior Anger Arousal
          as Determinants of Adult Aggressive Behavior." *Journal of Per-*
          sonality and Social Psychology 17: 236-243.
Bateson, G., D. D. Jackson, Haldy, and J. Weakland
   1956 "Toward a Theory of Schizophrenia." *Behavioral Sciences* 1: 251-264.
Becker, Howard S.
   1967 *Outsiders: Studies in the Sociology of Deviance.* Glencoe, Ill.: The
          Free Press.
   1967 "Whose Side Are We On?" *Social Problems* 14: 239-247.
Bell, Daniel
   1964 *The Radical Right.* New York: Doubleday.
Bennis, W. G., and P. E. Slater
   1968 *The Temporary Society.* New York: Harper & Row.

Berk, Richard A.
1972a "The Controversy Surrounding Analysis of Collective Violence: Some Methodological Notes," pp. 112-118, in James F. Short, Jr. and Marvin E. Wolfgang, *Collective Violence.* Chicago: Aldine.
1972b "The Emergence of Muted Violence in Crowd Behavior: A Case Study of an Almost Race Riot," pp. 309-328, in James F. Short, Jr. and Marvin E. Wolfgang, *Collective Violence.* Chicago: Aldine.
1972c "Patterns of Vandalism During Civil Disorder as an Indicator of Selection of Targets." *American Sociological Review* 37: 533-547.
1974a "A Gaming Approach to Crowd Behavior." *American Sociological Review* 39: 355-373.
1974b *Collective Behavior.* Dubuque: Wm. D. Brown.
Berkowitz, Leonard
1965 "Some Aspects of Observed Aggression." *Journal of Personality and Social Psychology* 12: 359-369.
1968 "The Study of Urban Violence: Some Implications of Laboratory Studies of Frustration and Aggression," in L. H. Masotti, and D. Bowen (eds.), *Riots and Rebellion: Civil Violence in the Urban Community.* Beverly Hills: Sage.
Bertalanffy, L. Von
1968 *General Systems Theory.* New York: George Braziller.
Birch D., and J. Veroff
1966 *Motivation: A Study of Action.* Belmont, Ca.: Brooks Cale.
Blalock, Hubert
1957 "Percent Non-White and Discrimination in the South." *American Sociological Review* 22: 677-682.
Blalock, H. M.
1962 "Evaluating Relative Importance of Variables." *American Sociological Review* 26: 866-874.
1965 *Causal Inference in Non-Experimental Research.* Chapel Hill: University of North Carolina Press.
1969 *Theory Construction: From Verbal to Mathematical Formulation.* Englewood Cliffs, N.J.: Prentice-Hall.
1972 *Social Statistics.* New York: McGraw-Hill.
Blatt, M.
1970 *The Effects of Classroom Discussion upon Children's Moral Judgment.* Unpublished doctoral dissertation, University of Chicago.
Block, J. H., N. Haan, and M. B. Smith
1969 "Socialization Correlates of Students' Activism." *Journal of Social Issues* 25: 143-178.
Bloombaum, Milton
1968 "The Conditions Underlying Race Riots." *American Sociological Review* 33: 76-91.
Blumer, Herbert
1946 "Elementary Collective Behavior," pp. 170-193, in A. M. Lee (ed.), *New Outline of Principles of Sociology.* New York: Barnes and Noble.
1971 "Elementary Collective Grouping," Chaps. 8-10, in A. M. Lee (ed.), *Principles of Sociology.*

Bogdan, Bovert
1969 "Youth Clubs in a West African City," pp. 223-239, in Paul Meadows and Ephraim Mizrucki (eds.), *Urbanism, Urbanization and Change: Comparative Perspectives.* Reading, Mass.: Addison-Wesley Publishing Co.

Bohannan, L.
1958 "Political Aspects of Tiv Social Organization," pp. 33-66, in J. Middleton, and D. Tart (eds.), *Tribes Without Rulers.* London: Routledge & Kegan Paul.

Bohrnstedt, George W.
1969 "Quick Method for Determining the Reliability and Validity of Multiple-Item Scales." *American Sociological Review* 34: 542-548.

Brentano, Lujo
1916 *Die Anfänge der Modernen Kapitalismus.* München: K. B. Akademie der Wissenschaften.

Breton, Albert, and Breton, Raymond
1961 "An Economic Theory of Social Movements." *American Economic Review* 59: 198-205.

Brinton, C.
1965 *The Anatomy of Revolution.* Englewood Cliffs, N.J.: Prentice-Hall.
1969 *The Changing Societies.* New Haven, Conn.: Yale University Press.

Brisset, Dennis
1968 "Collective Behavior: The Sense of a Rubric." *American Journal of Sociology* 74: 70-78.

Brooks, Russell R. Dynes, and E. L. Quarantelli
1972 "Police Department Planning for Civil Disturbances: Organizational Factors Involved in Changes," pp. 76-88, in Freda Adler, and G. O. H. Muellers (eds.), *Politics, Crime and the International Scene.* San Juan, P.R.: North South Center Press.

Brown, Roger
1965 *Social Psychology.* New York: Free Press.

Broyles, J. Allen
1963 "The John Birch Society: A Movement of Social Protest of the Radical Right." *Journal of Social Issues* 19: 51-62.

Buck, Gary, and Alvin L. Jacobson
1968 "Social Evaluation and Structural Functional Analysis: An Empirical Test." *American Sociological Review* 33: 343-355.

Buckley, W.
1967 *Sociology and Modern Systems Theory.* Englewood Cliffs, N.J.: Prentice-Hall.

Busia, K. A.
1950 *Social Survey of Sekondi-Takoradi Accra.* Gold Coast: Government Printer.

Bwy, D. P.
1968 "Political Instability in Latin America: The Cross-Cultural Test of a Causal Model." *Latin American Research Review* 3: 17-66.

Campbell, A., G. Gurin, and W. E. Miller
1954 *The Voter Decides.* Evanston, Ill.: Row Peterson.

Campbell, A., P. E. Converse, W. E. Miller, and D. E. Stoker
1960 *The American Voter.* New York: Wiley.

Campbell, E. Q., and T. F. Pettigrew
1959   *Christians in Racial Crisis.* Washington, D.C.: Public Affairs.
Campbell, O.
1965   "Variations and Selective Retention in Socio-Cultural Tradition,"
       pp. 19-49, in H. R. Barringer, G. L. Blankston, and R. W. Mack
       (eds.), *Social Change in Developing Areas.* Cambridge: Schinkman.
Canetti, Elias
1966   *Crowds and Power.* New York: Viking Press.
Cantril, Hadley
1973   *The Psychology of Social Movements.* New York: Robert E. Krieger
       Publishing Company.
Caplow, Theodore
1969   *Two Against One: Coalitions in Triads.* Englewood Cliffs, N.J.:
       Prentice-Hall.
Caser, Lewis A.
1956   *Function of Social Conflict.* New York: Free Press.
CELAP (Latin American Population Center)
1966- *Encuesta sobre la Familia y la Fecundidad en Poblaciones*
  67   *Marginales del Gran Santiago.* Santiago: CELAP/DESAL.
Chenery, H. B.
1960   "Patterns of Industrial Growth." *American Economic Review* 50:
       663-664.
Chernoff, Herman, and Lincoln E. Moses
1959   *Elementary Decision Theory.* New York: John Wiley.
Child, Irvin L., Thomas Storm, and Joseph Veroff
1958   "Achievement Themes in Folk Tales Related to Socialization Prac-
       tice," pp. 479-492, in John W. Atkinson (ed.), *Motive in Fantasy,
       Action and Sociology, A Method of Assessment and Study.* New York:
       D. Van Nostrand Co.
Christ, C. L.
1966   *Econometric Models and Methods.* New York: John Wiley.
Christie, R., J. Havel, and B. Seidenberg
1958   "Is the F Scale Irreversible?" *Journal of Abnormal and Social Psy-
       chology* 56: 143-159.
Clark, Terry N.
1969   *On Communication and Social Influence.* Chicago: University of
       Chicago Press.
1971   "Community Structure, Decision-Making, Budget Expenditures, and
       Urban Renewal in 51 American Communities," pp. 293-313, in
       Charles M. Bonglan, Terry N. Clark, and Robert L. Lineberry (eds.),
       Community Politics. New York: Free Press.
Clark, H. D., and A. Kornberger
1970   "A Note on Social Cleavages and Democratic Performance." *Com-
       parative Political Studies* 4: 69-90.
Clement, Pierre
1956   "Social Patterns of Urban Life," pp. 368-494, in Daryll Forde (ed.),
       *Social Implications of Industrialization and Urbanization in Africa
       South of the Sahara.* Paris: United Nations Educational, Scientific
       and Cultural Organization.

Cloward, Richard, and Lloyd Oklin
   1960   *Delinquency and Opportunity.* Glencoe, Ill.: The Free Press.
Cofer, Charles N., and Mortimer Appley
   1968   *Motivation: Theory and Research.* New York: John Wiley.
Cohen, Albert K.
   1955   *Delinquent Boys.* Glencoe, Ill.: The Free Press.
Cohen, Jerry, and William S. Murphy
   1966   *Burn Baby Burn!* New York: Avon Books.
Coleman, James S.
   1957   *Community Conflict.* Glencoe, Ill.: The Free Press.
   1968   "The Mathematical Study of Change," in N. M. Blalock, Jr., and
          A. B. Blalock (eds.), *Methodology in Social Research.* New York:
          McGraw-Hill.
Congressional Quarterly Service
   1967   *Urban Problems and Civil Disorder.* Special Report 36: 3-6.
Conot, Robert
   1968   *Rivers of Blood, Years of Darkness.* New York: Bantam.
Cooper, M. N.
   1974   "Reinterpretation of the Causes of Turmoil: The Effects of Culture
          and Modernity." *Comparative Political Studies* 7: 267-291.
CORHABIT (Housing Corporation of the Government of Chile)
   1969   *Encuesta Nacional Socio-Economica de Poblaciones Marginales.*
          Santiago: Consejeria Nacional de Promacion Popular.
Cummings, E., and W. Henry
   1961   *Growing Old.* New York: Basic Books.
Currie, Elliot, and Jerome Skolnick
   1972   "A Critical Note on Conceptions of Collective Behavior," pp. 60-71,
          in James F. Short, Jr., and Marvin E. Wolfgang (eds.), *Collective
          Violence.* Chicago: Aldine.
Cutright, P. E.
   1963a "National Political Development, Measurement and Analysis."
          American Sociology Review 28: 253-264.
   1963b "National Political Development, Social and Economic Correlates,"
          in D. Palsby et al. (eds.), *Politics and Social Life.* Boston: Houghton
          Mifflin.
Dahrendorf, F.
   1959   *Class and Class Conflict in Industrial Society.* Stanford: Stanford
          University Press.
   1967   "Conflict After Class: New Perspectives on the Theory of Social and
          Political Conflict." Third Noel Burton Lectures, University of Essex.
Dallard, J., L. Doob, N. Miller, O. Mowrer, and R. Sears
   1935   *Frustration and Aggression.* New Haven: Yale University Press.
Davies, James C.
   1962   "Toward Theory of Revolution." *American Sociological Review*
          27: 5-19.
   1969   "The J.-Curve of Rising and Declining Satisfactions as a Cause of
          Some Great Revolutions and a Contained Rebellion," pp. 690-
          730, in H. D. Graham, and T. R. Gurr (eds.), *Violence in America.*
          New York: Bantam.
   1971   *When Men Revolt and Why.* New York: Free Press.

De Fleur, Melvin L.
  1966 "Mass Communication and Social Change." *Social Forces* 44:
         314-365.
Demerath, Nicholas J., and Richard A. Peterson
  1968 *System, Change and Conflict, A Reader on Contemporary Socio-
         logical Theory and Debate over Functionalism.* New York: Free
         Press.
Denzin, Norman K.
  1968 "Collective Behavior in Total Institution." *Social Problems* 15:
         353-365.
De Schweinitz, C., Jr.
  1970 "On Measuring Political Performance." *Comparative Political
         Studies* 2: 503-511.
de Tocqueville, Alexis
  1946 *Democracy in America,* Vol. II. New York: Alfred A. Knopf.
  1955 *The Old Regime and the French Revolution.* Trans. by Stuart
         Gilbert. Garden City, New York: Doubleday and Co., Inc.
Deutsch, K. W.
  1953 *Nationalism and Social Communication.* New York: Wiley.
  1960 "Social Mobilization and Political Development." *American Political
         Science Review* 55: 34-57.
  1961 "Social Mobilization and Political Development." *American Political
         Science Review* 55: 493-514.
Downes, Bryan T.
  1968 "The Social Characteristics of Riot Cities: A Comparative Study."
         Social Science Quarterly 49: 504-520.
  1970 "A Critical Reexamination of the Social and Political Characteristics
         of Riot Cities." *Social Science Quarterly* 51: 349-360.
Drabek, Thomas, and E. L. Quarantelli
  1967 "Scapegoats, Villains and Disaster." *Trans-Action* 4: 12-17.
Duncan, O. D.
  1964 "Social Organization and the Ecosystem," pp. 37-82, in R. E. L.
         Faus (ed.), *Handbook of Modern Sociology.* Chicago: Rand-
         McNally.
  1966 "Methodological Issues in the Analysis of Social Mobility," pp. 51-
         58, in Neil J. Smelser, and S. M. Lipset (eds.), *Social Structure and
         Mobility in Economic Development.* Chicago: Aldine.
Durkheim, Emile
  1947a *The Division of Labor in Society.* George Simpson, trans. Glencoe,
         Ill.: The Free Press.
  1947b *The Elementary Forms of the Religious Life.* Joseph W. Swain,
         trans. Glencoe, Ill.: The Free Press.
Dynes, Russell, and E. L. Quarantelli
  1963 "Urban and Civil Disturbances." *American Behavioral Scientist* 16:
         303-440.
Dynes, Russell, E. L. Quarantelli, and James L. Ross
  1972 *Police Perspectives and Behavior in a Campus Disturbance.* Wash-
         ington: LEAA.
Ebony
  1969 "The Unity of Blackness." *Ebony* 24: 2.

ECLA (United Nations Economic Council for Latin America)
  1963   *La Participacion de las Poblaciones Marginales en el Crecimento Urbano.* Santiago: Latin Conference on Infancy and Youth.
Eckstein, H.
  1968   "Introduction: Toward the Theoretical Study of Internal Wars," pp. 1-32, in H. Eckstein (ed.), *Internal Wars, Problems and Approaches.* New York: Free Press.
Eibe, W.
  1968   "Social Involvement and Political Activity: A Replication and Elaboration." *American Sociological Review* 29: 189-226.
Eisenstadt, S. N.
  1959   "Primitive Political Systems: A Preliminary Analysis." *American Anthropologist* 61: 200-220.
  1964   "Institutionalization and Change." *American Sociological Review* 29: 235-247.
  1966   *Modernization: Protest and Change.* New York: Prentice-Hall.
Evans-Pritchard, E. E.
  1940   *The Ruler.* Oxford: Clarendon Press.
Fanfani, A.
  1930   *Catholicism, Protestantism and Capitalism.* London: Sheed and Ward.
Fanon, F.
  1963   *The Wretched of the Earth.* New York: Grove.
Feierabend, I. K., and R. L. Feierabend
  1966   "Aggressive Behavior Within Polities, 1948-1962: A Cross-National Study." *Journal of Conflict Resolution* 10: 249-276.
Feierabend, I. K., R. L. Feierabend, and B. A. Nesvold
  1969   "Social Change and Political Violence: Cross-National Patterns," pp. 632-687, in H. D. Graham, and T. R. Gurr (eds.), *Violence in America.* New York: Bantam.
Firestone, J. M.
  1971   "The Causes of Urban Riots: A New Approach and a Causal Model." State University of New York at Binghamton Center for Comparative Political Research Paper 12.
  1972a "A New Approach to Dynamics of Urban Civil Strife: Conceptual Framework and Causal Model." State University of New York at Binghamton. (Unpublished manuscript.)
  1972b "Some Theoretical Issues in Research on Urban Riots." State University of New York at Binghamton. (Unpublished manuscript.)
  1972c "Theory of Riot Process." *The American Behavioral Scientist* 15: 859-882.
Fisher, Belton M.
  1966   *The Economics of Delinquency.* Chicago: Quadrangle Books.
Fisher, Charles S.
  1972   "Observing a Crowd: The Structure and Descriptions of Protest Demonstrations."
Fishkin, J., K. Keniston, and C. MacKinnon
  1973   "Moral Reasoning and Political Ideology." *Journal of Personality and Social Psychology* 27: 109-119.

Fishman, J. A., V. C. Naherng, J. E. Hoffman, and R. G. Hayden
1966 *Language Loyalty in the United States.* The Hague: Mouton.
Fitzpatrick, John, J. Rick Ponting, and E. L. Quarantelli
1973 "A Social Control Organizational Perspective of Four Disturbances."
Columbus, Ohio: Disaster Research Center Preliminary Paper, No. 8.
Fogelson, Robert M., and Robert Hill
1968 "Who Riots? A Study of Participation in the 1967 Riots," pp. 217-
248, in *Supplementary Studies for the National Advisory Commission on Civil Disorders.* Washington, D.C.: U.S. Printing Office.
Fogelson, Robert M.
1971 *Violence in Protest.* New York: Doubleday.
Form, W., and J. A. Geschwender
1962 "Social Reference Basis of Job Satisfaction." *American Sociology
Review* 27: 228-237.
Fortes, M.
1940 "The Political Systems of the Tollensi of the Northern Territories of
the Gold Coast," pp. 239-271, in M. Fortes, and E. E. Evans-
Pritchard (eds.), *African Political Systems.* London: Oxford Uni-
versity Press.
Free, L. A.
1971 "Gauging Threshold of Frustration," in J. C. Davies (ed.), *When
Men Revolt and Why.* New York: Free Press.
Freud, Sigmund
1957 "Group Psychology and the Analysis of the Ego," pp. 169-209, in
A General Selection of the Works of Sigmund Freud. New York:
Anchor Books.
Fried, Robert C.
1967 "Urbanization and Italian Politics." *Journal of Politics* 29: 509-530.
Friedrich, P.
1972 "Political Homicide in Rural Mexico," in I. K. Feierabend et al.
(eds.), *Anger, Violence and Politics.* Englewood Cliffs, N.J.:
Prentice-Hall.
Fromm, Erich
1963 *Escape from Freedom.* New York: Holt, Rinehart and Winston.
Galliher, John
1971 "Explanations of Police Behavior, A Critical Review and Analysis."
Sociological Quarterly 12: 308-318.
Gallup Opinion Index
1969 Report No. 47. Princeton, N.J.
Gamson, William A.
1968 *Power and Discontent.* Homewood, Ill.: Dorsey.
Gastil, R. D.
1971 "Homicide and Regional Authors of Violence." *American Sociology
Review* 36: 412-427.
Gerlach, L. P.
1968 "People, Power, Change." A 16 mm sound/color film. University of
Minnesota.Audio-Visual.
1970a *People, Powers, Change: Movements of Social Transformation.*
Indianapolis: Bobbs-Merrill.

1970b "Corporate Groups and Movement Networks in Urban America." *Anthropological Quarterly* 43: 123-145.

1970c "People Eco-Action." A 16 mm sound/color film. University of Minnesota. Audio-Visual.

1970d "Wit, Wisdom and Woe." *Natural History.* October.

1970e "You and the Ecology Movement." *Natural History.* June/July.

1971 "Movements of Revolutionary Change: Some Structural Characteristics." *The American Behavioral Scientist* 14: 812-36.

1976 "Eco-Gemini." *Natural History.* May.

Gerlach, L. P., and V. H. Hine
1970 "The Social Organization of a Movement of Revolutionary Change: Case Study Black Power," in N. Whitten, Jr., and J. Szwed (eds.), *Afro-American Anthropology: Contemporary Perspectives.* New York: Free Press.

Germani, Gino
1966 "Social and Political Consequences of Mobility," pp. 368-394, in N. J. Smelser and Seymour M. Lipset (eds.), *Social Structure and Mobility in Economic Development.* Chicago: Aldine.

Geschwender, J. A.
1968 "Explorations in the Theory of Social Movements and Revolutions." *Social Forces* 47: 127-135.

Gilbert, Ben
1968 *Ten Blocks from the White House.* New York: Praeger.

Gluckman, M.
1959 *Political Institutions: The Institution of Primitive Sociology.* Glencoe, Ill.: The Free Press.

Goffman, Erving
1959 *The Presentation of Self in Everyday Life.* Garden City: Doubleday Anchor Books.

Goldberger, Arthur S.
1963 *Econometric Theory.* New York: Wiley International Association of Chiefs with Justice for All: A Guide for Law Enforcement Officers. Washington, D.C.: International Association of Chiefs of Police.

Goldrich, Daniel
1965 "Toward the Comparative Study of Politicization in Latin America," pp. 361-378, in D. Heath, and R. Adams (eds.), *Contemporary Culture and Societies in Latin America.* New York: Random House.

Goldrich, Daniel, Raymond B. Pratt, and C. R. Schuller
1967 "The Political Integration of Lower Class Urban Settlements in Chile and Peru." *Studies in International Comparative Development* 3: 1-22.

Gould, Julius, and William L. Kalb
1968 *A Dictionary of the Social Sciences.* New York: Free Press.

Greer, Thomas H.
1949 *American Social Reform Movements: Their Pattern Since 1865.* Englewood Cliffs, N.J.: Prentice-Hall.

Grindstaff, C. F.
1968 "The Negro, Urbanization, and Relative Deprivation in the Deep South." *Social Problems* 15: 342-352.

Grimshaw, Allen D.
  1968   "Three Views of Urban Violence, Civil Disturbance, Racial Revolt,
         Class Assault." *American Behavioral Scientist* 4: 2-7.
Grinshaw, M.
  1970   Article in *Annals of American Academy of Political and Social
         Science*. September, pp. 9-20.
Gude, E.
  1972   "Political Violence in Venezuela 1958-1964," pp. 259-273, in J. C.
         Davies (ed.), *When Men Revolt and Why*. New York: Free Press.
Guevara, Ernesto
  1970   "Message to the Latin American Solidarity Organization (Havana),"
         pp. 607-620, in L. L. Horowitz, J. de Castro, and J. Geressi (eds.),
         Latin American Radicalism. New York: Random House.
Gurr, T. R.
  1966   *New Error Compensated Measures for Comparing Nations*. Prince-
         ton: Princeton University Center for International Studies.
  1968   "A Causal Model of Civil Strife: A Comparative Analysis Using New
         Indices." *American Political Science Review* 62: 1104-1124.
  1969   "A Comparative Survey of Civil Strife," pp. 443-486, in H. D.
         Graham, and T. R. Gurr (eds.), *Violence in America*. New York:
         Bantam.
  1970a "Psychological Factors in Civil Violence." *World Politics* 20: 245-
         278.
  1970b "Sources of Rebellion in Western Societies: Some Quantitative
         Evidence." *Annals of American Academy of Political Science Review*
         62: 128-144.
  1970c *Why Men Rebel*. Princeton, N.J.: Princeton University Press.
  1974   *Nations Divided: Patterns and Causes of Political Conflict in the
         1960s*.
Gurr, T. R., and C. Ruttenberg
  1971   "The Conditions of Civil Violence: First Test of a Causal Model,"
         in J. Gillespie, and B. Nesvold (eds.), *Macro-Quantitative Analysis*.
         Beverly Hills: Sage.
Gusfield, Joseph R.
  1962   "Mass Society and Extremist Politics." *American Sociology Review*
         27: 19-30.
Haan, N.
  1965   "Coping and Defense Mechanisms Related to Personality Inven-
         tories." *Journal of Consulting Psychology* 29: 373-378.
  1971   "Moral Redefinition in the Family as the Fundamental Aspect of
         the Generational Gap." *Youth and Society* 2: 259-284.
  1974   "Changes in Young Adults after Peace Corps Experience: Political-
         Social Views, Moral Reasoning, and Perceptions of Self and Par-
         ents." *Journal of Youth and Adolescence* 3: 177-194.
  1975   "Hypothetical and Actual Moral Reasoning in a Situation of Civil
         Disobedience." *Journal of Personality and Social Psychology* 32:
         255-270.
Haan, N., M. B. Smith, and J. H. Block
  1968   "Moral Reasoning of Young Adults: Political-Social Behavior,

Family Background, and Personality Correlates." *Journal of Personality and Social Psychology* 10: 183-201.

Haan, N., J. Stroud, and C. Holstein
1973 "Moral and Ego Stages in Relationship to Ego Problems: A Study of 'Hippies.'" *Journal of Personality* 41: 596-612.

Haas, M.
1970 "Dimensional Analysis in Cross-National Research." *Comparative Political Studies* 3: 3-35.

Harbison, F., and C. A. Myers
1964 *Education, Manpower and Economic Growth.* New York: McGraw-Hill.

Hare, M.
1968 "New Role for Uncle Toms." *Negro Digest* 18, 10: 14-19.

Hauser, Phillip M.
1959 "Cultural and Personal Obstacles to Economic Development in the Less Developed Areas." *Human Organization* 18: 78-84.

Hayden, Thomas
1967 *Rebellion in Newark.* New York: Vintage.

Heberle, Rudolph
1951 *Social Movements.* New York: Appleton-Century Crofts.

Hirschman, A. O.
1964 *The Strategy of Economic Development.* New Haven, Conn.: Yale University Press.

Hoffer, Eric
1958 *The True Believer; Thoughts on the Nature of Mass Movements.* New York: Mentor Books.
1966 *The True Believer.* New York: Harper & Row.

Homans, George C.
1958 "Social Behavior as Exchange." *American Journal of Sociology* 63: 597-606.
1961 *Social Behavior: Its Elementary Forms.* New York: Harcourt, Brace and World.
1964 "Bringing Men Back In." *American Sociological Review.* 29: 809-818.

Hopper, Rex D.
1950 "The Revolutionary Process: A Frame of Reference for the Study of Revolutionary Movements." *Social Forces* 28: 270-279.

Hundley, James R.
1969 "The Dynamics of Recent Ghetto Riots," pp. 480-492, in Robert Evans (ed.), *Readings in Collective Behavior.* Chicago: Rand McNally.

Hurwitz, L.
1971 "Democratic Political Stability: Some Traditional Hypotheses Re-examined." *Comparative Political Studies* 4: 476-489.

Hyman, Herbert
1967 *Survey Design and Analysis.* New York: Free Press.

Hyman, H. H., and P. B. Sheatsley
1964 "Attitudes Toward Desegregation." *Scientific American* 211: 2-9.

INAP (National Institute of Communal Action of Chile)
1968 *La Junta de Vecinor, Principios de una Administracion Eficiente.* Santiago: INAP, Censos Para Dirigentes.

Inkeles, Alice
1966 "The Modernization of Man," pp. 138-150, in Myron Weiner (ed.), *The Dynamics of Growth.* New York: Basic Books.
International City Managers Association
1967 *The Municipal Yearbook.* Chicago.
Johnston, J.
1963 *Econometric Methods.* New York: McGraw-Hill.
Jonassen, Christen T.
1947 "The Proletariat Ethic and the Spirit of Capitalism in Norway." *American Sociological Review* 12: 676-685.
1973 "Ethical Systems and Economic Development." *Southeast Asian Journal of Social Science* 1: 117-131.
1974 "Functions of Voluntary Associations in Developing Nations." *Rural Sociology* 39: 529-535.
Jones, Edward E.
1964 *Ingratiation, A Social Psychological Analysis.* New York: Appleton-Century Crofts.
Kahl, Joseph A.
1959 "Some Social Concomitants of Industrialization and Urbanization." *Human Organization* 18: 53-74.
1969 *The Measurement of Modernism: A Study of Values in Brazil and Mexico.* Austin: University of Texas Press.
Kapsis, Robert et al.
1970 *The Reconstruction of a Riot: A Case Study of Community Tensions and Civil Disorder.* Waltham, Mass.: Brandeis University.
Kapytoff, I.
1964 "Classification of Religious Movements: Analytical and Synthetic." *Proceedings of the 1964 Annual Spring Meeting of the American Ethnological Society.* Seattle: University of Washington Press.
Keasey, C. B.
1973 "Experimentally Induced Changes in Moral Opinions and Reasoning." *Journal of Personality and Social Psychology* 26: 30-38.
Kennedy, Robert E., Jr.
1962 "The Protestant Ethic and the Poor." *The American Journal of Sociology* 28: 11-20.
Kerner Commission
(See National Advisory Commission on Civil Disorder, 1968.)
Kerner, Otto
1968 *Report of the National Advisory Commission on Civil Disorders.* New York: Bantam.
Killian, L.
1964 "Social Movements," pp. 426-455, in R. E. L. Faris (ed.), *Handbook of Modern Sociology.* Chicago: Rand McNally.
King, C. Wendell
1956 *Social Movements in the United States.* New York: Random House.
Klapper, J. T.
1960 *The Effects of Mass Communication.* New York: Free Press.
Kluckhohn, F. R., and F. L. Stradtveck
1961 *Variations in Value Orientations.* Evanston, Ill.: Harper & Row.
Kmenta, Jan
1971 *Elements of Econometrics.* New York: Macmillan.

Knopf, Terry Ann
  1969   *Youth Patrols: An Experiment in Community Participation.* Waltham, Mass.: Brandeis University.
Kohlberg, L. A.
  1969   "Cognitive Developmental Approach to Socialization," pp. 93-120, in D. Goslin (ed.), *Handbook of Socialization.* New York: Rand McNally.
Kohlberg, L., and R. Kramer
  1969   "Continuities and Discontinuities in Childhood and Adult Moral Development." *Human Development* 12: 93-120.
Kohlberg, L., P. Scharf, and J. Hickey
  1973   "Structure of the Prison: A Theory and Intervention." *The Prison Journal* 51: 3-14.
Kornhauser, William
  1959   *The Politics of Mass Society.* New York: Free Press.
Kuhn, T. S.
  1962   *The Structure of Scientific Revolution.* Chicago: University of Chicago Press.
Kuznets, S.
  1963   "Qualitative Aspects of the Economic Growth of Nations. Part VIII: Distribution of Income by Size."
Laidler, Harry W.
  1944   *Social-Economic Movements.* New York: Thomas Y. Crowell.
Landau, M.
  1969   "Redundancy, Rationality, and the Problem of Duplication and Overlapping." *Public Administration Review* 24: 346-358.
Lang, Kurt, and Gladys Engel Lang
  1961   *Collective Dynamics.* New York: Thomas Y. Crowell.
Langer, J.
  1969   "Disequilibrium as a Source of Development," in P. Mussen, J. Langer, and M. Covington (eds.), *Issues and Trends in Developmental Psychology.* New York: Holt, Rinehart & Winston.
Lasswell, H. D., and A. Kaplan
  1950   *Power and Society.* New Haven, Conn.: Yale University Press.
Lazarsfeld, P. F., B. Berelson, and H. Gaudet
  1948   *The People's Choice.* New York: Columbia University Press.
LeBon, Gustave
  1960   *The Crowd.* New York: Viking Press.
Lemberg Center for the Study of Violence
  1968a *Compilation of the 1967 Disorders.* Brandeis University. (Unpublished manuscript.)
  1968b *Riot Data Review.* Nos. 1-3. Brandeis University. (Mimeographed manuscript.)
Lenin, Vladimir I.
  1929   *What Is To Be Done?* New York: International Publishers.
Lerner, D.
  1958   *The Passing of Traditional Society.* New York: Free Press.
  1963   "Toward a Communication Theory of Modernization," pp. 327-350, in L. Pye (ed.), *Communication and Political Development.* Princeton, N.J.: Princeton University Press.

Lewin, K.
1947 "Frontier in Group Dynamics: Concept, Method and Reality in Social Science; Social Equilibrium and Social Change." *Human Relations* 1: 5-44.
Lewis, I. M.
1961 *A Pastoral Democracy: A Study of Pastoralism and Politics among the Northern Somali of the Horn of Africa.* London: Oxford University Press.
Lidz, Theodore, Stephen Fleck, and Alice R. Cornelius
1965 *Schizophrenia and the Family.* New York: International Universities Press.
Lieberson, Stanley, and Arnold K. Silverman
1965 "The Precipitants and Underlying Conditions of Race Riots." *American Sociological Review* 30: 887-898.
Life Magazine
1971 "Persons of Interest." 26: 21-27.
Lin, N.
1975 "McIntire March: A Study of Recruitment and Commitment." *Public Opinion Quarterly* 38: 562-573.
Lipset, Seymour N.
1959 "Some Social Requisites of Democracy: Economic Development and Political Legitimacy." *American Political Science Review* 53: 69-109.
1963 *Political Man.* Garden City, N.Y.: Anchor Books.
1969 *Rebellion in the University.* Boston: Little Brown.
Lipt, George K.
1949 *Human Behavior and the Principle of Least Effort: An Introduction to Human Ecology.* Cambridge: Addison-Wesley.
Little, Kenneth
1957 "The Role of Voluntary Associations in West African Urbanization." *American Anthropologist* 59: 579-596.
Llewellyn, Karl N.
1930 "Agency," pp. 483-485, in *Encyclopedia of the Social Sciences,* Vol. I. New York: Macmillan.
Locke, Hubert G.
1969 *The Detroit Riot of 1967.* Detroit: Wayne State University Press.
Lofland, John
1966 *Doomsday Cult.* Englewood Cliffs, N.J.: Prentice-Hall.
Lopreato, Joseph
"Upward Social Mobility and Political Orientation." *American Sociological Review* 32: 586-592.
Lowenthal, M. F., and D. Boler
1963 "Voluntary vs. Involuntary Social Withdrawal." *Journal of Gerontology* 20: 363-371.
Lupsha, P. A.
1971 "Explanation of Political Violence: Some Psychological Theories vs. Indignation." *Politics and Society* 2: 89-194.
Lyons, G.
1965 "The Police Demonstration: A Survey of Participants," in S. M. Lipset, and S. S. Wolin (eds.), *The Berkeley Student Revolt: Facts and Interpretation.* Garden City, N.Y.: Anchor Books.

Maddox, G. L.
  1965 "Fact from Artifact: Evidence Bearing on Disengagement Theory from the Duke Geriatrics Project." *Human Development* 8: 117-130.
Malinowski, Bronislaw
  1939 "The Group and the Individual in Functional Analysis." *American Journal of Sociology* 44: 938-964.
Mangin, William A.
  1967 "Latin American Squatter Settlements: A Problem and a Solution." *Latin American Research Review* 2: 65-68.
Manning, Peter K.
  1972 "Observing the Police," pp. 213-268, in Jack Douglas (ed.), *Research on Deviance*. New York: Random House.
Marugama, M.
  1968 "The Second Cybernetics: Deviation Amplifying Mutual Causal Processes." *American Scientist* 51.2: 164-179.
Marx, G. T.
  1970 "Issueless Riots," pp. 21-33, in M. Wolfgang, and J. F. Short (eds.), *Collective Violence, Annals of the American Academy of Political and Social Science*. Philadelphia: American Academy of Political and Social Science.
Mattick, Hans W.
  1968 "Form and Content of Recent Riots." *Midway* 9: 3-32.
Mayer, A.
  1966 "The Significance of Quasi-Group in the Study of Complex Societies: The Social Anthropology of Complex Societies," pp. 97-119, in M. P. Banton (ed.), *Association of Social Anthropologists Monograph*. New York: Frederick A. Praeger.
McClelland, David C.
  1961 *The Achieving Society*. New York: D. Van Nostrand Co.
  1966 "The Impulse to Modernization," pp. 28-39 in Myron Weiner (ed.), *Modernization: The Dynamics of Growth*. New York: Basic Books.
McClelland, David C., John W. Atkinson, Russell A. Clark, and Edgar L. Lowell
  1953 *The Achievement Motive*. New York: Appleton-Century-Crofts.
McGuire, W. J.
  1969 "Nature of Attitudes and Attitude Change," pp. 136-314, in G. Lindzey, and E. Aronson (eds.), *Handbook of Social Psychology* (second edition). Reading, Mass.: Addison-Wesley Publishing Co.
McKinney, J. C., and L. B. Boueque
  1971 "The Changing South: National Incorporation of a Region." *American Sociological Review* 36: 395-412.
Mcphail, Clark
  1969 "Student Walkout: A Fortuitous Examination of Elementary Collective Behavior." *Social Problems* 16: 441-455.
Meadows, Paul, and Ephraim H. Mizrucki
  1969 *Urbanism, Urbanization and Change: Comparative Perspectives*. Reading, Mass.: Addison-Wesley Publishing Co.
Mecklin, J. M.
  1970 "Fire and Steel for Palestine."
Merton, Robert K.
  1938 "Social Structure and Anomie." *American Sociological Review* 3: 672-682.

1957 *Theory and Social Structure* (revised edition). Glencoe, Ill.: The Free Press.
1963 *Social Theory and Social Structure.* New York: Free Press.

Meyer, P.
1967 *The Detroit Free Press.* August 20: 11.

Middleton, J., and D. Tart
1958 "Introduction," in *Tribes Without Rulers.* London: Routledge & Kegan Paul.

Midlarsky, M., and R. Tanter
1967 "Toward a Theory of Political Instability in Latin America." *Journal of Peace Research* 3: 209-227.

Milbraith, L. W.
1965 *Political Participation.* Chicago: Rand McNally.

Milgram, Stanley, and Hans Toch
1969 "Collective Behavior: Crowds and Social Movements," pp. 507-610, in Gardner Lindzey, and Elliott Aronson (eds.), *Handbook of Social Psychology* (second edition). Reading, Mass.: Addison-Wesley.

Miller, J. A.
1965 "Living Systems, Basic Concepts, Structure and Process: Cross-Level Hypotheses." *Behavioral Science* 10: 337-379.

Mitchell, E. J.
1969 "Some Econometrics of the Huk Rebellion." *American Political Science Review* 63: 1159-1171.

Mohr, Lawrence B.
1969 "Determinants of Innovation in Organizations." *American Political Science Review* 63: 111-126.

Morgan, W. R., and T. N. Clark
1973 "Causes of Racial Disorders: A Grievance-Level Explanation." *American Sociological Review* 38: 611-624.

Morgan, W. R., and Jack Sawyer
1967 "Bargaining, Expectations, and the Preference for Equality over Equity." *Journal of Personality and Social Psychology* 6: 139-149.

Morrison, Denton E.
1971 "Some Notes Toward Theory on Relative Deprivation, Social Movements, and Social Change." *American Behavioral Scientist* 14: 675-690.

Morrison, D. E., and A. Steeves
1967 "Deprivation, Discontent, and Social Movement Participation: Evidence on a Contemporary Farmers' Movement, the NFO." *Rural Sociology* 32: 414-434.

Municipal Yearbook
1966 Chicago: International City Manager's Association.

Murdock, George P.
1967 "Ethnographic Atlas." *Ethnology* 6: 109-236.

Myers, F. E.
1971 "Civil Disobediance and Organizational Change: The British Committee of 100." *Political Science Quarterly* 86: 92-112.

Myrdal, Gunnar
1968 *Asian Drama: An Inquiry into the Poverty of Nations.* New York: Pantheon.

Nardin, T.
1971 "Theories of Conflict Management." *Peace Research Review* 4.

National Advisory Commission on Civil Disorders
  1968   *A Report [by the Kerner Commission].* Washington, D.C.: U.S.
         Government Printing Office.
  1968   *Final Report.* New York: Bantam.
Nelson, Joan M.
  1969   *Migrants, Urban Poverty and Instability in Developing Nations.*
         Cambridge, Mass.: Harvard University Center for International
         Affairs.
Nesvold, B.
  1969   "Scalogram Analysis of Political Violence." *Comparative Political
         Studies* 2: 172-174.
Newsweek
  1970   "The FBI's Toughest Foes: The Kids." October 26, 22-23.
  1971   "The Decline and Fall of the Panthers." March 22, 26-28.
Nieburg, H. L.
  1962   "The Threat of Violence and Social Change." *American Political
         Science Review* 66: 965-973.
  1969   *Political Violence: The Behavioral Process.* New York: St. Martin's.
Nisbet, R. A.
  1970   "Developmentalism, A Critical Approach," in J. C. McKinney, and
         E. A. Tiryakian (eds.), *Theoretical Sociology.* New York: Appleton-
         Century-Crofts.
Odum, H.
  1967   *Southern Regions of the United States.* Chapel Hill: University of
         North Carolina Press.
Olson, M.
  1965   *The Logic of Collective Actions.* Cambridge, Mass.: Harvard Uni-
         versity Press.
Paige, J. M.
  1971   "Political Orientation and Riot Participation." *American Sociologi-
         cal Review* 36: 810-820.
Park, Robert E., and Ernest W. Burgess
  1924   *Introduction to the Science of Sociology.* Chicago: University of
         Chicago Press.
Parsons, Talcott
  1957   *Essays in Sociological Theory* (revised edition). Glencoe, Ill.: The
         Free Press.
  1960   *Structure and Process in Modern Societies.* New York: Free Press.
  1961   "An Outline of the Social System," pp. 36-42, in Talcott Parsons,
         Edward Shils, Kaspar D. Naegele, and Jesse R. Pitts (eds.), *Theories
         of Society,* Vol. I. New York: The Free Press of Glencoe.
  1966   *Societies: Evolutionary and Comparative Perspectives.* Englewood
         Cliffs: Prentice-Hall.
Parsons, Talcott, and Neil J. Smelser
  1956   *Economy and Society.* Glencoe, Ill.: The Free Press.
Parvin, M.
  1973   "Economic Determinants of Political Unrest: An Econometric Ap-
         proach." *The Journal of Conflict Resolution* 17: 271-296.
Petras, James, and Maurice Zeitlin
  1968   "Miners and Agrarian Radicalism," pp. 235-248, in James Petras,
         and Maurice Zeitlin (eds.), *Latin America, Reform or Revolution?*
         Greenwich, Conn.: Fawcett.

Pfautz, Harold W.
   1961 "Near-Group Theory and Collective Behavior: A Critical Reformulation." *Social Problems* 9: 167-174.
Pinard, M.
   1967 "Poverty and Political Movements." *Social Problems* 15: 250-263.
Portes, Alejandro
   1969 *Cuatro Poblaciones.* Santiago: Monograph Report to the University of Wisconsin Sociology of Development Program.
   1970 *Radicalism in the Slum: A Study of Political Attitudes in Chilean Lower-Class Settlements.* Unpublished doctoral dissertation, University of Wisconsin, Madison.
   1971 "Political Primitivism, Differential Socialization, and Lower-Class Leftist Radicalism." *American Sociological Review* 36: 820-835.
Quarantelli, E. L.
   1957 "The Behavior of Panic Participants." *Sociology and Social Research* 41: 187-194.
Quarantelli, E. L., J. Rick Ponting, and J. Fitzpatrick
   1974 "Police Department Perceptions of the Occurrence of Civil Disturbances." *Sociology and Social Research* 59: 30-38.
Quarton, G. C., T. Melnechuk, and F. O. Schmitt
   1967 *The Neurosciences.* New York: Rockefeller University Press.
Radcliffe Brown, A. R.
   1952 *Structure and Function in Primitive Societies.* Glencoe, Ill.: The Free Press.
Rokeach, M.
   1960 *The Open and Closed Mind.* New York: Basic Books. *Political and Religious Dogmatism: An Alternative to Authoritarianism.* Personality Psychology Monograph 70, No. 18.
Ransford, H. E.
   1968 "Isolation, Powerlessness, and Violence: A Study of Attitudes and Participation in the Watts Riot." *American Journal of Sociology* 73: 581-591.
Rao, C. R.
   1965 *Linear Statistical Inference and Its Applications.* New York: Wiley.
Rapoport, A.
   1968 "A Philosophical View," in J. H. Milsum (ed.), *Positive Feedback.* Oxford: Pergamon.
Richardson, L. F.
   1960a *Arms and Insecurity: A Mathematical Study of the Causes and Origins of War.* Nicolas Rashevsky, and Ernesto Trucco (eds.). Pittsburgh: Boxwood Press.
   1960b *The Statistics of Deadly Quarrels.* Pittsburgh: Boxwood Press.
Roche, John P.
   1968 "Distribution of Powers," pp. 300-307, in *International Encyclopedia of the Social Sciences,* Vol. 3. New York: Macmillan Co. and Free Press.
Rogers, Everett M., and Lynne Slenning
   1969 *Modernization among Peasants: The Impact of Communication.* New York: Holt, Rinehart and Winston.
Rosenau, J. W.
   1964 *International Aspects of Civil Strife.* Princeton: Princeton University Press.

Rosenbluth, Guillermo
1962   *Problemas Socio-Economico de la Marginalidad y la Integracion Urbana.* Santiago: University of Chile and Latin American Demographic Center.
Rudé, George
1964   *The Crowd in History.* New York: John Wiley & Sons, Inc.
Rummell, R. J.
1963   "Dimensions of Conflict Behavior Within and Between Nations." *General Systems Yearbook* 8: 1-50.
1964   *Dimensionality of Nations Project.* New Haven, Conn.: Yale University Press.
1966   "Dimensions of Conflict Behavior Within Nations, 1946-1959." *Journal of Conflict Resolution* 10: 65-73.
Russett, B. M., et al.
1964   *World Handbook of Political and Social Indicators.* New Haven, Conn.: Yale University Press.
Sahlins, Marshall R., and Elman Service
1960   *Evolution and Culture.* Ann Arbor: University of Michigan Press.
Sahlins, M. D.
1961   "The Segmentary Lineage: An Organization of Predatory Expansion." *American Anthropologist* 63: 322-345.
Samuelson, Kurt
1957   *Ekanomi och Religion.* Stockholm: Svenska Bokforlaget.
Sanders, Thomas G.
1970   "Chile—The Elections and After." *American Universities Field Staff Reports, West Coast South American Series 27.*
Schiller, H. I.
1969   *Mass Communications and American Empire.* New York: Kelly.
Schnore, Leo F., and David W. Varley
1955   "Some Concomitants of Metropolitan Size." *American Sociological Review* 20: 408-414.
Sears, D., and J. McCanahay
1967   "The Politics of Discontent." Institute of Government and Public Affairs. University of California, Los Angeles.
Shannon, Lyle W., and Magdaline Shannon
1968   "The Assimilation of Migrants to Cities," pp. 49-78, in Leo F. Schnore (ed.), *Social Science and the City.* New York: Frederick A. Praeger.
Shapiro, D., and A. Crider
1969   "Psychophysiological Approaches in Social Psychology," pp. 1-49, in G. Lindzey, and E. Aronson (eds.), *The Handbook of Social Psychology,* Vol. III (Second edition).
Sherif, M., and C. W. Sherif
1969   *Social Psychology.* New York: Harper & Row.
Shibutani, T.
1965   *Improvised News.* New York: Bobbs-Merrill.
Simmel, Georg
1902   "The Number of Members as Determining the Sociological Form of the Group." *American Journal of Sociology* 8: 1-46, 158-196.
Simon, H. A.
1957   *Models of Man: Social and Rational.* New York: John Wiley.

Singer, B. D.
1970   "Mass Media and Communication Processes in the Detroit Riot of 1967." *The Public Opinion Quarterly* 34: 236-245.
Singer, Melton
1956   "Cultural Values in India's Economic Development." *The Annals of The American Academy of Political and Social Science* 305: 81-91.
Skolnick, J. H.
1969   *The Politics of Protest: A Report to the National Commission on the Causes and Prevention of Violence.* New York: Ballantine.
Slater, Philip E., and Dori A. Slater
1965   "Maternal Ambivalence and Narcissism: A Cross-Cultural Study." *Merrill-Palmer Quarterly* 11: 241-259.
Smelser, Neil J.
1959   *Social Change in the Industrial Revolution.* Chicago: The University of Chicago Press.
1971   *Theory of Collective Behavior.* Glencoe, Ill.: The Free Press.
Smith, M. B., N. Haan, and J. H. Block
1970   "Social-Psychological Aspects of Student Activism." *Youth and Society* 1: 261-288.
Smith, O. H., and A. Inkeles
1966   "The OM Scale: A Comparative Socio-Psychological Measure of Individual Modernity." *Sociometry* 29: 353-377.
Smith, P.
1966   *The Age of the Reformation,* Vol. 2. New York and London: Collier Books. (Originally published in 1920.)
Smucker, M. J., and A. C. Zijderveld
1970   "Structure and Meaning: Implications for the Analysis of Social Change." *British Journal of Sociology* 21: 375-389.
Snow, P. G.
1966   "A Scalogram Analysis of Political Development." *American Behavioral Scientist* 9: 33-36.
Soares, Glaucio A.
1965   "Desarollo Economico y Radicalismo Politico," pp. 516-559, in J. A. Kahl (ed.), *La Industrializacion de America Latina.* Mexico, D.F.: Fondo de Cultura Economica.
Sombert, Weiner
1902   *Der Moderne Kapitalismus.* Leipzig: Duncker and Humbolt.
Sorokin, P. A.
1937   *Social and Cultural Dynamics.* New York: American Book.
Southall, A.
1959   *Social Change in Modern Africa.* London: Oxford University Press.
Spiegel, J. P.
1969a "Hostility, Aggression and Violence," in A. D. Grinshaw (ed.), *Patterns in American Racial Violence.* Chicago: Aldine.
1969b "Violence and the Social Order." *Zygon* 4: 222-237.
1970   "Campus Conflict and Professional Egos." *Trans-Action* 6: 41-50.
1971   "Theories of Violence: An Integrated Approach." *International Journal of Group Tensions* 1: 77-90.
Spilerman, Seymour
1970a "The Causes of Racial Disturbances: A Comparison of Alternative Explanations." *American Sociological Review* 35: 627-649.

1970b "Comment on Wanderer's Article on Riot and Its Correlates." *American Journal of Sociology* 75: 556-560.

1971a "The Causes of Racial Disturbances: Tests of an Explanation." *American Sociological Review* 36: 427-442.

1971b "Comments on a Comparison of Alternative Explanations." *American Sociological Review* 36: 515-517.

1975 "Forecasting Social Events," pp. 381-403, in Kenneth Land, and Seymour Spilerman (eds.), *Social Indicator Models.* New York: Russell Sage.

1976 "Structural Characteristics of Cities and the Severity of Racial Disorders." *American Sociological Review* 41: 771-793.

Stinchcombe, Arthur L.
1968 *Constructing Social Theories.* New York: Harcourt, Brace and World.

Sussman, M. B., and L. B. Burchenal
1962 "Kin Family Network: Unheralded Structure in Current Conceptualization of Family Functioning." *Marriage and Family Living* 24: 231-240.

Sutherland, Edwin H., and Donald R. Cressey
1960 *Principles of Criminology.* Philadelphia: Lippincott.

Swanson, Guy E.
1931 *Social Change, An Introduction to Explanations and Evidence.* Chicago: Scott-Foresman Co.

1959 "The Effectiveness of Decision-Making Groups." *Adult Leadership* 8: 48-52.

1967 *Religion and Regime, A Sociological Account of the Reformation.* Ann Arbor: University of Michigan Press.

1968 "On Sharing Social Psychology," pp. 20-52, in Sven Lundstedt (ed.), *Higher Education in Social Psychology.* Cleveland: Case Western Reserve University Press.

1969 *Rules of Descent, Studies in the Sociology of Parentage.* Ann Arbor: The Museum of Anthropology, The University of Michigan.

1970 "Toward Corporate Action, A Reconstruction of Elementary Collective Processes," pp. 124-144, in Tamotsu Shibutani (ed.), *Human Nature and Collective Behaviors.* Englewood Cliffs: Prentice-Hall.

1971a "Interpreting the Reformation." *Journal of Interdisciplinary History* (Spring): 419-446.

1971b "Organizational Analysis of Collectivities." *American Sociological Review* 36: 607-624.

Taeuber, Karl E., and Alma F. Taeuber
1968 *Negroes in Cities.* Chicago: Aldine.

Tanter, R.
1966 "Dimensions of Conflict Behavior Within and Between Nations, 1958-1960." *Journal of Conflict Resolution* 10: 41-65.

Tarde, Gabriel
1969 *On Communication and Social Influence.* Chicago: University of Chicago Press.

Tawney, H.
1926 *Religion and the Rise of Capitalism.* London: John Murray.

Tilly, C., and D. Snyder
1972 "Hardship and Collective Violence in France, 1830-1960." *American Sociological Review* 37:

Time
1968 "Rhetoric into Relevance." August 9, 92: 21.
1970 "Jordan: The King Takes On the Guerrillas." September 16-23.
1971 "Radicals: Destroying the Panther Myth." March 22, 19-20.

Tomlinson, T. M.
1968 "The Development of a Riot Ideology among Urban Negroes." *American Behavioral Scientist* 2: 27-31.

Troeltsch, Ernest D.
1931 *The Social Teaching of the Christian Churches.* Olive Wyon (trans.). New York: The Macmillan Co.

Turiel, E.
1966 "An Experimental Test of the Sequentiality of Developmental Stages in the Child's Moral Judgments." *Journal of Personality and Social Psychology* 3: 611-618.
1969 "Developmental Processes in the Child's Moral Thinking," in P. Mussen, J. Langer, and M. Covington (eds.), *Trends and Issues in Developmental Psychology.* New York: Holt, Rinehart and Winston.
1974 "Conflict and Transition in Adolescent Moral Development." *Child Development* 45: 17-29.

Turiel, E., and G. Rothman
1972 "The Influence of Reasoning on Behavioral Choices at Different Stages of Moral Development." *Child Development* 43: 741-756.

Turner, John F. C.
1968 "Uncontrolled Urban Settlement: Problems and Policies." *International Social Development Review* 1: 107-130.

Turner, Ralph H.
1958 "Needed Research in Collective Behavior." *Sociology and Social Research* 42: 461-465.
1969 "The Theme of Contemporary Social Movements." *British Journal of Sociology* 20: 390-405.

Turner, R. H., and L. M. Killian
1957 *Collective Behavior.* Englewood Cliffs, N.J.: Prentice-Hall.

Turner, R. H., and Samuel J. Surace
1956 "Zoot-Suiters and Mexicans: Symbols in Crowd Behavior." *American Journal of Sociology* 62: 14-20.

United States Bureau of the Census
1960 *Census Tracts for SMSA's.* Washington, D.C.: Government Printing Office.
1963 *1960 Census of Population: Volume 1. Characteristics of the Population.* Washington, D.C.: Government Printing Office.
1967a *County and City Data Book.* Washington, D.C.: Government Printing Office.
1967b *Finances of Municipalities.* Washington, D.C.: Government Printing Office.

Van der Kroef, Justus M.
  1956 "Economic Development in Indonesia: Some Social and Cultural
         Impediments." *Economic Development and Social Change* 4: 116-
         133.
Vander Zanden, James W.
  1959 "Resistance and Social Movements." *Social Forces* 37: 312-315.
Von Neumann, J.
  1956 "Probabilistic Logics and the Synthesis of Reliable Organizations
         from Unreliable Components," in C. E. Shannon, and J. McCarthy
         (eds.), *Automata Studies.* Cambridge: Princeton University Press.
Wanderer, J. J.
  1969 "Index of Riot Severity and Some Correlates." *American Journal of
         Sociology* 74: 500-505.
Warner, Wellman J.
  1930 *The Wesleyan Movement in the Industrial Revolution.* London:
         Longmans, Green and Co.
Warren, Donald
  1969 "Neighborhood Structure and Riot Behavior in Detroit: Some Ex-
         planatory Findings." *Social Problems* 16: 464-484.
Watzlawick, P., J. H. Beaven, and D. D. Jackson
  1967 *Pragmatics of Human Communication.* New York: Norton.
Weber, Max
  1930 *The Protestant Ethic and the Spirit of Capitalism.* Talcott Parsons
         (trans.). New York: Charles Scribner Sons.
  1947 *The Theory of Social and Economic Organization.* A. M. Anderson,
         and Talcott Parsons (trans.). Glencoe, Ill.: The Free Press.
  1963 *The Sociology of Religion.* Ephraim Fischoff (trans.). Boston:
         Beacon Press.
Weiner, Myron
  1966 *Modernization: The Dynamics of Growth.* New York: Basic Books.
Weinert, R. S.
  1966 "Violence in Pre-Modern Societies: Rural Columbia." *American
         Political Science Review* 60: 340-347.
Weiss, Robert Frank
  1963 "Defection from Social Movements and Subsequent Recruitment to
         New Movements." *Sociometry* 26: 1-20.
Welton, R. A.
  1972 "Peasants, Social Conflict and Correlation Analysis." *Comparative
         Political Studies* 4: 101-107.
Wheeler, Stanton
  1967 "Deviant Behavior," pp. 601-666, in N. J. Smelser (ed.), *Sociology.*
         New York: Wiley.
Williamson, R. C.
  1965 "Toward a Theory of Political Violence: The Case of Rural Colum-
         bia." *Western Political Organization* 43: 35-44.
Wilson, Godfrey, and Monica Wilson
  1945 *The Analysis of Social Change: Based on Observations in Central
         Africa.* London: Cambridge University Press.

Winch, Robert F., and Donald T. Campbell
1969 "Proof? No. Evidence? Yes. The Significance of Tests of Significance." *The American Sociologist* 4: 140-143.
Winsborough, H. H.
1965 "The Changing Regional Character of the South," in John C. McKinney and E. T. Thompson (eds.), *The South in Continuity and Change.* Durham, N.C.: Duke University Press.
Wright, Q.
1964 *A Study of War.* Chicago: University of Chicago Press.
Yinger, J. M.
1957 *Religion, Society and the Individual.* New York: Macmillan.
Zald, Mayer N., and Roberta Ash
1964 "Social Movement Organization Growth, Decay and Change." *Social Forces* 44: 327-341.
Zeitlin, Maurice
1968 "The Social Determinants of Political Democracy in Chile," pp. 264-288 in James Petras, and Maurice Zeitlin (eds.), *Latin America, Reform or Revolution?* Greenwich, Conn.: Fawcett.

Name Index

Subject Index

Acting crowd, 67; character, 68; common objective, 68; evaluation, 71–72; individual, 69; milling process, 68, 69; revolutionary movements, 124; suggestibility, 69
Activism, 183, 185
Actual moral reasoning, 182, 184, 186
AFL–CIO, 137
Agency, 298
Agent provocateurs, 165
Agitation, 80–81, 120
Agitators, 120, 121, 165; role in riots, 379, 380
Alcoholics Anonymous, 99
Alienation, 220, 257
American Civil Liberties Union, 265
American Public Health Association, 312
American Revolution, 110
Anabaptists, 229, 237
Anatomy of Revolution, 402
Animal crowd behavior, 28
Anti-Saloon League, 99
Antisemitism, 14
Antislavery movement, 78–79
Anti-systems, 332
Arbitration, 43, 44
Assimilation, 336
Associational groups, 425, 426, 427, 429; conflict regulation, 426
Aspiration, 205; level, 204
Aspirational deprivation, 205, 207
Audience, 93
Authoritarian Personality, The, 228

Bayesian analysis, 160; probability, 163
Behavior: collective, *see* Collective behavior; coordinated, 172–173; crowd, *see* Crowd behavior; culturally determined, 424, definition, 118; designating, 171; natural history approach, 118; prescribing, 171
Biological organisms: catastrophic changes, 395; communication, 392; environment, 395; feedback mechanism, 393, 394; information processing, 392, 393; learning, 394; memory, 394; social systems, 395–397; time span, 393
Birth control movement, 104

Black Death, 27
Black Muslims, 287
Black power movement, 284–285, 287
Blacks, *see* Negroes
B'nai B'rith, 137
Bolsheviks, 97, 99, 233, 269
British Committee of 100, 255, 281
Buddhism, 326, 329
Bureaucracies, 323, 324, 325; institutionalization, 331
Byzantium, 322, 323, 325, 330

Campaign for Nuclear Disarmament (CND), 276
Canada, social movements, 409
Canadian Commonwealth Federation, 97
Canton Commune incident, 232
Cargo cult, 231
Carnival, 70
Casual crowd, 67
Catholicism, 300, 201
Central city syndrome, 456
Centralism: balanced, 297; limited, 296–297; simple, 295, 296; unitary, 295–296; U.S. government, 297
Ceremonial behavior, 82, 101; collective behavior contrasted, 92
Change, analysis of, 318
Child Rearing Practices Report, 186
Chile, 224, 225, 227
Chilean Housing Corporation, 224
Charisma, 270
Christianity, 26
Circular interaction, 120
Circular reaction, 158
Civil disobedience, 182, 183, 275–281; groups, 255; illegal actions, 279–280
Civil Disorder Chronology, 464
Civil Rights movement, 264
Civil strife, *see* Turmoil
Coercive Potential (Coerp), 428; model, 430
Cognitive dissonance, 206, 207
Cold Water Army, 101
Collective behavior, 3; ceremonial behavior contrasted, 92; change in social values, 149; countermovements, 149; decision-

523

THE BOOK MANUFACTURE

Composition:	Fox Valley Typesetting
	Menasha, Wisconsin
Printing and Binding:	R. R. Donnelley & Sons Company
	Crawfordsville, Indiana
Internal Design:	F. E. Peacock Publishers
	art department
Cover Design:	Sandy Mead
Type:	Times Roman
	with Optima running heads